Tony Cowley

D0435848

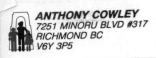

French Leave
Encore

Richard Binns

Chiltern House

**For
our granddaughters
Victoria and Alison**

in the hope that they, too, will
one day grow to love the country
which has given us so much pleasure.

The cover, a watercolour of Honfleur harbour, is by Denis Pannett. If you would like an almost identical print (image size 30 by 40 cm) send £5.95 (sterling cheque drawn on a UK bank or International sterling money order drawn on a UK bank payable to D. Pannett) to Heathers, 1 Woodland Drive, Beaconsfield, Bucks HP9 1JY. Readers living outside the UK should add £1.05 for extra surface-mail postage (making £7.00 in total).

The four pencil drawings on the front and back cover endpapers are by the author. These are also available in packs of 12 (three of each scene plus a dozen white envelopes). Each drawing is the same size as the endpaper illustration and is printed on stiff white card (14.5 cm deep by 10 cm wide which opens to 14.5 cm deep by 20 cm wide). For a pack of 12 send £2.95 (sterling cheque drawn on a UK bank or International sterling money order drawn on a UK bank payable to R. Binns) to Honeywood House, Avon Dassett, Leamington Spa, Warwickshire CV33 0AH. Readers living outside the UK should add 55p for extra surface-mail postage (making £3.50 in total). (The four scenes are: Château de Cordès – Auvergne (Massif Central); the D17 west of Châtillon-sur-Chalaronne – Lyonnais; Les-Baux-de-Provence – Provence; and St-Paul – Côte d'Azur.)

© Richard Binns 1992 (Text, Drawings and Maps)
Published in October 1992 by Chiltern House Publishers, Honeywood House, Avon Dassett, Leamington Spa, Warwickshire CV33 0AH

ISBN 0 9516930 1 8

Maps drawn by the author
Typeset in Century (text) and Gill (maps) by Art Photoset Limited, 64 London End, Beaconsfield, Bucks HP9 2JD
Printed by Butler & Tanner Limited, The Selwood Printing Works, Caxton Road, Frome, Somerset BA11 1NF

Contents

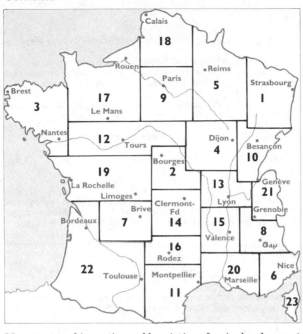

Please read both pages carefully: important changes

Maps

Regional maps identify hotels and restaurants in **four** ways:

- Autoroute hotel included for motorists' convenience: close to an autoroute exit; rarely closed; usually group owned; and frequently has bedrooms suitable for disabled clients

■ Base hotel: *sans restaurant* (no restaurant) and, with few exceptions, always in a quiet or secluded location

▲ Hotel with a restaurant or a restaurant with bedrooms

△ Restaurant only (with no bedrooms)

Text

Within each region the four recommendation types are grouped in **three** sections. Within each of the three sections entries are listed in alphabetical order by village/town name.

Autoroute Hotels Hotels near autoroute exits. If you have my *En Route* guide (ER) I give the exit map page number

Base Hotels Hotels with no restaurants

Hotels & Restaurants Hotels with restaurants; restaurants with bedrooms; and restaurants only (no bedrooms)

Cooking ratings

Since 1980 I have tried various ways of categorising cooking standards. I have often discussed the best way of presenting cooking ratings with Tom Jaine of the *Good Food Guide*. Like Tom, I am now using five ratings – but with four important variations which allow me to solve the problem where, from day to day, standards can vary between two ratings.

Cooking 1 Simple, straightforward cooking. Establishments serving basic fare which, more often than not, will consist of *cuisine Bourgeoise* specialities (see page 19). Many readers could do as well, or better, at home. Other factors count in making the recommendation: perhaps good value; or the site; or nearby attractive terrain; or friendly owners. (Most autoroute hotels are in this category: expect grills, buffets, "out-of-the-bag dishes", occasionally some classical, *Bourgeoise* and regional specialities, and commercial desserts.)

Cooking 2 Good, competent cooking. When standards vary, up or down, I use **Cooking 2-3** or **Cooking 1-2** as a rating.

Cooking 3 Very good level of cooking. Some faults but close or equal to Michelin one-star standard. If standards are sometimes higher I use **Cooking 3-4** as a rating. (See list on page 6.)

Cooking 4 Excellent cooking, often innovative and ambitious and rarely flawed. Two exceptionally inventive and individualistic chefs are rated as **Cooking 4-5**. (See lists on page 6.)

Cooking 5 Superb, flawless cooking. (See pages 6, 23 and 172.)

Key to Abbreviations and Price Bands

Abbreviations

Few abbreviations are used in *French Leave Encore*. Each entry has an introductory one to three line summary of the main facilities provided and a concluding section of up to six lines where essential information is shown as follows:

Menus range of cost of fixed-price menus (*prix-fixe*) or, if not available, the minimum cost of three courses from the à la carte menu; see price bands listed below

Rooms number of bedrooms (in brackets) and price band range (for the room). The word "Disabled" indicates that some bedrooms are accessible to guests in wheelchairs

Cards accepted: AE American Express; Access (Mastercard & Eurocard); DC Diners Club; Visa. Always check ahead

Closed annual holidays (if any) and days of the week closed. Always check ahead, as changes are often made. If no details provided then open all the year

Post post code, village/town name, *département* (page 479)

Tel telephone number

Telex telex number, where available

Fax fax number, where available

Mich page number/grid square on which the entry is located in Michelin spiral-bound *Motoring Atlas France*

Price Bands

A	under 100 Francs	D	300 to 400 Francs
B	100 to 200 Francs	E	400 to 500 Francs
C	200 to 300 Francs	F	over 500 Francs

F2, F3, F4: multiply F by figure indicated.
All price bands include service charges and taxes; wine and breakfasts are not included. Agree *pension* terms in advance.

Additional notes on Maps and Text

Important: almost half the entries offer good value for money; these are highlighted by the words **Good value**. In some regions (Côte d'Azur/Loire/Provence/Savoie/etc.) prices may be higher but will still represent good value. Towns and villages with a good value recommendation are shown on maps as follows: **Tours** (In addition, many of the comfortable and very comfortable hotels/restaurants offer clients good-value menus. Look for the letter "B" – 100 to 200 Francs – following the word "Menus".)

Many of the villages and towns and wine-producing areas referred to in the regional wine texts are identified on the regional maps, or on separate "Wines & Cheeses" maps, as follows: ○ Monbazillac (village)   *Côtes de Duras* (wine-producing area represented by light grey shading). The maps also show cheese-producing areas as follows: Iraty

To make identification easier on large-scale maps a limited number of places of interest (towns, villages, rivers, etc.) are shown on the regional maps in either light or black print (the latter when also the site of an hotel or restaurant recommendation); and in black on *France à la Carte* maps. They are also shown in **bold** print in regional and "themed" texts.

Map scales: 1/2,000,000: 1 cm is 20 km and 1 inch is 32 miles.

5

Top-rated Restaurants

Listed in region and page number order within each category (see page 4). Details include the region number (see page 3), the restaurant or hotel name and, in brackets, the chef's name, town or village location and page number of the entry.

Cooking 5
10 Girardet (Girardet, Crissier, 172)

Cooking 4-5
14 Michel Bras (Bras, Laguiole, 250)
22 L'Aubergade (Trama, Puymirol, 367)

Cooking 4
  1 Host. du Cerf (MM. Husser, Marlenheim, 43)
  4 Host. du Vieux Moulin (Silva, Bouilland, 84)
  6 Jean-François Issautier (Issautier, St-Martin-du-Var, 119)
10 Jean-Paul Jeunet (Jeunet, Arbois, 169)
10 La Gare (Wenger, Le Noirmont, 174)
12 Grand Hôtel Lion d'Or (Clément, Romorantin-Lanthenay, 212)
12 Bardet (Bardet, Tours, 213)
15 La Pyramide (Henriroux, Vienne, 261)
18 La Meunerie (Delbé, Téteghem, 294)
20 Serge Lanoix (Lanoix, Castillon-du-Gard, 324)
21 Albert 1er (Carrier, Chamonix, 341: see text)
22 Pain Adour et Fantaisie (Oudill, Grenade-sur-l'Adour, 364)

Cooking 3-4
  1 Au Père Rota (Kuentz, Fougerolles, 41)
  1 Château de Vauchoux (Turin, Port-sur-Saône, 44)
  2 La Cognette (Nonnet, Issoudun, 51)
  2 La Renaissance (Dray, Magny-Cours, 52)
  3 Le Goyen (Bosser, Audierne, 63)
  3 Auberge Grand'Maison (Guillo, Mur-de-Bretagne, 67)
  3 Bretagne (Paineau, Questembert, 68)
  3 Le Franklin (Abraham, St-Malo, 70)
  3 Régis Mahé (Mahé, Vannes, 71)
  4 Barnabet (Barnabet, Auxerre, 83)
  4 Les Millésimes (MM. Sangoy, Gevrey-Chambertin, 86)
  4 Host. de Levernois (MM. Crotet, Levernois, 87)
  5 Aux Armes de Champagne (Michelon, L'Epine, 101)
  6 Chênes Verts (Bajade, Tourtour, 120)
  7 Gindreau (Pélissou, St-Médard, 135)
  8 Les Santons (Abert, Moustiers-Ste-Marie, 146)
10 Auberge de Chavannes (Carpentier, Courlans, 171)
11 Léonce (Fabre, Florensac, 189)
11 Le Mimosa (Pugh, St-Guiraud, 190)
12 Auberge des Templiers (Les Bézards, 206)
12 Au Plaisir Gourmand (Rigollet, Chinon, 208)
13 La Fontaine (Jury, Châteauneuf, 227)
13 Auberge du Cep (Guérin, Fleurie, 229)
13 Greuze (Ducloux, Tournus, 231)
14 Radio (Mioche, Royat, 256)
15 Chabran (Chabran, Pont-de-l'Isère, 255)
15 Auberge des Cimes (Marcon, St-Bonnet-le-Froid, 257)
19 Bonne Auberge (Poiron, Clisson, 305)
19 Moulin de la Gorce (Bertranet, La Roche-l'Abeille, 308)
20 L'Escale (Clor, Carry-le-Rouet, 324)
21 Million (Million, Albertville, 340)
22 Relais de la Poste (MM. Coussau, Magescq, 365)
22 Pyrénées (Arrambide, St-Jean-Pied-de-Port, 369)

6

Chiltern House is back again

After a five-year break "Chiltern House" is alive and kicking again. Some of you will know that, at the end of 1987, Anne and I decided to close down the publishing enterprise we ran from our home, Chiltern House. We had researched, written, published and distributed seven books during the Eighties and, in addition, we had "packaged" an eighth title for a main-line publisher. Both research and production costs had become much too high and, to make matters worse, we found the task of getting bookshops to stock our titles more and more difficult. We had been living far too dangerously as **all** our annual income had come from the single book we published each year.

Ironically, at the start of 1988, our publishing venture would have ground to a halt anyway. Serious eye problems, including a messy case of detached retinas, laid me low and continued to dog me for three years. Thank heavens the eye problems didn't worry me during the years from 1980 to 1987. Every day counted during those busy eight years and any setbacks then would have meant financial disaster.

The health worries started two days before our move away from Buckinghamshire, the main benefit of which was to reduce our living expenses dramatically. Despite the eye problems I kept busy, writing numerous articles for national newspapers.

What didn't stop were readers' letters. We had got used to receiving about one thousand a year. But what did surprise us was that a vast number continued to arrive at our new home, forwarded on to us by the post office. We lost count of the times readers asked: "Is there a new *French Leave?*" Your invaluable feedback, on both existing entries and numerous suggestions on worthy contenders for inclusion in a new edition, has helped us enormously. Without that support this new edition most certainly could not have been written.

In February 1991 we decided to have another go. Why? My eyes had improved though the doctors could not guarantee a problem-free future. We also felt much wiser and more confident and we were itching to improve on *FL3*. This time all our financial eggs are not in one basket: our overheads are lower, for both living expenses and book production costs (doing all the maps and most of the typesetting myself has saved a five-figure sum); and income now comes from other writing sources as well. We are grateful for the help given by five friends (chefs and ex-guide book inspectors) who have checked out cooking standards at some of the new entries. My word processor, too, has been invaluable; without it *Encore* would not exist.

I've worked hard to improve one *FL3* weakness: the maps. Like all similar compact pocket guides I use small type sizes for the text pages; but, because I had crammed so much into the maps, I had to use even smaller type sizes. The new maps are also full of detail but, by adding many more maps and by using the larger text type sizes, I hope they are easier to read.

Few authors and publishers know the pleasure of doing **everything** from soup to nuts. Anne and I are the researchers, designers, editors, cartographers, indexers and proof-readers. There's no selling of souls and we relish the joy of **total** independence of both minds and time. I am not a gifted writer; I try to "speak" to you as I would to a friend, giving advice as honestly as I can. I also remind myself constantly that I'm asking you to spend your **own** hard-earned cash. This new guide is as fallible and idiosyncratic as its predecessors; please read the first four paragraphs on pages 450/451. We hope that *Encore*, once again, puts the best of France in your pocket.

What's new in French Leave Encore?

La guillotine

Of the 600-plus hotels and restaurants which I recommended in *French Leave 3* just over 200 have been dropped from this new edition. In all but 50 or so of the deletions the guillotine has fallen because critical reports from readers have been at an unacceptable level.

Following *French Leave 3* I adopted a different policy with my next book, *Best of Britain*. In the latter I didn't waste space in listing entries where my basic message was "Don't go!" The same philosophy has been applied to this new edition. Numerous Michelin one and two-star chefs, in *FL3*, have been omitted from *Encore*; so have many luxury hotels. First-time visits to other starred chefs were also miserable affairs (like Veyrat at Annecy); they, too, have not been included.

But what will cause far more controversy is my decision to drop all France's provincial three-star chefs.

Nothing has depressed me more over the years than the endless stream of readers' letters complaining about visits to the restaurants of the superstar chefs. Often the words "seething" and "abominations" would be the most appropriate labels to describe readers' feelings. None of this has surprised me. Those of you who bought *French Leave Favourites* will already know that only three three-star chefs qualified for inclusion (readers' favourites from 1980 to 1986).

During the last couple of years Anne and I have re-visited many of the provincial superstars. Without exception we were disappointed. After visiting half of them we gave up; we were wasting time and effort in confirming our readers' gripes.

Put simply we concluded that your hard-earned cash is better spent at restaurants where the chefs' reputations have not yet reached hyped-up levels and where cooking skills are a match for the three-star shrines. Dishes at the latter are often prepared by locums or fee-paying students, working to a "cooking-by-numbers" formula and operating on "automatic-pilot". Where's the boss? He's away, cashing in on his three-star fame. (It pays to have a son. Many do. Dad jets around the globe harvesting fees, leaving *le fils* to man the stoves.)

"Grand" and "glitzy" are the words that sum up the fixtures and fittings, cutlery and crockery, sundry works of art, wines and service. The whole wretched business is oppressive and ostentatious and is no more than a performing extravaganza; the "Enjoyment Factor" is often zero out of 10. Penguin-stiff service is frequently both supercilious and stuffy. You pay through the nose for the "show", often menus give you no choice, and you are taken to the cleaners for wines and "extras".

Some two-star chefs, striving for a third and in *Encore*, are too close for comfort to emulating their peers – for prices, "elegant surroundings" and idiotic snobbishness. A friend's three-year-old exclaimed, on rummaging through her mum's bag: "It's chock-a-block full of nothing!" That delicious, original thought is equally true of many multi-starred restaurants. Our cynicism is the child of disillusion and disappointment.

The "three-star spiral chase" is the bleakest part of the French culinary scene. Most three-star and too many two-star restaurants have become too precious, pretentious and pompous: you see the 3Ps on the plates, in the trappings and service, and in the owners, who change gradually as they ascend the spiral. (Read *Michelin stars* and *Michelin's inspectorate* pages 25/26; *Les Mères Merveilleuses* – pages 218/219; Michel Bras – pages 250/251; and Michel Trama – page 367.)

Hard-earned cash and rapport qualité-prix

Most two and some one-star chefs, trapped on the "three-star spiral chase", are having a hard time in recession-hit France. Those lower down the ambition scale, guided by the lifesaving culinary lighthouse of *rapport qualité-prix*, the all-important balance of both quality and price, have fewer problems.

Of many examples I could list, Jean-Pierre Battaglia of the Auberge Fleurie, Valbonne (Côte d'Azur), blazes like a beacon. His business is thriving. Earlier this year his 98-franc menu (a trio of choices at each of three courses) put to shame the no-choice or minimal-choice "economy" menus of three-star chefs (300 francs or more). And I don't mean just the price: his quality produce and preparation skills match those encountered on the superstars' "cheapie" menus.

Chefs, the lesson is simple: clients are fed up with having to pay for non-culinary frills; concentrate instead on *RQP*.

Entente Cordiale

In *French Leave 3* I asked the question: *"Entente Cordiale – Dead or Alive?"* I then went on to say that "Everyone has two countries – his own and France; but some of you dislike the French a great deal, finding them unacceptably hostile."

Are matters any better? Yes, if measured by the fewer complaints I receive from readers recalling nasty experiences. No, if judged by the disruptive action regularly taken by bolshie air-traffic controllers, seamen, farmers, lorry drivers, dockers and myriad other groups: they've all caused havoc for residents and tourists alike over the years. But one aspect of the *cordiale* needs a thoroughly good stirring.

We may all have two countries – our own and France. But the French have just one – France. The vast majority of the French make absolutely no effort at all to find out more about Britain – let alone actually experience what lies to the north of *la Manche*.

For the French, civilisation ends at Calais. Go into any small-town bookshop in France: if the shop stocks more than a handful of books about Britain and the beastly *rosbifs* you've made a rare find. Total ignorance of both Britain and the British is the rule though some may successfully locate London on a map. What about British cooking? Contempt is a charitable way of describing the usual Gallic shrug, grimace and finger across the jugular which one encounters when debating our culinary abilities. French gastronomic polls always place us at the bottom of the heap; we're considered the dustbin of Europe. Yet so few French ever cross the Channel to put our ever-improving culinary standards to the test.

Culinary differences

Sure, the French culinary pyramid is many times larger than the equivalent in Britain. At the very top of the pyramid in France there are probably many hundreds of top-notch chefs; in Britain possibly 100 and no more. Lower down, at the base of the pyramid, one can safely say that there are many, many more consistently good cafés, bistros, brasseries and simpler restaurants across the Channel in France.

But don't assume everything is better in France. In some culinary areas standards are higher in Britain.

We have left the French behind in many eating-out aspects: breakfasts in all parts of Britain are poles apart from most encountered in France (some there are fit only for the dustbin

– like French milk); so are the range and quality of vegetables, potatoes and fruit served in British restaurants (often in France you'll get just a single vegetable served during a meal and rarely does one encounter the humble potato in serious kitchens); and soups, breads and desserts are invariably better this side of the Channel.

The differences don't end there. British chefs (Marion Jones and Stephen Bull are typical examples) have developed eclectic repertoires, using culinary ideas from all over the globe. The latter is also true of wine lists in Britain. Consumers here have a much more varied eating-out choice: British, French, Italian, Indian, Chinese, Thai and numerous other ethnic styles are commonly available throughout the land. Other than in the biggest cities there's no similar choice in France. And why don't more French chefs make at least some effort to serve genuine vegetarian meals? So many readers complain about this. Finally, smoking in French restaurants is still a scourge; minimal effort is made to separate smokers from non-smokers.

France's simpler hotels: love them or hate them

In my last book, *French Leave Favourites*, I wrote: "There's a special appeal about France's simpler hotels which is sometimes hard to put one's finger on. For Anne and me, like the majority of our readers, there has always been a willing acceptance of anything that is a little decrepit, of down-at-heel fittings, of horrendously-styled wallpapers and decorations, of cheap, tatty plumbing and lighting, of threadbare carpets and spongy beds. That's part of the fun. Remember, above all, what value for money they provide."

Expectations have risen dramatically, not just during the last dozen years but also from previous decades when we all seemed happier to accept a lower standard of facilities. Even Michelin have adapted their standards to suit the times: unless a simple establishment has some bedrooms with *en suite* facilities then no mention is made of accommodation.

Some readers have given me fair old stick about bedrooms and bathrooms at simpler places. But I shall continue to include details of a handful of places, usually restaurants with rooms, with no *en suite* facilities. In these cases I have used the word **basic** in the introductory summary for each entry.

Bedroom prices

Over the last four decades French bedroom prices have risen by a greater margin than menu costs. At the bottom of the pyramid the ratio between bedroom and meal prices is only slightly different today from the early Fifties. In the middle the difference is more noticeable. However, at the top end the ratio has, in many cases, more than trebled.

I, for one, object to having to pay the fancy bedroom prices at the homes of some talented chefs. I always try to recommend a cheaper alternative and remember, too, that nearby Base or Autoroute hotels will save you many francs.

Some final advice

Thefts from cars have reached epidemic proportions, especially along the Med. Leave nothing in your car and watch where you park. Random police checks are rife: so don't drink and drive. Note too: traffic offences bring heavy on-the-spot cash fines. When exploring any region always try to travel from south to north; then the sun is behind you – essential for perfect views.

How to use French Leave Encore

I have made some important changes in the way I classify hotel and restaurant recommendations in *French Leave Encore*. They are now classified under four different types. Refer to page 4 for a detailed explanation of how the four classifications are shown on the regional maps.

Within each region the hotels and restaurants are listed alphabetically by village or town name in **three** sections:

1 The **first** section includes hotels situated close to autoroute exits. These are mainly group-owned hotels and, with very few exceptions, they all have restaurants or grills. Apart from a dozen or so none of them offers anything special in the culinary stakes. What they all do is to provide easy access for travellers using motorways to get to and from holiday regions. Importantly, most have bedrooms suitable for disabled clients.

2 The **second** section is for "Base hotels". These have no restaurants and all of them, with few exceptions, have quiet or secluded sites. What they provide is the freedom to eat out where and when you please. Use them for a stay of one night or several days; the latter is an especially good way to explore an area. Obviously no cooking ratings are given.

3 The **third** section includes hotels and restaurants which have accommodation and also restaurants without bedrooms. Cooking standards have been classified under five ratings ranging from one to five – with four further variations.

Please read page 4 for an explanation of the new **cooking ratings**. Remember, recommendations within the third section in each region range from the simplest to the greatest of places and they cover the complete spectrum of both price and skill levels. Some of the simpler restaurants have basic bedroom facilities (without showers, baths or toilets). Elsewhere I've written about the caveats you must take account of in these establishments, noting that when I use the word **basic** for bedrooms, that's just what I mean. Remember, too, that *pension* and low-price menus do not always provide "gastronomic experiences". Whenever specialities are listed bear in mind that chefs constantly change their repertoires.

Some entries offer value for money; these are identified by the words **Good value**. In many regions (Provence, Savoie, etc.) prices may be higher but will still represent good value. (In addition many of the more comfortable and very comfortable hotels and restaurants offer clients a less-expensive menu which also represents good value for money. Refer to the concluding lines for each entry and look out for the letter "B" – 100 to 200 Francs – following the word "Menus".)

A list of general **caveats**: in France a garden, a park, a lounge or a living room has many versions and do not always expect the British or American equivalents; always try to check closing dates, changes can and do occur; and please do remember that **simple** means what it says.

Some guidance on **prices**: price bands include service charges and taxes; wine is not included in meal price bands; room price bands do not include breakfasts, nor is it compulsory to have them (rarely do they represent good value); room price bands indicate the price for the bedroom, not per person.

Other **tips**: for good value choose a fixed-price menu; have no qualms about sharing dishes; cheapest menus are not always available on Sundays or public holidays; try always to book ahead; take a portable cold-box; take an insect killer aerosol; inspect rooms before accepting them; most petrol (gasoline) stations are modern and have toilet facilities.

Enjoying the best of France

I see no point in re-inventing the wheel: the advice I gave in *French Leave 3* still applies so forgive me for repeating the same message again. I can only hope that many of you will be reading this page for the first time.

Twelve years ago I wrote that "the next decade will be a better time than ever to explore France." Nothing has changed in the Nineties. France has everything: value-for-money hotels and restaurants to suit any budget; a vast range of beaches and coastlines; majestic mountains; lovely lakes; a variety of rivers and streams; endless tracts of forests and woodlands; and, to top it all, an immense larder of culinary delights.

Both the Channel Tunnel and Euro Disney (to the east of Paris) are certain to encourage a multitude of first-time visitors to France. These first-timers will soon get the bug for France and, before long, they, too, will start seeking out some of its more distant hidden corners.

The ferry companies, with their new super-large ships, will also fight back; they'll ensure prices are kept at the lowest competitive levels. One way and another France will become an even greater attraction to a new generation of visitors.

How can we all ensure that we get our fair share of France's myriad pleasures? The first golden rule applies as much as ever: maps are the essential key to open the door to any country. A good large-scale map will repay its small outlay a thousand times over. The finest investment that you can make is to go out and buy the spiral-bound Michelin *Motoring Atlas France*. The atlas will ensure you see the best of France (and will help you bypass any juggernaut blockades!). Whatever maps you buy immerse yourself in them; every hour spent studying them will be time profitably spent.

Remember *French Leave Encore* is for the motorist and recall, too, that **I deliberately do not direct you into the centres of large towns and cities**, where noise, traffic, thefts from cars, navigation and parking are a nightmare. Alas, I've still not found the time to research a full chapter on Corsica.

How does *French Leave Encore* help? There are various ways to explore each region. You may already have your own base: an hotel, a flat, a villa, a *gîte*, a caravan or a tent. If not, the three methods below will help you to select the best hotels and restaurants, at all price levels.

Method One Use a Base hotel whenever you can: all of them are *sans restaurant* (no restaurant); nearly all of them have quiet or secluded sites. You have the freedom to eat whenever or wherever you want, or not at all.

Method Two The second way of seeing a region would be to stay at an establishment with a dining room and bedrooms, moving on from place to place every day or two. Each entry in the guide shows where bedrooms are available.

Method Three You can permutate Base hotels and other establishments from region to region, staying a varying number of days at each. If you choose *pension* terms then agree them in advance (and don't expect the chef's best specialities).

How else does *French Leave Encore* help? I implore you to use the *Glossary of Menu Terms* (Anne's worked hard to extend it); I urge you to refer to the lists of specialities and cheeses detailed at the start of each region (easily spotted as they're in **bold** print); and may I remind you to make use of the *Index of Wines* and the *Index of Cheeses*, both in France and at home. Finally, may I suggest you read *So you think you know that road sign?*: the list is full of surprises.

Enjoying French cuisine (& British Cooking too)

Nothing is new in cooking. French cuisine still falls neatly into four different types, just as it did 70 years ago when Curnonsky, the French gastronome and writer, identified this quartet of categories: *la haute cuisine*; *la cuisine Bourgeoise*; *la cuisine Régionale*; and *la cuisine Improvisée*.

Whether 70 or 200 years ago, French cooks have always been introducing new ideas and techniques into their cuisine. Today, modern-day interpretations of *la cuisine Improvisée*, more than ever, rule the roost in the more glamorous French restaurants. *La haute cuisine* (classical cooking) survives in an ever decreasing number of top restaurants; even chefs who've spent 50 years mastering the difficulties of the repertoire are increasingly "modernising" specialities and making them lighter and less rich (neo-classical cooking). Will there be any first-class restaurants serving **authentic** classical cuisine by the year 2000? If not, blame Gault Millau. Ironically, at the lower levels of the culinary pyramid, classical cooking – with its hundreds of rich sauces and garnishes – is very much alive.

Throughout France *la cuisine Régionale* (regional cooking) continues to wither at an alarming rate. Some chefs, who have stayed loyal to their ancient regional specialities, have implored me not to over-emphasise this aspect of their repertoires. They plead: "Tell your readers about our modern specialities." Once again Gault Millau have a lot to answer for: they pay lip service to identifying those chefs who propose "traditional regional recipes" (or "revived versions") but the same *cuisiniers* know only too well that they're not going to get the gushing accolades and publicity given to their colleagues practising *la cuisine Improvisée*.

Nosing out chefs who are true and authentic disciples of regional cooking has become more difficult than ever. Most regional cuisine, usually under the banner of *cuisine terroir* (cooking of the local area or region, including both produce and ancient recipes), is more often than not a fraud. Add some lentils, fungi, or beans, cheat by tagging on some sacred culinary term which was never intended to be used and, hey presto, before you know where you are, the trendy guides will soon signpost you as a guardian of French culinary traditions. However, in defence of chefs, remember that their loyal clients do not always want to eat regional specialities. (Some French chefs make a similar point about the lack of vegetables. They claim when they do serve vegetables French clients turn their noses up and leave them uneaten.)

La cuisine Bourgeoise is still alive and kicking, as it always will be. More about this later on.

The notes above and those that follow are my own personal points of view. They are provocative, prejudiced and fallible. Don't take them too seriously. But before I devote some space to the four differing types of French cuisine let me introduce some tongue-in-cheek thoughts on British cooking.

The French fall about at any mention of "British Cooking". They simply don't believe that such an art form exists. Few cross the Channel and, invariably, they head for London. What a pity, as there are many great chefs elsewhere in the UK.

Take chef Betty Allen at Airds (Port Appin) as one example of what's possible with "British Cooking": a port and stilton flan or lightly grilled scallops from local waters, simple and subtle; cauliflower cheese soup – there's now't like that in France; succulent Scottish beef; and raspberry and Drambuie ice cream is as brilliant a "British" menu you'll ever encounter.

Her vegetable cookery is the essence of the art; what's more they are served the way all vegetables should be, on a platter in the middle of the table. Every Frenchman should be dragged screaming to restaurants like Betty's, and to others, too, in the wastelands beyond Watford.

Another is Kit Chapman's remarkable Castle Hotel at Taunton. His chef, Phil Vickery, has given a welcome new lease of life to numerous dishes in an authentic and traditional British repertoire; the French would drool over superb potted pigeon and rabbit and baked egg custard tart with nutmeg ice cream, just two of dozens of examples. Kit's record of encouraging and developing British chefs is incomparable: Chris Oakes (now at his own Oakes restaurant in Stroud); Ray Farthing (recently at Calcot Manor, near Tetbury); and Gary Rhodes (London's Greenhouse) all worked at The Castle.

(The art of "hotelkeeping" – the attention to detail, welcome, service and common sense – is flourishing in Britain; French hoteliers could learn so much from individuals like Kit Chapman and Martin Skan. Among luxury hotels I have yet to encounter any in France which beats the all-round excellence of Martin Skan's incomparable Chewton Glen at New Milton.)

Have the efforts of Britain's talented food and wine writers had no effect in increasing and informing public attitudes to cooking and eating out in the post-war years? Of course they have. And so have the vast number of superstores and specialist small stores dotted around Britain. The goods on offer today are a world away from what was available four decades ago. (Areas of weakness persist however: few butchers, fishmongers and cake shops stand comparison with their French counterparts. Many claim they try to introduce "fine tastes" to their clients, but with little success.)

Perhaps one reason why the French rubbish our cooking is that they are influenced too much by Michelin's UK ratings. Here, unbelievably, only 42 chefs win stars (one, two or three) and 53 are awarded an M accolade (do not equate this with the "Repas" (R) rating in France; good value for money is an additional criterion for the latter). This is a gross misrepresentation of how much standards have improved on this side of the Channel. Put bluntly, on home ground, French inspectors are an easier touch, despite the recent carnage among France's starred chefs (see *Santé Bibendum!*). I maintain they are still too many; Michelin should send its British inspectors across to France to sort their stars out.

Cuisine Moderne (la cuisine Improvisée)

I've grown to detest the term *nouvelle cuisine*. I shall use the label only once more, in a quote which I still consider is the best definition of *cuisine moderne (la cuisine Improvisée)*. Frédy Girardet, in conversation with Craig Claiborne, said this: "*La nouvelle cuisine* is nothing more than good taste. It is to prepare dishes to preserve their natural flavours and with the simplest of sauces." What did Curnonsky say all those decades ago? Good cooking resulted when "ingredients taste of what they are."

Yet foodie scribblers maintain that this particular branch of cooking is dead. Don't you believe it. I haven't seen any evidence on my French travels that *cuisine moderne* is dead and buried. Reworking old recipes or introducing some traditional local produce into a speciality does not convert them into authentic grandmother's cooking.

La cuisine Improvisée is flourishing more strongly than ever in France: spices, flavouring agents, herbs, mountain plants – everything under the sun is added to produce. Cooking in tea, cooking in endless varieties of oil, marinating in a range of juices and liquids; there's no end to the techniques used, many cribbed from the East. Amusingly, a few chefs are honest enough to admit that they discovered some of their "improvisations" in medieval cookery books. One debit: alas, sometimes combinations are hideous, *improvisée* gone gaga!

Simplicity and the quality and purity of produce are the keys. In its purest, simplest form, modern cooking allows the basic ingredients to count most; the emphasis is on highlighting one natural flavour at a time. For me, thankfully, portions do sometimes border on the frugal though I'm regularly stir-fried by readers that they hate this aspect of modern-day trends. Fast cooking is everything; steaming, poaching and baking are vital methods of preparation; slow cooking is out of fashion. Sauces, too, are a thing of the past; the reductions are no more than the concentrated juices of the food released during cooking. Flour is all but banned. Butter, cream and wine are still used, but not to any great excess. I've had meals where no butter or cream have been used at any point until the dessert stage.

It's then that "healthy modern cooking" goes out of the window. Dessert upon dessert, piled high and wide, are forced on all but the most strong-willed clients.

One aspect of modern cooking worries Anne and me enormously: undercooked food and dishes that are allowed to stand too long before serving. Since *FL3* both of us have been laid low with food poisoning at least six times; oysters, mussels and chicken have been the culprits. What's odd, too, is that it has always been at multi-starred restaurants.

Regional Cuisine (la cuisine Régionale)

I've had some tough things to say about the demise of French regional cooking. But that's not to say that chefs do not make use of local produce. (You would be surprised how much comes from abroad, especially Britain.) In each chapter I've listed some of the regional specialities you may encounter.

In the notes that follow I examine first the French regions with Atlantic seaboards, starting in the north and finishing at the Spanish frontier; then the regions bordering Belgium, Germany, Switzerland, Italy and the Mediterranean; and, finally, the regions of inland France. The numbers following each region's name are those used on the map on page 3 and at the start of each regional chapter.

In the following pages I do not refer to the cheeses of each region, though there is a short introduction to cheeses on page 19. I would also ask you to read, at the start of each region, the details listed on cheeses. Equally, the same goes for the country's wines, liqueurs and brandies; please read the comprehensive notes detailed in each regional introduction and elsewhere in the book (on pages 20 to 22 and 480).

Markets I have gone to some trouble in *Encore* to identify some of the best markets in France. At the end of the introduction to each region, before listing the cheeses, regional specialities and wines, I've included details of the locations of some of the better ones and, importantly, the day of the week each market is held (always mornings only).

North (18) Fish takes pride of place, freshly landed at the ports of Boulogne, Calais, and smaller ones like Le Crotoy. *Sole, turbot, maqueraux, barbue, lotte de mer, flétan, harengs, merlan, moules, crévettes*; all appear on menus. So do soups and stews, many with root vegetables: *waterzooï* – fish or chicken; *hochepot* – meat and vegetable *pot-au-feu; carbonnade* – beef stew with beer. Leeks are super; enjoy *flamiche aux poireaux* (*quiche*-like pastry). Seek out the *hortillonages* (water-gardens) of Amiens and their fine vegetables. Try *gaufres* (yeast waffles) and *ficelles* (variously stuffed pancakes). Beer, too, is good.

Normandy (17) Land of cream, apples and the pig. Vallée d'Auge gives its name to many dishes, including chicken, veal and fish; the term means cream, apples or cider, or apple brandy (Calvados) have been added. Cider is first class. Pork products are everywhere: *andouilles* – smoked tripe sausages, eaten cold; *andouillettes* – small grilled tripe sausages. Fish are superb: *sole à la Normande, à la Dieppoise, à la Fécampoise, à la Havraise* (the last three are ports); *plats de fruits de mer*; shrimps; oysters; *bulots* (whelks); mussels. Enjoy tripe; *ficelles* – pancakes; cow's milk cheeses; rich cream; butters, both salty and sweet; salad produce and potatoes from Caux; exquisite apple tarts; *canard à la Rouennaise*; and fish stews.

Brittany (3) Fish and shellfish are commonplace: lobsters, *huîtres, langoustes*, crabs, of varying sorts, *moules*, prawns, shrimps, *coquilles St-Jacques*; to name just a few. Enjoy *cotriade* – a Breton fish stew with potatoes and onions; *galettes* – buckwheat flour pancakes with savoury fillings; *crêpes de froment* – wheat flour pancakes with sweet fillings; *far Breton* – a batter mixture with raisins; *gâteau Breton* – a mouthwatering concoction; *agneau de pré-salé* – from the salt marshes near Mont-St-Michel (fine omelettes are also made there); and *poulet blanc Breton*. Brittany is one of France's market-gardens: enjoy artichokes, cauliflowers, cabbages, onions and strawberries.

Charentes/Vendée (19) western half of Poitou-Charentes. La Rochelle is a famed fishing port; consequently fish predominates. Oysters are glorious (see *Huîtres* in Glossary). The port of La Cotinière, on the island of Oléron, is renowned for its shrimps. Challans, in the Vendée, is reputed for its quality ducks. Charentes is second to none for butter, goat's milk cheeses, Charentais melons, Cognac, cabbages, mussels, *mojette* (white beans) and salt-marsh lamb from the Marais Poitevin.

Southwest (22) One of the great larders of France; can be divided into several distinct areas. From the countryside that lies in a semicircle to the north-west, west, south and south-east of Bordeaux comes: lamb from Pauillac; oysters (*gravettes*) from Arcachon; eels (*pibales*); beef (*entrecôte Bordelaise* is the best-known); onions and shallots; *cèpes; alose* (shad); and *lamproie* – lamprey (eel-like fish). The Garonne Valley is one vast orchard: try prunes from Agen; peaches; pears and dessert grapes.

South of the Garonne is **Gascony**: famed for *foie gras* (duck and goose); *confit* (preserved meat from both birds); jams and fruits; and Armagnac. Try a *floc* (see regional wine notes).

To the south and west of Gascony are **Béarn** and the **Landes**. From the latter came *palombes* and *ortolans*, ducks and chickens. Among traditional Béarn specialities are *garbue* – the most famous of vegetable soups; *poule au pot* – the chicken dish given its name by Henri IV; *tourin, ouliat* and *cousinette (cousinat)*. See the Southwest for further details.

West of Béarn is **Basque** country: tuna, anchovies, sardines and salmon (from Béarn also) are great; Bayonne ham, *piments* (peppers), *piperade, ttoro* (fish stew) and *gâteau Basque.*

Champagne-Ardenne (5) Ile de France (9) Many of the specialities listed earlier in the North appear in the former, renowned for its potatoes and turkeys. In the Ardenne you'll enjoy smoked hams, sold in nets; *sanglier; marcassin*; and red and white cabbages. West of Verdun, at Ste-Menehould, try *pieds de cochon* (pig's trotters); *petits gris* (snails); and the many differing sweets and sugared almonds (Verdun is famous for them). Troyes is renowned for pork and *andouillettes.*

Regional specialities and produce are all but non-existent in the Ile de France. Look out for cherries from Poissy, beans from Arpajon and tomatoes from Montlhéry. Enjoy *pâtés* and *terrines* and tempting *pâtisseries* and *galettes.*

Alsace (l) There is a strong German influence in much of the cooking; pork, game, goose and beer are common. *Foie gras* (fattened goose liver) is superb. So, too, is a range of tarts; *flammekuchen* – flamed open tart; and some with fruit (*linzertorte* – raspberry or bilberry open tart); jams, fruit liqueurs and *eaux-de-vie* (see Alsace wines). Stomach-filling *choucroute* and local sausages are on most menus; as are *kougelhopf, beckenoffe* and *lewerknepfle* (see Alsace specialities). Enjoy *tourte Alsacienne* – pork pie. Use *winstubs* (wine bars).

Lorraine on the north-west borders is known for its *madeleines* (tiny sponge cakes), *macarons*, mouthwatering *quiche Lorraine*, fruit tarts, omelettes and *potée.*

Jura (10) This is dairy country; witness the cheeses in the regional introduction. Try *Jésus de Morteau* – a fat pork sausage smoked over pine and juniper; *brési* – wafer-thin slices of dried beef; and many local hams. *Morilles* and other fungi are common; so are freshly-caught trout and other freshwater fish.

Savoie (21) Hautes-Alpes (8) *Plat gratiné* applies to a wide variety of dishes; in the Alps this means cooked in breadcrumbs; *gratins* of all sorts show how well milk, cream and cheese can be combined together. Relish *fondue* and *gougère.* Freshwater lake fish are magnificent (see the regional specialities for Savoie). Walnuts, chestnuts, all sorts of fruits and marvellous wild mushrooms are other delights.

Côte d'Azur (6) Provence (20) A head-spinning kaleidoscope of colours and textures fills the eyes: aubergines, peppers, beans, tomatoes, cauliflowers, asparagus, olives, garlic, artichokes, courgettes; the list is endless. Fruit, too, is just as appealing: melons from Cavaillon; strawberries from Monteux; cherries from Remoulins; glacé fruit from Apt; truffles from Valréas and Aups. Fish from the Med are an extra bonus: *bar* and *loup de mer, daurade, St-Pierre*, monkfish and mullet; these are the best. Lamb from the foothills of the Alps near Sisteron; herbs of every type from the *département* of Var; nuts from Valensole; honey and olive oil; *ratatouille*; sardines; *saucisson d'Arles; bouillabaisse* and *bourride; soupe de poissons* and *soupe au pistou*; what memories are stirred as I write.

Corsica (23) Savour game and charcuterie: *prisuttu* – raw ham, like Italian *prosciutto; figatelli* – grilled pig's liver sausage; *lonzu (lonza)* – slice of pork pickled is salt and herbs; *coopa (copa)* – pork sausage or shoulder of pork. Chestnut flour is used in many ways, particularly in desserts. Fine citrus fruits and, befitting the island of the *maquis*, superb herbs.

Languedoc-Roussillon (11) Cevennes (16) The same products and dishes listed under Provence are available here. Also oysters and mussels (*les coquillages*) from the lagoons (particularly the Bassin de Thau; visit Mèze and Bouzigues).

17

Excellent shellfish; cherries from Céret; anchovies; apricots and pumpkins. Enjoy *brandade de morue* (salt cod), *confit d'oie* (and *canard*), *cassoulet* and *saucisses de Toulouse*.

Loire (12) The river and its many tributaries provide *alose*, *sandre*, *anguille*, carp, perch, pike, salmon and *friture*. A tasty *beurre blanc* is the usual sauce with fish. *Charcuterie* is marvellous: *rillettes*, *rillons*, *andouillettes*, *saucissons*, *jarretons* and other delights. Cultivated mushrooms come from the limestone caves near Saumur.

The **Sologne** is famous for asparagus, frogs, game, fungi, lake and river fish and wildfowl. You'll be offered, too, many a *pâté*, fruit tarts (it's the home of *tarte Tatin*) and pies.

Burgundy (4) Refer to the often seen regional specialities. Many dishes are wine based: *coq au Chambertin* and *poulet au Meursault* are examples. Enjoy hams, freshwater fish, vegetables, *escargots*, mustard and gingerbread from Dijon and blackcurrants (used for *cassis*, the term for both the fruit and the liqueur made from them).

Lyonnais (13) The culinary heart and stomach of France. There is a variety of top-class produce on hand: Bresse poultry (*chapons* – capons – are unforgettable treats); *grenouilles* and game from Les Dombes; Charolais cattle from the hills west of Beaujolais; fish from the rivers and pools (pike *quenelles* appear everywhere); *charcuterie* from Lyon, particularly sausages called *sabodet*, *rosette*, *saucisson en brioche* and *cervelas*; and chocolates and *pâtisseries* from Lyon.

Auvergne (14) Ardèche (15) Both areas which keep alive old specialities. Refer to the regional lists but here are some of the best: *potée Auvergnate* – a stew of cabbage, vegetables, pork and sausage; *friand Sanflorin* – pork meat and herbs in pastry; *aligot* – a purée of potatoes, cheese, garlic and butter; *pounti* – a small egg-based savoury soufflé with bacon or prunes; and delectable *charcuterie*, hams, *saucisson*, *saucisses sèches* (dried sausages), *pâtés* and so on. The quality and variety of cheeses are second to none. Cabbages, potatoes, bacon and cheese feature on menus. The area around Le Puy is famed for its lentils and Verveine du Velay – yellow and green liqueurs made from over 30 mountain plants. The Ardèche is renowned for its sweet chestnuts (relish *marrons glacés*).

Berry-Bourbonnais (2) Poitou (19) – eastern half of Poitou-Charentes. The flat terrain of Berry-Bourbonnais is dull country, the granary of France. The area is renowned for beef, deer, wild boar, rabbits, hares, pheasants and partridge.

Much of Poitou lies in the deserted, wooded hills of Limousin (as do the western edges of Auvergne). Apart from the specialities listed look out for *mique* – a stew of dumplings; *farcidure* – a dumpling, either poached or sauteed; and *clafoutis* – pancake batter, poured over fruit (usually black cherries) and baked. Limousin is reputed for its *cèpes* – fine, delicate, flap mushrooms; and also for its reddish-coloured cattle.

Dordogne (7) A land of truffles, geese, ducks, walnuts, *cèpes*, chestnuts, sunflowers and fruit. *Foie gras* (goose and duck) is obligatory on menus; as are *confits* of both birds (preserved in their own fat) and *magrets* (boned duck breasts which have become so popular in the last decade throughout France). *Pâtés* incorporating either poultry or game, and truffles, are common place. If you see *miques* (yeast dumplings) or *merveilles* (hot, sugar-covered pastry fritters) on menus, order them. In the south, in the Lot Valley and towards the Garonne, it's a land of orchards: plums, prunes, figs, peaches, pears and cherries.

Classical Cuisine (la haute cuisine)

Henri Gault once claimed that classical cuisine was based on recipes and techniques developed in order to conserve food without the help of refrigeration and to mask food that had already gone bad. *Cuisine moderne* requires fresh quality produce; menus are consequently short and revolve around the chef's purchases each day. Compare that approach with old menus which offered clients scores, if not hundreds, of dishes. How fresh could some of that produce have been?

Classical French cuisine was established 450 years ago when Catherine de Medici came to France to become Queen; she brought with her a dozen or so Italian chefs from Florence. Just over 250 years later the developing art came to a standstill with the storming of the Bastille. In 1800 *la grande cuisine* (or *la haute cuisine*) re-emerged when Carême perfected the art and then re-established its prestige. In his day raw materials were either smoked, salted or preserved in vinegar; there was no refrigeration to keep food fresh. At the start of the 20th century Escoffier, with the advantage of refrigeration, took classical cuisine to its supreme peak.

The basic repertoire of hundreds of sauces and garnishes remains relatively unchanged. Some chefs have worked hard to bring a lighter touch to classical cooking (neo-classical). The Roux brothers have done wonders in this respect; their book, *New Classical Cuisine* (Macdonald), is a masterpiece.

Cuisine Bourgeoise

This is the simple, family, home cooking which most French chefs offer clients; to their credit it is invariably well done, using good produce, either from the locality or elsewhere. More often than not it represents value for money. The repertoire sometimes appears to revolve around 20 to 30 dishes – wherever you are in France: *terrine, jambon, truite, escalope, côte de veau, entrecôte, gigot, côte d'agneau, poulet* and so on. Rarely do you see a *navarin* or a *blanquette*; these are costly to prepare and must be thrown away if not ordered. Often the more enjoyable alternative is to picnic; then you have the chance to try the appetising alternatives (often authentic regional dishes) of the *pâtissier, boulanger* and *charcutier*. Take a portable cold box to keep food cool.

Cheeses

Within each region I have listed most of its cheeses; the best-known varieties appear on menus throughout the country. They are made from the milk of cows (*vaches*), goats (*chèvres*) or ewes (*brebis*). Try all types and don't be prejudiced about cheeses. In any restaurant follow a good French custom of selecting small portions of several varieties (ask for *une bouchée*, a mouthful, or *une petite tranche*, a small slice). Make waiters identify every cheese. Eat the mildest, freshest cheeses first, the strongest last. Soft cheeses should be soft and creamy (not runny) and if they smell of ammonia, they are off. Blue cheese that is crumbling is unacceptable. The right season for the best cheese will depend on when the cows are put out to pasture and how long it takes to make the cheese. Wherever possible, I indicate the best season. For more detail buy Patrick Rance's *The French Cheese Book*, a superb work published by Macmillan (H/B 1988; P/B 1991).

I repeat: don't be prejudiced. Tuck into French cheeses, described by Prince Charles as "gloriously unhygienic" in his stirring attack against the EC's "bacteriological police".

Map showing main wine-producing areas

Your appreciation and enjoyment of French wines will be greatly enhanced if you understand some basic bits of knowledge.

Grape types and soil

One wine will differ from another because it has been made from a different variety of grape. Through hundreds of years of selection and development, each region has its own best single or group of grape varieties. Red Burgundy is made of one grape type, the Pinot Noir. The best white Burgundy is made from the Chardonnay grape (the second rank Burgundy white grape is the Aligoté). Red Bordeaux can come from a variety of grape types: among them the Cabernet Sauvignon grape, the Cabernet Franc grape, the Merlot and the Malbec. Cabernets give wine which matures later; Merlot is ideal for quick-developing wine. Blending allows wines to be produced which provide either characteristic: clearly, when long-lasting potential is wanted (particularly for the great Médoc wines), the Cabernet vines predominate; in Saint Emilion the Merlot is widely used.

You should recognise some of the important grape types: the two kinds of Cabernet, Gamay and Pinot Noir (red wine grapes); Riesling, Sauvignon Blanc, Sémillon, Chardonnay, Muscat and Gewürztraminer (Traminer) – six white wine grapes. I refer to these ten, plus several others, throughout the regions.

In some regions you will see a few wines described by their grape type name. These are *varietal* wines: Gamay (the Beaujolais grape) will appear in Savoie, in the Ardèche and elsewhere; Chardonnay will be seen in the Lyonnais, in Champagne country and in obscure wine areas like Poitou. All the wines of Alsace take their names from the grape type used.

Apart from the differing grape vines, the type of soil in which they are grown plays the major part in determining the quality and status of French wines (climate plays another important part). That is why in Burgundy there are so many differing AC classifications; soil can vary from one acre to the next. That's the reason, too, why Gamay and other varietal wines can vary so much from one part of France to another.

The main classifications
In every region I list the local wines. Most are AC (or AOC: *Appellation d'Origine Contrôlée*) or VDQS (*Vin Délimité de Qualité Supérieure*) wines. These classifications are clearly identified on bottle labels – the AC is shown as *Appellation Contrôlée* – and they mean that the authenticity of each wine is guaranteed by the French Government; in addition, the AC or VDQS identifies each wine to its precise birthplace. There are many hundreds of wines with the AC and VDQS guarantee and all but one or two of them are mentioned within the pages of this book. To win these classifications each wine must match its pedigree: specific area, specific grape type or types, maximum yield per acre, minimum alcohol content and so on. Liken the AC wines to soccer clubs in the Premier League and First Division (they can vary from the very best of the premier clubs to the worst teams in the First Division). The VDQS wines are the next division down; and, believe me, a few of these lower division wines, on their home grounds, are perfectly capable of soundly beating some of their big brothers.

Identifying the wines of France
I have tried to make it as simple as possible for you to identify all the wines of France. You may be in a French restaurant (**or anywhere else in the world**) with a wine list in your hand, or, you may be back home, wanting perhaps to locate a specific wine before buying it. **Use the index at the back of the guide**; this lists hundreds of wines (page 468). The list includes all the AC and VDQS wines of France, together with most of the more common *Vins de Pays* (explained later). It also includes many of the important village names which, themselves, take the AC or VDQS classification of the region (this is particularly true in the south). Throughout France you can often be confused by this method of description. Reference to many of the starred restaurants in the Michelin guide will illustrate what I mean: do you know **Bruley, Bué, Mareuil** or **Taradeau** wines?

In the regional texts on wines all these hundreds of varieties have been shown in **bold** print; so, whenever you see a label name on a wine list, it will be easy for you to quickly indentify it and to find its birthplace on the regional map.

How does the Appellation Contrôlée system work?
Let us consider Beaujolais wines as a way of explaining the AC system; the same logic applies in the other wine-making areas of France. Beaujolais is an area north of Lyon and south of Mâcon, on the west side of the River Saône (see page 220). From the Beaujolais hills come fresh, fruity, light red wines, all made from the Gamay grape. If you see a bottle with an **Appellation Beaujolais Contrôlée** label, the wine could have originated in any part of the area. It will be a *generic* wine, both cheaper and of a lesser quality than the following wines.

If the label states **AC Beaujolais Villages**, the wine will have been made in one of the three dozen or so villages in the north of the region which have not yet earned their own AC status. The wine will usually be superior to the previous one.

If the words say **AC Brouilly**, the wine will have come from the *commune* of Brouilly itself (one of the nine Beaujolais villages which have their own AC classification); if the wine has originated from the hillsides of Mont Brouilly, the label would say **AC Côte de Brouilly**, the tenth individual AC of the area. Often the best vineyards are on the *côtes* (sides). Finally, if the label has the addition of **Château Thivin** to the words **AC Côte de Brouilly**, this will be wine from the best estate on the *mont*. Generally speaking, the larger the geographic area described on the label, the cheaper and less superior the wine will be.

VDQS wines

There are plenty of other good wines in France without the AC classification which are just as appealing and enjoyable and less expensive. The main category below AC is VDQS, made by producers who are working hard to earn their own AC status. Among many examples are the **Haut-Poitou**, various **Vins de Bugey** and **Sauvignon de St-Bris** wines.

Vins de Pays and Vins de Table

Below the VDQS classification are *Vins de Pays* (liken them to the bottom division of football clubs) scattered throughout the country. These meet strict French Government controls: the labels specify precisely from which *département* or, in some cases, from which tiny area they come; and the wines must be made from the grape varieties designated by Government order. They must meet minimum alcohol levels (not less than 10 per cent in the south; 9 or 9.5 per cent elsewhere). There are some one hundred or so *Vins de Pays* classifications throughout France, over half of them in the *départements* of Aude, Hérault, Gard and Pyrénées-Orientales (Languedoc-Roussillon). I have tried to identify and locate the most common ones.

Vins de Table is the lowest category of all; your non-league wines or your supermarket plonk. Some of them, bottled by the best producers, like Listel, are really good; but most are rubbish. Many of these wines, grown in the vast vineyards of the Midi, are blended with Italian wine (France buys huge quantities), or are turned into alcohol, or are poured into the bottomless wine lake financed by the CAP, from taxes conned out of taxpayers.

What to order

Whatever the restaurant, always order local or regional wines. If you explore each region in the way this guide suggests, it will follow, without fail, that you will gain some basic idea of where the main wine-producing areas are situated, the villages within them, and the varying types of wine coming from the local vineyards. It is not imperative to order a wallet-breaking bottle of the very finest Burgundy or Bordeaux vintages when you eat at any of the great restaurants. Alsace, Loire, Lyonnais, Savoie, Provence, the Southwest and the Côte d'Azur have their own marvellous local wines and the best of these are on the wine lists of all the best restaurants in each of those regions. It is significant that, during the last decade, many restaurants have been doing far more to promote the unknown, local wines; with the high prices being asked world-wide for Burgundy and Bordeaux vintages this promotional effort was inevitable.

At the best restaurants take the advice of the *sommelier*. Look for their small lapel badge (a bunch of grapes); they have worked and studied hard to acquire their knowledge of wines.

Essential terms you should understand are: **brut** very dry; **sec** dry (Champagne, medium sweet); **demi-sec** medium sweet; **doux** or **moelleux** sweet; **mousseux** sparkling; **crémant** a little less sparkle; **pétillant** a slight sparkle; **perlant** (**perlé**) a few bubbles; **cru** growth, as in first growth, meaning vineyard status; **blanc de blancs** any white wine made exclusively from white grapes, rather than white and red. (Also read page 480.)

Who's who in French cuisine

Jean-Anthelme Brillat-Savarin (1755–1826) Born at Belley (see Lyonnais), he was the greatest of all French gastronomes. A lawyer by profession, a linguist, an inventor and violinist; and a do-it-yourself publisher. His book *La Physiologie du gout* (published by Penguin as *The Philosopher in the Kitchen*) had a profound influence on gastronomic thinking.

Antonin Carême (1784–1833) Some claim he was the greatest cook of all time. By the end of the 18th century, during the French Revolution, *la haute* or *la grande cuisine* had ground to a halt. Carême, more than any other chef, through his writings and his genius for creating sauces, took classical cuisine to new levels of excellence and excess. He came from the poorest of families, one of 25 children. The first "superstar" chef.

Auguste Escoffier (1846–1935) Became known as "the king of chefs and the chef of kings". Born at Villeneuve-Loubet (near Nice), he worked for over 40 years in various kitchens, mainly in London; he was one of the founders of the Savoy Hotel. Through his books and creative talent he did much to simplify and record classical recipes; all modern masters admit that they owe much to the principles laid down by Escoffier.

Les Mères Arguably the Lyonnais has more first-class chefs than any other region of France. This priceless legacy was conceived over 200 years ago by a series of talented, skilled women. For further details see the Lyonnais introduction.

Fernand Point (1899–1956) The father of *cuisine moderne* and the first to sense, 60 years ago, that eating habits were changing. He built his menus each day around his purchases at the market; he began the move towards lightness and simplicity. Another contribution to the new ways was his training of Bocuse, Vergé, the Troisgros brothers and others.

Alexandre Dumaine A simple man who won a world-wide reputation. He retired in 1963 after working 50 years in kitchens, 30 of them at his Hôtel de la Côte-d'Or in Saulieu (Burgundy). He, too, trained many of today's famous chefs.

Paul Bocuse The modern-day "Emperor of Chefs". Described by one foodie scribbler as "the occasional cook and gastrobiz celebrity". Won his first Michelin star in 1961, his third in 1965; a record. Said to have been the greatest advocate of *cuisine moderne*, though that hardly applies today. The family *auberge*, near Lyon, started life in 1765; Paul Bocuse is the seventh generation to carry on the tradition.

Michel Guérard One of the greatest of the modern innovators. The inventor of *cuisine minceur*, his rejuvenation, as a chef and man, came 20 years ago when he married Christine Barthélémy and moved to her family's thermal resort hotel at Eugénie-les-Bains in Gascony.

Frédy Girardet Towers head and shoulders above the other modern greats. A brilliant Swiss chef, a talented restaurateur (which cannot be said of all chefs), an inspiring leader and a loyal family man; he stays at home in his kitchens and, despite not having the guarantee to fame that a three-star Michelin rating brings, he is considered by other chefs, critics and sceptics to be the world's greatest "French" chef.

Joël Robuchon In the early Eighties Gault Millau were slow to recognise his genius. By the Nineties he was one of their three *cuisiniers du siècle* (with Bocuse and Girardet). The epitome of what a Michelin three-star chef ought to be.

Michel Bras Like Robuchon an extraordinary innovator. His rise to fame at Laguiole (see Massif Central) has been a culinary miracle. Bras will become the superstar chef of the Nineties.

Santé Bibendum!

My admiration for Michelin's guides and maps is stronger than ever. For 25 years, prior to 1980, I had studied, used and relied on their products for our annual holidays. In the last 13 years, as I've beetled away producing my own series of guides, I've discovered, first-hand, the trials and tribulations of what is needed to produce and publish guide books and to compile accurate maps.

Monsieur Bibendum's guides and maps set the standards of clarity and information by which all others are judged. That's not to say that everything is perfect; we are all fallible. Later, I have some constructive comments to make on Michelin's inspection methods for the red guides, the most famous of their products. First, readers may like to know a bit more about the tyre company's illustrious history and how the "Tourism" division came into being. In addition I'll also explain their inspectorate's *modus operandi*.

The company
Robert William Thomson, a Scotsman, invented the pneumatic tyre in 1845; another Scot, John Boyd Dunlop, found a way, in 1888, of glueing a rubber tube onto a solid tyre and then applying it to a tricycle. But it was left to the Michelin brothers, André (1853-1931) and Edouard (1859-1940), to mastermind a method of making the invention practical: they combined a tyre with an inner tube which could be pushed on and off a rim without the dirty and exceptionally time-consuming business of glueing and drying.

The fledgling company started life at Clermont-Ferrand (Auvergne) in 1889. Michelin's first patent for a removable tyre was filed two years later. It proved difficult at first to persuade the cycling public to accept the principle of "floating" along on air even though a Michelin-tyred bike beat all 200-odd competitors in the Paris-Brest-Paris race that year. But the relative ease of overcoming punctures soon became apparent to even the most pessimistic doubters.

Apart from his business nose, André also had a flair for public relations. He commissioned the brilliant posters, designed by the artist O'Galop, for which the company became renowned in its early years. In 1894, after seeing a pile of different-sized tyres lying haphazardly on top of each other at a fair in Lyon, André conceived "Bibendum".

The first poster designed for the roly-poly tyre man was a masterpiece of advertising subtlety. "Bibendum" loomed over a table at an imaginary feast, holding an oversized goblet overflowing with all the nasty, jagged metalware which made punctures an everyday nightmare in those early motoring days (nails from horseshoes were the main hazard). Below him cowed two deflated competitors. Michelin man was pictured making a taunting Latin toast: *"Nunc est bibendum!!"* ("Now is the time to drink!!") The message conveyed in that superlative 1898 poster proved to be an inspired advertising success.

Services de Tourisme
There was a third streak of genius in André's makeup. In 1900 he wrote these words in the foreword of the first Michelin red guide: "This guide appears with the new century; it will last as long as the century." And: "Motoring is in its infancy; it will develop each year as will the tyre, for the tyre is an essential part without which the car cannot run." Despite those visionary words even he could never have envisaged how vast

Michelin's *Services de Tourisme* would become.

The 1900 guide was solely a promotional exercise, full of adverts and fatherly homilies. Today, 92 years on, Michelin's red guides are still faithful in numerous ways to the original. Some of the symbols can be traced back to the first guide and the system still works like a reliable Swiss timepiece. But one caveat: to extract the most rewarding dividends from any red guide, it is imperative you spend an hour or so swotting up the few pages of explanatory English text if you want to crack the shorthand symbols' code.

The France red guide is one of several similar versions, all of which use the same system of 150 or so symbols and aids. In 1989 colour was introduced for the first time for the French guide; last year the British edition got the same treatment. Another recent and invaluable introduction to the French guide has been scores of "local" maps which show all recommended hotels and restaurants within a 30-minute drive of 89 selected cities and towns. This new innovation is very useful indeed.

The hotel and restaurant guides, together with the invaluable *Camping Caravaning France* Guide, are only part of Services de Tourisme sales. More than 50 touring "Green Guides", from a total of over 70 alternatives published in various languages, are available in UK and US bookshops. They cover nations as far apart as Austria and Mexico, cities like Paris, London and New York, and regions as different as Brittany, New England and Scotland. Among the most recently published are: Euro Disney; Ireland; and Great Britain.

The touring guides started in 1901 when Michelin published a booklet giving details of what to see in Clermont-Ferrand and its environs. The modern-day green guides (the colour format appeared for the first time in 1939) are further evidence of Michelin's thoroughness and professionalism.

Last but not least is the superb range of Michelin maps, now numbering well over 100.

André published the company's first map in 1906 and, by the start of World War I, 47 had been introduced, covering all France. He was the inventor of the "accordion" fold.

Five years ago Michelin introduced a hardback *Road Atlas of France* and a paperback *Motoring Atlas France*. Two years later a spiral-bound paperback version appeared.

Michelin stars

The red guides are renowned for their "stars", awarded to chefs for culinary prowess. The word "star" is always used now, even by Michelin, although in 1926, when André introduced the one-star accolade for the first time, the symbol was meant to be a flower (*marguerite*: white daisy).

When the Michelin three-star award was first introduced in 1931, the criterion for success was simple: "One of the best tables in France; worth a special journey." Six decades later the requirements are more demanding: "Exceptional cuisine, worth a special journey. Superb food, fine wines, faultless service, elegant surroundings. One will pay accordingly!"

Those additional criteria cover aspects which have nothing to do with cooking skills. In the Thirties the consequences of Michelin's pragmatism was that a *cuisinière* genius, Marie Bourgeois, won three stars at a seedy-looking, down-at-heel *auberge* in Priay, north-east of Lyon. Wild flowers graced her tables; the wines amounted to a few regional vintages; service was provided by her husband and a couple of local ladies; the dining room was simplicity itself; and the bill, by any standards, was exceptionally modest.

Today, Marie, however superb her cooking talents, would have to engage a huge *équipe* of skilled staff, spend a fortune on her "cellar" and invest heavily in the "elegant" trappings of the modern age. Winning a third star is arguably a gateway to fame and fortune. Alas, the accolade seems also to guarantee that most three-star restaurants rapidly become soulless vacuums of idiotic snobbery.

Michelin's inspectorate

Those of you who bought *French Leave 3* in the mid Eighties will remember my oft-repeated warnings, made about dozens of starred restaurants, that Michelin's ratings, in France, had become more than a little unreliable.

At the beginning of 1986 Michelin's long-established French editor, André Trichot, retired, to be replaced by the younger Bernard Naegellen. He has a taste for blood. From 1987 onwards the Ides of March, when Michelin France is published, have been notable for the numerous blades stuck into the backs of France's starred chefs. The carnage has been particularly savage at one-star level, where over a third of chefs have seen their accolades hacked away. In 1991 the number of one-star chefs fell to an all-time low of 495. Yet despite the on-going blood-letting at both one and two-star levels (10% of both categories got the chop in 1992), Michelin's three-star chefs appear to wear knife-proof vests. Why?

Michelin's "inspection" operation is staggering. In France the company employs about 20 full-time, professionally trained inspectors; in the UK there are nine, two of them women. I estimate an inspector's full overhead cost amounts to at least £45,000 a year and that more than 200 overnight hotel and 400 restaurant bills are paid for every year by each inspector.

Let me now give you, in note form, some "insider" clues to various facets of Michelin's *modus operandi*, many of which are grossly misunderstood by foodie scribblers around the world.

When chefs change their premises and take existing staff to new kitchens then stars move with them. I can give you a score of examples (Michel Bras is the latest). It is nonsense to claim that this merits some sort of special treatment.

One important tip about Michelin red guides is to understand the significance of the *couvert* (knife and fork) symbol, the one used for restaurants. You would think that this requires the *cuisinier* to be put on trial at least once every year. True in the UK but most definitely not so in France. (Over the years I've talked to scores of chefs about "inspections".) However, if a chef is being considered for a star, additional stars or a demotion, then many, many visits are made in the year before the crucial decision is made.

Hotel entries are categorised by a series of *pavillon* (tent) symbols. But do not assume that an inspector has eaten in the establishment's dining room. My guess is that only a nominal number of hotel dining rooms are put to the test. The result is that far too many hotel dining rooms are disaster areas. On the other hand, some, without any Michelin culinary accolade, do have highly competent chefs and their dining rooms are well worth a visit; they should be highlighted with a separate *couvert* entry (which is the norm for large cities). This failure to identify the better hotel dining rooms is by far the most serious flaw in the Michelin system.

Michelin's Aladdin's Cave

I would like to bring to your attention, in a little more detail, some of Michelin's magical mix of mapoholic gems .

I've already referred to the famous red guides, published annually. So is the brilliantly practical *Camping Caravaning France*; this fits the bill perfectly for those readers who have asked me to provide details of nearby camping sites for my restaurant and hotel dining room recommendations.

Over 30 "green guides" are available in English. Ten are for French regions. One of the newest is a 320-page version for France itself . Like the other "new" editions, the combination of text with colour illustrations and maps is superb.

I wonder how many of you are aware that Michelin now publish a range of "I-Spy" books for children? The range of subjects is wide: from creepy crawlies to cars. One is a *Mini-Atlas* for France, so good it would suffice for adults.

Of the huge range of maps there are several series and individual maps which you should know about. You will already know of the "detailed maps", the famed "yellows", numbered 51 to 90, which cover all France in 40 sheets (1 cm to 2 km). But have you seen 171 (replaces 71): *La Rochelle / Bordeaux*?

The front of 171 retains the same format as 71; the reverse is an identical, lighter-shaded version but is overprinted with particulars of sports, leisure and tourist facilities and details scores of useful local phone numbers. Further examples have recently been published: 166 (66); 170 (70); 189 (89) .

There are 17 "regional maps" of France, numbers 230 to 246; these have the same scale as the "detailed" versions. They are more expensive but cover, on average, the same terrain as three of the cheaper maps. I do strongly recommend two "green" maps with a scale of 1 cm to 1 km: No 106, *Environs of Paris*; and No 115, *Côte d'Azur*. Michelin also publish a couple of specials: *Les Chemins du Roy Soleil* (The Treasure Houses of the Sun King), based on the Environs of Paris map but with photographs and other tourist details; and *La Vallée des Rois* (The Valley of the Kings), Loire territory and based on three of the 200 series maps (also with colour photos) .

Of the eight main road maps of France, 989 (with red cover and 1 cm to 10 km) and 911 (showing all the *bison futé* bypass routes) are the most useful . I've already mentioned the France atlases published for the first time five years ago (same scale as all yellow maps: 1 cm to 2 km). There are also atlases for Europe and the British Isles and Ireland.

What else? There are maps of the world, of Africa, of Europe, of the British Isles and Ireland and most European countries. There are "golf" maps: France (199), Germany, Austria & Benelux (197) and Ireland (198), which show the location of many courses . There's a 300-page gazeteer which lists the names of every *commune* in France, together with its postcode and grid reference on the 40 "detailed maps".

There are a dozen atlases and "plans" for Paris and Lyon: I find No 11 (*Paris Atlas*), in pocket size format, especially useful . One treasure, now almost sold out, so move fast, is the reprint of a 1947 map (1 cm to 2 km), numbered 102 (582); published in 1984, the 40th anniversary of D-Day, this tells the story of the *Battle of Normandy* in an innovative way.

All in all, Michelin is one of the four cornerstones of French touring. The other three? France's man-made treasures; its varied scenic delights; and the nation's myriad culinary treats. Each one of the four is indispensable. Agreed?

Specimen Letters of Reservation & Useful Phrases

To reserve bedrooms; options on right (in brackets)

1 Would you please reserve a room	(2 rooms, etc.,)
2 with a double bed	(with 2 single beds) (one room with) (each room)
3 and bathroom/WC	(and shower/WC)
4 for one night	(2 nights, etc.,)
5 *(indicate day, date, month)*	
6	(We would like *pension* (half-*pension*) terms for our stay)
7 Please confirm the reservation as soon as possible and please indicate the cost of the rooms	(your *pension* terms for each person)
8 An International Reply Coupon is enclosed	
9 Yours faithfully	
1 Pouvez-vous, s'il vous plaît, me réserver une chambre	**(2 chambres, etc.,)**
2 avec un lit à 2 places	**(avec 2 lits à une place) (une chambre avec) (chaque chambre)**
3 avec salle de bains/WC	**(et douche/WC)**
4 Pour une nuit	**(2 nuits, etc.,)**
5 le *(indicate day, date, month)*	
6	**(Nous voudrions pension complète (demi-pension) pour notre séjour)**
7 Veuillez confirmer la réservation des que possible, et indiquer le tarif des chambres	**(le tarif de pension par personne)**
8 Ci-joint un coupon-réponse international	
9 Je vous prie, Monsieur, d'accepter l'expression de mes salutations distinguées	

If appropriate: Can I have a room/table overlooking the water
Puis-je avoir une chambre/une table qui donne sur l'eau

To reserve tables; options (in brackets)
Would you please reserve a table for __ persons for lunch (dinner) on *(indicate day, date, month)*. We will arrive at the restaurant at *(use 24 hour clock)* hours. (We would like a table on the terrace.) Please confirm the reservation. An International Reply Coupon is enclosed. Yours faithfully
Pouvez-vous me réserver une table pour __ personnes pour déjeuner (dîner) le. Nous arriverons au restaurant à heures. (Nous aimerons une table sur la terrasse.) Veuillez confirmer la réservation. Ci-joint un coupon-réponse international. Je vous prie etc., (see 9 above)

Useful general phrases
Can I have **Puis-je avoir** Can we have **Pouvons-nous avoir** an (extra) pillow (**encore**) **un oreiller** a blanket **une couveture** a towel **une serviette** some soap **du savon** heating **le chauffage** a laundry service **une blanchisserie** some hot (cold) milk **du lait chaud (froid)** a plate **une assiette** a knife **un couteau** a fork **une fourchette** a spoon **une cuiller** a bottle of **une bouteille de** a half-bottle of **une demi-bouteille de** the wine list **la carte des vins** a glass **une verre**
Get a doctor. **Appelez un médicin**
Fill the tank up (fuel). **Faites le plein** Check the oil. **Vérifiez l'huile** May I park here? **Puis-je me garer ici?**

28

Useful phrases at the hotel
Can I have **Puis-je avoir** Can we have **Pouvons-nous avoir**
I would like **Je voudrais** We would like **Nous voudrions**
May I see the room? **Puis-je voir la chambre?**
No, I don't like it. **Non, elle ne me plaît pas**
What's the price? **Quel est le prix?**
Do you have anything...? **Avez-vous quelque chose...?**
    better **de mieux**; bigger **de plus grand**;
    quieter **de plus tranquille**; cheaper **de moins cher**
Haven't you anything cheaper please? **N'avez-vous rien de moins cher, s'il vous plaît?**
Fine, I'll take it. **D'accord, je la prends**
What is the price for full board (half-board)? **Quel est le prix pour la pension complète (demi-pension)?**
I would like a quiet room, please. **Je voudrais une chambre tranquille, s'il vous plaît**
Can we have breakfast in our room? **Pouvons-nous prendre le petit déjeuner dans la chambre?**
Please telephone this hotel/restaurant and reserve a room/a table for me. **Pouvez-vous, s'il vous plaît, téléphoner a cet hôtel/ce restaurant et me réserver une chambre/une table**
Would you recommend the best local *pâtissier/charcutier/*baker? **Pouvez-vous me recommander le meilleur pâtissier/charcutier/boulanger du coin?**

Useful phrases in the restaurant
Can I have **Puis-je avoir** Can we have **Pouvons-nous avoir**
I would like **Je voudrais** We would like **Nous voudrions**
Could we please have **Pouvons-nous avoir, s'il vous plaît**
We would like to have a look at the fixed-price menu, please. **Nous voudrions voir le menu à prix-fixe, s'il vous plaît**
What's this? **Qu'est-ce que c'est que ça?**
Would you please recommend your regional specialities? **Pourriez-vous nous recommander les spécialités de la région, s'il vous plaît?**
We would like to share this speciality between us, please. **Nous aimerions partager cette spécialité entre nous, s.v.p.**
May we change this speciality for another one? **Est-ce que nous pouvons changer cette spécialité pour une autre?**
Which local wines would you recommend that we try? **Quels vins du pays nous recommanderiez-vous d'essayer?**
Please do not serve us big portions. **Ne vous servez pas de trop grosses portions, s'il vous plaît**
That is not what I ordered. I asked for... **Ce n'est pas ce que j'ai commandé. J'ai demandé...**
rare **saignant**; medium-done **à point**; well-done **bien cuit**
Could you please bring another plate, please? **Pourriez-vous apporter une autre assiette, s'il vous plaît**
Would you please identify your local cheeses? **Pouvez-vous nous donner les noms de vos fromages du coin, s.v.p?**
May we have decaffeinated coffee, please? **Pouvons-nous avoir du café décaféiné, s'il vous plaît**
May we please see your kitchens after our meal? **Serait-il possible de visiter les cuisines après le repas, s.v.p?**
May we please see your wine cellar after our meal? **Serait-il possible de visiter la cave après le repas, s'il vous plaît?**
Would you give us the address of your wine merchant? **Pourriez-vous nous donner l'adresse de votre marchand de vins?**
Would you give us the name of your cheese supplier? **Pourriez-vous nous donner le nom de votre fournisseur en fromages?**

ALSACE

Legend:
- Autoroute hotel
- Base hotel
- ▲ Hotel/Rest (rooms)
- △ Restaurant only

0   10   20 Miles

Contz
Sierck
A30
Vin de Moselle
A4   A32
Metz   **St-Avold**
A31
Sarre-Union
Côtes de Toul
A4   **Brumath**
Nancy
N4   **Marlenheim**   **Strasbourg**
Carré-de-l'Est
Ottrott-le-Haut   Obernai
N420   N83
A31   N57   Rhin
Contrexéville   Moselle
Vittel
Epinal△   ALLEMAGNE
see page 92
Bains-les-Bains
D417
Plombières   Murbach
Fougerolles   Grand
Luxeuil   Ballon d'Alsace   Ballon
Ronchamp   A36   A35   **Mulhouse**
Port-sur-Saône
N19   BALE
Vesoul   Sochaux   **Belfort**   SUISSE
Saône   ▼ see page 162

N59   St-Dié
Haut-Koenigsbourg   △**Sélestat**
Vosges   △
Baldenheim
N415   Ribeauvillé ○
Riquewihr■   **Illhaeusern** ■
△**Mittelwihr**
■**Kaysersberg**
Gérômé   **Lapoutroie** ▲   **Artzenheim**
▲**Orbey**   **Colmar** ▲
Ammerschwihr ▲
Crêtes   **Les Trois-Epis** ▲   Wintzenheim
Gérardmer   Le Linge   ○
Hohneck   Munster   **Eguisheim**   **Herrlisheim**
▲**Bas-Rupts**   ▲**Muhlbach**   N83   A35
Route des
▲**La Bresse**   N415

30

I'll start the first of my extended regional introductions by explaining that the area names I've used are very much my own choice. I haven't slavishly followed the "official" tourist office definitions of the country's regions. I think my versions make more sense for the tourist.

I've called this first regional chapter "Alsace". Normally the official label is Alsace and Lorraine. I've only included part of Lorraine, the countryside to the east of the River **Moselle**. The western half of Lorraine, the Meuse Valley, is incorporated in the chapter entitled Champagne-Ardenne.

Alsace appeals throughout the year. I've spent happy days there during each of the four seasons. I'm always pleased to absorb the man-made elixirs of the famed wine villages, hemmed in between the **Rhine** and the **Vosges**, a long line of high, dark peaks which run, spine-like, from north to south. And I've always been more than willing to escape the hordes of tourists milling around the wine villages and head west to the woods, streams and lakes of the refreshing Vosges mountains.

For example, December is a month when I would be more than content to return to **Kaysersberg**. The small town, birthplace of Albert Schweitzer, is the home of the most endearing Christmas market in France. Every Friday, Saturday and Sunday during the four weekends prior to Christmas (11 a.m. to 8 p.m.) Kaysersberg buzzes and sparkles.

The "buzz" comes from the carefully selected 28 stalls, dotted among the narrow cobbled streets and courtyards, where hand-made, quality products, most locally produced and all associated with Christmas in Alsace, are on sale.

The "sparkle" comes free, every evening throughout the period. Almost every window, balcony and tower in the town is garlanded with traditional festive decorations and lights. The townspeople make an enormous effort; not just with the authentic decorations but also in organising an exhibition based on a Christmas theme and in laying on a varied programme of concerts and *animations*, both musical and cultural.

The long procession of exceedingly prosperous wine villages on the Route des Vins d'Alsace (my favourites are **Obernai**, **Riquewihr**, Kaysersberg and **Eguisheim**) are at their best, and quietest, during the winter months.

Two wine *viticulteurs* are worth nosing out: Colette Faller at Kaysersberg – her *vendanges tardives* vintages deserve their *cuvée exceptionelle* labels; and English-speaking Olivier Humbrecht at the Domaine Zind-Humbrecht at **Wintzenheim** – many consider his Alsace Grand Cru wines the region's best.

The high slopes of the Vosges offer plenty of opportunities for skiing. Try your hand at *ski de fond* (the cross-country variety) on the many trails near **Gérardmer**.

In spring numerous mountain streams are at their best and a large-scale map will help you to identify many small lakes and cascades. The extensive forests are mixed woods and the new greens of the broadleaved varieties are an eye-pleasing pleasure. Equally colourful are the pastures of wild daffodils found in a rough 10 km circle around Gérardmer.

Summer brings swarms of tourist bees to the wine *villages fleuris*. This is the time to drive the **Route des Crêtes**, a north-south mountain run along the ridge of Vosges peaks. Two summits offer panoramic viewpoints: **Hohneck** and **Grand Ballon**. South-east of the latter is the First World War Memorial at Vieil Armand. Another renowned viewpoint is the **Ballon d'Alsace**, above the Col du Ballon.

The Vosges is a walkers' paradise. Energetic visitors can hire mountain bikes, lap up the watersport facilities on the Gérardmer lake or play golf on a course at **Ammerschwihr**.

Autumn is a benevolent season. This is the best time to explore the northern Vosges: seek out the unique 50-yard high boat and barge lift (*Plan incliné* on maps) near Lutzelbourg, built in 1969 to replace 17 canal locks; and the St-Léon chapel at Dabo, perched atop a rocky cone and accessed by a corkscrew road (both north-west of **Marlenheim**).

Seek out, too, the gentler pace of the spas to the west: **Vittel**, among the most famous of watering holes; busier **Luxeuil**; and the smaller resorts of **Contrexéville**, **Bains-les-Bains** and **Plombières**. Don't fret if you bypass the climb to the Colline Inspirée (north of Vittel), the site of Barrès' novel *La Colline inspirée*.

Drive the forest roads (RF) to the south-east of Gérardmer; relish the trees, the views and the unspoilt lakes of Longemer and Rétournemer. The roads between **Munster** and **Orbey** are especially colourful, particularly around **Le Linge**.

The latter is a football pitch-sized hilltop where, in 1915, 17,000 French and German soldiers lost their lives. The opposing trenches have been left as they were, rusty barbed wire and all. A small museum tells the story of the massacre: some of the finds unearthed from the site are chilling; others are both morbid and poignant human effects.

There are scores of man-made sites that compete for your attention. If you can stand the effort needed to drive into **Strasbourg** and **Nancy** then marvel at the former's glorious cathedral and both the old town and La Petite France (contained within two arms of the River Ill), and the latter's majestic Place Stanislas and Palais Ducal. **Colmar** is full of timber houses from the 16th century; the Maison Pfister is said to be the most beautiful in the world.

Other man-made sites are more easily reached: **Murbach** church; the perched castle at **Haut-Koenigsbourg**, restored in 1900 by Kaiser Bill; and Le Corbusier's controversial modern church with its concave roof at **Ronchamp**, north-west of **Belfort**. No other region in France is so endowed with such a variety of museums. Four are great personal favourites: the Musée National de l'Automobile (containing the Schlumpf collection) and Musée Français du Chemin de Fer at **Mulhouse**; the Musée Peugeot at **Sochaux** (a minute away from the A36 south of Belfort); and the Musée d'Unterlinden, with its lovely treasures, in Colmar.

Markets Colmar (Thurs and Sat); Epinal (Wed and Sat); Gérardmer (Thurs and Sat); Munster (Tues and Sat); Strasbourg (Tues, Wed, Fri and Sat); Vittel (Wed and Sat). Michelin green guide: Alsace et Lorraine.

Cheeses Cow's milk

Carré-de-l'Est soft, edible white rind, made in a small square; milder than Camembert. Bland taste. Available all year

Gérardmer same cheese as Gérômé, alternative name

Gérômé soft, gold-coloured cheese, a little more solid than Munster, often covered with fennel or caraway. Made as a thick disk. Spicy taste and at its best in summer and autumn. Good with full-bodied red wines

Munster soft, gold-coloured, stronger taste than Gérômé, made as a small disk. Munster *laitier* (made by commercial dairies) available all year; *fermier* (made by farms) at its best in summer and autumn. Try them with Traminer wines. Munster *au cumin* (with caraway seeds)

Regional Specialities

Beckenoffe (Baeckeoffe) (Baeckaoffa) "baker's oven"; a stew, or hotpot, of potatoes, lamb, beef, pork and onions, cooked in a local wine
Choucroute garnie sauerkraut with peppercorns, boiled ham, pork, Strasbourg sausages and boiled potatoes. Try it with a beer (*bière*)
Chou farci stuffed cabbage
Flammekueche (Tarte flambée) bacon, onion and cream tart
Foie gras goose liver
Kougelhopf a round brioche with raisins and almonds
Krapfen fritters stuffed with jam
Lewerknepfle (Leber Knödel) liver dumpling (pork liver dumpling)
Matelote Alsacienne in Alsace made with stewed eels (in the past from the River Ill) – sometimes with freshwater fish
Pflutters Alsacienne potato puffs
Potage Lorraine potato, leek and onion soup
Schifela shoulder of pork with turnips
Tarte (aux mirabelles) golden plum tart. Also with other fruits
Tarte à l'oignon Alsacienne onion and cream tart

Wines (Great vintages: **83 85 88 90**)
Until recently there was a single Appellation Contrôlée (AC) for the region, **AC Alsace** (or **Vin d'Alsace**). In October 1975 an additional AC was announced, **AC Alsace Grand Cru**; these are the wines from the best vineyards.

The wines of Alsace take their names from the type of grapevine; followed by the village or wine producer's name.

    AC Alsace – Traminer d'Ammerschwihr (village name)
    AC Alsace Grand Cru – Riesling Hugel (producer's name)

Some restaurants will identify the best wines to their precise birthplace by indicating vineyard names: examples are **Kaefferkopf** (south of Ammerschwihr); **Schoenenbourg** (near Riquewihr); **Schlossberg** (east of Kaysersberg).

Almost all the wines are white but some are pink or light red. They are dry, fresh and fruity. Some are dessert wines (*vendanges tardives*: late harvested). The grape types are:

    Riesling for dry white wine
    Gewürztraminer (Traminer for short) dry white wine, with a spicy scent and flavour
    Sylvaner a light, tart, workhorse grape for white wine
    Pinot Blanc or **Klevner** related to the Chardonnay grape, but not as good; a fresh, aromatic white wine
    Muscat dry, white wine and with a perfume fit for your handkerchief
    Tokay d'Alsace spicy, full-bodied white wine: also known as **Pinot Gris** and **Auxerrois**. Needs ageing
    Pinot Noir for rosés and light red, full-bodied wines
    Chasselas (Gutedel) inferior white grape

Wines with the **AC Vin d'Alsace – Edelzwicker** label are the most basic of Alsace wines, made from a mixture of grape types, usually Sylvaner and Pinot Blanc; these are fruity, light whites. Rarely seen is a white **Crémant d'Alsace**. Alsace wines are sold in distinctive green bottles, called *flûtes*.

For details of the VDQS **Côtes de Toul** and **Vin de Moselle** wines see the notes in Champagne-Ardenne.

Don't miss any of the Alsace brandies – called *eaux-de-vie*. These are colourless liqueurs distilled from fermented fruit juices: *kirsch* – cherry; *framboise* – raspberry; *prunelle* – sloe; *mirabelle* – golden plum; *quetsche* – purple plum; and *myrtille* – bilberry (blueberry). Look out for brightly-coloured fruit liqueurs; these are macerated – hence their lovely colours.

33

BELFORT   Campanile

Simple hotel/Cooking 1
Parking/Good value

Leave A36 Belfort Nord exit. Drive south from autoroute, use
bridge over D419; hotel on left, opposite Euromarché.
Menus A-B. Rooms (46) C. Disabled. Cards Access, Visa.
Post 90160 Bessoncourt, Ter.-de-Belfort. (En Route p 140)
Tel 84 29 94 42. Telex 361687. Fax 84 29 83 84. Mich 77/D2.
(Bookings: UK freephone 0800 897863)

BELFORT   Mercure

Very comfortable hotel/Cooking 1
Quiet/Terrace/Swimming pool/Lift/Parking

Leave A36 Belfort Sud/Danjoutin exit. Hotel to east of both
A36 autoroute and N19.
Menus B. Rooms (80) E-F. Disabled. Cards All.
Post 90400 Danjoutin, Ter.-de-Belfort. (En Route p 139)
Tel 84 57 88 88. Telex 360801. Fax 84 21 32 12. Mich 76/C2.
(Bookings: UK 071 724 1000; US toll free 800 221 4542)

COLMAR   Campanile

Simple hotel/Cooking 1
Parking/Good value

On N83, 2 km north of town (east side). South A35/N83 junc.
Menus A-B. Rooms (50) C. Disabled. Cards Access, Visa.
Post rue de Frères-Lumière, 68000 Colmar, H.-Rhin.
Tel 89 24 18 18. Telex 880867. Fax 89 24 26 73. Mich 61/D3.
(Bookings: UK freephone 0800 897863)

COLMAR   Novotel

Very comfortable hotel/Cooking 1
Terrace/Gardens/Swimming pool/Parking

On N83, 3km north of town (west side). South A35/N83 junc.
Menus B. Rooms (66) D-E. Cards All.
Post 68000 Colmar, H.-Rhin.
Tel 89 41 49 14. Telex 880915. Fax 89 41 22 56. Mich 61/D3.
(Bookings: UK 071 724 1000; US toll free 800 221 4542)

CONTREXEVILLE   Campanile

Simple hotel/Cooking 1
Quiet/Terrace/Parking/Good value

Leave A31 exit 9. 6 km towards Contrexéville (D164). By lake.
Menus A-B. Rooms (31) C. Disabled. Cards Access, Visa.
Post rte du Lac de la Folie, 88140 Contrexéville, Vosges.
Tel 29 08 03 72. Telex 960333. Mich 59/D3.
(Bookings: UK freephone 0800 897863)

METZ   La Bergerie

Comfortable hotel/Cooking 1-2
Secluded/Terrace/Gardens/Parking/Good value

Leave A4 Argancy exit (11 km north of Metz). Hotel 800m
north of A4, in Rugy (east of D1). Privately owned by Michel
and Michèle Keichinger. Part 16th-cent house. *Relais du
Silence*; not so silent when celebration parties held at hotel.
Menus B. Rooms (43) C-D. Cards Access, Visa.
Post Rugy, 57640 Argancy, Moselle. (En Route p 40)
Tel 87 77 82 27. Fax 87 77 87 07. Mich 24/B3.

METZ   Climat de France

Simple hotel/Cooking 1
Parking/Good value

Leave A31 (5 km north of A4) Talange exit. Hotel west of A31.
Menus A-B. Rooms (38) C. Disabled. Cards AE, Access, Visa.
Post rue des Alliés, 57300 Talange, Moscllc. (En Route p 127)
Tel 87 72 13 11. Telex 861731. Fax 87 70 22 85. Mich 24/B3.
(Bookings: UK 071 287 3181)

METZ   Mercure

Very comfortable hotel/Cooking 1
Terrace/Lift/Parking

Leave A31 (6 km south of A4) La Maxe exit. Hotel west of A31.
Menus B. Rooms (83) E-F. Disabled. Cards All.
Post Z.I. Metz Nord, 57140 Woippy, Moselle. (En Route p 128)
Tel 87 32 52 79. Telex 860891. Fax 87 32 73 11. Mich 24/B3.
(Bookings: UK 071 724 1000; US toll free 800 221 4542)

METZ   Novotel

Very comfortable hotel/Cooking 1
Terrace/Gardens/Swimming pool/Lift/Parking

A31 (2 km north of A4) Maizières-lès-Metz exit. Hotel to west.
Menus B. Rooms (132) D-E. Disabled. Cards All.
Post 57210 Maizières-lès-Metz, Moselle. (En Route p 127)
Tel 87 80 41 11. Telex 860191. Fax 87 80 36 00. Mich 24/B3.
(Bookings: UK 071 724 1000; US toll free 800 221 4542)

MULHOUSE   Ibis

Simple hotel/Cooking 1
Terrace/Lift/Parking/Good value

Leave A36 Ile Napoléon exit (just east A35). Hotel to north.
Menus A. Rooms (76) C. Disabled. Cards Access, Visa.
Post Ile Napoléon, 68390 Sausheim, H.-Rhin. (En Route p 141)
Tel 89 61 83 83. Telex 881970. Fax 89 61 78 10. Mich 77/E1.
(Bookings: UK 071 724 1000; US toll free 800 221 4542)

MULHOUSE   Novotel

Very comfortable hotel/Cooking 1
Terrace/Swimming pool/Parking

Leave A36 Ile Napoléon exit (just east A35). Hotel to north.
Menus B-C. Rooms (77) D-E. Cards All.
Post Ile Napoléon, 68390 Sausheim, H.-Rhin. (En Route p 141)
Tel 89 61 84 84. Telex 881673. Fax 89 61 77 99. Mich 77/E1.
(Bookings: UK 071 724 1000; US toll free 800 221 4542)

NANCY   Novotel Nancy Ouest

Very comfortable hotel/Cooking 1
Terrace/Gardens/Swimming pool/Lift/Closed parking

Just east A31/A33 junction (west of Nancy). From A31
(heading south) and A33 (heading north) Nancy-Gentilly exit;
from A31 (heading north) Nancy Centre exit. Hotel north side N4.
Menus B. Rooms (119) D-E. Disabled. Cards All.
Post rte de Paris, 54520 Laxou, M.-et-M. (En Route p 130)
Tel 83 96 67 46. Telex 850988. Fax 83 98 57 07. Mich 41/D4.
(Bookings: UK 071 724 1000; US toll free 800 221 4542)

ST-AVOLD   Novotel

Very comfortable hotel/Cooking 1
Terrace/Gardens/Swimming pool/Parking

Leave A4 St-Avold exit. South of A31, east side N33.
Menus B. Rooms (61) D-E. Disabled. Cards All.
Post 57500 St-Avold, Moselle. (En Route p 41)
Tel 87 92 25 93. Telex 860966. Fax 87 92 02 47. Mich 41/F1.
(Bookings: UK 071 724 1000; US toll free 800 221 4542)

SARRE-UNION   Au Cheval Noir

Simple hotel/Cooking 1-2
Parking/Good value

Leave A4 Sarre-Union exit. Left at N61. In village, on right.
Menus A-C. Rooms (20) B-C. Cards All.
Closed 1st 3 wks Oct. Restaurant: Mon.
Post rue Phalsbourg, 67260 Sarre-Union, B.-Rhin. (ER p 43)
Tel 88 00 12 71. Fax 88 00 19 09. Mich 42/B2.

STRASBOURG   Aigle d'Or

Simple hotel (no restaurant)
Good value

Leave A4 Reichstett exit (7 km north Strasbourg). Hotel east of
A4, south of D63; in Reichstett village (by church).
Rooms (18) C-D. Cards All.
Post 67116 Reichstett, B.-Rhin. (En Route p 46)
Tel 88 20 07 87. Fax 88 81 83 75. Mich 43/E4.

EPINAL   Le Colombier

Simple hotel
Lift/Parking/Good value

Grotty exterior but adequate enough. Two minute drive to Les
Abbesses rest. Use N57 Razimont exit from eastern bypass.
Rooms (32) B-C. Cards All.
Closed Mid July to mid Aug. Xmas to New Year.
Post 104 fg Ambrail, 88000 Epinal, Vosges.
Tel 29 35 50 05. Fax 29 35 22 14. Mich 59/F3.

GERARDMER   Echo de Ramberchamp

Very simple hotel
Quiet/Gardens/Parking/Good value

Chalet-style, west of town, on southern banks of lake.
Rooms (16) B-C. Cards Access, Visa.
Closed Nov to mid Dec. 2nd half Jan. Mon.
Post Ramberchamp, 88400 Gérardmer, Vosges.
Tel 29 63 02 27. Mich 60/B3.

GERARDMER   Bains

Simple hotel
Gardens/Parking

Scores of window boxes give the hotel a colourful, bright look.
Owners, the Leonards, speak excellent English.
Rooms (56) B-D. Cards Access, Visa.
Closed Nov to mid Dec.
Post 16 bd Garnier, 88400 Gérardmer, Vosges.
Tel 29 63 08 19. Mich 60/B3.

HERRLISHEIM   Au Moulin

Comfortable hotel
Secluded/Gardens/Lift/Parking

Old mill. On D1 east of village, alongside River Thur.
Rooms (17) C-D. Cards Visa.
Closed Mid Nov to March.
Post 68420 Herrlisheim-près-Colmar, H.-Rhin.
Tel 89 49 31 20. Fax 89 49 23 11. Mich 61/D4.

ILLHAEUSERN   La Clairière

Very comfortable hotel
Secluded/Tennis/Lift/Parking

Elegant rooms, stylish building; west of village (D106).
Rooms (26) F-F2. Cards Access, Visa.
Closed Jan. Feb.
Post rte Guémar, 68150 Illhaeusern, H.-Rhin.
Tel 89 71 80 80. Fax 89 71 86 22. Mich 61/D3.

KAYSERSBERG   Remparts

Comfortable hotel
Quiet/Garage/Parking

The Remparts is one of the best "base" hotels in France. Why?
Not for its convenient site or modern amenities, but because
the owner, Christiane Keller, a lively, intelligent lady, who
speaks excellent English, makes the place zing. And, in
addition, ensures that Kaysersberg zings along with her; she's
the driving force behind the Xmas market and the "Horizons
d'Alsace" venture – a group of 12 hoteliers where clients can
permutate overnight stops between any of the hotels, walking
from one to another in the knowledge that their luggage is
taken to the next base. The 12 are in a semi-circle to the west
of Kaysersberg. Details from 20, r. Ch. de Gaulle, 68370 Orbey
(Tel 89 71 25 25; Fax 89 71 30 75) or Christiane. The Remparts
has been extensively refurbished during the last few years. I
commend both the hotel and Mme Keller to you.
Rooms (31) C-D. Cards AE, Access, Visa.
Post 68240 Kaysersberg, H.-Rhin.
Tel 89 47 12 12. Fax 89 47 37 24. Mich 61/D3.

RIQUEWIHR   Couronne

Comfortable hotel
Quiet/Parking

Within the walls of the superb medieval village. South of the
main street. 16th-cent, plenty of beams, plenty of character,
modern fittings. English-speaking owner, Danielle Claudel.
Rooms (36) C-D. Cards Access, Visa.
Post 5 rue de la Couronne, 68340 Riquewihr, H.-Rhin.
Tel 89 49 03 03. Fax 89 49 01 01. Mich 61/D3.

RIQUEWIHR   Le Riquewihr

Comfortable hotel
Quiet/Lift/Parking

Newly-built, east of village; facing Schoenenbourg vineyards.
No grumbles from readers about Philippe Dubick's base.
Rooms (49) B-C. Cards All.
Post rte Ribeauvillé, 68340 Riquewihr, H.-Rhin.
Tel 89 47 83 13. Fax 89 47 99 76. Mich 61/D3.

RIQUEWIHR   Le Schoenenbourg

Comfortable hotel
Quiet/Lift/Parking

Recently extended; just outside village, below Schoenenbourg
vineyards. Next door to François Kiener's Aub. Schoenenbourg
restaurant; the hotel is managed by his brother.
Rooms (45) D-E. Disabled. Cards Access, Visa.
Post rue de la Piscine, 68340 Riquewihr, H.-Rhin.
Tel 89 49 01 11. Fax 89 47 95 88. Mich 61/D3.

AMMERSCHWIHR   Aux Armes de France

**Very comfortable restaurant with rooms/Cooking 3
Parking**

All readers agree about one aspect of this family enterprise:
service is unhurried and is performed with both precision and
panache. Pierre Gaertner, trained by Fernand Point himself, is
partnered these days by his two sons, Philippe and François
(the *pâtissier* of the trio). An enterprising mix of classical,
regional (the ultimate *foie gras*) and modern. One fan reckoned
his meal was the best of the holiday; others found the food
disappointing. Excellent large bedrooms. Formidable *cave*.
Menus C-E. Rooms (10) D-E. Cards All.
Closed January. Wed. Thurs midday.
Post 68770 Ammerschwihr, H.-Rhin.
Tel 89 47 10 22. Fax 89 47 38 12. Mich 61/D3.

ARTZENHEIM   Auberge d'Artzenheim

**Comfortable restaurant with rooms/Cooking 2
Quiet/Terrace/Gardens/Parking**

Typical Alsace *auberge*: built-in rustic ambiance with beams
and flowers. Some bedrooms smallish. Cooking is *Bourgeoise*
banal, redeemed by spectacular sorbets and ice-creams.
Menus B-C. Rooms (10) C-D. Cards Access, Visa.
Closed Mid Feb to mid Mar. Mon evg.
Tues. Post 68320 Artzenheim, H.-Rhin.
Tel 89 71 60 51. Fax 89 71 68 21. Mich 61/E3.

BALDENHEIM   Couronne

**Very comfortable restaurant/Cooking 2-3
Parking**

Chefs Angèle Trébis and her son-in-law, Daniel Rubiné, marry
regional and modern styles. Particularly pleasant is their
matelote du Ried (the name for the marshy Rhine plain):
sandre, brochet et anguille in a Riesling sauce. Marcel Trébis
and Daniel's wife, Chantal, look after the flower-filled and
panelled dining rooms with flair and courtesy. On the D209
north-west entrance to the village.
Menus B-D. Cards AE, Access, Visa.
Closed 1st wk Jan. Last wk July. Sun evg. Mon.
Post 67600 Baldenheim, B.-Rhin.
Tel 88 85 32 22. Fax 88 85 36 27. Mich 61/E2.

BAS-RUPTS   Host. Bas-Rupts/Chalet Fleuri

**Comfortable hotel/Cooking 3
Fairly quiet/Terrace/Gardens/Tennis/Parking**

Those of you who have *Favourites* will know of the tragic death
of 25-year-old Thierry Philippe. His father, Michel, has had to
return to the kitchens: he's especially fond of Scottish lamb
and smokes his own salmon. Michel's repertoire spans all

39

French styles. His English-speaking daughter, Sylvie, is a helpful hostess. One severe groan about inattentive service when the place was taken over by a large private party (a common problem); but, by and large, no other grumbles. The chalet annexe is super. Bikes provided free of charge.
Menus B-E. Rooms (32) D-F. Cards All.
Closed 9 to 20 Dec.
Post Bas Rupts, 88400 Gérardmer, Vosges.
Tel 29 63 09 25. Telex 960992. Fax 29 63 00 40. Mich 60/B4.

BELFORT   Host. du Château Servin

Very comfortable restaurant with rooms/Cooking 3
Quiet/Terrace/Gardens/Lift

Common sense eventually prevailed: the two Michelin stars awarded here and at Ammerschwihr were pruned back to one. Interesting that Dominique Mathy has switched tracks; he's happier now with a classical range of dishes. Sweets are first class. Lucie Servin looks after guests supremely well. An ugly house in a quiet side street.
Menus B-E. Rooms (10) D-E. Cards All.
Closed August. Fri. Sun evg. (En Route p 139)
Post 9 r. Gén.-Négrier, 90000 Belfort, Ter.-de-Belfort.
Tel 84 21 41 85. Fax 84 57 05 57. Mich 76/C2.

LA BRESSE   Vallées et sa Résidence

Very comfortable hotel/Cooking 1-2
Quiet/Gardens/Swimming pool (indoor)/Tennis/Lift
Garage/Parking/Good value

Considering the facilities prices are not unreasonable at the huge Rémy family business. Amazingly a *Logis de France*; 54 bedrooms and 60 studios (with small kitchens). Cuisine? Cheap and cheerful *Bourgeoise*: who's grumbling? Warm welcome.
Menus A-C. Rooms (54) C-D. Studios D. Disabled. Cards All.
Post 88250 La Bresse, Vosges.
Tel 29 25 41 39. Telex 960573. Fax 29 25 64 38. Mich 60/B4.

BRUMATH   Ecrevisse

Comfortable restaurant with rooms/Cooking 2
Gardens/Garage/Parking

I first came across this unprepossessing inn at the end of a hot summer's day when I was researching my autoroute guide. I was exhausted. Twelve hours later I was happy at my lucky dip choice. Over the top décor, modest but acceptable rooms, an eclectic (French that is) cellar and the competent talents of Jean Orth and his son, Michel, the seventh generation to man the stoves at Brumath. Hearty Alsace and classical fare. And a sauna to burn off any excess indulgence.
Menus B-D. Rooms (21) B-D. Cards All.
Closed 2nd half July. Mon evg. Tues. (En Route p 45)
Post 4 av. Strasbourg, 67170 Brumath, B.-Rhin.
Tel 88 51 11 08. Fax 88 51 89 02. Mich 43/E3.

EGUISHEIM   Le Caveau

Comfortable restaurant/Cooking 2

There's nothing prissy about either the cooking or the décor at Pascal and Suzanne Schubnel's historic flower-bedecked inn, at the heart of picture-postcard Eguisheim. Robust portions require belts to be eased back a notch or two. *Tarte à l'oignon*, pile-it-high *choucroute* and a nostalgic *baeckaoffa* (must be ordered in advance) are typical regional treats.
Menus B-D. Cards All.
Closed Mid Feb to mid Mar. 2nd wk July. I wk at Christmas. Tues evg. Wed.
Post 68420 Eguisheim, H.-Rhin.
Tel 89 41 08 89. Fax 89 23 79 99. Mich 61/D3.

EPINAL   Les Abbesses

Very comfortable restaurant/Cooking 3
Terrace/Gardens

Jean-Claude and Francine Aiguier's new home, a few miles downstream on the Moselle from their previous restaurant in Remiremont. Ask to see the photographs of the house when they bought the wreck six years ago. Modern cooking: no mingy portions, great use of local produce, clever adaptations of herbs and a cascade of both vegetables and menus are plus points; over-seasoning and lack of delicacy are debits. One novelty: a menu based entirely on *le cochon*. Dining rooms are both airy and stylish (with some terrific paintings). A summer lunch in the shady garden would be an alternative delight.
Menus C-F. Cards AE, Access, Visa.
Closed Last wk Aug. Sun evg. Mon.
Post 23 rue Louvière, 88000 Epinal, Vosges.
Tel 29 82 53 69. Mich 59/F3.

FOUGEROLLES   Au Père Rota

Very comfortable restaurant/Cooking 3-4
Parking

What significant changes at this longtime favourite, in an old town renowned for its *eaux-de-vie* distilleries and surrounded by orchards. Jean-Pierre and Chantal Kuentz, a young couple from nearby Plombières-les-Bains, have transformed the staid dining room into an oasis of pastel shades and light. There's nothing flashy or exotic about J-P's skills. He bridges both the classical and modern banks of cooking. I recall the elaborate depth of a *petite nage de turbot* in a flavoursome sauce of *vin jaune* (from the Jura) and ginger. One couple so enjoyed an accomplished *biscuit des champignons de bois* that they would have been happy to have sat there all evening savouring the intensity of that single dish. Try the famous local cherries (*griottes* and *griottines*) for dessert.
Menus B-D. Cards All. (Rooms? Métropole at nearby Luxeuil.)
Closed Xmas to mid Jan. Ist wk July. Sun evg. Mon.
Post 70220 Fougerolles, H.-Saône.
Tel 84 49 12 11. Mich 76/A1.

GERARDMER   Chalet du Lac

Simple hotel/Cooking 1
Gardens/Parking/Good value

Alain Bernier's family chalet, one km west of the town, sits
among pine trees and above the road alongside the northern
shore of the Gérardmer lake. Invigorating views across the
water to wooded hills beyond. *Cuisine Bourgeoise (quenelles*
and *côte de porc* are typical) takes a back seat to the
spectacular vista from the *salle à manger* panoramique.
Several bedrooms have balconies with the same lake views.
Menus A-C. Rooms (11) B-C. Cards Access, Visa.
Closed Oct. Fri (except in summer).
Post 88400 Gérardmer, Vosges.
Tel 29 63 38 76. Mich 60/B3.

GERARDMER   La Réserve

Very comfortable hotel/Cooking 3
Terrace/Lift/Parking

Completely refurbished and at the eastern end of the lake.
(The hotel was out of action for a year after a fire in December
1988.) Chef and owner Patrick Marchal is the brother of
Jacques Marchal who has made such a success of his Chez Nous
restaurant in Plymouth. Patrick's a consummate classicist:
witness his own *foie gras de canard*, an *escalope de saumon à*
la vapeur aux aromates, bursting with flavour, and a luscious
filet de boeuf aux trois moutardes. Desserts are of a high
standard: among them *oeuf à la neige, nougat glacé, Bavarois*
aux poire caramélisées and a memorable honey ice-cream.
Menus B-C. Rooms (24) C-F. Cards All.
Closed Mid Nov to Palm Sun. Tues midday (out of season).
Post esplanade du Lac, 88400 Gérardmer, Vosges.
Tel 29 63 21 60. Fax 29 60 81 60. Mich 60/B3.

LAPOUTROIE   Les Alisiers

Comfortable restaurant with rooms/Cooking 2
Secluded/Terrace/Gardens/Parking

At an altitude of 2300 ft above sea-level, Jacques and Ella
Degouy's *logis* has a refreshing, panoramic vista, a
Chartreuse-shaded distillation of the Vosges' varied scenic
charms. In these northern climes the weather is not always
suited to outdoor eating. So if it's wet no matter: the dining
room, with walls of glass, allows the emerald view to dazzle
just as brilliantly. English-speaking Jacques; his smiling wife
Ella; three acres of woods; and a mixture of both Alsace and
Bourgeois dishes (*choucroute à l'ancienne, tarte à l'oignon,*
faux-filet, cotelettes d'agneau grillées and *truite aux amandes*):
all combine to please any reader who makes the winding three
km climb south-west from the village.
Menus B-C. Rooms (13) C-D. Cards Access, Visa.
Closed Dec. Mon evg. Tues.
Post 68650 Lapoutroie, H.-Rhin.
Tel 89 47 52 82. Mich 60/C3.

LAPOUTROIE   du Faudé

Comfortable hotel/Cooking 2
Terrace/Gardens/Swimming pool/Good value

A thoroughly happy family atmosphere: Jean Marie and
Mariette Baldinger, their chef and son, Thierry, his English-
speaking wife, Chantal, and other son Eric, are much-loved
readers' favourites. No wonder: nothing is too much trouble for
the willing, friendly family. Thierry was the proud winner of
the *1991 le meilleur plat national des Logis de France*. He's
equally proud of his regional repertoire, backed up by a mix of
grills and *Bourgeoise* specialities. No culinary fireworks, no
midget portions and no clichés. Breakfasts, sadly, are not that
hot. The indoor pool is heated.
Menus A-D. Rooms (29) B-D. Cards AE, DC, Visa.
Closed 2nd half Mar. Mid Nov to mid Dec.
Post 68650 Lapoutroie, H.-Rhin.
Tel 89 47 50 35. Fax 89 47 24 82. Mich 60/C3.

MARLENHEIM   Host. du Cerf

Very comfortable restaurant with rooms/Cooking 4
Terrace/Gardens

Stars and *toques* have brought fame for Robert Husser (the
second Michelin star arrived on his 50th birthday, in March
1986) and his confident chef son, Michel, now 37. But both the
Hussers and their wives, Marcelle and Catherine (Cathy),
have their feet planted firmly on the ground. What a delightful
family enterprise the Cerf is; Irmgard, Robert's mother, still
takes an active part in the business. Cooking standards are
impeccable with many modern creations and a virtuoso menu
of regional classics. Cathy and English-speaking Daniel Krier
are unfussy, top-notch *maîtres-d'hôtel*. The courtyard is a
flower-bedecked picture. Try the fine Marlenheim wines.
Menus D-F. Rooms (15) E-F. Cards AE, Access, Visa.
Closed One wk Feb. Tues. Wed.
Post 67520 Marlenheim, B.-Rhin.
Tel 88 87 73 73. Fax 88 87 68 08. Mich 43/D4.

MITTELWIHR   A La Maison Blanche

Comfortable restaurant/Cooking 3
Terrace/Gardens/Parking

The Marchal brothers, each of whom has a Michelin star, gave
me the nod about this up-and-coming chef, Marc Decker. He's
worked at several of the top Alsace shrines, including the
three-star homes of Jung and Haeberlin. Previously he and his
wife, Janine, were based at Turckheim. Marc's clever with fish:
a *bouillabaisse terrine*, *marmite de pêcheur* and *langoustines
aux épices* are aromatic and confident examples of the chef's
contrasting range of modern culinary styles.
Menus B-D (B menu good value). Cards AE, Access, Visa.
Closed Mid Dec to mid Jan. Sun evg. Mon.
Post 68630 Mittelwihr, H.-Rhin.
Tel 89 49 03 04. Fax 89 49 01 07. Mich 61/D3.

MUHLBACH   Perle des Vosges

Comfortable hotel/Cooking 1
Quiet/Terrace/Lift/Good value

A handsome *Logis de France* in a splendid setting; high above
the village with extensive views south to the Ballon peaks. The
Benz and Ertle families have many fans. Cooking? Readers are
far less happy: basic *Bourgeoise* which most of you could better
handsomely at home. A regular *Logis de France* problem.
Menus A-C. Rooms (40) C-D. Disabled. Cards None.
Closed 2nd half Nov. Jan. Mon.
Post 68380 Muhlbach, H.-Rhin.
Tel 89 77 61 34. Mich 60/C4.

ORBEY   Croix d'Or

Simple hotel/Cooking 1
Good value

The Thomann family celebrated their centenary of ownership
in 1992: Jean Bertin Thomann is the third generation
chef/patron. Regional dishes. One highlight is the *baeckaoffa*
evening (Thurs in high season); see regional specialities.
Menus A-C. Rooms (19) C. Cards All.
Closed Mid Nov to Xmas. Mon. Wed.
Post 13 r. de l'Eglise, 68370 Orbey, H.-Rhin.
Tel 89 71 20 51. Fax 89 59 33 00. Mich 60/C3.

OTTROTT-LE-HAUT   Beau Site

Very comfortable hotel/Cooking 2-3
Terrace/Garage/Parking/Good value (see text)

Martin and Brigitte Schreiber have extensively refurbished
their family hotel. The beamed dining room ("Spindler") is
noted for its marquetry and classical and Alsace offerings
(*gibier* especially good). Superb cellar. "Les 4 Saisons" is a
glass-fronted restaurant where simpler meals are available.
Menus A-D. Rooms (15) C-F. Cards All.
Closed Sun evg and Mon (rest. only).
Post 67530 Ottrott-le-Haut, B.-Rhin.
Tel 88 95 80 61. Fax 88 95 86 41. Mich 61/D1.

PORT-SUR-SAONE   Château de Vauchoux

Very comfortable restaurant/Cooking 3-4
Gardens/Swimming pool/Tennis/Parking

On his day Jean-Michel Turin is one of the best chefs in
Alsace. But survival at Vauchoux is a tricky business. Readers
of *Favourites* will recall how he risked all to start a
supplementary enterprise to help finance his restaurant: a
weekly trip to Rungis market and, back home, a delivery run
made by an employee to J-M's chef *copains* in eastern France.
Vachouxfrais, the name of the venture, has been a great
success. The trouble is his cooking skills have stood still. But

he and his adorable wife, Franceline, are content with their lot. And why not? A handsome Louis XV hunting lodge, gorgeous dining room, stunning *cave* and tranquil park, complemented by delicate neo-classical cooking.

Jean-Michel seduces in all sorts of ways: examples are a simple *pigeonneau rôti rosé*; and a flamboyant *profiteroles amandines glacées*, ten tiny "mushrooms" of ice-cream, topped with crushed almond hats and a chocolate sauce.

Menus C-E. Cards Access, Visa. (Rooms? See Vesoul entry.)
Closed February. Mon. Tues.
Post Vauchoux, 70170 Port-sur-Saône, H.-Saône.
Tel 84 91 53 55. Telex 361476. Fax 84 91 65 38. Mich 75/F2.

SELESTAT　　　　　　　　　　　　　　　　Edel

Very comfortable restaurant/Cooking 3
Terrace

The omnipresent English-speaking Jean-Frédéric Edel, a chef with an immaculate pedigree, mixes classical, Alsace and modern. He's more at home with the former two styles (*suprême de volaille à la Sélestadienne*, a *volaille fourrée de choucroute*; and a gossamer-thin topped *crème brûlée au sucre cassonnade*) than his fussy, over-ambitious personal creations (*ravioles tièdes de homard et saumon, sauce aux herbes*; alas, with stale, smelly fish). Aline Edel is a charming *patronne*.

Menus B-E. Cards All. (Just off pl. du marché aux choux.)
Closed 26 July-17 Aug. 21 Dec-6 Jan. Sun evg. Tues evg. Wed.
Post 7 rue Serruriers, 67600 Sélestat, B.-Rhin.
Tel 88 92 86 55. Fax 88 92 87 26. Mich 61/D2.

LES TROIS-EPIS　　　　　　　　　　　　Croix d'Or

Simple hotel/Cooking 2
Terrace/Good value

New owners, Catherine Bruley and Marianne Gebel, at the modest Croix d'Or, 2000 ft above sea-level. Numerous walks from the front door. *La table Hans em Schnoleloch*, a vast buffet-style *hors d'oeuvre*, remains the best *Bourgeois* highlight.

Menus A-C. Rooms (12) B-C. Cards None.
Closed Mid Nov to mid Dec. 23-28 Mar. Wed.
Post 68410 Les Trois-Epis, H.-Rhin.
Tel 89 49 83 55. Fax 84 49 87 14. Mich 61/D3.

VESOUL　　　　　　　　　　　　　　　　Hôtel du Nord

Comfortable hotel/Cooking 2
Terrace/Good value

Owned by the Turins (Port-s-Saône). Completely refurbished. *Bourgeoise* cooking adequate. But use as a base for the Château de Vauchoux; transport laid on in evening for clients.

Menus A-B. Rooms (32) C-E. Appts (3) F. Cards Access, Visa.
Closed Mon evg (rest. only).
Post 7 rue de l'Aigle Noir, 70000 Vesoul, H.-Saône.
Tel 84 75 02 56. Telex 361476. Fax 84 91 65 38. Mich 75/F2.

BERRY-BOURBONNAIS

This second chapter gives me an early chance to admit how prejudiced I can be about flat terrain. Ten years ago, when introducing the region in *French Leave 82/83*, I wrote: "my preference is for countryside where a mountain aspect fills the eye." Since then, I have made an effort to find out more about the heartland of France, rather than ignore it.

The landscape hasn't changed: most of the north-western quarter is flat, unexciting country, the plentiful wheat fields of Berry. Further south is the Normandy-like "bocage" (see Normandy) of Bourbonnais where gentle hills and forests add extra interest. But, primarily, the most significant topographical attractions are man-made sites. I'll start by identifying the numerous architectural treasures of Berry.

Bourges is the most splendid of French medieval towns. Despite shocking traffic congestion I do recommend you make the effort to see, first hand, the St-Etienne Cathedral (with stunning stained glass); the adjacent Jardins de l'Archevêché; the elaborate and flamboyant Palais Jacques-Coeur; the nearby streets with striking half-timbered houses (the 16th-century Hôtel Cujas houses the Musée du Berry); and, finally, the French-style Jardins des Prés-Fichaux.

There's a series of ancient sites, both north and south of Bourges. Start at **Aubigny-sur-Nère**, on the D940 Bourges-Gien road: sumptuous half-timbered façades are the highlights. A semicircle of seven châteaux are to the east of the D940: Argent-sur-Sauldre; the brick-built **Blancafort** (so typical of the Sologne; see Loire); the lakeside La Verrerie with its spires, turrets, gables and towers (you can stay here – at one of France's most renowned Château Accueil); **La Chapelle d'Angillon**; the moated Boucard; Maupas (with a museum of earthenware); and **Menetou-Salon**, rebuilt in the 19th century

46

and with a collection of carriages and cars.

To the south-east and south is a second set of châteaux: the brick and stone Jussy-Champagne; my personal favourite, picturesque **Meillant**; another great favourite, the moated **Ainay-le-Vieil** (a miniature Carcassonne) and its "English" garden (including a collection of roses cultivated from 1420 to the present day); and **Culan**, a medieval castle in the English sense of the word, atop a small mound.

Between Meillant and Ainay is the Cistercian **Noirlac** Abbey, founded in 1150 by St-Bernard; the building is a majestic example of medieval monastic architecture. All the sites above are on the celebrated Route Jacques-Coeur.

Further west, in the **Indre** Valley and just north of La Châtre, is George Sand's house at **Nohant**. It was here that she lived and worked, where her two children were born and where, at the age of 35, she began her affair with Chopin. She died there in June 1876, aged 72. **Lignières**, west of Meillant, is the home of another château, rebuilt in the 17th century; the village has Calvin associations.

Where better to start your exploration of Bourbonnais than the magnificent Forêt de Tronçais. I first saw this remarkable oak forest three decades ago. Its future will be as interesting as its past; careful regeneration and thinning-out in the decades to come, will ensure that some handsome specimens will be flourishing in future centuries.

Let Nature have some more of your time. The **Allier** Valley has two horticultural treats: at **Apremont-sur-Allier**, south of the river's confluence with the Loire, is the Parc Floral, a recent creation, part of which was inspired by the gardens at Sissinghurst in Kent; and the **Balaine** Arboretum, 70 acres of mixed trees and shrubs with, again, an English influence.

Heading south, man-made sites now compete to catch your eye. The Allier and **Sioule** valleys are notable for numerous churches along its banks: Châtel-de-Neuvre, Saulcet, **St-Pourçain**, Jenzat and Ebreuil are just some of them. The finest highlight though is the ancient Prieuré (Priory) St-Pierre at **Souvigny**; especially intriguing is the 12th-century *calendrier*. The **Besbre** Valley is notable for a handful of châteaux: Toury, Beauvoir, Jaligny, Vieux-Chambord, Chavroches and the renowned Renaissance version at **Lapalisse**. (Follow the Besbre upstream to the wooded Monts de la Madeleine - deserted, unspoilt terrain.)

Vichy is world renowned for two reasons: the debit is its association with the German occupation of France during the last war; the credit is the spa town, described by Robin Yapp as being "caught in a *fin de siècle* time-warp". The parks alongside the Allier are the town's best attractions.

Junction 12 of the A71 autoroute, which now cuts like a knife across Berry-Bourbonnais, provides easy access for both Vichy and the Gorges de la Sioule, at their best from Ebreuil, upstream to Châteauneuf-les-Bains, the smallest of small spas but with a couple of dozen sources.

Finally, spare time for **La Charité-sur-Loire**, on the western border of Burgundy and the site of one of the finest examples of the region's rich heritage of Romanesque churches, the Eglise Notre-Dame; it's claimed the interior could once house a congregation of 5,000 worshippers.

Markets Bourges (every day; best weekends); La Charité (Sat); Cosne-s-Loire (Wed & Sun); Nevers (Sat); Pouilly (Fri). Michelin green guides: Berry/Limousin and Auvergne.

Cheeses **Cow's milk**

Chambérat fruity-tasting; made as a flat, pressed disk

Goat's milk

Chevrotin du Bourbonnais a truncated cone and creamy tasting. Best in summer and autumn. Also know as **Conne**

Crézancy-Sancerre small ball, similar taste to Chavignol (see Loire cheeses). **Santranges** is a related, similar cheese

Graçay nutty, soft cheese; made as a dark, blue-coloured cone

Regional Specialities

Bignons small fritters

Bouquettes aux pommes de terre grated potato, mixed with flour, egg white and fried in small, thick pieces

Brayaude (gigot) lamb cooked in white wine, onions and herbs

Chargouère (Chergouère) pastry turnover of plums or prunes

Cousinat (Cousina) chestnut soup (*salée* – salted) with cream, butter and prunes; served with bread

Gargouillau a *clafoutis* of pears

Gouèron a cake of goat cheese and eggs

Gouerre (Gouère) a cake of potato purée, flour, eggs and *fromage blanc* (fresh cream cheese), cooked in an oven as a *tourtiére*

Lièvre à la Duchambais hare cooked slowly in a sauce of cream, chopped-up shallots, vinegar and pepper

Milliard (Millat) (Milla) a *clafoutis* of cherries

Pâté de pommes de terre a tart of sliced potatoes, butter, bacon and chopped-up onions, baked in an oven. Cream added to hot centre

Poirat pear tart

Pompe aux grattons a cake, in the shape of a crown, made up of a mixture of small pieces of pork, flour, eggs and butter

Sanciau thick sweet or savoury pancake; made from buckwheat flour

Truffiat grated potato, mixed with flour, eggs and butter and baked

Wines

At first glance a small wine area but, nevertheless, there are a handful of good, unknown varieties to seek out. First, I'll describe what they are and where to find them. Then, I'll take a sentence or two to introduce you to my favourite British wine supplier, a small company operating very much in the same way that Chiltern House has done for the last dozen years.

Both **Châteaumeillant** and **St-Pourçain-sur-Sioule** are VDQS wines. The former's reds, made from the Gamay grape, are passable enough; the latter's reds and whites are much better. The fruity red is mainly Gamay, topped up with Pinot Noir; so is the quaffable rosé. The St-Pourçain white – a blend of Chardonnay, Aligoté, Sauvignon and a rarity, Tresallier – is a particularly pleasant hot weather drink.

Anne and I first fell for the **Sancerre** white 30 years ago, long before this super Sauvignon wine became so chic and so costly. Nowadays, in both Britain and France, we regularly delight over the **Menetou-Salon**, **Quincy** and **Reuilly** (north and west of Bourges) whites, all made from the Sauvignon grape. All three have an AC classification. The reds and rosés (made, like the Sancerre versions, from the Pinot Noir) are also high-quality wines; don't ignore them.

Back home, write to Yapp Bros for their annual catalogue – written with the same enthusiasm and passion that I try to put into my work. Robin and Judith Yapp have nosed out a selection of Rhône, Loire and Provence wines; all reminders, during cold winter months, of sunny summer holidays. Yapp Bros, Mere, Wilts BA12 6DY. Tel (0747) 860423.

Autoroute Hotels followed by Base Hotels

BOURGES
Confortel

Simple hotel/Cooking 1
Terrace/Parking/Good value

Leave A71 exit 7. On N151 towards centre of Bourges.
Menus A-B. Rooms (42) C. Disabled. Cards Access, Visa.
Post rte de Châteauroux, 18000 Bourges, Cher.
Tel 48 67 00 78. Telex 760280. Fax 48 67 95 87. Mich 84/C2.
(Note: a new Novotel is open on the west side of A71.)

MONTLUCON
Campanile

Simple hotel/Cooking 1
Terrace/Parking/Good value

Leave A71 exit 10. West on D94 (northern bypass of Montluçon)
for 8½ km; St-Victor exit. North on N144; hotel on right.
Menus A-B. Rooms (50) C. Disabled. Cards Access, Visa.
Post 03410 St-Victor, Allier.
Tel 70 28 48 48. Telex 393004. Fax 70 28 51 04. Mich 99/D2.
(Bookings: UK freephone 0800 897863)

Base Hotels

BOURBON-LANCY
La Roseraie

Simple hotel
Gardens/Good value

Woods and calm appeal in this modest small spa.
Rooms (11) B-C. Cards Access, Visa.
Closed Mid Dec to mid Jan.
Post r. Mart.-de-la-Libération, 71140 Bourbon-Lancy, S.-et-L.
Tel 85 89 07 96. Mich 100/C1.

ST-PIERRE-LE-MOUTIER
Vieux Puits

Simple hotel
Quiet/Garage/Good value

Even quieter, now that village has N7 bypass. Near church.
Rooms (11) C. Cards Access, Visa.
Closed 11 to 25 Jan.
Post 58240 St-Pierre-le-Moutier, Nièvre.
Tel 86 37 41 96. Mich 85/F4.

SANCOINS
Parc

Comfortable hotel
Quiet/Gardens/Garage/Parking/Good value

An old house in a garden dominated by fir trees.
Rooms (11) B-C. Cards None.
Closed 1st half Jan.
Post rue M. Andoux, 18600 Sancoins, Cher.
Tel 48 74 56 60. Mich 85/E3.

AMBRAULT   Commerce

Very simple restaurant with basic rooms/Cooking 1
Parking/Good value

A very modest *Logis de France*, alongside the D918 and
between Issoudun and Georges Sand's home at Nohant. Still in
the hands of the Maleplate family; these days Jean François is
le patron. Cuisine Bourgeoise with the odd regional dish.
Menus A-B. Rooms (7) B. Cards Access, Visa.
Closed 1-15 Oct. 1-15 Jan. Sun evg. Mon. Evgs on pub. hols.
Post 36120 Ambrault, Indre.
Tel 54 49 01 07. Mich 84/A4.

BANNEGON   Aub. Moulin de Chaméron

Comfortable restaurant with rooms/Cooking 2
Secluded/Terrace/Gardens/Swimming pool/Parking

English-speaking Jacques and Annie Candoré (they lived in
California for years) look after the bedrooms at the 18th-cent
mill. Born in Bannegon, Jacques' great-grandfather once
worked at the *moulin*. Son-in-law, chef Jean Merilleau, runs
the rest. Mix of neo-classical and modern. Standards can vary,
from super to indifferent. A few grumbles about surly service.
Menus B-C. Rooms (13) D-E. Disabled. Cards AE, Access, Visa.
Closed Mid Nov to Feb. Tues (out of season). Mich 85/D4.
Post 18210 Bannegon, Cher. (3 km south-east of village.)
Tel 48 61 83 80 (H). 48 61 84 48 (R). Fax 48 61 84 92.

BOURBON-L'ARCHAMBAULT   Thermes

Comfortable hotel/Cooking 2-3
Terrace/Gardens/Garage/Good value

Guy Barichard is the chef, Roger is both *maître-d'hôtel* and
sommelier. Classical cuisine with fungi spiking many elaborate
dishes: *ris de veau à la crème et aux morilles* and *foie gras d'oie
poêlé aux morilles farcies* are two. Chambres *coquettes*.
Menus A-C. Rooms (21) B-D. Cards AE, Access, Visa.
Closed Nov to 20 Mar.
Post 03160 Bourbon-l'Archambault, Allier. (Opp. spa baths.)
Tel 70 67 00 15. Mich 99/F1.

LA CHARITE-SUR-LOIRE   Grand Monarque

Comfortable restaurant with rooms/Cooking 2
Gardens/Garage/Good value

James and Monique Grennerat's restaurant with rooms over-
looks the Loire and the town's 16th-century bridge. Happily,
the N7 now bypasses La Charité. Classical and *Bourgeoise*
cooking with, alas, no evidence of any regional specialities.
Menus B-C. Rooms (9) B-C. Cards All.
Closed 2nd half Nov. 2nd half Jan. Fri (Nov to Mar).
Post 33 quai Clémenceau, 58400 La Charité-s-Loire, Nièvre.
Tel 86 70 21 73. Mich 85/E1.

CHOUVIGNY   Gorges de Chouvigny

Very simple restaurant with rooms/Cooking 2
Secluded/Terrace/Parking/Good value

Recommended by many readers. West of both junc. 12 (A71)
and Ebreuil, on the right bank of the Sioule and the wooded
Gorges de Chouvigny; a super spot. Young owners Eric and
Sylvie Fleury do a great job. *Cuisine Bourgeoise*: *truites*, *filet
de boeuf*, *jambon sec* and *petite friture*. The restaurant is
beside the river and the vine-covered "hotel" across the road.
Menus A-B. Rooms (7) B. Disabled. Cards Access, Visa.
Closed Xmas. Feb sch. hols. Tues evg & Wed (not high season).
Post Chouvigny, 03450 Ebreuil, Allier.
Tel 70 90 42 11. Mich 99/F4.

COULANDON   Le Chalet

Comfortable hotel/Cooking 1
Secluded/Terrace/Gardens/Parking/Good value

Between Moulins and Souvigny (don't miss the 12th-century
calendrier). Henry and Nicole Hulot's 19th-century hunting
lodge has a handful of natural bonuses: a fish-filled *étang*,
handsome old trees, gardens and park. Good-value classical
meals and typically French-decorated bedrooms. The odd dish
has a *Bourbonnaise* twist, like a *tourte* and *pommes de terre*.
Auvergne cheeses and a tasty *rosette d'Auvergne*.
Menus A-B. Rooms (25) C-D. Cards All.
Closed Rest. at midday. Mid Nov to Jan.
Post Coulandon, 03000 Moulins, Allier.
Tel 70 44 50 08. Fax 70 44 07 09. Mich 100/A1.

DIGOIN   Gare

Comfortable hotel/Cooking 2-3
Gardens/Parking

Billoux has moved on to Dijon. New owners, Jean-Pierre and
Jacqueline Mathieu, have filled the previous patrons' shoes
admirably. Jean-Pierre is a classical fan with, alas, a tendency
to over-richness. The lowest-price menu, 125 francs in early
1992, is fantastic value: plenty of choice and a memorable
consommé de canard. Some bedrooms are noisy.
Menus B-D. Rooms (13) C-D. Cards Access, DC, Visa.
Closed Mid Jan to mid Feb. Wed (not July & Aug).
Post 79 av. Gén. de Gaulle, 71160 Digoin, S.-et-L.
Tel 85 53 03 04. Fax 85 53 14 70. Mich 101/D2.

ISSOUDUN   La Cognette

Very comfortable restaurant with rooms/Cooking 3-4
Quiet/Gardens/Garage

What a treat. An almost over-the-top corner of France - as she
used to be. Anne and I would return willingly tomorrow, for a
dozen reasons. The family Nonnet make the cosy dining room

tick (the inn was a Balzac favourite from 1830 to 1836): Alain, with an infectious "Roger Royle" laugh, is an English-speaking font of culinary know-how; his wife, Nicole, is a delight and has the most attentive eye for detail we've encountered; and the duo are helped by their daughter, Isabelle, and her chef husband, Jean-Jacques Daumy. Cooking is a mix of skills: a dozen *Berrichonne* regional specialities and both modern and classical pleasures. Savour "forgotten" vegetables, like *pommes de terre noires* with scallops; *râble de lièvre rôti* carved at the table; and finish with perfectly-balanced desserts. And, in autumn, delight in fresh, locally-picked fungi. There's nothing anaemic about Alain, his cooking or his restaurant. Old fashioned virtues and values. Three cheers. (The "hotel" is a short 50-yard walk away.)

Menus C-E. Rooms (11) D-F. Disabled. Cards All.
Closed Jan. Sun evg. Mon.
Post bd Stalingrad, 36100 Issoudun, Indre.
Tel 54 21 21 83. Fax 54 03 13 03. Mich 84/A3.

MAGNY-COURS   La Renaissance

Very comfortable restaurant with rooms/Cooking 3-4
Quiet/Terrace/Parking

What a coincidence that Jean-Claude Dray's restaurant should follow on the heels of La Cognette. Those final sentences for Alain are just as valid here. Restrained good taste sums up the cooking, the staff and the décor. Nothing flashy, nothing hackneyed, just a master at work. Born in 1941, J-C spent his early years in Charolais terrain and then trained in the kitchens of several grand Parisian hotels. No wonder then his repertoire is authentically classical with regional produce counting above all: pigeons from Puisaye, Charolais beef, naturally, local ducks and *ris de veau*. Try, too, his *tapinaude Morvandelle*, a local *gratin Dauphinois*. Cheaper rooms? See Base hotels. N7 bypasses village.

Menus C-F. Rooms (9) F-F2. Cards AE, Access, Visa.
Closed 24 Feb to 16 Mar. 1st 3 wks Aug. Sun evg. Mon.
Post 58470 Magny Cours, Nièvre.
Tel 86 58 10 40. Fax 86 21 22 60. Mich 85/F3.

MOULINS   Paris-Jacquemart

Very comfortable hotel/Cooking 3
Lift/Garage/Parking

Saved by the bell. The Laustriat's hotel (see *FL3*) went into liquidation in early 1991. Nine months later new owners, Louis and Anne-Françoise de Roberty re-opened the place: the clue in the name is that the couple used to run the Jacquemart restaurant, just down the road. Louis controls *la cuisine*; Anne-Françoise the front of house. What a refreshing breeze now blows through the Paris and a modern cooking style brings freshness to the once dead-on-its-feet hotel.

Menus B-E. Rooms (22) D-F. Cards All.
Closed 3 wks Jan. 15 days May. Sun & Mon (rest.).
Post 21 rue de Paris, 03000 Moulins, Allier
Tel 70 44 00 58. Fax 70 34 05 39. Mich 100/A1.

POUILLY-SUR-LOIRE L'Espérance

Comfortable restaurant with rooms/Cooking 3
Gardens/Parking/Good value

During the last few years I've had groans about the Relais
Fleurie, moans about the Bouteille d'Or (not in *FL3* but
described by one reader as a dump with a surly owner), and
bleats about L'Espérance in the days of the previous owner,
Jacques Raveau. All that has changed under the stewardship
of young Patrick Léger; what effort he's put into beefing-up the
restaurant's good name. A bevy of value-for-money menus, the
epitome of light *cuisine moderne* at its best: dishes like *rouget
sur tartare de légumes frais, gâteau d'agneau aux tuiles d'ail
doux* and *terrine d'épices maison et glace cannelle*. Modern
rooms? Use English-speaking Robert Fischer's brand new
Hôtel de Pouilly (Relais Grillade) beside the Loire. Rooms (23)
D. Cards AE, Access, Visa. Tel 86 69 07 00. (3 km S.)
Menus A-C. Rooms (3) C. Cards AE, Access, Visa.
Closed 1-15 Jan. 1-15 Feb. Sun evg & Mon.
Post 17 rue R.-Couard, 58150 Pouilly-sur-Loire, Nièvre.
Tel 86 39 07 69. Mich 85/E1.

ST-POURCAIN-SUR-SIOULE Chêne Vert

Comfortable hotel/Cooking 2
Terrace/Garage/Good value

Yet another hotel with new owners and a welcome wind of
change blowing away old cobwebs. Martine Siret is *la patronne*
and husband, Jean-Guy, mans the stoves. A mix of *Bourgeoise*
and classical cooking with a toothsome number of local treats:
andouillette St-Pourçinoise and *salade Bourbonnaise* are two.
One pleasant surprise at the very heart of France: an *omble
chevalier aux lardons et noix*. Do try the St-Pourçain wines.
Menus A-C. Rooms (32) B-D. Cards All.
Closed 2nd half Jan. Sun evg & Mon (ex. high season).
Post bd Ledru-Rollin, 03500 St-Pourçain-sur-Sioule, Allier.
Tel 70 45 40 65. Fax 70 45 68 50. Mich 100/A3.

SANCERRE La Tour

Very comfortable restaurant/Cooking 3

One of England's most able cookery writers led me to this most
unusual restaurant with two dining rooms: a 14th-century
salon and, on the first floor, a modern room with views of the
town's rooftops and, beyond, Sancerre's distant vineyards. The
architecture is intriguing but that's not the *raison d'être* for
your visit. Daniel Fournier is an able classical technician:
witness his *pavé de daurade royale aux épices*, the *tête et
langue de veau sauce ravigote* and an ethereal *filet de sandre
poché à la Sancerroise*. Both wines and cheeses show off the
wares of the local *pays* to perfection.
Menus B-D. Cards AE, Visa. (Rooms? Use nearby Panoramic.)
Closed 15 Dec–15 Jan. 1-15 Mar. Mon evg/Tues (ex. July/Aug).
Post pl. Halle, 18300 Sancerre, Cher.
Tel 48 54 00 81. Mich 85/E1.

BRITTANY

3

Brignogan-Plages Roscoff **Ploumanach** ▲
Trébeurden ▲ Perros-
Guirec

Ile d'
Ouessant

Morlaix ● *N12* Guingamp

BREST ● Guimiliau • St-Thégonnec

Monts d'Arrée Huelgoat

Camaret **Le Faou** ■ ▲ **Locmaria-Berrien**
Morgat △ Ménez-Hom • Pleyben **Carhaix-Plouguer**
Plomodiern ■ *Aulne* △ *N164*

Douarnenez **Ste-Anne-la-Palud** ▲ • Locronan **Montagnes Noires**

Audierne ▲ **Quimper** ■ ▲ **Rosporden** Pontivy
Pouldreuzic ■ **Fouesnant** *N165*
Bénodet ■ ▲ ▲ Riec-s-Belon
Concarneau **Moëlan-sur-Mer** ▲
Pont-Aven ▲▲ **Hennebont** ▲
Raguenes-Plage Lorient **Branderion** *N24*

Auray

Carnac

Quiberon

Belle-Ile

● Autoroute hotel
■ Base hotel
▲ Hotel/Rest (rooms)
△ Restaurant only

0   10   20 Miles

One of the inexplicable oddities of my publishing enterprise is
that I have received fewer letters about Brittany and its hotels
than any of the other major French regions. Why is that?
I would have expected to receive far more about a region which
is renowned as a home from home for Britons.

France has a long, scenically varied coastline: Brittany's
share, about 750 miles, is the most dramatic and spectacular.
Despite that, for me, it doesn't compare with the incomparable
Scottish coastline, arguably one's of Europe's greatest natural
glories. On the other hand, the weather is warmer and
Brittany's beaches and coves are absolutely perfect for
children, as my family discovered many times decades ago.

I'll start by describing the Breton coastline, travelling in an
anti-clockwise direction from **Le Mont-St-Michel** to **La
Baule**. Later, I'll head inland and highlight some of the

largely-ignored pleasures well away from the beaches.

Le Mont-St-Michel is an exhilarating, enthralling sight. Tourists make this three-star wonder the most sticky of honeypot attractions; the narrow steep *rue* winding to the top of the rocky cone is always packed, making even Stratford seem like an off-the-beaten-track attraction. Climb every step to the summit of the *mont* where the famous abbey silently snoozes 300 ft above the sea. The bay is badly silted-up now and the huge, racing tides are rarely seen these days.

To the west, from Cancale to **Le Val-André**, is the "Emerald Coast". What happy memories our children have of **Dinan**, high above the Rance, with its ramparts and old houses; of the hard working, rewarding river – literally as a tour of the tidal power station, east of **Dinard**, will prove; of elegant, sheltered Dinard where both of them learned to swim in the sea-water pool; and of walled, atmospheric **St-Malo**, a granite fortress and bustling port combined. Beaches for kiddies abound: at the resorts of Dinard, **Sables-d'Or**, Erquy (especially well-sheltered) and Le Val-André. Other beaches we have used in the past are those just west of the Pointe du Grouin and at **Rothéneuf**. The scenic highlight of the Côte d'Emeraude is **Cap Fréhel** with its high cliffs, lighthouse and distant view of the Breton coast; a near neighbour is the man-made, almost impregnable Fort La Latte.

Continuing anti-clockwise, as the rocky coast sweeps north-west to **Paimpol**, we recall other beaches from times past: at St-Quay-Portrieux; the deserted Plage Bonaparte, just north of **Plouha**; and the neighbouring minute version at Bréhec-en-Plouha. Beyond Tréguier, renowned for St-Tugdual Cathedral, is the Corniche Bretonne, from **Perros-Guirec** to **Trébeurden**. This is the colourful Granit-Rose (pink granite) coast, which abounds with sheltered coves and beaches. On my own, without Anne and our two children, I've seen the rose-tinted rocks north of **Ploumanach**; enjoyed walking the many beaches at Trébeurden; and have been thrilled by the ever-changing seascapes glimpsed from the D788.

Beyond **Roscoff** I have seen little of the remote northern coast of Finistère; readers have spoken warmly of the beaches at **Brignogan-Plages** and others have relished the lanes that link one cape to another in this isolated terrain. South of **Brest**, however, is an area I know extremely well. Headland after headland, *pointe* after *pointe*, there's a multitude of sea views. But the most thrilling extravaganzas – flamboyant shows of cliffs, rocks, birds, sea noise and whistling wind – are at the Pointe de Penhir and the Pointe du Raz, to the west of **Douarnenez**. An easier alternative detour, without the overture of sound and spectacle, is the road up to the summit of **Menez-Hom**; the reward is a 360-degree panorama of sea, beaches, bays, headlands and inland moors.

There's a beach at **Camaret** but the one at **Morgat** is better as it's sheltered from the windy west. There's an isolated long stretch of sand at **Ste-Anne-la-Palud**, across the Baie de Douarnenez from Morgat; and another with the name of Les Sables Blancs just west of the port of Douarnenez.

From **Quimper** right down to **St-Nazaire**, Brittany's coast changes dramatically from the cliffs and high rocky headlands along the northern shores. Now the landscape is flat, the scenery is softer and there's a warm, southern feel in the air – no wonder as beaches face south; the only common factor is that every Bretonne house seems to be whitewashed. There's no shortage of beaches but really there are only a couple which deserve the very top rating: the expanse of white sand across the bay from **Carnac**, named literally "Sables Blancs"; and the three-mile immaculate sweep of sand, with fashionable backing promenade, at elegant, sophisticated La Baule.

What else is there to enjoy on this southern, sunny side of Brittany? Immediately behind La Baule is the Parc Régional de **Brière**. Much of it is deserted marshland, criss-crossed by canals and channels. Use the D50 across the marshes and detour to one of several "islands", the Ile de Fédrun.

The **Golfe du Morbihan** is another essential *déviation*. The "little sea" (from the Breton *Mor-bihan*) is peppered with islands and edged with inlets. The gulf is ideal for painters, ornithologists and small-boat sailors. A leisurely boat trip from either **Vannes** or **Auray** is the ideal way to enjoy the ever-changing light, solitude and almost sub-tropical environment. North of Carnac are thousands of megalithic monuments which lie in long lines, for all the world resembling giant granite soldiers on the march. Why were they hauled into these lines by Stone Age man 5,000 years ago? I have yet to visit **Belle-Ile**, reached by ferry from **Quiberon**, a one-hour crossing. Readers have spoken highly of the Plage de Bordardoué and the Côte Sauvage on the western side of the island. I've not seen them but I have enjoyed the sea vistas from the other "wild coast", north of Quiberon (D186).

Paul Gauguin brought fame to **Pont-Aven** a century ago. Still enjoying a flourishing artistic reputation the picture postcard village is always buzzing with tourists. **Concarneau** is one of France's busiest fishing ports; you'll also be fascinated by the tiny island walled *cité*, called "Ville Close". Quimper and **Locronan** are the *portes* to Cornouaille (Cornwall), the south-western corner of Finistère: in the former there's a cathedral and medieval streets; in the latter dark, granite-stoned Renaissance houses.

What of inland Brittany? In centuries past Bretons called the coast the "Armor" (land of the sea); the inland, forested heights were named "Argoat" (land of the woods). Inland Brittany is hardly wooded any longer; centuries ago there were huge expanses of oak and beech covering the hills and plateaux. Small pockets still exist; the best place to get a feel for the past is around **Huelgoat**. Forests of oak, beech, spruce and pine lie to the north-east, with huge outcrops of granite hidden among the trees. There's a small lake and, most pleasing of all, many a stream flows along rock strewn beds. The *pays* is best in late spring, when golden splashes of broom and gorse and new tints of green illuminate the landscape.

Here, you are at the heart of the Parc Régional d'Armorique. To absorb the extent of the remote, inland plateaux climb the 1197-ft-high summit of Roc Trévezel, a rocky rampart easily reached on foot. The views include the **Monts d'Arrée**, surrounding you, and the **Montagnes Noires** to the south.

To the north of the regional park is an enclave of *enclos paroissiaux*, parish closes. A typical example might include a church, calvary, triumphal arch and charnel house; each contains hundreds of ornate, centuries-old sculptures. The two most striking are at **St-Thégonnec** and **Guimiliau**, south-west of **Morlaix**. On the southern slopes of the Monts d'Arrée there's a terrific church and calvary at **Pleyben**.

At the heart of Brittany, between the regional park and Rennes, is **Lac de Guerlédan**, a glorious coil of water. On the southern banks is the Forêt de Quénécan, with walks, viewpoints, gorges, old villages, *ètangs* (pools) and forests.

Both **Nantes** and **Rennes** are traffic nightmares, the scourge of all French towns in the Nineties. If you can endure the traffic the castle in the former and the old town in the latter will reward your efforts. Finally, don't bypass three man-made specials: the gigantic castle at **Fougères**; the medieval streets and castle with its fairy-tale outline at **Vitré**; and the most handsome of feudal fortresses at **Josselin**, rising sheer from the left bank of the River Oust.

Markets Carnac (Wed & Sun); Concarneau (Mon & Fri); Dinard (Tues, Thurs & Sat); Dol-de-Bretagne (Sat); Guingamp (Fri & Sat); Quimper (Wed & Sat); Riec-s-Belon (Wed); Rosporden (Thurs); St-Malo (Mon, Wed, Thurs, Fri & Sat). Michelin green guide: Brittany (English).

Cheeses Cow's milk

Campénéac a pressed, uncooked cheese. Strong smell and main in thick disks. Good all the year

Meilleraye de Bretagne at its best in summer. Light smell, ochre-yellow rind, made in large squares

Nantais dit Curé (Fromage du Curé) (Nantais) strong smell, supple, small square of cheese. Good all the year

Port-Salut is a semi-hard, mild cheese, good all the year. Port-du-Salut was the monastery where the cheese was originally made – at **Entrammes** (Mayenne); the name was sold to a dairy company, though a variety of the type is still produced there. St-Paulin is a related cheese

St-Gildas-des-Bois a triple-cream cheese with a mushroom smell; cylinder shape and available throughout the year

St-Paulin semi-hard, yellow, mild, smooth-textured with a washed, bright orange rind. Made commercially throughout northern France: in Brittany, the Loire Valley, Normandy and Champagne-Ardenne

Try any of these cheeses with the reds from the Coteaux d'Ancenis or the whites of Muscadet or Gros Plant du Pays Nantais

Regional Specialities

Agneau de pré-salé leg of lamb, from animals pastured in the salt marshes and meadows of Brittany

Bardatte cabbage stuffed with hare, cooked in white wine and served with chestnuts and roast quail

Beurre blanc sauce for fish dishes; made from the reduction of shallots, wine vinegar and the finest butter (sometimes with dry white wine)

Cotriade fish soup with potatoes, onions, garlic and butter

Crêpes Bretonnes the thinnest of pancakes with a variety of sweet fillings; often called **Crêpes de froment** (wheat flour)

Far Breton batter mixture; vanilla-flavoured sugar, rum, dried prunes

Galette takes various forms: can be a biscuit, a cake or a pancake; the latter is usually stuffed with fillings like mushrooms, ham, cheese or seafood and is called a **Galette de blé noir** (buckwheat flour)

Gâteau Breton rich cake with butter, flour, egg yolks and sugar

Gigot de pré-salé same as *agneau de pré-salé*

Kouign-amann crisp, flaky pastries of butter, sugar and yeast

Palourdes farcies clams in the shell, with a *gratiné* filling

Poulet blanc Breton free-range, fine quality white Breton chicken

Wines

Whites (Great Muscadet vintages: **79 82 90**)
Let me be charitable and allow this region to claim **Muscadet** wines, grown on the southern banks of the Loire, near Nantes. The white, very dry and inexpensive white wines are made from the Muscadet grape (the best are *sur lie*) and are ideal with fish. The AC wines are **Muscadet, Muscadet de Sèvre-et-Maine** and **Muscadet des Coteaux de la Loire**. A junior VDQS cousin is **Gros Plant du Pays Nantais**, made from the acidy Folle Blanche grape. The VDQS **Coteaux d'Ancenis** Malvoisie white (same as Tokay in Alsace) is a sweet, honey-tasting gem. Enjoy, too, the marvellous Breton cider.

Reds
A fruity VDQS red comes from Ancenis (**Coteaux d'Ancenis**), made from the Gamay grape; the area is east of Nantes, on the northern bank of the Loire. (All Coteaux d'Ancenis labels, reds and whites, show the grape type used to make the wine.)

Vins de Pays
Not as good as the Muscadet whites and Ancenis reds: they are classified by *département*, **Maine-et-Loire** and **Loire-Atlantique**, or **Vin de Pays des Marches de Bretagne**.

NANTES   Novotel

Very comfortable hotel/Cooking 1
Quiet/Terrace/Gardens/Swimming pool/Parking

2 km east of A11 with junction of N23 (Nantes-Est exit).
Follow signs Angers par RN; hotel on north side of N23.
Menus B. Rooms (98) E. Disabled. Cards All.
Post à la Belle Etoile, 44470 Carquefou, Loire-Atl.
Tel 40 52 64 64. Telex 711175. Fax 40 93 70 78. Mich 64/C4.
(Bookings: UK 071 724 1000; US toll free 800 221 4542)

Base Hotels

BENODET   Menez-Frost

Very comfortable hotel
Secluded/Gardens/Swim pool/Tennis/Garage/Parking

Several buildings, old and new. Central situation. Much liked.
Rooms (43) D-F. Cards Acccos, Visa.
Closed Oct to Easter.
Post près poste, 29950 Bénodet, Finistère.
Tel 98 57 03 09. Mich 45/D3.

BRANDERION   L'Hermine

Comfortable hotel
Quiet/Parking

Modern hotel with an unusual roof. Friendly, talkative hosts.
L'Hermine has been a great favourite with readers.
Rooms (9) D. Cards Visa.
Post Brandérion, 56700 Hennebont, Morbihan. (West of village)
Tel 97 32 92 93. Mich 46/B3.

DINARD   Manoir de la Rance

Comfortable hotel
Secluded/Gardens/Parking

Terrific spot on left bank of Rance. South of D168.
Rooms (7) D-F. Cards Access, Visa.
Closed Jan. Feb.
Post La Jouvente, 35730 Pleurtit, I.-et-V.
Tel 99 88 53 76. Fax 99 88 63 03. Mich 29/F2.

DINARD   Reine Hortense

Very comfortable hotel
Quiet/Parking

Dear, idiosyncratic, luxurious; overlooks Plage de l'Ecluse.
Rooms (10) F-F2. Cards All.
Closed Mid Nov to March
Post 19 rue Malovine, 35800 Dinard, I.-et-V.
Tel 99 46 54 31. Fax 99 88 15 88. Mich 29/F2.

MOELAN-SUR-MER   Manoir de Kertalg

Very comfortable hotel
Secluded/Gardens/Parking

Gorgeous: the long drive is a copy of Wales' Llyfnant Valley.
Palatial bedrooms in manor house. Overlooks Belon estuary.
Owner's English-speaking son, "Brann", is a talented artist.
Rooms (9) F-F2. Cards Access, Visa.
Closed Nov to mid April.
Post 29350 Moëlan-sur-Mer, Finistère. (D24, 3km west)
Tel 98 39 77 77. Mich 45/E3.

LE MONT-ST-MICHEL   Les Terrasses Poulard

Comfortable hotel
Quiet

Great views. Park outside *mont*; steep walk and lots of steps.
Part of Mère Poulard empire, a tourist trap *par excellence*.
Rooms (29) F-F2. Cards All.
Post 50116 Le Mont-Saint-Michel, Manche.
Tel 33 60 14 09. Telex 170197. Fax 33 60 37 31. Mich 30/C4.

MORLAIX   Menez

Comfortable hotel
Secluded/Gardens/Parking/Good value

Modern stone building, immaculate gardens, views south-west.
Rooms (10) C. Cards None. (6 km north-east of Morlaix)
Closed Mid Sept to Mar. May. Sat and Sun (out of season).
Post St-Antoine-Plouézoch, 29252 Plouézoch, Finistère.
Tel 98 67 28 85. Mich 27/E2.

PLOMODIERN   Relais Porz-Morvan

Simple hotel
Secluded/Gardens/Tennis/Parking/Good value

Restored farm, small bedrooms, minutes from beach.
Rooms (12) C. Cards Visa.
Closed Nov to Easter.
Post 29550 Plomodiern, Finistère.
Tel 98 81 53 23. Mich 44/C1.

POULDREUZIC   Manoir de Brénizenec

Comfortable hotel
Quiet/Gardens/Parking

Old, stone-built mill. Woods, pool, fields; all extra pluses.
Rooms (10) D-E. Cards None.
Closed 25 Sept to Easter.
Post rte Audierne, 29710 Pouldreuzic, Finistère.
Tel 98 91 30 33. Mich 44/C2.

QUIMPER La Coudraie

Comfortable hotel
Quiet/Gardens/Parking/Good value

For once, a building without a whitewashed coat. Quiet side
road in Pluguffan, west of Quimper. Walnut tree too.
Rooms (11) B-C. Cards Visa.
Closed School hols Nov & Spring. Sat & Sun (out of season).
Post impasse du Stade, 29700 Pluguffan, Finistère.
Tel 98 94 03 69. Mich 44/C2.

QUIMPER Sapinière

Simple hotel
Tennis/Parking/Good value

For budget-conscious. Unattractive site, on D34 to Bénodet.
Rooms (40) B-C. Cards All.
Closed Mid Sept to mid Oct.
Post rte Bénodet, 29000 Quimper, Finistère.
Tel 98 90 39 63. Telex 940034. Mich 45/D2.

RAGUENES-PLAGE Men Du

Comfortable hotel
Secluded/Parking

A great delight for many readers. Isolated site, alongside beach
and with super views. French spoken fast!
Rooms (14) C-D. Cards Access, Visa.
Closed 28 Sept to 2 Apl.
Post Raguenès-Plage, 29139 Névez, Finistère.
Tel 98 06 84 22. Mich 45/E3.

ROTHENEUF Terminus

Simple hotel
Quiet/Parking/Good value

North of busy D201; 2 min. walk to popular Centre rest.
Rooms (30) C. Cards Access, Visa.
Closed 15 Nov to 27 Dec. 15 Jan to 15 Feb. Tues (Oct to Mar).
Post 16 rue des Goélands, 35400 Rothéneuf, I.-et-V.
Tel 99 56 97 72. Mich 30/A4.

ST-MALO (PARAME) Alba

Comfortable hotel
Quiet/Parking

Behind beach and *digue* (promenade). Helpful, friendly owners.
Rooms (22) E-F. Cards Access, Visa.
Closed Mid Nov to mid Dec. 5 Jan to 6 Feb.
Post 17 rue des Dunes, 35400 St-Malo, I.-et-V. (Paramé)
Tel 99 40 37 18. Mich 30/A4.

ST-MALO (ST-SERVAN) La Korrigane

Very comfortable hotel
Quiet/Gardens/Limited closed parking

Elegant, stylish rooms in 19th-century *Belle Epoque* mansion.
Rooms (10) E-F. Cards All.
Closed Mid Nov to mid March.
Post 39 rue Le Pomellec, 35403 St-Malo, I.-et-V. (St-Servan)
Tel 99 81 94 76. Telex 740802. Fax 99 40 40 50. Mich 30/A4.

ST-MALO (PARAME) Logis de Brocéliande

Comfortable hotel
Fairly quiet/Parking

Colourful, small hotel behind beach and *digue* (promenade).
Rooms (9) C-E. Cards Access, Visa.
Closed Dec. Sun evg (mid Nov to Jan).
Post 43 chaussée du Sillon, 35400 St-Malo, I.-et-V. (Paramé)
Tel 99 56 86 60. Mich 30/A4.

ST-MALO (ST-SERVAN) Valmarin

Very comfortable hotel
Quiet/Gardens/Closed parking

Hereabouts a château is called a "Malounière"; this one, a stern
18th-century version, has a pleasing interior and gardens.
Rooms (10) E-F. Cards AE, Access, Visa.
Closed Mid Nov to mid Feb (except Xmas & New Year).
Post 7 rue Jean XXIII, 35400 St-Malo, I.-et-V. (St-Servan)
Tel 99 81 94 76. Fax 99 81 30 03. Mich 30/A4.

STE-ANNE-D'AURAY Le Myriam

Comfortable hotel
Quiet/Lift/Parking/Good value

Modern, three storeys; off D17 Auray road (turn opp. post).
Rooms (30) C. Cards None.
Closed Oct to Apl.
Post 56400 Ste-Anne-d'Auray, Morbihan.
Tel 97 57 70 44. Fax 97 57 50 61. Mich 46/C4.

VANNES Moulin de Lesnuhé

Simple hotel
Gardens/Parking/Good value

In wooded valley, beside mill race. To south-east of D126, 2 km
north St-Avé; ideal for Régis Mahé restaurant in Vannes.
Rooms (12) C. Cards Access, Visa.
Closed Mid Dec to mid Jan.
Post Plumelec, 56890 St-Avé, Morbihan.
Tel 97 60 77 77. Mich 47/D4.

AUDIERNE   Le Goyen

Very comfortable hotel/Cooking 3-4
Lift/Parking

Let's get the bad news out of the way first. If I had to rate
readers' favourite ·hoteliers and restaurateurs the Bossers
would get the wooden spoon with a score of zero out of 10. Will
the 1992 acceptance of the hotel by the Relais & Châteaux
chain bring about a transformation in the Bossers attitude to
clients? Some grumbles about small bedrooms but certainly no
gripes on the all-important matter of cooking skills. In this
area Adolphe Bosser does a fine job. Fish and shellfish
predominate, as you would expect at an hotel overlooking a
busy port and just down the road from the major fishing port of
Douarnenez. Modern interpretations using Breton oysters and
lobsters, sea-bass, scallops, salmon and much else to great
effect. Two *plats*, a *civet de la mer au Gamay en meurette* and a
bar in a Chambertin sauce are both champion creations. The
Grand Plateau (fruits de mer) is a seafood extravaganza.
Menus B-E. Rooms (25) D-F. Cards Access, Visa.
Closed Jan. Feb. Mon/Tues midday (ex high season & pub. hols).
Post 29770 Audierne, Finistère.
Tel 98 70 08 88. Fax 98 70 18 77. Mich 44/B2.

CARHAIX-PLOUGUER   Auberge du Poher

Comfortable restaurant/Cooking 2
Gardens/Parking/Good value

Robert Le Roux's modern *auberge* is at Port de Carhaix, south
of the town and beyond the Brest-Nantes canal. Four classical/
Bourgeois menus with a good choice for each course: *soupe de
poissons*, *saumon grillé au Roquefort*, *gigot grillé* and *turbot
sauce mousseline* are typical. Gardens and a stream.
Menus A-B. Cards Access, Visa. (Rooms? D'Ahès in Carhaix.)
Closed Feb. 1-15 Sept. Sun evg. Mon.
Post Port de Carhaix, 29270 Carhaix-Plouguer, Finistère.
Tel 98 99 51 18. Mich 45/F1.

DINAN   Caravelle

Comfortable restaurant with basic rooms/Cooking 2-3
Good value

Jean-Claude Marmion has found it hard to maintain standards
during the last few years; predictably his Michelin star was
extinguished two years ago. Like others elsewhere in France,
he's cut his cloth to fit clients' needs: good value and quality
have become his motto. Christiane Marmion will present you
with three neo-classical menus. The middle one, F165 in early
1992, is a bargain: some *amusettes*; delicate smoked salmon
par la maison; a *marmite aux trois poissons au coulis de
crustacés*; cheeses; and a quality dessert.
Menus B-D. Rooms (10) C. Cards All.
Closed 12 Nov-4 Dec. 1 wk Mar. Sun evg & Wed (Dec-Mar).
Post 14 place Duclos, 22100 Dinan, C.-d'Armor.
Tel 96 39 00 11. Mich 29/F3.

DINAN   D'Avaugour

Comfortable hotel/Cooking 2-3
Terrace/Gardens/Lift

Built of Breton granite, D'Avaugour shelters behind Dinan's
ramparts. The solid old town squats on a rocky spur above the
Rance. Solid is the adjective which also best describes the
cooking. These days Georges Quinton is aided and abetted by
Christian Doré, who once worked for André Surmain at Le Relais
à Mougins (see Côte d'Azur). Regularly praised by readers,
who appreciate the dependable standards, the welcome from
Gisèle Quinton and the well-judged menus. On one hand a
modern, light *feuilleté de homard et coquilles St-Jacques*; on
the other an appetite-quenching classical *filet de boeuf poêle au
vin de Chinon*. (There's a second restaurant, La Poudrière,
serving grills cooked over an open fire.) I like the gardens and
outlook at the rear. Park in the place du Champ-Clos or even
bigger place Du Guesclin, both opposite D'Avaugour.
Menus B-C. Rooms (27) D-E. Disabled. Cards All.
Closed Rest: Tues.
Post 1 pl. Champ-Clos, 22100 Dinan, C.-d'Armor.
Tel 96 39 07 49. Fax 96 85 43 04. Mich 29/F3.

DOL-DE-BRETAGNE   La Bresche Arthur

Comfortable restaurant with rooms/Cooking 2
Gardens/Garage/Parking/Good value

Disaster struck the new owner, Philippe Martel, not long after
he bought the restaurant: fire damaged much of the interior.
The refurbished La Bresche Arthur is better than ever and
arguably the culinary skills of Martel have given the place a
revitalising pick-me-up; he's well named. Two accomplished
menus studded with modern touches: *rouget-barbet grillés,
beurre de fenouil bronze*; and a duo of desserts, one a plate of
caramel concoctions, the other a mango tart and *sa glace*,
remain sharp memories. A wide selection of meat dishes
provide tasty alternatives to non-fish fans.
Menus B. Rooms (24) C. Cards Access, Visa.
Closed Mid Jan to mid Feb. 2nd half Nov. Mon evg. Tues.
Post 36 bd Deminiac, 35120 Dol-de-Bretagne, I.-et-V.
Tel 99 48 01 44. Fax 99 48 16 32. Mich 48/B1.

DOL-DE-BRETAGNE   Bretagne

Simple hotel/Cooking 1
Good value

A dependable whitewashed *Logis de France*. For some a touch
dour but for families looking for good value (like us 25 years
ago) then Catherine and Patrick Haelling-Morel's Bretagne is
the answer. *Bourgeoise* cuisine with plenty of choice, big
helpings and some Breton *plats*, all cooked by Catherine.
Menus A-B. Rooms (29) B-C. Cards Access, Visa.
Closed Oct. Sch hols Feb. Sat (Oct to Mar).
Post pl. Chateaubriand, 35120 Dol-de-Bretagne, I.-et-V.
Tel 99 48 02 03. Mich 48/B1. (Park in the *place* opp. hotel.)

LE FAOU   **Relais de la Place**

**Comfortable hotel/Cooking 1-2
Good value**

Michelin has always rated the cooking at the Relais above its
neighbour, Vieille Renommée. Yet of the many readers who
have tried both, the latter usually gets the top vote. Competent
Bourgeois menus: *assiette de fruits de mer, coquilles St-
Jacques, langoustines* and *moules marinières* are typical.
Menus A-C. Rooms (35) B-C. Cards Access, Visa.
Closed 25 Sept to 19 Oct. Sat (Nov to June).
Post 29580 Le Faou, Finistère. (Park in the huge *place*.)
Tel 98 81 91 19. Mich 26/C4.

LE FAOU   **Vieille Renommée**

**Comfortable hotel/Cooking 1-2
Lift/Good value**

Readers have rarely been let down by Yves Philippe. Like its
neighbour the hotel is a modern building with parking opposite
both of them in the football field-sized *place*. A roll call of
Bourgeois dishes with odd highlights like *truite saumonée au
coulis de crustacés* and *pot-au-feu de la mer*.
Menus A-C. Rooms (38) B-D. Cards Access, Visa.
Closed Last wk June. Nov. Sun evg & Mon (not July/Aug).
Post 29580 Le Faou, Finistère.
Tel 98 81 90 31. Mich 26/C4.

FOUESNANT   **Armorique**

**Comfortable hotel/Cooking 1-2
Quiet (annexe)/Gardens/Parking/Good value**

High praise is consistently lavished on Jacques and Huguette
Morvan's *logis* (3rd generation). As good value as ever is the
regular cry; children, too, are made welcome. The annexe has
the more comfortable rooms. In May camellias are a riot of
colour. *Bourgeoise* cooking with strong emphasis on a wide
range of fish dishes. All-in-all a cracking winner.
Menus A-B. Rooms (32) B-C. Cards Access, Visa.
Closed Oct to Mar. Mon (ex. school holidays).
Post 33 rue de Cornouaille, 29170 Fouesnant, Finistère.
Tel 98 56 00 19. Mich 44/D3.

LA GOUESNIERE   **Hôtel Tirel-Guérin**

**Very comfortable hotel/Cooking 3
Gardens/Tennis/Swimming pool/Parking/Good value**

The ultimate family closed shop. Previously called La Gare,
I've seen the once modest hotel, surrounded by cabbage fields,
grow into a sizeable business operation over three decades. My
first visit was in the days when Robert and Adélaïde Tirel ran
the show. Now a family quartet pluck the strings: Roger, the
Tirel's son, married Annie Guérin; Marie-Christiane, Roger's

sister, married Annie's brother, Jean-Luc Guérin. Got that? Roger and Jean-Luc are the *cuisiniers*, M-C and Annie are the animated hostesses. Progress has been made on all fronts, year-in, year-out. The indoor, heated pool complex is a real hunky dory asset; kids will adore the *piscine*.

A mix of classical and modern and, thankfully, a quintet of menus which all earn the accolade *rapport qualité-prix*: try the likes of a *terrine aux trois poissons, suprême de bar au beurre blanc* and a *fricassée de volaille fermière aux langoustines*. No wonder then that the hotel gets busy, especially on a Sunday when locals and tourists pack the huge dining rooms. I said the enterprise was sizeable; it's successful too. Get quality and price in balance and you cannot go wrong: cut the prices and the clients come.

Menus B-C. Rooms (60) C-D. Cards All. (2 km north on D76.)
Closed Mid Dec to mid Jan. Rest: Sun evg (not high season).
Post Gare de la Gouesnière, 35350 La Gouesnière, I.-et-V.
Tel 99 89 10 46. Telex 740896. Fax 99 89 12 62. Mich 30/A4.

HENNEBONT   Château de Locguénolé

Very comfortable hotel/Cooking 3
Secluded/Gardens/Swimming pool/Tennis/Parking

This must be the ugliest château in Brittany, more akin to a V2 rocket-firing blockhouse. Yet the site is pure enchantment, encircled by splendid woods and grounds alongside the River Blavet. The interior is typical R&C: laced with sumptuous furniture and gigantic tapestries. Owner Alyette de la Sablière's son, Bruno, a passionate and highly-successful sailor, steers the land-based craft these days. Chefs tack to and fro; cooking, often inconsistent, follows a modern course. Francis Bonneau proposes a variety of personal creations; for example a fussy *millefeuille glacé de saumon mariné et ses mousselines de légumes* and a more endearing duo, *rouget de petit bateau en civet* and *noisettes de colin au vin de Graves*.
Menus C-E. Rooms (20) F-F2. Cards All.
Closed Jan to mid Feb. Rest: Mon (Oct to Apl).
Post 56700 Hennebont, Morbihan. (On D781, south of town.)
Tel 97 76 29 04. Telex 950636. Fax 97 76 39 47. Mich 46/B4.

LOCMARIA-BERRIEN   Auberge de la Truite

Comfortable restaurant with rooms/Cooking 2
Gardens/Garage/Parking/Good value

A tiny corner of old-fashioned France. Mme Le Guillou's restaurant is a Breton-furnished house, surrounded by trees. Long renowned for its cuisine, the *auberge*, modest as it is, leaves impressions which also linger long in readers' memories. The trout come from the Aulne behind the restaurant; the unctuous *gâteau Breton* is as good as any in Brittany; and the 20 or so *plats* on the various menus are authentically classical. But don't expect great miracles.
Menus B-D. Rooms (6) B. Cards Access, Visa.
Closed Jan to 18 Apl. Sun evg & Mon (not July/Aug).
Post 29690 Locmaria-Berrien, Finistère. (Sth-east Huelgoat.)
Tel 98 99 73 05. Mich 27/E3.

MOIDREY   Au Vent des Grèves

Comfortable restaurant/Cooking 2
Terrace/Parking/Good value

English-speaking Jean-Claude Pierpaoli was the director of
the legendary Mère Poulard at Mont-St-Michel for part of the
20 years he worked at the hotel. I've dropped that rip-off
honeypot hotel because so many readers have been badly stung
there. Jean-Claude, too, has jumped ship. Now he has his own
small craft. Modest, yes, but fair prices, a likeable personality
and sound classical cooking work well: so much so this is
where the locals flock at weekends. Nothing frivolous: *gigot
d'agneau pré-salé*, of course; a few tasty Normandy cheeses;
and a *fine tarte tiède aux pommes* are the sort of things I mean.
Rooms? Use the nearby bases (see Normandy chapter).
Menus B-C. Cards Access, Visa.
Closed Jan to mid Feb. Tues evg & Wed (not July/Aug).
Post 50170 Moidrey, Manche. (On D976, 6 km S of Mont-St-Mich.)
Tel 33 60 01 63. Mich 30/C4.

MUR-DE-BRETAGNE   Auberge Grand'Maison

Very comfortable restaurant with rooms/Cooking 3-4

No arguments: for many, many readers this is the jewel in the
French crown. Arguably the Grand'Maison is the biggest
favourite in Brittany, by a long way. What fantastic progress
has been made. Jacques Guillo is an unassuming *cuisinier*
with a passion for both his *pays* and his kitchen; Brigitte, his
wife, is an unruffled, smiling *patronne*. An assured couple, a
much refurbished *auberge*, and a cooking repertoire which
capitalises on the produce from both the "Armor" and "Argoat"
(see the Brittany introduction); no wonder the end result is
"ace". Memorable modern and neo-classical dishes include
*galettes de pommes de terre en crème océane, feuillantine
d'araignée de mer sauce Newburg* and *le dessert de Sophie*. If
only more French hoteliers were like Jacques and Brigitte:
such a generous, involved, helpful and amiable duo.
Menus B-D. Rooms (12) C-F. Cards All.
Closed Sch hols Feb. 25 Sept to 25 Oct. Sun evg. Mon.
Post 22530 Mur-de-Bretagne, C.-d'Armor.
Tel 96 28 51 10. Fax 96 28 52 30. Mich 28/B4.

PLOUMANACH   Rochers

Very comfortable restaurant with rooms/Cooking 2-3

Alas, a chequered record at Mme Justin's attractively sited
restaurant overlooking Ste-Anne's bay. No moans about the
bracing views, but constant drips of cold water comments on
the classical cooking of Gérard Tanvier. The régime needs
tightening up. It's safe to stick with the quality fish and
shellfish and keep to the relatively simpler offerings.
Menus B-E. Rooms (13) D-E. Cards Access, Visa.
Closed Oct to mid April. Wed (not high season).
Post Ploumanach, 22700 Perros-Guirec, C.-d'Armor.
Tel 96 91 44 49. Mich 28/A1.

QUESTEMBERT Bretagne

Luxury restaurant with rooms/Cooking 3-4
Gardens/Parking

A varied record: a much-fancied restaurant (with numerous *toques* and stars) which has failed to please many readers; yet has also managed to earn a greater number of glowing observations. Most don't like the traffic, despite the double glazing. Some reckon the puds lack distinction. Others feel the menus are so lack lustre they force you to order *à la carte*. Less of the gloom: what are the strengths? Chef-patron, English-speaking Georges Paineau, has both a sense of humour and a modern innovative bent (he's assisted in the kitchen by son-in-law, Claude Corlouër). Some specialities are three-star beaters: potato *galettes*; *tête de veau* with a *gribiche* sauce (cream rather than *vinaigrette* based); and cheek of beef in a luscious dark Chinon-based sauce. The wood-panelled dining room is liked by all readers; so, too, is Michèle Paineau (now helped by her daughter, Nathalie). Ultra modern rooms.
Menus B-E. Rooms (15) E-F. Cards AE, Access, Visa.
Closed Jan to 15 Feb. Sun evg/Mon (not July/Aug nor pub hols).
Post 13 rue St-Michel, 56230 Questembert, Morbihan.
Tel 97 26 11 12. Telex 951801. Fax 97 26 12 37. Mich 63/D2.

RAGUENES-PLAGE Chez Pierre

Comfortable hotel/Cooking 2
Quiet/Gardens/Parking/Good value

Universally appreciated with many a letter complimenting the efficient, charming owners, Xavier and Dany Guillou. A quiet spot, just a few hundred metres from the coast and beach. Holder of a Michelin Repas (R) award for 20+ years. Classical *plats* such as grilled lobster with tarragon, turbot in a Champagne sauce and *lieu jaune au beurre blanc*. The gardens are much improved. (Note: nearby Pont Aven's Moulin Rosmadec has been dropped as a result of many grumbling letters.)
Menus B-C. Rooms (29) B-D. Disabled. Cards Access, Visa.
Closed Oct to Easter. Rest: Wed (mid June to mid Sept).
Post Raguenès-Plage, 29920 Névez, Finistère.
Tel 98 06 81 06. Mich 45/E3.

RENNES Germinal

Comfortable hotel/Cooking 1-2
Quiet/Terrace/Lift/Good value

A converted mill on an island site in the River Vilaine, 6 km east of Rennes at Cesson-Sévigné. The *moulin* has been owned by Louis and Danielle Goualin's family for three generations; flour was milled as recently as 1970. Both the terrace and glass-walled dining room are beguiling pluses. A vast choice of both *Bourgeois* and classical dishes.
Menus A-C. Rooms (20) C-D. Cards Access, Visa.
Closed 1st 3 wks Aug. Xmas to New Year. Rest: Sun.
Post 9 cours de la Vilaine, 35510 Cesson-Sévigné, I.-et-V.
Tel 99 83 11 01. Fax 99 83 45 16. Mich 48/C3.

ROSPORDEN   Bourhis

Very comfortable hotel/Cooking 3 (see text)
Lift/Good value (Le Jardin)

Marcel Bourhis has overcome the disaster which struck his
family hotel in 1982: fire reduced the building to a blackened
shell. Alas, his marriage to Maryvonne hit rocky ground; they
separated a few years back. Not many of you like the new,
modern structure. But it's functional and one rare benefit (for
France that is) is that it has rooms for the disabled.

The Michelin star came; the Michelin star went. Why? My
visits and dozens of letters have all praised Marcel's neo-
classical talents. Painstaking detail, inventive thinking and
quality produce are his culinary hallmarks. But to survive in
Rosporden you must get clients into the restaurant. Perhaps
Le Jardin, a low-cost grill, has spread Marcel's efforts too
thinly and thus prejudiced the Restaurant Gastronomique?
Skills must wane in those circumstances; but at least you
survive. (Cooking rating applies to the restaurant only.)
Menus Rest: B-E. Rooms (27) C-D. Disabled. Cards All.
Menus Le Jardin: A-B. (Park in the *place* opp. the hotel.)
Closed Rest & Grill: Sun evg & Mon (Oct to May).
Post 3 place de la Gare, 29140 Rosporden, Finistère.
Tel 98 59 23 89. Telex 941808. Mich 45/E2.

ROTHENEUF   Centre et du Canada

Very simple hotel/Cooking 1
Gardens/Good value

There's now't simpler in *Encore* but no other hotel can boast
such big-hearted owners (M. and Mme Filliette), for whom
nothing is too much trouble (including one tale of chasing
clients all the way to the ferry with their left-behind credit
card). Guests get a warm welcome. Good value all round,
bargain wines and copious *cuisine traditionelle*. My family fell in
love with this whitewashed, unpretentious gem more than two
decades ago; readers continue to be bowled over 20 years later.
Menus A. Rooms (23) B-C. Cards Access, Visa.
Closed Xmas to end Jan. Sun & Mon (not in high season).
Post 7 place du Canada, Rothéneuf, 35400 St-Malo, I.-et-V.
Tel 99 56 96 16. Mich 30/A4.

ST-MALO   Le Chalut

Comfortable restaurant/Cooking 2

Go once and you'll return night after night. What better
compliment can I pay this bustling congenial fish restaurant.
Fresh fish is laid out on an open-air counter alongside the
pavement; shellfish are in a central tank in the dining room.
On our visit at least a dozen varieties were on offer on the
various classical menus. Not for carnivores.
Menus B-C. Cards AE, Access, Visa.
Closed 3 wks Jan. 2 wks Oct. Sun evg (out of season). Mon.
Post 8 rue Corne de Cerf, 35400 St-Malo, I.-et-V.
Tel 99 56 71 58. Mich 30/A4. (NE corner of walled town.)

ST-MALO
Le Franklin

Very comfortable restaurant/Cooking 3-4

Jonathan Meades marked my card about this inspired newcomer, by coincidence on the day before I was told I faced an immediate operation for detached retinas. Two years passed before I eventually nosed out Robert Abraham at his restaurant overlooking the sea outside the old walled town.

Like Michel Trama (Puymirol, Southwest), Robert started working life as a *maître-d'*; he only took up cooking in 1982, at the age of 40. Like Michel Bras (Laguiole, Massif Central), he has an uncluttered, original and open mind on all aspects of culinary concoctions (with no exposure to catering colleges and concepts fixed in concrete). Like both Michels his tune is *cuisine moderne* counterpoint: spices and herbs, plants and flowers, flavouring agents and infusions of flowers; invention is manifest. He's developed a fruitful partnership with Nadia Romé who cultivates rare plants and flowers for him. His great good fortune, too, is that Brittany's bountiful larder is on his doorstep. Superb fish and shellfish play a big part in his work. The results are exciting, work well and leave you itching to return. Don't bypass Robert and Lyliane's magical box of culinary tricks. (Public parking nearby.)
Menus B-D. Cards All.
Closed Mid Jan to end Feb. Sun evg & Mon (not July & Aug).
Post 4 chausée Sillon, 35400 St-Malo, I.-et-V.
Tel 99 40 50 93. Fax 99 40 19 19. Mich 30/A4.

STE-ANNE-D'AURAY
L'Auberge

Comfortable restaurant with basic rooms/Cooking 2
Parking/Good value

The *logis*, on the Dl9 Vannes road, has an unappetising exterior. What arrives on the plate is most certainly the opposite. Neo-classical specialities with both fish and other alternatives: *filet de St-Pierre dans sa soupe d'ail* and *grillade de canard aux abricots epicés* are tasty treats.
Menus A-D. Rooms (7) A-B. Cards Access, Visa.
Closed 3 wks Jan. 3 wks Oct. Tues evg. Wed.
Post 56 rte de Vannes, 56400 Ste-Anne-d'Auray, Morbihan.
Tel 97 57 61 55. Mich 46/C4.

STE-ANNE-LA-PALUD
Plage

Very comfortable hotel/Cooking 3
Secluded/Gardens/Swimming pool/Tennis/Lift/Parking

No changes at this most idyllic of settings, on the sands of the Baie de Douarnenez and protected by a headland where, in June, azaleas and rhododendrons bathe the hillside with colour. Indefatigable Manick Le Coz, now 70, is still the boss. Her son, Jean-Milliau, and Marie, the friendliest of receptionists, both speak excellent English. Cooking remains in the hands of Jean-Pierre Le Goloanec, now 40 but the chef here for nearly 20 years. A mix of ultra-light and classically sauced dishes with an emphasis on fish and shellfish. Dear?

Yes: but few regret a stay at this Breton hideaway.
Menus C-D. Rooms (26) F. Cards All.
Closed Mid Oct to end March.
Post Ste-Anne-la-Palud, 29127 Plonevez-Porzay, Finistère.
Tel 98 92 50 12. Telex 941377. Fax 98 92 56 54. Mich 44/C1.

TREBEURDEN   Ti al-Lannec

Very comfortable hotel/Cooking 2
Secluded/Gardens/Parking

For many readers this is a little piece of heaven on earth.
Almost hidden behind massive fir trees at the front, and with
pretty, sea-view gardens at the rear, the handsome hotel sits
contentedly 50 metres above the shore. Danielle and Gérard
Jouanny are ideal hoteliers; their personal touch is a vital
ingredient. There's even a daily *gazette* for guests. Popular
with VFB clients. Ever-improving neo-classical cooking.
Menus A-D. Rooms (29) D-F. Cards All.
Closed 12 Nov to end Feb.
Post 22560 Trébeurden, C.-d'Armor.
Tel 96 23 57 26. Telex 740656. Fax 96 23 62 14. Mich 27/F1.

LE VAL-ANDRE   Cotriade

Comfortable restaurant/Cooking 2-3

Jean-Jacques Le Saout retains an entry by a wafer-thin fish
skin. Many complaints almost outweighed positive feedback.
Inattentive service by amateurs and a *panaché* of fish with
several sauces is too fussy and complicated. Classical fish
cooking; small dining room with invigorating sea vistas.
Menus B-C. Cards Access, Visa. (Rooms? Clemenceau, *sans rest.*)
Closed Mid Jan to mid Feb. 11-26 June. Mon evg & Tues.
Post Port de Piégu, 22370 Pléneuf-Val-André, C.-d'Armor.
Tel 96 72 20 26. Mich 29/D2.

VANNES   Régis Mahé

Very comfortable restaurant/Cooking 3-4
Good value

Robert Abraham is the surfacing talent on the north Brittany
coast. Here, on the southern *côte*, Régis Mahé is the rising
young, modern master. Wife Edith is an attentive hostess.
Mahé's two lowest-priced menus (under F200) are dazzling
examples of *rapport qualité-prix*. A year ago the 170 franc
menu was as follows: *grillade de saumon et pommes de terre
écrasées (vinaigrette huile de noisette)*, a toothsome treat; a
light and flavoursome *raie au coulis de tomates et au thym*,
with a touch of the Med; *rizotto de volaille aux poivrons et
safran*, an explosion of colour; and a lick-the-lips-for-more
terrine *chocolat et banane*. (Rooms? See the Vannes base.)
Menus B-D. Cards AE, Access, Visa.
Closed Last 2 wks Feb. Last 2 wks Nov. Sun evg. Mon.
Post pl. de la Gare, 56000 Vannes, Morbihan. (Opp. station.)
Tel 97 42 61 41. Mich 47/D4.

BURGUNDY

see page 148 **St-Florentin** see page 92

Joigny
Armançon D905 Seine Langres
Serein Tanlay
Auxerre ○△ ▲**Chablis** Ancy-le-Franc
Vaux △ Noyers ▲**St-Rémy**
Montbard ●Fontenay
Mailly-le- Alise-Ste-Reine ●Bussy-Rabutin
Chateau Vézelay **Semur-en-** **Til-Châtel**
Clamecy ●St-Père △**Avallon** **-Auxois** **Val-Suzon**
Chastellux **Velars-sur-** DIJON
Quarré-les-Tombes △ Saulieu **Ouche**
Corbigny **Morvan** **Gevrey-Chambertin**■
Montsauche-les-Settons **Châteauneuf** ▲ **Nuits-St-**
Lac des Settons **Bouilland**▲ **Georges**
Alligny-en- **Aloxe-Corton**■ A36
Morvan **Beaune**■ ■ ▲
Nevers Château- **Levernois**
Chinon Mont Sène △
Mont Beuvray △ **Autun** **Chagny** ■
Mercurey ▲ **Chalon-**
sur-Saône
Loire Digoin **Taizé**●
Cluny● Mâcon ● A40

● Autoroute hotel
■ Base hotel
▲ Hotel/Rest (rooms)
△ Restaurant only

0   10   20 Miles

see page 214
see page 193
see page 46
see page 162

Don't make the same mistake that Anne and I made for so many decades. In our headlong rush south across France, first on the N6 and, later, the A6, we were quite oblivious of the endless pleasures to each side of the busy highways.

I would be the first to encourage you to visit the two world famous Burgundian towns of **Dijon** and **Beaune**. But I would also urge you to head elsewhere, through the lanes of Burgundy, to other sites – some famous, some totally ignored.

Dijon is a treasurehouse full of architectural jewels, including the Palais des Ducs et des Etats de Bourgogne with its glorious Musée des Beaux Arts, the Rue des Forges (an old street with noble houses), the Cathedral of St-Bénigne, the 13th-century Gothic Notre-Dame church, the archeological museum and the area around the Palais de Justice.

Beaune is another man-made treat. The Hôtel-Dieu with its superb kaleidoscopic roof of multi-coloured tiles is the first essential port of call; next the wine museum and the Collégiale Notre-Dame with its display of fabulous tapestries. Enjoy, too, the town's unusual and colourful flower displays.

Where next? Go to the heights of **Vézelay** (west of Avallon), to the inspiring Basilica of Ste-Madeleine. Whether you stand and admire the tympanum sculpture, the majestically-rounded arches of the interior, or the view from the tree-shaded terrace, you'll most certainly be filled with a strong sense of history past: this is where St-Bernard called for the Second Crusade; where Richard the Lionheart and Philippe Auguste, arch-

72

enemies, undertook jointly the Third Crusade; and where, in 1166, Thomas à Becket took refuge and pronounced the excommunication of Henry II. You'll return often.

Avallon, too, has a vibrant feel of history past: Napoléon came this way, as did Mrs Simpson a century or so later. Be sure to take in the views from the south gate, high above the River **Cousin**; behind you is the old walled part of the town with medieval houses and the Church of St-Lazare. Now explore the Cousin; follow the river downstream through a small wooded valley which is as pretty as a picture. Shortly after the Cousin joins the **Cure** are the Grottes d'Arcy, 500 metres of underground caves carved out millions of years ago by the river. At the end of the caves, the floor looks as if the surface of the moon has been transported back to earth.

Now head east to two largely ignored river valleys. First to the **Armançon** and splendid **Semur-en-Auxois**. The river loops in a circle around the town's massive walls; the combination of the latter, many narrow streets and pleasing views is hard to resist. To the east is a trio of man-made treats: the idyllic small château at **Bussy-Rabutin**; the mixture of medieval eye-catchers within Flavigny-sur-Ozerain; and the legendary Roman hilltop citadel of **Aliso-Sainte-Reine**.

I'm always happy to give my time to **Fontenay**, lost in the woods to the east of **Montbard**. Founded in 1118, though greatly restored in later centuries, its a perfect example of the hugely important Cistercian influence on Burgundy many centuries ago. Six kilometres downstream from Montbard is the Taylor-Whitehead's restored forge at Buffon, another spot I would hate to miss. Further north are the well-known châteaux at **Tanlay** and **Ancy-le-Franc**, both "worth a detour".

Between the Armançon and Avallon lie the **Serein** Valley. **Epoisses** is renowned for its strong-smelling cheese and château; Montréal's perched site gives the village extra appeal; and **Noyers** is a romantic medieval gem, a tiny place with narrow streets and 500-year-old buildings, contained within a fortified wall with 16 towers. **Chablis**, further downstream, is a name instantly recognised by all wine buffs.

Less well known are the small wine villages of **St-Bris** and **Irancy**, south of **Auxerre** and in the **Yonne** Valley. St-Bris' white wines, made from Sauvignon and Aligoté grapes, are particularly good value; Irancy is the home of both rosés and reds (Palotte is a wine from the best slopes). Auxerre, a busy cathedral town, has particularly pleasing river views and shaded promenades alongside the Yonne's left bank.

Further upstream enjoy **Mailly-le-Château**. Seek out the medieval church and a 400-year-old lime tree and then relish the view from the terrace around the corner: tree-lined arms of the Yonne, a canal, wooded hills and the lower half of Mailly lie below you. The roads will be quiet as you head upstream through **Clamecy**, Dornecy and **Corbigny**.

I've said nothing about the hills that line the west side of the *route nationale* which connects Dijon, Beaune and **Chagny**. The slopes are some of our planet's most expensive real estate; they also produce many of the world's most sumptuous, wallet-busting wines. The Route des Grands Crus starts at **Marsannay**, near Dijon, and winds south through prosperous, handsome villages, a roll-call of household wine names.

In those same hills, to the west, are a series of deserted visual tonics: Montculot and its château; Pont-de-Pany alongside the Canal de Bourgogne; the abbey in landscaped grounds at Bussière-sur-Ouche; further west the perched village of **Châteauneuf** with extensive views, narrow streets and ancient houses; La Rochepot, another château with a mosaic roof; and **Mont Sène** (signposts call the peak Montagne des 3 Croix) with extensive panoramas of southern Burgundy.

See the Lyonnais chapter for details of the attractions that lie to the south of Mont Sène: places like **Cluny** and **Taizé**. But what I'm always impatient to do is to head west into the mystical **Morvan**. I'll try to persuade you to do the same.

Head west from Chagny to **Autun**; *en route* make a detour to Sully's marvellous château and park. Roman Autun, once called the "sister of Rome" by Julius Caesar, is a busy town; the 800-year-old St-Lazare Cathedral is its special treasure. Enter the Parc Naturel Régional du Morvan at St-Léger. The "park", 40 miles long by 30 miles wide, is extensively wooded, in the main with broadleaved trees, and is notable for its many rivers, much loved by "white water" enthusiasts.

Climb out of the village and follow signs to the 2695-ft-high **Mont Beuvray**. Once the Gallic *oppidum* of Bibracte, the fortified camp commands extensive views south and covers a large part of the Beuvray summit. At several points on the mountain archeological digs continue.

The woods to the north are a rejuvenating sight; in late October the panoramas are stunning. From afar the tops of beech, oak, sweet chestnut and silver birch resemble giant cobblestones of differing hues. Explore the valleys of the infant Yonne and the Touron, before visiting **Château-Chinon**, which has fine views in all directions, the best being from the *calvaire* high above the town.

Both the **Lac des Settons** and the lake at Pannesière-Chaumard are attractive and the roads encircling them are cool, rewarding drives. Between the two man-made reservoirs is the tiny hamlet of Planchez, alongside the D37. Be sure to nose out the most unpretentious and rustic café in France, Chez Millette, where Morvan fare is both cooked and served by *la patronne*: *jambon du Morvan*, *rosette* (pork sausage), *boudin blanc*, *crapinauds* (bacon pancakes) and *fromage blanc*.

During the last war the Morvan was renowned for its formidable Resistance groups (*maquis*). Among them was the Maquis Bernard, a pseudonym for its leader, Louis Aubin, a *gendarme* before hostilities started. The group operated in the wooded hills around **Montsauche**.

Give an hour or so of your time to the following itinerary. Head south-west from Montsauche on the D977; at Le Boulard follow the sign "Maquis Bernard Cimitière Franco-Anglais". In 1982, when I first "discovered" this unusual cemetery, the track was rough and there wasn't a clue, anywhere, to tell me the story of the *cimitière*. Today the lane is smooth and surviving members of the *maquis* have erected several signs along the route which explain the events of 1943/44.

During the last ten years hundreds of readers, urged on by me, have visited the poignant spot. The site and the "story" have made a dramatic impact on all those who sought out the cemetery. What the new signs do not tell you, and something I've only recently established, is that the bodies of the 21 *maquis* and seven British airmen, initially buried in the sacred ground, were moved some years after the war to other cemeteries in France. Nevertheless there remains an overpowering air of pride in this secret woodland corner. I know many of you have sensed a human "presence" at this most overwhelming of memorials: "souls are still there".

In the days after the D-Day landings there was a huge increase in Resistance activity in the Morvan. The *maquis* groups were joined by ten officers of the SAS. German soldiers were ambushed and killed; revenge was horrific. Montsauche was put to the torch; at Dun-les-Places 17 villagers were murdered; and Planchez was destroyed. The story of the Morvan Resistance is told at a museum based at the Maison du Parc at St-Brisson, north-east of Montsauche.

Before leaving the Morvan seek out the Saut de Gouloux, a modest waterfall north-east of Montsauche; the panorama from the observation table of hand-painted tiles atop the Rocher de la Pérouse (towards **Quarré-les-Tombes**); the picturesque château at **Chastellux** (en route to Vézelay); the old bridge over the Cure at Pierre-Perthuis; and, finally, the unusual *église* at **St-Père**, in the shadow of Vézelay.

Markets Arnay-le-Duc (Thurs); Autun (Wed and Fri); Auxerre (Tues, Fri and Sat); Avallon (Sat); Beaune (Sat); Chablis (Sun); Chagny (Thurs and Sun); Château-Chinon (Sat); Cluny (Sat); Dijon (Tues, Fri, Sat and Sun); Gevrey-Chambertin (Tues); Montbard (Fri); Noyers (Wed); Nuits-St-Georges (Fri); St-Florentin (Mon); Saulieu (Thurs and Sat).

Michelin green guide: Burgundy (in English).

Cheeses Cow's milk

L'Ami du Chambertin salty, washed in Marc de Bourgogne

Aisy-Cendré cured in Marc and stored in wood ashes. Firm, strong-smelling, fruity taste; good with full-bodied red wines

Boulette de La Pierre-Qui-Vire amusingly named; made at the abbey of the same name near St-Léger-Vauban. Small, firm herb-flavoured ball

Chaource to the west of Les Riceys. At its best in summer and autumn; a creamy cheese, made in cylinders; mushroom smell

Cîteaux thick disk, very rare and made by the monks at Cîteaux Monastery - once a rival of Cluny. Cîteaux is to the east of Nuits-St-Georges (11 km from the A31 autoroute exit)

Ducs made near Tonnerre; a soft cylinder ideal with St-Bris whites

Epoisses soft, orange-dusted, made as a flat cylinder. At its best in the summer, autumn and winter; goes well with full-bodied red wines

Langres small, cone-shaped and strong. Related to Epoisses and is made north of Dijon. Try it with red Burgundy

Les Riceys from the borders of Champagne and Burgundy; a still Rosé des Riceys comes from the same area and is classified as a Champagne wine. Try it with this soft, fruity-tasting, small disk of cheese

Rouy related to Epoisses. Strong smell, soft and made as a square

St-Florentin related to Epoisses. Smooth, red-brown appearance with spicy taste. Season summer to winter

Soumaintrain strong tasting, russet crust, brine washed

Goat's milk

Dornecy just west of Vézelay. Small, firm, upright cylinder

Lormes south of Avallon, related to both Dornecy and Vézelay

Montrachet soft, mild and creamy; made as a tall cylinder

Pourly slight nutty flavour, soft and made as a small cylinder

Vézelay a farm-produced cheese, at its best in summer and autumn. Soft, and in the form of a cone, with a bluish rind

Regional Specialities

Boeuf Bourguignon braised beef simmered in red wine-based sauce

Charolais (Pièce de) steak from the excellent Charolais cattle

Garbure heavy soup; mixture of pork, cabbage, beans and sausages

Gougère cheese pastry, based on Gruyère cheese

Jambon persillé parsley-flavoured ham, served cold in its jelly
Jambon en saupiquet, Jambon à la crème, Jambon à la Morvandelle
ham with a piquant cream sauce, wine and wine vinegar
Matelote freshwater fish soup, usually based on a red wine sauce
Meurette red wine-based sauce with small onions. Accompanies fish or
poached egg dishes
Pain d'épice spiced honeycake from Dijon
Pochouse (Pouchouse) stew of freshwater fish and garlic, usually
white wine based. Rarely seen on restaurant menus
Potée see *Garbure*

WINES & CHEESES

Wines

I have asked you to always try local wines; the only difficulty in
this region is that some of the "locals" are the most famous and
expensive in the world. Some *Grand Cru* wines, dating back to
the best vintage years, could cost as much as you are paying for
your whole holiday. The simple reason for this is that the Côte
d'Or, where the best Burgundy wines come from, produces less
than one-tenth of the AC wines of Bordeaux; yet, there is a
complex patchwork of many dozens of Appellation Contrôlée
classifications, every one of them listed here. All the famous
Burgundies, those at the very top of the pyramid, both in quality
and price, will have labels that identify them down to the
commune, followed by the vineyard, *domaine* or *clos* itself,
some no bigger than a pocket handkerchief. Most of them will
have their own AC, whereas in Bordeaux, the famous châteaux

share the AC for the local *commune* or region. In Burgundy, the term *Premier Cru* means the second rank vineyards – below the *Grand Cru* top level (these days they're called simply *Cru*).

The best red Burgundy is usually less dry and is sweeter than a claret, warm and more full-bodied. The great white Burgundies, rich and dry, are far and away the best whites to drink with food, but most of them are priced out of reach of us all. The groups of AC classifications which follow have all been listed in **north** to **south** order; this will help you to locate and identify each village, and the estates within them, more readily.

Famous Reds (Great vintages: 49 61 64 69 71 76 78 85 90)

This first group lists the great red wine *communes*, each with their own AC; in brackets are shown the individual Appellation Contrôlée estates within each village. These are the great wine-producing estates, the *Grand Cru* vineyards:

Gevrey-Chambertin	(Mazis-Chambertin, Ruchottes-Chambertin, Chapelle-Chambertin, Griotte-Chambertin, Chambertin Clos de Bèze, Chambertin, Charmes-Chambertin, Latricières-Chambertin Mazoyères-Chambertin)
Morey-Saint Denis	(Clos de la Roche, Clos Saint Denis, Clos de Tart, Clos des Lambrays)
Chambolle-Musigny	(Bonnes Mares, Musigny)
Vougeot	(Clos de Vougeot)
Vosne-Romanée	(Echézeaux, Grands Echézeaux, Richebourg, Romanée-Saint Vivant, Romanée, Romanée-Conti, La Tâche: these are some of the world's finest vineyards)
Nuits-Saint Georges	
Aloxe-Corton	(Corton, Charlemagne)
Pernand-Vergelesses	
Savigny-lès-Beaune	
Beaune	
Pommard	
Volnay	(Volnay-Santenots; not a *Grand Cru* and sited in Meursault)
Monthélie	
Auxey-Duresses	
Santenay	

Famous Whites (Great vintages: 69 71 73 76 79 89 90)

The following are the famous white wine villages with AC classifications (estates with their own AC are shown in brackets):

Chablis	To the east of Auxerre; **Grand Cru** and **Premier Cru** classifications
Aloxe-Corton	(Corton-Charlemagne)
Meursault	
Puligny-Montrachet	(Chevalier-Montrachet, Bienvenues Bâtard-Montrachet, Montrachet, Bâtard-Montrachet, Criots-Bâtard-Montrachet)
Chassagne-Montrachet	
Pouilly-Fuissé	Well to the south, near Mâcon

Rosés

Perhaps the best rosé in France comes from Marsannay, the village at the northern end of the Route des Grands Crus. But that's not the only rosé. A host of more general rosés have their own AC classifications – all starting with the word **Bourgogne**:

Grand Ordinaire Rosé; Ordinaire Rosé; Rosé; Rosé Hautes Côtes de Nuits; Rosé Hautes Côtes de Beaune; and a new AC **Rosé Côtes Chalonnaise**.

Less-Famous Wines

The ordinary traveller will have to be content with the wines carrying humbler labels, and thankfully, among the dozens of *appellations*, there are many really fine, inexpensive wines like the following examples:

Reds

Bourgogne Ordinaire. Bourgogne Grand Ordinaire (made from the Gamay grape – the lowest Burgundy *appellation*; *clairet* – this term, if applied to any Burgundy wines, means they will be light red wines). **Bourgogne Passetoutgrains** (a mixture of Gamay – two-thirds – and Pinot Noir – one-third; slightly further up the quality scale). **Bourgogne** – made from Pinot Noir - is an even more highly thought of *appellation* and is produced in much the greatest quantities among the reds of the area. **Bourgogne Marsannay** and **Bourgogne-Marsannay-la-Côte. Fixin. Bourgogne Hautes Côtes de Nuits. Côtes de Nuits (Vins Fins). Côte de Nuits-Villages. Bourgogne Hautes Côtes de Beaune. Ladoix. Chorey-lès-Beaune. Côte de Beaune. Côte de Beaune-Villages** (13 can add their names). **Blagny. Maranges** (previously three ACs). **Mercurey. Givry. Mâcon (rouge). Mâcon Supérieur**.

Whites

Petit Chablis. Bourgogne. Bourgogne Aligoté (the second rank grape type, but the most common white). **Bourgogne Bouzeron Aligoté. Auxey-Duresses. Saint Romain. Saint Aubin. Rully. Montagny** (including **Buxy**). **Bourgogne Côtes Chalonnaise. Mâcon (blanc)**; over 40 villages can add their names. **Mâcon-Villages. Pinot Chardonnay-Mâcon** (a *varietal* wine example). **Pouilly-Loché. Pouilly-Vinzelles** (these last two villages, just east of Fuissé, are cheaper alternatives to Pouilly-Fuissé; they do not have the right to that famous name). **Saint Véran** (see Lyonnais: several villages straddling Pouilly-Fuissé and including Saint Vérand – note the spelling – have the right to this AC; again, a similar wine to its famous namesake). Many restaurants describe Mâconnais wines by village names: two of the best of the 40+ are **Vire** and **Lugny**.

Many of the villages in the lists produce both red and white wines. Remember also that many of the well-known *communes* in the first two lists will have vineyards in them that have the right to claim the AC for the village, but, nevertheless, do not have the reputation of some of their famous neighbours; many of those villages will have excellent wines at much lower prices.

Other wines

If you are based at Avallon, or anywhere in the north of the region, look out for the red **Irancy**, the light **Rosé Irancy** and the crisp, dry white wine called **Sauvignon de St-Bris**, made in two tiny villages on the eastern bank of the Yonne. Other local villages are **Chitry** and **Coulanges**; their names are often seen on wine lists. Look out, too, for a **Crémant de Bourgogne** or a **Bourgogne mousseux**. Try a **Marc de Bourgogne**, pure spirit, distilled from grapes after the final pressing. Dijon is where Cassis is produced – that rich syrup made from blackcurrants and, when added to white wine (particularly good with Aligoté), it becomes **Kir**, named after Canon Kir, a mayor of Dijon and a Resistance hero. Mixed with Crémant de Bourgogne it's called **Royal Kir**. Relish, too, Liqueur de Poires William.

AUXERRE   Les Clairions

Comfortable hotel/Cooking 1
Swimming pool/Tennis/Lift/Parking

Leave A6 Auxerre-Nord exit. On left-hand side of N6 towards
Auxerre. Useful for Barnabet restaurant.
Menus B. Rooms (60) C-D. Disabled. Cards All.
Post av. Worms, 89000 Auxerre, Yonne. (En Route p 51)
Tel 86 46 85 64. Telex 800039. Fax 86 48 16 38. Mich 72/A2.

AUXERRE   Mercure

Comfortable hotel/Cooking 1-2
Gardens/Swimming pool/Parking

Leave A6 Auxerre-Nord exit. Hotel, in large park, on south
side of A6; turn right after passing through toll.
Menus B-C. Rooms (82) E. Disabled. Cards All.
Post 89380 Appoigny, Yonne. (En Route p 51)
Tel 86 53 25 00. Telex 800095. Fax 86 53 07 47. Mich 72/A1.
(Bookings: UK 071 724 1000; US toll free 800 221 4542)

BEAUNE   Campanile

Simple hotel/Cooking 1
Swimming pool/Parking/Good value

Leave A6 Beaune exit. Left after toll, towards Montagny.
Menus A-B. Rooms (42) C. Disabled. Cards Access, Visa.
Post Montagny-lès-Beaune, 21200 Beaune, Côte-d'Or.
Tel 80 22 65 50. Telex 350156. Fax 80 24 73 98. Mich 88/A2.
(Bookings: UK freephone 0800 897863)

BEAUNE   Climat de France

Simple hotel/Cooking 1
Terrace/Parking/Good value

Leave A6 Beaune exit. Through toll, on left towards Beaune.
One of several hotels near A6. English-speaking manager.
Menus A-B. Rooms (48) C. Disabled. Cards AE, Access, Visa.
Post av. Ch. de Gaulle, 21200 Beaune, Côte-d'Or. (ER p 54)
Tel 80 22 74 10. Telex 351384. Fax 80 22 40 45. Mich 88/A2.
(Bookings: UK 071 287 3181)

BEAUNE   Ibis

Simple hotel/Cooking 1
Terrace/Gardens/Swimming pool/Lift/Parking

Leave A6 Beaune exit. Through toll towards Beaune.
Menus A-B. Rooms (103) C-D. Disabled. Cards Access, Visa.
Post av. Ch. de Gaulle, 21200 Beaune, Côte-d'Or.
Tel 80 22 46 75. Telex 351410. Fax 80 22 21 16. Mich 88/A2.
(Bookings: UK 071 724 1000; US toll free 800 221 4542)

Autoroute Hotels

BEAUNE   Novotel

Very comfortable hotel/Cooking 1
Terrace/Gardens/Swimming pool/Lift/Parking

One of the newest Novotels, a multi-storey affair. Leave A6
Beaune exit, through toll and on right towards Beaune.
Menus B. Rooms (127) D-E. Disabled. Cards All.
Post av. Ch. de Gaulle, 21200 Beaune, Côte-d'Or.
Tel 80 24 59 00. Telex 352237. Fax 80 24 59 29. Mich 88/A2.
(Bookings: UK 071 724 1000; US toll free 800 221 4542)

CHALON-SUR-SAONE   Ibis

Simple hotel (no restaurant)
Parking

A6 Chalon-Nord exit. On left towards town. Court Paille grill.
No rest (see above). Rooms (61) C-D. Cards Access, Visa.
Post 71100 Chalon-sur-Saône, S.-et-L. (En Route p 54)
Tel 85 46 64 62. Telex 800381. Mich 88/A3.
(Bookings: UK 071 724 1000; US toll free 800 221 4542)

CHALON-SUR-SAONE   Mercure

Very comfortable hotel/Cooking 1-2
Terrace/Gardens/Swimming pool/Lift/Parking

Leave A6 Chalon-Nord exit. On right past toll.
Menus B-C. Rooms (85) E. Disabled. Cards All.
Post av. Europe, 71100 Chalon-sur-Saône, S.-et-L. (ER p 54)
Tel 85 46 51 89. Telex 800132. Fax 85 46 08 96. Mich 88/A3.
(Bookings: UK 071 724 1000; US toll free 800 221 4542)

NUITS-ST-GEORGES   St-Georges

Simple hotel/Cooking 1
Terrace/Swimming pool/Tennis/Lift/Garage/Parking

Leave A31 exit 1 (Nuits-St-Georges). Past toll on right. New,
modern hotel, not far from railway line.
Menus A-B. Rooms (47) C-D. Disabled. Cards All.
Post 21700 Nuits-St-Georges, Côte-d'Or.
Tel 80 61 15 00. Telex 351370. Fax 80 61 23 80. Mich 88/B2.

TIL-CHATEL   Poste

Simple hotel/Cooking 1
Garage/Good value

Leave A31 exit 5. 3 km S on N74. In Til (which is bypassed).
Menus A-B. Rooms (9) B-C. Cards Access, Visa.
Closed Last wk Oct. Xmas-New Year. 20 Feb to 8 Mar. Sat (not
evgs May to Oct). Sun evg (Nov to Apl).
Post 21120 Til-Châtel, Côte-d'Or. (En Route p 134)
Tel 80 95 03 53. Mich 74/B3.

ALOXE-CORTON
Clarion

Comfortable hotel
Secluded/Gardens/Parking

Regularly praised by readers: for the "protected" village of
Aloxe-Corton, surrounded by vines; and the breakfasts served
by Edmée and Christian Voarick, among the best in France.
Rooms (10) E-F. Disabled. Cards All.
Post 21420 Aloxe-Corton, Côte-d'Or.
Tel 80 26 46 70. Fax 80 26 47 16. Mich 88/A2.

AUXERRE
Hôtel Le Maxime

Very comfortable hotel
Lift/Garage

Overlooking the Yonne and in the shadow of the cathedral. An
ideal base for the Barnabet restaurant, a two min. walk away.
Rooms (25) D-F. Cards All.
Post 2 quai Marine, 89000 Auxerre, Yonne. (En Route p 51)
Tel 86 52 14 19. Fax 86 52 21 70. Mich 72/A2.

AVALLON
Moulin des Templiers

Simple hotel
Secluded/Gardens/Parking

The old mill has an idyllic setting, alongside the tree-lined
Cousin. Much loved, but frequent groans about small bedrooms.
Rooms (14) C-D. Cards None.
Closed Nov to mid March.
Post 89200 Avallon, Yonne.
Tel 86 34 10 80. Mich 72/B3.

AVALLON
Vauban

Comfortable hotel
Fairly quiet/Gardens/Lift/Parking

Though alongside the N6 and in town centre most rooms, at the
rear, are fairly quiet. Two min. walk from Morvan restaurant.
Rooms (26) C-D. Cards None.
Post 53 rue de Paris, 89200 Avallon, Yonne. (En Route p 52)
Tel 86 34 36 99. Fax 86 31 66 31. Mich 72/B3.

BEAUNE
Le Cep

Very comfortable hotel
Fairly quiet/Lift/Garage/Parking

A tremendous restoration job: handsome stonework at rear;
fine furnishings. Bernard Morillon restaurant in same building.
Rooms (49) F-F2. Disabled. Cards All.
Post 27 rue Maufoux, 21200 Beaune, Côte-d'Or.
Tel 80 22 35 48. Telex 351256. Fax 80 22 76 80. Mich 88/A2.

BEAUNE La Closerie

Comfortable hotel
Quiet/Gardens/Swimming pool/Parking

Modern, busy and on the N74 south-west of Beaune.
Rooms (46) D-F. Disabled. Cards All.
Closed Xmas to mid Jan.
Post rte Autun, 21200 Beaune, Côte-d'Or.
Tel 80 22 15 07. Telex 351213. Fax 80 24 16 22. Mich 88/A2.

CHAGNY Poste

Simple hotel
Quiet/Gardens/Garage/Parking/Good value

Ideal for those on a tight budget. In town centre.
Rooms (11) C. Cards Access, Visa.
Closed 20 Nov to mid March.
Post rue Poste, 71150 Chagny, S.-et-L.
Tel 85 87 08 27. Mich 88/A3.

GEVREY-CHAMBERTIN Les Grands Crus

Comfortable hotel
Quiet/Gardens/Parking

New owners, the Farniers, ensure the hotel continues to be
well liked. Two minute walk to Les Millésimes restaurant.
Rooms (24) D-E. Cards Access, Visa.
Closed Dec to Feb.
Post 21220 Gevrey-Chambertin, Côte-d'Or.
Tel 80 34 34 15. Fax 80 51 89 07. Mich 88/B1.

GEVREY-CHAMBERTIN Les Terroirs

Comfortable hotel
Gardens/Parking

Strongly recommended by readers. On N74 but don't be put
off; the stylish 17 bedrooms at the rear are surprisingly quiet.
Rooms (20) D-E. Disabled. Cards All.
Closed Dec to Jan.
Post route de Dijon, 21220 Gevry-Chambertin, Côte-d'Or.
Tel 80 34 30 76. Fax 80 34 11 79. Mich 88/B1.

LEVERNOIS Parc

Simple hotel
Secluded/Gardens/Parking

Much liked. Book ahead. Next door to Crotet restaurant.
Rooms (25) B-E. Cards Visa. (East of A6 autoroute.)
Closed Mid Nov to mid Dec.
Post Levernois, 21200 Beaune, Côte-d'Or. (En Route p 54)
Tel 80 24 63 00. Mich 88/A2.

ALLIGNY-EN-MORVAN   Auberge du Morvan

Very simple restaurant with basic rooms/Cooking 1-2
Good value

Jean Branlard's rustic little *auberge* is on the eastern fringes
of the Morvan Regional Park. Humble is the word; but a smile
is guaranteed when you come to settle the bill. Stick with the
local dishes: *terrine maison, rosette, jambon persillé, jambon en
saupiquet, jambon cru du Morvan* and *crêpe Morvandian* (a
dessert). Note carefully when closed.
Menus A-B. Rooms (5) B. Cards Visa.
Closed Nov to Feb. Mon to Fri (Mar, Apl, Oct). Thurs & every
evg except Sat (May, June, Sept). (Open every day July/Aug.)
Post 58230 Alligny-en-Morvan, Nièvre.
Tel 86 76 13 90. Mich 87/D1.

AUTUN   Chalet Bleu

Comfortable restaurant/Cooking 2
Good value

Modern cooking from the hands of Philippe Boucher, who once
worked for François Mitterrand. Fish specialities and desserts
are absolutely terrific. Good to see, too, among the lighter
personal creations, a *saupiquet de jambon vieux Morvan* and a
jambon persillé. Philippe's father, and owner of the restaurant,
looks after the front of house. Père Boucher was once the chef
at the French Embassy in London.
Menus A-B. Cards All. (Rooms? Nearby Arcades.)
Closed Feb. Mon evg. Tues.
Post 3 rue Jeannin, 71400 Autun, S.-et-L.
Tel 85 86 27 30. Mich 87/E3

AUXERRE   Barnabet

Very comfortable restaurant/Cooking 3-4
Terrace

Readers of the first edition of *French Leave* will recall that
Jean-Luc and Marie Barnabet's first restaurant was at nearby
Vaux, south of Auxerre and on the left bank of the Yonne. The
big-hearted, sunny couple have a new home now, once again
alongside the Yonne. We saw the empty shell, previously a
garage, a couple of years ago when, delayed by endless
problems, the couple were nervously waiting to fire off again.
The finished job is a restrained success. So, too, is Jean-Luc's
modern cooking. He has a sure touch and makes much use of
local wines: Chablis, of course, but also the Irancy Gamay and
the not-well-known Epineuil and Auxerre's Clos de la
Chaînette. More good news: handsome, English-speaking Jean-
Claude Mourguiart (he once worked for Raymond Blanc at
Summertown) is *sommelier*, *M-D* and a partner. Ask to see the
Menu Enfant, written by Julie Barnabet, now an 11-year-old.
Menus B-C. Cards Access, Visa. (Rooms? See A/R & Base hotels.)
Closed Xmas to mid Jan. Sun evg. Mon.
Post 14 quai de la République, 89000 Auxerre, Yonne.
Tel 86 51 68 88. Mich 72/A2.

AVALLON
Morvan

Very comfortable restaurant/Cooking 2
Terrace/Gardens

If your tastes are exclusively influenced by lightness and
brightness and food served on black octagonal plates, then
don't visit the Morvan. Jean and Marinette Breton soldier on,
loyal to classical and regional traditions. Reports vary wildly:
most relish Jean's substantial and numerous home-made
terrines and *pâtés*. A caveat though: I said substantial. One
reader gave the football-sized mound of butter the bird: "Brits
breathe over it, unhealthily." The Morvan gives you the chance
to step back a few decades; France as she used to be.
Menus B-C. Cards All. (Rooms? See Base hotels.)
Closed Jan. Feb. 12-22 Nov. Sun evg & Mon (not pub. hols).
Post 7 rte de Paris (N6), 89200 Avallon, Yonne.
Tel 86 34 18 20. Mich 72/B3.

BEAUNE
Bernard Morillon

Very comfortable restaurant/Cooking 3
Terrace

Here's one of the supreme outposts of authentic French
classical cuisine. Here, too, is one of my readers' most loved,
most praised culinary couples. In their days at the
Castel de Valrose, Montmerle, they were, after Alain and
Nicole Rayé, the most popular French favourite. Bernard,
trained by the legendary Eugénie Brazier at the Col de la
Luère (see *Les Mères Merveilleuses,* Lyonnais), is a supporter
of classical skills: glories described as *rognon de veau
Alexandre Dumaine, gratin de barbue Brillat-Savarin, homard
façon Mère Brazier, pigeonneau de Bresse Souvaroff* and sauces
such as *beurre blanc* and *sauce Périgueux*. Martine Morillon
plays a vital part in the client seduction: is there a more
vivacious, larger than life extrovert with such a bubbling,
expansive welcome for guests anywhere else in France? She
tells me that 1993 may see them move to another Beaune
home, this one their own restaurant with rooms. (The present
set-up is part of the 17th-century Le Cep; see Base hotels. Do
look at the rear courtyard and its stunning stonework.)
Menus B-D. Cards All. (Rooms? See various A/R & Base hotels.)
Closed Feb. Mon. Tues midday.
Post 31 rue Maufoux, 21200 Beaune, Côte-d'Or.
Tel 80 24 12 06. Fax 80 22 66 22. Mich 88/A2.

BOUILLAND
Host. du Vieux Moulin

Very comfortable restaurant/Cooking 4
Secluded/Terrace/Swimming pool(indoor)/Tennis/Parking

I first visited the Vieux Moulin 10 years ago, just after Jean
Pierre and Isabelle Silva bought the mill from the illustrious
Raymond Heriot. Still only in his mid-thirties, J-P has
graduated into an accomplished chef. On our last three visits
Anne and I have had a succession of specialities which made
three-star chefs' efforts seem like kindergarten rip-offs. The

second Michelin star arrived two years ago; and, at last, Gault
Millau have seen the light as well.

What is exceptionally welcome is that Silva rarely makes
use of any cream, butter and flour. He's fond of tampering with
centuries-old recipes and his innovative work is both unfussy
and assured. What has intrigued me is that, among the scores
of readers who have sung his praises, many British chefs rated
their meals as among the best they had eaten in France. Among
a dozen or more highlights we savour memories of a *suprême
de chapon au lait lardé, sa cuisse en jambonneau*, a dish
involving painstaking technique; and a *millefeuille* of thin
ginger-bread slices interleaved with vanilla ice cream. All has
not been rosy however. One serious complaint concerned a
hostile welcome from Isabelle; this occurred in the period after
her daughter, Laura, was recovering from a terrible car
accident. And another reader spoke of two courses as *nouvelle*
gone gaga: tiny pieces of *canette* under a cabbage leaf and a
chocolate cannon-ball dessert.

June 1992 saw the completion of 14 extra bedrooms, an
indoor swimming pool, gym, sauna and billiards room.

Menus C-E. Rooms (27) E-F2. Disabled. Cards Access, Visa.
Closed 15 Dec-15 Jan. Rest: Wed/Thurs midday (not pub. hols).
Post 21420 Bouilland, Côte-d'Or.
Tel 80 21 51 16. Fax 80 21 59 90. Mich 88/A2.

CHABLIS   Hostellerie des Clos

Very comfortable restaurant with rooms/Cooking 3
Quiet/Gardens/Lift/Parking

I first encountered Michel and Marié Vignaud at the Aub. de
l'Atre (see Quarré-les-Tombes) in 1985, shortly after they won
their first Michelin star. A year later they moved to Chablis
and the old town hospice. Originally trained by Marc Meneau,
the chef is a modern cooking fan; many of his creations make
use of Chablis white and Irancy red wines. Lack of consistency
is the only debit featuring in readers' feedback. Over 200
northern Burgundy wines are listed; from a Petit Chablis half-
bottle at 50 francs to a bottle of 1964 Le Clos at 1,650 francs.
Menus B-E. Rooms (26) C-F. Cards Access, Visa.
Closed 9 Dec to 10 Jan. Wed. Thurs midday (Oct to May).
Post rue Jules Rathier, 89800 Chablis, Yonne. (VFB base.)
Tel 86 42 10 63. Telex 351752. Fax 86 42 17 11. Mich 72/B2.

CHATEAUNEUF   Host. du Château

Simple hotel/Cooking 1-2
Secluded/Terrace/Gardens

Anne and I first stayed at this 15th-century presbytery, with
its westerly views from the evocative perched village of
Châteauneuf, in 1976. The village, with centuries-old houses,
has been saved from dereliction by private individuals, not by
the State. Classical and *Bourgeoise* cooking.
Menus C. Rooms (16) B-F. Cards AE, Access, Visa.
Closed Mid Nov-mid Feb. Mon evg & Tues (15 Sept-15 June).
Post 21230 Châteauneuf, Côte-d'Or.
Tel 80 49 22 00. Fax 80 49 21 27. Mich 87/F1.

GEVREY-CHAMBERTIN   Les Millésimes

Very comfortable restaurant/Cooking 3-4
Parking

How's this for an involved family sextet? Jean Sangoy and his
sons, Denis and Laurent, work in the kitchen; Monique, the
elegant mother, runs the front-of-house, assisted by daughter
Sophie and son Didier, a top-notch *sommelier*. I cannot praise
the family enough. I've known the restaurant (an old below-
the-ground *cave*) for most of the nine years since the Sangoy
family returned to France from Argentina; progress has been
remarkable. The dining room is as opulent a cellar as you can
ever imagine. The furnishings are lavish: Limoges crockery,
crystal glasses, candelabra, an exceedingly handsome wine list
and menu (both printed on heavy, rich paper), attractive small
flower arrangements on the tables, lots of greenery and the
family dressed in a manner which complements the serious
restaurant Les Millésimes undoubtedly is.

The classical and neo-classical cooking is faultless and
assured. Among many sumptuous specialities a *canette de
Barbarie au miel et aux épices* (7 of them) *en deux service*,
purée pomme poire, petite salade deserves an Oscar. There are
also many lighter, simpler dishes: witness a *langoustines rôties
au beurre léger*. And surely there's no more superb wine cellar
(40,000 bottles) in provincial France? Study the wine *carte* and
drool over the glorious roll-call of vintages; for most of us
reading the contents will have to suffice as some of the prices
will make you shudder.

Menus C-E. Cards All. (100-yard walk from Grands Crus base.)
Closed Christmas to New Year. Tues. Wed midday.
Post 25 rue Eglise, 21220 Gevrey-Chambertin, Côte-d'Or.
Tel 80 51 84 24. Fax 80 34 12 73. Mich 88/B1.

GEVREY-CHAMBERTIN La Rôtisserie du Chambertin

Very comfortable restaurant/Cooking 3
Parking

How good to see Pierre Menneveau recover his zest for life
again after Céline, his chef wife, died in May 1985. The new
chef, and partner too, is Jean-Pierre Nicolas who, among many
stints in famed kitchens, spent a dozen years working for
Outhier at La Napoule. One important change: Pierre, a fluent
English speaker, now displays a menu outside the door in the
corner of the courtyard. J-P's cooking is a mix of styles but
essentially classical: an olden days *pâte en croûte*; a dark and
sweetish *coq au vin à l'ancienne comme Céline Menneveau*; a
succulent *suprême de volaille, sauce à l'Ami du Chambertin*
(local cheese); and a modern-day *pigeon entier rôti au four, aux
épices et au miel* are typical. The wine *carte* is a roll call of
Gevrey-Chambertin's finest vintages. You can buy direct from
Pierre; there's no better expert on the village's ruby wines.
He's also thinking about opening a less-expensive restaurant
in the rooms upstairs; let's hope he does.

Menus C-D. Cards Access, Visa.
Closed Feb. 1st wk Aug. Sun evg & Mon (not pub. hols).
Post 21220 Gevrey-Chambertin, Côte-d'Or.
Tel 80 34 33 20. Fax 80 34 12 30. Mich 88/B1.

JOIGNY   Modern'H Frères Godard

Very comfortable hotel/Cooking 3
Gardens/Swimming pool/Tennis/Garage/Parking

We first stayed at the Modern 30 years ago. Renovated,
repainted and refurbished, the Modern, today, is just that.
Jean-Claude and Nicole Godard are the owners; brother Charles
runs the Paris et Poste in Sens. Cooking is neo-classical: try
J-C's father's elaborate creation, *le fameux canard à la Gaston
Godard aux deux façons et son gratin Morvandiau*. A local
reader prefers the nearby Paris Nice rest (owned by the
Godards). One snag: if you eat out you pay more for bedrooms.
Menus C-D. Rooms (21) E-F. Cards All.
Closed 1st 3 wks Feb. (On N6, S of town, opposite station.)
Post 17 rue Robert Petit, 89300 Joigny, Yonne. (ER p 50)
Tel 86 62 16 28. Telex 801693. Fax 86 62 44 33. Mich 71/E1.

LEVERNOIS   Hostellerie de Levernois

Luxury restaurant with rooms/Cooking 3-4
Secluded/Terrace/Gardens/Tennis/Parking

Things are looking up for Jean Crotet and his son, Christophe.
The family has left the Côte d'Or in Nuits-St-Georges (see
FL3) and encamped in a heavenly setting east of the A6 and
Beaune. Light, spacious and airy dining rooms with fine
flagstones and bedrooms in a single storey annexe at the heart
of a park-like garden; there's even a stream. Cooking has
changed to an exclusively modern style which, when compared
with Jean's Nuits days, often disappoints. His *foie gras*
remains Burgundy's best. Christianne, Jean's wife, still
masterminds the huge *cave* with its superb *vins du pays*. Her
daughter-in-law, Gabrielle, is an English girl. Golf next door.
(Cheaper rooms? Use the adjacent Levernois base hotel.)
Menus C (lunch, Mon-Fri); D-F. Rooms (12) F2. Cards All.
Closed 20 Dec-10 Jan. Tues & Wed midday.
Post Levernois, 21200 Beaune, Côte-d'Or.
Tel 80 24 73 58. Telex 351468. Fax 80 22 78 00. Mich 88/A2.

MAILLY-LE-CHATEAU   Le Castel

Comfortable restaurant with rooms/Cooking 2
Quiet/Gardens/Good value

Readers adore this old-world corner of France: the village, the
site and view of the Yonne below, the church, the Trumpton
Town Hall clock (now gagged at night), the 400-year-old lime
tree, Le Castel and, above all, the friendliest of owners, Michel
and Janet Breerette. A fluent English speaker, Michel worked
on the French Line and in Britain for many years. Menus are a
mix of *Bourgeois* and classical. The Prégilbert trout come from
a hamlet up the road. Try the Irancy Palotte wine. Furnishings
and décor, too, are old-fashioned traditional.
Menus A-B. Rooms (12) B-D. Cards Access, Visa.
Closed Mid Nov to mid Mar. Wed.
Post 89660 Mailly-le-Château (Le Haut), Yonne.
Tel 86 81 43 06. Fax 86 81 49 26. Mich 72/A3.

MERCUREY Hôtellerie du Val d'Or

Comfortable hotel/Cooking 3
Gardens/Garage

I can pay this family hotel no better compliment by repeating the opening words I used in *Favourites*. Here in Mercurey is an example which epitomises the thousands of dedicated, hardworking French hotelier families. The Cogny family is in every way typical of the very best of the breed. Jean-Claude Cogny is at the heart of this happy home; self-effacing, with a ready smile and eager to help clients. Wife Monique is a quiet, unassuming soul, always ready to be involved. The couple welcome you as if you were old friends. The menus are studded with authentic Burgundian specialities, not prissy, tarted-up interpretations: *jambon persillé, oeufs en meurette, le vrai coq au vin* and others. But both classical and modern also have their place. Jean-Claude is anxious to ensure clients know about the latter: an example is *rouget barbet rôti à la coriandre et au thym.* Many super Rully and Mercurey wines; the Delorme and Juillot vintages are notable examples.
Menus B-D. Rooms (13) D. Cards Access, Visa.
Closed 1 wk May. 1st wk Sept. 15 Dec-15 Jan. Mon. Tues midday.
Post 71640 Mercurey, S.-et-L.
Tel 85 45 13 70. Fax 85 45 18 45. Mich 88/A3.

MONTSAUCHE-LES-SETTONS Idéal

Very simple hotel/Cooking 1
Quiet/Gardens/Garage/Parking/Good value

Montsauche was put to the torch in 1944; the Mariller hotel was no exception. The Idéal was rebuilt in 1950. Alice Mariller has run the hotel single-handedly since her husband died 23 years ago. Enjoy modest local and *Bourgeoise* fare like Morvan *charcuterie, omelette Morvandelle* and *truite de pays.*
Menus A-B. Rooms (15) C. Cards Access, Visa.
Closed Nov to Easter.
Post 58230 Montsauche-les-Settons, Nièvre.
Tel 86 84 51 26. Mich 87/D1.

QUARRE-LES-TOMBES Auberge de l'Atre

Very comfortable restaurant/Cooking 2-3
Gardens/Parking/Good value

I implore you to make the effort to seek out the 18th-century granite farmhouse, 5 km south of Quarré (an easy 20-minute drive on the D10 from Avallon). The Morvan is irresistible; the garden is a colourful *palette*; the owners, Odile and English-speaking Francis Salamolard, are accomplished hosts; and the cooking is an exuberant mix of styles. Top marks to Francis: for the numerous Morvan-grown herbs he uses; his tremendous efforts to offer 30 desserts; a *cave* of 350 wines (and rare in France for their *rapport qualité-prix*); and tasty regional cheeses. Specialities include many surprises (for the heart of the Morvan that is): *eventails de turbot légérement safrané, et au Crémant de Bourgogne*; *salade de truite saumonée*

fumée au citron vert et aux pétales de fleurs; and *les filets de sandre à la sariette et au serpolet*. If you cannot manage lunch or dinner then why not try afternoon tea?
Menus B-C. Cards All. (Rooms? See Avallon base hotels.)
Closed 26 Nov-7 Dec. 25 Jan-10 Mar. Tues evg/Wed (Sept-June).
Post Les Lavaults, 89630 Quarré-les-Tombes, Yonne.
Tel 86 32 20 79. Mich 72/C4. (On D10, 5 km south of town.)

QUARRE-LES-TOMBES   Auberge des Brizards

Comfortable hotel/Cooking 1-2
Secluded/Terrace/Gardens/Tennis/Parking

Odd-ball and quirky: perhaps even unique? You have to work hard to find the place; follow signs from Quarré, heading east and south-east on the D55, D355 and V7 to Les Brizards, hidden in a wooded, remote corner of Morvan. This is time travel: Tardis takes you back through the decades to an old farm (tarted up in a salmon-pink wash these days); to hearty, anything but frivolous Burgundian fare; and to a formidable family trio. Boss is 75-year-old Odette Arfeux, *cuisinière extraordinaire*; she's helped in the kitchen by her grandson, Jérôme Besancenot; and his mother, glamorous Françine, runs the dining room. The farm and its *étang* are put to good use: the pigs, turkeys, rabbits, chickens, ducks and geese come through no middle man here, but straight from farmyard to cooking pot; eggs are still warm fresh; hams are cured and dried *sur place*; and *charcuterie* and *le vrai boudin* are both home-made. Here, too, you can relish a Morvan version of a *crapinaud de blé noir aux petits lardons* (bacon pancake).
Menus B-C. Rooms (25) C-F. Cards AE, Access, Visa.
Closed Jan to mid Feb.
Post Les Brizards, 89630 Quarré-les-Tombes, Yonne.
Tel 86 32 20 12. Fax 86 32 27 40. Mich 72/C4.

ST-FLORENTIN   Grande Chaumière

Very comfortable restaurant with rooms/Cooking 3
Quiet/Terrace/Gardens/Parking

There are four Michelin three-star Burgundian shrines. Shed no tears if you bypass them. Head instead to the homes of chefs like Morillon (Beaune), Barnabet (Auxerre), Cogny (Mercurey) and this one: each restaurant has a high enjoyment factor, a genuine family atmosphere and reward you with great quality-price bargains. Jean-Pierre and Lucette Bonvalot do a super job: the handsome, quietly-situated restaurant is the first big plus; the camera-pleasing garden and terrace is the second credit; Madame's warm welcome is a third bonus; but the most rewarding benefit comes from the English-speaking chef's assured neo-classical cooking. Faultless, intense saucing in treats such as *filet de boeuf à l'estragon* and *grenadin de veau à la crème de morilles* contrast with modern interpretations like *filet de loubine* (see Southwest) *au gingembre*.
Menus A-E. Rooms (10) D-F. Cards All.
Closed 20 Dec to 17 Jan. 1st wk Sept. Wed (out of season).
Post 3 rue des Capucins, 89600 St-Florentin, Yonne.
Tel 86 35 15 12. Fax 86 35 33 14. Mich 56/A4.

ST-FLORENTIN

Tilleuls

Simple hotel/Cooking 2
Quiet/Terrace/Gardens/Parking/Good value

Like the grander Grande Chaumière (a near neighbour) the
logis is tucked away in a quiet side street (three cheers for the
new N77 bypass to the east). Monsieur Lestriez is the cook;
Madame and her daughter do the serving. A typical classical
Bourgeois meal, in the low 100s, could include some choux
pastry appetisers, smoked haddock with lentils, salmon in a
white wine sauce with a selection of vegetables, cheeses and a
dessert. A much above average *Logis de France*.
Menus B-C. Rooms (10) C-D. Cards Access, Visa.
Closed Feb school holidays. Sun evg. Mon.
Post 3 rue Decourtive, 89600 St-Florentin, Yonne.
Tel 86 35 09 09. Mich 56/A4.

ST-REMY

St-Rémy

Very comfortable restaurant/Cooking 2
Parking/Good value

FL3 readers will recall that Madeleine and Jean Clara's pretty
little restaurant was recommended by the Taylor-Whiteheads
(their home is a *monument historique*, a fascinating restored
forge at nearby Buffon). Thoroughly satisfying Burgundian
and classical *plats*: *oeufs en meurette, jambon persillé,
saupiquet Montbardois de M. Belin* (the late majestic chef at
the Gare in Montbard, once a much-loved favourite *cuisinier*),
daube de boeuf en gelée and *coupe Bourguignonne*.
Menus B-C. Cards All. (4 km NW of Montbard, on D905.)
Closed Xmas to June. Mon (not pub. hols). Evgs (but not Sat).
Post St-Rémy, 21500 Montbard, Côte-d'Or.
Tel 80 92 13 44. Mich 73/D3.

SEMUR-EN-AUXOIS

Côte d'Or

Simple hotel/Cooking 1
Garage/Good value

An endearing town, hotel and hosts. Nothing is too much
trouble for M. and Mme Christian Chène. Burgundian cooking
and excellent breakfasts with unlimited real coffee.
Menus A-C. Rooms (14) B-D. Cards AE, Access, Visa.
Closed 24 Nov to 17 Jan. Sun evg (Jan to Apl). Wed.
Post 3 place Gaveau, 21140 Semur-en-Auxois, Côte-d'Or.
Tel 80 97 03 13. Fax 80 97 29 83. Mich 73/D3.

SEMUR-EN-AUXOIS

Lac

Comfortable hotel/Cooking 1-2
Quiet/Terrace/Parking/Good value

The tag "quiet" only applies during the week. South of Semur
(an ancient town with the most impressive river meander in
France), Michel Laurençon's *logis* is alongside a lake and near

a camping site; at weekends youngsters can stir up quite a racket. *Bourgeoise* cuisine with only the odd Burgundian *plat*. Hotel 3 km S of the town; 6 km N of A6 Bierre-lès-Semur exit.
Menus A-B. Rooms (23) B-D. Cards Access, DC, Visa.
Closed Mid Dec to end Jan. Sun evg & Mon (not July & Aug).
Post Lac de Pont, 21140 Semur-en-Auxois, Côte-d'Or. (ER p 53)
Tel 80 97 11 11. Mich 73/D3.

VAL-SUZON   Host. Val-Suzon

Very comfortable restaurant with rooms/Cooking 2-3
Quiet/Terrace/Gardens/Parking

An attractive, wooded valley setting with owners Yves and Chantal Perreau winning universal praise for their welcome; and generous acclaim, too, for both the ambience and cuisine. A chalet annexe, with 9 more comfortable rooms, lies behind the main building. Modern classical specialities: especially notable are *gibier*, a *fricassée de volaille de Bresse aux pleurottes* and *noisettes de lapin à la graine de moutarde*.
Menus B-D. Rooms (16: 9 of which in annexe). Cards All.
Closed Dec to 20 Jan. Wed & Thurs midday (not July & Aug).
Post 21121 Val-Suzon, Côte d'Or.
Tel 80 35 60 15. Telex 351454. Fax 80 35 61 36. Mich 74/A4.

VAUX   La Petite Auberge

Very comfortable restaurant/Cooking 2
Parking/Good value

New owners, M. and Mme Mansour, took over the tiller here in late 1989, after Jean-Luc and Marie Barnabet paddled downstream to Auxerre. Classical cuisine with not a complaint to date from readers: *canard sauvage au Gamay d'Irancy* and *rable de lièvre sauce poivrade* are typical examples.
Menus A-C. Cards Access, Visa. (Rooms? See Auxerre hotels.)
Closed sun evg & Mon.
Post Vaux, 89290 Auxerre, Yonne. (6 km S of Auxerre, on D163.)
Tel 86 53 80 08. Mich 72/A2.

VELARS-SUR-OUCHE   Auberge Gourmande

Very comfortable restaurant/Cooking 2-3
Terrace/Parking/Good value

Rustic yet refined, the stone-built, flower-bedecked *auberge* is 12 km west of Dijon, immediately south of an exit on the toll-free A38. Louise and chef André Barbier survive by attention to detail and with an ungreedy eye for knock-down prices. A mixture of classical and regional on the quartet of menus, one of which is *Bourguignon*: *un kir, jambon persillé Dijonnais, 6 escargots, oeuf poché en meurette, coq au vin*, Burgundian cheeses and *poire au sorbet cassis*. (Rooms? See line below.)
Menus B. Cards Access, Visa. (Relais Arcade; 10 km E–A38/N5.)
Closed 2 wks Jan. Sun evg & Mon.
Post 21370 Velars-sur-Ouche, Côte-d'Or.
Tel 80 33 62 51. Mich 74/A4.

CHAMPAGNE-ARDENNE

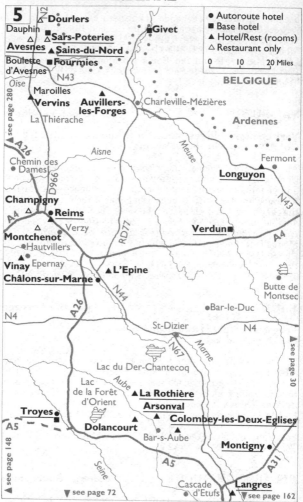

5

Dourlers

Dauphin
△

Sars-Poteries
Avesnes ▲ Sains-du-Nord
Boulette
d'Avesnes ■ Fourmies

Givet

● Autoroute hotel
■ Base hotel
▲ Hotel/Rest (rooms)
△ Restaurant only

0   10   20 Miles

N43

BELGIQUE

Oise

Maroilles

Vervins Auvillers-
les-Forges

La Thiérache

Charleville-Mézières

Ardennes

see page 280

Aisne

Chemin des
Damès

Meuse

Fermont

A26

D966

Longuyon

Champigny

△ ● Reims

A4 △   Verzy

Montchenot
● Hautvillers

RD77

Verdun ■

A4

Vinay Epernay
Châlons-sur-Marne ●

▲ L'Epine

N44

Butte de
Montsec

N4

● Bar-le-Duc

N4

St-Dizier

see page 30

A26

N67

Marne

Lac du Der-Chantecoq

Aube

Lac
de la Forêt
d'Orient

▲ La Rothière
Arsonval

Troyes ●

■

A5

Dolancourt

▲

Colombey-les-Deux-Eglises

see page 148

Bar-s-Aube

Montigny ●

Seine

A5

A31

Cascade
d'Etufs

Langres

see page 72   *see page 162*

The huge American monument on the summit of the **Butte de
Montsec**, south-east of **Verdun** and at the heart of the Parc
Régional de Lorraine, is a graceful, proud structure. By
coincidence, Anne and I visited the memorial, an apt reminder
of our American ally's formidable strength, on the 75th
anniversary of the start of the Battle of the Somme. Both the
day and setting were entirely appropriate for us to quietly
grieve over the unrelenting futility of war. Northern France
has endured more than it's fair share of bloody fighting over
the centuries. We reflected, too, on the happier fact that war
had been absent from these killing lands for almost half-a-
century: we prayed that those 50 years would multiply time
and time again over the centuries to come.

I can't say the region is one of my favourites. Much of the

landscape is flat – never-ending prairies which, year by year, add their share to the EC mountains of cereals and grain. The only breaks on the horizon are the cathedral-sized silos, their concrete walls rising high into the sky.

Not all is doom and gloom. I've spent pleasant hours in Le Pays de l'Aube, to the east of **Troyes**. Here you'll find two vast man-made lakes. On the 12,000-acre **Lac du Der-Chantecoq**, edged with woods and beaches, there is swimming, water-skiing and sailing. The 5,750-acre **Lac de la Forêt d'Orient** is part of a wooded regional park; there's sailing and bathing at Mesnil-St-Père and a wildfowl nature reserve in the north-east corner of the lake.

Heading towards **Colombey-les-Deux-Eglises** on the N19, you're given plenty of notice that you are nearing the village where Charles de Gaulle maintained a home for almost 40 years. High on a hill, appropriately facing Paris, is the mammoth granite Cross of Lorraine, the stirring symbol associated with the general. You can visit his old family home, La Boisserie, every day except Tuesday. Spare an hour for the pastoral Blaise Valley, to the north of Colombey; and, to the south, the wooded hills of the upper **Aube**, where you should seek out the unusual stepped waterfall, the **Cascade d'Etufs**. All this is a world away from the crush of tourism.

Troyes has many architectural treasures to capture your attention: the Cathedral of St-Pierre-et-St-Paul; several churches; the ancient streets of Le Vieux Troyes; and, among many museums, the notable Musée d'Art Moderne. A different celebration of man's skills is the village of Bayel, south of **Bar-sur-Aube**, where you can see various stages in the production of the world-renowned crystal glassware at the Cristalleries Royales de Champagne; there's also a shop.

Heading north other man-made sites merit a detour. Bustling **Châlons-sur-Marne** has the Cathedral of St-Etienne with fine 16th-century windows, the Romanesque Eglise Notre-Dame-en-Vaux and adjacent Muséee du Cloître and another Romanesque church, the Eglise St-Alpin. The Basilica of Notre-Dame at **L'Epine** is a flamboyant medieval church, the size of a cathedral.

Champagne lovers will not want to bypass the **Marne** Valley to the west of Châlons-sur-Marne. The wine map which follows will give you the clues needed to the numerous Champagne villages, names synonymous with the magical, sparkling liquid. **Epernay** is a must: explore one of the underground caves (try the Moët & Chandon version; Napoléon and Wellington are just two of the many illustrious visitors who've walked some part of the 25 km of cellars). Cross the Marne to the Abbey of **Hautvillers**, where the blind Dom Pérignon discovered how to put the bubbles into Champagne and keep them there. Some of you will be keen to navigate the lanes on the Montagne de Reims, especially those running through the beech woods south of **Verzy**. Autumn is much the best season to be in Champagne country, for both the obvious visual and essential *dégustation* reasons.

Reims must not be missed. The 13th-century Gothic cathedral is a masterpiece; the west front façade is among the world's greatest man-made creations. See the adjoining Palais du Tau and the Basilica and Museum of St-Rémi. Visit, among several options, the Pommery château to the south-east, one of the great Champagne houses built above *les crayères*, a network of underground chalk galleries and "pyramids".

To the far east, in the **Meuse** Valley and part of Lorraine, is Verdun – a unique, symbolic name that means so much to

France, a symbol of French valour and suffering. Spare moments for the Fort de Vaux, the Fort de Douaumont and the battlefields, cemeteries and monuments to the north-east. See, too, the amazing fort at **Fermont** and its underground "town", part of the Maginot Line in 1940 (east of **Longuyon**).

The **Chemin des Dames** (D18) is to the north-west of Reims. This famous road runs along the top of the hills between the rivers **Aisne** and Ailette, the scene of more bitter fighting during the First World War. Visit the cemeteries, monuments and the Caverne du Dragon, a museum devoted to the battles. More reminders of fighting in centuries past are the fortified churches of **La Thiérache**. There are dozens, built of brick with multi-coloured patterns in their walls, in the valleys of the Oise and Brune. Those nearest the A26 are south of **Vervins**: Prisces, Burelles, Hary and Gronard.

Last year I revisited the Meuse and Semoy valleys north of **Charleville-Mézières** (don't miss the Place Ducale, reminiscent of my favourite square in Paris, the Place des Vosges) and was most disappointed. Crowded and not especially attractive, the wooded **Ardennes** hill and river views are hardly worth the effort needed to seek them out. There are scores of much nicer valleys elsewhere in France.

Finally, if you stay overnight in the area around **Avesnes**, spare a little time for the lake and lanes in the undulating, wooded hills to the east of the town: the Lac du Val Joly will please both adults and children alike.

Markets Avesnes (Fri); Bar-le-Duc (Tues, Thurs and Sat); Chaource (every day); Reims (Wed, Fri, Sat and Sun); St-Dizier (Thurs and Sat); Troyes (Sat and Sun).

Michelin green guides: Champagne and Alsace et Lorraine.

Cheeses Cow's milk

Barberey from the area between Chaource and Les Riceys. A soft, musty-smelling, small cylinder. Best in summer and autumn

Boulette d'Avesnes soft, pear-shaped and pungent bouquet. Sharp and strong. Try it with Genièvre (see the North region)

Caprice des Dieux soft and mild, packed in oval-shaped boxes

Cendré d'Argonne from north of Châlons-s-Marne; soft, ash coated

Cendré de Champagne (Cendré des Riceys) mainly from Châlons-s-Marne and Vitry-le-François area. Flat disk and coated with ashes

Chaource at its best in summer and autumn; a creamy cheese, made in cylinders and with a mushroom smell. From the borders of Burgundy

Chaumont related to Epoisses and Langres cheeses (see Burgundy); cone-shaped, soft cheese with strong smell

Dauphin from the Avesnes area. Soft, seasoned, crescent-shaped, heart or loaf. Is related to Boulette d'Avesnes

Evry-le-Châtel truncated cone; firm with a mushroom smell

Igny made by monks at the Igny monastery; a pressed flat disk

Maroilles soft, slightly salty and gold. Appears in many regional dishes

Les Riceys from the area south of Troyes, home also of the good Rosé des Riceys wine. Best seasons, summer and autumn. Flat disk, no strong smell and fruity taste. Try the local wine with the cheese

Saint Rémy a spicy-tasting, strong-smelling, reddish-coloured square

Regional Specialities

Flamiche aux Maroilles see *Tarte aux Maroilles*

Flamiche aux poireaux puff-pastry tart with cream and leeks

Goyère see *Tarte aux Maroilles*

Rabotte (Rabote) whole apple wrapped in pastry and baked

Tarte aux Maroilles a hot creamy tart based on the local cheese

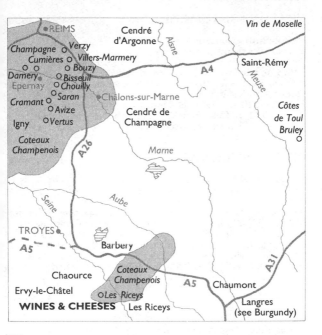

Wines (Great vintages: **61 70 71 72 79 82 83 85 88 90**)

Champagne is the only area in France where the AC classification does not have to be shown on the labels of bottles.

A **Crémant de Cramant** (*crémant* means about half the normal bubbles) is a delicious alternative to Champagne. There are many non-sparkling wines from the Champagne area worth looking out for; the broadest AC classification is **Coteaux Champenois**. Whites from **Cramant**, **Villers-Marmery**, **Avize** and **Chouilly** and a **Rosé des Riceys** (with its own AC – see map) are good. You may also see a **Chardonnay** (the Champagne area white grape), usually carrying a merchant's name (**Saran** – made by Moët & Chandon is one). Other fine wines are the reds: a delicate **Bisseuil**; a light **Bouzy**; and those from **Vertus**, **Damery** and **Cumières** (all made from the other important Champagne grape – the red Pinot Noir). The term **ratafia** describes a mixture of brandy and unfermented Champagne.

Don't, under any circumstances, miss out on the free guided tours of the world-famous Champagne houses at Epernay and Reims. The guides usually speak English. Of my favourites I would rate the most enjoyable as Moët & Chandon and Mercier in Epernay, and Pommery and Taittinger in Reims. Bear in mind you will be underground a great part of the time – so take something warm to cover your arms. One benefit at Mercier is that a train takes you around. (Note: all closed in winter.)

To the north-east of the region – in Lorraine country – are two VDQS areas: **Côtes de Toul** (the village name **Bruley** is often used on local lists); and **Vin de Moselle** (from the Metz area; wines made in the spas of **Contz** and **Sierck** appear on menus). Wines of all shades are made in both areas but the dry **Vin Gris** (a pale pink) is the most common. See Alsace wine map.

CHALONS-SUR-MARNE   Campanile

Simple hotel/Cooking 1
Terrace/Parking/Good value

Leave A4 Châlons-Nord exit. South to N44. At Châlons ignore
N44 bypass to left; continue towards town, hotel on left.
Menus A-B. Rooms (47) C. Disabled. Cards Access, Visa.
Post rte de Reims, 51520 St-Martin-sur-le-Pré, Marne.
Tel 26 70 41 02. Telex 842137. Fax 26 66 87 85. Mich 38/C2.
(Bookings: UK freephone 0800 897863)

CHALONS-SUR-MARNE   Ibis

Simple hotel/Cooking 1
Quiet/Parking

A4 Châlons-Nord exit (from west); south on N44, then RD77 (A4
Metz signs). A4 Châlons-Est exit (from east); towards town.
Menus A-B. Rooms (40) C-D. Disabled. Cards Access, Visa.
Post rte de Sedan, 51000 Châlons-s-Marne, Marne. (ER p 37)
Tel 26 65 16 65. Telex 830595. Fax 26 68 31 88. Mich 38/C2.
(Bookings: UK 071 724 1000; US toll free 800 221 4542)

MONTIGNY   Moderne

Comfortable hotel/Cooking 1-2
Garage/Parking/Good value

Leave A31 exit 8. West 2 km to junc. D417/D74; hotel on left.
Menus A-C. Rooms (26) C. Disabled. Cards All.
Post Montigny-le-Roi, 52140 Val de Meuse, H.-Marne. (ER p 133)
Tel 25 90 30 18. Telex 830349. Fax 25 90 71 80. Mich 58/B4.

REIMS   Campanile-Sud

Simple hotel/Cooking 1
Terrace/Parking/Good value

Leave A4 Reims-St-Rémi exit. South on N51, hotel on left.
Menus A-B. Rooms (60) C-D. Disabled. Cards Access, Visa.
Post av. G.Pompidou, 51100 Reims, Marne. (En Route p 36)
Tel 26 36 66 94. Telex 830262. Fax 26 49 95 40. Mich 38/B1.
(Bookings: UK freephone 0800 897863)

REIMS   Ibis

Simple hotel/Cooking 1
Gardens/Parking

A4 Reims-Tinqueux exit (just east A4/A26 junc). N31 towards
Reims; hotel on right. Rest open evgs only (and not Sun).
Menus A. Rooms (75) C-D. Disabled. Cards Access, Visa.
Post 51430 Tinqueux, Marne. (En Route p 36)
Tel 26 04 60 70. Telex 842116. Fax 26 84 24 40. Mich 38/A1.
(Bookings: UK 071 724 1000; US toll free 800 221 4542)

REIMS   Mercure

Very comfortable hotel/Cooking 1-2
Terrace/Swimming pool/Lift/Parking

A4 Reims-Cormontreuil exit. North to N44; hotel towards Reims.
Menus B. Rooms (103) E-F. Disabled. Cards All.
Post 51100 Reims, Marne. (En Route p 36)
Tel 26 05 00 08. Telex 830782. Fax 26 85 64 72. Mich 38/B1.
(Bookings: UK 071 724 1000; US toll free 800 221 4542)

REIMS   Novotel

Very comfortable hotel/Cooking 1
Terrace/Gardens/Swimming pool/Parking

Leave A4 Reims-Tinqueux exit (just east of A4/A26 junc). N31
towards Reims; hotel on right.
Menus B. Rooms (127) E. Disabled. Cards All.
Post 51430 Tinqueux, Marne. (En Route p 36)
Tel 26 08 11 61. Telex 830034. Fax 26 08 72 05. Mich 38/A1.
(Bookings: UK 071 724 1000; US toll free 800 221 4542)

REIMS   Relais Bleus

Simple hotel/Cooking 1
Parking

A4 Reims-Cormontreuil exit. North towards N44; hotel on left.
Menus A-C. Rooms (40) D. Disabled. Cards Access, Visa.
Post 12 rue G.Voisin, 51100 Reims, Marne. (En Route p 36)
Tel 26 82 59 79. Telex 842121. Fax 26 82 53 92. Mich 38/B1.

TROYES   Campanile

Simple hotel/Cooking 1
Terrace/Parking/Good value

Leave A5 Troyes-Sud exit (just west A5/A26 junc). North on
N71 towards Troyes. Hotel on left of N71 in one km.
Menus A-B. Rooms (55) C. Disabled. Cards Access, Visa.
Post 10800 Buchères, Aube.
Tel 25 49 67 67. Telex 840840. Fax 25 75 17 31. Mich 56/C3.
(Bookings: UK freephone 0800 897863)

TROYES   Pan de Bois

Simple hotel/Cooking 1
Quiet/Terrace/Parking/Good value

A5 Troyes-Sud exit (just west A5/A26 junc). North on N71 for 5
km. Hotel at Bréviandes. Restaurant: mainly grills.
Menus A-B. Rooms (31) C. Disabled. Cards Access, Visa.
Closed Sun. Rest also on Mon.
Post av. Gén-Leclerc, 10800 Bréviandes, Aube.
Tel 25 75 02 31. Fax 25 49 67 84. Mich 56/C3.

Base Hotels

FOURMIES
Ibis

Simple hotel
Secluded/Parking

South-east of Fourmies, north of D964. Beside the Etang des Moines, in wooded terrain. Useful for Sains-du-Nord rest.
Rooms (29) C-D. Cards Access, Visa.
Post 59610 Fourmies, Nord.
Tel 27 60 21 54. Telex 810172. Fax 27 57 40 44. Mich 10/A3.
(Bookings UK 071 724 1000; US toll free 800 221 4542)

GIVET
Val St-Hilaire

Comfortable hotel
Parking

Modern, newly-built hotel, in pleasant site alongside River Meuse. Owner, Madame Dardenne, speaks English.
Rooms (20) C-D. Cards Access, Visa.
Post 7 quai des Fours, 08600 Givet, Ardennes.
Tel 24 42 38 50. Mich 11/D3.

SARS-POTERIES
Hôtel Fleurie

Simple hotel
Quiet/Gardens/Tennis/Parking/Good value

An old farm, behind the Aub. Fleurie restaurant, run as a separate business by Claudine and Thérèse Carrié-Guinot.
Rooms (11) B-C. Cards Access, Visa.
Closed 20 Dec to 12 Jan.
Post 59216 Sars-Poteries, Nord.
Tel 27 61 62 72. Mich 10/A2.

TROYES
Chantereigne

Comfortable hotel
Quiet/Parking/Good value

Horseshoe-shaped modern hotel, on N60 west of Troyes.
Rooms (30) C. Disabled. Cards Access, Visa.
Closed Xmas to New Year.
Post 128 av Gén.-Leclerc, 10300 Ste-Savine, Aube.
Tel 25 74 89 35. Fax 25 74 47 78. Mich 56/B3.

VERDUN
Montaulbain

Very simple hotel
Good value

As basic as they come. Fairly quiet, behind rue Mazel, to the north-east of both the cathedral and post office (on N3).
Rooms (10) B. Cards Access, Visa.
Post 4 r. Vieille-Prison, 55100 Verdun, Meuse. (ER p 38)
Tel 29 86 00 47. Mich 40/A1.

ARSONVAL   La Chaumière

Comfortable restaurant with basic rooms/Cooking 1-2
Terrace/Gardens/Parking/Good value

Bernard Guillerand is the chef; wife Susan is a Leamington Spa
lass. A mixture of classical and *Bourgeois* dishes: *tournedos
Périgourdin* and *filet de cabillaud au champagne* are examples.
Equally tasty are the home-made treats: *saumon fumé, terrine
de canard* and *foie gras de canard* demonstrate Bernard's
skills. Arsonval is on the N19, seven km north-west of Bar-sur-
Aube. Well worth the detour from the A5/A26.
Menus B. Rooms (3) B-C. Cards AE, Access, Visa.
Closed Annual not fixed. Sun evg & Mon (not pub. hols).
Post Arsonval, 10200 Bar-sur-Aube, Aube.
Tel 25 27 91 02. Mich 57/E3.

AUVILLERS-LES-FORGES   Host. Lenoir

Very comfortable restaurant with rooms/Cooking 3
Quiet/Gardens/Lift

Brave, diligent and hard-working Jean and Maryse Lenoir,
helped by his sister, Ginette, battle on in their family home.
From a modest bistro in 1955 the Lenoirs have transformed Le
Paix (the original name) into one of France's finest outposts of
classical cooking. But there's also many a modern gem lurking
on the menus: steamed fillets of sole with bean sprouts, soya
sauce and vegetables (just one dish influenced by Jean's
annual Far Eastern working holiday) is typical.
Menus B-E. Rooms (21) B-E. Cards All.
Closed Jan. Feb. Fri (not pub. hols).
Post 08260 Auvillers-les-Forges, Ardennes.
Tel 24 54 30 11. Fax 24 54 34 70. Mich 21/D1.

AVESNES-SUR-HELPE   La Crémaillère

Comfortable restaurant/Cooking 2
Good value

A new lease of life for this town-centre restaurant (which I
criticised so hard in *FL3*) after Francis Lelaurain took over the
kitchens, following his father's death. Classical stuff with a
welcome Menu de la Mer: salmon *rillettes*, scallop soup, two
fish courses, cheese and a dessert.
Menus B-C. Cards All. (Rooms? See nearby Base hotels.)
Closed Mon evg & Tues (not public holidays).
Post 26 pl. Gén. Leclerc, 59440 Avesnes-sur-Helpe, Nord.
Tel 27 61 02 30. Mich 10/A3.

CHAMPIGNY   La Garenne

Comfortable restaurant/Cooking 3
Parking

On the N31, just west of Reims and the A4/A26 junc. A famous
building on the apex of the infamous Thillois hairpin, part of

99

the legendary Reims motor racing circuit. A Boyer student, Laurent Laplaige has made a fast start from the grid. His forté is fish: among emphatic modern creations are *St-Pierre grillé au coulis d'etrilles, lotte rôtie en crépine* and *fricassée de gambas à l'embeurrée de choux* (see Poitou-Charentes).
Menus B-D. Cards AE, Access, Visa. (Rooms? See A/R hotels.)
Closed 1st 3 wks Aug. Sun evg & Mon.
Post Champigny, 51370 St-Brice-Courcelles, Marne.
Tel 26 08 26 62. Fax 26 84 24 13. Mich 38/A1.

COLOMBEY-LES-DEUX-EGLISES Aub. Montagne

Comfortable restaurant with rooms/Cooking 2
Quiet/Gardens/Parking/Good value

I first wrote about this humdinger in a national newspaper. Several readers have written to applaud chef Gérard Natali, his wife Arlette and their sons, the *cave*, the quality of service and the classical and *Bourgeoise* offerings. Menus include *andouillette au petit blanc, pigeonneau et son beurre de choux, carré d'agneau au poivre vert, côte de Marcassin père Renato* and desserts like *tarte au citron* and *galette Haut Marnaise*. Well worth the not-too-long detour from the A5/A26.
Menus B-D. Rooms (9) B-D. Cards AE, Access, Visa.
Closed Mid Jan to mid Feb. Mon evg & Tues.
Post 52330 Colombey-les-Deux-Eglises, H.-Marne.
Tel 25 01 51 69. Fax 25 01 53 20. Mich 57/F3.

DOLANCOURT Moulin du Landion

Comfortable hotel/Cooking 1-2
Gardens/Parking

A watermill built in 1872 and restored a century later. Since 1975 the *moulin* has been owned by Paul and Marie-France Bajolle. The mill race still flows, noisily. Cuisine is classical with trout from the river and salmon from Scotland.
Menus B-C. Rooms (16) C-D. Cards All.
Closed Dec. Jan. (Just off N19, north-west of Bar-sur-Aube.)
Post Dolancourt, 10200 Bar-sur-Aube, Aube.
Tel 25 27 92 17. Fax 25 27 94 44. Mich 57/E3.

DOURLERS Auberge du Châtelet

Comfortable restaurant/Cooking 2
Gardens/Parking

Sadly, Yolande Carlier, a talented *cuisinière*, died in 1990. Pierre, her English-speaking husband, battles on – helped now by his son, François, in the kitchen. A neo-rustic *auberge* on the N2, north of Avesnes. Classical and neo-classical menus, one based entirely on fish. *La Marmite Yolande* (with fish and vegetables) remains a tasty and satifying appetite buster.
Menus C-E. Cards All. (Rooms? See Sars-Poteries Base hotel.)
Closed 1-15 Jan. 15 Aug-15 Sept. Wed. Evgs (Sun & pub. hols).
Post Dourlers, 59440 Avesnes-sur-Helpe, Nord.
Tel 27 61 06 70. Mich 10/A2.

Hotels and Restaurants

L'EPINE   Aux Armes de Champagne

Very comfortable hotel/Cooking 3-4
Gardens/Parking

On my last-but-one call on Jean-Paul and Denise Pérardel the
couple were excited about their new chef signing. Rightly so,
too, as Patrick Michelon has made a resounding impact at the
old family coaching inn, across the road from the flamboyant,
over-the-top Gothic basilica. Refurbished bedrooms and a
freshly-decorated, restyled dining room have also done
wonders. Cuisine is Nineties style with a distinctive Michelon
touch: _lasagnes de grenouilles aux cèpes au chardonnay et jus
de poulet; poêlée de sole et de langoustines aux artichauts,
aromates et huile d'olive._ First-class cellar (and shop); Pérardel
label champagnes are very drinkable. VFB base.
Menus C-E. Rooms (39) E-F. Cards Access, Visa. (ER p 37)
Closed Jan to mid Feb. Sun evg & Mon (Nov to Mar).
Post 51460 L'Epine, Marne. (Cheaper rooms? See A/R hotels.)
Tel 26 66 96 79. Telex 830998. Fax 26 66 92 31. Mich 38/C2.

LANGRES   Auberge des 3 Jumeaux

Comfortable restaurant with rooms/Cooking 2
Terrace/Good value

For goodness sake don't be put off by the plastic armchairs and
the basic bedrooms. Jean-Claude Thomassin, the chef/patron,
has earned a hatful of plaudits from readers who saw a piece I
did about his restaurant in a national newspaper. Value for
money with meat and grills featuring on each of four classical
menus: _faux filet maître-d'hôtel, tournedos aux baies roses_ and
mixed grill d'agneau are a representative selection.
Menus A-C. Rooms (10) C. Cards Access, Visa.
Closed 3 wks Jan. Sun evg (Oct to Apl). Mon.
Post Saints Geosmes, 52200 Langres, H.-Marne.
Tel 25 87 03 36. Mich 74/C1. (4 km south of Langres.)

LONGUYON   Lorraine et Rest. Le Mas

Comfortable restaurant with rooms/Cooking 3
Good value

There's nothing twee or precious about the Lorraine. One
reader described Gérard and Viviane Tisserant's out-of-the-
way home as: "A feast for the eyes. The restaurant, the service,
the food, everything was right. And the choice on the sweet
trolley: how do they do it?" How? English-speaking Gérard has
three essential character strengths: ability, an Everest-sized
sense of humour and he's a workaholic. Self-taught, his
repertoire is a mix of styles; home-grown vegetables are grown
by _père_ Maurice; and fish comes by overnight train from
Boulogne. Trains? The clue is in the postal address: it can be
noisy during the night; ask for rooms at the rear.
Menus B-D. Rooms (12) B-C. Cards All.
Closed Jan. Feb sch hols. Mon (not pub. hols; not July-Sept).
Post face gare, 54260 Longuyon, M.-et-M.
Tel 82 26 50 07. Fax 82 39 26 09. Mich 22/C3.

MONTCHENOT   Aub. du Grand Cerf

Comfortable restaurant/Cooking 2-3
Gardens

A roller-coaster record; the stag (*cerf*) squeaks an entry by a
nose. Alain Guichaoua, a Breton, is an able chef (helped these
days by his son Yannick) but some readers suspect that too
much is prepared in advance. A mix of *plats*: clever use of
Maroille cheese in a *feuillantines doux*; a meaty Ardennaise
pâté en croûte; a champagne sauce with turbot; and again in a
gratin de sabayon de champagne aux fruits rouges. A tip for
elegant Françoise: make sure your waiters clean their nails.
Menus B-D. Cards AE, Access, Visa. (Rooms? See A/R hotels.)
Closed Feb. Aug. Sun evg. Wed. (On N51, 10 km S of Reims.)
Post Montchenot, 51500 Rilly-la-Montagne, Marne.
Tel 26 97 60 07. Fax 26 97 64 24. Mich 38/B1.

REIMS   L'Assiette Champenoise

Very comfortable hotel/Cooking 3
Quiet/Terrace/Gardens/Swimming pool(indoor)/Parking

Jean-Pierre and Colette Lallement's sizeable new home, built
originally as a farm, is only a mile from the cathedral. J-P was
really motoring at his previous Châlons-s-Vesle base; now he's
freewheeling. My last visit, on Guy Fawkes night, was a damp
squib. Classical and modern sit cheek by jowl: *filet de biche
poêlé et sa sauce au sang*; *rouget et son émulsion à la noisette*.
Effervescent owners and cellar (200 sparklers and 50 halves).
On N31 at Tinqueux, west of Reims. Cheaper rooms? See A/R
hotels; just minutes away to the west.
Menus D-E. Rooms (60) F. Disabled. Cards All.
Post 40 av. P. Vaillant-Couturier, 51430 Reims, Marne.
Tel 26 04 15 56. Telex 830267. Fax 26 04 15 69. Mich 38/A1.

LA ROTHIERE   Aub. de la Plaine

Simple restaurant with rooms/Cooking 1
Parking/Good value

A *Logis de France*, in a lonely site on the D396 south of
Brienne-le-Château (links with Napoléon). Jean-Pierre Galton
and his family do the basics well. *Bourgeoise* cooking and
appetite-quenching grills (including an excellent Dover sole).
Menus B. Rooms (18) B-C. Cards All.
Closed Xmas to New Year. Fri evg (mid Sept to mid Mar).
Post La Rothière, 10500 Brienne-le-Château, Aube.
Tel 25 92 21 79. Mich 57/D2.

SAINS-DU-NORD   Centre

Simple restaurant with rooms/Cooking 2
Parking/Good value

From the D951 follow signs for Parc du Val Joly. Murielle
Vitoux is *la cuisinière*, husband Guy the *maître-d*. Some

regional specialities: *tarte au Maroilles* and *ficelle Picarde*. *Bourgeoise* and classical alternatives such as *charollais sauce Béarnaise* (loosen your belt). Sains is no bundle of laughs.
Menus A-B. Rooms (7) B. Cards Access, Visa.
Closed 2nd half Feb. 2nd half Aug. Fri. Sun evg. Pub. hols.
Post rue Leo Lagrange, 59177 Sains-du-Nord, Nord.
Tel 27 59 15 02. Mich 10/A3. (Also see Fourmies base.)

SARS-POTERIES   Auberge Fleurie

Very comfortable restaurant/Cooking 3
Parking

Alain and Josette Lequy are the second generation hosts at this old favourite of ours; we first visited the farmhouse (built 1700) 30 years ago when his parents were *les patrons*. Alain wears his mother's classical clogs with no stinting on cream and butter. His *demi homard au beurre blanc* is an unbeatable, inspirational *plat*. No less than nine shellfish and fish alternatives are normally on the menus. At pudding time a gallon bowl of cream is left at the table to tempt you. Definitely not for the cholesterol "scweamish".
Menus B-D. Cards All. (Rooms? See Sars-Poteries base.)
Closed 2nd half Jan. 2nd half Aug. Sun evg. Mon.
Post 59216 Sars-Poteries, Nord.
Tel 27 61 62 48. Fax 27 59 32 16. Mich 10/A2. (S side D962.)

VERVINS   Tour du Roy

Comfortable hotel/Cooking 3
Terrace/Gardens/Closed parking

An extrovert hotel (ask to see the two tower bedrooms) run by an extrovert, English-speaking owner, Claude Desvignes. His wife, Annie, is an exceptional *cuisinière*; she's Alain Lequy's sister (see above). Classical cooking, some hearty regional favourites and great use of local Thiérache produce.
Menus B-D. Rooms (16) C-F. Cards All.
Closed Rest only: Sun evg & Mon midday (out of season).
Post 02140 Vervins, Aisne.
Tel 23 98 00 11. Fax 23 98 00 72. Mich 20/B1.

VINAY   La Briqueterie

Very comfortable hotel/Cooking 3
Quiet/Gardens/Swimming pool(indoor)/Garage/Parking

Substantial progress has been made by Catherine and Georges Guillon at their ultra-swish, neo-rustic hotel complex, set in large, pretty grounds. There's a gym too. Cooking is a *mélange* of classical and neo-classical. Readers speak highly of polished saucing and top-class produce. Alas, hiked prices spike nasty holes in holiday budgets these days.
Menus D-E. Rooms (42) F-F2. Disabled. Cards All.
Closed Xmas.
Post Vinay, 51200 Epernay, Marne.
Tel 26 59 99 99. Telex 842007. Fax 26 59 92 10. Mich 38/A2.

COTE D'AZUR

I regret starting this chapter with several bleak paragraphs. I first saw this once magical part of France almost 40 years ago; what horrific changes have occurred in four decades.

Much of the coastal strip is appalling: concrete mutations litter the landscape, a grim memorial to the planners (aided by backhanders) who conceived and continue to extend this 20th-century nightmare; pollution in both sea and atmosphere is rampant; the sound of traffic is deafening – in an environment where cars seem to outnumber people; burglaries have reached epidemic proportions, from both property and vehicles (never leave anything in a car); and where burglars, con-men and rip-off merchants thrive. One writer has tagged the coast "Côte d'Excess". Another renamed it "Côte d'Usure" (usury) and asked: "Has the Riviera reached its Rubicon?"

The Nineties will see even more man-made slaughter of the

landscape. There's a great legal battle going on to decide the fate of the projected TGV across Provence and an equally fierce war is being raged over the precise line of the "relief" autoroute for the **A8**. This new motorway will cut through the hills between **Draguignan**, **Grasse** and **Vence**. *Métro* systems, extensions to airports at **Nice** and **Cannes**, and other projects are also in hand.

As much as I admire France's transport infrastructure I do deplore the rape of the coast: does nobody care? During the Eighties half the area's agricultural land vanished; the population increased by 20% and will continue to grow at the same rate in the Nineties. All the new public works are being built to "service" the ever-growing population, pouring into what is already a grossly overcrowded corner.

Forgive me, then, if I devote little space to the narrow coastline. I'll concentrate instead on *l'arrière-pays*; but more about just where that is later on.

I've painted a dreary picture of the coast. But I must not overstate the horror story; many pockets of interest and beauty still survive. Recall that this was a landscape where the light and vistas inspired master artists: the talents of Matisse, Renoir, Picasso and Chagall were awakened on the Côte d'Azur. Visit the Picasso Museum in **Antibes**; Renoir's old home at Les Collettes in **Cagnes-sur-Mer**; the Chapelle du Rosaire at Vence; and the Maeght Foundation at **St-Paul-de-Vence**, the home of fine contemporary art.

Cannes has always been a great favourite of ours; both La Croisette, alongside the Mediterranean, and the long, narrow rue Meynadier still have a magnetic attraction. Nice has never appealed much, though the flower market is an explosively colourful sight. Monaco and its Oceanographic Museum are musts; so is **Monte-Carlo** across the harbour with its casino, gardens and twisty Grand Prix circuit. **Menton** is relatively quieter and less hemmed-in than the rest of the eastern end of the Côte d'Azur coastline.

Both Beaulieu, a smaller resort, and **Villefranche**, with crowded, bustling ports, should not be missed; nor should the unique wooded headland of **Cap Ferrat**. Drive the famous Corniche roads between Nice and Menton and gasp at the views. Drive the not quite so impressive coast road from **La Napoule** to **St-Raphaël**, with the red, craggy Esterel mountains to the north. Further west, "fight" to get your car into **St-Tropez**. I remember, far more vividly, the mountain-top road high above **Le Lavandou** and Le Royal where carpets of wild-flowers remain a sharp memory. Explore, too, the vast cork forests covering the Massif des Maures; from Bormes to Collobrières and beyond to La-Garde-Freinet.

Near the packed A8, north-east of Cannes, are two quite different attractions: **Vallauris**, a town made famous by Picasso, will appeal to any of you interested in pottery; and, nearby, a handsome new motor museum, financed by Adrien Maeght – a must for all motoring "nuts".

I'm always impatient to flee north. But I can hear you asking the question: *"L'arrière-pays*: where on earth is that?"* Simply, all the land to the north of the coastline.

For me, one village, **Peillon**, embodies the true essence of the French Mediterranean. Peillon and Nice epitomise the juxtaposition of the two worlds; and the dangers to the former. An air of timelessness pervades Peillon's huddle of houses, an oasis of calm perched atop huge vertical slabs of rock. The village is minutes from the coast yet remains hidden from the ever-creeping, ever-nearing tentacles of Nice's ghastly suburbs and from the local quarries where gargantuan mouthfuls are gouged from the hillsides.

The coastal "menace" has crept close to Peillon. Film-set **Mougins** has already been engulfed; Grasse and Vence are close to the same fate. Don't bypass either of these two hill "stations", so cool on hot days; narrow streets, markets and parks give them both seductive personalities. But don't linger; continue instead to a series of hill villages, many of which are "perched". From east to west they include: Tourrettes-sur-Loup, **Gourdon**, **Opio**, Cabris, **Spéracèdes**, **Montauroux**, Callian, **Fayence**, Seillans, Bargemon, **Tourtour** (the village in the "sky"), **Fox-Amphoux** (a tiny jewel) and **Cotignac** (seek out Notre Dame de Grâces).

At any time of the year the wooded hillsides between the villages are an enchantment. In spring every inch of ground seems to be a splash of differing colours. Gardens, terraces and villa walls are blanketed with roses, oleander, bougainvillea, veronica, hibiscus and countless other plants. Climb the roads that zig-zag up from the villages and delight at the variety and profusion of wild flowers; one example is the Col du Bel Homme, north of **Bargemon**.

The villages have narrow streets; ancient houses almost seem to touch in places. Their shaded "squares" vary from the minute at Bargemon to biggish ones at Fayence and Montauroux; all have "umbrellas" of chestnuts and plane trees and cool, twinkling fountains. Is this heaven?

As you wind through the necklace of villages, make detours to others too: **Aups**, north of Cotignac, is famed for its ham and truffles and has a particularly large, shaded *place*; Salernes, to the south of Aups, is renowned for the production of coloured enamel tiles; Entrecasteaux, further south, is dominated by a part 11th/part 17th-century château; and medieval Bargème, north of Bargemon, is a step back in time to an isolated ruined castle, church and tiny hamlet.

I have left to the end the best of *l'arrière-pays*. From this point on Mother Nature reigns supreme. Get out your large-scale maps, do some navigating, and try to follow as many of the suggested drives as you can.

First the terrain to the north of Nice. Drive north up the **Var** Valley and, just beyond Plan-du-Var, turn right, heading north-east through the Gorges de Vésubie (Michelin reckon them *vaut le voyage*: no way). Detour up to the celebrated viewpoint at **Madone d'Utelle**, a 15 km run that climbs from 285 metres above sea-level to 1174 metres (3852 ft). At the end of the road there's an observation platform under a weird umbrella roof. If you're lucky you may see Corsica.

Descend and continue up the Vésubie Valley, past St-Martin and then north-east to **Le Boréon**. Here you're at the door of the Parc National du Mercantour. Continue until the road peters out. It's a walkers' paradise; set off up the valley and who knows, you may be fortunate enough to spot chamois, marmots and, at higher altitude, the *lièvre variable*.

On another day try the exciting **Col de Turini**; the turn is halfway up the Vésubie. This is the Monte-Carlo Rally's most famous stage: held on closed icy roads in January, the testing timed climb runs from the perched village of La Bollène to Moulinet on the D2566. At the summit of the Turini, turn north and complete the anti-clockwise tour of L'Authion. Try again for that elusive view of Corsica.

Now follows what I've tagged a "Tour de Force". From Grasse, head north-east on the D2085 towards Nice, and after six km, use the D3 to Gourdon. Stop at the village for its aeroplane panorama of the mighty Gorges du Loup far below. Continue on the D3 to the D2; turn left towards Gréolières. Continue to Les Quatre-Chemins; then climb the **Col de Bleine** (Bleyne). At the summit, detour on the narrow, steep track to the right and continue to the radio mast. A surprise awaits you: distant views north of snow-capped peaks.

Descend to the north and then east on the D10. Exciting for drivers and geologists too. Gasp at Le Mas on its dizzy perch; but even more so at the Clue d'Aiglun, an orange and grey gash slashed through slabs of rock hundreds of metres high. Some seven km later you'll spot the village of Sigale high above you, clinging on by its fingernails to the mountain.

Use the D17 through the village. Now another *clue*, the Clue du Riolan. Then west on the D2211A to a third "rift", the Clue de **St-Auban**; here the road and stream share the narrow, deep slit in the rocks.

Retrace your steps to Briançonnet and climb north on the Col du Buis and then on to **Entrevaux**. As you descend you have a remarkable aspect of the medieaval village and its citadel towering above it, linked together by an umbilical zigzag wall. Explore the old village on the Var's left bank.

To finish the tour, head east for 15 km, to the point where the River Cians joins the Var. Drive north up the D28 for a Disney-like adventure, the **Gorges du Cians**. Steep cliffs, they almost touch, overhang the narrow road; dark rocks add extra splendour to the rushing torrent as it falls steeply down towards the Var and the distant Mediterranean.

There's still more exhilarating mountain terrain to see. Three high cols lead north from the Var: France's highest pass, the **Col de la Bonette** (9193 ft); the **Col de la Cayolle** (7634 ft); and the **Col d'Allos** (7349 ft). I prefer the Allos, because, at the village of the same name, you can head east up a fantastic "dead-end" to the Lac d'Allos (7313 ft). Allow 45 minutes each way for the pulsating (literally!) walk from the car park to the azure lake.

Finally, do not miss the circuit of the **Grand Canyon du Verdon**, one of Europe's great natural wonders. Starting at the western end, near Moustiers-Ste-Marie, I suggest the circuit is driven in a clockwise direction. The gorge is then always on your right, making parking much easier at the viewpoints. At many places on the circuit the Verdon River is nearly 2,000 ft below you; you require little imagination to visualise the tremendous vistas. The gorge is heavily wooded with deciduous trees and is particularly colourful in late autumn. Please be very careful if you do any walking.

In addition to all those suggestions there are numerous other roads and villages to explore, all of which are a world away from the frenetic pace on the coast.

Markets Antibes (Tues, Wed, Thurs, Sat and Sun); Aups (Wed and Sat); Barjols (Tues and Sat); Cannes (Tues to Sun); Cotignac (Tues); Digne (Wed, Thurs and Sat); Fayence (Tues and Sat); Grasse (Tues to Sat); Menton (every day); St-Tropez (Tues and Sat); Valbonne (Fri); Vallauris (Wed and Sun); Vence (Tues and Fri); Villefranche-sur-Mer (Wed and Fri).

Michelin green guide: French Riviera (English).
Michelin "green" map 115 recommended (1 cm: 1 km).

Cheeses **Goat's milk**
Banon a soft cheese made in a small disk, usually wrapped in chestnut leaves; sometimes *au poivre* (covered with black pepper)
Poivre-d'Ane flavoured with rosemary or the herb savory (*sarriette*). Aromatic taste and perfume

Ewe's milk
Brousse de la Vésubie from the Vésubie Valley, north of Nice; a very creamy, mild-flavoured cheese

Regional Specialities
Aïgo Bouido garlic and sage soup – with bread (or eggs and cheese)
Aïgo saou fish soup (no *rascasse* – scorpion fish) with *rouille*
Aïoli (ailloli) a mayonnaise sauce with garlic and olive oil
Anchoïade anchovy crusts
Berlingueto chopped spinach and hard-boiled eggs
Bouillabaisse a dish of Mediterranean fish (including *rascasse, St-Pierre, baudroie, congre, chapon de mer, langoustes, langoustines, tourteaux, favouilles, merlan* and, believe it or not, many others) and a soup, served separately with *rouille, safran* and *aïoli*
Bourride a creamy fish soup (usually made with big white fish), thickened with *aïoli* and flavoured with crawfish
Brandade (de morue) à l'huile d'olive a mousse of salt cod with cream, olive oil and garlic
Capoum a large pink *rascasse* (scorpion fish)
Pain Bagna bread roll with olive oil, anchovies, olives, onions, etc.
Pieds et paquets small parcels of mutton tripe, cooked with sheep trotters and white wine
Pissaladière Provençal bread dough with onions, anchovies, olives, etc.
Pistou (Soupe au) vegetable soup bound with *pommade*
Pollo pépitora Provençal chicken *fricassée* thickened with lemon-flavoured mayonnaise
Pommade a thick paste of garlic, basil, cheese and olive oil
Ratatouille aubergines, courgettes, onion, garlic, red peppers and tomatoes in olive oil
Rouille orange-coloured sauce with hot peppers, garlic and saffron
Salade Niçoise tomatoes, beans, potatoes, black olives, anchovy, lettuce and olive oil. Sometimes tuna fish
Tapénade a purée of stoned black olives, anchovy fillets, capers, tuna fish and olive oil
Tarte (Tourte) aux blettes open-crust pastry with filling of Swiss chard (not unlike Chinese cabbage) and pine nuts
Tian Provençal earthenware dish

Wines
In the west of this region and in the Var Valley, lie several wine-producing areas. The wines are fresh and fragrant; they have two per cent more alcohol than their northern cousins.

The wines are usually white or rosé; some reds are produced, notably the excellent full-bodied **Château Vignelaure**. **Cassis**, **Bandol**, **Bellet** (near Nice), **Coteaux d'Aix-en-Provence** and **Côtes de Provence** are among the AC classifications; **Coteaux Varois** is a new VDQS. Many of the wines carry village names on labels: **Pierrefeu**, **Cuers** and **La Londe** (all near Hyères); **Le Beausset** and **La Bégude** (near Aix-en-Provence); **Vidauban**, **Taradeau**, **Les Arcs** and **Trans** (south of Draguignan); **Gassin** (**Château Minuty** is a Gassin property), near St-Tropez. In Nice you'll certainly see **Villars-sur-Var** and **Château de Cremat** (the best Bellet wine). Menus often show producers' names – like Listel or L'Estandon. Also refer to Provence: for its regional wine map and details of *Vins de Pays*.

BRIGNOLES   Ibis

Simple hotel/Cooking 1
Terrace/Swimming pool/Parking

A8 Brignoles exit. Keep going left after toll; Ibis off D554.
Menus A-B. Rooms (41) D. Disabled. Cards Access, Visa.
Post route du Val, 83170 Brignoles, Var.
Tel 94 69 19 29. Telex 404556. Fax 94 69 19 90. Mich 161/D2.
(Bookings: UK 071 724 1000; US toll free 800 221 4542)

CANNES   Campanile

Simple hotel/Cooking 1
Swimming pool/Parking

A8 Cannes-Ouest exit. South, hotel on other side N7.
Menus A-B. Rooms (98) D. Disabled. Cards Access, Visa.
Post 06150 Cannes-la-Bocca, Alpes-Mar. (En Route p 74)
Tel 93 48 69 41. Telex 461570. Fax 93 90 40 42. Mich 163/F3.
(Bookings: UK freephone 0800 807863)

DRAGUIGNAN   Climat de France

Simple hotel/Cooking 1
Parking/Good value

A8 Le Muy exit. North on N555. Hotel to right in 8 km.
Menus A-B. Rooms (34) C. Disabled. Cards AE, Access, Visa.
Post 83720 Trans-en-Provence, Var. (En Route p 72)
Tel 94 70 82 11. Telex 970625. Fax 94 67 77 70. Mich 161/F1.
(Bookings: UK 071 287 3181)

FRÉJUS   Climat de France

Simple hotel/Cooking 1
Parking/Good value

A8 Fréjus exit (from west); Puget-sur-Argens exit (from east).
N7 towards Fréjus; hotel on left, just past airport.
Menus A-B. Rooms (47) C. Disabled. Cards AE, Access, Visa.
Post 83600 Fréjus, Var.
Tel 94 53 34 97. Telex 970973. Fax 94 44 27 43. Mich 163/E3.
(Bookings: UK 071 287 3181)

NICE   Campanile

Simple hotel/Cooking 1
Lift/Garage

A8 Nice-Aéroport/Promenade des Anglais exits. South on N202
to prom. des Anglais; hotel on left, just past airport.
Menus A-B. Rooms (170) D. Disabled. Cards Access, Visa.
Post 459 prom. des Anglais, 06200 Nice, Alpes-Mar.
Tel 93 21 20 20. Telex 461640. Fax 93 83 83 96. Mich 165/D4.
(Bookings: UK freephone 0800 897863)

Autoroute Hotels

NICE

Climat de France

Simple hotel/Cooking 1
Parking/Good value

A8 Nice St-Augustin exit. East to N202, left, hotel on right.
Menus A-B. Rooms (72) C. Disabled. Cards AE, Access, Visa.
Post 232 rte de Grenoble, 06200 Nice, Alpes-Mar. (ER p 77)
Tel 93 71 80 80. Telex 461929. Fax 93 18 14 22. Mich 165/D4.
(Bookings: UK 071 287 3181)

NICE

Holiday Inn

Very comfortable hotel/Cooking 1
Terrace/Swimming pool/Lift/Garage

A8 Nice-Aéroport/Promenade des Anglais exits. South on
N202; under rail bridge, join N7 heading east; hotel on right.
Menus B. Rooms (150) F. Disabled. Cards All.
Post 179 bd R.Cassin, 06200 Nice, Alpes-Mar. (ER p 77)
Tel 93 83 91 92. Telex 970202. Fax 93 21 69 57. Mich 165/D4.

NICE

Novotel

Very comfortable hotel/Cooking 1
Terrace/Gardens/Swimming pool/Lift/Closed parking

A8 St-Laurent-du-Var exit (west of Nice & River Var). South,
under bridges for railway, N7 & N78 to Cap 3000. On left.
Menus B. Rooms (103) E-F. Disabled. Cards All.
Post Cap 3000, 06100 Nice, Alpes-Mar. (En Route p 77)
Tel 93 31 61 15. Telex 470643. Fax 93 07 62 25. Mich 165/D4.
(Bookings: UK 071 724 1000; US toll free 800 221 4542)

VALBONNE

Ibis

Simple hotel/Cooking 1
Terrace/Gardens/Swimming pool/Parking

A8 Antibes/Juan-les-Pins exit. West on D35. Under A8 and
straight on (D103). Shortly right to Sophia Antipolis.
Menus B. Rooms (99) D-E. Disabled. Cards AE, Access, Visa.
Post Sophia-Antipolis, 06560 Valbonne, Alpes-Mar. (ER p 75)
Tel 93 65 30 60. Telex 461363. Fax 93 95 83 99. Mich 165/D4.
(Bookings: UK 071 724 1000; US toll free 800 221 4542)

VALBONNE

Novotel

Very comfortable hotel/Cooking 1
Quiet/Terrace/Gardens/Swim pool/Tennis/Lift/Parking

Follow directions for Ibis above.
Menus B. Rooms (97) E-F. Disabled. Cards All.
Post Sophia-Antipolis, 06560 Valbonne, Alpes-Mar. (ER p 75)
Tel 93 65 40 00. Telex 970914. Fax 93 95 80 12. Mich 165/D4.
(Bookings: UK 071 724 1000; US toll free 800 221 4542)

CAGNES-SUR-MER   Les Collettes

Comfortable hotel
Swimming pool/Tennis/Parking

Small, modern building. Some rooms have small kitchens.
Rooms (13) D-E. Cards All.
Closed Nov to Xmas.
Post 38 ch. des Collettes, 06800 Cagnes-s-Mer, Alpes-Mar.
Tel 93 20 80 66. Mich 165/D4.

CAGNES-SUR-MER   Hamotel

Comfortable hotel
Quiet/Lift/Garage/Parking

On D6 towards St-Paul. Modern building, part of a new
purpose-built complex of attractive flats and villas.
Rooms (30) D. Cards All. (En Route p 76)
Post Hameau du Soleil, 06270 Villeneuve-Loubet, Alpes-Mar.
Tel 93 20 86 60. Telex 970944. Fax 93 73 33 94. Mich 165/D4.

LA COLLE-SUR-LOUP   Marc Hély

Comfortable hotel
Quiet/Gardens/Parking

Provençal style; gardens are the highlight. On D6, to south.
Rooms (13) D-F. Cards AE, Access, Visa.
Closed 10 Nov to 5 Dec.
Post rte de Cagnes, 06480 La Colle-sur-Loup, Alpes-Mar.
Tel 93 22 64 10. Fax 93 22 93 84. Mich 165/D3.

LA CROIX-VALMER   Parc

Comfortable hotel
Quiet/Gardens/Lift/Parking

A huge, old mansion, built originally as a school. Handsome
palm trees. On D93, east of D559 to St-Tropez.
Rooms (33) D-E. Cards DC, Visa.
Closed Oct to March.
Post 83420 La Croix-Valmer, Var.
Tel 94 79 64 04. Mich 161/F3.

FREJUS   L'Oasis

Simple hotel
Quiet/Terrace/Parking

Well-named, a real oasis. Tucked away in a narrow side lane,
south of the N98 to St-Raphaël. Beach just minutes away.
Rooms (27) C-E. Cards Access, Visa.
Closed Feb.
Post rue H.Fabre, 83600 Fréjus Plage, Var.
Tel 94 51 50 44. Mich 163/E3.

Base Hotels

GRIMAUD Athénopolis

Comfortable hotel
Quiet/Gardens/Swimming pool/Parking

On the D558 north-east of Grimaud. All rooms face north and
have either balconies or terraces.
Rooms (10) E-F. Cards All.
Closed Nov to Easter.
Post 83990 Grimaud, Var.
Tel 94 43 24 24. Fax 94 43 37 05. Mich 163/D4.

JUAN-LES-PINS Mimosas

Very comfortable hotel
Quiet/Gardens/Swimming pool/Parking

The gardens and pool have been much appreciated by readers.
Rooms (37) E-F. Cards None.
Closed Nov to March.
Post rue Pauline, 06160 Juan-les-Pins, Alpes-Mar.
Tel 93 61 04 16. Mich 165/D4.

JUAN-LES-PINS Welcome

Comfortable hotel
Quiet/Gardens/Lift/Closed Parking

A great favourite. New owners, Annick and Dominique Pollet,
are well liked. Both rooms and gardens "refurbished".
Rooms (29) E-F. Cards All.
Closed Nov to March.
Post 7 av. Dr Hochet, 06160 Juan-les-Pins, Alpes-Mar.
Tel 93 61 26 12. Fax 93 61 38 04. Mich 165/D4.

MANDELIEU Acadia (Sant'Angelo)

Simple hotel
Quiet/Gardens/Swimming pool/Tennis/Lift/Parking

Was called Sant'Angelo. Much liked; for the man-made benefits
(plus nearby golf course) and river almost encircling hotel.
Rooms (34) E-F. Cards Access, Visa. (*Cuisinettes* available.)
Post 681 av. de la Mer, 06210 Mandelieu, Alpes-Mar. (ER p 74)
Tel 93 49 28 23. Fax 92 97 55 54. Mich 163/F3.

MENTON Princess et Richmond

Very comfortable hotel
Lift/Parking

On prom. Roof terrace alternative to sardine-packed beach.
Rooms (43) E-F. Cards All.
Closed 5 Nov to 20 Dec.
Post 617 prom. du Soleil, 06500 Menton, Alpes-Mar.
Tel 93 35 80 20. Fax 93 57 40 20. Mich 165/F3.

PEGOMAS   Le Bosquet

Simple hotel
Secluded/Gardens/Swim pool/Tennis/Parking/Good value

There's no doubt about the fact that this base is absolutely the number one favourite of readers and has been consistently for a dozen years. Anne and I, and our children (now 30 and 28!), first discovered Le Bosquet and the utterly lovable Bernardi family a year or so after they opened their little gem in 1965. Like us, and hundreds of readers, fall in love with the fastidious, hard-working and friendly family: the locomotive of the family, Simone, and her wise, self-effacing husband, Jean Pierre; daughter Chantal, a look-alike of her mother; and Romain, Chantal's son, now nine. (Alas, Françoise, Simone's mother, died in Jan 1992, aged over 90.) The older building has been improved during the last 12 months.
Rooms (18) B-C. Studios with kitchen (7) D. Cards None.
Closed 7 Jan to 7 Feb.
Post 74 ch. des Perissols, 06580 Pégomas, Alpes-Mar.
Tel 93 42 22 87. Mich 163/F2.

PLAN DE LA TOUR   Mas des Brugassières

Comfortable hotel
Secluded/Gardens/Swimming pool/Tennis/Parking

A heavenly spot: gardens and pool are especially enticing.
Rooms (14) E-F. Cards Access, Visa.
Post rte Grimaud (D44), 83120 Plan de la Tour, Var.
Tel 94 43 72 42. Mich 163/D4.

PLAN DE LA TOUR   Parasolis

Simple hotel
Secluded/Gardens/Parking

Friendly *patron*; reasonable prices; all rooms on one level.
Rooms (15) C-D. Cards None.
Closed mid Oct to mid March. (4 km south on D44)
Post Courruères, 83120 Plan de la Tour, Var.
Tel 94 43 76 05. Mich 163/D4.

RAMATUELLE   Ferme d'Hermès

Comfortable hotel
Secluded/Gardens/Swimming pool/Parking

Delectable! Your first welcome will be from Hermès, a Welsh terrier; the second from the delightful, English-speaking owner, Françoise Verrier. Encircled by vines (protected ground). Rooms have clever, space-saving small kitchens.
Rooms (10) E-F. Cards Access, Visa.
Closed Nov to Mar. (Winter bookings: Tel Paris 1 48 28 75 75 or write to Françoise at 15 rue Peclet, 75015 Paris)
Post rte l'Escalet, 83350 Ramatuelle, Var. (South of D93)
Tel 94 79 27 80. Fax 94 79 26 86. Mich 161/F3.

ST-JEAN-CAP-FERRAT   Brise Marine

Comfortable hotel
Quiet/Gardens/Garage

Sensational views east from elevated site. Yves Maîtrehenry is
a helpful owner. Expensive garaging, almost 60 francs a day.
Rooms (16) F. Cards Access, Visa.
Closed Nov to Jan.
Post 58 av. J.Mermoz, 06230 St-Jean-Cap-Ferrat, Alpes-Mar.
Tel 93 76 04 36. Fax 93 76 11 49. Mich 165/E3.

ST-JEAN-CAP-FERRAT   Clair Logis

Simple hotel
Quiet/Gardens/Parking

Ochre-coloured villa in largish park with firs and both palm
and fig trees. Free parking in grounds. Annexe cramped.
Rooms (16) D-F. Cards Access, Visa.
Closed Nov to mid Dec.
Post 12 av. Centrale, 06230 St-Jean-Cap-Ferrat, Alpes-Mar.
Tel 93 76 04 57. Mich 165/E3.

ST-PAUL   Le Hameau

Comfortable hotel
Quiet/Gardens/Swimming pool/Parking

Old buildings; fragrant gardens. Xavier Huvelin is attentive,
English-speaking owner. Air conditioning in some bedrooms.
Rooms (14) D-F. Cards All.
Closed Mid Nov to 22 Dec. 6 Jan to mid Feb.
Post rte de la Colle, 06570 St-Paul, Alpes-Mar. (ER p 76)
Tel 93 32 80 24. Fax 93 32 55 75. Mich 165/D3.

VENCE   Le Floréal

Very comfortable hotel
Gardens/Swimming pool/Lift/Parking

Modern; popular with coach tours. West of old town.
Rooms (43) F. Cards Access, Visa.
Post 440 av. Rhin & Danube, 06140 Vence, Alpes-Mar.
Tel 93 58 64 40. Telex 461613. Fax 93 58 79 69. Mich 165/D3.

VENCE   Miramar

Comfortable hotel
Quiet/Gardens/Parking

Older building, not too dear and east of old Vence.
Rooms (17) D-E. Cards AE, Access, Visa.
Closed 25 Oct to Feb.
Post plateau St-Michel, 06140 Vence, Alpes-Mar.
Tel 93 58 01 32. Mich 165/D3.

AURIBEAU   **Auberge Nossi-Bé**

**Comfortable restaurant with rooms/Cooking 2-3
Terrace**

Jean-Michel Retoré hails from Arras; dark-eyed Anne-Marie,
his wife, is a Cannes girl. Consistently praised (quite excellent
still is a run-of-the-mill plaudit) but the record is spoilt by
some readers expressing disappointment and regular grumbles
about prices. Pity. Neo-classical, modern and local specialities
with a wide choice. A typical permutation could be: *pistou de
légumes aux raviolis de crabe et goujounettes de sole*; *saumon
frais en couscous à la coriandre fraîche*; and *crème brulée
vanille aux figues*. The couple are motoring addicts: ask them
about their interest in classic cars.
Menus C. Rooms (6) C. Cards Access, Visa.
Closed Jan. Feb. Mon midday & Wed midday (season). Tues,
evg & Wed (rest of the year).
Post 06810 Auribeau-sur-Siagne, Alpes-Mar.
Tel 93 42 20 20. Mich 164/C4.

LA COLLE-SUR-LOUP   **La Belle Epoque**

**Comfortable restaurant/Cooking 2
Terrace/Gardens/Parking/Good value**

The clue to the décor is in the name: old-world charm with a
seductive terrace and clever exterior lighting come darkness.
New owners Jean-Pierre and Michelle Frédéric are doing a
good job. Primarily classical cooking with many an original
plat: saumon de Norvège au gros sel, tian de courgettes and *le
carioca* (coffee ice cream, rum and raisin ice cream and
caramel sauce) are a couple of examples.
Menus B-C. Cards All.
Closed Jan. Tue. Mon evg (ex Jul/Aug). Wed midday (Jul/Aug).
Post 06480 La Colle-sur-Loup, Alpes-Mar.
Tel 93 20 10 92. Mich 165/D4. (2 km south-east, on D6.)

COTIGNAC   **Lou Calen**

**Comfortable hotel/Cooking 1-2
Quiet/Terrace/Gardens/Swimming pool**

Readers of *Favourites* will know that this was a much liked
hotel. But not long after publication the place went to the dogs.
Letters brought news of several disasters. Happily the owners
took a firm grip of the leash a couple of years ago and they
seem to have the wayward beast under control again. My spies
have been busy: tasty food (*Bourgeoise* with some Provençale
and classical dishes); excellent welcome; helpful, friendly staff;
and the setting have all earned brownie points. Debits? Some
rooms are far too basic; and the poolside furniture is tatty. But
is the place still tacky, as several readers have suggested?
Please tell me. In by a pip squeak.
Menus B-C. Rooms (8) C-F. Cards All.
Closed Jan to Mar. Rest: Wed (not July & Aug).
Post 1 cours Gambetta, 83570 Cotignac, Var.
Tel 94 04 60 40. Mich 162/B3.

FAYENCE   France

Simple restaurant/Cooking 1
Terrace/Good value

Not long after *FL3* was published Marcel and Rosette Choisy
threw in the towel and retired. What a sad day indeed. For so
long a family favourite and, for five years, loved by every
reader who sought out this evocative spot. A *copain* of Marcel,
Guy Boury, took over but didn't last long. Now Pierre and
Claudine Le Sec'h are making a go of trying to meet the
difficult objective of *la cuisine d'autrefois*. Classical mixed with
Provençale. The *hors d'oeuvre* remains a favourite.
Menus B. Cards Access, Visa.
Closed 15 Nov-15 Feb. Tues evg/Wed (out of season). Pub hols.
Post 83440 Fayence. Var.
Tel 94 76 00 14. Mich 164/B4.

FOX-AMPHOUX   Aub. du Vieux Fox

Comfortable restaurant with rooms/Cooking 1-2
Secluded/Terrace/Parking/Good value

If you receive a three-figure number of reports on any
recommendation you can expect a handful or so of moans. True
enough, this was no exception: so-so service, a casual, "tired"
welcome and ordinary food were the thumbs-down markers.
What of the rest? A unanimous thumbs-up from everyone else.
Jean-Charles Martha, the fluent English-speaking host and
self-taught chef, still shows the fighting spirit that made him
such a formidable Competitions Manager for Ford
International during the 60s. The hamlet is narcotic; the
auberge was once the presbytery of the church (mainly 16th
century, part 900 years old); J-C is a gentle, kind *patron*; and
his cooking (classical and regional) has improved.
Menus B. Rooms (10) B-C. Cards AE, Access, Visa.
Closed Mid Dec to mid Feb. Wed midday. Thurs midday.
Post Fox-Amphoux, 83670 Barjols, Var.
Tel 94 80 71 69. Fax 94 80 78 38. Mich 162/B3.

GRASSE   Maître Boscq

Very simple restaurant/Cooking 1-2
Good value

Patrick Boscq, the Stormin' Norman of French cuisine, has the
girth that all chefs should have. An engaging sense of humour,
good English (his card reckons "Tries hard to speak English"),
and a fierce loyalty to Grassoise recipes makes his minuscule,
300-year-old restaurant a must. Odile, too, is a lovable, down-
to-earth *patronne*. Where else can you savour *lou fassum*? Or
tourteau Grassois aux herbes? Or *fricot de cacho-fuou*? Herbs,
vegetables, game: everything's authentically Provençal. Enjoy
let-your-hair-down informality in magical Grasse.
Menus B. Cards Access, Visa. (Be sure to book ahead.)
Closed 1st 2 wks Nov. Sun. Pub hols. Evgs (Nov to Easter).
Post 13 r. Fontette, 06130 Grasse, Alpes-Mar.
Tel 93 36 45 76. Mich 164/C4. Off pl. aux Aires (market).

LES ISSAMBRES Chante-Mer

Simple restaurant/Cooking 2
Terrace/Good value

The names Mario and Nanette Battaglia will immediately ring
bells for some readers. Mario is the elder brother of Jean-Paul
(Feu Follet, Mougins) and Jean-Pierre (Auberge Fleurie,
Valbonne). A talented trio providing lucky clients with quality
produce, cooked expertly, at knock-down prices. A small but
light and airy dining room, off the N98 at Les Calanques (turn
opposite Hôtel Les Calanques). Nanette is a delight and so is
Mario's cooking: fish features in a universally liked *soupe de
poisson* and in a *filet de rascasse à la tapenade*. Order
bouillabaisse and *chapon farci* (fish) in advance. A mix of
classical and Provençale cuisine.
Menus B-C. Cards Access, Visa.
Closed 15 Dec-15 Jan. Sun evg (Oct-Mar). Mon (not July/Aug).
Post Village Provençal, 83380 Les Issambres, Var.
Tel 94 96 93 23. Mich 163/E4.

MONS Auberge Provençale

Very simple restaurant/Cooking 1-2
Good value

Be sure to breathe-in the heady, sensual delights of the string
of perched villages west of Grasse: Cabris, Montauroux,
Callian, Fayence, Seillans and Bargemon among them. But be
certain, too, to head north to ancient Mons. Follow signs for
table d'orientation (stunning views) to the tiny *auberge*,
clinging by its nails to the hillside. Claude Reveau will not
fail to please: among classical and Provençal *plats* are
quenelle de brochet à la Nantua, sublime *gigot d'agneau aux
herbes* and a huge platter of *charcuterie*. Good value? No,
fabulous value. Note that only lunch is served.
Menus A-B. Cards None.
Closed Nov. Wed. Every evening.
Post 83440 Mons, Var.
Tel 94 76 38 33. Mich 164/B4.

MONTAUROUX Aub. du Puits Jaubert

Comfortable restaurant with rooms/Cooking 2
Secluded/Terrace/Gardens/Parking

Brothers Henri and Fabien Fillatreau bought the 15th-century
bergerie (sheepfold) five years ago and what a welcome new
fillip they've given its ancient timbers and stonework. All
rooms were refurbished last year. Classical cooking with the
odd Provençale touch: *tournedos de boeuf sauce à l'estragon*,
filet de canard à la réduction de porto and *filet d'agneau à
la crème d'ail* are three of the menu alternatives. Near to but
not overlooking the man-made Lac de St-Cassien.
Menus B-C. Rooms (8) C-D. Cards Access, Visa.
Closed Mid Nov to mid Dec. Tues.
Post Callian, 83440 Fayence, Var.
Tel 94 76 44 48. Mich 164/C4. (Due S of Montauroux & D562.)

MOUGINS   Ferme de Mougins

Very comfortable restaurant/Cooking 3
Terrace/Gardens/Parking

An old *mas*, hidden in a quintessential Provençal garden, yet
only a hop-step-and-jump from Mougins. This is where we first
encountered the brilliance of Patrick Henriroux (see Vienne,
Massif Central). The owners, Henri Sauvanet and his son, and
new chef Jean-Louis Vosgien, a modern and neo-classical *maître*
(he once worked in Scotland), have sharp eyes for fine detail.
Superb flowers and bread and intense, flavoursome creations:
witness *assiette de moules*, *ravioles et galinette au safran* (with
red mullet and goat's cheese) and *aiguillettes de magret de
canard en bigarade* (a light, not-too-sweet sauce). (Ask J-L if
he's yet risked putting Yorkshire pudding on his menus.)
Menus C-D Cards Access, DC, Visa. (On D35 Valbonne road.)
Closed Sun evg & Mon (Nov to Apl).
Post St-Basile, 06250 Mougins, Alpes-Mar.
Tel 93 90 03 74. Fax 92 92 21 48. Mich 165/D4.

MOUGINS   Feu Follet

Comfortable restaurant/Cooking 2-3
Terrace/Good value

Michelin took years to wake up to what I had been telling
readers for a decade. Here in film-set Mougins (the most
expensive real estate on the *côte*) a talented young couple,
Jean-Paul and Micheline Battaglia (both speak English), are
working wonders: despite sky-high overheads clients can relish
quality produce, prepared with precision, at sensible prices.
Anne and I are thrilled by their progress: a new extension and
kitchen, new loos and a non-smoking dining room. No wonder
Feu Follet is always busy. But it needs to be, to make financial
sense. Classical and Provençale specialities. Super sweets.
Menus B. Cards Visa.
Closed Last 3 wks Mar. 1st wk Apl. Sun evg & Mon.
Post pl. Mairie, 06250 Mougins, Alpes-Mar.
Tel 93 90 15 78. Mich 165/D4.

MOUGINS   Relais à Mougins

Very comfortable restaurant/Cooking 3
Terrace

André Surmain (trained by Dumaine and once owner of the
Big Apple's Lutèce) has got his grin back and is in there,
fighting the recession with a knock-out Menu Bistro (F140 a
few months ago; inclusive of VAT at 18.6% and service at 15%).
The Dumaine pedigree means classical cuisine: *chartreuse de
pigeonneau de ferme braisée aux laitues* and *noisettes d'agneau
en chemise aux herbes de Provence* are typical. (André is a
motoring nut: quiz him about his cars and Bugey wines.)
Menus B-E. Cards AE, Access, Visa.
Closed November. Mon. Tues midday (not pub. hols).
Post pl. Mairie, 06250 Mougins, Alpes-Mar.
Tel 93 90 03 47. Telex 462559. Fax 93 75 72 83. Mich 165/D4.

OPIO   Mas des Géraniums

Very simple hotel/Cooking 2
Quiet/Terrace/Gardens/Parking/Good value

What a relief. Anne and I have known this little gem, hidden among the olive groves, for 30 years (now with a new vista of a golf course 300 yards away). The *mas* was due for the chop. But then I got the welcome news that Michel and Colette Creusot (both worked for Surmain at Mougins) had bought the property. Life's tough for them: they have little help so the small details aren't always spot on. But classical and Provençale cooking appeals: typical of both are *suprême de volaille farci aux morilles* and *rouget grillé à l'Opidoise*. Let's hope they succeed and return the *mas* to past heights.
Menus B. Rooms (8) C. Cards Access, Visa.
Closed Jan. Tues evg & Wed.
Post San Peire, 06650 Opio, Alpes-Mar.
Tel 93 77 23 23. Mich 165/D4. (On D7, south of D2085.)

PEILLON   Aub. de la Madone

Comfortable hotel/Cooking 2
Secluded/Terrace/Gardens/Tennis/Parking

Abandon the ghastly coastal strip and wind your way up the zig-zags to this flower-bedecked, perched haven of peace. The Millo family provides a lively buzz: Aimée is *mère*; her son Christian, the chef, and his English-speaking wife, Carine; and her daughter, Marie-Josée, a charismatic, lovable smasher. And let's not forget Roger, the perpetual-motion waiter. Everything is the very essence of the Med, including the authentic Provençale cuisine. Savour all the tastes of the south, sensibly prepared and served. Sit among the olive trees on the sunny, flower-fringed terrace and breathe in the scent of herbs. Order *le tourton des Pénitents*, an omelette of pine nuts, almonds, chives, onions and a dozen herbs. More likely than not, Marie-Josée (her English is engagingly infectious) will pick the latter from the beds around you. "Aphrodisiacs" she claims. See her face when you ask her why?
Menus B-C. Rooms (15) E-F. Cards None.
Closed Jan. 20 Oct to 20 Dec. Wed.
Post 06440 Peillon, Alpes-Mar.
Tel 93 79 91 17. Mich 164/E3.

ST-MARTIN-DU-VAR   Jean-François Issautier

Very comfortable restaurant/Cooking 4
Parking

Anne and I first encountered Jean-François and Nicole Issautier almost 20 years ago, at their isolated home in St-Etienne-de-Tinée. (How isolated? Follow the Var north, then north again on the D2205 to the village, at the foot of France's highest pass, the Col de la Bonette.) We already knew the Auberge de la Belle Route at St-Martin. Fifteen years ago the couple decided enough was enough and moved south, buying the *auberge* from the Costes, the previous owners. What a transformation; now the Provençale *auberge* fairly sparkles.

Jean-François, in his mid-forties, remains a humble, happy man; Nicole, too, has lost none of her unspoilt charm. Chef J-F mixes neo-classical with modern and his repertoire includes as much local produce as possible. Two examples: *fleur de courgette de Gattières farcie* (a village down the valley); and *nougat glacé au miel de la Haute-Tinée* (his old *pays*). Some Eastern mystery finds a place on his menus (very much the vogue in culinary France these days): *langoustines rôties aux herbes Thai* and *canette aux poivres Sechuan*.

Menus B-F. Cards All. (Book ahead.)

Closed Mid Feb to mid Mar. 1st 2 wks Nov. Sun evg. Sun midday (July and Aug). Mon.

Post Aub. de la Belle Rte, 06670 St-Martin-du-Var, Alpes-Mar. Tel 93 08 10 65. Fax 93 29 19 73. Mich 165/D3.

SPERACEDES   La Soleillade

Simple restaurant with basic rooms/Cooking 1-2
Terrace/Good value

Michel Forest is a dry-humoured, loquacious chef/patron with a cynical sense of humour. 25 years ago he turned his back (no wonder) on a circus career (ask to see the photographs of his strong-arm balancing act), preferring instead to juggle pots and pans. Appetite-quenching Provençale fare: one menu includes a first course of *panier de crudités*, *tourte fermière*, *cochonnailes variées*, *jambon cru* and an *amuse-gueule*; *côtes d'agneau aux herbes* and *canard aux olives* are typical second courses; and four desserts of *le Turinois*, *tarte à l'orange*, *délice de la Martinque* and *gâteau de Michel* (you get the quartet).

Menus A-B. Rooms (8) B-C. Cards None.

Closed October. Wed.

Post Spéracèdes, 06530 Peymeinade, Alpes-Mar. Tel 93 60 58 46. Mich 164/C4.

TOURTOUR   Chênes Verts

Comfortable restaurant/Cooking 3-4
Gardens/Parking

How does Paul Bajade survive? Well, he's a single-minded, shy individual, is quite content with his hassle-free lot in his remote home and, importantly, is a damn good chef. A small dining room where, on weekday evenings, you're likely to be on your own. Classical cuisine with a not-too-heavy but getting expensive touch. A typical meal could include a *feuillantine de caille* with *foie gras* and *jus de truffes*, *gambas* in a lobster sauce, *blanc de volaille à la creme de morilles* and a wild strawberry *millefeuille*. But for a truly exotic meal, extravagant and quite unbeatable, save the pennies (about 700 francs to be exact) for his unique six-course Menu Special Truffes. Paul knows his truffles and nearby Aups is renowned for the quality of its delicate black fungi.

Menus C-D. (Menu Truffes F.) Cards None. (Rooms? Petite Aub.)

Closed Jan. 1st 2 wks Feb. Tues evg & Wed.

Post rte Villecroze, 83690 Tourtour, Var. (2 km W, on D51.) Tel 94 70 55 06. Mich 162/C3.

VALBONNE   Auberge Fleurie

Comfortable restaurant/Cooking 2-3
Terrace/Parking/Good value

Anne and I first came across Jean-Pierre Battaglia 17 years
ago when the young chef, then in his mid-twenties, was based
in a seedy Mouans-Sartoux restaurant. The impact of the meal
was dramatic: our family re-visited each evening for the
following three. Trained at Noves and by Outhier at La
Napoule, the youngster's talents were immediately obvious:
classical precision and high-class produce at charity prices.

For over a decade I've been pestering readers to seek out
this supreme example of *rapport qualité-prix*. Today, Jean-
Pierre has been "discovered"; shame on Michelin for taking so
long. As a consequence the tables are always crowded, the
auberge is looking extra smart, but the formula remains the
same: polished preparation using quality produce, of whatever
sort. The pleasure factor is high, *l'addition* pain is low – facts
confirmed by hundreds of satisfied readers.
Menus B. Cards Access, Visa.
Closed 2nd half Dec. Wed.
Post 06560 Valbonne, Alpes-Mar. (On D3, south of Valbonne.)
Tel 93 42 02 80. Fax 93 40 22 27. Mich 165/D4.

VALBONNE   Bistro de Valbonne

Comfortable restaurant/Cooking 2
Good value

Raymond Purgato has made many friends at the tiny bistro,
lost in a criss-cross of lanes, during his ten-year tenure. (His
latest venture is the nearby Royal Pub, a wine bar with a
difference.) Classical menus: *pâté Périgourdin au foie gras
truffé, boeuf Strogonoff, filet de boeuf au poivre vert* and
marquise au chocolat illustrate what I mean.
Menus B-C. Cards All.
Closed Mar. Nov. Sun. Mon.
Post 11 rue Fontaine, 06560 Valbonne, Alpes-Mar.
Tel 93 42 05 59. Mich 165/D4.

VENCE   Auberge des Templiers

Comfortable restaurant/Cooking 2
Terrace/Good value

Sue Lopez, a Scottish lassie, once ran the front of house with
Micheline Battaglia at Mougins' Feu Follet; Patrice, her
husband, worked for 14 years as a *sommelier* at Vergé's Moulin
de Mougins. Now he's slipped on chef's whites and handles
pots and pans, rather than bottles. (His vast knowledge is put
to good use. Study the formidable wine list; and the menu front
cover.) Neo-classical and Provençale cuisine.
Menus B-C. Cards Access, Visa.
Closed 15 Dec to 5 Jan. 5-20 Mar. Sun evg & Mon (out of
season). Mon midday, Thurs midday & Sat midday (July/Aug).
Post 39 av. Joffre, 06140 Vence, Alpes-Mar.
Tel 93 58 06 05. Mich 165/D3. (Near Post Office, W of Vence.)

DORDOGNE

see page 297

7

- ■ Base hotel
- ▲ Hotel/Rest (rooms)
- △ Restaurant only

0   10   20 Miles

Coussac-Bonneval

Vieux-Mareuil ▲
Brantôme ▲

St-Jean-de-Côle ▲
Champagnac-de-Belair ▲

Hautefort

Objat
Gimel-les-Cascades

Périgueux

Varetz

Tulle ● ▲ Sédière
Brive

St-Pardoux

Montignac ▲ ▲ Coly

Aubazine

Lascaux

Collonges-la-Rouge

Souillac

Argentat

Martel ● Beaulieu
● St-Céré

Trémolat

Bergerac

Dordogne

Bretenoux ●

Sousceyrac

Gouffre de Padirac

Les Eyzies

Tamniès

Rocamadour ●

Le Bugué ▲

Monpazier

Gourdon ●

Sarlat-la-Canéda

Biron ●
Bonaguil ●

Goujounac ▲
St-Médard

Pech-Merle ●

St-Cyprien

▲ Vézac

Lot

Cabrerets ▲

Dordogne
Beynac ● Domme ●

Cahors

St-Cirq-Lapopie

see page 347

see page 346

see page 232

Who would disagree with Benjamin Franklin's assertion that "Everyone has two countries – his own and France." Ask any Anglo-Saxon which corner of France he would claim to be a home from home and the response is likely to be the "Dordogne".

Long before the area became so popular with the British both Anne and I fell in love with Périgord; we first saw the area at the start of our married life, over 30 years ago. The "Dordogne" is very much a British label. Tell a Breton that you're off to the Dordogne and he'll assume you mean the river or *département* of the same name. For a Frenchman the map above shows two regions: Périgord and Quercy (the latter, primarily, the area north and south of the River Lot).

Anne and I have scores of vivid memories of this most pastoral of French regions. **Sarlat**, a few kilometres north of the River **Dordogne**, has changed much since we first saw the small medieval town three decades ago. Most of the centuries-old houses have been restored and their golden stonework cleaned up. The outskirts are more commercial these days, as they are everywhere, but not to an overwhelming extent; the heart of the town, squeezed into a long, narrow valley, is where your heart is certain to be captured.

We recall the terrain to the south of the town: a landscape of glistening brown earth, huge chestnuts, ancient oaks and twisted walnut trees, drooping giant sunflowers, drying tobacco, mellow old houses, perched castles and an exquisite river flowing peacefully through this earth-bound Eden. We remember, too, getting up early one flawless autumn morning. The sky was dark in the west, pink in the east and mists shrouded the valleys below us. A heavy dew carpeted fields, hedges and the verges; the bushes sparkled as the rising sun created shimmering lights on thousands of spiders' webs.

One spot, more than any other, is the perfect entry to this captivating land. Seek out the dead-end lane leading to the

Château de **Sédière**. Here, lost in the *département* of Corrèze, a natural cocktail refreshes the senses: silence; cool, still air, broken only by a cock's crow or a bird's song; mixed woods of oaks, beeches, silver birch, sweet chestnuts and pines; and ferns, royal purple heather, butterflies and *étangs*. An austere small château sits contentedly in the middle of the uplifting watercolour. Yes, start at Sédière.

Where do you go next? To nearby **Gimel-les-Cascades**. Three separate waterfalls combine, particularly after heavy rain, to put on an extrovert show of fury and foaming sound. Walk the steep steps to the bottom; but remember that a long, steep return awaits you. Corrèze remains quite unspoilt. Its tiny and numerous lanes are as inviting as ever, like myriad veins spreading through some of the finest forests in France.

Before going south to the River Dordogne aim south-west to **Collonges-la-Rouge**, literally "red" as the houses and Romanesque church are built of red sandstone. Then east to photogenic **Argentat** and **Beaulieu**-sur-Dordogne, both alongside the river. Spare time for a quick *déviation* to the Tours de Merle, a ruined château in the most stunning of settings among the wooded hills to the east of Argentat.

Beaulieu is the southern *porte* to Corrèze. Downstream from the town, on either side of the river's banks, are scores of appealing treats, both man-made and natural.

The first man-made attraction is the red sandstone château at Castelnau-Bretenoux, once a vast medieval fortress. A number of notable caves are all on the left bank of the river: Presque, west of **St-Céré**, is renowned for stalagmites; Lacave, south-east of **Souillac**, is famed for both its underground streams and hundreds of stone formations resembling animals, people and buildings; and Cougnac, east of **Domme**, has cave paintings rivalling both Pech-Merle and Lascaux.

One cave is a must. The **Gouffre de Padirac** is to the west of St-Céré; you can travel for several kilometres on a subterranean river which flows through the most spectacular of caves, hollowed out of the limestone below the *causse* (plateau). Take warm clothes.

Another must is nearby **Rocamadour**, built, house upon house, church upon church, tower upon tower, on the side of a vertical cliff. Before exploring this most remarkable of small towns, drive up to the viewpoint on the D32 across the valley. For centuries Rocamadour has been one of the most legendary pilgrimage sites in Christendom; kings, saints, sinners and pilgrims have all come this way. So did Poulenc, one of my favourite composers; he rediscovered his Christian faith here in 1935 on a visit to the shrine of the Black Virgin (a statue of the Virgin Mary carved from walnut).

Of the many small towns and villages, St-Céré, Carennac, hidden Gluges and Creysse (use the D114 and D43 east of Souillac), Souillac (see the 14th-century abbey and its carved, twisted pillars), Domme, La Roque-Gageac, Castelnaud and **Beynac**-et-Cazenac (the last four are especially evocative) should not, under any circumstances, be missed.

Domme is a "perched" dream of a *bastide* (fortified village); the river panorama is a three-star marvel. La Roque-Gageac is a beauty too: the old houses with their roofs of *lauzes* (lines of local stone tiles laid on wooden slats) are reflected in the waters below the steep cliffs. The château at Castelnaud, high above the Dordogne, glowers northwards at the equally remarkable site of Beynac, where the castle walls sit majestically atop high vertical rock faces.

Several isolated châteaux are located along both banks of the Dordogne downstream from Beaulieu: Belcastel, La Treyne, Fénelon, Montfort, Fayrac and Les Milandes (owned earlier this century by Josephine Baker, the American cabaret singer).

No wonder then that the River Dordogne is loved by so many. But further south, not visited by anything like as many tourists to the area, many of whom treat the Dordogne as France's southern border, is another equally gorgeous length of river terrain, the **Lot**. The lower reaches of the river are especially idyllic: numerous meanders, tranquil fields and wooded hillsides combine to please both the eye and soul.

Start in one of its tributaries, at the **Pech-Merle** caves; here there are the most amazing stone formations, shapes like saucers, plates and wheels, and the most vivid of wall paintings. Around the corner is one of my favourite French villages: medieval **St-Cirq-Lapopie** on a spectacular perched site above the left bank of the Lot. Downstream is **Cahors**, enclosed within a mighty meander: the most famous landmark is the Pont Valentré, the most handsome of medieval fortified bridges; equally interesting is the Cathédrale St-Etienne and the antique lanes adjacent to the building.

From Cahors drive in a westerly arc, first along the Lot Valley, then circling north to join the Dordogne again at its confluence with the **Vézère**. On the journey seek out three man-made creations. First **Bonaguil** castle (seen it at its best from the lane to the south); the lofty walls marry grace with formidable strength. Disney, near Paris or in the States, cannot better this most elegant of 15th-century strongholds. Continue to the sullen château at **Biron**. With an elevated perch commanding extensive views in all directions, the castle must have been the ideal site for a fortress. Within the walls are an intimidating *donjon*, a chapel and a grass-covered *place*. Finally, to **Monpazier**, one of many *bastides* between the two rivers. Built in 1284 by Edward I, King of England and Duke of Aquitaine, Monpazier is much the best. The arcaded square at the heart of the fortified village is a gem with perfectly proportioned stone buildings.

The Vézère is the third of the exceptional river valleys in Périgord-Quercy. **Les Eyzies** is the "University of Prehistory". The skull of Cro-Magnon man was found in the cave-riddled limestone walls above the village. But the most magnetic site is the cave at **Lascaux**. I regret bitterly that Anne and I, in the early 60s, didn't visit the cave before it was closed to the public on April 30, 1963. Today, there's a fantastic facsimile called Lascaux II, built underground 300 metres away from the original (closed Mondays).

The wall paintings fill me with a massive feeling of mystery. What made the Magdalenian hunters enter the subterranean cave? What were the gigantic problems facing early man in the harsh world outside the sanctuary of the dark cavern? It must have been a world of unimaginable danger and an unbearably lonely one at that. Yet early man, 17,000 years ago, had the ingenuity to create those paintings, full of vitality and technical wizardry. What a treasure the four boys from Montignac opened up for the world on September 12, 1940; all because a small dog, Robot, fell down a hole.

After Lascaux II other sights tend to pale. But head north from **Montignac** to **Hautefort**. Dominating the horizon is a huge château with pepperpot towers and, tumbling down the hill below it, is the village of Hautefort.

Finally, detour to the north-western corner of the area. **Brantôme** first charmed us three decades ago; the abbey with a riverside setting, alongside the **Dronne**, is a spellbinder. Just downstream from the town is Bourdeilles where a château, part Renaissance, part medieval, snoozes above the river.

Seek out other spots. First, to the north-east of **Champagnac** is **St-Jean-de-Côle**. Drive off the D707, along a street the width of a car, and marvel at the most evocative of Périgord villages. A small square – flanked by an unusual 11th-century church, an ancient covered market and a modest château – is today just what it looked like in the Middle Ages, with the addition now of two humble cafés with terraces. Walk down to the Gothic bridge that spans the Côle and continue for 100 metres for a view of the church's cloisters.

The Dronne changes its nature upriver from Champagnac. Park the car at Champs-Romain and walk to the Saut du Chalard where the stream cascades over rocks in a steep wooded valley. Beware: it's an easy downhill walk; the opposite coming back. On your way visit two different attractions: the château at Puyguilhem, with its lone, sentry-like pepperpot tower; and the Grottes de Villars, open in the high season only.

Downstream on the Dronne, west of Ribérac, is the hillside village of **Aubeterre**, stuffed full of character. The site, narrow streets, a *place* and the Eglise St-Jacques will please; but even more so perhaps will be the *église monolithe*, carved out of rock and similar to the St-Emilion version.

The countryside is lovely in May: unploughed green fields; wooded hills, the newly-opened tints a joy; and flowers everywhere – lilac, bluebells, cowslips and many others.

I would like to finish the chapter with some reflections about one role played by the French Resistance (*maquis*) during the Second World War.

It is often claimed that, south of the River Loire, the Resistance liberated France in the weeks following the D-Day landings. Elsewhere in this book, I've written about one of the great tragedies which unfolded during the summer of 1944; see Hautes-Alpes and the Vercors. But one classic example demonstrates perfectly how the *maquis* did make a major contribution to the success of the Normandy landings.

Hitler ordered his 22nd SS Panzer Division to proceed post-haste from Montauban (south of Cahors) to Normandy. Their journey was expected to take three to four days; in fact the trip took over a fortnight. Small, lightly-armed groups of Resistance fighters held up the crack division at point after point on the **N20** and other roads as the long column headed north, through the wooded, switch-back hills of the region.

Two of the most horrific aspects of that much-thwarted rush north were the hideous acts of revenge meted out by the Panzers at **Tulle** and Oradour-sur-Glane, north-west of Limoges. There's no more effective way of absorbing this most recent of wartime actions than by first reading the story told so well by Max Hastings in his book *Das Reich* (Pan paperback); and then following the route north across Périgord.

Markets Brantôme (Fri); Bretenoux (Tues and Sat); Brive (Tues, Thurs and Sat); Cahors (Wed and Sat); Domme (Thurs); Gourdon (Tues and Sat); Martel (Wed and Sat); Montignac (Wed and Sat); St-Céré (Tues and Sat); St-Cyprien (Sun); Sarlat (Wed and Sat); Souillac (Mon, Wed and Fri).

Michelin green guide: Dordogne (in English).

Cheeses Cow's milk

Most of these are Massif Central cheeses (see that region's maps):

Auvergne (Bleu d') when made on farms at its best in summer and autumn. Strong smell, soft, made in the same way as Roquefort

Cantal from the Auvergne. Semi-hard, nutty flavour. Praised by Pliny. The best comes from Salers (**Fourme de Salers**). Also known as **Cantalon** and **Fourme de Rochefort**. *Fourme* is an old word describing how the cheeses were formed

Causses (Bleu des) a blue cheese with parsley-like veins, hence the term *persillé* – often used to describe a blue cheese. At its best in summer and autumn. **Bleu du Quercy** is a related cheese

Echourgnac pressed, uncooked, small disk – made by monks

Fourme-d'Ambert a summer and autumn season. A blue cheese from the Auvergne and in the shape of a tall cylinder

Laguiole related to Cantal. Big cylinders, penetrating bouquet

Murol a semi-hard cheese, like St-Nectaire. Made in small disks with a hole in the centre, mild with no special smell

St-Nectaire a purply-brown skin, made in larger disks than Murol. Semi-hard, mild cheese

Thièzac (Bleu de) at its best in summer and autumn. A blue cheese related to Bleu d'Auvergne

Tomme de Cantal a fresh, softish, cream-coloured, unfermented cheese; used in many Auvergne regional dishes

Goat's milk

Cabécou de Rocamadour gets its name from the patois for little goat. Very small size with nutty taste. At its best in summer and autumn

Ewe's milk

Roquefort the best blue cheese of all. Sharp and salty. See notes in Massif Central. Try it with a local red Cahors wine – or surprise yourself with an accompanying sweet Sauternes

Regional Specialities

Bourrioles d'Aurillac sweet pancakes, made from buckwheat flour

Cèpes fine, delicate mushrooms. Sometimes dried

Chou farci stuffed cabbage. Sometimes *aux marrons* – with chestnuts

Confit de canard (d'oie) preserved duck (goose)

Cou d'oie neck of goose

Foie de canard (gras) duck liver (goose)

Friands de Bergerac small potato cakes

Merveilles hot, sugar-covered pastry fritters

Mique stew or soup with dumplings

Pommes à la Sarladaise potatoes, truffles, ham or *foie gras*

Rilletes d'oie soft, potted goose

Sobronade soup with pork, ham, beans and vegetables

Tourin Bordelais (Ouillat) onion soup

Tourin Périgourdine vegetable soup

Truffes truffles; black and exotic tubers or fungi, as large as walnuts, which grow on the roots of certain oak and hazelnut trees

Truffes sous les cendres truffles, wrapped in paper (or bacon) and cooked in ashes

Walnut oil As you explore the quiet, sunny lanes you'll soon realise that the walnut tree thrives in the benevolent Dordogne. Eight years ago Lucien and Solange Gardillou, owners of the Moulin du Roc at Champagnac de Belair (a restored 17th-century walnut oil mill – see Hotels and Restaurants), let me into the secret of where they got their superb walnut oil (*huile de noix*). In centuries past there were a couple of dozen walnut oil mills in the Dronne and Côle valleys, upstream from Brantôme. The oil used by Solange Gardillou in her cooking is pressed at the sole remaining mill, owned by the Debord family, at Rochevideau, eight km east of Brantôme and between the D78 and the River Côle (no signposts make the *moulin* hard to locate).

Wines
Reds
There are many good local wines made in the region. From **Bergerac** and the **Côtes de Bergerac** (encircling the town, both north and south of the River Dordogne) come some fine wines, light-weight, claret-type reds. Similar wines are produced in the **Pécharmant** area and in the **Côtes de Duras** (south of Bergerac). **Sigoulès** and **Leparon** are Côtes de Bergerac wines.
Whites
Among the whites, look out for **Bergerac sec**, **Côtes de Bergerac**, **Côtes de Duras** and **Rosette** – all ideal for fish dishes and entrées. Across the Dordogne from Bergerac is the commune of **Monbazillac**, where the famous, sweet, heady dessert wine is made; another sweet white is **Côtes de Bergerac moëlleux**. From the **Côtes de Montravel**, **Montravel**, **Haut-Montravel** (three areas north of the Dordogne) and **Saussignac** come medium-sweet and a few dry whites.
Other wines
From the Lot, south of the River Dordogne, come the full-bodied dark reds of **Cahors** and the white Blanc du Lot.

North-west of Agen is the AC **Côtes du Marmandais** area with its reasonably good light reds and whites.

Most restaurant lists will include wines, of all types and shades, from **Gaillac** on the Tarn (see Languedoc). Particularly pleasing are the medium sweet and sparkling varieties.

All the wines of **Bordeaux**, detailed in my description of the Southwest, can be enjoyed here in the Dordogne. Many of the best are in fact made on the banks of the River Dordogne, just before it flows into the Gironde.
Vins de Pays
Examples include wines of all shades from the **Coteaux du Quercy**; *département* labels will say **Lot** and **Lot-et-Garonne**.

LES-EYZIES-DE-TAYAC Les Roches

Comfortable hotel
Gardens/Swimming pool/Parking

All new, attractive gardens, shady terrace and small stream.
Rooms (28) C-D. Cards Access, Visa.
Closed Dec to March.
Post rte Sarlat, 24620 Les Eyzies-de-Tayac, Dordogne.
Tel 53 06 96 59. Fax 53 06 95 54. Mich 123/F3.

MONPAZIER Edward ler

Comfortable hotel
Quiet/Gardens/Swimming pool/Parking

My favourite *bastide*, built by Edward 1st, hence the name of
this evocative, mini 19th-century château (opened in 1990).
Rooms (13) D-F. Cards AE, Access, Visa.
Closed Mid Nov to 25 March.
Post 24540 Monpazier, Dordogne.
Tel 53 22 44 00. Fax 53 22 57 99. Mich 123/E4.

SARLAT-LA-CANEDA Mas de Castel

Simple hotel
Quiet/Gardens/Swimming pool/Parking/Good value

Mostly on one level; 2 km south of the town.
Rooms (13) C-D. Cards All.
Closed 11 Nov to March.
Post Sudalissant, 24200 Sarlat-la-Canéda, Dordogne.
Tel 53 59 02 59. Mich 124/B3.

SARLAT-LA-CANEDA Salamandre

Comfortable hotel
Swimming pool

In quietish side street, just south of old Sarlat. Originally a
distillery. Recommended by several readers.
Rooms (35) D. Cards All.
Post rue Abbé Surguier, 24200 Sarlat-la-Canéda, Dordogne.
Tel 53 59 35 98. Telex 571587. Mich 124/B3.

SOUILLAC Le Quercy

Comfortable hotel
Gardens/Swimming pool/Garage/Good value

Fairly quiet site; to the west of the busy N20 and on the right
bank of the River Borrèze.
Rooms (25) C. Cards Access, Visa.
Closed Mid Dec to mid March.
Post 1 rue de la Récège, 46200 Souillac, Lot.
Tel 65 37 83 56. Fax 65 37 07 22. Mich 124/C3.

AUBAZINE   de la Tour

Simple hotel/Cooking 2
Good value

A captivating corner of Corrèze: the village is high above the
Corrèze Valley; and, opposite the *logis*, is the fine façade of a
12th-century Cistercian abbey. Jacques Lachaud juggles
regional (*confits* galore: *canard*, *oie* and *poule*), *Bourgeoise* and
classical balls. Readers have relished the *hors d'oeuvre* trolley;
and have spoken warmly of *patronne* Arlette Lachaud.
Menus A-B. Rooms (20) B-C. Cards Access, Visa.
Closed Feb. Sun evg & Mon (out of season).
Post Aubazine, 19190 Beynat, Corrèze.
Tel 55 25 71 17. Mich 124/C2.

BRANTOME   Moulin de l'Abbaye

Very comfortable hotel/Cooking 3
Secluded/Terrace/Gardens/Garage

In *FL3* I described how, in 1979, Régis and Cathy Bulot had
transformed a 15th-century mill (not the most endearing of
buildings), alongside the Dronne, into one of the region's finest
hotels. The *moulin* is consistently praised by readers: for the
furnishings, the cuisine and, above all, for the style, service
and comfort, where the client is both right and revered. Régis
is the President of the Relais & Châteaux chain; consequently
he's away for much of the time but his managers, Bernard and
Yvette Dessum, have a natural rapport with clients, and chef
Christian Ravinel does a supremely good job. He's a modern
master, capitalising on the bountiful produce from his *pays*:
ducks, truffles, *cèpes*, walnut oil, goat's cheese, *foie gras*,
confits, fruit and veg. One fault: some raw materials are
excessively coated in herbs. Ten rooms are in two nearby
annexes, both ancient houses. Cathy, too, is busy elsewhere,
running another new Bulot venture: the Hôtel St-Paul at the
heart of St-Paul (Côte d'Azur).
Menus C-E. Rooms (17) F-F2. Cards All.
Closed 22 Oct to 5 May. Rest: Mon midday.
Post rte de Bourdeilles, 24310 Brantôme, Dordogne.
Tel 53 05 80 22. Fax 53 05 75 27. Mich 109/D4.

LE BUGUE   Royal Vézère

Very comfortable hotel/Cooking 1-2
Terrace/Lift/Swimming pool/Garage

The modern hotel makes a return to *Encore* after being
dropped from *FL3*. Much the most appealing features are the
terraces: one's on the roof, where the pool is situated; the other
is adjacent to the restaurant and alongside the River Vézère.
Cuisine? Regional (*boeuf en croûte à la Périgourdine*) and
classical (*paupiettes de saumon à l'oseille*).
Menus B-C. Rooms (49) D-F. Cards All.
Closed Oct to Apl.
Post 24260 Le Bugue, Dordogne.
Tel 53 07 20 01. Telex 540710. Mich 123/E3.

CABRERETS
Auberge de la Sagne

Simple hotel/Cooking 1-2
Quiet/Terrace/Gardens/Swim pool/Parking/Good value

Readers have rightly bullied me into seeking out the Labrousse's small *auberge*, tucked away as it is in one of the most scenically intoxicating corners of the Lot *département*. Three words sum up the owners, always anxious to please, the terrain, the hotel and the cooking: unpretentious and unfussy. The cuisine is down-to-earth regional and *Bourgeoise*: *bloc de foie gras de canard au naturel* and *magret de canard au miel d'acacia* with a *tarte de légumes* are typical.
Menus A-B. Rooms (10) C. Cards All.
Closed Oct to Apl. Rest: Wed midday/Fri midday (not Jul/Aug).
Post 46330 Cabrerets, Lot.
Tel 65 31 26 62. Mich 138/C2.

CAHORS
Château de Mercuès

Very comfortable hotel/Cooking 2-3
Secluded/Terr/Gardens/Swim pool/Tennis/Lift/Parking

Three words summed up the Labrousse *auberge* (above). Two words sum up the benefits here: top notch. That applies to the view of the River Lot; the majestic site, facing west and high above the valley; the striking 13th-century château; the champion cellar; the luxury you'd expect from a R&C member; and the prices. Cooking? No, not top notch, just competent classical. If you want to spoil yourself rotten then this is the ultimate B&B (bed and breakfast and busted budgets); eat in once but then try the skills of Alexis Pélissou at nearby St-Médard and Gilles Marre at Cahors (see next entry).
Menus C-D. Rooms (25) F-F3. Cards All.
Closed Mid Nov to mid Mar.
Post Mercuès, 46090 Cahors, Lot. (NW of Cahors, on D911.)
Tel 65 20 00 01. Telex 521307. Fax 65 20 05 72. Mich 138/B2.

CAHORS
Terminus & Rest. Le Balandre

Comfortable hotel/Cooking 3
Terrace/Lift

I imagine I must know several dozen members of the Jeunes Restaurateurs de France group. I made good use of these contacts in quizzing them about which new members I should nose out. Appropriately, one of the most recommended couples were Gilles and Jacqueline Marre, who work at the heart of truffle country. Gilles' repertoire is primarily classical and regional but there's many a modern creation among his specialities. Savour the best of the local *pays*: *oeufs Pierre Marre* (*oeufs pochés, escalope de foie gras, sauce truffe*); *pièce de boeuf poêlée, fondue d'échalote et sauce au vin*; and one of several chocolate desserts.
Menus B-C. Rooms (31) C-D. Cards Access, Visa.
Closed Rest: 15-28 Feb. 1-8 Jul. Sat lun. Sun evg/Mon (ex Aug).
Post 5 av. Ch. de Freycinet, 46000 Cahors, Lot. Mich 138/B2.
Tel 65 30 01 97 (H). 65 30 01 97 (R). Fax 65 22 06 40 (H).

CHAMPAGNAC-DE-BELAIR   Moulin du Roc

Very comfortable hotel/Cooking 3
Secluded/Terr/Gardens/Swim pool(indoor)/Tenn/Parking

I've had an enormous number of letters since 1980 about the
17th-century walnut oil mill. A handful more of the slash
across the jugular variety and the mill would have been
drowned in the River Dronne. Feedback has fallen into two
categories, depending on whether readers have never been
before or if they saw the mill at its best, pre-1987. Gripes? An
over-prettified garden, small rooms, young wines, silk flowers
and plastic banana decorations have all been hammered. And
serving the same vegetables evening after evening means the
kitchen is working in a vacuum. The most apt description
came from a reader who reckoned the premises had recently
been vacated by a crazed German antique dealer.

Solange and Lucien Gardillou (now joined by son Alain) have
fiddled around much too much of late, in more ways than one.
She's also changed her cooking style to a more regional and
neo-classical base. Tell me how you find the *moulin*.
Menus C-D. Rooms (10) E-F. Cards All.
Closed 15 Nov-15 Dec. 15 Jan-15 Feb. Rest: Tues/Wed midday.
Post 24530 Champagnac-de-Belair, Dordogne.
Tel 53 54 80 36. Fax 571555. Fax 53 54 21 31. Mich 109/D4.

COLY   Manoir d'Hautegente

Very comfortable hotel/Cooking 1-2
Secluded/Gardens/Swimming pool/Parking

I've been itching for years to tell you about this adorable,
creeper-covered manor house in a delectable woodland setting.
In centuries past the site has been both a forge and mill, water
power being provided by the pool and river. There's an
overwhelming sense of peace about the place. Astonishingly
the property has been in the Hamelin family for over 300
years. Edith Hamelin does the cooking, *Bourgeoise*, classical
and regional; Patrick, her son, runs the front of house.
Menus (Dinner) C. Rooms (10) F-F2. Cards AE, Access, Visa.
Closed Nov to Mar. Rest: every midday.
Post Coly, 24120 Terrasson, Dordogne. (E of Montignac.)
Tel 53 51 68 03. Fax 53 50 38 52. Mich 124/B2.

COUSSAC-BONNEVAL   Voyageurs

Comfortable restaurant with rooms/Cooking 2
Gardens/Good value

The vine-covered *logis* of Henri Robert, an English speaker
who has made many trips to the UK promoting his beloved
Limousin, snoozes in the shadow of a 15th-century castle.
Classical (*tournedos Rossini*) and regional cooking, both
Périgord (*confits* and *foies*) and Limousin (*cèpes* and *clafoutis*).
Menus A-C. Rooms (9) B-C. Cards Access, Visa.
Closed Jan. Sun evg & Mon (out of season).
Post 87500 Coussac-Bonneval, H.-Vienne.
Tel 55 75 20 24. Mich 110/B3.

LES EYZIES-DE-TAYAC

Centre

Comfortable hotel/Cooking 2
Terrace/Good value

A mixed record for Gérard and Claudine Brun and their well-named hotel. The shady terrace appeals to everyone, either at lunchtime or, better still, on a balmy summer evening when the market square's trees, the sounds of fountain and river and the gathering darkness (illuminated by the floodlit crag across the road) puts paid to any feeling of depression. No wonder then the place gets busy; consequently service can be slow and forgetful and, as far as the mechanics of ordering and serving wine are concerned, is almost non-existent. Few complaints about the grub which is generally good; primarily regional (*cèpes* and walnut oil feature often), classical and *Bourgeoise* with the odd Nineties creation which seems so out of place (*homard à la saveur de vanille* would you believe).
Menus A-D. Rooms (20) C. Cards Access, Visa.
Closed Nov to Mar.
Post 24620 Les Eyzies-de-Tayac, Dordogne.
Tel 53 06 97 13. Fax 53 06 91 63. Mich 123/E3.

LES EYZIES-DE-TAYAC

Cro-Magnon

Very comfortable hotel/Cooking 2-3
Terrace/Gardens/Swimming pool/Parking

Anne and I have known, and loved, the Cro-Magnon all our married lives, almost 33 years now. We took our children too, when they were, literally, toddlers. Many is the time our family rested and played in the large, informal garden that surrounds the annexe. We recall, too, on many hot days, sitting under the chestnut and plane trees that shade the hotel's terrace, when the gently rustling leaves and the azure sky above would hypnotise us into sleep.

During the last three decades we have got to know the owners of Cro-Magnon, Jacques and Christiane Leysalles, very well. However appealing the man-made and natural features of this unspoilt hotel, at the end of the day human beings mean far more. That's why Cro-Magnon is one of the most liked readers' favourites: a genuine welcome, a traditional old-fashioned family and personal service; as the years whistle by we all recognise that these virtues are priceless. (Sadly, since 1987, when *Favourites* was published, I've not had a decent report about the Centenaire; appalling and German Bierkeller were two jibes. All the culinary accolades in the world mean nothing if clients sense they are being taken to the cleaners. The Centenaire could learn a lot from Cro-Magnon.)

Chefs come and go (the present incumbent is Xavier Davoust) but cooking standards remain consistently good. A mix of all styles: you can vary your diet between Périgord, classical and many a light modern creation. Any debits? Yes, there's a railway line and a busy road between the hotel and annexe; the road bothers some readers more than others.
Menus B-D. Rooms (20) D-F. Cards All.
Closed 11 Oct to end Apl. Rest: Wed midday (not pub. hols).
Post 24620 Les Eyzies-de-Tayac, Dordogne.
Tel 53 06 97 06. Fax 53 06 95 45. Mich 123/E3.

LES EYZIES-DE-TAYAC   **Moulin de la Beune**

Comfortable hotel/Cooking 1-2
Quiet/Terrace/Gardens/Parking

If you bought *Favourites* you'll recall I spoke warmly of this, then, *sans restaurant* hotel. The Dudicourts sold the hotel (with airy modern bedrooms) in 1988 to Georges and Annick Soulié, owners of the adjoining Vieux Moulin restaurant, once a walnut oil mill. Cooking is mainly Périgord and classical and with the unheard-of-option of a low-calories menu. Main dishes, like a bison *civet* (the meat is imported from Canada), are dull. The River Beune and its many streamlets in the grounds play a major part in the mill's appeal.
Menus A-D. Rooms (20) C-D. Cards Access, Visa.
Closed Nov to Mar.
Post 24620 Les Eyzies-de-Tayac, Dordogne. Mich 123/E3.
Tel 53 06 94 33 (H). 53 06 93 39 (R). Fax 53 06 98 06 (H).

GIMEL-LES-CASCADES   **Host. de la Vallée**

Simple hotel/Cooking 1-2
Terrace/Good value

Readers of *Hidden France* will know full well the great love I have for Corrèze, the greenest of green French *départements*. Here, at both Gimel and the immediate east, is the most seductive corner within Corrèze. Read the first few paragraphs of the introduction to grasp just why.

How marvellous then to be able to include in *Encore* a *Logis de France* which complements the terrain to a tee. Marie-Thérèse Calis, Corrèzienne born, spent 20 years in the States and speaks fluent English; there she married Bernard, a Washington hotelier. The couple bought the *logis* in 1988. The village is at the head of the valley, above the sparkling falls; the hotel has its own panoramic view of both scenic attractions. Cooking is Périgord, *Bourgeoise* and classical.
Menus A-C. Rooms (9) C. Cards Access, Visa.
Closed Jan. Sun evg & Mon (Oct to Mar).
Post Le Bourg, 19800 Gimel-les-Cascades, Corrèze.
Tel 55 21 40 60. Mich 125/D1.

GOUJOUNAC   **Host. de Goujounac**

Very simple restaurant with basic rooms/Cooking 1-2
Good value

Well, who would have thought this most modest and earthy *FL3* recommendation would, one day, make the Michelin guide? The rustic dining room and endearing Costes family offer clients authentic Quercy and Périgord fare: *foie gras, mique, poularde aux cèpes, confit de canard, cous farcis, civet de poireaux aux Cahors, omelette aux cèpes, rillettes* and *poule farci*. Enjoy Monpazier and Bonaguil; then top them both here.
Menus A-B. Rooms (7) A-B. Cards Access, Visa.
Closed 1st wk Feb. Oct. Sun evg & Mon (Nov to June).
Post 46250 Goujounac, Lot.
Tel 65 36 68 67. Mich 138/A1.

Hotels and Restaurants

MONTIGNAC
Château de Puy Robert

Luxury hotel/Cooking 3
Secluded/Gardens/Swimming pool/Lift/Parking

The enterprising, impressive and likeable chef cum hotelier entrepreneur, Albert Parveaux (see Varetz), has added a fourth charmer to his existing trio of hotels. The Napoléon III château is a mile or so from Lascaux and is at the heart of the Périgord Noir. Crunchingly expensive but both the château and the adjacent, modern Gentilhommière are cossetting, if a touch artificial, luxuries. Cooking? Neo-classical, regional and some modern *plats* from Jean-Marc Delepine: a *rose de saumon à la crème de fenouil*, followed by a *duo de confit et magret de canard* are examples of contrasting and assertive courses on Le Grand Menu. Relais & Châteaux member.
Menus C-E. Rooms (33) F-F2. Cards All.
Closed Mid Oct to Apl. Rest: Wed midday.
Post rte de Valojoux, 24290 Montignac, Dordogne. (S, on D65.)
Tel 53 51 92 13. Telex 550616. Fax 53 51 80 11. Mich 124/A2.

OBJAT
Pré Fleuri

Comfortable restaurant with rooms/Cooking 2
Terrace/Gardens/Good value

The Pré Fleuri is behind a ring of trees, on the road to the "horse" town of France, Arnac-Pompadour. Jacques and Ingrid Chouzenoux have stopped chasing culinary stars; now they are content to sit back a bit in the saddle, to concentrate on a repertoire of neo-classical and regional specialities: *soupe aux truffes et tartinettes de foie gras*, *marbré de foie gras*, *omelette aux truffes* and *croustade de père Marcel* are the sort of hurdles currently being jumped by Jacques.
Menus B-C. Rooms (7) B. Cards AE, Access, Visa.
Closed Jan. Mon (out of season).
Post rte Pompadour, 19130 Objat, Corrèze.
Tel 55 25 83 92. Mich 124/B1.

ST-CIRQ-LAPOPIE
La Pélissaria

Simple hotel/Cooking 2
Secluded/Gardens

The ancient village, high above the Lot, is a photographer's dream; sadly, for the motorist, parking is a nightmare. The medieval hotel is just off the eastern approach to the village, where parking is marginally easier. The views are breathtaking; some rooms are smallish and some have their own terrace. Marie-Françoise Matuchet is an able *cuisinière*; regional, classical and *Bourgeoise* cooking with sorbets which match, if not beat, any three-star chef's efforts. A typical *plat* is *pâtes fraîches maison aux cèpes*. Husband François looks after the front of house. English spoken.
Menus (Dinner) B. Rooms (7) D-F. Cards Access, Visa.
Closed Mid Nov to Mar. Thurs. Every midday.
Post 46330 St-Cirq-Lapopie, Lot.
Tel 65 31 25 14. Mich 138/C2.

134

ST-MEDARD   Gindreau

Comfortable restaurant/Cooking 3-4
Terrace/Good value

What startling progress has been made at the old school house, with its shady terrace, overlooking the Vert Valley. Since my first visit, a decade ago, I've received an ever-increasing number of readers' letters expressing delight at having made the effort to seek out Alexis and Martine Pélissou's unspoilt home, where standards, both culinary and non-culinary, are high and where no corners are cut. Alexis uses local produce (even lamb) and his style is best described as neo-classical and regional. Depth of flavour is his cooking signature: a superlative *noix d'agneau fermier du Quercy rôtie et tranchée* and a champion *croustillant de volaille au fumet de cèpes* (a heavenly concoction) epitomise his conviction for both his *pays* and his individualistic *métier*. Martine is an elegant *patronne* and a happy, contented mum. The couple's Cahors wine list is exemplary. Rooms? Use the nearby Campanile at Cahors (junction D911 and N20; 46000 Cahors; Tel 65 22 20 21).
Menus B-C. Cards AE, Access, Visa.
Closed 21 Feb-5 Mar. 1-15 Nov. Mon. Sun evg (not high season).
Post St-Médard, 46150 Cahors, Lot. (NW Cahors, N of D911.)
Tel 65 36 22 27. Fax 65 36 24 54. Mich 138/B1.

ST-PARDOUX-LA-CROISILLE   Beau Site

Comfortable hotel/Cooking 2
Quiet/Gardens/Swimming pool/Tennis/Parking/Good value

The Bidault family, after a brief shaky start, has established a sound reputation with readers. Consistent praise for the friendly welcome from the trio of Madame Bidault, her son Dominique and his wife, Catherine; for the picnic lunches; and the mix of classical and regional cooking from *le père*, Jean-Claude. His desserts are rated highly by everyone.
Menus B-C. Rooms (32) B-C. Cards Access, Visa.
Closed Oct to Apl.
Post 19320 St-Pardoux-la-Croisille, Corrèze.
Tel 55 27 79 44. Mich 125/E1.

SARLAT-LA-CANEDA   St-Albert et Montaigne

Comfortable hotel/Cooking 1-2
Lift/Good value

English-speaking Jean-Michel Garrigou is a proud ambassador: for his hotel (both the St-Albert and its spanking new annexe, the Montaigne); his town and *pays*; and for the copious *Bourgeoise* and Périgord fare served to clients. The place is busy, coping with individual tourists and coachloads of Germans and Dutch holidaymakers. (Park in the *place* Pasteur adjacent to both hotels.)
Menus B-C. Rooms (56) C. Cards All.
Closed Sun evg (out of season). Rest: Mon (out of season).
Post pl. Pasteur, 24200 Sarlat-la-Canéda, Dordogne.
Tel 53 59 01 09. Fax 53 59 19 99. Mich 124/A3.

SOUSCEYRAC   Au Déjeuner de Sousceyrac

Comfortable restaurant with rooms/Cooking 2-3
Terrace/Good value

All change at this out-of-the-way village, to the east of the
Dordogne and lost in the invigorating wooded terrain between
St-Céré and Aurillac. I first came across the run-down bistro
and its amazing chef/patron, M. Espinadel, two decades ago.
New young owners, Richard and Laurence Piganiol, are a welcome
gale of fresh air: the place sparkles; the dining room has a
light, airy feel (helped no end by flowers); and readers rave
about Richard's value-for-money cooking, a mix of regional,
modern and neo-classical. Support the enterprising young duo.
Menus B. Rooms (10) B-C. Cards Visa.
Closed Feb. Mon (not July & Aug).
Post 46190 Sousceyrac, Lot.
Tel 65 33 00 56. Mich 125/E3.

TAMNIES   Laborderie

Comfortable hotel/Cooking 2
Secluded/Terr/Gardens/Swim pool/Parking/Good value

Much of the *FL3* entry hasn't changed a jot. The hotel has a
hilltop site with fine views over the Beune Valley. An *étang* or
two in the valley provide extra interest with boating, fishing
and swimming facilities. What has changed is that the
Laborderie is now always busy, popular as it is with
independent travellers and tour operators like VFB. Too busy
is a regular gripe; but that's the norm now in Dordogneshire.
Pluses on the credit side of the P&L A/C are as varied as
praise for the swish, outshine-the-Swiss geraniums and the
appetite-quenching Périgord cuisine. I'll add my own credit:
the village is ideally placed to explore the best of Périgord Noir
with peace and quiet as a gilt-edged bonus.
Menus B-C. Rooms (31) C-D. Cards Access, Visa.
Closed Nov to Mar.
Post 24620 Tamniès, Dordogne.
Tel 53 29 68 59. Fax 53 29 65 31. Mich 124/A3.

TREMOLAT   Vieux Logis

Very comfortable hotel/Cooking 3
Secluded/Terrace/Gardens/Swimming pool/Parking

I know many of you consider this evocative spot to be your
favourite Dordogne hotel. In the same family's hands for over
400 years (Giraudel-Destord), the Vieux Logis is a magical
mixture of stone, timbers, plants and trees; the River
Dordogne provides the perfect backdrop.
   Pierre-Jean Duribreux, the chef, is an inventive modern
master and his estimable cooking has a sure touch and good
taste. Particularly welcome is his ability to use Périgord's
larder in a sensible way: you don't finish meals feeling as if
ballast has pinned you down in your dining room chair.
Examples? A *terrine d'alose au vert à ma façon* and a *poulet
fermier simplement rôti et son jus* are commonsense joys. The

136

hotel is a member of the Relais & Châteaux chain.
Menus C-D. Rooms (14) F-F2. Disabled. Cards All.
Closed 7 Jan to 18 Feb. Rest: Tues & Wed midday (Oct to May).
Post 24510 Trémolat, Dordogne.
Tel 53 22 80 06. Telex 541025. Fax 53 22 84 89. Mich 123/E3.

VARETZ   Château de Castel Novel

Luxury hotel/Cooking 3
Secluded/Terr/Gardens/Swimming pool/Tenn/Lift/Parking

The turreted, red sandstone Castel Novel was the home of
Colette, a quintessential Frenchwoman, from 1911-23; she
wrote *Chéri* at Varetz (1920). Today, the hilltop hotel, hidden
by woods and overlooking the Vézère Valley, is one of four
owned by Albert Parveaux. (Varetz and Montignac keep him
busy in the summer; and his two hotels at Courchevel is where
he hibernates during the winter.) I can't say the château has
been a whopping success with readers. The best summary I
can conjure up is that it is run in typical R&C fashion. Cuisine
is safe neo-classical with many Périgord touches.
Menus C-E. Rooms (32) F-F2. Cards All.
Closed Mid Oct to Apl.
Post 19240 Varetz, Corrèze. (NW of Brive-La-Gaillarde.)
Tel 55 85 00 01. Telex 590065. Fax 55 85 09 03. Mich 124/C1.

VEZAC   Oustal de Vézac

Comfortable hotel/Cooking 1
Quiet/Gardens/Swimming pool/Parking

A modern, single-storey building in an isolated spot with views
west to the perched Beynac castle. The hotel was a base in *FL3*
(*sans restaurant*); it now has a grill which is not recommended.
I suggest you continue to use it as a base.
Menus A-B. Rooms (20) D. Cards Access, Visa.
Closed Nov to Easter.
Post 24220 Vézac, Dordogne. (South of the village.)
Tel 53 29 54 21. Mich 124/A3.

VIEUX-MAREUIL   Château de Vieux Mareuil

Comfortable hotel/Cooking 2-3
Secluded/Gardens/Swimming pool/Parking

Many readers badgered me to visit English-speaking Jean-Pierre
and Annie Lefranc's new hotel (previously he owned the Aub. de
Vendeuil, south of St-Quentin, for many years). What a gem: a
15th-century château; over 40 acres of woods and meadows;
and a young chef, Michel Cadieu (trained by both Jacques Le
Divellec and Michel Rostang; see earlier editions of *FL*). His
repertoire is pleasing neo-classical, a welcome relief from the
relentless Périgord cooking encountered further south.
Menus B-C. Rooms (12) E-F. Cards All.
Closed Mid Jan to Feb. Sun evg & Mon (Oct to Easter).
Post 24340 Vieux-Mareuil, Dordogne.
Tel 53 60 77 15. Fax 53 56 49 33. Mich 109/D4.

HAUTES-ALPES

▲ see page 330

8

La Buffe · GRENOBLE
Claix · Chamrousse · Col du Galibier · **ITALIE**
St-Jean- · **Bresson** · Col du Lautaret
en-Royans · Villard- · **Varces** · N91
· ▲ **La** · de-Lans · Massif des
Chapelle · **Monestier-de** · Ecrins
Col de la · **-Clermont** · Briançon
Machine · **St-Agnan** · **Corps** · Col d'Izoard
Vercors · △ Mont Aiguille · **Molines-en-Queyras**
· Cirque d'Archiane · St-Véran Mont
Crest · **Die** Die○ · La Jarjatte · Viso
Châtillon- · Col de
Col de · **en-Diois** · Gap · Vars
Pennes · Luc-en-Diois
Picodon · Lac de Serre-Ponçon
Col de · · Barcelonnette
Carabès · **Serres** · Durance · Col de la Bonette
Buis-les-Baronnies · Col d'Allos
Orpierre · Col de la
Mont Ventoux · Cayolle
△ · **Sisteron** · **Château-Arnoux** · Annot
· Sault · **St-Auban** · Digne · **St-André-les-Alpes** ▲ **Annot**
Forcalquier · N202 Var
· **Moustiers-** · Castellane
Valensole · **Ste-Marie**
Aiguines · Verdon

● Autoroute hotel
■ Base hotel
▲ Hotel/Rest (rooms)
△ Restaurant only

0   10   20 Miles

▼ see page 104

The map above overlaps with two other regions: Provence and the Côte d'Azur, the topography of which I describe in more detail in the respective introductions to those two chapters. Here I'm going to concentrate, in some depth, on the top half of the map (north of **Gap** and **Serres**), mountainous terrain in the French Alps and part of a larger area called Dauphiné. Hautes-Alpes is an appropriate title.

As you travel north, across the length of the area shown above, the landscape changes dramatically. To the south of Serres and **Sisteron** the light and shades of Provence are unmistakable: olive trees, soil the colour of rust, regimented rows of lavender (at their best in July) and the rich hues of terracotta roof tiles are just a few of the visual clues. Your sense of smell, awoken by the perfume of herb-scented fields, will also tell you that this is Provence.

To the north of Serres the landscape is alpine, similar in most respects to the mountainous country that arcs, first north and then east, across a great swathe of Europe. Though I always feel a twinge of disappointment on leaving Provence there is, nevertheless, much to awaken your interest: not just scenic attractions but terrain which will capture your heart too. I hope I can persuade you to head to a mountainous corner which I love as much as any in France: the **Vercors**.

The inspiring Vercors *massif* (between **Die** and **Grenoble**) is a natural fortress, full of the majestic handiwork of Mother Nature at her most ferocious and spectacular. Tragically, it was in those high, rampart-topped peaks and deep gorges that the most emotional saga of the French Resistance unfolded almost fifty years ago, during the summer of 1944.

The Vercors is a limestone mass of mountains, 30 miles long by 20 miles wide. Access is unusually difficult: a few, tortuous lanes climb up in steep zig-zags from the encircling river valleys, the roads often blasted out of precipitous mountain sides. Within the *massif* two torrents, the Bourne and Vernaison, create an even more remote inner sanctuary. This secret heart of the Vercors wears a coat of dense pines, cool in summer but an enveloping dark cover in winter.

No wonder then that the Vercors became a citadel of the Resistance and, later, such a legend; its stirring story deserves the attention of all those who love France.

Two days after the D-Day landings in June 1944 the tricolour flew on numerous flag-poles in the Vercors. One fluttered above St-Nizier, in full view of Grenoble far below. The Germans were incensed and, during the weeks which followed, sent 20,000 troops into the mountain fortress.

The *maquis* (Resistance) had counted on relief coming from the air and, additionally, from the anticipated Allies' landing in Provence. The uprising came too soon, help came too late. Hundreds died defending the citadel which they proudly called the "Free Republic of the Vercors". By the end of July the overwhelming German force had full control of the *massif*.

As you travel the mountain roads you'll see a great number of monuments in memory of those who gave their lives in 1944: *mort pour la France* say the carved words on the simple monuments; no finer words can be used for any epitaph. On the narrow D215 and D221 which wind west from **Villard-de-Lans**, through the pine forests towards Valchevrière, are many monuments to those who died in the last critical days of the 1944 battle. But perhaps the most moving of all is the one at the entrance to the Grotte de la Luire (south of **La Chapelle**), used by the Resistance as a hospital.

What scenic sights should you seek out? Enter the *massif* by one of three spectacular roads. The first is the best northern approach. Leave the **A48** at the point the autoroute becomes toll-free, at Veurey-Voroize, climb the lane up to **La Buffe** and, just before the Tunnel du Mortier, admire the view below you. Nearby is a grassy plateau called La Molière with extensive views east towards the **Chamrousse** (worth a visit for its own three-star panoramas). Under your feet is the Gouffre Berger, the deepest and most dangerous pot-hole in France.

A second exciting access to the Vercors is a southerly one: starting from Die in the **Drôme** Valley, the Col de Rousset is a memorable climb of numerous hairpin bends.

The third entrance is via an engineering marvel. From **St-Jean-en-Royans**, a sleepy village, climb the Combe Laval, a vast *cirque* (amphitheatre) of rocks which rises sharply above the Cholet stream. The final stretch, before you reach the summit at the **Col de la Machine**, is a series of tunnels gouged out of the vertical mountain face.

Within the *massif* are other man-made wonders, combining with some of Nature's most violent sculptures. One is the amazing Grands Goulets where the tiny, but powerful Vernaison punches through a rocky barrier at Les Barraques. Somehow man has built a leech-like road alongside the torrential stream as it hurtles down the narrow ravine. Equally unusual is the road through the Gorges de la Bourne, west of Villard.

The Germans made the Vercors pay a cruel price for the uprising. Villard-de-Lans, La Chapelle and Vassieux were almost razed to the ground. The National Cemetery, north of Vassieux, is a more emotional reminder of the hundreds of patriots who lost their lives in 1944.

What of other scenic pleasures? Explore the huge Forêt de Lente which helped to hide so many of the *maquis*; visit the underground caves at Chorance; and relish the isolation of the dead-end road that leads you through the Gorges d'Omblèze.

The mountains to the south of the Vercors will entertain in different ways. Here's an itinerary that shows them off well. Start at Serres, on the N75 between Grenoble and Sisteron. Head north-west, up the D27, over the **Col de Carabès** into the *département* of the Drôme, then picking up the D106 which, within a few km, has the infant River Drôme as a neighbour. The waters alongside both the D27 and the D106 are cracking fishing streams (details from Fifi Moulin, Serres).

Continue north. Four km beyond **Luc-en-Diois** turn left at the D140. This is the first of several detours into the mountains straddling the Drôme. As you near the top of the **Col de Pennes** (a renowned Monte-Carlo Rally stage) note the dramatic change from the Mediterranean scrub to the cool, north-facing woods. In late October, on halogen bright days, the trees' autumn coats shine like shimmering torches. 200 metres from the summit, stop, and soak in a fabulous vista.

Bernard Levin, in one of the most vivid pieces of descriptive travel writing I've ever read, recalled the view in his classic *Hannibal's Footsteps*. The book is a splendid read; buy or borrow a copy before you set out.

Return to the Drôme and cross the river to **Châtillon**. From here make three "Diois" *déviations*. First head up the D539 to the Gorges des Gats, a gigantic slice through the mountains. Hannibal and his Carthaginian army were ambushed here 2,000 years ago. The legendary general masterminded a surprise night manoeuvre to save his great army.

For the second detour retrace your steps and drive up the D120 to the Col de Menée. As you come out of the far end of the summit tunnel stop. To the north is the hypnotic, tilted, table-top mass of **Mont Aiguille**, one of the most startling sights in France. Descend back again on the D120 and at Menée turn right up the D224. This, my third detour, is one of France's finest dead-end roads, the **Cirque d'Archiane**. A tremendous sight confronts you: a vast semicircle stone wall rears high above the valley. It's best seen in the afternoon when the setting sun makes the rock faces glow.

The Drôme is perhaps at its best west of Die. Enjoy minute Ste-Croix with its vineyards and walnut trees and the river view from Pontaix. Use the new roads on the left bank of the Drôme but don't rush past either Saillans or Aouste-sur-Sye; relish the colourful village vistas from the southern banks of the river. The ridge of hills south of Saillans is well named: "les Trois Becs" look for all the world like "beaks". The climb up the Col de la Chaudière will not disappoint.

The rest of the Hautes-Alpes is richly endowed with scenic pleasures. Almost any road will reward you handsomely; not just scenically but with peace and quiet too. I'll list some ideas for you; the possibilities are endless.

A perfect example is the dead-end valley of **La Jarjatte**. Leave Serres to the north and, six km south of the Col de la Croix-Haute, turn off the N75 to Lus-la-Croix-Haute and follow the signs. It's a miniature Chamonix valley: a jagged jaw of sharply-pointed peaks and the crystal-clear Buëch.

From Eyguians, 11 km south of Serres, head west through Orpierre and across the Col de Perty. At the summit climb to the *table d'orientation*: to the east snow-capped peaks; to the west the sulking hulk of **Mont Ventoux**.

On the eastern bank of the **Lac de Serre-Ponçon**, east of Gap, marvel at the "Demoiselles coiffées", needles of rock 50 to 80 ft high, topped with flat rocks that look like hats.

Detour to the attractive Forêt de Boscodon, due east from the same lake. Use forestry roads that climb to the Fontaine de 'Ours; enjoy refreshing mixed woods and terrific views.

North-east of Embrun, an old fortified town, is a rarely visited mountainous enclave: the Parc Régional du **Queyras**. The imposing Château-Queyras is the gateway to the unspoiled Queyras Valley; Hannibal used this route. Detour south to **St-Véran**, the highest *commune* in Europe. Then follow the River Guil as far as the road allows (alas, a bridge collapsed some years ago); the views of **Mont Viso** are superb.

Briançon, the highest town in Europe and with triple rows of Vauban fortifications, is the eastern entrance to the **Massif des Ecrins**, a National Nature Park; high peaks (Barre des Ecrins is the second highest in France), quiet valleys and a botanists' paradise are the great pluses. The best of the *massif* is the beautiful Vallée du Vénéon, from Bourg d'Oisans, on the **N91**, to La Bérarde. High passes there are a plenty. I described a trio in the Côte d'Azur; others include the **Col de Vars**, the **Col d'Izoard**, the **Col du Galibier** and the **Col du Lautaret**. Grand Canyon du **Verdon**: see Côte d'Azur.

For a break from driving and walking spend a day on parts of the metre-gauge railway line which runs from Nice to Digne, owned by the Chemin de Fer de la Provence.

Markets Barcelonnette (Wed and Sat); Buis-les-Baronnies (Wed); Castellane (Wed and Sat); Crest (Tues, Wed and Sat); Die (Wed and Sat); Digne (Wed and Sat); Forcalquier (Mon); Saillans (Sun); Sault (Wed); Sisteron (Wed and Sat).

Michelin green guides: Alpes du Nord; Alpes du Sud.

Cheeses **Goat's milk**

See also the cheeses listed in the Savoie region

Annot (Tomme d'Annot) a nutty-flavoured, pressed disk; made from ewe's or goat's milk

Picodon is a goat cheese; soft, mellow taste and doughnut size. Various sources – Diois (see map) and Rhône Valley

Regional Specialities

See those listed in the Savoie region

Wines

You will encounter wines from Provence (see both the Provence and Côte d'Azur chapters), from Savoie and the Rhône Valley (see both the Massif Central and Provence chapters). But don't, under any circumstances, order any of the above in preference to the super value-for-money vintages from the Diois area around Die. They travel well too.

Two "sparklers" are especially drinkable **Clairette de Die mousseux** – a *brut* (dry) wine produced by the *méthode champenoise* from Clairette grapes; and a fragrant **Clairette de Die tradition** – primarily Muscat grapes with some Clairette, created by a unique two-stage filtering technique, the *méthode Dieoise*. Wines of all shades are made around the town of **Châtillon-en-Diois** (see the map).

141

Autoroute Hotel followed by Base Hotels

SISTERON

Ibis

Simple hotel/Cooking 1
Parking/Good value

At northern end of A51 (junction with N75/N85). Brand new.
Menus A-B. Rooms (44) C. Disabled. Cards Access, Visa.
Post Le Plan Roman, 04200 Sisteron, Alpes-de-H.-Prov.
Tel 92 62 62 00. Fax 92 62 62 10. Mich 146/A3.
(Bookings: UK 071 724 1000; US toll free 800 221 4542)

Base Hotels

CLAIX

Manoir des Matitis

Very comfortable hotel
Secluded/Gardens/Swimming pool/Parking

Amazing: over the top *manoir* and extrovert bathrooms; wooded
grounds; extensive views: Grenoble, Chartreuse, Chamrousse.
Rest, run as separate business, minutes away (see Varces).
Rooms (12) F. Cards All.
Post rte d'Allières, 38640 Claix, Isère. (South-west Claix)
Tel 76 98 84 55. Telex 320161. Fax 76 98 35 19. Mich 131/E2.

MOUSTIERS-STE-MARIE

Le Colombier

Simple hotel
Quiet/Gardens/Tennis/Parking/Good value

Fairly new, south of village. Ideal base for the delectable Les
Santons restaurant and the Grand Canyon du Verdon.
Rooms (22) C-D. Disabled. Cards Access, Visa.
Post 04360 Moustiers-Ste-Marie, Alpes-de-H.-Prov.
Tel 92 74 66 02. Mich 162/C1.

ST-ANDRE-LES-ALPES

Monge

Simple hotel
Gardens/Parking/Good value

As basic as they come; at the door of majestic countryside.
Rooms (25) B-C. Cards Access, Visa.
Post 04170 St-André-les-Alpes, Alpes-de-H.-Prov.
Tel 92 89 01 06. Mich 147/D4.

ST-AUBAN

Villiard

Comfortable hotel
Gardens/Parking

A tatty exterior but adequate enough to save francs for rooms
if you eat at La Bonne Etape (Ch. Arnoux). West side of N96.
Rooms (20) C-E. Cards Access, Visa.
Closed Xmas and New Year. Sat (Oct to Mar). (On Sat use Ibis)
Post 04600 St-Auban, Alpes-de-H.-Prov
Tel 92 64 17 42. Fax 92 64 23 29. Mich 146/B4.

AIGUINES Altitude 823

Simple restaurant with rooms/Cooking 1
Terrace/Good value

I first came across this humble little place at lunchtime one
wet day, after getting soaked sketching the pencil drawing on
page 181 in *Favourites* (Aiguines château and church). 1,000 ft
above the distant (3 km) Lac de Ste-Croix and at the western
entrance to the Verdon Canyon. Modest *Bourgeoise* grub.
Menus A-B. Rooms (13) B-C. Cards Access, Visa.
Closed Nov to Mar. Wed (out of season).
Post 83630 Aiguines, Var.
Tel 94 70 21 09. Mich 162/C2.

ANNOT Avenue

Simple hotel/Cooking 1-2
Good value

Ideally placed to explore the high cols to the north. A warm
welcome and enterprising *Bourgeoise* and classical cooking
(*millefeuille de truites rosées*) from Jean-Louis Genovesi.
Menus A-B. Rooms (12) B-C. Cards AE, Access, Visa.
Closed Mid Nov to Mar.
Post 04240 Annot, Alpes-de-H.-P.
Tel 92 83 22 07. Mich 147/E4.

BRESSON Chavant

Very comfortable restaurant with rooms/Cooking 2-3
Quiet/Terrace/Gardens/Swimming pool/Lift/Parking

Seriously classical, and seriously dear cuisine from Jean-Pierre
Chavant; his sister Danièle is the hostess. Five miles from the
centre of Grenoble means lots of business functions each week:
the end result is noise and service suffers too. Despite that
Chavant remains a better bet than any Grenoble hotel.
Menus C-D. Rooms (7) F. Cards All.
Closed Xmas. Rest: Sat midday. Mon (Oct to May).
Post 38320 Bresson, Isère. (SE of Grenoble; D269C, off D5.)
Tel 76 25 25 38. Telex 980882. Fax 76 62 06 55. Mich 131/E2.

LA CHAPELLE-EN-VERCORS Bellier

Simple hotel/Cooking 2
Quiet/Terrace/Gardens/Swimming pool/Parking

The Bellier family played an important part in the Vercors
Resistance. During a short summer season (winter sees them
at their hotel in Val d'Isère) M. and Mme Bellier offer clients
old-fashioned service in their small modern chalet. Cooking?
Classical and *Bourgeoise* with fine use of local produce.
Menus A-C. Rooms (12) D-E. Cards All.
Closed 25 Sept to 18 June.
Post 26420 La Chapelle-en-Vercors, Drôme.
Tel 75 48 20 03. Fax 75 48 25 31. Mich 131/D3.

CHATEAU-ARNOUX

La Bonne Etape

Very comfortable hotel/Cooking 3
Quiet/Gardens/Swimming pool/Parking

No other entry in *Encore* has had such dramatically contrasting feedback from readers. My acid comments in *FL3* brought a stream of letters, taking me to task for being so acerbic: readers wrote highly of the warm welcome, the stylish interior and the extrovert cooking from the smiling Pierre Gleize and his son, Jany. The duo are Anglophiles (both have worked in London); Jany, particularly, gets unanimous praise from readers. Alas, Arlette Gleize is regularly freeze-dried for her frosty style. Cooking is bravura modern with imaginative, sometimes bizarrely so, personal creations using Provençal produce. Herbs and many of the vegetables are grown by the family. Arguably, there's nothing insipid about tastes here. Yet horror stories still bubble to the surface. One flim-flam lamb creation was treated like a Chinese duck dish, shredded before the reader's eyes; all that was required were pancakes and sauce. The meat, overcooked, burnt and stringy, was inedible Best of luck: tell me how you get on.

Menus C-E. Rooms (18) F-F2. Cards All.
Closed 1-9 Dec. 5 Jan-16 Feb. Sun evg & Mon (15 Sept-15 June).
Post 04160 Château-Arnoux, Alpes.-de-H.-P.
Tel 92 64 00 09. Fax 92 64 37 36. Mich 146/B4.

COL DE LA MACHINE

du Col

Simple hotel/Cooking 1
Secluded/Swimming pool/Garage/Parking/Good value

A remarkable site and a remarkable family. What a view, too Jacques and Eliane Faravellon are the fifth generation of the family based at their hotel on top of the col; their son, already in the kitchen, will be the sixth. The business was started in 1848; the fantastic, exciting access road from the north-west with many tunnels, was finished in 1896. Basic *Bourgeoise* with a *gratin Dauphinois à la crème* and *pommes Dauphines* on all four menus. The present-day hotel is a modern *Logis de France*; ask to see photographs of the original.

Menus A-B. Rooms (16) B-C. Cards Access, Visa.
Closed 12 Nov to 15 Dec. (11 km SE of St-Jean-en-Royans.)
Post Col de la Machine, 26190 St-Jean-en-Royans, Drôme.
Tel 75 48 26 36. Fax 75 48 29 12. Mich 130/C3.

CORPS

Poste

Comfortable restaurant with rooms/Cooking 2
Terrace/Garage/Good value

My many contacts in the Jeunes Restaurateurs de France group gave me the tip about Gilbert and Christiane Delas at their outpost on the Route Napoléon. What a colourful outpost too on a sunny day enjoy a lunch under the petunia-striped umbrellas on the terrace. Gilbert, once chef on the liner *France*, is a classical *maître*. He promotes his *pays*: even the cheapest 4-course menu has a *gigot d'agneau à la broche*, mated

with the ubiquitous *gratin Dauphinois*. Mouthwatering stuff.
Menus A-C. Rooms (20) B-C. Cards Access, Visa.
Closed Dec. Jan.
Post 38970 Corps, Isère.
Tel 76 30 00 03. Fax 76 30 02 73. Mich 131/F3.

DIE   La Petite Auberge

Simple hotel/Cooking 2
Terrace/Parking/Good value

Perfectly placed to drive and ramble through the under-rated
Drôme Valley and the mountain terrain to all sides. Patrick
and Mme Montero have earned scores of well-done comments.
Readers have enthused about the welcome, the high standard
of classical fare (*noix de St-Jacques sous croûte de beurre
saumoné* and *le meilleur du boeuf poêlé à la moelle* are two
highlights; one chuckle is that chopped chives can appear with
every course) and, of course, the very quaffable local Die
sparklers and still wines. Read the introduction wine notes.
Menus B-C. Rooms (11) B-C. Cards Access, Visa.
Closed 1 wk Sept. Mid Dec to mid Jan. Sun evg & Wed (Sept to
June). Rest only: Mon (July & Aug).
Post 13 av. Sadi-Carnot, 26150 Die, Drôme. (Opposite station.)
Tel 75 22 05 91. Mich 131/D4.

MOLINES-EN-QUEYRAS   L'Equipe

Simple hotel/Cooking 1
Quiet/Terrace/Parking/Good value

Hannibal country and on the road to St-Véran, the highest
commune in Europe. Fabulous mountain terrain with many a dead-
end road and invigorating walks galore. Simple *Bourgeoise*
nosh (enlivened no end by *fondues* and a *raclette* served in the
evening) and modest accommodation in a chalet-styled *Logis
de France*. The site is the *raison d'être* for the entry.
Menus A-B. Rooms (22) C. Cards All.
Closed 27 Apl to 26 May. 20 Sept to 20 Dec.
Post 05350 Molines-en-Queyras, H.-Alpes.
Tel 92 45 83 20. Mich 133/E4.

MONESTIER-DE-CLERMONT   Au Sans Souci

Simple hotel/Cooking 2
Secluded/Gardens/Tennis/Garage/Parking/Good value

Anne and I enjoyed a wholesome, tasty lunch at this away-from-
the-main-road (N75) *logis* in the shadow of the eastern wall of
the Vercors. The Maurice family have been at the helm here for
almost 60 years. Classical and *Bourgeoise* fare. We tucked into
ravioles du Royans (to the west of the Vercors), *omble belle
meunière* and *fromage blanc*; all hearty mountain treats.
Menus A-B. Rooms (15) B-C. Cards Access, Visa.
Closed Mid Dec to end Jan. Sun evg & Mon (not July/Aug).
Post St-Paul-lès-Monestier, 38650 Monestier-de-Cler't, Isère.
Tel 76 34 03 60. Mich 131/E3. (N of Monestier, W of N75.)

MOUSTIERS-STE-MARIE   Les Santons

Comfortable restaurant/Cooking 3-4
Terrace

Enjoyment factor? 10 out of 10. What more can we say to get
you to visit the minute home, buzzing with vitality (and some
luminous paintings), of English-speaking André Abert and
Claude Fichot. A contented duo, cutting no corners and
satisfying all who make the short, steep climb to Les Santons,
overlooking a stream. This is *la vraie France*. Nothing grates:
olive bread, caviare of aubergines, profiteroles of Scottish
salmon in a *beurre blanc* sauce, consumate *lapereau* stuffed
with herbs, a wide selection of tasty veg and potatoes, wild
mushroom *raviolis* in a consommé, a three-star *nougat glacé aux
noisettes et amandes de Valensole* (to the west) and sorbets
served as a colourful terrine. Just a few examples of
harmonious cooking served in a cottagey setting. Simple but
perfect with a lot of thought going into the little details.
Anne and I cannot return to Les Santons soon enough.
Menus C. Cards Access, DC, Visa. (Rooms? Use Base hotel.)
Closed Dec. Jan. Mon evg (mid Sept to mid July). Tues.
Post pl. Eglise, 04360 Moustiers-Ste-Marie, Alpes-de-H.-P.
Tel 92 74 66 48. Mich 162/C1.

ST-AGNAN-EN-VERCORS   Le Veymont

Simple hotel/Cooking 1
Quiet/Good value

Englishman Martyn Jones and his family bought the hotel, in
a tiny village and opposite a church and fountain, in 1989.
Cooking is basic *Bourgeoise* (*ravioles du Royans, gigot
d'agneau, gratin Dauphinois and fromage blanc à la crème* all
feature on menus). An English oasis, popular with British
ramblers. The Vercors is perfect for mountain bikers and
Nordic ski-ing; not surprisingly Martyn is making much of
both. He hires out bikes and has sorted out many runs.
Menus A-B. Rooms (17) B. Cards Access, Visa.
Closed Mon (not July & Aug).
Post 26420 St-Agnan-en-Vercors, Drôme.
Tel 75 48 20 19. Fax 75 48 10 34. Mich 131/D3.

SERRES   Fifi Moulin

Comfortable hotel/Cooking 2
Quiet/Gardens/Swimming pool/Garage/Good value

We're not too many years away from the 40th-anniversary of
our first visit to this deliciously-named hotel (don't ask why;
the answer is a let down). In the 50s the owners were the
Martin family; today Philippe and Isabelle Frenoux are the
capable patrons. English-speaking Philippe is a winner and is
universally admired for his friendliness and willingness to go
to any lengths to help clients. Classical and *Bourgeoise*
cuisine is less skilled and not so ambitious these days; the
highlight remains the *tranche de gigot grillée crème d'ail*,
accompanied by an only average *gratin Dauphinois*. The glass-

panelled dining room is appreciated, especially on hot summer days when the panels are drawn back. The annexe rooms are less popular. Some readers reckon Fifi needs a facelift.
Menus B. Rooms (25) B. Cards All.
Closed Dec to mid Mar. Wed (Oct to May).
Post rte de Nyons, 05700 Serres, H.-Alpes.
Tel 92 67 00 01. Fax 92 67 07 56. Mich 145/F2.

VALENSOLE   Piès

Comfortable hotel/Cooking 2
Quiet/Terrace/Gardens/Parking/Good value

A smart, modern stone *logis*, high above the Riez road. An ambitious family enterprise, run by two generations of Piès. Classical and *Bourgeoise* cooking, making use of local produce. Less meaty bits of the pies are cold baked potatoes in their jackets, some *hors d'oeuvre* tasting suspiciously like tinned titbits, poor service and lack of attention to detail.
Menus A-B. Rooms (16) B. Cards Access, Visa.
Closed Feb.
Post 04210 Valensole, Alpes-de-H.-P.
Tel 92 74 83 13. Mich 162/B1.

VARCES   Les Matitis

Very comfortable restaurant/Cooking 2-3
Terrace/Parking

In the lanes between Varces and Claix (W of N75 and two-ticks from the Manoir des Matitis base hotel). The panorama is dramatic: the Chartreuse and Chamrousse dominate the skyline. Gilles Hubert (I hope now fully recovered from his accident) is an inventive modern *cuisinier*. Ironically a couple of classical *plats* appealed more: *consommé clair de caille et sa quenelle* and *noisette de chevreuil sauce poivrade*. Don't miss the exotic dessert *le Carthusien* (the clue is the view to the north p 333).
Menus B-E. Cards All. (Rooms? See Claix Base hotel.)
Closed Sun evg & Mon.
Post allée des Chênes, 38760 Varces, Isère.
Tel 76 98 15 46. Telex 320161. Fax 76 98 35 19. Mich 131/E2.

VARCES   Relais l'Escale

Very comfortable restaurant with rooms/Cooking 2
Quiet/Terrace/Gardens/Garage/Parking

Three cheers: L'Escale has new owners, Frédéric and Géraldine Buntinx. The individual chalets remain the unusual means of overnight accommodation and the terrace still has its imposing plane trees. Frédéric is a classical fan: a *chausson de turbot et St-Jacques au cerfeuil* is assured; and a succulent *petite pièce de boeuf aux morilles farcies* is a gutsy main course.
Menus B-D. Rooms (7) E. Cards AE, Access, Visa.
Closed Jan. Sun evg & Mon (Oct-15 May). Tues (15 May-30 Sept).
Post 38760 Varces, Isère. (On east side of N75.)
Tel 76 72 80 19. Fax 76 72 92 58. Mich 131/E2.

ILE DE FRANCE

▲ see page 280

The Ile de France is a mixture of ancient towns, superb châteaux and palaces, glorious cathedrals, prairie-like flat farmlands and an outer ring of huge forests. The Ile de France was the birthplace of the nation and, today, is very much the financial and commercial heart of France.

Access to the historic towns of the Ile de France from **Paris** is easy. The magnificent RER (Regional Express Trains) rail system provides fast, comfortable and modern services in every direction from the capital. Driving in Paris is as hellish as ever but, in the Ile de France, hundreds of kilometres of toll-free motorways and dual-carriageways, backed up by several new autoroutes, have made getting about by car a great deal easier. The transport infrastructure of the Paris basin is light years better than the one London has to endure. And, what is more, there are many additional projects underway, including the ambitious eastern TGV "bypass" of Paris.

First, let me briefly outline some of the natural pleasures surrounding Paris. The great forests are especially welcome at any time of the year. When the weather is kind there's nothing more pleasant than to head for the wooded glades of a dozen or more *forêts*. I adore them most in the autumn when, on balmy, benevolent days, there's no better way of recharging batteries than walking along the forest paths. Autumn cloaks envelop you; underfoot dry leaves crackle; and blackberries, plump and ripe, plead to be picked. Not surprisingly, at weekends the Ile de France is overrun by Parisians fleeing the crowded, noisy city. Try to explore the area during the week.

148

▲see page 281

● Beauvais

Aisne

A1

▲Bazincourt-sur-Epte

Oise

Compiègne

Soissons

N14

Chantilly

Senlis

N2

Lys-Chantilly▲

▲Fontaine-Chaalis

A4

Seine

Mantes

Ch-de-Gaulle
St-Denis

Marne

A15

Meaux

▲Germigny-l'Evèque

Orgeval▲

A104

△La Ferté-sous-
Jouarre

PARIS

A3

A86

Euro Disney

Versailles●

A13

La Francilienne

Fontenay-Trésigny

Châteaufort

△

Orly

Senlisse▲

Varennes-Jarcy ▲

▲

N4

Rambouillet

A10

Melun

△Le Châtelet-en-Brie

A11

Ablis

▲
St-Vrain

◀see page 263

Chartres

Samois-sur-Seine

Fontainebleau

Seine

A5

▲Recloses

▲Flagy

Sens

see page 92 ▶

Yonne

A6

▲ Hotel/Rest (rooms)
△ Restaurant only

0   10   20 Miles

▼see page 193   ▼see page 72

N7

   To the north of Paris are several forests: the Forêt de
Montmorency, Forêt de l'Isle-Adam and Forêt de Carnelle are
all north of **St-Denis** and south of the River **Oise**; the forests
of **Chantilly**, Halatte and **Ermenonville** encircle **Senlis**;
and, further north, the giant forest of **Compiègne** and the
smaller Forêt de Retz lie to the east and south-east of the town
of Compiègne. To the west of Paris is the much loved forest at
St-Germain-en-Laye; and to the south-west are the woods of
the Parc Naturel Régional de la Haute Vallée de Chevreuse
and the extensive Forêt de **Rambouillet**. South-east of Paris
is my own favourite, the Forêt de **Fontainebleau**.
   Painters have long loved the forest and river country
surrounding the capital. They include the Oise to the north,
the **Seine** and the Loing to the south-east, the latter a magnet
for Sisley, Monet and other Impressionists. **Barbizon**, north-
west of Fontainebleau, was made famous by the landscape
artists of the 19th century. The former homes of Rousseau and
Millet are now museums. Seek out **Samois**-sur-Seine and
Moret-sur-Loing; both towns inspired many painters.
   Though not sharing the same fame as the Impressionist
landscapes further east, I like the valleys and woods near
Dampierre, between Paris and Rambouillet. The Yvette and
Ru des Vaux streams flow through pleasing woodland valleys
and are complemented by fine châteaux at both Dampierre and
Rambouillet. There are also many golf courses nearby.
   Some of France's finest châteaux, cathedrals and gardens
are in the Ile de France. I'll identify some of the best by

149

following a circle around Paris, starting in the north. The name **Chantilly** will conjure up visions of cream or lace for most people. Chantilly's moated château, with many flamboyant touches and an extensive park created by the ubiquitous Le Nôtre, has a terrific site alongside the racecourse. Not so well known is the Musée Vivant de Cheval, literally a "living" horse museum with many live demonstrations.

Beauvais, to the north-west of Chantilly, is renowned for its cathedral and particularly the sublime Gothic choir, the double flying buttresses, tapestries and glorious windows. Senlis, east of Chantilly, is a handsome town with a cathedral, ruined castle, medieval houses and cobbled streets. To the south of Senlis are the ruins of two ancient abbeys, both impressive even today: the 700-year-old Abbaye de Royaumont and the Abbaye de Chaalis, founded in 1136.

South-east of Paris are two exceptional châteaux: near **Melun** is the 17th-century **Vaux-le-Vicomte**, a perfectly balanced structure and the model for what came later at Versailles; Fontainebleau is a Renaissance palace and much the most atmospheric of the Ile de France versions.

The cathedral at **Chartres**, south-west of Paris, is one of the wonders of France: gigantic twin spires, one early Gothic, the other Romanesque, and fabulous stained-glass windows are inspiring sights. A dozen or so old bridges over the Eure and the ancient cobbled streets of Vieux Chartres, to the south of the cathedral, deserve the time of all visitors.

Versailles' colossal palace, majestic and flamboyant, is a household name around the world. You could make several visits and still not absorb all the grandiose apartments, the exquisite 250-acre gardens and the two Trianons. The château at St-Germain, in its present form, was the brainchild of Henri IV: the interior, the gardens, the terrace above the Seine and the old town captivate all. Something quite different is the wildlife park at Thoiry, to the west of Versailles. Hundreds of animals can be seen from your car as you drive through the reserve or from an aerial walkway; lesser attractions are the 16th-century "château of the sun" and the Le Nôtre park (he worked as hard as Capability Brown) where, believe it or not, cricket is often played.

I have left one of the sweetest pleasures to the end of our clockwise tour: Claude Monet's Water-Lily Garden at **Giverny**, north-west of **Mantes**. The artist bought the property in 1883, long before he became so renowned. He was 42 at the time; during the next 43 years he painted some of his most famous canvases in the delectable gardens. In the 50 years that followed his death in 1926, the gardens became derelict but, today, thanks to the French Académie des Beaux Arts and many private donors, you can visit Monet's old home and its eye-catching grounds. Open April to October (closed Mondays).

Euro Disney

Earlier this year saw the opening of the 4,800-acre Euro Disney site in the **Marne** Valley, 20 miles east of Paris (between the River Marne and the A4 autoroute). Everything about the theme park is gigantic in scale: six Disney-owned hotels with 5,200 bedrooms (by the end of the decade 18,000 bedrooms); 29 attractions; a giant lake; a golf course; 12,000 employees; and over 10 million visitors expected in year one.

An RER line from Paris gives fast rail access and, by 1994, a TGV rail link with the rest of France (and Britain) will be in place. For Britons, in their cars, the simplest access will be to leave the A1 at Senlis, take the N330 to Meaux, and then use the A4 to the site. Over one million Brits are expected in year one: will those that don't use the rail and air links get the bug for France and venture further south in their cars? I hope so: France is big enough for them all and can certainly beat anything to be found in the fantasy land of Euro Disney. For further information phone 071 287 6558 (US 818 543 3435).

Markets Beauvais (Wed and Sat); Chantilly (Sat); Chartres (Wed and Sat); Compiègne (Wed and Sat); Fontainebleau (Tues, Fri and Sun); Meaux (Sat); Moret-sur-Loing (Tues and Fri); Rambouillet (Wed to Sun); St-Germain-en-Laye (Tues, Fri and Sun); Versailles (Tues and Thurs to Sun).

Michelin green guide: Ile de France (in English).
Michelin "green" map 106 recommended (1 cm: 1 km).

Bypassing Paris

Thank heavens there are now several ways of bypassing that most tortuous of tortures, the Boulevard Périphérique.

1 If you are heading for the Med from the northern channel ports, then the newly-completed A26 autoroute from Calais to Troyes, A5 from Troyes to Langres, and A31 from Langres to Beaune is much the best "Run to the Sun".

2 Another newly-completed route, called **La Francilienne**, connects the **A1**, **A6** and **A10**. This bypass starts at the A1 3 km south of **Charles-de-Gaulle** airport and, heading east around Paris, uses the **A104**, **A4**, N104, N446 & N447. La Francilienne is either an autoroute or dual-carriageway run over its entire length from the A1 to A10. (One caveat: the A4 section is just 3½ km long. Ignore exit 12 on the A4, which is midway between La Francilienne's junctions with the A104 and N104.)

3 A third bypass, a few miles east of the Périphérique, starts at the **A1** 4½ km south of Charles-de-Gaulle airport. This makes use of the **A3**, **A86** (care exit off A3), **A4**, A86 again and N186 to connect with the **A6** north of **Orly** airport. (Two caveats: the short A4 section requires care in both directions – keep to the right; and heading north on the A6, nearing Orly, keep to the extreme right of the autoroute, the Paris Est side.)

Cheeses Cow's milk

Brie soft, white rind, the size of a long-playing record. It will frequently be described with the addition of the name of the area in which it is made: **Brie de Coulommiers**; **Brie de Meaux**; **Brie de Melun**; and **Brie de Montereau** are the best known. Faint mushroom smell
Chevru similar in size and taste to Brie de Meaux
Coulommiers like Brie, but a smaller, 45 rpm disc. At its best in summer, autumn and winter. Both cheeses are ideal with Côte de Beaune reds
Délice de Saint Cyr a soft, triple-cream cheese – nutty-tasting and made in small disks
Explorateur a mild, triple-cream cheese – made in small cylinders
Feuille de Dreux fruity-flavoured, soft disk. Ideal with fruity red wines
Fontainebleau a fresh cream cheese with whipped cream; add a dusting of sugar and it really is great

Regional Specialities

Refer to the five regions elsewhere in *French Leave Encore*: Normandy to the west; the North; Champagne-Ardenne to the east; and Burgundy and the Loire on the southern borders of the Ile de France.

Wines

Refer again to the chapters of Champagne-Ardenne to the east; and Burgundy and the Loire to the south of the Ile de France.

CHARTRES   Novotel

Very comfortable hotel/Cooking 1
Terrace/Gardens/Swimming pool/Lift/Parking

A11 Chartres/Chartres Est (from Le Mans) exits. West on N10.
Menus B. Rooms (78) E. Disabled. Cards All.
Post 28630 Chartres, E.-et-L. (En Route p 104)
Tel 37 34 80 30. Telex 781298. Fax 37 30 29 56. Mich 53/D2.
(Bookings: UK 071 724 1000; from US toll free 800 221 4542)

CHATEAU-THIERRY   Ibis

Simple hotel/Cooking 1
Terrace/Lift/Tennis/Parking/Good value

Leave A4 Château-Thierry exit. South on D1. Use western bypass
of town. Before Marne bridge right on D969 (river right bank).
Menus A. Rooms (55) C. Disabled. Cards All.
Post 68 av. Gén de Gaulle, 02400 Essomes-sur-Marne, Aisne.
Tel 23 83 10 10. Telex 140616. Fax 23 83 45 23. Mich 37/E2.
(Bookings: UK 071 724 1000; from US toll free 800 221 4542)

CHATEAU-THIERRY   Ile de France

Comfortable hotel/Cooking 1
Gardens/Lift/Parking

Leave A4 Château-Thierry exit. South on D1. Hotel on left.
Menus B-C. Rooms (53) D. Cards AE, Access, Visa.
Post 02400 Château-Thierry, Aisne. (En Route p 35)
Tel 23 69 10 12. Telex 150666. Fax 23 83 49 70. Mich 37/E2.

CORBEIL   Campanile

Simple hotel/Cooking 1
Terrace/Parking/Good value

A6 Corbeil-Nord exit (from south); Evry-Lisses (from north).
Use road on east side A6 to head north to D26; right to hotel.
Menus A-B. Rooms (79) C. Disabled. Cards Access, Visa.
Post av. P.Maintenant, 91100 Corbeil-Essonnes, Essonne.
Tel (1) 60 89 41 45. Telex 600934. Mich 54/B1. (ER p 47)
(Bookings : UK freephone 0800 897863)

EVRY   Ibis

Simple hotel/Cooking 1
Lift/Parking

A6 Evry-ZI exit (from north); Evry-Courcouronnes exit (from
south). Hotel on west side of A6 (Courcouronnes).
Menus B. Rooms (132) D. Disabled. Cards Access, Visa.
Post 1 av. du Lac, 91000 Evry, Essonne. (ER p 47) Mich 54/B2.
Tel (1) 60 77 74 75. Telex 601728. Fax (1) 60 78 06 03.
(Bookings: UK 071 724 1000; from US toll free 800 221 4542)

EVRY　　　　　Novotel

Very comfortable hotel/Cooking 1
Terrace/Gardens/Swimming pool/Lift/Closed parking

Follow exit instructions for previous Ibis entry.
Menus B. Rooms (174) E. Cards All. (En Route p 47)
Post 3 rue de la Mare-Neuve, 91000 Evry, Essonne. Mich 54/B2.
Tel (1) 60 77 82 70. Telex 600685. Fax (1) 60 78 14 75.
(Bookings: UK 071 724 1000; US toll free 800 221 4542)

MANTES-LA-JOLIE　　　　　Climat de France

Simple hotel/Cooking 1
Parking

A13 exit 12 (Mantes-Sud). D928 N to Seine. Left. (ER p 112)
Menus A-B. Rooms (41) D. Disabled. Cards AE, Access, Visa.
Post r. M.Tabu, 78200 Mantes-la-Jolie, Yvelines. Mich 35/D3.
Tel (1) 30 33 03 70. Telex 689174. Fax (1) 30 63 03 54.
(Bookings: UK 071 287 3181)

MEAUX　　　　　Climat de France

Simple hotel/Cooking 1
Terrace/Parking

A4 St-Jean-les-2-Jumeaux (from Paris) and Meaux (from
Reims) exits. Head towards Meaux on N3; hotel on left.
Menus A-B. Rooms (60) D. Disabled. Cards AE, Access, Visa.
Post 32 av. Victoire, 77100 Meaux, S.-et-M. Mich 36/C3.
Tel (1) 64 33 15 47. Telex 690020. Fax (1) 60 23 11 64.
(Bookings: UK 071 287 3181)

MELUN　　　　　Ibis

Simple hotel/Cooking 1
Parking/Good value

Use northern bypass (N105). Ibis at junc. of N371/N36/N105.
Menus A. Rooms (74) C. Disabled. Cards Access, Visa.
Post 81 av. Meaux, 77000 Melun, S.-et-M. Mich 54/C1
Tel (1) 60 68 42 45. Telex 691779. Fax (1) 64 09 62 00.
(Bookings: UK 071 724 1000; US toll free 800 221 4542)

MEULAN　　　　　Mercure

Very comfortable hotel/Cooking 1-2
Quiet/Terrace/Gardens/Lift

An exceptional site, on an island in the Seine. A13 Meulan/Les
Mureaux exit. D43 north. At T left; on left after 1st bridge.
Menus B-C. Rooms (65) F. Disabled. Cards All.
Post 78250 Meulan, Yvelines. (En Route p 111) Mich 35/E2.
Tel (1) 34 74 63 63. Telex 695295. Fax (1) 34 74 00 98
(Bookings: UK 071 724 1000; US toll free 800 221 4542)

Autoroute Hotels

NEMOURS   Altéa

Comfortable hotel (no restaurant)
Gardens/Parking

Previously Euromotel. Direct access A6 (going north). Or leave
A6 Nemours exit. South to D225 (Sens), left, under A6, left.
Menus Use A6 service facilities. Rooms (102) D-E. Cards All.
Post 77140 Nemours, S.-et-M. (En Route p 49) Mich 54/C3.
Tel (1) 64 28 10 32. Telex 690243. Fax (1) 64 28 60 59.
(Bookings: UK 071 724 1000; US toll free 800 221 4542)

NEMOURS   Ibis

Simple hotel/Cooking 1
Parking/Good value

A6 Nemours exit. South from toll; on left. Closed Sun lun.
Menus A. Rooms (41) C. Disabled. Cards Access, Visa.
Post 77140 Nemours, S.-et-M. (En Route p 49)
Tel (1) 64 28 88 00. Telex 694212. Mich 54/C3.
(Bookings: UK 071 724 1000; US toll free 800 221 4542)

POISSY   Climat de France

Simple hotel/Cooking 1
Terrace/Parking

A13 Poissy exit. East on N13 towards St-Germain-en-Laye.
Menus A-B. Rooms (87) D. Disabled. Cards AE, Access, Visa.
Post 78240 Chambourcy, Yvelines. (En Route p 110)
Tel (1) 30 74 42 61. Telex 689095. Mich 35/E3.
(Bookings: UK 071 287 3181)

POISSY   Novotel

Very comfortable hotel/Cooking 1
Terrace/Gardens/Swim pool/Tennis/Lift/Closed parking

Leave A13 Poissy exit. Hotel on N13, south of autoroute.
Menus B. Rooms (119) E. Cards All.
Post 78630 Orgeval, Yvelines. (En Route p 110) Mich 35/E3.
Tel (1) 39 75 97 60. Telex 697174. Fax (1) 39 75 48 93.
(Bookings: UK 071 724 1000; US toll free 800 221 4542)

RAMBOUILLET   Ibis

Simple hotel/Cooking 1
Tennis/Parking/Good value

Leave A11 at Ablis/Rambouillet exit. Head north on N10. South
of Rambouillet; use D936 to cross N10 to hotel. (ER p 104)
Menus A. Rooms (62) C-D. Disabled. Cards Access, Visa.
Post 78120 Rambouillet, Yvelines. Mich 53/E1.
Tel (1) 30 41 78 50. Telex 698429. Fax (1) 34 85 66 45.
(Bookings: UK 071 724 1000; US toll free 800 221 4542)

SENLIS   Campanile

Simple hotel/Cooking 1
Parking/Good value

Leave A1 exit 8 (Senlis). N324 towards Senlis; on left.
Menus A-B. Rooms (75) C-D. Disabled. Cards Access, Visa.
Post 60300 Senlis, Oise. (En Route p 23)
Tel 44 60 05 07. Telex 155028. Fax 44 53 27 68. Mich 36/B1.
(Bookings: UK freephone 0800 897863)

SENLIS   Ibis

Simple hotel/Cooking 1
Parking

Leave A1 exit 8 (Senlis). N324 towards Senlis; on left.
Menus B. Rooms (92) D. Disabled. Cards Access, Visa.
Post 60300 Senlis, Oise. (En Route p 23)
Tel 44 53 70 50. Telex 140101. Fax 44 53 51 93. Mich 36/B1.
(Bookings: UK 071 724 1000; US toll free 800 221 4542)

SURVILLIERS   Mercure

Very comfortable hotel/Cooking 1-2
Fairly quiet/Terrace/Swimming pool/Lift/Parking

Leave A1 exit 7 (Survilliers/Ermenonville). Hotel on north side
of D126, to the east of the A1.
Menus B-C. Rooms (115) F. Disabled. Cards All.
Post 95470 Survilliers, Val-d'Oise. (ER p 23) Mich 36/B2.
Tel (1) 34 68 28 28. Telex 605917. Fax (1) 34 68 22 81.
(Bookings: UK 071 724 1000; US toll free 800 221 4542)

SURVILLIERS   Novotel

Very comfortable hotel/Cooking 1
Terrace/Gardens/Swimming pool/Closed parking

Leave A1 exit 7 (Survilliers/Ermenonville). Hotel on west side
of A1, towards Survilliers village.
Menus B. Rooms (79) E-F. Cards All.
Post 95470 Survilliers, Val-d'Oise. (ER p 23) Mich 36/B2.
Tel (1) 34 68 69 80. Telex 605910. Fax (1) 34 68 64 94.
(Bookings: UK 071 724 1000; US toll free 800 221 4542)

URY   Novotel

Very comfortable hotel/Cooking 1
Quiet/Terr/Gardens/Swim pool/Tennis/Closed parking

Leave A6 Ury exit. North-east of A6, on N152. Wooded site.
Menus B. Rooms (127) E-F. Disabled. Cards All.
Post 77116 Ury, S.-et.-M. (En Route p 49) Mich 54/B2.
Tel (1) 64 24 48 25. Telex 694153. Fax (1) 64 24 46 92.
(Bookings: UK 071 724 1000; US toll free 800 221 4542)

Base Hotels

CHANTILLY   Parc

Very comfortable hotel
Gardens/Lift/Parking

An ideal site for the forest, racecourse and the château and its
park. Bypass the dreadful Relais du Coq Chantant restaurant.
Rooms (58) E-F. Disabled. Cards AE, Access, Visa.
Post 36 av. Mar. Joffre, 60500 Chantilly, Oise.
Tel 44 58 20 00. Telex 155007. Fax 44 57 31 00. Mich 36/A1.

ERMENONVILLE   Le Prieuré

Comfortable hotel
Gardens/Parking

No wonder readers recommend this jewel of a base, in the
shadow of a church. Jean-Pierre and Marie-José Treillon have
every right to be proud of their house and *jardin anglais*.
Rooms (11) E-F. Cards AE, Access, Visa.
Closed February.
Post 60950 Ermenonville, Oise.
Tel 44 54 00 44. Telex 145110. Mich 36/B2.

ST-CYR-L'ECOLE   Aérotel

Comfortable hotel
Quiet/Closed parking/Good value

Much appreciated by readers. On east side of D7; west of
Versailles, opposite small aerodrome. Close to A12 & A13.
Rooms (26) C-D. Cards Access, Visa.
Post 78210 St-Cyr-l'Ecole, Yvelines. (En Route p 110)
Tel (1) 30 45 07 44. Fax (1) 34 60 35 96. Mich 35/E4.

VERSAILLES   Home St-Louis

Simple hotel
Fairly quiet/Good value

Quietish side street. Save francs. One km to château. Street
parking. Near RER station. Adequate; no readers' complaints.
Rooms (27) C-D. Cards Access, Visa.
Post 28 rue St-Louis, 78000 Versailles, Yvelines.
Tel 39 50 23 55. Fax 30 21 62 45. Mich 35/E4.

VOISINS-LE-BRETONNEUX   Port Royal

Simple hotel
Quiet/Gardens/Closed parking/Good value

A thoroughly useful base. Near Châteaufort restaurant and
numerous golf courses. Not too expensive either.
Rooms (36) C. Cards Access, Visa.
Post 20 r. H.Boucher, 78960 Voisins-le-Bretonneux, Yvelines.
Tel (1) 30 44 16 27. Fax (1) 30 57 52 11. Mich 35/E4.

ABLIS   Château d'Esclimont

Luxury hotel/Cooking 2-3
Secluded/Gardens/Swimming pool/Tennis/Lift/Parking

One of a select chain called Grandes Etapes Françaises. The label is spot-on: serious bucks is the grand setback here. Not surprisingly when you tot up the benefits: 150 acres of woods, gardens, *étangs*, moats and a 15th-century château fit for a king. I first encountered the busy R&C enterprise when researching *En Route* some years ago; then a weekday lunch was the least expensive way of absorbing the sensuous setting. That's still true today. Cooking is a palette of classical and modern classical with a Provençal brush run over many a dish. *Pignons de pin* are sown on various *plats*: with roasted Scottish salmon and again on *carré d'agneau primeur*.
Menus D-E. Rooms (48) F-F3. Cards Visa.
Post 28700 St-Symphorien-le-Château, Eure-et-Loir. (ER p 104)
Tel 37 31 15 15. Telex 780560. Fax 37 31 57 91. Mich 53/E1.

BAZINCOURT-SUR-EPTE   Château de la Rapée

Comfortable hotel/Cooking 2
Secluded/Gardens/Parking

Built in 1825, the château style is Anglo-Norman baroque. In an isolated site, on the edge of woods and with extensive views north, both the setting and the approach to the hotel would not be out of place in a Brontë novel. Roger Bergeron, owner of the château since 1973, has worked as a chef for 45 years. Classical and Normandy cooking prevails though modern touches are likely to surface soon; his two sons (trained by Guy Savoy and Gérard Vié) now work alongside him.
Menus B-D. Rooms (12) D-E. Cards All.
Closed Mid Jan to mid Feb. Rest: Wed.
Post 27140 Bazincourt-sur-Epte, Eure. (NW of village.)
Tel 32 55 11 61. Telex 771097. Mich 17/D4.

CHATEAUFORT   La Belle Epoque

Comfortable restaurant/Cooking 3
Terrace

La Belle Epoque's terrace is tiny; the view of the Mérantaise Valley (part of the Parc Naturel Régional de la Haute Vallée de Chevreuse) is a scenic bonus; the rustic restaurant is well named, full of odd-ball bric-à-brac; and, in the shapes of Michel and Josette Peignaud, has patrons who are capable restaurateurs. Michel's repertoire is schizophrenic: a classical note or two (*tournedos Rossini*); some modern tunes played with a Chinese bow (*canette du Berry à la façon du Chinois*); and an odd-ball regional melody mix (*une cotriade Audiernaise à la Berrichonne*, featuring both Brittany and Berry). Rooms? See Voisins base, just five km to the west.
Menus C-E. Cards All.
Closed Xmas to New Year. 9 Aug to 7 Sept. Sun evg. Mon.
Post 78117 Châteaufort, Yvelines.
Tel (1) 39 56 21 66. Mich 35/E4.

LE CHATELET-EN-BRIE   Auberge Briarde

Comfortable restaurant/Cooking 2-3

Jean and Monique Guichard have headed north from their Aub.
Velay at St-Didier-en-Velay (south-west of St-Etienne) and set
up shop in Brie terrain. They brought some Le Puy lentils and
Verveine du Velay (see end of Ardèche intro.) with them; both
feature on the menus. Jean's a classicist: witness a *jambon à
l'os cuit au foin, blanc de turbot au Champagne* and *filet de
boeuf grillé Béarnaise*. Some dishes are lighter versions of the
great classics. In the autumn there's a *menu dégustation des
gibiers*; the chef's especially proud of the latter and his home-
made *foie gras*, breads, sorbets and *pâtisseries*.
Menus C-D. Cards All. (Rooms? See Melun Autoroute hotel.)
Closed 1st 3 wks Aug. Sun evg. Mon. Wed evg.
Post Les Ecrennes, 77820 Le Châtelet-en-Brie, S.-et-M.
Tel (1) 60 69 47 32. Mich 54/C1. (On D213, east of village.)

LA FERTE-SOUS-JOUARRE   Auberge de Condé

Very comfortable restaurant/Cooking 3
Terrace/Parking

The heroic Emile Tingaud manned the kitchens at the *auberge*
(which he opened in 1947) until his death, in 1989, aged 81.
(His son, Jean-Claude, who originally succeeded him, died at
the early age of 38 in 1973.) Now his grandson, Pascal, in his
early 30s, strives hard to protect the formidable Tingaud
reputation. Authentic classical cooking is mixed with regional
and one or two lighter dishes: *filet de biche en Rossini* is a page
from the past; *poularde de Bresse à la Briarde* has a Brie
streak; and *saumon légèrement fumé à l'auberge sur un lit de
pommes tièdes* is a very much in-fashion modern creation.
Menus C-E. Cards All. (Rooms? See Meaux Autoroute hotel.)
Closed Mon evg and Tues.
Post 1 av. Montmirail, 77260 La Ferté-sous-Jouarre, S.-et-M.
Tel (1) 60 22 00 07. Fax (1) 60 22 30 60. Mich 37/D3.

FLAGY   Hostellerie du Moulin

Very comfortable restaurant with rooms/Cooking 1-2
Secluded/Terrace/Gardens/Parking/Good value

Claude Scheidecker, an involved and attentive English-speaking
host, hails from Alsace. His 13th-century mill, alongside the
River Orvanne, is a charmer; breakfast on the terrace is
particularly pleasant. Cooking is straightforward classical (the
ubiquitous *sauce Béarnaise* pops up three times on the menu)
and *Bourgeoise*. Curry powder, too, is a popular flavouring
agent; both pork and lamb get the treatment. There's no
chance here of taking away your bedroom key inadvertently,
attached as it is to a miniature sack of grain.
Menus B. Rooms (10) B-E. Cards All.
Closed 2nd half Sept. 20 Dec to 22 Jan. Sun evg & Mon (except
Easter and Whitsun when closed Mon evg & Tues).
Post 77940 Flagy, S.-et-M. (South of Montereau-Faut-Yonne.)
Tel (1) 60 96 67 89. Mich 55/D3.

FONTAINE-CHAALIS   Auberge de Fontaine

Comfortable restaurant with rooms/Cooking 1-2
Terrace/Good value

I've dropped the quiet tag at this stone-built, rustic family-run
Logis de France. Readers reckon the road can be noisy
sometimes; pity. Chef/patron Jacques Campion's cooking is
unambitious, safe as stone-built houses stuff: *Bourgeoise* and
classical with an appetite-quenching *andouillette sauce grain
de moutarde* (Meaux is down the road) winning a AAAAΛ accolade
n its menu description. AAAAA? Association Amicales des
Amateurs d'Authentiques Andouillettes. Now you know.
Menus B. Rooms (8) C. Cards Access, Visa.
Closed Feb school hols. Tues evg & Wed.
Post 60300 Fontaine-Chaalis, Oise.
Tel 44 54 20 22. Mich 36/B1.

FONTENAY-TRESIGNY   Le Manoir

Very comfortable hotel/Cooking 2
Secluded/Terrace/Gardens/Swim pool/Tennis/Parking

An isolated creeper-covered, Normandy-style mansion, to the
east of the village and well clear of the N4. Woods and gardens
entice as do the richly-styled furnishings. The Relais
& Châteaux hotel is superbly placed for Euro Disney, just over
20 km to the north. Equally, Fouquet's 17th-century
masterpiece, the château at Vaux-le-Vicomte, is as close, but to
the south. If you want to visit either, or both, and insist on
some luxury, then this is the ideal base. Cooking? Classical,
straight from the pages of Larousse. One sour note: room
prices were given a real hike in 1992. I wonder why?
Menus C-D. Rooms (15) F2. Cards All.
Closed Mid Nov to 21 Mar. Rest: Tues.
Post 77610 Fontenay-Trésigny, S.-et-M. Mich 36/C4.
Tel (1) 64 25 91 17. Telex 690635. Fax (1) 64 25 95 49.

GERMIGNY-L'EVEQUE   Le Gonfalon

Very comfortable restaurant with rooms/Cooking 2
Secluded/Terrace

This is where I would head for if our children were 20 years
younger and Euro Disney was on the itinerary. On the left
bank of the River Marne, north-east of Meaux, the modern
restaurant has delectable river views and the enviable plus of
being away from through traffic. Line Colubi is a chef who
loves working with fish and shellfish; the latter come straight
from a dining room tank which holds 1,600 litres of sea-water.
Classical *plats*: just dive straight into the piscatorial pool
or treats like *langouste grillée*, *roulé de saumon au coulis*
and a *marmite courte-nage*; assured, conviction cooking. Some
bedrooms have individual riverside terraces.
Menus C-D Rooms (10) C-D. Cards All.
Closed Jan. Sun evg & Mon.
Post 77910 Germigny-l'Evèque, S.-et-M. (En Route p 34)
Tel (1) 64 33 16 05. Mich 36/C2.

LYS-CHANTILLY
Hostellerie du Lys

Comfortable hotel/Cooking 1-2
Secluded/Terrace/Gardens/Parking

Modern buildings in wooded grounds, south-west of Chantilly; the neighbouring terrain is an Ascot look-alike (woods and luxury homes). Service is excellent but food is not so hot. Classical menus with little imagination but vast choice. Grills and text-book sauces: *Béarnaise, Choron*, etc.
Menus B-D. Rooms (35) D-E. Cards All.
Closed Rest: Xmas to New Year.
Post Lys-Chantilly, 60260 Lamorlaye, Oise.
Tel 44 21 26 19. Telex 150298. Fax 44 21 28 19. Mich 36/A1.

ORGEVAL
Moulin d'Orgeval

Comfortable hotel/Cooking 1-2
Secluded/Terrace/Gardens/Swimming pool/Parking

The Orgeval stream is the big star here: its waters flow alongside the covered terrace and a couple of bridges allow you to cross to extended island gardens. The wooded setting and gardens share second billing. Classical cuisine with some flickers of flair (*l'amandine du pâtissier*) comes third.
Menus B-E. Rooms (14) F. Cards All.
Post 78630 Orgeval, Yvelines. (En Route p 110) Mich 35/E3.
Tel (1) 39 75 85 74. Telex 689036. Fax (1) 39 75 48 52.

RECLOSES
Casa del Sol

Simple hotel/Cooking 1
Secluded/Terrace/Gardens/Parking/Good value

Go if you are looking for a rustic *logis* in a tranquil site on the edge of the Forêt de Fontainebleau. Abundant flowers, inside and out, are much appreciated. *Bourgeois* meals cooked by the friendly and attentive *patronne*, Colette Courcoul.
Menus B. Rooms (10) C-D. Cards All. (5 km E A6 Ury exit.)
Closed 20 Dec to end Jan. Tues (not high season).
Post 77760 Recloses, S.-et-M. (SW of Fontainebleau.)
Tel (1) 64 24 20 35. Telex 692131. Mich 54/C2.

ST-VRAIN
Hostellerie de St-Caprais

Comfortable restaurant with rooms/Cooking 1-2
Terrace/Gardens/Good value

I refer you to Mirabel Osler's "She said it used to be a sad place" on pages 400/401. Arlette Malgras is *la patronne*, her husband is *le cuisinier*. Classical and *Bourgeois* dishes: the likes of *sole grillée meunière* and *crème caramel*. The odd Normandy touch: *côte de veau Normande*. And *tarte Tatin*.
Menus B. Rooms (5) C. Cards AE, Access, Visa.
Closed 2nd half July. 1st wk Aug. Sun evg & Mon.
Post 30 rue St-Caprais, 91770 St-Vrain, Essonne.
Tel (1) 64 56 15 45. Mich 54/A1.

SAMOIS-SUR-SEINE   Hostellerie Country Club

Comfortable hotel/Cooking 1-2
Quiet/Terrace/Tennis/Parking/Good value

An ugly-looking building with the more than compensating
benefit of a site in a slightly elevated position on the left bank
of the Seine. Samois is north-east of Fontainebleau.
Patron/chef, Eric Plamçon, is no great Impressionist: expect
classical and *Bourgeois* canvases of the *fines de claires* and
truite au vin de Loire variety. Not forgetting the Ile de France
essential dessert, *tarte Tatin*.
Menus B-C. Rooms (16) B-D. Cards Access, Visa.
Closed Xmas to New Year. Sun evg & Mon.
Post 11 quai F.-D. Roosevelt, 77920 Samois-s-Seine, S.-et-M.
Tel (1) 64 24 60 34. Fax (1) 64 24 80 76. Mich 54/C2.

SENLISSE   Le Gros Marronnier

Comfortable restaurant with rooms/Cooking 2
Quiet/Gardens

The Trochon family's *auberge* is a restored presbytery,
adjacent to an old church and with a pretty *jardin de curé*. I
first came across both this restaurant and the hotel above
when assembling material for a major magazine feature, *A
Passing Interest for Paris*. Senlisse is at the heart of the Parc
Naturel Régional de la Haute Vallée de Chevreuse; what an
exhilarating surprise this wooded wonderland is, with streams,
étangs and other natural and man-made diversions. Cooking is
a touch more ambitious under the new owners: classical,
Bourgeoise and a number of grills. Some dishes? *Filet de biche
Grand Veneur*, *contrefilet poêlé au poivre*, *gratin de coquilles
St-Jacques* and *tarte Tatin* are a representative quartet.
Menus B-D. Rooms (18) C-D. Cards All.
Post 3 pl. de l'Eglise, 78720 Senlisse, Yvelines.
Tel (1) 30 52 51 69. Mich 35/E4.

VARENNES-JARCY   Moulin de Jarcy

Comfortable restaurant with basic rooms/Cooking 1
Secluded/Terrace/Parking/Good value

Gilles and Claudine Le Moign own an amazing old *moulin*. The
minute mill is an island within two arms of the River Yerres;
the valley is wooded; to the north the tree-lined stream
meanders away into the distance; on the eastern bank are
pastures where geese, ducks, cows and ponies sun themselves;
and yet all this is only 25 miles from the heart of Paris.
Cooking is humdrum *Bourgeoise* with no second mortgages
needed: run-of-the-mill basics like *poulet rôti*, *gigot d'agneau
rôti*, *entrecôte grillée* and *pêche Melba*. (From the N6 Croix de
Villeroy traffic lights, head north-east on the D33 and pass
under rail bridge; mill 200 metres east of Bricorama.)
Menus A-B. Rooms (5) B. Cards Access, Visa.
Closed 1-21 Aug. 20 Dec-15 Jan. Mon/Tues (rooms). Wed/Thurs.
Post 50 rue Boieldieu, 91480 Varennes-Jarcy, Essonne.
Tel (1) 69 00 89 20. Mich 36/B4 (shown on the Michelin map).

10   ▲ see page 92   ▲ see page 30

The map shows locations including:

- Montbéliard
- Belfort
- Vesoul
- St-Hippolyte
- Cirque de Consolation
- Goumois
- Aubigney
- Besançon
- Maîche
- Le Noirmont
- Bonnevaux-le-Prieuré
- Fuans
- Saut du Doubs
- Mouthier-Haute-Pierre
- Arc-en-Senans
- Source du Lison
- Source de la Loue
- SUISSE
- Salins-les-Bains
- Arbois
- Oye-et-Pallet
- Pontarlier
- Poligny
- Cirque du Fer à Cheval
- Malbuisson
- Passenans
- Forêt de la Joux
- Cirque de Baume
- Champagnole
- Châtillon
- Courlans
- Hérisson
- St-Laurent-en-Grandvaux
- Crissier
- Lausanne
- Lons-le-Saunier
- Bonlieu
- Morez
- Montreux
- Lac de Vouglans
- Lac Léman
- St-Claude
- Col de la Faucille
- Ferney-Voltaire
- Divonne-les-Bains
- Gex
- GENEVE
- Charix
- Echallon
- Lac Genin
- Bourg-en-Bresse

Legend:
- ● Autoroute hotel
- ▲ Hotel/Rest (rooms)
- △ Restaurant only

0   10   20 Miles

▼ see page 330

The late Jean Robertson, at one time travel editor of the *Sunday Times*, penned these telling words over two decades ago: "France is, for me, the First Lady of Europe."

Nothing has changed. France remains as beguiling as ever, a country both deeply rural and highly civilised. An added plus is that the tourist "industry" is run by individuals for individuals. And, joy of joys, the seductive First Lady still clutches to her ample breasts endless delights – hidden corners where Nature's priceless legacies are ignored by all but a handful of enterprising visitors.

Please don't mistake the Jura for a rival of the Alps; at its highest the "mountain" range rises to 5636 ft. The hills are thickly wooded, carpeted with green pastures and interlaced with dozens of streams and rivers. As a bonus there are a few attractive lakes, varying in size from the tiniest pool to large man-made sheets of water.

The Jura is a tonic at any time. We've seen the hills in all seasons but it was on our last trip, during the mellow days of late October when the weather was warm, dry and kindly, that we saw the region at its best. The landscape dazzled. The primarily broadleaved forests were gigantic swathes of autumn colours, Kaffe Fassett designs of random hues and shades: bronze, saffron, old gold, ochre, russet, chilli red and copper. The bird life was amazing: buzzards, red kites, herons, peregrines, kingfishers and dippers commonplace.

I have divided the introduction into two parts: I'll start by describing the terrain in the southern half of the Jura, in the *département* of the same name; then I'll recall, in some detail, our most recent autumn exploration of the northern half of the region, a drive through the delicious *département* of the Doubs, named after the river of the same name.

Part one Start at the most minute of lakes. **Lac Genin** is an unspoilt emerald, protected by a circular couch of wooded cushions – beech, pines and spruce. A display board tells you about the local flora and fauna. During the week you're likely to have the lake to yourself; or you may have to share it with some goldcrests hovering around your head like humming birds. Lac Genin is a few kilometres north of the **A40** autoroute (junction 9, then east and north on the D95 to Charix).

Continue on to **St-Claude**. 200 years ago the town prospered because of its reputation for making the world's finest pipe briars. St-Claude tumbles down from the hills to the floor of the Bienne Valley; it was much loved by the author Nevil Shute. There's a pipe museum and a fine Gothic cathedral.

Explore a small semicircle of terrain to the east of St-Claude. First use the narrow lanes heading upstream through the Gorges de la Bienne; the D126 is perhaps the best choice. **Morez**, at the head of the valley, also prospered two centuries ago when the town became famous for the production of spectacle frames. Note how the railway line loops and climbs high above Morez through tunnels and across viaducts.

Now head south from Morez, first using the D25 and, later, the N5. The **Col de la Faucille** crosses the long eastern escarpment of the Jura; hereabouts are the highest summits of the range. The views east towards the Alps are great but they cannot compare with the panorama from the summit of Mont-Rond. Keen walkers can make the peak on foot; for others there's an easier hike up the mountain, courtesy of a *télécabine*. If **Lac Léman** has its all too regular hazy smog obscuring the views then don't bother with the ascent of Mont-Rond.

To the west of St-Claude the River **Ain** has been made to work for its living; along its length are several man-made lakes. The largest is **Lac de Vouglans**. The snaking lake is nothing to shout about scenically but is a magnet for watersports enthusiasts: sailing, water-skiing and swimming facilities are all available, as are a couple of excellent camp sites.

Much more rewarding, and seen at its best on foot, is the **Hérisson** Valley. Small the valley may be, only 20 km or so, but what a punch it packs. The short-lived river is at the heart of a triangle of country called the Région des Lacs; the smallest of them are at the western end of the Hérisson. Use the D326 south-east from Doucier and you'll pass a couple on the right. At the end of the road park your car and walk upstream. If you walk the entire valley to Ilay you'll be bowled over by a score or so of cascades; the Hérisson falls over 250 metres in three kilometres. For the lazy a 400-metre amble takes you from the car park to the best of the falls, the multi-stepped Cascade de l'Eventail. Of course the falls are at their very best after heavy rain.

The biggest of the lakes in the triangle is Lac de Chalain. In summer, watersports of all kinds ensure it's busy; but walks in the woods on the southern banks (alongside the D39E) are quiet enough. To the east, near the N5, is the Cascade de la Billaude, a thundering sight after heavy rain.

The next scenic "show" is the **Cirque de Baume**, the first of several *cirques* (amphitheatres) you'll encounter in the Jura. View this *cirque* from the belvedere at its southern end, high above the valley floor. Then descend to Baume-les-Messieurs, a tiny village where, from the 6th-century abbey, monks went west to establish the abbey at Cluny. At the head of the valley a waterfall gushes out of the rock face and tumbles over mossy rocks. This is the first of the many resurgent streams (*reculées*) you'll see – where water disappears underground miles away, high above the top of the *cirque*, to reappear in caves or falls at the bottom of the steep rock faces. They, too, are at their best after heavy rain.

Two further *cirques* await you nearby, the Cirque de Ladoye and the **Cirque du Fer à Cheval**. The latter is most certainly worth a detour; here you'll witness resurgent streams at their finest. Visit the Grande Source de la Cuisance at the Grottes des Planches, where man-made subterranean pathways share space with the turbulent, roaring stream.

Arbois, at the mouth of the Cirque du Fer à Cheval, is the town where Pasteur worked. It's celebrated, too, for its rosé and sparkling white wines and its own version of the legendary *vin jaune*. There will be plenty of chances for a *dégustation* (tasting) in the town; perhaps the best is at the shop of Henri Maire, the most famous of the Jura wine-making firms.

Two unusual small towns lie to the north of Arbois: **Salins-les-Bains**, a spa where salt has been mined since pre-Roman times and, a few kilometres to the north-west, the "salt" town of **Arc-en-Senans**, where you can still see the few buildings that remain of what, once, was going to be an 18th-century planned town, La Saline Royale – built by the visionary architect Claude-Nicolas Ledoux.

To the east of Salins-les-Bains and Arbois is the **Forêt de la Joux**, one of France's largest pine forests. Hidden within the 6,000 acres is an arboretum and the Sapin Président, a giant pine tree with a circumference of four metres (it's a long walk from the road). You'll note from the map that a railway runs through the forest: this is the main Paris, Dijon, Lausanne line and you're likely to see an express or TGV flash through the pine trees. Detour, too, to Nozeroy, a medieval village south of the forest.

Part two What follows is the topography within the Doubs *département*. I'll describe our last trip there which included the best of the sights and sounds (and smells).

Start the tour with a bang: aim for a startling viewpoint, the Roche du Prêtre, 35 miles east of **Besançon** and close to the junction of the D461 and D41. To your right is the dramatic **Cirque de Consolation**; far below, nestling under an eiderdown of tree tops, is the 17th-century Abbey of Notre Dame de Consolation. If luck is with you you may spot a *milan royale* (kite) gliding in the swirling thermals of the *cirque*. (On one day alone we counted over 30 birds of prey on our drive through the Jura forests.) Don't linger; retrace your steps on the D461 and use the D39 to descend to the abbey grounds, the source of the delectable **Dessoubre**, for me the most captivating of small French rivers.

"River" is an over-statement; the Dessoubre is no more than a 20-mile long stream, flowing north to join the River **Doubs** at **St-Hippolyte**. I defy any visitor not to be bewitched by first the abbey park, a wonderland of springs, waterfalls, grottoes and woodland paths, and then the Dessoubre Valley as the stream winds its way through meadows and under hillsides, wooded for almost every foot of the way to the Doubs.

The Dessoubre is tempting enough at any time of the year. You'll pass few houses and only one hamlet of any size, Rosureux. There are also one or two *auberges*, happy to serve you a *truite*, or some *brési* or a *saucisse* from Morteau. Occasionally you'll see newly-felled pine trees, their bark scraped away, and the air full of pine-smoke from the fires that foresters have lit to burn the surplus trimmings. There are a couple of small workshops alongside the river where furniture is made or where timber is cut into endless varieties of planks. And there's many a spot where you can paddle unseen. Why not put all your senses to the test? What is certain, too, is that you'll have the valley to yourself.

At St-Hippolyte head south-east to the Corniche de Goumois. Two km south of **Goumois** park in a viewpoint on your left, just as the D437 turns sharp right. The vista below and to the front of you is I think one of the most rejuvenating in France. Breathe in pure air as you take in the panorama: a combination of distant humming river, lush emerald pastures and huge duvets of trees, cascading down both sides of an immense, deep valley. Is this not an image of eternity?

In the Doubs you'll notice the huge chimneys that dominate most farms. Do visit one of them: La Ferme des Guinots, owned by the Guillaume family. You'll find it south-east of the cross-roads at Les Cerneux-Monnots, on the D414 from Charquemont to Le Russey (both south of **Maîche**); it's the first farm on the right-hand side of the D457. The chimney is called a *tué* or *tuyé*; you'll gasp at the size of the structure and the sheer number of hams and sausages that can be smoked within the high, dark cavern. You'll have the chance to try some Jura wine and to savour a tasty morsel or two (even a lunch perhaps) of *saucisse de Morteau* (also called *Jésus de Morteau*) – a super pork concoction; *jambon de tuyé* – smoked ham; and *brési* – wafer-thin slices of dried beef.

Don't miss the 30-metre high waterfall, the **Saut du Doubs**, where the river shoots forth a cascade of foaming water between steep walls of rock. An unmarked road takes you to within 200 metres of the cascade. Upstream the river changes its character. The Doubs takes the form of a narrow, winding lake, the Lac de Chaillexon; you can take boat trips from Villers-le-Lac at the southern end of the lake.

From Morteau to **Pontarlier** the Doubs is a gentle, relaxing river. The Lac de St-Point is a long lake with numerous restful vistas; use the road on the left bank, the D129. As a contrast take the steep road that climbs to the 4800-ft summit of Mont d'Or. On our last October visit, an hour before sunset, we were fortunate enough to see the 100-mile-long range of the Swiss and French Alps at their breathtaking best: the setting sun illuminated the entire mountain wall and the snow-topped peaks glowed pink as if a decorator had run a roller brush across the eastern horizon.

Two intriguing family businesses lie at the foot of Mont d'Or. First the Sancay Richard Fromagerie du Mont d'Or at Metabief (to the north of the village). Arrive at 9.30 a.m. any morning, except Sunday, and witness, from specially constructed galleries, the making of three superb Jura cheeses: Comté, a huge hard wheel; Morbier, an LP-sized record with an ash streak through the middle; and Mont d'Or, a creamy CD-sized fromage, made only from November to March.

Second, the Obertino Fonderie de Cloches (bell foundry) on the D437, three km south-west of **Malbuisson**. I guarantee that anyone entering their octagonal-shaped shop will not come out empty-handed; the range and types of bell are fascinating.

Finish your Doubs tour with a pulsating finale. The **Source du Lison**, west of Pontarlier, is a classic example of a Jura resurgent stream. Two caves feed the river; one, the Grotte Sarrazine, is a ten-minute walk from the road. The thundering roar of water blasting from the base of vertical rock slabs is a dramatic sight. A similar, less stunning version, is the "stepped" **Source de la Loue**, north of Pontarlier.

Track the Loue downstream, past **Mouthier-Haut-Pierre** and Ornans, to its confluence with the Lison, sparing a moment for the remarkable river reflection, the Miroir de Scey, just before Cléron. Use the D103 to Lizine and then the D135 north. Under no circumstances drive past the two *belvédères* north of Lizine: the first, the Piquette, a five-minute walk from the road, overlooks the luminous, bowling-green waters of the Loue hundreds of feet under the viewpoint; the other, the Moulin Sapin, is high above the Lison. I hope you have the luck, as we did, to watch a heron "fishing" far below you in the clear waters of the Loue. The spectacle was a fitting reminder that the Doubs is a land where Nature reigns supreme.

(Of the towns and resorts **Divonne-les-Bains** is a handsome, flower-filled spa, famed for its casino; **Lons-le-Saunier** has several old architectural treats; and Besançon has a fine site, old town, *citadelle* and museums.)

Markets Arbois (Tues and Fri); Champagnole (Sat); Divonne (Tues and Fri); Gex (Sat); Lons-le-Saunier (Thurs and Sat); Maîche (Wed and Sat); Morez (Sat); Morteau (Sat); Poligny (Mon and Fri); Pontarlier (Thurs and Sat); St-Claude (Thurs and Sat); Salins-les-Bains (Thurs and Sat).

Michelin green guide: Jura Franche-Comté.

Cheeses Cow's milk
Cancoillotte very fruity flavour, prepared from **Metton** (an unmoulded, recooked cheese) and looks like a cheese spread. It is available all through the year and is eaten warm in sandwiches or on slices of toast
Comté a hard, cooked cheese, made in great disks. Has holes the size of hazelnuts. Best seasons are summer, autumn and winter
Emmental Français – the French version; another hard, cooked cheese, also made in huge disks but with holes the size of walnuts
Gex (Bleu de) a *fromage persillé*, with blue veins, like the pattern of parsley. Made in large disks; at its best in summer and autumn
Morbier strong-flavoured thick disk with ash stripe through middle
Septmoncel (Bleu de) made in thick disks; blue veins, slightly bitter
Vacherin Mont-d'Or soft, mild and creamy; made in cylinders
Goat's milk
Chevret faint goat smell; small flat disk or square-shaped cheese

Swiss Cheeses
The main types of **Emmental** and **Gruyère** have many varieties – all superb; so is **Tête de Moine** (made north-east of Le Noirmont); others are **Vacherin Mont-d'Or**, **Tomme de Valbroye** and **Chèvre de Valois**

Regional Specialities
Brési wafer-thin slices of dried beef
Gougère hot cheese pastry – based on Comté cheese
Jésus de Morteau fat pork sausage smoked over pine and juniper
Poulet au vin jaune chicken, cream and *morilles*, cooked in *vin jaune*

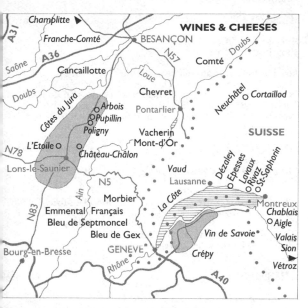

Wines

Whites and Rosés

The broadest AC classification is **Côtes du Jura**. Among the best wines are the refreshing rosés from **Arbois**, brownish-pink in colour, and the whites of **Poligny**, fragrant and light. Another AC is **L'Etoile** (just north of Lons-le-Saunier), where nice dry and sweet whites are made. There is also an **AC Arbois-Pupillin**, a small village to the south of Arbois.

The brightest star is a *vin jaune*, **AC Château-Châlon**, a rare wine, deep yellow, very dry and made from the Savagnin (Traminer) grape. **L'Etoile** and **Arbois** have their own versions of this *vin jaune*. A *vin de paille* (grapes dried on straw mats) is a very sweet, heady wine; *vin gris* is a pale rosé. Look out for the apéritif *macvin* – grape juice and *marc*.

Sparkling wines

Sparkling wines include **L'Etoile mousseux**, the **Côtes du Jura** and **Arbois mousseux** and the *vin fou* (mad wine) from Arbois.

Vins de Pays

Jura and **Franche-Comté** labels (**Champlitte** is a village).

Swiss Wines

Swiss wines are known by grape, place and type names. Chasselas is the main white grape: in **Valais** it's used to make **Fendant**; in **Vaud** it's **Dorin**; around Geneva **Perlan**.

Little red wine is made (Pinot Noir and/or Gamay grapes). Valais reds are called **Dôle**; Vaud reds are named **Salvagnin**.

Fine Valais wines come from **Sion**, **Vétroz** and, best of all, the **Domaine du Mont d'Or**. The best Vaud wines are from **Lavaux** (between Lausanne and Montreux) and its principal villages of **Dézaley**, **Rivaz**, **Epesses**, **St-Saphorin** and **Aigle**; **La Côte** (Vaud) is the area south-west of Lausanne. **Neuchâtel** makes reds and whites (best village – **Cortaillod**).

167

Autoroute Hotels

BESANCON

Simple hotel/Cooking 1
Parking/Good value

Leave A36 Besançon Centre exit. Hotel on south side of A36.
Menus A-B. Rooms (55) C. Disabled. Cards Access, Visa.
Post ZAC de Valentin, 25048 Besançon, Doubs. (En Route p 137)
Tel 81 53 52 22. Telex 361172. Fax 81 88 12 56. Mich 75/F4.
(Bookings: UK freephone 0800 897863)

BESANCON
Climat de France

Simple hotel/Cooking 1
Parking/Good value

A36 Besançon Centre exit. Hotel south of A36 and west of N57.
Menus A-B. Rooms (43) C. Disabled. Cards AE, Access, Visa.
Post Ecole Valentin, 25480 Misery-Salines, Doubs.
Tel 81 88 04 11. Telex 361651. Mich 75/F4.
(Bookings: UK 071 287 3181)

CRISSIER
Novotel

Very comfortable hotel/Cooking 1
Quiet/Terrace/Gardens/Swimming pool/Parking

Leave N1 autoroute Lausanne-Crissier exit. Hotel north-west
of exit, at Bussigny. Two-minute drive from Girardet rest.
Menus A (Swiss francs). Rooms (99) B (Swiss frs). Cards All.
Post CH1030 Bussigny, Switzerland.
Tel 21 701 28 71. Telex 459531. Fax 21 702 29 02. Mich 105/D1.
(Bookings: UK 071 724 1000; US toll free 800 221 4542)

FERNEY-VOLTAIRE
Novotel

Very comfortable hotel/Cooking 1
Terrace/Gardens/Swimming pool/Tennis/Parking

N1 (Swiss autoroute) Ferney-Voltaire exit. Head west, under
runway; after customs turn left (D35); hotel on right.
Menus B. Rooms (79) E. Disabled. Cards All.
Post 01210 Ferney-Voltaire, Ain.
Tel 50 40 85 23. Telex 385046. Fax 50 40 76 33. Mich 104/B3.
(Bookings: UK 071 724 1000; US toll free 800 221 4542)

MONTBELIARD
Ibis

Simple hotel/Cooking 1
Parking/Good value

Leave A36 Montbéliard exit. Hotel on west side of A36.
Menus A. Rooms (62) C. Disabled. Cards Access, Visa.
Post rue J.Foillet, 25200 Montbéliard, Doubs. (ER p 139)
Tel 81 90 21 58. Telex 361555. Fax 81 90 44 37. Mich 76/C3.
(Bookings: UK 071 724 1000; US toll free 800 221 4542)

ARBOIS   Jean-Paul Jeunet

Very comfortable hotel/Cooking 4
Gardens/Garage/Lift

What dramatic changes Anne and I found on our most recent visit to this Jura culinary shrine. The first change is the least important: the name Le Paris has been dropped. Next, the 17th-century building has been refurbished from chimney top to front doorstep; bedrooms have been modernised; restored stone and timber have given the ground floor a cosmetic face-lift and, most important of all, Jean-Paul Jeunet has taken over from his larger-than-life father, André.

How rewarding it is to watch a formidably talented son climbing far loftier culinary peaks than those scaled by his father. In this J-P is like his pal, Pierre Carrier at Chamonix. I'll stick my neck out and guarantee that the young chef will emerge as one of France's best by the year 2000.

His invention is manifest, his conviction is total and the complicated execution is faultless; this is *cuisine moderne* at its best. Many subtle touches impress: among them *foie de canard* in a caramelised *macvin jus* (local *marc* plus grape juice); a *crépinette de truite Fario rôtie* accompanied by a *galette de fanes* (a tricky assembly; ask Jean-Paul to explain how he does it and to list the ingredients); grilled *langoustines* with a *galette de céréales*; a magical modern-day version of *poularde en gigot au vin jaune et morilles* with a mound of basmati rice laced with herbs and spices; and a *galette moëlleuse de noisettes et glace pistache*.

What else appeals? There's a superb cellar and a *caveau de dégustation* where you can sample and buy the Jura's best wines. And, last but not least, there's Jean-Paul's wife, Nadine, who speaks fluent English (she worked for a long time in London and, by coincidence, went to school with Pierre Carrier in Chamonix); and Claude, a super English-speaking manageress, as professional as any you'll encounter.

Menus B-F. Rooms (17) C-E. Cards Access, DC, Visa.
Closed Dec. Jan. Tues. Wed midday (not sch. hols & Sept).
Post 9 rue de l'Hôtel de Ville, 39600 Arbois, Jura.
Tel 84 66 05 67. Fax 84 66 24 20. Mich 89/E3.

AUBIGNEY   Auberge du Vieux Moulin

Comfortable restaurant with rooms/Cooking 2
Quiet/Gardens/Parking

The mill was built in 1794 and, after seeing service as a sawmill for almost a century, was converted to a *restaurant avec chambres* in 1967. The property has been owned by the same family since day one. Today Louise Mirbey and her *cuisinière* daughter, Elisabeth, are *les patronnes*. Cooking encompasses both classical and regional dishes. Bearing in mind the *moulin* is on the borders of both Burgundy and the Jura you'll then grasp why regional classics as diverse as *matelote* (see Burgundy specialities; here with *anguilles*) and *escargots* will appear side by side with *morilles à la creme au vin jaune*.

Menus B-D. Rooms (7) D. Cards All.
Post 70140 Aubigney H.-Saône. (Between Gray and Pesmes.)
Tel 84 31 61 61. Fax 84 31 21 75. Mich 75/D4.

BONLIEU   La Poutre

Comfortable restaurant with rooms/Cooking 2-3
Parking

Our lunch was a nostalgic memory of the Jura we first fell in love with 30 years ago. Old fashioned traditions and skills in a timbered dining room and cooking, from the capable hands of Denis Moureaux, which pleased with both regional and classical delights. *Morilles* seem to accompany everything: sautéed scallops, *tournedos à la crème*, a *filet de canette rôti* and a *ragoût d'escargots* all get the treatment. We opted for a locally-caught *truite aux morilles* and an appetite satisfying combination of *langoustines aux choux et lentilles et son saucisson de Morteau*. We needed to walk off the latter dish. What better than the short drive north to the Hérisson (the lane by the restaurant) where we parked and walked from the Saut de la Forge downstream to the Grand Saut; an exhilarating head clearer and far more effective than an Alka-Seltzer.
Menus B-E. Rooms (10) B-D. Cards Access, Visa.
Closed 11 Nov to 10 Feb.
Post 39130 Bonlieu, Jura.
Tel 84 25 57 77. Mich 89/F4.

BONNEVAUX-LE-PRIEURE   Le Moulin du Prieuré

Comfortable restaurant with rooms/Cooking 2
Quiet/Gardens/Parking

North of Ornans and alongside the River Brème, the mill dates back to the 13th-century. Bedrooms are in bungalows. Cooking is classical and regional: one satisfying surprise was to see *boeuf Angus poêlé* on the handsome menu. Ask Renée and Marc Gatez to send you details of what must be the finest fly fishing break in France: at their remote Lodge de la Piquette. The beat is on the most deserted and idyllic stretch of the Loue. Piquette: where have you read the word? I refer you to the last couple of paragraphs of the Jura introduction. Why not share the fish in the Loue with a heron?
Menus C-D. Rooms (8) D. Cards All.
Closed 11 Nov to 10 Mar. Sun evg. Mon.
Post 25620 Bonnevaux-le-Prieuré, Doubs.
Tel 81 59 21 47. Fax 81 59 28 79. Mich 90/A1.

CHARIX   Auberge du Lac Genin

Very simple hotel/Cooking 1
Secluded/Terrace/Parking/Good value

If you have *Hidden France* turn to page 26: Jean Godet's *auberge* is reflected in the waters of the emerald gem, Lac Genin. (Read the introduction for details of the exquisite lake.) The *auberge* was originally a farm, built by Jean's father, Gustave. *Bourgeoise* basics and grills *au feu de bois*.
Menus A. Rooms (7) A-C. Cards Access, Visa.
Closed Mid Oct to end Nov. Sun evg. Mon.
Post Lac Genin, 01130 Charix, Ain.
Tel 74 75 52 50. Mich 103/F3.

CHATILLON   Chez Yvonne

Simple restaurant with rooms/Cooking 1-2
Secluded/Terrace/Swimming pool/Good value

When we first visited the little *logis*, 25 years ago, Yvonne Peltier was *la cuisinière*. Born in 1901, she worked for 50 years as a chef winning, not just a Michelin star, but also, in 1977, an *Ordre National du Mérité*. She died a few months after receiving the award. Madeleine Garnier continued the traditions started by Mme Peltier. Chez Yvonne was a big favourite with readers from 1980 to 1986. Then, with new owners, standards went up in smoke. In 1989 the dynamic duo of Renée and Jean-Louis Darbos bought the property; they've injected a lifesaving transfusion into the veins of the white-washed *auberge*, alongside the Ain. Cooking is *Bourgeoise* and regional: *morilles* feature, of course, as do *friture* from the river and *truite au vin jaune*. Service can be sloppy.
Menus A-C. Rooms (8) C. Cards Access, Visa.
Closed Dec to mid Mar. Mon.
Post 39130 Châtillon, Jura. (On D39, east of village.)
Tel 84 25 70 82. Mich 89/F4 (Village E of Lons-le-Saunier.)

CIRQUE DE CONSOLATION   Hôtel de la Source

Simple restaurant with rooms/Cooking 1-2
Secluded/Parking/Good value

Hidden among the woods above the abbey park. The dining room is on stilts, perched above a stream feeding the Dessoubre; after heavy rain the water is a cascading cacophony. M et Mme Faivre have retired; Mlle Marie-Jo Joliot is the new owner. She's made many improvements. *Bourgeois* and regional *plats*.
Menus A-B. Rooms (10) B-C. Cards Access, Visa.
Closed Mon (Oct to May).
Post Cirque de Consolation, 25390 Orchamps-Vennes, Doubs.
Tel 81 43 55 38. Mich 90/C1 (just off D39; marked on map).

COURLANS   Auberge de Chavannes

Very comfortable restaurant/Cooking 3-4
Terrace/Gardens/Parking

At last the French foodie Mafia is waking up to the polished, assured skills of Pierre Carpentier, a master of classical traditions but confident enough to introduce a slightly lighter personal style to his specialities. Examples such as a punchy *terrine de lapin fermier, pickles de légumes*; an intense, spiky *canêton rôti au caramel d'épices, chutney de pommes*; and a tantalisingly tasty *soufflé au chocolat amer*. Monique Carpentier is as elegant as her dining room; she has an encyclopaedic knowledge of Jura wines so accept her advice. (Rooms? Nouvel Hôtel, a 5-min. drive away, at 50 rue Lecourbe, 39570 Lons-le-Saunier: Tel 84 47 20 67; Rooms B-C.)
Menus B-D (book ahead). Cards Access, Visa.
Closed Feb. Sun evg. Mon.
Post RN78, Courlans, 39570 Lons-le-Saunier, Jura.
Tel 84 47 05 52. Mich 89/D4. (On N78, 6 km west of Lons.)

Hotels and Restaurants

CRISSIER   Girardet

Very comfortable restaurant/Cooking 5

In the previous four editions of *French Leave* I devoted more space to Girardet than any other *cuisinier*. Any of you who bought one or all of the quartet will know already that, for both Anne and me, the peerless Frédy Girardet is our favourite chef, a *cuisinier extraordinaire*. A reader expressed our dilemma succinctly: how can you explain perfection?

Arguably two certain facts have emerged during the 12 years since I published the initial *French Leave*. First, I've received more letters about readers' visits to Crissier than any of the French three-star Gods; my guess is that I've had several hundred reports, a figure which is many times more than the feedback for any of the French superstars. Second, and even more revealing, I've only ever received one sour letter about Girardet, this from an American about ten years ago. I can't say that for any of the French greats.

Well, how do you explain perfection? I'm certainly not up to the impossible task. All I can attempt to do is to list just a few of the ingredients that make Girardet the world's greatest "French" chef and his restaurant such an acclaimed success. When you talk to the man you instinctively sense honesty, humility and a deep love for his *métier*; his eyes, his hands and his deep, calm voice are instantly reassuring and his character and strength of personality are like the sun. (He's a man of few words. One couple, when he came to their table at the end of the meal, explained that they were on honeymoon. *"Bon"* was the single word response. A year later they returned to celebrate their anniversary. Once again they explained the reason to Frédy. Can you guess his one word reply? In replying to my questionnaire I received a single sentence response: *"Je vous fais savoir qu'il n'y à aucun changement pour mon établissement."* That's Frédy to a tee: efficient, economical and precise; and you don't take offence.)

Frédy's always *in situ*. As a business entrepreneur he's the antithesis of Paul Bocuse. His staff, led by the incomparable Louis Villeneuve, adore him. Frédy's a notoriously tough boss; but employees stay with him for years, always the acid test. By French standards the restaurant is quite dour. But there's an animated buzz in the air, helped no end by a largely Swiss clientele and waiters who are neither supercilious nor stuffy. There's none of that penguin stiffness, nose-in-the-air pomposity and precious pretentiousness which afflicts most three-star shrines. Another plus is the pace of serving the meal; here it's spot-on, not rushed as it so often is.

Girardet is the supreme *cuisine moderne* chef. He's an inventor and technician second to none, a scientist able to turn his innovative concepts into reality and an artist *par excellence*. He's the chef who, almost without exception, is most respected by his peers. I've asked enough of them to be certain as I can be of that statement of fact.

Expensive? Yes, crunchingly so. But you'll not regret the financial sacrifice. Rooms? Use the Autoroute hotel (Novotel), a two-minute drive away. A final caveat: book months ahead.
Menus B-C (Swiss francs). Cards None accepted.
Closed Xmas to mid Jan. 3 wks Aug. Sun. Mon.
Post CH1023 Crissier, Switzerland. (North-west of Lausanne.)
Tel 21 634 05 05 or 21 634 05 06. Mich 105/D1.

172

ECHALLON   Auberge de la Semine

Very simple restaurant with basic rooms/Cooking 2
Terrace/Parking/Good value

Simple? Yes, but what a terrific job Bernard Roux does; and
his wife, Françoise, is a friendly soul. A classical meal of
*terrine de canard, gâteau de foies de volaille, volaille à la crème
et morilles* and *framboises Melba* was perfection.
Menus A-B. Rooms (11) B. Cards Access, Visa.
Closed 1st 3 wks Dec. Sun evg. Tues (not high season).
Post 01490 Echallon, Ain. (North of St-Germain-de-Joux.)
Tel 75 76 48 75. Mich 104/A3. (On D49, off D55.)

FUANS   Patton

Simple hotel/Cooking 1-2
Parking/Good value

Claude and Marie-Madeleine Gaiffe are value-for-money fanatics
at their smart *logis*; and what a happy welcome clients get.
Bourgeoise, classical and regional cuisine. Great favourite.
Menus B-C. Rooms (10) B-C. Cards All.
Closed 10 Nov to 9 Dec. Mon (Oct to June).
Post Fuans, 25390 Orchamps-Vennes, Doubs.
Tel 81 43 51 01. Mich 90/C1. (East of Orchamps-Vennes.)

GOUMOIS   Taillard

Comfortable hotel/Cooking 2-3
Secluded/Terrace/Gardens/Swimming pool/Parking

A blissful spot, much loved by my family and readers. Alas,
many nigglish reports have surfaced of late. Readers feel
there's a lack of warmth and stand-offishness about Jean-
François (he's the artist and chef) and his second wife, Eliane;
they took over in 1987. The Taillard family have owned the
hotel since 1875. Classical and regional fare.
Menus B-D. Rooms (17) C-E. Cards All.
Closed Mid Nov to Feb. Wed (Mar, Oct and Nov).
Post 25470 Goumois, Doubs.
Tel 81 44 20 75. Fax 81 44 26 15. Mich 77/D4.

MALBUISSON   Jean-Michel Tannières

Comfortable restaurant with rooms/Cooking 3
Garage/Parking

Jean-Michel and Fabienne have run the family *pension* since
1982. What changes: a new name (was Bellevue); classical and
regional *plats*; refurbished rooms; and, in 1992, a new dining
room and kitchen. A *supreme de sandre au vin jaune* (crisp,
grilled skin and a luscious sauce) remains a vivid memory.
Menus B-D. Rooms (6) C-D. Cards All.
Closed Xmas. 5-23 Jan. 20-30 Apl. Mon. Tues *midi* (Sept-June).
Post 25160 Malbuisson, Doubs.
Tel 81 69 30 89. Fax 81 69 39 16. Mich 90/B3.

MOUTHIER-HAUTE-PIERRE   La Cascade

Comfortable hotel/Cooking 2
Fairly quiet/Parking/Good value

Built in 1981 the *logis* is over 100 metres above the River
Loue; views of the wooded valley are superb. In summer the
dining room gets stuffy as windows stay closed (to keep flies
out). Helpful René Savonet juggles *Bourgeoise*, classical and
regional balls: *truite belle meunière* and *croûte aux morilles à
la crème* are typical. Service can be slow. Popular VFB base.
Menus B-C. Rooms (23) C. Disabled. Cards Access, Visa.
Closed Mid Nov to mid Feb.
Post 25920 Mouthier-Haute-Pierre, Doubs.
Tel 81 60 95 30. Fax 81 60 94 55. Mich 90/B2.

LE NOIRMONT   La Gare

Very comfortable restaurant with rooms/Cooking 4
Terrace/Parking

Much the most enjoyable part of our publishing enterprise is
the satisfaction which comes from rooting-out burgeoning
culinary talent. Innovation, excitement, enthusiasm and
workaholic effort are the clues which distinguish young men
and women with their feet planted firmly on the success
ladder. One such culinary genius is the Swiss Georges Wenger.
    Wenger was born in Le Noirmont in 1954; his father was the
village baker. After compulsory military service he spent long
training stints in Switzerland, Germany, Britain and France.
He returned with his sweet German wife, Andrea, to Le Noirmont
in 1982. At first the new enterprise was no more than a café
with Georges cooking upstairs on a wood-burning stove in the
couple's tiny kitchen. But he soon made an impact, despite the
remote site. Today the dining room, the three luxury bedrooms
(new in 1992) and his modern repertoire are all a world away
from his early days. Both Georges and Andrea speak English.
    He's as creative and subtle as any young French chef and his
technical wizardry matches that of the local watchmakers at
La Chaux. The most striking aspect of his craft is the care the
gentle, quietly-spoken chef takes over small details. You see
and taste the precision in his breads; in his appetisers; in his
petits fours; in his delicately contrived vegetables; and in the
clever use he makes of local produce and unfashionable local
fruits (like crab apples, *fleurs de sureau*, *damassine*, sloes and
bourgeons (buds) *de sapin*). La Gare is one of our greatest
favourites. We have just one word of advice: GO.
Menus A-B (Sw F). Rooms (3) B-C (SF). Cards AE, Access, Visa.
(Room prices include super Swiss bkfts. Simpler, cheaper
rooms available at Hôtel du Soleil. Wengers will book if asked.)
Closed Mid Mar to mid Apl. Sun evg. Monday.
Post CH2725 Le Noirmont, Switzerland. (NE La Chaux-de-Fonds.)
Tel 039 53 11 10. Fax 039 53 10 59. Mich 91/D1.
(An idea. Dinner & room at La Gare. Next morning take marked
walk to La Goule on the Doubs; allow 1½ hrs for descent. Lunch
at Eric Wenger's remote riverside rest (Georges' brother). His
wife, Marlies, is the chef: relish *truite*, *ombre*, *brochet* and
jambon. 2-hr walk to Goumois; Swiss post bus to Saignelégier;
train back to Le Noirmont. Dinner & room at La Gare. Heaven!)

174

OYE-ET-PALLET   **Parnet**

Comfortable hotel/Cooking 1-2
Gardens/Swim pool/Tennis/Garage/Parking/Good value

A spick and span fourth generation family *logis* where Yvette
and Christian Parnet are friendly hosts. The pool is heated
(28C in summer, 31C in winter). Classical and regional dishes;
Jésus de Morteau vignerone is mouthwatering and champion.
Menus A-C. Rooms (18) C-D. Cards Access, Visa.
Closed 20 Dec to end Jan. Sun evg & Mon (not sch. hols).
Post 25160 Oye-et-Pallet, Doubs.
Tel 81 89 42 03. Mich 90/B3.

PASSENANS   **Revermont**

Comfortable hotel/Cooking 2
Secluded/Terrace/Gardens/Swimming pool/Tennis/Lift
Garage/Parking/Good value

The facilities are endless at this unattractive, modern *relais*
recommended in both *Hidden France* and *FL3*. Cooking (regional,
classical and *Bourgeoise*) is on the up-and-up; especially good
is Bresse poultry with *vin jaune et morilles*.
Menus A-C. Rooms (28) C-D. Cards Access, Visa.
Closed Jan & Feb. Sun evg & Mon (Oct to Mar).
Post 39230 Passenans, Jura. (South-west of Poligny.)
Tel 84 44 61 02. Fax 84 44 64 83. Mich 89/E3.

ST-CLAUDE   **Au Retour de la Chasse**

Comfortable hotel/Cooking 1-2
Quiet/Tennis

A chalet-style hotel five km south of St-Claude. Smartish
exterior but banal interior. One additional plus: there's an
entertaining pitch and putt course behind the hotel. Cooking?
Bourgeoise and the odd Jura *plat*. Some rooms have *cuisinettes*.
Menus B-D. Rooms (16) B-D. Cards All.
Closed 19-29 Dec. Sun evg & Mon (mid Sept to mid June).
Post Villard-St-Sauveur, 39200 St-Claude, Jura.
Tel 84 45 44 44. Fax 84 45 13 95. Mich 104/A2. (On D290.)

ST-LAURENT-EN-GRANDVAUX   **Moulin des Truites**
Bleues
Very comfortable restaurant with rooms/Cooking 1-2
Parking

Pluses? River, *cascade* (the Lemme falls 15 metres) and an
historical site (remains of Roman watchtower). The tag Rococo
could apply to both the décor (extravagant and fussy) and the
classical cooking, brightened up by Jura dishes: *truite grillée
aux amandes*, *écrevisses au vin jaune* (both trout and crayfish
come from the mill's fish farm) and *tarte Tatin*.
Menus B-D. Rooms (20) E-F. Cards All.
Post 39150 St-Laurent-en-Grandvaux, Jura. (On N5, 6 km to N.)
Tel 84 60 83 03. Telex 360443. Mich 104/B1.

175

LANGUEDOC-ROUSSILLON

I'll start this regional introduction with an acerbic aside. Dive off briefly from the **A9** autoroute and you'll grasp immediately why the European Community's Common Agricultural Policy (CAP) should be renamed "Conman Agricultural Policy".

Draw a parallel line 25 miles or so to the north-west of the Mediterranean beaches. In that mass of *pays* vines grow everywhere, seemingly in every nook and cranny. I call it *"Vinsee"*, Europe's vast sea of wine and just one of the bottomless lakes into which our taxes are poured. Europe's 10 million farmers benefit by an average of £7,000 a year each from the CAP. A large slice of that largesse, conned from taxpayers, lands up in this region, where much of the wine is turned into alcohol.

For most motorists the same strip of coastal country is Languedoc-Roussillon. Usually holidaymakers will head for the Med beaches, packing themselves like sardines on the crowded sands. (The vast majority will not be aware that burglaries from cars and property have reached epidemic proportions: so beware.) Visitors from northern climes start their summer breaks with skins the colour of vanilla, quickly passing through the strawberry stage and, by the end of their holiday, will hope to return home with chocolate tans: the three phases resemble the layers of a Neapolitan ice cream.

The coastline is not my cup of tea. The hideous concrete bunkers which line the shore are a world apart from the "real" Languedoc-Roussillon which lies to the west of the A9. The juxtaposition of the two contrasting areas is a startling revelation. I'm always impatient to head inland.

The region is made up of five *départements*: Lozère, Gard,

Within the map image the following labels appear:

▲ see page 232 — Grotte des Demoiselles — see page 312 ▶
Rogeret des Cévennes — Pélardon — **St-Martin-de-Londres** — NIMES — Costières de Nîmes
• Sylvanès — Montpeyroux — St-Guilhem — ○Pic-St-Loup — Clairette○
• Brusque — St-Saturnin○ — ○ St-Drézery — St-Christol○ — de — Bellegarde
St-Guiraud △ — Vérargues○ — ▲9 Lunel
Mourèze ← — • Aniane — ○La Méjanelle
Clermont-l'Hérault — Gignac — St-Georges — **Montpellier**
Cabrières ○ — -d'Orques ○Mireval — ● Aigues-
Clairette du — ○Frontignan — Mortes
Languedoc — **Bouziques** ▲ — Sète
N112 — Picpoul de Pinet○ — ▲**Florensac** — ● Autoroute hotel
Béziers — Agde○ — ■**Marseillan** — ■ Base hotel
A9 — ▲ Hotel/Rest (rooms)
A61 Narbonne● — △ Restaurant only
Méditerranée — 0   10   20 Miles

Hérault, Aude and Pyrénées-Orientales. Languedoc derived from the name of the Provençale language where "*oc*" meant "yes", rather than the northern "*oui*". Roussillon is the terrain south of **Carcassonne** and **Narbonne**.

I'll not be too brutal about the coastline and the immediate hinterland. I described **Nîmes** and **Aigues-Mortes** in Provence; don't bypass either. Neither must you miss **Montpellier**, the "Oxford of France": see the Promenade du Peyrou; the equally inspiring Le Vieux Montpellier to the immediate east – narrow medieval lanes with ancient houses; and, on the eastern boundary of the old town, the celebrated Musée Fabre, the home of many memorable paintings.

Carcassonne, too, is another man-made thriller. The Cité was restored by Viollet-le-Duc as recently as the last century; but don't be put off, the walled fortifications are a superb sight, especially so in the evenings when they are brilliantly floodlit. The view from the **A61** is as good as any.

Perpignan, overwhelmed by traffic these days, reminds you vividly that it is a Catalane city: cope with the traffic and you'll be caught up in the throbbing vitality of the place. To the north of the city, alongside the A9, is **Salses** "castle"; once this was a vital strategic site and the fortress design has more of a Spanish influence than French.

The coastal town which particularly appeals to me is the fishing port of **Collioure**, close to the Spanish border. Famed for its clear light, the place became, at the turn of the century, a favourite of the Fauvist artists (vivid colours; from *fauve* – literally "wild beast") and Braque, Chagall, Matisse and Picasso all painted here.

I'll now highlight some other sights, both man-made and natural, in the hidden "green" corners of the rich inland tapestry of treasures. I'll start in Languedoc.

Let's assume you are based at or near **Clermont-l'Hérault**, west of Montpellier, for a few days. One day you could drive north from Lamalou-les-Bains, a spa with modern baths and a casino. Use the D180, west of Lamalou.

The climb of the **Monts de l'Espinouse** is a delight at any time of the year: in spring wild flowers abound; in high summer heather sparkles on the Sommet de l'Espinouse; and, in the autumn, thousands of sweet-chestnut trees cover the hills, their unopened nuts glistening in the sun like a million yellowy-green tennis balls.

Shortly after the Col des Princes turn left on to a small crescent-shaped lane which leads to the Forêt des Ecrivains Combattants. In March 1930 the woods here were literally washed away by rain. The new forest commemorates the lives of 560 writers killed during the 1914-18 war.

Detour to tiny Douch, at the head of an emerald valley; in October drifts of lilac-tinted autumn crocuses shine brightly. Carry on, using the D12 which snakes down to **Brusque**.

The Cistercian abbey at **Sylvanès** is an austere yet graceful building. The abbey took 100 years to complete, work finishing in 1252. Many of you will already know the inspiring story of how a cathedral-sized organ was built in the small Gascony town of Plaisance. Now Daniel Birouste, the young builder of that glorious organ, has made a start on an even more ambitious project at Sylvanès; the work will be carried out at his ten-person strong workshop in Plaisance.

The abbey is already renowned for the highly successful musical events held in the acoustically perfect, high-vaulted interior. Michel Wolkowitsky, the artistic director, is the charismatic engine behind the fund-raising organ project, an instrument which will have no less than 58 stops and over 5,000 pipes. Like us, you can have your name engraved on one of the pipes; all you have to do is part with 300 francs. Write to Michel, Abbey de Sylvanès, 12360 Camarès.

A second day could be put to good use exploring the area near Clermont. Two vineyards merit your attention: the first the now celebrated Mas de Daumas Gassac (between **Gignac** and **Aniane**) – its humble *vin de pays* bottle label makes nonsense of the quality of the contents; the second an up and coming young wine-maker, Jullien Olivier, at the Mas Jullien, Jonquières, north-west of Gignac.

Just west of Clermont are a couple of unusual sites. Villeneuvette is a tiny, 17th-century planned "new town"; built for workers weaving woollen cloth, the place is in a time-warp. The Cirque de **Mourèze** is a battlefield of gigantic, dolomitic-shaped rocks; one needle has a fort on the top.

A third day could be spent heading north from Clermont: stopping first at the Grotte de Clamouse, full of curious formations and some unusually-coloured stalactites; then at the Romanesque abbey church and perched village of **St-Guilhem-le-Désert**; and, finally, at the "cathedral" of the **Grotte des Demoiselles**, perhaps France's most spectacular example of subterranean formations.

The final day will be a dramatic contrast from the Midi *garrigue* (scrub). Start at the **Gorges d'Héric**. The concreted walk from the car park is long and steep. A river weaves a tortuous path between massive boulders. In spring, after heavy rain, the jumping-jack waters spit and sizzle; in summer and autumn the gentle trickle is a lifeless squib.

From **St-Pons** use the D907 north to the Col du Cabaretou. The views south are sensational. So is the change in scenery. This is cool, green alpine terrain, the road running through forests of proud trees. The two lakes to the east and west of **La Salvetat** are extra pleasures. The countryside north to **Lacaune** (reputed for its *charcuterie*) is like being in Wales; slate roofs help the illusion. In late spring the road verges on the D607 are ribbons of wild flowers.

The run west from La Salvetat, through the wooded Agout Valley and past Brassac brings you to the **Sidobre**, a small ring of hills just east of **Castres**. There you'll find, among the trees, all sorts of oddly-shaped rocks; the strangest is the amusingly named Peyro-Clabado, an oversize tank sitting on top of a couple of Minis. Only the Goya Museum makes a detour to Castres worthwhile. Then head for **Albi**.

The massive, fortress-like cathedral, built of red brick and dominating the town, is a must. The exterior gives no clue to the surprises awaiting you in the glorious interior: frescoes, statuary, a fine choir and stone screen are just some of the highlights. The Palais de la Berbie, alongside the Tarn, houses many of Toulouse-Lautrec's paintings; the artist was born in the town. The new bypass is a welcome bonus.

Roussillon, too, provides a wide spectrum of largely-ignored treats. First, visit the 800-year-old Abbaye de **Fontfroide** in an isolated setting south-west of Narbonne, once a Cistercian monastery, now privately owned. Then head south to the small village of **Tautavel**, about 25 km north-west of Perpignan. In 1971, in a cave near the village, the skull of a 20-year-old man was discovered, an individual who had lived 450,000 years earlier. A skilfully-designed museum, above the village, explains the story of Europe's first *Homo erectus*.

West of Tautavel make the short trip north from the D117 to two ruined Cathar fortresses: **Peyrepertuse** is atop a high granite ridge; **Quéribus** resembles a fingernail stuck to a rocky finger. (Other Cathar castles are **Quérigut**, in the Aude Valley; isolated, lofty Termes, north of Peyrepertuse; and **Montségur**, the last fortress to fall.) Neither the Gorges de Galamus nor the Grau de Maury are worth the detour.

Don't miss unnerving **Rennes-le-Château** (north of **Quillan**), a hill-top village which played such an important part in the controversial book, *The Holy Blood and the Holy Grail*; and modern-day **Montaillou** (south-west of Quillan), a high-altitude hamlet which was the subject of the classic *Montaillou* (Penguin), a fascinating story of the Cathars in this remote spot during the period 1294-1324.

The country encircling the **Pic du Canigou**, west of Collioure, includes **Céret** with a Museum of Modern Art (the Tech Valley is renowned for cherry blossom); **Prades**, famed for an annual music festival; the priory at Serrabone, noted for its interior; and **Vernet-les-Bains**, a small pleasant spa and perched high above it, the exquisite remote abbey of St-Martin-du-Canigou. Further west is the Cerdagne, a verdant, mountain plateau: **Font-Romeu** is a high-altitude modern summer and winter resort. Use the exciting *Canari* metre-gauge train from Villefranche (427m) to reach the Cerdagne (1592m).

To the north-west and south of **Foix** are a handful of celebrated underground caves. The most famous are: the Grotte de **Niaux**; the **Lombrives** caves, Europe's largest (both near Ussat); the subterranean river at **Labouiche**; and the Grotte du **Mas-d'Azil**, towards the **Garonne** Valley.

I have left until last what one reader described as "the finest 100-mile drive in France." I did this same drive one April day a decade ago. From just north of **Tarascon**-sur-Ariège take the D20 "Route des Corniches", high above the River Ariège; past Montaillou and then, just before **Belcaire**, drop down into the Gorges du Rebenty (D20 and D107); and, from **Axat**, south up the Haute Vallée de l'Aude.

Markets Agde (Thurs); Carcassonne (Tues, Thurs & Sat); Céret (Sat); Collioure (Wed & Sun); Frontignan (Thurs & Sat); Quillan (Wed & Sat); Sète (Wed & Fri).

Michelin green guides: Gorges du Tarn & Pyrénées Roussillon.

Cheeses Cow's milk
Chester Français French Cheshire cheese from Castres and Gaillac
Montségur bland, pressed and uncooked disk
Les Orrys strong-flavoured, big disk; drink with fruity Corbières
Goat's milk
Pélardon a *generic* name; small disks, nutty-tasting and soft. A similar, related cheese is **Rogeret des Cévennes**

Regional Specialities
Aïgo Bouido garlic soup. A marvellous, aromatic dish; the garlic is boiled, so its impact is lessened. Served with bread
Boles de picoulat small balls of chopped-up beef and pork, garlic and eggs – served with tomatoes and parsley
Bouillinade a type of *bouillabaisse*; with potatoes, oil, garlic and onions
Boutifare a sausage-shaped pudding of bacon and herbs
Cargolade snails, stewed in wine
Millas cornmeal porridge
Ouillade heavy soup of bacon, *boutifare*, leeks, carrots and potatoes
Touron a pastry of almonds, pistachio nuts and fruit

Wines
This is the land of *Vins de Pays* and *Vin Ordinaire*. The vast majority of table wines which French people drink with their everyday meals come from this huge area, part of the Midi.
Reds
Some good, strong reds are made: **Côtes du Roussillon**, **Côtes du Roussillon Villages** (25 villages share this AC; they make wines with a higher alcohol content and yield less wine per acre),

Caramany and **Latour-de-France** (these two villages can couple their own names to the general AC) have AC classifications. Other AC wines include **Corbières** (soft and fruity), **Minervois** (dry), **Fitou** (near the coast and the same AC is shared by the countryside encircling Tuchan) and **Collioure**. VDQS reds include **Cabardès**, **Côtes du Cabardès et de l'Orbiel** and **Côtes de la Malepère**; whites and rosés are also made.

A vast AC area to the north is the **Coteaux du Languedoc**: scattered throughout it are many individual *communes*, taking either the general classification or their own AC; among the latter are **St-Chinian** and **Faugères**. Among the former, coupling their village names to the AC Coteaux du Languedoc, are: **Cabrières**, **La Clape**, **Montpeyroux**, **Picpoul-de-Pinet**, **Pic-Saint-Loup**, **Quatourze**, **St-Drézéry**, **St-Georges-d'Orques** (just west of Montpellier), **St-Saturnin**, **La Méjanelle**, **St-Christol** and **Vérargues** (the last three can also have **Côteaux de** with the village name).

Wine classified as Languedoc-Roussillon but in territory within my Provence region is **Costières de Nîmes** (mainly reds and rosés); an area previously called Costières du Gard.

Whites

Mainly sparkling wines are produced in the Aude Valley around Limoux: the ACs are **Blanquette de Limoux** (*méthode champenoise*), **Blanquette Méthode Ancestrale** (made in traditional, local way), **Crémant de Limoux** and **Limoux** (still). Other ACs are **Clairette du Languedoc** and **Clairette de Bellegarde** (east of Nîmes); these get their names from the Clairette grape (used for many French vermouths). A white **Picpoul de Pinet** is made from Picpoul, the Armagnac grape. A *vin vert*, from Roussillon, is a light, refreshing white.

Natural Sweet Wines (Vins Doux Naturels)/Liqueur Wines

Unusual AC wines to look out for are the rich, golden **Muscats** of **Lunel**, **Rivesaltes**, **Frontignan**, **Mireval** and **St-Jean-de-Minervois**; fortified wines, rich in sugar and with alcohol added – they are ideal *apéritifs* (made from Muscat grapes). Similar wines, but darker in colour, like port, and made principally from the Grenache and Malvoisie grapes, are **Banyuls**, **Banyuls Grand Cru**, **Maury**, **Rivesaltes**, **Frontignan** and **Grand Roussillon** (the general AC for the VDN wines of the area). Those kept for a long time are called **Rancio**.

Other wines

Far to the north-west (usually classified by the French as wines from the Sud-Ouest) are the wines from the area around **Gaillac**. Gaillac makes reds, rosés, whites, plus the sparkling whites, **Gaillac mousseux** and **Gaillac perlé**. **Gaillac Premières Côtes** and **Gaillac doux** are both medium-sweet whites.

Vins de Pays

Most of it is red and some of it is good wine. If you see it called **Vin de Pays d'Oc** it will have come from any part of the four *départements* that follow (on the other hand it may indicate just the *département* name): **Vin de Pays des Pyrénées-Orientales** or **de l'Aude** or **de l'Hérault** or **du Gard**. Or the label may show a small, specific area within those *départements* (there are more than 50). Space does not provide the chance to list them all but a few are worth a mention: **Coteaux de Peyriac** (from the Minervois); **Haute Vallée de l'Orb** (north of St-Chinian); **Haute Vallée de l'Aude** (Limoux); **Les Sables du Golfe du Lion** (see Provence); and **Pays Catalan**, **Côte Catalane**, and **Val d'Agly** (a Roussillon trio). Wines of all shades take the **Côtes du Tarn** label. **Mas de Daumas Gassac**? Read the introduction.

BEZIERS
Climat de France

Simple hotel/Cooking 1
Terrace/Swimming pool/Tennis/Parking/Good value

Leave A9 Béziers-Est exit. Left after toll, cross autoroute and
hotel on right of N112, south of the A9.
Menus A-B. Rooms (79) C. Disabled. Cards All.
Post rte Valras, 34420 Villeneuve-lès-Béziers, Hérault.
Tel 67 39 40 00. Telex 485912. Fax 67 39 39 61. Mich 173/E1.
(Bookings: UK 071 287 3181)

LE BOULOU
Néoulous

Comfortable hotel/Cooking 1-2
Swimming pool/Tennis/Lift/Parking

Unusual styling. Leave A9 Le Boulou exit. Left at D115, over
A9 and hotel on right. No brownie points for site.
Menus A-C. Rooms (47) C-E. Disabled. Cards Access, Visa.
Post 66160 Le Boulou, Pyr.-Or. (En Route p 88)
Tel 68 83 38 50. Fax 68 83 13 40. Mich 177/E3.

CARCASSONNE
Climat de France

Simple hotel/Cooking 1
Parking/Good value

A61 Carcassonne-Est exit. West on N113; hotel on left.
Menus A-B. Rooms (26) C. Disabled. Cards Access, Visa.
Post 8, r. des Coteaux, 11000 Carcassonne, Aude. (ER p 161)
Tel 68 71 16 20. Telex 506050. Fax 68 71 47 27. Mich 172/A2.
(Bookings: UK 071 287 3181)

CARCASSONNE
Ibis

Simple hotel/Cooking 1
Parking/Good value

A61 Carcassonne-Est exit. West on N113; hotel on right.
Menus A. Rooms (60) C. Disabled. Cards Access, Visa.
Closed Rest: Sat lunch (mid Oct to March). Sun lunch.
Post rte de Berriac, 11000 Carcassonne, Aude. (ER p 161)
Tel 68 74 98 35. Telex 500554. Fax 68 47 10 47. Mich 172/A2.
(Bookings: UK 071 724 1000; US toll free 800 221 4542)

MONTPELLIER
Ibis

Simple hotel/Cooking 1
Terrace/Lift/Parking

A9 Montpellier-Sud exit. Hotel on right, north side of A9.
Menus A. Rooms (165) D. Disabled. Cards Access, Visa.
Post 164 av. Palavas, 34000 Montpellier, Hérault. (ER p 82)
Tel 67 58 82 30. Telex 480578. Fax 67 92 17 76. Mich 156/C3.
(Bookings: UK 071 724 1000; US toll free 800 221 4542)

MONTPELLIER　　　　　　　　　　　　Novotel

Very comfortable hotel/Cooking 1
Terrace/Swimming pool/Lift/Closed parking

Leave A9 Montpellier-Sud exit. Hotel on right, on north side of
A9 (right at island and then right again).
Menus B. Rooms (162) E. Disabled. Cards All. (En Route p 82)
Post 125 bis av. Palavas, 34000 Montpellier, Hérault.
Tel 67 64 04 04. Telex 490433. Fax 67 65 40 88. Mich 156/C3.
(Bookings: UK 071 724 1000; US toll free 800 221 4542)

NARBONNE ·　　　　　　　　　　Climat de France

Simple hotel/Cooking 1
Parking/Good value

Leave A9 Narbonne-Sud exit. N113 west; hotel on right.
Menus A-B. Rooms (40) C. Disabled. Cards AE, Access, Visa.
Post ZI La Plaisance, 11100 Narbonne, Aude. (En Route p 86)
Tel 68 41 04 90. Telex 505085. Fax 68 41 34 13. Mich 173/D2.
(Bookings: UK 071 287 3181)

NARBONNE　　　　　　　　　　　　Novotel

Very comfortable hotel/Cooking 1
Terrace/Gardens/Swimming pool/Lift/Closed parking

A9 Narbonne-Sud exit. Right after toll; on right of N9.
Menus B. Rooms (96) E. Disabled. Cards All.
Post rte de Perpignan, 11000 Narbonne, Aude. (En Route p 86)
Tel 68 41 59 52. Telex 500480. Fax 68 41 32 12. Mich 173/D2.
(Bookings: UK 071 724 1000; US toll free 800 221 4542)

PERPIGNAN　　　　　　　　　　　　Novotel

Very comfortable hotel/Cooking 1
Terrace/Gardens/Swimming pool/Closed parking

A9 Perpignan-Nord exit. Use A9 to north; hotel on left.
Menus B. Rooms (85) E. Disabled. Cards All.
Post 66600 Rivesaltes, Pyr.-Or. (En Route p 87)
Tel 68 64 02 22. Telex 500851. Fax 68 64 24 27. Mich 173/D4.
(Bookings: UK 071 724 1000; US toll free 800 221 4542)

TOULOUSE　　　　　　　　　　　　Campanile

Simple hotel/Cooking 1
Terrace/Parking/Good value

Leave A612 (eastern autoroute bypass of Toulouse, linking A61/
A62) exit 14 (Croix-Daurade). North on N88, hotel on right.
Menus A-B. Rooms (71) C. Disabled. Cards Access, Visa.
Post rte d'Albi, 31240 L'Union, H.-Gar.
Tel 61 74 00 40. Telex 533884. Mich 152/C3.
(Bookings: UK freephone 0800 897863)

Base Hotels

ALBI

**Simple hotel
Lift/Parking/Good value**

On Tarn right bank, two-minute walk to Quatre Saisons rest.
Rooms (33) C. Cards AE, Access, Visa.
Closed Xmas to New Year.
Post 9 rue Cantepau, 81000 Albi, Tarn.
Tel 63 60 75 80. Fax 63 47 57 91. Mich 153/F1.

CARCASSONNE

Aragon

**Comfortable hotel
Swimming pool/Parking**

South of the N113 and close to the eastern walls of La Cité.
Rooms (29) D-E. Cards All.
Post 15 montée Combéléran, 11000 Carcassonne, Aude.
Tel 68 47 16 31. Telex 505076. Fax 68 47 33 53. Mich 172/A2.

CERET

Les Arcades

**Simple hotel
Lift/Garage**

A few paces from Les Feuillants restaurant, in a shady *place*.
Tech Valley is famous for cherry blossom (end Apl/start May).
Rooms (26) C-D. Cards AE, DC, Visa.
Closed Second half Nov.
Post 1 pl. Picasso, 66400 Céret, Pyr.-Or.
Tel 68 87 12 30. Mich 177/D4.

COLLIOURE

Casa Païral

**Very comfortable hotel
Quiet/Gardens/Swimming pool/Parking**

The interior garden is an emerald of delight. But Madame
Pons wins the wooden spoon for popularity with readers.
Rooms (28) D-F. Disabled. Cards AE, Access, Visa.
Closed Nov to March.
Post impasse Palmiers, 66190 Collioure, Pyr.-Or.
Tel 68 82 05 81. Fax 66 82 52 10. Mich 177/F3.

COLLIOURE

Madeloc

**Comfortable hotel
Quiet/Gardens/Parking**

Bedrooms on the top two floors have welcome and useful
terraces. Note: no lift.
Rooms (21) C-D. Cards All.
Closed Mid Oct to mid April.
Post rue R.-Rolland, 66190 Collioure, Pyr.-Or.
Tel 68 82 07 56. Fax 68 82 55 09. Mich 177/F3.

MARSEILLAN Château du Port

Simple hotel
Garage/Parking

Noilly Prat and *coquillages pays*. The 100-year-old quayside château (built for a wine *négociant*) has views of the Bassin de Thau. Bikes for hire; a splendid idea.
Rooms (15) C-F. Cards AE, Access, Visa.
Closed Nov to Feb (except weekends).
Post 9 quai Résistance, 34340 Marseillan, Hérault.
Tel 67 77 65 65. Telex 521216. Fax 63 61 67 52. Mich 156/A4.

MOUREZE Hauts de Mourèze

Simple hotel
Secluded/Gardens/Swimming pool/Parking/Good value

Wonderful location; very friendly *patronne*, Mme Navas.
Rooms (16) C-D.
Closed Mid Oct to March.
Post 34800 Mourèze, Hérault.
Tel 67 96 04 84. Mich 156/A3.

NARBONNE La Résidence

Comfortable hotel
Lift/Garage

A richly-furnished town house; just west of the cathedral.
Rooms (26) D-E. Cards Access, Visa.
Post 6 rue ler Mai, 11000 Narbonne, Aude.
Tel 68 32 19 41. Fax 68 65 51 82. Mich 173/D2.

VERNET-LES-BAINS Rés. des Baüs & Mas Fleuri

Comfortable hotel
Quiet/Gardens/Swimming pool/Parking

Gardens are the highlight of this much-liked base.
Rooms (35) D-F. Cards All.
Closed Nov to March.
Post bd Clemenceau, 66820 Vernet-les-Bains, Pyr.-Or.
Tel 68 05 51 94. Fax 68 05 50 77. Mich 176/C3.

VIEILLE TOULOUSE La Flânerie

Comfortable hotel
Secluded/Gardens/Swimming pool/Garage/Parking

The fifth of five exceptional bases on this page. Fine views west over the Garonne. Only 9 km from noisy Toulouse.
Rooms (15) C-F. Cards All.
Closed Xmas to New Year.
Post rte Lacroix-Falgarde, 31320 Vieille-Toulouse, H.-Gar.
Tel 61 73 39 12. Fax 61 73 18 56. Mich 152/C3.

ALBI
Jardin des Quatre Saisons

Comfortable restaurant/Cooking 2
Terrace/Good value

Georges Bermond, after an absence of 20 years, has returned to his *pays*. Lucky Albi. The young chef, an inventive modern *maître*, together with his blond wife, Martine, weaves a *rapport qualité-prix* cloth of gold. The menu offers a choice of 7 starters, 12 main courses and 9 desserts. Bravo.
Menus B. Cards AE, Access, Visa.
Closed Mon. (Rooms? See Albi Base hotel; a long-jump away.)
Post 19 bd Strasbourg, 81000 Albi, Tarn.
Tel 63 60 77 76. Mich 154/A1. (North bank of Tarn.)

ALBI
La Réserve

Very comfortable hotel/Cooking 2
Secluded/Terrace/Gardens/Swimming pool/Tenn/Parking

Few hotels have such a blissful setting; a handsome villa in five acres of grounds on the right bank of the Tarn. The Rieux family (they own both this hotel and the Host. St-Antoine in Albi; see *FL3*) are fifth-generation hoteliers. Classical and regional dishes (like *canard confite Languedocienne*).
Menus B-D. Rooms (24) F-F2. Cards All.
Closed Nov to Apl. (A Relais & Châteaux hotel.)
Post rte de Cordes, 81000 Albi, Tarn. (On D600.)
Tel 63 47 60 22. Telex 520850. Fax 63 47 63 60. Mich 154/A1.

AMELIE-LES-BAINS-PALALDA
Castel Emeraude

Comfortable hotel/Cooking 1-2
Secluded/Terrace/Gardens/Lift/Parking

Twin turrets from the last century give this otherwise largish and modern *Relais du Silence* an odd-ball look. On the left bank of the Tech and with a wooded backdrop. Classical and *Bourgeoise* cooking which does not meet advertised claims.
Menus A-D. Rooms (59) C-D. Disabled. Cards Access, Visa.
Closed Dec. Jan. (West of spa, on north bank of Tech.)
Post rte Corniche, 66112 Amélie-les-Bains-Palalda, Pyr.-Or.
Tel 68 39 02 83. Fax 68 39 03 09. Mich 177/D4.

BELCAIRE
Bayle

Very simple restaurant with rooms/Cooking 1-2
Terrace/Parking/Good value

A simple, clean *logis* at the heart of glorious wooded Cathar country. Massive Guy Bayle, once a formidable Rugby forward, provides copious *Bourgeois*, classical and regional *plats*. Readers' regular advice: scrum down for the dearer menus.
Menus A-B. Rooms (14) A-C. Cards Access, Visa.
Closed Nov to mid Dec. Mon (not June to Sept).
Post 11340 Belcaire, Aude.
Tel 68 20 31 05. Mich 176/A2.

BOUZIGUES   Motel Côte Bleue

Very comfortable hotel/Cooking 3
Quiet/Terrace/Gardens/Swimming pool/Parking

The Bassin de Thau is famed for *coquillages*. There must be hundreds of roadside stalls in the towns and villages encircling the inland lagoon, all piled high with oysters and mussels. Don't be put off by the name of the hotel: some motel, some restaurant. The latter is a revelation, especially at lunch when the pleasant terrace overlooking the *étang* provides both a sunny and shady setting for savouring the modern cuisine of Pascal Jacquinot. Naturally shellfish and fish predominate: *moules, huîtres, palourdes, oursins, St-Pierre, turbot, langoustines, rougets, saumon, morue*; the possibilities are a roll-call of *poissons* and *coquillages*. The chef is keen on herbs, spices, olive oil, light sauces and keeping things simple. The wine list is an all white affair.
Menus B-E. Rooms (32) C-D. Cards Access, Visa.
Closed Rest: Jan. Tues evg & Wed.
Post 34140 Bouzigues, Hérault. (En Route p 83). Mich 156/B4.
Tel 67 78 31 42 (H). 67 78 30 87 (R). Fax 67 78 35 49.

CARCASSONNE   La Vicomté

Very comfortable hotel/Cooking 1-2
Quiet/Terrace/Gardens/Swimming pool/Lift/Parking

Ideal for those of you wanting a bit more comfort, and welcome air-conditioning, than that provided by the Autoroute hotels listed earlier. Cooking? A mix of regional, classical and *Bourgeoise* and, welcome once more, some fish-based dishes.
Menus B. Rooms (58) D-E. Disabled. Cards All.
Closed Rest: Sun (Nov to Mar). (E of La Cité and S of N113.)
Post rue C. St-Saëns, 11000 Carcassonne, Aude.
Tel 68 71 45 45. Telex 500303. Fax 68 71 11 45. Mich 172/A2.

CASTRES   Grand Hôtel & Rest. La Caravelle

Comfortable hotel & restaurant/Cooking 1-2
Terrace & Gardens (Rest)/Lift/Garage/Good value

Micheline Fabre is the third generation *patronne* of the Grand, next door to the Musée Goya and on the right bank of the Agout. The hotel has its own rest. Most rooms look out on to the river and the old *maisons de tanneurs* lining the banks.
   La Caravelle is also owned by Mme Fabre but this restaurant, with a delectable terrace overlooking the same river, is one km upstream. Alas, a short summer season only. Cooking at both restaurants is classical, *Bourgeoise* and regional. Examples of the three types are *tournedos Rossini, omelette au choix* and, inevitably, *cassoulet maison au confit de canard*.
Menus (both rests) A-B. Rooms (40) B-C. Cards All.
Closed La Caravelle: Mid Sept to mid June. Fri evg & Sat.
Closed Hôtel: Mid Dec to mid Jan. Hôtel rest: Fri evg & Sat.
Post La Caravelle: 150 av. Roquecourbe, 81100 Castres, Tarn.
Post Hôtel: 11 rue de la Libération, 81100 Castres, Tarn.
Tel La Caravelle 63 59 27 72. Hôtel 63 59 00 30. Mich 154/A3.

CERET Les Feuillants

Very comfortable restaurant with rooms/Category 3
Terrace/Lift/Garage

First, I'll list the pluses: English-speaking *patronne*, Marie-Louise Banyols, a knowledgeable *sommelière*; an exceptional *cave* with some terrific *vins de pays*; lots of pleasing details (appetisers, fish and bread are especially good); and modern cooking capitalising on Roussillon's bountiful and varied larder. Alas, some debits grate: a rubbery *poularde de Bresse* (pre-cooked?) and silly artificial dishes of caviar and *petits fours* on the tables; and hardly a vegetable in sight. But overall, three cheers that Marie-Louise and Didier, her chef husband, left their small Perpignan restaurant two years ago and set up home in an ochre house in a shady corner of Céret.
Menus C-D. Rooms (3) F-F2. Cards All.
Closed Feb. Sun evg & Mon.
Post 1 bd La Fayette, 66400 Céret, Pyr.-Or.
Tel 68 87 37 88. Telex 505165. Fax 68 87 44 68. Mich 177/D4.

CLERMONT-L'HERAULT Sarac

Simple hotel/Cooking 1
Terrace/Parking/Good value

On the west side of the N9 and south of the town. The helpful Dunands' modest hotel is ideal for overnight accommodation if you're eating at the Pughs' Mimosa in St-Guiraud. Modest *Bourgeois* dinners available here, if you want them: *rumsteak*, *côte d'agneau*, *crème caramel maison* are representative *plats*.
Menus A-B. Rooms (22) C. Cards Access, Visa.
Closed Rest only: Dec. Midday. Sat & Sun (Oct to mid Apl).
Post rte de Nébian, 34800 Clermont-l'Hérault, Hérault.
Tel 67 96 06 81. Mich 156/A3. (Junction of N9 & D909D.)

COLLIOURE La Frégate

Comfortable hotel/Cooking 2-3
Terrace/Lift/Good value

Those of you who have *Favourites* will already know that Yves Costa, a talented chef, gave up chasing culinary accolades in the mid-Eighties. A fiery maverick (he really is his own man), Yves has managed to fall out with both the main French guides. But he remains a readers' favourite. These days he cuts his cloth to suit clients: value for money comes first. An intense mixture of *cuisine Catalane* (be sure to savour *le jambon Serrano* and *la crème Catalane à la cassonade*, a cold dessert), his own modern creations and a handful of classical dishes (*filet de boeuf Rossini au Banyuls* is one example). I'll repeat my *FL3* caveat: don't go if you put great store on polish, style and swish trappings; but do go if you want a buzz from an animated dining room, the odd culinary firework and, above all, if you put value on value for money.
Menus B. Rooms (24) C-E. Cards Access, Visa.
Post 24 quai Amirauté, 66190 Collioure, Pyr.-Or.
Tel 68 82 06 05. Telex 505072. Fax 68 82 55 00. Mich 177/F3.

FLORENSAC   Léonce

Comfortable restaurant with rooms/Cooking 3-4
Good value

So many readers (including a British doctor now based in the States and his chef son, Matthew Tivy, making a big name for himself in the Big Apple) and regional chefs (like Claude Giraud, whose Réverbère restaurant in Narbonne went bust two years ago) implored me to seek out Josette and Jean-Claude Fabre (a third generation chef) at their modest family *auberge* in the centre of Florensac. Each year, bit by bit, the building is renovated and refurbished, as I saw for myself at the end of 1991. J-C is a bubbly, joyous man with a passion for his *pays* and its produce. His repertoire is a combination of modern inventiveness and loyalty to *haute cuisine* classics. A supreme elixir of a dessert is his own creation, *Sublime Léonce*, an extra bitter mousse made with Valrhona chocolate and served with an *agrumes* (citrus fruits) sauce.
Menus B-D. Rooms (12) C. Cards All.
Closed 15 Feb-15 Mar. Last wk Sept. 1st wk Oct. Sun evg (not high season). Mon. (En Route p 84; 5 km from A9 Agde exit).
Post pl. République, 34510 Florensac, Hérault.
Tel 67 77 03 05. Mich 156/A4.

LACAUNE   Hôtel Fusiès

Comfortable hotel/Cooking 1-2
Terrace/Good value

In 1990 Pierre Fusiès celebrated a unique anniversary: his family first set up shop in Lacaune 300 years earlier. In addition, he also owns the casino where there's a swimming pool and tennis court (hotel guests can use them). The menus appear to have 300 choices; and, unusually, some soups too. Specialities are mainly classical but I'd head for the *Menu Terroir* which includes all the renowned Lacaune *charcuterie*. One other culinary note: the only formal training Michel Bras (Laguiole, Massif Central) ever had was here at the Fusiès.
Menus A-D. Rooms (52) C. Cards All.
Closed 20 Dec-20 Jan. Fri evg & Sun evg (Nov to mid Mar).
Post rue de la République, 81230 Lacaune, Tarn.
Tel 63 37 02 03. Fax 63 37 10 98. Mich 154/C2.

QUILLAN   Cartier

Comfortable hotel/Cooking 1
Lift/Good value

Henri Cartier's smart *Logis de France* is hidden behind a curtain of trees. Grills and classical, *Bourgeois* and regional *plats*: especially tasty are *rouzolle* (eggs and *jambon* in a vegetable soup) and *cèpes sautés Provençale*. And be sure to savour the local Blanquette de Limoux vintages.
Menus A-B. Rooms (30) B-D. Cards AE, Access, Visa.
Closed Mid Dec to mid Mar. Rest: Sat (Oct to Dec).
Post bd Ch. de Gaulle, 11500 Quillan, Aude.
Tel 68 20 05 14. Telex 505082. Fax 68 20 22 57. Mich 171/F3.

REALMONT   Noël

Comfortable restaurant with rooms/Cooking 2
Terrace/Good value

Another amazing Tarn family dynasty. Noël Galinier, a fifth
generation chef, worked for over 50 years as a *cuisinier*. A
sixth generation chef/patron, Jean-Paul, is now at the piano,
with his wife Michèle turning the pages. The green-shuttered
house and shady terrace remain the same, as does the classical
and regional fare: dishes like *jambonnette de volaille
Périgourdine* (*filet d'agneau* gets the same treatment),
coquilles St-Jacques au beurre blanc and *cassoulet fermier*.
Menus B-C. Rooms (8) C-D. Cards All.
Closed 3 wks Feb. Sun evg & Mon (mid Sept to mid June).
Post rue H. de Ville, 81120 Réalmont, Tarn.
Tel 63 55 52 80. Mich 154/A2.

ST-GUIRAUD   Le Mimosa

Comfortable restaurant/Cooking 3-4
Terrace

Those of you who have *Favourites* will already know, in some
detail, the story of how Bridget and David Pugh came to open
their restaurant on February 29, 1984. Bridget, a prima
ballerina and once a member of the Royal Ballet, is *la
cuisinière*; husband David, in days past a violinist with the
same company's orchestra, runs the front of house and
supervises the superb cellar (includes Languedoc's best).

After a rocky start the Pughs have earned themselves a
tremendous reputation in the Midi and they've now won
entries in the leading guides. To hear three tables of French
clients say to David: "We leave what we eat and drink to you"
is the single most gratifying compliment any Anglo-Saxon chef
and *sommelier* can ever win. The enjoyment factor is 10 out of
10 and Bridget has become as good a *cuisinière* as any I know
(she only started cooking in her thirties); my rating reflects her
ability. Her modern touch is the epitome of common sense and
good taste and she makes a supreme effort to use fresh
produce, prepared in a natural, satisfying way. David is the
friendliest of hosts; he's also become a Languedoc wines
mastermind. The dining room (decorated in mimosa hues),
terrace, pool and adjoining *cave* are all man-made pluses.
Menus C-D (book ahead). Cards Access, Visa.
Closed Jan. Feb. Midday (not Sun, not pub. hols). Sun evg (not
July & Aug). Mon (not midday on pub. hols).
Post St-Guiraud, 34150 Gignac, Hérault.
Tel 67 96 67 96. Mich 156/A2. Rooms? See Mourèze & Clermont.

ST-LAURENT-DE-LA-SALANQUE   Auberge du Pin

Simple hotel/Cooking 2
Gardens/Parking/Good value

Readers like this good-value *auberge*, now run by Philippe Got
who recently took over from his parents. Enterprising *Catalane
cuisine*, with a light touch, and complemented by some
190

neo-classical treats. Especially tasty are *chiffonade de Serrano (jambon) aux mangues* and *selle d'agneau en croûte de pommes de terre*. Ask for rooms away from the road.
Menus B. Rooms (20) B. Cards Access, Visa.
Closed Jan. Sun evg & Mon (not July & Aug).
Post 66250 St-Laurent-de-la-Salanque, Pyr.-Or.
Tel 68 28 01 62. Mich 173/D4.

ST-MARTIN-DE-LONDRES   Les Muscardins

Very comfortable restaurant/Cooking 3

Multi prize-winning *cuisinier* Georges Rousset, seconded by his son Thièrry, have moved from La Crèche, hidden in the *garrigue* to the north-west, to a new village site. An expert on Languedoc cuisine, Georges marries classical, neo-classical and regional cleverly: an *agneau en trilogie* (*noisettes, poitrine farcie et navarin*) is a rare, tasty speciality. How rare, too, to encounter *omble chevalier fumé avec toast* (new to me) in deepest Languedoc. If you're in a nearby *gîte* make use of the duo's *"traiteur Bourgeois"* home delivery service.
Menus B-D. Cards All.
Closed Feb. Mon & Tues midday (not pub. hols).
Post 19 rte Cévennes, 34380 St-Martin-de-Londres, Hérault.
Tel 67 55 75 90. Fax 67 55 70 28. Mich 156/B2.

ST-PONS-DE-THOMIERES   Auberge du Cabaretou

Comfortable restaurant with rooms/Cooking 2
Gardens/Parking/Good value

Hidden France readers have adored Liliane Dubost's (both chef and hostess) isolated *auberge* atop the Col du Cabaretou (spectacular southern panorama and exhilarating woods to the north). A pleasing formula of *Bourgeoise*, classical, modern (Troisgros' *saumon à l'oseille*) and regional (using local produce such as Lacaune ham, St-Chinian red wine, *chèvre* cheese, mushrooms and *myrtilles* in a mouthwatering sorbet).
Menus A-D. Rooms (9) B-C. Cards All.
Closed Nov to Jan. Sun evg & Mon (not Apl to mid Sept).
Post Col du Cabaretou, 34220 St-Pons-de-Thomières, Hérault.
Tel 67 97 02 31. Mich 155/D3.

ST-PONS-DE-THOMIERES   Château de Ponderach

Comfortable hotel/Cooking 2
Secluded/Terrace/Gardens/Parking

Small is beautiful at this green oasis of calm. Has any Relais & Châteaux hotel fewer bedrooms? Has any other R&C 400 acres of grounds? Mireille Counotte's 18th-century home is a congenial charmer. The handsome trees, after the dry *garrigue* to the south, are a treat. Cooking is classical and neo-classical.
Menus B-D. Rooms (9) E. Cards All.
Closed Mid Oct to Mar.
Post rte Narbonne, 34220 St-Pons-de-Thomières, Hérault.
Tel 67 97 02 57. Fax 67 97 29 75. Mich 155/D4. (On D907.)

LOIRE

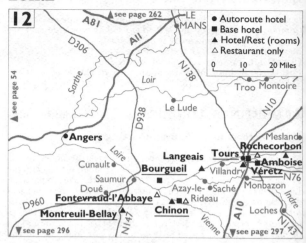

see page 262
see page 54
see page 296
see page 297

The Loire is a stunning region, filled with treasures created centuries ago, when France was the greatest cultural power in the civilised world. Man's architectural and artistic skills abound; the evidence, seemingly, is around every corner.

Nature competes in a self-effacing way. The River **Loire** itself has little to offer. The river's tributaries provide more restful, alluring vistas: the **Vienne**, **Indre**, Indrois, **Cher**, Sauldre, Beuvron, Cosson and **Loir** are examples. You'll discover, too, the **Sologne**, the eastern half of the region, a land of woods and pools.

First I'll pay due homage to the famous tourist attractions, the honeypot sights which Michelin rate as "worth the journey" or "worth the detour". Arguably Michelin is right: I've seen them all and I'll not quibble with their star ratings.

Where do you start? Three châteaux are thrilling glories: **Chambord** (from afar resembling a compact city: it was here that *son et lumière* was conceived by Paul-Robert Houdin); **Chenonceaux**, straddling the Cher so gracefully; and moated **Azay-le-Rideau**, a small structure and visual perfection (sadly now showing signs of neglect). The château at **Blois** and the "castle" at **Angers** also earn 3-star ratings.

But others attract too: the brick and stone **La Bussière**, surrounded by water and a Le Nôtre park (north-east of **Gien**); the stern castle at **Fougères**-sur-Bièvre (south of Blois); the red brick Château du Moulin, west of **Romorantin**; **Valençay** with pepper-pot towers and alluring gardens; elegant **Cheverny** and neighbouring Beauregard where the park is as appealing (both south-east of Blois); **Chaumont** and **Amboise**, both dominating the Loire's left bank between Blois and **Tours** (the small Château du Clos-Luce at Amboise, Leonardo da Vinci's last home, is a must); **Villandry**, where the French-style garden upstages the château; the brooding fortress at **Langeais**; picturesque Ussé, the inspiration for Perrault's *Sleeping Beauty*; the unfortress-like fortress at **Saumur**; the many-floored Brissac and the moated Serrant (south and west of Angers).

I have deliberately omitted two châteaux from the above list: **Chinon** and **Loches**. The French word "châteaux" is an

inappropriate word for these proud, majestic castles. Chinon fires the imagination: the Plantagenets, such a formidable force in both France and England, made the small town the centre of their considerable empire; here, too, in 1429, Joan of Arc met her Dauphin for the first time and, as Hammond Innes so aptly put it, the death knell of English power in France was sounded. Loches is a gigantic fortress: within its walls are towers, churches, a keep and museum.

Man didn't just erect châteaux. Close to the Loire's banks are three ecclesiastical treasures: the abbey at **St-Benoît**, north-west of Gien – revel at the glory of the belfry porch; the great abbey at **Fontevraud** (west of Chinon), where some of the Plantagenets are buried; and the graceful Romanesque abbey at **Cunault**, north-west of Saumur on the Loire's left bank.

Most visitors to the Loire give little if any time to the Loir, a northern tributary of France's premier river. In years gone by Anne and I have spent happy hours enjoying **Châteaudun** (the château sits high above the river); the old streets of central **Vendôme**, an "island" between two arms of the Loir; the quiet valley roads downstream from Vendôme, past **Montoire** and **Troo**; and finishing at **Le Lude** château (many say this one has the best of all *son et lumière* spectacles). Further north is **Le Mans**; the town gave me a surprise a few years back when, for the first time, I walked the streets of the old quarter, south of the Cathédrale St-Julien. (For details of Le Mans hotels see Normandy.)

I'll devote all my attention now to some of the unheralded sites in the region. I'll start in the east. From the handsome **Sully** castle, which had close links with Joan of Arc, cross the river and head north into the heart of the giant Forêt d'Orléans – to the "Carrefour de la Résistance"; here large sequoias shade a memorial to the Lorris *maquis*. In August 1944 over 50 patriots died in the woods, just days before Patton liberated **Orléans**. Crosses mark the spots where they fell and a map shows where each one died in the forest.

Some years ago, during the burning summer of 1985, I took an hour off from my autoroute research and headed the short distance east from junction 2 on the **A71** to the cool, refreshing

193

Parc Floral (south of Orléans). What a rare treat; commonplace in the UK but a surprise in France.

My favourite part of the Loire is La Sologne: a land of silver birch, chestnut and pine, *étangs* (ponds), streams, sandy soil, heather and broom. The combination of water and woodland make the area a wildlife paradise, famed for fish, wildfowl and game and renowned for asparagus, *pâtés* and the celebrated *tarte Tatin*. Use your large-scale Michelin maps and navigate along as many of the "whites" and "yellows" as you can. For example: seek out the Etang de Marcilly and Etang de la Grands Corbois, west of both **Nouan-le-Fuzelier** and the A71. North-west of Romorantin you'll find the Etang de Batarde: note the sluice gate alongside the road, which enables the large pool to be drained and cleaned periodically – a common occurrence for all the *étangs*.

The Indrois Valley, east of Loches, is a treat: **Montrésor** has a picturesque château overlooking the river; nearby is the Chartreuse du Liget, a Carthusian monastery built by Henry II to make amends for the murder of Becket.

Alongside the **N10**, north of Tours, is the massive Grange de Meslay, built 700 years ago. The 190-ft-long stone barn hides within its interior the most amazing maze of wooden rafters, beams and pillars; made of chestnut, some of the pillars are as thick as very sizeable tree trunks.

Near Chinon, to the west, is La Devinière, where Rabelais was born. Seek out, too, to the east of the town, the old church at Tavant, enriched by Romanesque frescoes. One km south-west of Montsoreau (between Chinon and Saumur) is La Herpinière with its ancient, restored windmill (there used to be scores in the area). Nearby Candes-St-Martin has a fine 12th-century church, full of character.

The Indre Valley has a handful of unusual attractions. **Saché** is known for two reasons: Balzac spent great periods of time at the château, from his childhood to his death in 1850 (the house has much of his memorabilia); and Alexander Calder lived nearby for many years – one of his steel mobiles is in the village square. Villaines-les-Rochers is five km south-west of Saché; the village is renowned for wickerwork products (*vannerie*) – chairs, baskets and other products are made by 60 local families. Cheillé is west of Azay-le-Rideau; marvel at the oak tree that literally grows out of a wall in the village church. Don't miss, too, the collection of 50 Cadillacs at St-Michel-sur-Loire (3 miles west of Langeais).

The banks of the Loire and Loir are studded with caves. Tunnelled out of tufa stone, they provide folk with homes (at Troo); with restaurant dining rooms (**Rochecorbon**); and they're ideal for the cultivation of *champignons de Paris*. Visit the Musée du Champignon, on the D751 at St-Hilaire, near Saumur; and the troglodyte village at Rochemenier, just north of **Doué-la-Fontaine**. Old quarries to the west of Doué have been used to provide shelter for the animals at the Parc Zoologique des Minières. Finally, detour to Château-Gontier (on the River Mayenne, north of Angers) and the remarkable Refuge de l'Arche. The refuge of rescued animals is run by an angel among men, Christian, helped by dozens of children, volunteers all. A truly heart-warming *déviation*.

Markets Blois (Tues, Wed & Sat); Langeais (Sun); Loches (Wed & Sat); Montbazon (Tues); Montoire-sur-le-Loir (Wed); Montrichard (Fri); Romorantin (Wed); Vendôme (Fri).

Michelin green guide: Châteaux of the Loire (English).

Romorantin Market

Market day in **Romorantin** is Wednesday. It's probably no different from the weekly markets held in hundreds of French towns but, by choosing the Romorantin version as a typical example, it allows me to write, briefly, on what is one of the great pleasures of France. I'm always tempted by the sight of a bustling provincial market; lack of time usually prevents me from stopping but, if I can, I'm happy to spend an hour looking, chatting, enquiring and perhaps buying, too.

The centre of Romorantin is alive and busy from the crack of dawn on market morning. Scores of traders bring goods of every description into the town, taking over the streets and squares. But these are travelling marketeers, moving from one place to another every day. They are of little interest to me. What I get excited about is when I wander among the stalls of the local producers: the asparagus and vegetable growers, mushroom pickers, sausage-stuffers, cake-bakers and many others. You'll find them in the covered market.

The first stallholder I met proved to be the formidable Madame Barboux, a local legend. I saw her unloading trays of cheeses from an ancient Peugeot estate car, which, anywhere else but in France, would have been despatched to the scrap heap long ago. I'm not joking when I tell you the headlamp bulbs were hanging from their reflector holders; the glass covers had long since disappeared. It must be a frightening experience to encounter Madame's motor in thick fog. She's from Billy, a northern neighbour of Selles-sur-Cher; the clue in the address is that she makes her own goat's milk cheeses. On display is a range of different types, six in all; from tingling fresh to very, very dry.

Near her, in a corner, was an older woman, renowned for the quail eggs she had in baskets in front of her. These are the same eggs you will relish when you try the Lion d'Or's appetisers. Alongside her was the amazing Elisa Bouleau, mother of twelve; her eldest daughter, Annick, is the receptionist who welcomes you at the hotel. It seems unnecessary to say how hard Elisa works to keep her brood alive; she does it so successfully that she wins many of the local horticultural prizes for the quality of her produce: cheeses (goat's and cow's milk), chickens and vegetables.

Next came Lucien Carré, from Pruniers, eight km to the south-west of the town; he's considered by the Cléments as the best *charcutier* in the Loire Valley. What a display: *boudins blancs*, *boudins noirs*, hams tasting quite different from the supermarket "plastic" varieties, *saucisses*, both garlic and *sec* versions, *andouillettes*, and *rillettes* and *rillons*. Both the latter derive from the word *rille* (lard). (During the hunting season, *la chasse*, you'll also be beguiled by several stalls offering their "catch" of wild boar, roe-deer, hares, pheasants and wild fowl from the Sologne.)

A few metres away from the butchers and *charcutiers* was a small dark woman, in front of her a table with both white and grey examples of *champignons de Paris*. Later that day I visited her "caves" where the townspeople of Bourré, at the eastern entrance to **Montrichard**, alongside the Cher, earn their laboriously hard living. The caves were cut centuries ago, in tiers one above the other; the tufa stone was used to build the Loire châteaux. Pass through Bourré during the day and the place is deserted; everyone is underground using miners' lamps to illuminate their task of picking, at just the right time, the never-ending harvest of mushrooms.

Madame Terreau, aptly named, earns her living differently, above ground near Cour-Cheverny. She is famed for her bedding plants and home-grown fruit. I counted at least 30 varieties of colourful plants ready to brighten up local gardens.

Across the aisle was a super ten-metre-long "display" of mouthwatering *pâtisseries*, of a much higher standard than is normal at markets. The family running the stall have made it such a hit that they now own their own *pâtisserie* in the town, the one immediately across the road from the Lion d'Or. Apart from the four dozen different cakes on display the thing that took my eye was a *galette aux pommes de terre*, a shining pastry-like surface with an amazing rubbery flexibility and a rough, earthy taste; you can bend and roll it as you like.

Near the *pâtisserie* was Monsieur Gaullier's "stand", perhaps the biggest in the market. On the floor, in a square around him, was a huge assortment of vegetables; I counted over 40 different sorts. There was also a selection of six different types of potato, looking so good you could have eaten them on the spot. Everything was of first-class quality but the *haricots verts*, *haricots beurres*, cabbages, different sorts of lettuce, radishes, chicory and courgettes looked particularly appetising. In May and June you will also see in the market stack upon stack of the famed Sologne asparagus.

My last call was to meet Madame Leloup, surrounded by her small, but so interesting, selection of produce. She's a real character; tall, with sparkling eyes, and skin shining with good health. She must be over 60; later I was to meet her remarkable family at their simple two-acre farm (you'll understand soon why I'm not locating the site precisely).

Around her in a circle was the evidence of the family's hard labour: courgettes, *cornichons*, *ciboules*, *laitues*, *échalotes*, *groseilles* and other vegetables and fruit; freshly-picked herbs like *menthe*, *marjolaine*, *absinthe*, *ciboulettes*, *estragon*, *sariette*, *persil* and others; dried herbs such as *thym*, *camomille*, *mélisse*, *laurier*, *basilic* and *thym citronelle*; and colourful "everlasting" flowers.

I was taken by her striking personality and amazing energy. Fortunately Marie-Christine Clément was with me and, on the spot, she agreed to accompany me to the Leloup smallholding. Fifteen minutes later we met Madame Leloup's daughter, working in the fields, her granddaughter and her mother, still active and full of vitality. The whole family mucked in.

Our walk through the rows of plants, flowers, fruit bushes and herbs was a revelation. The profusion of herbs was an eye-opener; some unknown and some considered "weeds" by the Leloup family but not by the Cléments. *Pourpier* is one; it's used by Didier in a *grenouilles* speciality, the weed being perhaps the only one he knows which stands cooking in butter. There was tarragon, so strong smelling it was more like *anis*. Wild garlic, *rocambole*, was evident; in late evening its heavy perfume fills the air. What gave me the greatest surprise was to be shown *ache*, the original celery. Last but not least were the rows of bright "everlasting" flowers, of all types, hanging in the family kitchen for final drying.

Finally, can I ask you to keep a secret? Madame Leloup has a sense of humour. During the "season" she collects edible wild fungi from the woods bordering her land. She then sells some of them to the owner of the self-same woods. That demonstrates an admirable survival instinct. Agreed?

The Pottery at Mesland   **Owen Watson**

The Prior of Mesland laid out vineyards here in the eleventh century, for wine for his altar, his guests, his monks and for himself. **Mesland** is now at the northern limit of the vine in France, producing fine wines (*appellation contrôlée* Touraine Mesland) if the long maturing season is kind. It also produces a certain kind of man: hard working, convivial, not well off, full of human kindness. Puritanism and social snobbishness cast no shadows here in this corner of the Loire Valley.

I had the good fortune to come to this place 32 years ago (I was then 37), and also had the luck of finding a small farmhouse to live in just right for my work, my temperament, and my standard of life. It is a small clearing on a wooded hillside, with room for Alpine goats, peacocks, fantails, bantams, and for old roses in profusion. The house lies in a little valley where poplars grow beside the tiny Cisse. Oaks, hornbeams and acacias cover the low northern slope of the valley, alongside chestnut and wild cherry.

Now all this is not so far removed from potting as it may seem. A craftsman lives a solitary life, much shut in on himself in his workshop. William Morris taught me that liking to work where you work is of the first importance: that as the body is to the soul, so is his place of work to the craftsman.

At Mesland I make ash-glazed stoneware for the table, in the Hamada-Leach tradition. For me it involves a certain refinement of form and appearance, rather tight throwing, and care over finish: these are sources of beauty, but can make for feeble ware. Now the old tradition in the centre of France is of vigorous peasant salt-glazed stoneware, wood-fired, the clay dominant, the finish minimal. (You can see it at its best in **Bourges** Museum. **St-Amand-en-Puisaye** is at the heart of the tradition.) Of course stoneware in France is as much a middle class affair now as it is in the rest of Europe, and no longer a peasant concern. But I have found that attention to this reference has improved my pots greatly. St-Amand pots are collected, prized, merchandised, catalogued, displayed, in a way their creators would probably not have thought well of, if ever the idea that it could happen had occurred to them.

In common with most French stoneware potters, I get my clay from the same seam that these old potters used. It not only throws supremely well, it fires to a lovely colour, has a dense, beautiful texture, and is immensely strong. (For 50 cm high slab pots I add no sand or grog.) Even going to get it is a pleasure, with an early-morning drive through **Sologne**, and back home for tea: twice a year, two tons each time.

The ashes I use for glaze are apple ash (from the Normandy cider orchards near Caen), lavender ash (from the distilleries in the Drôme), oak ash (from my fireplace: in this part of France oak is still what you burn to keep warm) and vine ash (from the Mesland vineyard prunings). I think of the vine ash glaze as my main glaze. It is beige on a single dipping, bluey white on double dipping, yellow on iron, and flows well without running off the pot. The vines are pruned in the dead of the year, and I burn the stacks reserved for me in the spring. They make wonderful fires, all crackle and spit, with sheets of flame leaping and veering. Generally boys from the village share this work with me, liking bonfires as much as I do. The ashes are cold enough by nightfall to be collected, and in due course they are sieved, sacked and stored away.

In England I had a small experience of gas kilns and electric

197

kilns, but promised myself a wood kiln when I could reasonably have one. My first care after settling in Mesland was to visit the studio potters using wood kilns at La Borne (near St-Amand-en-Puisaye), get a design from the porcelain factory at Sèvres, have refractory bricks of the first quality sent up from Bordeaux, and build a fine kiln of 1.3 cubic metres capacity that I had no idea how to fire. I did eight firings without success (each involving 50 hours of sawing and splitting wood, but there are other designs that do not call for such a load of work). Then with the advice from Leach and Hamada, and 24 hours of help from Michel Lavice, a French ex-potter who happened to pay a call at the critical moment and whom I had never met, I got to know how to make the kiln climb to 1300 degrees, and the pots were wonderful.

The point about a wood kiln is the extreme variety of the atmosphere in which the pots bathe. Flame, smoke and fly ash play freely over the pots. They modify the clay and glazes in a thousand ways. The presence of so much carbon and silica changes the colours and quality of the glazes fundamentally. A potter who uses wood can well cultivate a certain humility: much of his achievement is the gift of the kiln.

My 60th birthday was celebrated by an exhibition in the Grand Renaissance Salle des Conférences in Blois Château of 220 of these wood-fired pieces, whilst the walls were hung with splendid embroidered patchworks made by my friend Jacqueline Hauser at Castlebridge in Co. Wexford, Ireland.

A wood kiln is exhausting. Besides, mine is currently bedevilled by the roots of an ash tree that refuse to be killed. I rely largely on a second kiln now, fired by propane and wood together. In both kilns I burn oak and hornbeam from local sources up to 1000 degrees, and silver birch from Amboise Forest, 20 km away, from 1000 to 1300 degrees. The birch gives less heat but makes very little ash, so the fireboxes do not get clogged. I find longer firings are better (for the pots) than shorter ones, so I don't try to see how fast I can get to temperature. Young friends come in and help. Indeed, it is one of the happiest aspects of my life here that the work brings me friendship of the young people in the village. Their generation has had a harder start in adult life than mine did, and I like their sturdy, life-loving attitudes.

I will end with a word on sales. I suppose it has always been hard to make a living out of a small workshop. It is hard now, and as hard here in France as anywhere else. Sales are precarious, costs and dues are hefty. There are probably fewer outlets for selling pots in France than in England. On the other hand, French people tend to be great present givers, and to buy generously for their own needs. My own practice is to sell direct to customers, and to work a great deal to order. I like best of all working to order for people I've watched grow up. But what puts the butter in spinach is selling to summer visitors, and singularly to the happy devotees of *French Leave*: who in one go discover Richard Binns, Owen Watson and the Prior of Mesland's true descendants.

(How do you find Owen Watson – a publisher and lexicographer turned potter? Mesland is midway between **Blois** and **Amboise**, on the northern or right bank of the Loire. Half a kilometre south of the village, on the D65 and on the western side of the road, you'll pass Owen's *"poterie"*, a cottage called Les Fraisiers. St-Amand-en-Puisaye is on the borders of Burgundy and the Loire – south-east of Gien.)

Sologne Maquis

There is a strong sense of tranquillity and determination in both the landscape and people of La **Sologne**. So it comes as no surprise that, throughout the last war, the area was a Resistance stronghold, one of the most formidable in France.

A wonderfully poignant book by Stella King, *Jacqueline: Pioneer Heroine of the Resistance* (Arms and Armour Press), tells the story of Yvonne Rudellat, known as Jacqueline, the first British woman SOE agent sent into German-occupied France – to the secretive Sologne. Like many SOE stories this one was suppressed for far too long. Stella's superbly researched book relates Yvonne's heroic mission and captures both the spirit and bravery of the people and the essence of the landscape. Highly recommended. (Also see the Huisseau-sur-Cosson entry.)

(An interesting link is that the late Moune Gardnor-Beard, part of the "Jacqueline" story, was Owen Watson's wife. Note: a memorial to the SOE agents who died behind enemy lines was unveiled by the Queen Mother at **Valençay** in May 1991.)

Cheeses Cow's milk

Olivet Bleu small disk, often wrapped in leaves. A fruity taste and a light scent of blue mould. Try it with a red Bourgueil

Olivet Cendré savory taste. Cured in wood ashes. Same size as Olivet Bleu. **Gien** is a related cheese

Frinault a soft, small disk; ideal with light Loire wines

Pithiviers au Foin also known as **Bondaroy au Foin**. A soft cheese, made in thin disks and protected by a covering of bits of hay

Saint-Benoît a fruity, soft, small disk

Saint-Paulin semi-hard, yellow, mild, smooth-textured with a washed, bright orange rind. Made commercially throughout northern France

Vendôme Bleu (Vendôme Cendré) related to the Olivet cheeses

Make sure you try some of the delicious fresh cream cheeses called **Crémets**, eaten with sugar and fresh cream

Goat's milk

Crottin de Chavignol from the area just west of Sancerre, which, with Chavignol, makes the ideal wine to accompany it. Takes the form of a small, flattened ball. In grilled form it now appears regularly throughout France as a hot cheese course. The best season is winter. Please also refer to the cheeses listed in the Berry-Bourbonnais region)

Levroux identical to Valençay. Nutty flavour

Ste-Maure summer and autumn season. Soft cylinders, full goat flavour cheese. Try it with dry Vouvray or Montlouis wines or the reds of Chinon and Bourgueil. **Ligueil** is a similar related cheese

Selles-sur-Cher from the Sologne; also known as **Romorantin**. Dark blue skin, pure white interior with mild, nutty flavour. Both **Montoire** and **Troo** are similar related cheeses

Valençay pyramid shaped; usual best seasons for all goat's milk cheeses – summer and autumn. Mild, soft and nutty taste. Often called **Pyramide**

Regional Specialities

Alose à l'oseille grilled shad with a sorrel sauce

Bardette stuffed cabbage

Beuchelle à la Tourangelle kidneys, sweetbreads, morels, truffles, cream

Bourdaines apples stuffed with jam and baked

Rillauds chauds strips of hot bacon

Rillettes potted pork

Sandre freshwater fish, like perch

Tarte à la citrouille pumpkin tart

Tarte Tatin *upside-down* tart of caramelised apples and pastry

Truffiat potato cake

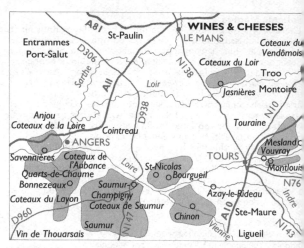

Wines (Great vintages: Anjou and Touraine **47 49 53 55 59 69 71 75
76 78 82 85 90**; Pouilly and Sancerre **73 75 76 85 90**)

Whites

All the Loire wines are charming, light and quite dissimilar in
character from each other. The various **Muscadet** wines
which I let Brittany claim as its own, are dry and fruity.

Wines from the huge areas of **Anjou**, **Anjou-Villages** and
Touraine can be sweet, medium-sweet or dry (check wine lists
and read *Wines of France* on pages 20-22). Among the numerous
whites worth recording is a personal favourite, **Vouvray**, made
just east of Tours from the Chenin Blanc grape, the most
important of the Loire white grape types; it is a particularly
delicate wine. South of Angers is the **Coteaux du Layon**
with its own very broad AC. Here some fine sweet whites are
made: **Quarts-de-Chaume**, **Coteaux du Layon Chaume** and
Bonnezeaux (all three are sweet) have their own *appellations*.
Savennières (dry whites), near Angers, lies on the north bank
of the Loire; within that tiny area is **Savennières-Roches-aux-
Moines** and **Savennières-Coulée-de-Serrant**, both small
vineyards and both making magnificent dry wines.

Look out for the medium-sweet whites of **Jasnières**, from the
Coteaux du Loir, to the north of Tours; good-value wines of
all shades are made here. In the neighbourhood of Tours, the
Sauvignon grape is used for a **Sauvignon de Touraine** wine; a
much cheaper alternative to Sancerre and nearly equal in quality.
A **Touraine Azay-le-Rideau** (Chenin Blanc grape again) is a
super dry white. Dry and semi-sweet wines are **Saumur**,
Coteaux de Saumur, **Coteaux de l'Aubance** and **Anjou
Coteaux de la Loire**. There's a never-ending choice.

Sparkling Wines

Particularly good are all the dry, sparkling wines; the words
mousseux and **pétillant** are added to the AC areas. The **Vouvray**
sec and *demi-sec* **pétillant** whites are superb; others to enjoy are
Montlouis, across the river from Vouvray, **Anjou**, **Touraine**,
Saumur and a delicious **Crémant de Loire**.

Other Whites

From the Upper Loire, well to the east of the region, come
some lovely white wines, made from the Sauvignon Blanc grape:

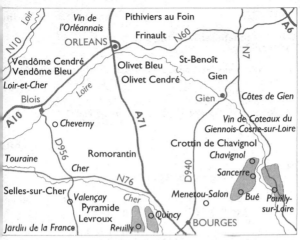

Pouilly-Fumé and **Sancerre**, both flinty and smoky flavoured.
Another white is **Quincy**, from an area south of Vierzon, dryer
than Fumé. **Pouilly-sur-Loire** wines are made from a different
and not as good grape type, Chasselas. An unknown AC is
Menetou-Salon, just north of Bourges; dry wines of all shades
are made. **Reuilly**, **Valençay** and **Cheverny** (a VDQS duo)
wines are dry and fragrant. The last four whites are made
from the Sauvignon grape. The same grape is used in the
VDQS **Coteaux du Giennois-Cosne-sur-Loire**, **Vin de
Coteaux du Giennois** and **Côtes de Gien**.

Rosés
There are some notable rosés from **Saumur** and **Anjou** – and
their respective **Coteaux** – from **Touraine**, **Touraine Mesland**,
Touraine Amboise and from the **Coteaux de l'Aubance**, on the
south bank of the Loire, opposite Angers. Look out for **Rosé
d'Anjou**, **Rosé de Loire** and a rosé made from two different
grape types, **Cabernet d'Anjou** (Cabernet Franc and
Sauvignon). The **Cabernet de Saumur** is lighter in colour
and dryer than the Anjou wine. There is also a sparkling **Rosé
d'Anjou pétillant**. From the Sancerre area come fine rosés –
often described on wine lists as **Rosé de Bué** and **Rosé de
Chavignol**. VDQS rosés are the **Coteaux du Vendômois** and
Vin de l'Orléanais (a *vin gris* – light, pale and fragrant).

Reds
Among the good Loire Cabernet reds are **Chinon**, **Bourgueil**,
Saint Nicolas-de-Bourgueil, **Anjou** and **Saumur-Champigny**.
Sancerre produces a small amount of excellent red wine,
made from the Pinot Noir grape. A **Gamay de Touraine** is a
red made from the same grape type used in Beaujolais; other
Gamay wines are **Anjou Gamay** and the VDQS trio of
Cheverny, **Valençay** and **Coteaux d'Ancenis**. The VDQS
Vin du Thouarsais is a sound red – as are the whites and
rosés. Remember, too, that Angers is the home of **Cointreau**.

Vins de Pays
These will have labels showing either the *département* or the
general area name: examples are **Vin de Pays de Loir-et-Cher**
or, in the second case, a **Vin de Pays du Jardin de la France**.
Often the labels will also describe the grape type used.

ANGERS   **Altéa Lac de Maine**

Comfortable hotel/Cooking 1
Lift/Parking

Leave N23 (links both ends A11) at Lac de Maine exit. S side.
Menus B. Rooms (80) D-E. Disabled. Cards All.
Post 49000 Angers, M.-et-L.
Tel 41 48 02 12. Telex 721111. Fax 41 48 57 51. Mich 65/F3.
(Bookings: UK 071 724 1000; US toll free 800 221 4542)

BLOIS   **Campanile**

Simple Hotel/Cooking 1
Terrace/Parking/Good value

Leave A10 Blois exit. Through toll on to N252. Ignore road left
to Blois; keep turning right. (En Route p 93)
Menus A-B. Rooms (54) C. Disabled. Cards Access, Visa.
Post rue de la Vallée-Maillard, 41000 Blois, L.-et-Ch.
Tel 54 74 44 66. Telex 751628. Fax 54 74 02 40. Mich 68/C3.
(Bookings: UK freephone 0800 897863)

BLOIS   **Ibis**

Simple hotel/Cooking 1
Parking/Good value

A10 Blois exit. Past toll, keep going right. See above.
Menus A. Rooms (61) C-D. Cards Access, Visa. (En Route p 93)
Post 3 rue Porte-Côte, 41000 Blois, L.-et-Ch.
Tel 54 74 60 60. Telex 750959. Fax 54 74 85 71. Mich 68/C3.
(Bookings: UK 071 724 1000; US toll free 800 221 4542)

ORLEANS   **Campanile**

Simple hotel/Cooking 1
Parking/Good value

Leave A71 exit 2 (Orléans-La Source). East on N271 to N20.
South for 3½ km. Left on D326; hotel on left. (ER p 92)
Menus A-B. Rooms (42) C. Disabled. Cards Access, Visa.
Post rue Chateaubriand, 45100 Orléans-La-Source, Loiret.
Tel 38 63 58 20. Telex 781228. Fax 38 69 02 60. Mich 69/E1.
(Bookings: UK freephone 0800 897863)

ORLEANS   **Climat de France**

Simple hotel/Cooking 1
Parking/Good value

Exit as above entry. East on N271; over N20, hotel on left.
Menus A-B. Rooms (42) C. Disabled. Cards Access, Visa.
Post 20 rte de Bourges, 45160 Olivet, Loiret.
Tel 38 69 20 55. Telex 783451. Fax 38 63 17 72. Mich 69/E1.
(Bookings: UK 071 287 3181)

ORLEANS   Ibis

Simple hotel/Cooking 1
Terrace/Parking/Good value

Leave A10 Orléans-Nord exit. Past toll, take first exit off A701 (Saran); hotel on north side of this short autoroute.
Menus A. Rooms (104) C-D. Cards Access, Visa.
Post ch. des Sablons, 45770 Saran, Loiret. (En Route p 91)
Tel 38 73 39 93. Telex 760902. Fax 38 74 05 78. Mich 69/E1.
Bookings; UK 071 724 1000; US toll free 800 221 4542)

ORLEANS   Novotel Orléans La Source

Very comfortable hotel/Cooking 1
Terrace/Swimming pool/Tennis/Lift/Closed parking

See Campanile exit details previous page. Hotel on left N20.
Menus B. Rooms (119) E. Disabled. Cards All.
Post rue H. de Balzac, 45100 Orléans, Loiret. (ER p 92)
Tel 38 63 04 28. Telex 760619. Fax 38 69 24 04. Mich 69/E1.
Bookings; UK 071 724 1000; US toll free 800 221 4542)

TOURS-NORD   Ibis Nord

Simple hotel/Cooking 1
Parking/Good value

Leave A10 Tours-Nord exit. N10 towards Tours; Ibis on right.
Menus A. Rooms (62) C-D. Disabled. Cards Access, Visa.
Post La Petite Arche, 37100 Tours, I.-et-L. (En Route p 94)
Tel 47 54 32 20. Telex 751592. Fax 47 41 67 17. Mich 67/F4.
Bookings; UK 071 724 1000; US toll free 800 221 4542)

TOURS-SUD   Ibis Sud

Simple hotel/Cooking 1
Parking/Good value

Leave A10 exit 14: Montbazon (from north); Chambray (from south). South on N10. Hotel on right. Old maps say exit 15.
Menus A. Rooms (80) C-D. Cards Access, Visa.
Post 37170 Chambray-lès-Tours, I.-et-L. (ER p 94)
Tel 47 28 25 28. Telex 751297. Fax 47 27 84 26. Mich 67/F4.
Bookings; UK 071 724 1000; US toll free 800 221 4542)

TOURS-SUD   Novotel

Very comfortable hotel/Cooking 1
Terrace/Swimming pool/Lift/Parking

See exit instructions for Ibis Sud hotel above.
Menus B. Rooms (125) E-F. Disabled. Cards All.
Post 37170 Chambray-lès-Tours, I.-et-L. (ER p 94)
Tel 47 27 41 38. Telex 751206. Fax 47 27 60 03. Mich 67/F4
Bookings; UK 071 724 1000; US toll free 800 221 4542)

Base Hotels

BOURGUEIL
Le Thouarsai

Very simple hotel
Fairly quiet/Gardens/Good value

Much loved: the hotel, the gardens and the Caillaults.
Rooms (29) B-C.
Closed 14-23 May. Sch. hols Feb & Xmas. Sun (Oct to Easter)
Post pl. Hublin, 37140 Bourgueil, I.-et-L.
Tel 47 97 72 05. Mich 81/E1.

CHINON
Didero

Simple hotel
Quiet/Closed parking

Vine-covered, 18th-cent town house. Cypriot owner, Théodor
Kazamias. Five-minute walk to Au Plaisir Gourmand restaurant
Rooms (24) C-E. Disabled. Cards All.
Closed Mid Dec to mid Jan.
Post 4 rue Buffon, 37500 Chinon. I.-et-L.
Tel 47 93 18 87. Mich 81/F1.

NOUAN-LE-FUZELIER
Charmille

Simple hotel
Quiet/Gardens/Parking

Dominique Sené's popular base. One black mark when a client
becoming ill, wanted to leave early; M. Sené was not pleased.
Rooms (14) C-E. Cards Access, Visa.
Closed Mid Dec to mid March.
Post rte D122, 41600 Nouan-le-Fuzelier, L.-et-Ch.
Tel 54 88 73 55. Mich 69/E3.

ONZAIN
Château des Tertre

Comfortable hotel
Quiet/Gardens/Parking

Elevated position in large park; west of the village (D58).
Rooms (19) D-E. Cards AE, Access, Visa.
Closed 10 Nov to Easter.
Post rte de Monteaux, 41150 Onzain, L.-et-Ch.
Tel 54 20 83 88. Fax 54 20 89 21. Mich 68/B3.

ORLEANS
Orléans Parc Hôte

Comfortable hotel
Secluded/Gardens/Closed parking

Modern, 7 acres of parkland, right bank Loire; off N152, 1 kr
west of A71, exit 1 (Orléans-Ouest). Restaurant in grounds.
Rooms (34) D-E. Disabled. Cards AE, Access, Visa.
Post 55 rte d'Orléans, 45380 La Chapelle St-Mesmin, Loiret.
Tel 38 43 26 26. Telex 760823. Fax 38 72 00 99. Mich 69/E1.

ST-BENOIT-SUR-LOIRE   **Labrador**

Simple hotel
Quiet/Gardens/Parking/Good value

Beside the abbey. Enjoy the latter and the Gregorian chants.
Rooms (47) B-D. Disabled. Cards AE, Access, Visa.
Closed Jan to mid Feb.
Post 45730 St-Benoît-sur-Loire, Loiret.
Tel 38 35 74 38. Fax 38 35 78 33. Mich 70/A2.

TOURS   **Cèdres**

Comfortable hotel
Quiet/Gardens/Swimming pool/Lift/Garage/Parking

A flower-bedecked modern building, 11 km west of Tours and
six km from Villandry (D7). Restaurant in grounds.
Rooms (40) D-E. Cards AE, Access, Visa.
Post rte de Villandry, 37510 Savonnières, I.-et-L.
Tel 47 53 00 28. Telex 752074. Fax 47 80 03 84. Mich 67/E4.

TOURS   **Chantepie**

Comfortable hotel
Quiet/Closed parking /Good value

Modern building; just to the north of the D751 (Chinon road);
west of A10 exit 14. Care: old maps say exit 15.
Rooms (28) C. Cards Access, Visa.
Closed Xmas.
Post rue Chantepie, 37300 Joué-lès-Tours, I.-et-L.
Tel 47 53 06 09. Fax 47 67 89 25. Mich 67/F4.

TOURS   **Les Fontaines St-Georges**

Simple hotel
Fairly quiet/Gardens/Parking/Good value

On the north bank of the Loire, to the east of Tours, at
Rochecorbon (N152). Roland Lafaye is a mine of tourist info.
Rooms (15) C-D. Cards All.
Closed Mon (during winter).
Post 6 quai Loire, 37210 Rochecorbon, I.-et-L.
Tel 47 52 52 86. Mich 67/F4.

VERETZ   **Grand Repos**

Simple hotel
Swimming pool/Garage/Parking/Good value

Modern building, east of village, south of N76.
Rooms (25) B-C. Disabled. Cards AE, Access, Visa.
Closed Mid Oct to March.
Post 18 ch. Acacias, 37270 Véretz, I.-et-L.
Tel 47 50 35 34. Fax 47 50 58 58. Mich 67/F4.

AMBOISE

Novotel

Very comfortable hotel/Cooking 1-2
Secluded/Terrace/Gardens/Swim pool/Tenn/Lift/Parking

One of the most striking and pleasantly situated Novotels, in an isolated, elevated position. Cooking, a mix of styles, is of a slightly higher standard than most Novotels.
Menus B-C. Rooms (121) E-F. Disabled. Cards All.
Post rte de Chenonceaux, 37400 Amboise, I.-et-L. (D31 bypass.)
Tel 47 57 42 07. Telex 751203. Fax 47 30 40 76. Mich 68/A4.
(Bookings; UK 071 724 1000; US toll free 800 221 4542)

LES BEZARDS

Auberge des Templiers

Luxury hotel/Cooking 3-4
Quiet/Terrace/Gardens/Swim pool/Tenn/Garage/Parking

England's Chewton Glen is one of the finest luxury hotels on this side of the Channel. The Auberge des Templiers earns the same accolade in France. There's a common link that makes the two hotels so exceptional. In Martin and Brigitte Skan there's no finer hotelkeeping duo in the UK; the same is true of Phillipe and Françoise Depée at their ultimate *auberge*.

Phillipe, a handsome host, is proud that the Templiers is the only one of the 1954 founding eight members of the Relais & Châteaux chain which is still owned by the same family and occupies the same site. Arguably, Françoise is the most elegant hostess at any hotel I know. She, like Phillipe, is deeply involved in all aspects of running the business. Most of the 32 bedrooms and suites are located in buildings scattered around the 15-acre grounds. The gardens are magnificent and furnishings are lavish (recently the dining rooms have been completely refurbished). Staff, mostly long-established regulars, are supreme professionals.

Chefs come and go but the Depées know what they want from their *cuisiniers*. Standards are high and, whoever the chef, specialities reflect both modern and neo-classical styles.
Menus D-F. Rooms (32) F-F3. Disabled. Cards All.
Closed Feb.
Post Les Bézards, 45290 Boismorand, Loiret.
Tel 38 31 80 01. Telex 780998. Fax 38 31 84 51. Mich 70/C2.

BLOIS

La Péniche

Comfortable restaurant/Cooking 1-2
Good value

Some of you will recall Gérard Bosque at his Botte d'Asperges in Contres (first editions of *FL*). For the last ten years he's been afloat, on a handsome, renovated barge tied-up on the right bank of the Loire. Classical cooking with an emphasis on fish and shellfish (there's a sea-water tank for the latter in the dining room); *blanquette de la mer* is a blockbuster.
Menus B. Cards All. (On N152, between the two Blois bridges.)
Closed Sun (not pub. hols). (Adjacent quayside parking.)
Post promenade Mail, 41000 Blois, L.-et-Ch.
Tel 54 74 37 23. Mich 68/C3.

BLOIS   Au Rendez-vous des Pêcheurs

Very simple restaurant/Cooking 2-3
Good value

A reader gave me the nod, in early 1992, about young Eric
Reithler, the new chef/patron at a modest bistro just off the
Loire's right bank, near the château. What a find; what value
for money. Eric worked for Guy Savoy in Paris and how that
shows: modern inventiveness, demonstrated to perfection in his
mainly fish-based specialities and masterful desserts.
Menus B. Cards Access, Visa. (Off N152, Loire right bank.)
Closed Sun. Mon evg. (Park off quayside 200 m. upriver.)
Post 27 rue du Foix, 41000 Blois, L.-et-Ch.
Tel 54 74 67 48. Fax 54 74 47 67. Mich 68/C3.

BRINON-SUR-SAULDRE   La Solognote

Comfortable hotel/Cooking 3
Quiet/Gardens/Parking/Good value

Andrée and Dominique Girard's hotel is typical of the red-brick
buildings throughout the Sologne. The atmosphere is homely,
the welcome warm and both the hotel and Dominque's cooking
are unpretentious. The latter is classical with a lighter touch
applied to several fish dishes. The chef smokes his own
Scottish salmon and, come the autumn, shows off his cooking
skills with the Sologne's varied game. Falling leaves also see
him capitalising on the forests' larder of fungi: *cèpes*, *girolles*
and *champignons sauvages*.
Menus B-D. Rooms (13) C-D. Cards Access, Visa.
Closed 15 Feb to 15 Mar. 12 to 20 May. 8 to 24 Sept. Tues evg
(Oct to June). Wed.
Post 18410 Brinon-sur-Sauldre, Cher.
Tel 48 58 50 29. Fax 48 58 56 00. Mich 69/F3.

CANDE-SUR-BEUVRON   Hostellerie de la Caillère

Comfortable restaurant with rooms/Cooking 3
Terrace/Gardens/Parking/Good value

There's no disputing the fact that during the last five years
this entrancing spot (vine-covered cottages hidden behind
chestnut trees in the Beuvron Valley) has emerged as one of
the most popular favourites in the Loire. Jacky Guindon is a
fine chef, breakfasts are great and readers, like me, cannot
explain the loss of his Michelin star. "We loved it" and "Best
meal of the holiday" are commonplace plaudits. Cooking is
mainly modern (one example is an anything but insipid *sandre
aux agrumes et gingembre*), the odd gutsy classical *plat* (*pièce
de boeuf à la moelle*) and some modern classical alternatives
(*rognon de veau en papillote de poitrine fumée*). Nine new
bedrooms have recently been built in a separate block. Top
marks to both Jacky and Françoise.
Menus B-D. Rooms (9) C-D. Cards DC, Access, Visa.
Closed Mid Jan to Feb. Rest: Wed. (On D7, east of village.)
Post rte Montils, 41120 Candé-sur-Beuvron, L.-et-Ch.
Tel 54 44 03 08. Fax 54 44 05 95. Mich 68/B3.

CHINON   Au Plaisir Gourmand

Very comfortable restaurant/Cooking 3-4
Gardens

FL3 readers will recall that Jean-Claude Rigollet left the
Auberge des Templiers at Les Bézards to take up teaching.
Chalking blackboards didn't last long; in 1984 he and Danielle
opened their own restaurant in a 17th-century house near the
castle walls. Standards are superlative in this pleasure trove
of authentic classical cooking. Saucing is consumate, especially
those based on red Chinon wine. Whichever way you turn
haute cuisine gems sparkle: *matelote d'anguille au Chinon* and
sandre au beurre blanc (both locally caught); *cuissot de
lapereau à l'ancienne* (*jambon de canard* gets the same
treatment; the dish is worth ordering for the sauce alone); and
highly polished desserts with many a flattering facet like
crème grand-mère à la cassonade. The *cave* of Chinon wines is
a *tour de force*, among them numerous L'Echo vintages, from
Jean-Claude's very own vineyard. Note the Wedgwood crockery.
Menus B-D. Cards Access, Visa. (Rooms? Base & next but one.)
Closed 3 wks Feb. 2nd half Nov. Sun evg & Mon.
Post 2 rue Parmentier, 37500 Chinon, I.-et-L.
Tel 47 93 20 48. Mich 81/F1. (Not far from Vienne right bank.)

CHINON   Château de Marçay

Very comfortable hotel/Cooking 3
Secluded/Terrace/Gardens/Swim pool/Tenn/Lift/Parking

For once advertising blurbs match reality: 20th-century luxury
in a 15th-century setting. This is, I imagine, what comes to
mind if you picture the archetypal Relais & Châteaux hotel.
Expensive but super luxury at the heart of Rabelais' *pays*.
Modern and neo-classical cooking is often praised but, alas, is
often thumped: sleepy soufflés which refuse to rise; and meat
courses which arrive barely cooked.
Menus B-D. Rooms (34) F-F3. Cards All.
Closed 10 Jan to 10 Mar. (7 km south of Chinon; use D116.)
Post Marçay, 37500 Chinon, I.-et-L.
Tel 47 93 03 47. Telex 751475. Fax 47 93 45 33. Mich 81/F2.

CHINON   La Giraudière

Simple hotel/Cooking 1
Secluded/Terrace/Gardens/Parking/Good value

Fluent English-speaking Jean-Jacques Daviet is universally
appreciated; he's an attentive, friendly owner. Readers like the
peaceful atmosphere. I don't envy J-J his continuing battle to
refurbish and maintain the 17th-century manor house. Highly
recommended as an overnight base. I'm less sure about the
new dining room/kitchen. Chefs have changed, cooking is
classical: the jury is out. (NW of Chinon; 1 km off D749.)
Menus B. Rooms (25) B-E. Cards All. (*Cuisinettes* available.)
Closed Rest: Jan. Tues & Wed (mid Sept to mid May).
Post Beaumont-en-Véron, 37420 Avoine, I.-et-L.
Tel 47 58 40 36. Fax 47 58 46 06. Mich 81/E1.

CHITENAY   **Auberge du Centre**

Comfortable hotel/Cooking 2
Terrace/Gardens/Parking/Good value

Gilles Martinet was born in the *auberge* in the year his
grandmother started the business (1951). She was the first
cook and Gilles' mother followed her into the kitchen. What a
transformation the English-speaking chef and his blond wife,
Brigitte, have masterminded in their four-year tenure: a
colourful freshness permeates the *auberge*, both inside and
out. Ambitious classical and *Bourgeoise* cooking.
Menus B-C. Rooms (23) C-D. Disabled. Cards Access, Visa.
Closed Feb. Sun evg & Mon (Oct to Apl).
Post 41120 Chitenay, L.-et-Ch.
Tel 54 70 42 11. Fax 54 70 35 03. Mich 68/C3.

COUR-CHEVERNY   **Trois Marchands**

Comfortable hotel/Cooking 2
Parking/Good value

The Bricault family has owned the hotel for over a century.
The annexe is disliked by all; rooms in the main hotel cause no
problems. Classical cooking which, one suspects, has remained
unchanged for a century too. Some menu permutations provide
perfect meals: asparagus, chicken breast in a cream sauce and
strawberries. Keep it simple; you'll not go wrong.
Menus B-C. Rooms (38) B-D. Cards All.
Closed Feb-15 Mar. Mon midday (Easter-June). Mon (Oct-Easter).
Post 41700 Cour-Cheverny, L.-et-Ch.
Tel 54 79 96 44. Fax 54 79 25 60. Mich 68/C3.

FONTEVRAUD-L'ABBAYE   **Abbaye**

Very simple restaurant/Cooking 1-2
Parking/Good value

There's now't simpler in *Encore*; but what satisfaction André
Côme has provided readers exploring the village which has
such important links with English history. Grills, *Bourgeois*
and classical *plats*: *côte d'agneau grillée*, *saumon grillé beurre
blanc* and *poire belle-Hélène* are typical.
Menus A-B. Cards Access, Visa. (Rooms? See Base hotels.)
Closed Feb. Oct. Tues evg. Wed.
Post 8 av. des Roches, 49590 Fontevraud-l'Abbaye, M.-et-L.
Tel 41 51 71 04. Mich 81/E1.

GIEN   **Rivage**

Comfortable hotel/Cooking 3
Parking

The Rivage has changed out of all recognition in the decade
since I first visited the riverside *relais*. Christian Gaillard has
an eye for both hotelkeeping and what's needed to be a
successful restaurateur. Light and airy modern rooms, plenty

209

of flowers, stylish service and a professional, sure touch in the kitchen; the ingredients gel well and please enormously. Classical, neo-classical and regional specialities. A typical example is a rich *jambonnette de poularde au foie gras et jus de truffes*. A more modern and easily digestible dish, trout with spinach in olive oil, is just as pleasing. Spanking fresh cheeses and several local wines (see wine notes).

Menus B-D. Rooms (19) C-E. Cards All.
Post 1 quai Nice, 45500 Gien, Loiret. (Right bank of Loire.)
Tel 38 67 20 53. Fax 38 38 10 21. Mich 70/B2.

HUISSEAU-SUR-COSSON   Château de Nanteuil

Simple hotel/Cooking 1-2
Quiet/Terrace/Gardens/Parking/Good value

Read Stella King's masterpiece, *Jacqueline*, and you'll grasp why this château, which has a well-worn look about it, is in *Encore*. The château played a major part in the heroic story of Yvonne Rudellat, an SOE agent during the last war. (Another intriguing twist, which I didn't know about until I read the book, is that Moune Gardnor-Beard married Owen Watson; read *The Pottery at Mesland* in the regional introduction.)

Anglophile Frédéric Théry is the third generation owner; his English grandfather bought the château earlier this century. The terrace, which overlooks the River Cosson, is a dream; another bonus is the seven acres of wooded grounds. Classical and *Bourgeoise* cooking, plus one or two regional offerings: representative of the spectrum are *emincé de boeuf au vinaigre de Xéres*, *faux-filet grillé sauce Roquefort* and both *salade Tourangelle* (which includes *rillons*) and *tarte Tatin*.

Menus B. Rooms (10) B-D. Cards Ac's, Visa. Dinner compulsory.
Closed Jan. One wk Nov. Rest: Mon. Tues midday.
Post Huisseau-sur-Cosson, 41350 Vineuil, L.-et-Ch.
Tel 54 42 61 98. Fax 54 42 37 23. Mich 68/C3.

LANGEAIS   Hosten & Rest. Langeais

Comfortable hotel/Cooking 3
Garage

Anne and I were happy to return to a much loved favourite (our first visit was 30 years ago). In the early Eighties the hotel closed temporarily; as a consequence there was no entry in earlier *FL* editions. Jean-Jacques and Joëlle Hosten have restored the reputation of the vine-covered family hotel (opened in 1904) with a vengeance. Classical cooking is not dead in France; far from it. (You may think otherwise studying the top Gault Millau awards: those go to inventive chefs; most classical masters get the cold shoulder for the big gongs.) Jean-Jacques style is immaculate *haute cuisine*. His menu includes obvious classics like *tournedos Rossini*, *homard Cardinal* and *crêpes au Grand Marnier*. But mouthwaterers from other regions tempt too: *bourride* and *mouclade* are just two.

Menus C-D. Rooms (11) D-F. Cards All.
Closed 10 Jan to 10 Feb. 20 June to 10 July. Mon evg. Tues.
Post 2 rue Gambetta, 37130 Langeais, I.-et-L.
Tel 47 96 82 12. Fax 47 96 56 72. Mich 67/E4.

MONTREUIL-BELLAY   Splendid et Relais du Bellay

Comfortable hotel/Cooking 1
Gardens & Swimming pool (annexe)/Parking/Good value

What a mixed saddle bag of reports: the hotel and modern annexe (Relais du Bellay) squeak in by the thickness of this page (60 gsm for your interest). Gripes about disinterested and insolent reception and average food are some of the debits. Credits? Rooms are reckoned to be well appointed. One reader's son (22), who hated France, spent a happy week here and became an instant Francophile. Readers point out that the hotel is a popular base for a British cycling tour operator. Cooking? *Bourgeoise* & grills. The hotel leaflet claims light, creative local cuisine. Puncture that claim pronto M. Berville.
Menus A-C. Rooms (40) B-D. Cards Access, Visa.
Closed Rest: Sun evg (mid Oct to mid Mar). Mich 81/D2.
Post rue Dr Gaudrez, 49260 Montreuil-Bellay, M.-et-L.
Tel 41 52 30 21 (H). 41 52 35 50 (Annexe). Fax 41 52 45 17.

NOUAN-LE-FUZELIER   Le Dahu

Comfortable restaurant/Cooking 2-3
Terrace/Gardens/Parking/Good value

I must have received a couple of dozen letters or more telling me in no uncertain terms to pay a call on Jean-Luc and Marie-Thérèse Germain at their colourful little restaurant (once a Solognote farm with fine timbers) where flowers play such an eye-catching part both inside and out. Jean-Luc continues the theme in his cooking. Modern, light specialities, often just as flavoursome and bright as *le jardin* outside, tickle both the palate and pupils: examples like a subtle *soupe de moules à la fleur de thym* and a *saumon au beurre rouge*.
Menus B-C. Cards AE, Access, Visa. (Short walk to Base hotel.)
Closed 20 Feb to 20 Mar. Tues evg & Wed (not July & Aug).
Post 14 r. H.-Chapron, 41600 Nouan-le-Fuzelier, L.-et-Ch.
Tel 54 88 72 88. Mich 69/E3.

NOUAN-LE-FUZELIER   Moulin de Villiers

Simple hotel/Cooking 1
Secluded/Gardens/Parking/Good value

The ancient *moulin*, once a watermill used to grind wheat, is a mini version of the Sologne. Everyone who seeks out the 17 acres of private woodland is bowled over by the setting. Surrounded by the Sologne forests, the mill has its own very sizeable *étang*, streams and marshes. Two friendly and good-humoured angels, Gérard and Gladys Andrieux, care over you. (Her grandfather bought the property in 1929). As one reader wrote: at breakfast on the terrace you're just as likely to encounter a guest introducing a still wriggling 2 kg perch, caught in the *étang*. Cooking is basic *Bourgeoise*.
Menus A-B. Rooms (20) B-D. Cards Access, Visa.
Closed 4 Jan-20 Mar. 1-15 Sept. Tues evg & Wed (Oct to Dec).
Post 41600 Nouan-le-Fuzelier, L.-et-Ch.
Tel 54 88 72 27. Mich 69/E3. (On D44, 3 km NE of village.)

ONZAIN
Pont d'Ouchet

Very simple restaurant with basic rooms/Cooking 1-2
Parking/Good value

Simple and small in every way yet massive in spirit and hugely popular with readers. Go once and return often. For 30 years the Cochets have enchanted clients. Louisette, who speaks English, is reckoned by many to be better entertainment than the copious meals. Antonin's repertoire is *Bourgeois* and grills with the odd local dish. Madame rates her husband's *moules marinière* as the best in the world.

Menus A-B. Rooms (9) B. Cards Access, Visa.
Closed Dec-Feb. Sun evg & Mon. (Also see Onzain Base hotel.)
Post 50 Grande Rue, 41150 Onzain, L.-et-Ch.
Tel 54 20 70 33. Mich 68/B3.

ROCHECORBON
L'Oubliette

Comfortable restaurant/Cooking 2
Terrace/Parking/Good value

New owners, Thierry and Anne-Marie Duhamel, have maintained the exacting standards set by Carole and Jean-Paul Chevreuil (see *FL3*). This unusual restaurant is *taillé dans le roc*; the Duhamels have added a second troglodyte dining room. Thierry has carved out a modern repertoire: there's nothing bland or prissy about a *filet de turbot au curry et riz basmati aux fruits secs*. The odd neo-classical interpretations are less Impressionist: an emphatic, well-sauced *canard du Marais au Chinon* is typical of his polished skills and technique.

Menus B-C. Cards Access, Visa.
Closed Sun evg & Mon. (Rooms? See base, Les Fontaines St-G'.)
Post 37210 Rochecorbon, I.-et-L.
Tel 47 52 50 49. Mich 67/F4. (In village, north of N152.)

ROMORANTIN-LANTHENAY Grand Hôtel Lion d'Or

Luxury hotel/Cooking 4
Terrace/Lift/Parking

Emphatically, without any question, this superb family hotel is one of three supreme readers' favourites. During the last decade I've received a three-figure number of reports praising the family foursome: Colette and Alain Barrat; their daughter, Marie-Christine; and her husband, chef Didier Clément.

Didier is a gentle giant with a subtle sense of humour. Like his wife and her parents, he wears no false airs or graces. If ever a cooking style matched a personality then here is the perfect example: delicate, unassertive and with the odd chuckle here and there. Remember that you lovers of classical cuisine. Fluent English-speaking Marie is an intelligent, gifted girl and is deeply involved in her husband's *métier*. Her studies of medieval cooking have played a huge part in Didier's inventive modern repertoire; his use of spices (commonplace centuries ago), *aromates* and flavouring agents is exceptional. Occasionally a marriage combination hits the rocks: for one reader snails in liquorice were inedible, like rubber all-sorts.

Few thumbs-down bleats have come my way. Those that do are about ever-climbing prices. Luxury is the word I now use to describe the stunning interior, with prices to match. One tip: bypass the cheapest, little-choice, poor-value three course menu (D). Almost every one of the three dozen à la carte specialities can be "shared" between two clients. Use this clever method to tailor-make your own multi-course meal; but still budget on breaking the F band barrier.
Menus D-F. Rooms (13) F-F3. Disabled. Cards All.
Closed Jan to mid Feb.
Post 69 r. G. Clémenceau, 41200 Romorantin-Lanth'y, L.-et-Ch.
Tel 54 76 00 28. Telex 750990. Fax 54 88 24 87. Mich 69/D4.

TOURS   Bardet

Luxury hotel/Cooking 4
Secluded/Gardens/Swimming pool/Parking

Everything about Jean Bardet's spacious new home is larger than life, complementing to a tee the hugely likeable and sizeable English-speaking chef and his extrovert wife, Sophie. All is now set for star three: 7½ acres of grounds; luxury lounges and dining rooms; romantic bedrooms; and top-notch staff. Cooking is opulent modern. *Foie gras poêlé* (blackish exterior but soft inside) *aux pommes acidulées et navets confits* (sliced so thin they're transparent) is an 18-carat gem. Bardet claims that beautiful recipes come from poverty and not from luxury. Do scallops sandwiched between slices of black truffle and sitting atop a mush of celery and truffle come from poverty? The succulent scallops, strangled to death, cried out to be served on their own. *Faites simple* Jean.
Bardet is a big-bucks business. Witness the catalogue on your table listing wines, cognac, chocs, sweets, crystal, pots and pans, silverware, linen, jewellery and goodness knows what else. Buy them in his shop or mail-order when you get home.
Menus D-F. Rooms (16) F-F3. Cards All. (N of Loire, E of N10.)
Closed 21 Feb-9 Mar. Rest: Sun evg(No-Mar).Mon(ex evg Ap-Oct).
Post 57 rue Groison, 37100 Tours, I.-et-L.
Tel 47 41 41 11. Telex 752463. Fax 47 51 68 72. Mich 67/F4.

TOURS   Hôtel de Groison & Rest. Jardin du Castel

Very comfortable hotel/Cooking 3
Quiet/Terrace/Gardens/Garage

The new home of Guy Tricon and Jean André who beguiled *FL3* readers at their Aub. Mourrachonne (Côte d'Azur). The new setting can't match that seductive spot; nevertheless, a lunch in the garden, shaded by massive trees, is a pleasure. Guy's repertoire is modern and neo-classical: savour exotic dishes like a *brochet croustillant au vinaigre et légumes caramélises* (crisp on one side, the pike is the ideal mate for caramelised vegetables) and a *compote de canard de Challans* in a red wine sauce and served with *navets* tasting more like pears.
Menus B-E. Rooms (10) F. Cards All. (Superb breakfasts.)
Closed 15 Jan-15 Feb. Sat midday. Wed. (N of Loire; E of N10.)
Post 10 rue Groison, 37100 Tours, I.-et-L.
Tel 47 41 94 90. Fax 47 51 50 28. Mich 67/F4.

LYONNAIS

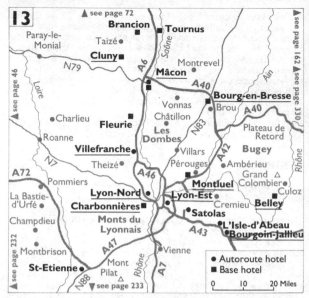

see page 72

13

Paray-le-Monial

Brancion ▪ **Tournus**

Taizé •

Cluny ▪

Montrevel

Mâcon

Saône

A6

A40

Ain

Bourg-en-Bresse

Vonnas •

Brou ▪ A40

Châtillon •

N83

Fleurie ▪

Charlieu •

Les Dombes

Plateau de Retord

Roanne

• Villars

Bugey

Villefranche •

Théizé •

Pérouges ▪ • Ambérieu

A72

A46

Grand △ Colombier

Pommiers

Lyon-Nord •

Montluel

La Bastie-d'Urfé •

Lyon-Est

Culoz

Champdieu •

Charbonnières ▪

Cremieu • **Belley**

• Satolas

Monts du Lyonnais

L'Isle-d'Abeau

A47

A43

Bourgoin-Jallieu

Montbrison •

Rhône

A7

• Vienne

St-Etienne •

Mont Pilat △

N88

see page 233

see page 46 · see page 232 · see page 162 · see page 330

N79

Loire

N7

• Autoroute hotel
▪ Base hotel

0   10   20 Miles

Many years ago I was berated by a reader for suggesting that **Les Dombes**, a flat landscape peppered with *étangs* (pools) and north-east of **Lyon**, was well worth exploring. The reader maintained his detour had been a waste of time. I asked what map he had used. "Michelin 989" was the reply.

Any map with a scale of 10 km to one cm is useless if you are to get the best out of a small enclave of terrain. That's as true of Les Dombes as it is of another upturned triangle of mountain country called **Bugey**. I would like to use what follows, described in some detail, as a classic example of "Hidden France" at its best; get out the large-scale maps and escape the hordes. Visit Bugey once and you'll return often.

Where is Bugey? Part of the *département* of Ain, Bugey is to the east of Lyon. It's borders are the River **Ain** to the west and, to the south and east, the great "V" formed by the energy creating powerhouse of the River **Rhône**.

Most tourists only ever see the grim works of man on or alongside the Rhône: giant dams, cement works, power stations and vast viaducts. Only "insiders" know of the numerous surprises awaiting those who venture into the mountains.

Where do you start? Simple, on the D120 at **Culoz**. The road scrambles up steep, rocky slopes and then through the shade of beech and pine to the 5003-ft-high **Grand Colombier**. Detour first to the Grand Fenestrez, a window 3000 ft above Culoz. The view is a stunner. Far more entertaining are the acoustics: you may hear, clearly, the chimes of a church, a dog barking, a car starting or a boat chugging along the Rhône. All are miles away but appear to be 20 ft below you.

The views from Grand Colombier are among the finest in the Alps: to the east a series of great lakes and high snow peaks; to the west the wishbone-shaped valley of a tiny area, within Bugey, called Valromey. Only 100 square miles in size, the valley is an intriguing haven of content and pleasure.

see page 72

Tournus

Cluny ▲

Charolles

Châteauneuf △

Fuissé △
Chénas △
Fleurie △

Montmerle-sur-Saône

Roanne

Blaceret △

Theizé ▲

Pont-de-Vaux

Mâcon

A6

A40

Bourg-en-Bresse

A40

Ochiaz ▲

Dompierre-▲
sur-Veyle

Méximieux
Artemare

Belley

LYON

Montrond-
▲les-Bains

Vienne

Faverges-de-
▲ la-Tour

ST-ETIENNE

see page 46
see page 162
see page 331
see page 232
see page 233

N79 · A6 · A40 · N83 · A46 · A42 · A72 · N7 · A47 · A43 · A7 · N88 · Saône · Loire · Rhône · Ain

| ▲ | Hotel/Rest (rooms) |
| △ | Restaurant only |

0   10   20 Miles

When is the best time to visit Valromey? Arguably in April,
May or June when some of Nature's greatest treats are laid
out at your feet. In April gigantic eiderdowns of yellow jonquils
flood the pastures on the **Plateau de Retord**; in May and
early June equally gargantuan duvets of white narcissi take
their place (Anne and I have picked armfuls in minutes). Other
wild flowers, less numerous in number, fight their corner to
catch your eye: dog-tooth violets, gentians, trollius and
cranesbill geraniums among them. The best displays are from
the Crêt du Nu to the northern slopes of the Col de Bérentin.

Make the most of the lanes that tumble down from the Grand
Colombier and twist north again to the Col de Richemont. The
gentle vale immediately south-west of the latter is a visual
tonic: a combination of pastures, woods and peaks combine to
refresh and satisfy. Walks abound hereabouts.

At the Col de Richemont you'll spot the first of numerous
reminders of the Bugey *maquis*. The Valromey underground
was one of the most courageous. Their poignant memorial is on
the D8 just west of Luthézieu. The monument's few words
strike a telling truth: *"Nous avons combattu avec un tronçon
d'epée."* ("We fought with a broken sword.") Nearby St-Maurice
was totally destroyed by the Germans.

To discover some of the reasons why the Valromey patriots
fought so valiantly seek out the marvellous Musée Rural du
Valromey at Lochieu. (Their ancestors included Saracens; note
the Arabic influence in some village names ending with "az"
and "oz".) The *musée* is the epitome of just what a rural
museum should be in unearthing, from the past, a rare
collection of intriguing treasures.

Originally the museum was a 16th-century fortified house
with unusual medieval windows. There's a living room; cellars
which show how Bugey wines were produced; a costume room;
an archaeological room; a children's room; and outside annexes

with harvesting, threshing and dairy machinery.

Centuries ago every Valromey village had a *seigneur* and one of his many perks was the right to own the sole oven. Many ovens can still be seen. There's one at Don, which is put to good use at the village's annual festival held during the second weekend in August. There's another *four* at Vaux-Morets on the D31D north of Dom; and others at Belmont, south of Luthézieu, and at Ouche, east of Don.

Water and wine have always played an important part in the life of both Valromey and Bugey. First water. Three spots should be sought out. The Source du Groin is easily found on the map. Park at Vaux-Morets, walk to the source and wonder at the weird 30-metre deep hole in the ground, from which gushes forth water absorbed elsewhere in Valromey. The cascade at Cerveyrieu is a more conventional 200-ft-high waterfall; access is from the D31 west of Don. The Pain Sucre is another unusual sight, a stalagmite formed by a waterfall below the D30, south-west of Brénaz. Happy navigating.

In centuries past Bugey wines were highly regarded, especially by the greatest of all French gastronomes, Brillat Savarin (born in **Belley** in 1755). Visit Flaxieu, where Camille Crussy supplies many a famous French restaurant, and the *caves* of Le Caveau Bugiste; and Eugene Monin et fils at Vongnes. Savour sparklers, Chardonnay whites, and both reds and rosés. One illustrious vineyard made Brillat-Savarin's favourite tipple, Manicle. The Miraillet family is working hard to restore the famed vineyard; you'll spot the vines from the N504 just east of Cheignieu-la-Balme. Buy the wines from the house behind the church, to the west of the phone box.

If you visit Bugey during the first weekend in August then don't miss the mechanical organ fair at Contrevoz, north-west of Belley. Everyone in the village is involved; organs come from all over Europe; and the village oven works non-stop, baking special breads and *galettes*.

Nose out, too, the Château d'Andert, just off the D32 from Contrevoz to Belley. The 360-degree panorama is pleasure number one; the second is the 17th-century château; and the third is the fine range of home-made *cassis* products, especially the *jus naturel* (no sugar and no alcohol).

There's a lot more in the Lyonnais to interest and please. I'll pinpoint a handful of areas, all of which deserve to be explored – with the right maps. I'll describe them briefly.

Les Dombes is a strange, alluring landscape, one which is now encircled by a quartet of autoroutes: the **A6** to the west; the **A40** to the north; the **A42** to the east; and the new Lyon bypass, the **A46**, to the south. The plain is spotted with a couple of thousand *étangs*. These, and the marshy fields that surround them, are full of wildlife: my family and I have often idled away many pleasurable hours on the edges of some of the ponds, watching the endless varieties of birds.

If time doesn't allow such dallying, head for the Slimbridge equivalent at **Villars**-les-Dombes. Notable, too, are the *villages fleuris*: **Vonnas** is a 4-star stunner; **Châtillon**-sur-Chalaronne is equally colourful (the medieval timbered buildings are eye-catching pluses).

On the bottom edge of Les Dombes is **Pérouges**, a small village on top of one of the low hills that line the right bank of the Rhône. Four centuries ago this atmospheric hilltop citadel was a busy, thriving place; 300 years later it had all but fallen into ruin. At the turn of this century it was even threatened with demolition. Walk the narrow streets, soak up the dream-like atmosphere that shrouds its stone and timbered houses, and seek out the lime tree at its heart.

An exceptional architectural magnet on the north-eastern borders of Les Dombes is the Eglise de **Brou**, a Gothic structure full of rich treasures. Enjoy the cool cloisters and the adjoining monastery which now houses the Ain Museum.

In the triangle formed by **Tournus, Mâcon** and **Bourg-en-Bresse** are more than 30 Bressane farms with *cheminées Sarrasines* (Saracen chimneys). Three of the best are: Grange des Planons, north of St-Cyr-sur-Menthon (on the N79); Ferme de Sougey, west of **Montrevel** (on the D975); and Ferme de la Forêt, east of St-Trivier-de-Courtes (north of Montrevel).

In the hills between Tournus and Mâcon, and the river valleys of the Grosne and **Saône**, are numerous Romanesque churches: the great pink abbey of St-Philibert at Tournus; the simple structure of the church of St-Pierre at **Brancion**; the striking, high-towered Eglise St-Martin at Chapaize; the now sad remains of **Cluny** Abbey but once a fantastic sight – second only to St-Peter's in Rome – and radiating enormous influence throughout Europe; and smaller examples at Ougy, Malay, Blanot, Berzé-la-Ville and elsewhere.

Taizé, north of Cluny, was founded by Brother Roger in 1940; each year about 100,000 young people, of all nationalities and denominations, spend time at the tented village camp. The "church" resembles a concrete bunker; but the interior has an overwhelming sense of peace and faith.

The name Beaujolais is primarily associated with a pleasant enough red wine but there's much else to capture your attention. Start in the south, in *au pays des pierres dorées*. Villages here are constructed from the local stone, a golden-textured, warm material, much darker than the Cotswold variety. Seek out both **Theizé** and Oingt. To the north is "Clochmerle" country, made famous by Gabriel Chevallier; Vaux-en-Beaujolais is a must for all his fans.

Follow the string of Beaujolais villages, from Brouilly to St-Amour. Detour to two terrific viewpoints: one atop Mont Brouilly (descend to the east, to St-Lager); and La Terrasse, above **Fleurie**. Cross the Beaujolais hills to **Charlieu** with a 1,000-year-old Bénédictine abbey and the 15th-century Cloîtres des Cordeliers. Between Charlieu and **Paray-le-Monial** (the impetus to build Sacré-Coeur in Paris came from this pilgrimage town and its Romanesque basilica) is Le Brionnais. Several villages have Romanesque churches: the best two are at Semur-en-Brionnais and Anzy-le-Duc.

Do you need any more ideas? There's **Cremieu** to the east of Lyon where I've often marvelled at the huge covered market halls; **Vienne** with many Roman ruins, cathedral and several old churches; **Mont Pilat** and its regional park, a lung for dreary **St-Etienne** and with notable panoramas; and the cool, quiet hills (during weekdays) to the west of Lyon, known by the ambitious name of **Monts du Lyonnais** (the area around Yzeron is especially pleasant). And there's Lyon itself: it has been a long time since Anne and I endured the noise and bustle of the busy city but we have fond memories of old Lyon, on the right bank of the River Saône.

Markets Ambérieu-en-Bugey (Wed, Fri & Sat); Bourg-en-Bresse (Wed & Sat); Belley (Sat); Châtillon-sur-Chalaronne (Sat); Paray-le-Monial (Fri); Tournus (Sat); Vonnas (Thurs). Michelin green guide: Vallée du Rhône.

Les Mères Merveilleuses

Ask any Francophile gastronome which region of France is the culinary tops and I'll wager the answer will be "Lyonnais".

Arguably, the Lyonnais has more skilled chefs than any other French region. However, the present-day cooking styles of the famed Lyonnais chefs bear no resemblance whatsoever to the repertoires of the cooks who, during the last couple of centuries, laid the foundations for the region's worldwide fame. For a start, modern cooking today is somewhat different from the classical and regional traditions of the past. But, more fundamentally than that, it was a large number of lady chefs, *cuisinières*, who originally established the culinary reputation of the region. They were known as *les mères*.

La Mère Guy is said to be the lady who, 200 years ago, started it all. At the turn of this century, Françoise Fillioux was among the most famous of *les mères* working in the Lyonnais. Her repertoire was small but each speciality was honed to perfection (in this she was not alone; all of them shared the same characteristic).

Madame Fillioux's contemporaries included Elisa Blanc at Vonnas, Marie Bourgeois at Priay and the remarkable Madame Eugénie Brazier, the latter trained by Françoise herself. They were many others; but what is remarkable is that each of these four won either two or three Michelin stars.

(One intriguing aside: "outsiders" marrying into a family can protect and improve culinary skills. The Bressane family Blanc is a culinary dynasty. Georges Blanc is the fourth generation chef at the world-famous Vonnas restaurant. His great-grandmother, Virginie Gervais, was the first to graft on real cooking talent to the Blanc tree; she had passed on her magical touch to her daughter, Elisa Blanc (née Gervais), who won her first Michelin star in 1929 and a second in 1931. Another outsider, Pauline, married Elisa's son, Jean Blanc; she preserved her mother-in-law's second star from 1934 until 1968, when her son, Georges, took over. He won a third Michelin star in 1981 and, 11 years later, he retains the ultimate accolade, so revered by all chefs.)

Indeed, during the Thirties, there was the exceptional situation where Madame Brazier ran two restaurants, each with three stars: one in Lyon itself, the other at her "bungalow" on the Col de la Luère. After the war she retained the third star for many years at her home in the hills to the west of Lyon. Just as amazingly, Marie Bourgeois, too, was the holder of three Michelin stars at her seedy *auberge* in Priay (north-east of Lyon), classified by Bibendum at the time as a "small hotel without modern comforts". There's no way that either Eugénie or Marie would win a third star today when so much emphasis is put on non-culinary criteria.

Anne and I count ourselves lucky that, from the late Fifties to the early Eighties, we had the chance to discover why *les mères* had won such legendary reputations. By the Eighties almost all traces of their unique styles had disappeared.

We made single visits to the Col de la Luère and to Vonnas, when Paulette Blanc was *la cuisinière*. The two meals were memorable affairs but it was a series of visits to La Mère Bourgeois at Priay which opened our eyes to just what levels "old" culinary skills could reach.

By 1960, when we made our first visit, Marie Bourgeois had passed on but not before she had taught Georges Berger her entire repertoire and not before he had absorbed her awesome array of skills. Georges and his delectable wife, Jannie (the most gorgeous hostess we've ever encountered), ran the same bistro in Priay for 30 years and, believe it or not, before retiring, they had retained a Michelin two-star award for most of their tenure of La Mère Bourgeois.

When asked what has been our most loved restaurant, Anne and I need only a nano-second to provide the answer: Georges and Jannie Berger's La Mère Bourgeois. A trio of his specialities, all passed on by Marie, remain among our choice of the top ten dishes we've relished on our many travels over the decades: *pâté chaud de Madame Bourgeois sauce aux truffes*, a spectacular recipe and said by Fernand Point to be one of the greatest dishes of all time; *omble chevalier au beurre moussant*, the pinnacle of freshwater specialities, where a huge char is cooked in a modest amount of butter but, at the point of final preparation in the kitchen, copious amounts of fresh butter, which has been creamed, beaten and heated, is poured on; and *île flottante aux pralines* served with tasty *petits choux* (*profiteroles* stuffed with confectioner's custard and topped with crisp caramel), an incomparable dessert which bears no resemblance to the normal floating islands.

(Twenty-five years ago, in 1967, a bedroom, breakfast, dinner, wine, coffee, Evian, tax and service cost a total of 95 francs at Priay – for two people.)

Other dishes cooked by Georges were replicas of the classics made famous by the band of ladies tagged *les mères*: *fonds d'artichauts* with truffled *foie gras*, *terrine de volaille pistachée, loup braisée au Chablis, poulet de Bresse pochée aux morilles* (and in numerous other forms), *quenelles au gratin au beurre d'écrevisses, la glace pralinés*; and simpler delights like *haricots verts* and *fromage blanc crème de la maison* – both, to this day, unmatched anywhere else.

Isn't it revealing, that despite all the modern creations of today, both Anne and I can recall those classics of the past with much greater pleasure. For many of us, fortunate enough to have known La Mère Bourgeois during its finest days, this was indeed "the greatest restaurant in the world".

Cheeses Cow's milk

Bresse (Bleu de) available all the year. A mild, soft, blue cheese, made in small cylinders. One of the poorest French blue cheeses

Mont-d'Or from just north of Lyon; small disks, delicate, savory taste

Goat's milk

Bressan a small, truncated cone – also known as **Petit Bressan**

Charolais (Charolles) soft, nutty-flavoured, small cylinder

Chevreton de Mâcon if made of pure goat's milk it is at its best in summer and autumn. A light blue rind and slightly nutty taste

Without fail try **fromage blanc**; a fresh cream cheese, eaten with sugar and fresh cream. If you've never tried some, you've missed a treat

Regional Specialities

Bresse (Poulet, Poularde, Volaille de) the best French poultry. Fed on corn and, when killed, bathed in milk. Flesh is white and delicate

Gras-double ox tripe, served with onions

Poulet demi-deuil *half-mourning*; called this because of the thin slices of truffle placed under the chicken breast; cooked in a *court-bouillon*

Poulet au vinaigre chicken, shallots, tomatoes, white wine, wine vinegar and a cream sauce

Rosette a large pork sausage; (**Sabodet** see *Glossary of Menu Terms*)

Tablier de Sapeur *gras-double* coated with flour, egg-yolk, breadcrumbs

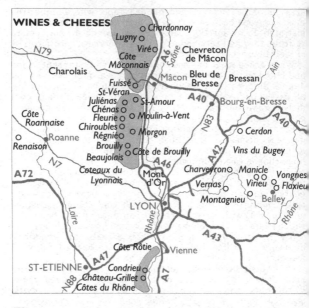

WINES & CHEESES

Chardonnay
Lugny
Viré
Chevreton de Mâcon
Côte Mâconnais
Charolais
Bleu de Bresse
Mâcon
Bressan
Fuissé
St-Véran
Juliénas
St-Amour
Bourg-en-Bresse
Chénas
Côte Roannaise
Fleurie
Moulin-à-Vent
Chiroubles
Régnié
Morgon
Cerdon
Renaison
Roanne
Brouilly
Beaujolais
Côte de Brouilly
Vins du Bugey
Coteaux du Lyonnais
Charveyron
Manicle
Vongnes
Mont d'Or
Vernas
Virieu
Flaxieu
Montagnieu
Belley
LYON
Côte Rôtie
Vienne
ST-ETIENNE
Condrieu
Château-Grillet
Côtes du Rhône

Wines (Great vintages **90**)

In Lyon they say there are three rivers: the Rhône, the Saône and the Beaujolais. Beaujolais reds are made from the Gamay grape. The best wines (growths) are from the AC *communes* of **Moulin-à-Vent**, **Brouilly**, **Fleurie** and **Morgon**; for me the **Côte de Brouilly** is the best of all. Other notable AC *communes* are **Chiroubles**, **St-Amour**, **Chénas**, **Juliénas** and the newly-promoted **Régnié**. Wines not classified among those best 10 are bottled under the **AC Beaujolais**, **AC Beaujolais-Supérieur** (not in quality, just alcohol strength) or **AC Beaujolais-Villages** grades. Three dozen or so villages make up the general latter category or they can couple their names to the AC Beaujolais: among them **Quincié**, **Lancié**, **St-Etienne-la-Varenne**, **St-Lager**, **Romanèche**, **Beaujeu**, **Vaux** and **Charentay**. In southern Beaujolais wines from villages like Lachassagne and Theizé take the inferior, catch-all AC Beaujolais classification.

Near Roanne, look out for VDQS **Côte Roannaise** reds and a **Renaison** rosé. See Burgundy for **Côte Mâconnais** wines. The **AC Côteaux du Lyonnais**, just outside the Beaujolais area, are light reds, made from the Gamay and Syrah grapes.

South of Lyon is the start of the **Côtes du Rhône**. Lyon claims for itself the **Côte Rôtie** (roasted), the home of some superb reds. Two world-famous whites are made here, from the rare Viognier grape: **Condrieu** and **Château-Grillet** (a 3½-acre vineyard – the smallest of all AC properties).

On the eastern borders of the region you'll find some tasty, inexpensive, and not well-known Bressan wines, VDQS **Vins du Bugey**: they include the whites of **Montagnieu** and **Manicle**; the reds of **Charveyron**, **Vernas** and a **Gamay**; the sparklers of **Cerdon**, **Bugey pétillant** and **mousseux**; and a **Cerdon rosé**. Other whites include **Roussette de Virieu** and **du Bugey**. Best producers are in Flaxieu and Vongnes.

BOURGOIN-JALLIEU   Campanile

Simple hotel/Cooking 1
Parking/Good value

Leave A43 L'Isle d'Abeau-Est exit. Right after toll, towards
L'Isle d'Abeau. Cross A43. Hotel to left, beyond island.
Menus A-B. Rooms (50) C. Cards Access, Visa.
Post 38080 Bourgoin-Jallieu, Isère. (En Route p 154)
Tel 74 27 01 22. Telex 308232. Fax 74 27 06 08. Mich 116/C3.
(Bookings: UK freephone 0800 897863)

BOURGOIN-JALLIEU   Climat de France

Simple hotel/Cooking 1
Terrace/Parking/Good value

See above but left after toll, towards Bourgoin. On right.
Menus A-B. Rooms (42) C. Disabled. Cards All.
Post 38300 Bourgoin-Jallieu, Isère. (En Route p 154)
Tel 74 28 52 29. Fax 74 43 94 81. Mich 116/C3.
(Bookings: UK 071 287 3181)

L'ISLE-D'ABEAU   Mercure

Very comfortable hotel/Cooking 1-2
Terrace/Gardens/Swimming pools/Tennis/Lift/Parking

A43 L'Isle d'Abeau Villefontaine exit; past toll, on left.
Menus B. Rooms (146) F. Disabled. Cards All.
Post 38090 Villefontaine, Isère. (Note: one pool indoors)
Tel 74 96 80 00. Telex 308100. Fax 74 96 80 99. Mich 116/C3.
(Bookings: UK 071 724 1000; US toll free 800 221 4542)

LYON-EST   Ibis Bron Eurexpo

Simple hotel/Cooking 1
Parking/Good value

From east: A43 Parc de Parilly (takes you south, use return
loop). From Lyon: Eurexpo Visiteurs. North of A43, on left.
Menus A. Rooms (50) C-D. Disabled. Cards Access, Visa.
Post rue M.Bastié, 69500 Bron, Rhône.
Tel 72 37 01 46. Telex 306073. Fax 78 26 65 43. Mich 116/B2.
(Bookings: UK 071 724 1000; US toll free 800 221 4542)

LYON-EST   Novotel Lyon Bron

Very comfortable hotel/Cooking 1
Terrace/Gardens/Swimming pool/Lift/Closed parking

See Ibis Bron above for exits. North of A43, on right.
Menus B. Rooms (191) E. Disabled. Cards All.
Post rue L-Terray, 69676 Bron, Rhône. (En Route p 153)
Tel 78 26 97 48. Telex 340781. Fax 78 26 45 12. Mich 116/B2.
(Bookings: UK 071 724 1000; US toll free 800 221 4542)

LYON-NORD   Campanile

Simple hotel/Cooking 1
Parking/Good value

Leave A6 exit 22 (Limonest). Hotel to west of A6.
Menus A-B. Rooms (51) C. Disabled. Cards Access, Visa.
Post 69570 Dardilly, Rhône. (En Route p 58)
Tel 78 35 48 44. Telex 310155. Fax 78 64 96 12. Mich 116/A2.
(Bookings: UK freephone 0800 897863)

LYON-NORD   Ibis Lyon Nord

Simple hotel/Cooking 1
Terrace/Swimming pool/Parking

Leave A6 exit 22 (Limonest). Hotel to west on left of road.
Menus B. Rooms (69) D. Disabled. Cards Access, Visa.
Post 69570 Dardilly, Rhône. (En Route p 58)
Tel 78 66 02 20. Telex 305250. Fax 78 47 47 93. Mich 116/A2.
(Bookings: UK 071 724 1000; US toll free 800 221 4542)

LYON-NORD   Novotel Lyon Nord

Very comfortable hotel/Cooking 1
Terrace/Gardens/Swimming pool/Lift/Closed parking

Leave A6 exit 22 (Limonest). Hotel to west of A6.
Menus B. Rooms (107) E. Cards All.
Post 69570 Dardilly, Rhône. (En Route p 58)
Tel 78 35 13 41. Telex 330962. Fax 78 35 08 45. Mich 116/A2.
(Bookings: UK 071 724 1000; US toll free 800 221 4542)

MACON   Altéa Mâcon

Very comfortable hotel/Cooking 1-2
Terrace/Lift/Parking

Previously called Frantel. Leave A6 Mâcon-Nord exit. South on
N6 to Mâcon; hotel on left. Leave A40 (from east) exit 1,
Mâcon-Nord exit; then south on N6, hotel on left.
Menus A-C. Rooms (63) E-F. Cards All.
Post 26 rue Coubertin, 71000 Mâcon, S.-et-L. (En Route p 56)
Tel 85 38 28 06. Telex 800830. Fax 85 39 11 45. Mich 102/B2.
(Bookings: UK 071 724 1000; US toll free 800 221 4542)

MACON   Climat de France

Simple hotel/Cooking 1
Parking/Good value

See Altéa exit details above. South of A40, left side N6.
Menus A-B. Rooms (42) C. Disabled. Cards AE, Access, Visa.
Post 71000 Mâcon, S.-et-L. (En Route p 56)
Tel 85 39 21 33. Telex 351076. Mich 102/B2.
(Bookings: UK 071 287 3181)

MACON   Ibis

Simple hotel/Cooking 1
Terrace/Gardens/Swimming pool/Parking

Leave A6 Mâcon-Sud exit. Left at N6. Hotel on left.
Menus B. Rooms (62) D. Disabled. Cards Access, Visa.
Post 71570 La Chapelle-de-Guinchay, S.-et-L. (ER p 56)
Tel 85 36 51 60. Telex 351926. Fax 85 37 42 40. Mich 102/B3.
(Bookings: UK 071 724 1000; US toll free 800 221 4542)

MACON   Novotel

Very comfortable hotel/Cooking 1
Terrace/Gardens/Swimming pool/Parking

Leave A6 Mâcon-Nord exit. On left, past toll.
Menus B. Rooms (115) E. Disabled. Cards All.
Post 71000 Mâcon, S.-et-L. (En Route p 56)
Tel 85 36 00 80. Telex 800869. Fax 85 36 02 45. Mich 102/B2.
(Bookings: UK 071 724 1000; US toll free 800 221 4542)

ST-ETIENNE   Novotel

Very comfortable hotel/Cooking 1
Terrace/Gardens/Swimming pool/Lift/Closed parking

From north: A72 exit 8, Andrezieux; hotel to south, west of
A72. From south: A72 exit 8a Andrezieux; hotel west of A72.
Menus B. Rooms (98) E. Disabled. Cards All.
Post 42160 Andrezieux-Bouthéon, Loire. (En Route p 173)
Tel 77 36 55 63. Telex 900722. Fax 77 55 09 05. Mich 115/D3.
(Bookings: UK 071 724 1000; US toll free 800 221 4542)

SATOLAS   Sofitel

Very comfortable hotel (no restaurant)
Lift

At Lyon Satolas Aéroport. Use A430 north from A43. Hotel at
terminal buildings. Restaurants and parking at airport.
No restaurant. Rooms (120) F. Cards All.
Post 69125 Lyon Satolas Aéroport, Rhône.
Tel 72 22 71 61. Telex 380480. Fax 72 22 81 25. Mich 116/B2.
(Bookings: UK 071 724 1000; US toll free 800 221 4542)

VILLEFRANCHE   Ibis

Simple hotel/Cooking 1
Terrace/Lift/Parking/Good value

Leave A6 Villefranche exit. Hotel to east of A6, on D70.
Menus A. Rooms (115) C. Cards Access, Visa.
Post 69400 Villefranche, Rhône. (En Route p 57)
Tel 74 68 22 23. Telex 370777. Fax 74 60 41 67. Mich 102/B4.
(Bookings: UK 071 724 1000; US toll free 800 221 4542)

Base Hotels

BELLEY Urbis

Simple hotel
Lift/Good value

In the town centre with plenty of nearby parking.
Rooms (36) C. Disabled. Cards Access, Visa.
Post bd du Mail, 01300 Belley, Ain.
Tel 79 81 01 20. Telex 319107. Mich 117/E2.
(Bookings: UK 071 724 1000; US toll free 800 221 4542)

BOURG-EN-BRESSE Le Logis de Brou

Comfortable hotel
Lift/Garage/Parking/Good value

Flowers everywhere. On west side of N75, north of Eglise de
Brou. A40 exit 7: then eight km to north. Near Aub. Bressane.
Rooms (30) C-D. Cards All.
Post 132 bd de Brou, 01000 Bourg-en-Bresse, Ain.
Tel 74 22 11 55. Fax 74 22 37 30. Mich 103/D3.

BOURG-EN-BRESSE Prieuré

Very comfortable hotel
Fairly quiet/Gardens/Lift/Garage/Parking

East side N75, north of Eglise de Brou (see above). Colourful
gardens, handsome furniture. Some rooms with terraces.
Rooms (14) E-F. Cards All.
Post 49 bd de Brou, 01000 Bourg-en-Bresse, Ain.
Tel 74 22 44 60. Fax 74 22 71 07. Mich 103/D3.

BRANCION Montagne de Brancion

Comfortable hotel
Secluded/Gardens/Swimming pool/Parking

New young, English-speaking owners, Jacques and Nathalie
Million. A much-appreciated base. Extensive views east over
Saône Valley; Romanesque churches in all directions.
Rooms (20) E-F. Cards All.
Closed Nov to mid March.
Post Brancion, 71700 Tournus, S.-et-L.
Tel 85 51 12 40. Fax 85 51 18 64. Mich 102/B1.

CHARBONNIERES-LES-BAINS Beaulieu

Comfortable hotel
Lift/Parking/Good value

A small, green spa town in the hills west of Lyon. The latter is
only eight km away; it could be one thousand.
Rooms (40) C. Cards All.
Post 19 av. G. de Gaulle, 69260 Charbonnières-les-B, Rhône.
Tel 78 87 12 04. Fax 78 87 00 62. Mich 116/A2.

CLUNY   St-Odilon

Simple hotel
Gardens/Parking/Good value

Robert Berry's new, unusually-styled hotel is just across the river from the abbey (D15). Not far from TGV line.
Rooms (36) C. Disabled. Cards AE, Access, Visa.
Closed 20 Dec to 5 Jan.
Post rte Azé, 71250 Cluny, S.-et-L.
Tel 85 59 25 00. Fax 85 59 06 18. Mich 102/B2.

FLEURIE   Grands Vins

Comfortable hotel
Secluded/Gardens/Swimming pool/Parking

Adequate enough. South of village, between D68 and D119E.
Rooms (20) D. Disabled. Cards Access, Visa.
Closed 1st wk Aug. 12 Dec to 7 Jan.
Post 69820 Fleuric, Rhône.
Tel 74 69 81 43. Fax 74 69 86 10. Mich 102/B3.

MACON   Nord

Simple hotel
Lift/Good value

Alongside both the Saône and N6. Only plus is good value.
Rooms (21) B-C. Cards AE, Access, Visa.
Closed Sun evg. (200 metres north of Saône bridge.)
Post 313 quai J.-Jaurès, 71000 Mâcon, S.-et-L.
Tel 85 38 08 68. Fax 85 39 01 92. Mich 102/B2.

MONTLUEL   Le Petit Casset

Simple hotel
Fairly quiet/Gardens/Parking/Good value

New owners, Mireille and Bernard Kiehl. North of N84, two km south-west of village. Close to A42 exit 5.
Rooms (15) C-D. Cards Access, Visa.
Post La Boisse, 01120 Montluel, Ain.
Tel 78 06 21 33. Mich 116/B1.

TOURNUS   Hôtel de Greuze

Very comfortable hotel
Quiet/Lift/Parking

An exceptional hotel in a splendid building. Elegantly furnished. Next door to Greuze restaurant. Noisy church clock. English-speaking receptionist.
Rooms (19) F-F2. Disabled. Cards All.
Post 5 rue A.Thibaudet, 71700 Tournus, S.-et-L. (ER p 55)
Tel 85 40 77 77. Telex 351055. Fax 85 40 77 23. Mich 102/C1.

ARTEMARE   Au Vieux Tilleu**l**

Simple hotel with basic rooms/Cooking 1-2
Quiet/Terrace/Parking/Good value

The credits first: glorious views east across the secret land o**f**
Valromey; a family affair, led by brothers Jean-Paul an**d**
Michel Pras (both champion *boules* players; hence the floodli**t**
jeux de boules); and *Bourgeoise* and regional fare (*lavaret*
sanglier, poulet aux morilles and so on). Debits? Basic room**s**
with odd-ball plumbing (hot water from cold taps).
Menus B. Rooms (10) B. Cards Access, Visa.
Closed Jan. Tues & Wed (except 21 June to 10 Sept).
Post Luthézieu, 01260 Belmont-Luthézieu, Ain.
Tel 79 87 64 51. Mich 117/E1. (On D8, 8 km NW of Artemare.)

BLACERET   Beaujola**is**

Simple restaurant/Cooking 2
Terrace/Good value

Don't judge this *Clochemerle* terrain restaurant by its façade**.**
Jacques and Monique Mayançon are the salt of the earth**.**
Lip-smacking classical, *Bourgeoise* and Lyonnaise cuisine**:**
nostalgic *poulet à la creme, crêpes Parmentier* (potat**o**
pancakes) and, every Thursday (15 Oct-15 Apl), *pot au feu.*
Menus B. Cards All. (Rooms? Use Villefranche A/route hotel.)
Closed Xmas. Mon. Tues. (Arrive early for lunch & dinner.)
Post 69460 Blaceret, Rhône. (On D43, 10 km NW Villefranche**.**
Tel 74 67 54 75. Mich 102/B4.

BOURG-EN-BRESSE   Auberge Bressan**e**

Very comfortable restaurant/Cooking 2-3
Terrace/Parking

FL3 readers will not be surprised to see the stars have bee**n**
extinguished above Jean-Pierre and Dominique Villin's *auberge*
Uninspired yes: but fine classical and Lyonnaise cooking wit**h**
one menu devoted to Brillat-Savarin and six alternativ**e**
specialities on the à la carte list devoted to *les poulardes d**e**
Bresse*. Rooms? Two Base hotels are a two-minute walk away.
Menus B-E. Cards All.
Closed Mon evg & Tues.
Post 166 bd Brou, 01000 Bourg-en-Bresse, Ain.
Tel 74 22 22 68. Mich 103/D3. (On N75, opp. Eglise de Brou.)

BOURG-EN-BRESSE   France & Rest. Jacques Gu**y**

Comfortable hotel/Cooking 3
Lift/Garage

Readers who visited Jacques Guy at Coligny (*FL3*) will need n**o**
persuading to seek him out in his new restaurant home, par**t**
of the Hôtel de France. I liked the old *relais* better bu**t**
survival there was hard work. Classical, neo-classical an**d**
Lyonnaise cuisine: savour a spiky *fricassée de volaille d**e***
226

Bresse au gingembre and an inspired *tarte chaude aux pommes*.
Menus B-D. Rooms (46) C-D. Cards All. (Parking next door.)
Closed Rest: 9-24 Mar. 5-20 Oct. Sun evg. Mon.
Post 19 pl. Bernard, 01000 Bourg-en-Bresse, Ain. Mich 103/D3.
Tel 74 45 29 11 (R). 74 23 30 24 (H). Fax 74 23 69 90 (H).

BOURG-EN-BRESSE   Mail

Comfortable restaurant with rooms/Cooking 2
Gardens/Garage/Parking/Good value

On the D936 at the point the road passes under the railway
line on the west side of Bourg. Nevertheless, not noisy and
certainly you're assured of a pleasant welcome from Bernadette
Charolles. Chef Roger's repertoire is classical and Lyonnais.
His *poulet de Bresse rôti* is simple and succulent; a reader
reckoned he didn't realise chicken could taste so good.
Menus B-C. Rooms (9) B-C. Cards All.
Closed 12-28 July. 21 Dec-12 Jan. Sun evg & Mon.
Post 46 av. Mail, 01000 Bourg-en-Bresse, Ain.
Tel 74 21 00 26. Fax 74 21 29 55. Mich 103/D3.

CHAROLLES   Poste

Comfortable restaurant with rooms/Cooking 2-3
Garage/Good value

An attractive, colourful *maison Bourgeoise* with a collection of
antique clocks. Classical cuisine. This is Charollais terrain so
what better than a rare and meaty *terrine de boeuf en gelée* or
a hard-to-beat *entrecôte Charollaise à la plaque* (the meat
served sizzling on a cast-iron plate). Even the 120-franc menu
offers *la dinette des desserts* (two separate sweets plus biscuits
and *petits fours*). Terrific value.
Menus B-D. Rooms (9) C. Cards AE, Access, Visa.
Closed Mid Nov to mid Dec. Sun evg. Mon midday.
Post av. Libération, 71120 Charolles, S.-et-L.
Tel 85 24 11 32. Mich 101/E2. (Parking nearby.)

CHATEAUNEUF   La Fontaine

Simple restaurant/Cooking 3-4
Parking/Good value

Readers of earlier *FL* guides will recall the impact Yves Jury
made at his family hotel in nearby Chauffailles. But off he
went to find fame and fortune; he didn't find either so he and
his wife, Anne, are back at square one. The tiny restaurant
may be oddball but not Yves' cooking, a sparkling mix of
modern and neo-classical: sumptuous is the word for *tourte de
pigeon fermier au foie gras et pommes de terre* and superlative
describes a *framboises en tartelette de fraises*. Rooms? Relais
de l'Abbaye at 42190 Charlieu (Prices C): Tel 77 60 00 88.
Menus B-D. Cards Access, Visa.
Closed 25 Jan to 20 Feb. Tues evg & Wed.
Post 71740 Châteauneuf, S.-et-L.
Tel 85 26 26 87. Mich 101/E3. (10 km north-east of Charlieu.)

CHENAS   Daniel Robi◄

Comfortable restaurant/Cooking 2
Terrace/Gardens

Many of you urged us to visit the restored *Beaujolaise* farr
with views over the vines to the valley beyond. Daniel Robi
hops between classical and regional cooking perches: a tast
poulet de Bresse rôti au four or, as a contrast, *à la crème*; fis
grilled *au vieux Chénas*; *pièce de Charollais sauc
Bourguignonne* and an *andouillette de Chénas aux fines herbe*
A touch dear but you'll not be disappointed.
Menus C-D. Cards All. (Rooms? See Fleurie Base hotel.)
Closed Feb to mid Mar. Wed. Evgs (not Fri & Sat).
Post 69840 Chénas, Rhône.
Tel 85 36 72 67. Telex 351004. Fax 85 33 83 57. Mich 102/B3.

CLUNY   Bourgogn◄

Comfortable hotel/Cooking 2-3
Garage

Alongside the abbey and ideally placed to explore the man
fine Romanesque churches in the hills to the east. Ancier
stonework and timbers and period furnishings complemer
Bruno Dupasquier's cuisine: classics matched by the od
lighter delight (*galette de saumon mariné*); and, to finish,
formidable, Cluny Abbey-sized *chariot de desserts*.
Menus B-E. Rooms (12) D-E. Cards All. (Also see Base hotel.)
Closed Mid Nov to end Feb. Mon. Tues midday.
Post 71250 Cluny, S.-et-L.
Tel 85 59 00 58. Fax 85 59 03 73. Mich 103/B2.

DOMPIERRE-SUR-VEYLE   Auber◄

Very simple restaurant with basic rooms/Cooking 1
Gardens/Good value

Down-to-earth in every way. *Bourgeoise* and *Bressane* cookin◄
grenouilles, truites, poulet à la crème, vacherin praliné an
fromage blanc. Full? Play it off with a game of *boules*.
Menus B-C. Rooms (2) A. Cards Access, Visa.
Closed Feb. Last wk July. Sun evg. Wed evg. Thurs.
Post 01240 Dompierre-sur-Veyle, Ain.
Tel 74 30 31 19. Mich 103/D4.

FAVERGES-DE-LA-TOUR   Château de Faverge◄

Luxury hotel/Cooking 2-3
Secluded/Terrace/Gardens/Golf (9 holes)/Swimming poo◄
Tennis/Lift/Parking

Ten years ago the château was in ruins. A courageous coup◄
restored the shambles to what is now one of the most luxuriou◄
in the Relais & Châteaux chain. Ask Cathérine Tournier (sh
and Jo own the Lana and Tournier hotels in Courchevel) ◄
show you photographs of the restoration work. The hall, doub◄

staircase and upper landing (galleried on three sides) are remarkable: the first two structures appear to be made of marble; not so, the plaster is painted. Chefs come and go but cooking pitches between classical and neo-classical greens.
Menus C-E. Rooms (34) F-F3. Cards All. (En Route p 155)
Closed Nov to mid May. Rest: Mon (not July & Aug).
Post 38110 Faverges-de-la-Tour, Isère. (NW junc. N75/N516.)
Tel 74 97 42 52. Telex 300372. Fax 74 88 86 40. Mich 117/D3.

FLEURIE   Auberge du Cep

Comfortable restaurant/Cooking 3-4
Terrace

What an invigorating and happy restaurant this is, so long a favourite of mine and scores of readers. Sadly, two years ago, Gérard Cortembert died, still in his 40s. His widow, Chantal, aided by her daughter Hélène and chef, Michel Guerin, have gone from strength to strength. Nothing fancy or too comfy; just an endearing and estimable mix of classical and regional cooking (a roll call of Bourgogne, Beaujolais and Bresse brilliance). Simply reading the mouthwatering menus sets off Pavlovian bells. How satisfying to see Chantal, the daughter of a *vigneron*, prosper in the enterprise she helped Gérard to set up two decades and more ago.
Menus D-F. Cards AE, Access, Visa. (Rooms? See Base hotel.)
C'd 9-16 Mar/8-15 June/7-14 Sept/15 Dec-15 Jan. Sun evg/Mon.
Post pl. Eglise, 69820 Fleurie, Rhône.
Tel 74 04 10 77. Mich 102/B3.

FUISSE   Au Pouilly Fuissé

Comfortable restaurant/Cooking 2
Terrace/Good value

Eric and Dominque Point (she's the fourth generation owner) entice with lick-your-lips classical and *Bressane* cuisine at charitable prices: *saucisson chaud, poulet à la crème aux crêpes Parmentier* (potato pancakes), *soufflé de saumon, filet de boeuf au vin de Fleurie* and *fromage blanc à la crème*.
Menus A-B. Cards Access, Visa. (Rooms? Use A/R Ibis hotel.)
Closed Mid to end Feb. 1st wk Aug. Tues evg. Wed.
Post Fuissé, 71960 Pierreclos, S.-et-L.
Tel 85 35 60 68. Mich 102/B3.

MEXIMIEUX   Claude Lutz

Comfortable restaurant with rooms/Cooking 2-3
Terrace/Gardens/Parking

No change at this reliable *Bressan* rest. A warm welcome from Madame and an in-the-tramlines consistency from Claude. Mainly classical with many a supporting, diet-ruining regional *plat*.
Menus B-D. Rooms (17) B-D. Cards AE, Access, Visa.
Closed Feb. 20 Oct to 7 Nov. Sun evg. Mon.
Post 17 rue Lyon, 01800 Meximieux, Ain.
Tel 74 61 06 78. Fax 74 34 75 23. Mich 116/C1.

MONTMERLE-SUR-SAONE   Rivage

Comfortable hotel/Cooking 1-2
Terrace/Garage/Parking/Good value

No prizes for guessing what readers fancy most: the shady, paved terrace (which, at night, is lamplit) overlooking the river and suspension bridge. We've always enjoyed an evening walk downstream on the left bank from the hotel. Breakfasts are poor but no gripes about helpful Emile Job's classical, *Bourgeoise* and regional fare: *petite friture* from the Saône is a tasty treat; *grenouilles* and *poulet à la crème* are ubiquitous Bresse alternatives; and *filet de sole Duglère* (*Dugléré*) and *tournedos grillé beurre maître d'hôtel* are a classic twosome.
Menus A-C. Rooms (21) C-D. Cards AE, Access, Visa.
Closed Sun evg. Mon (not June to mid Sept when midday only).
Post 01090 Montmerle-sur-Saône, Ain. (En Route p 57)
Tel 74 69 33 92. Fax 74 69 49 21. Mich 102/B4.

MONTROND-LES-BAINS   Hostellerie La Poularde

Very comfortable hotel/Cooking 3
Gardens/Garage

Gilles and Monique Etéocle run the show now at this most family of family hotels. Remember why? Gilles' father-in-law is Joannès Randoing (a lovely man); his mother is the latter's second wife, Yvonne; so he's also the old chef's step-son. Got it? Monique wins an absolutely unanimous vote from readers for her warm welcome and caring attention. Service is efficient and friendly and the *sommelier* is given top marks. Part old, part modern, the rooms and furnishings are always praised. Gilles' cooking, when he's on song, is as good as anyone's. When it's not, or when he's not at home (which happened on our last visit), *la cuisine* is far too ordinary and really does not merit the major guides' gongs. His menus are both numerous and extensive and his style has changed of late: a mixture of classical, neo-classical, regional and the odd modern flash.
Menus B-E. Rooms (11) D-E. Cards All. (En Route p 174).
Closed 2-15 Jan. Mon evg and Tues midday (not pub. hols).
Post 42210 Montrond-les-Bains, Loire.
Tel 77 54 40 06. Telex 307002. Fax 77 54 53 14. Mich 115/D3.

OCHIAZ   Auberge de la Fontaine

Comfortable restaurant with rooms/Cooking 2-3
Quiet/Terrace/Gardens/Parking/Good value

The Plateau de Retord forms a wooded backdrop for this rustic, flower-bedecked *logis*. Colette Ripert is a friendly, involved hostess. Husband Claude is a loyal classicist: one clue to his training is *filet de turbot champagne Fernand Point*; other assured examples from culinary history books are *quenelle de brochet à la Nantua* and *grenadin de veau au Madère*.
Menus B-C. Rooms (7) B-C. Cards All. (En Route p 143)
Closed Jan. 7-17 June. Sun evg Mon
Post Ochiaz, 01200 Châtillon-en-Michaille, Ain
Tel 50 56 57 23. Mich 104/A3.

PONT-DE-VAUX   Commerce

Comfortable restaurant with rooms/Cooking 2-3
Garage/Good value

Competition is murderous in this little *Bressane* town: just
2,000 souls and three cracking restaurants. What makes the
Commerce my favourite, as true now as it was a decade ago, is
a *patronne*, Monique Patrone. Attentive and attractive,
Monique battles on on her own these days; she and Jean-Claude
separated a couple of years ago. Chef André Dunisi gives
Monique and her beloved *pays* loyal support. His repertoire is
a combination of the classics and dishes built around local
produce: *volaille de Bresse en surprise rôtie* is a winner by a
beak from a rare and gusty *matelotte de poissons de Saône*.
Menus B-C. Rooms (10) C. Cards All.
Closed 23 Nov to 18 Dec. Tues & Wed (not July & Aug).
Post 5 place Joubert, 01190 Pont-de-Vaux, Ain.
Tel 85 30 30 56. Mich 102/C2. (Handy for both A6/A40 A/rtes.)

THEIZE   Espérance

Very simple hotel/Cooking 1
Good value

Theizé is at the heart of *au pays des pierres dorées*, terrain
where buildings are constructed of the local stone, a golden-
textured material, darker than Cotswold or Hornton varieties;
hence the name. Take undemanding hopes with you to Espérance.
In the days of Louis Clavel the *logis* was a big favourite.
Since his death, in 1984, his widow, Marie-Louise, has
courageously carried on. Meals complement the hotel: simple,
copious, cheap and entirely Lyonnais in content. Wash them
down with an Antoine Pein red (his *cave* is across the road).
Menus A-B. Rooms (9) A-B. Cards AE, Access, Visa.
Closed 20 Sept to 20 Oct. Tues evg. Wed.
Post 69620 Theizé, Rhône. (By village church; see *Favourites*.)
Tel 74 71 22 26. Mich 115/F1.

TOURNUS   Greuze

Very comfortable restaurant/cooking 3-4

No praise is high enough for the indefatigable, illustrious
cuisinier, Jean Ducloux. Now over 70, he was an apprentice
cook in 1933, opened this restaurant in 1947, won his first
Michelin star 45 years ago, and the second in 1977. Unbeatable
depth of flavour is the hallmark of his classical expertise.
Many a dish has a simple, distinctive flair. Typical tempters
are *pâté croûte Alexandre Dumaine* (he worked for the famous
Saulieu chef in the late 30s), *quenelles de brochet* and an
understated stunning *poulet sauté nature*. Crown jewel
confections from the hands of *pâtissier*, Jean Léopold; and
English-speaking Claude Bouillet is a master *maître-d'hôtel*.
Menus C-F. Cards AE, Access, Visa. (Rooms? See Base hotel.)
Closed 1-10 Dec. (En Route p 55)
Post 1 rue A. Thibaudet, 71700 Tournus, S.-et-L.
Tel 85 51 13 52. Fax 85 40 75 42. Mich 102/C1.

MASSIF CENTRAL

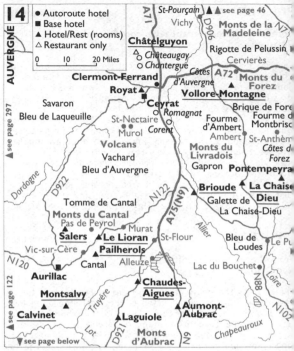

14

AUVERGNE

- ● Autoroute hotel
- ■ Base hotel
- ▲ Hotel/Rest (rooms)
- △ Restaurant only

0   10   20 Miles

St-Pourçain ▲ ▲ see page 46

Vichy

Monts de la Madeleine

D906

Rigotte de Pelussin

Cervierès

A72

Châtelguyon
△ Châteaugay
○ Chantergue

Côtes d'Auvergne

Monts du Forez ▲

Clermont-Ferrand

Royat ▲

Vollore-Montagne

Ceyrat

Romagnat

Brique de Fore
Fourme d
Montbriso

Savaron
Bleu de Laqueuille

St-Nectaire
Murol   Corent

Fourme d'Ambert

Ambert   St-Anthèm

Côtes d
Forez

Volcans
Vachard
Bleu d'Auvergne

Monts du Livradois

Gapron   **Pontempeyra**

Dordogne   D922

N122

A75(N9)

Brioude ▲ **La Chais**

Galette de **Dieu**
La Chaise-Dieu

Tomme de Cantal

Monts du Cantal
Pas de Peyrol

Murat   St-Flour

Bleu de
Loudes   Le Pu

Salers ▲**Le Lioran**
Pailherols

Vic-sur-Cère   Cantal   Alleuze

Lac du Bouchet ●

N120

Aurillac

Montsalvy ▲ ▲

Truyère

Chaudes-Aiguès

Aumont-Aubrac

Calvinet

Laguiole

Lot

Monts d'Aubrac

D921

Chapeauroux

N9

N88

Loire

N102

▼ see page below

The Massif Central, a huge geographical mass of country,
really several separate regions. What I've done is to divide th
Massif Central into three parts and, to emphasise th
division, I've drawn three separate maps: **Auvergne (14**
Ardèche (15); and **Cévennes (16)**.

I've described the topography for each of the three area
separately; see the pages which follow. But I've groupe
together the cheeses, regional specialities and wines; as yo
travel through the Massif Central you'll encounter them all

16

CEVENNES

▲ **Conques**
Vin d'Estaing
Marcillac

▲ see page above

Vin d'Entraygues
et du Fel

Mende ●

N88

N140

Aveyron

Lot

Ste-Enimie

Belcastel

Rodez

**Bleu des
Causses**

Gorges du Tarn

D911

Le Rozier

Najac

Salles-Curan

Millau ▲▲

Meyrueis

St-Jean
du-Gar

Cordes

N88

Tarn

Mont Aigoual

▲**St-Jean-du-Bru**

Albi

Roquefort

Le Vigan ●

N112

**Brousse-
le-Château**

▲ Roquefort-sur-Soulzon

St-Affrique

Cirque de
Navacelles

Hérault

▼ see page 176

▼ see page 177

each of the three areas. I've also included all the hotels and restaurants in one or other of the usual three groups.

A few days spent in each of the three magnificent, unspoilt areas will provide the ideal method of seeing something, in turn, of each part of the Massif Central. Explore them in a leisurely way: high mountains, green pastures, numerous river valleys and ancient, historical towns and villages will entice you to linger as you meander slowly over a multitude of deserted minor roads. Here, more than anywhere else in France, is where you must take the advice running throughout this guide: the more you get off the beaten track, and the more

you run the risk of getting lost, then the more certain you are of seeing the best of France. Large scale maps are a must.

The three maps on these two pages and the seven pages of text which follow show clearly how the areas relate to each other and how they can be explored as separate units.

Auvergne (14) is the northernmost area, stretching from **Vichy** on the edge of the mountains to the valley of the **Lot**. In the north, from east to west, several groups of mountainous terrain have magnetic appeal: the **Monts de la Madeleine** and **Monts du Forez**, to the north and south of the **A72**; the **Monts du Livradois**; and the Parc Régional des **Volcans**. Further south are the equally pleasing **Monts du Cantal** and **Monts d'Aubrac**.

Ardèche (15) is the exhilarating line of densely wooded mountains which guard the right bank of the River **Rhône**. The area is virtually ignored by the vast majority of motorists speeding down the **A7** and N7 towards the Med and the sun.

Cévennes (16) is the area centered on **Millau**. Nature has endowed the Cévennnes with a glorious legacy: fantastic underground caves and grottoes; carved, tortuous gorges and valleys; spectacular rivers; and thickly forested mountains.

Auvergne (14)

All the Massif Central, not just the Auvergne, is at its most beguiling during the spring and autumn. For both Anne and me the huge *massif* is synonymous with wild flowers. We have many vivid memories of days spent among the high mountains when pastures shone with luminous displays of wild flowers.

One hot Midsummer's Day, on the narrow and steep D106, near Perrier (north-east of **Ambert**), we stopped – startled by the colourful meadows straddling the road. Anne was able to identify, within just a few minutes, a score of wild flowers: yellow crosswort, various-hued field scabious, fox-glove, dog rose, marguerites, orchids, pink campions, white bladder wort, broom, columbine, white polygonum, tricolour violas, purple vetch, forget-me-nots, bugloss and many others. An hour later, at the Col des Supeyres a few miles to the east, above the tree line, we thrilled at the sight of pastures whitewashed with wild narcissi and speckled with blue violas, wild geranium cranesbill, cornflowers and pink polygonum.

We recall, too, an October day, spent among the gale-whipped volcanic cones of the Monts du Cantal, when the tiniest of tricolour pansies, campion, scabious, harebells, verbascum, hardy cranesbill, wild lavatera, dianthus and spiraea glistened and waved in the halogen-bright autumn light. No wonder then that the coronation dress for Queen Elizabeth was based on a design of the hundreds of wild flowers of France.

Nature teases the senses in other ways during both the spring and autumn months. For example, one of our favourite small French rivers is unknown to even Monsieur Bibendum; Michelin's green guide for the Auvergne makes no mention of the **Chapeauroux**, an eye-tickling visual confection. Anne and I discovered it by accident almost 30 years ago. We were on our way north from **Mende**, in the Lot Valley, to **Le Puy**. The obvious route was the N88 but, instead, we chugged up the D988 in our little Mini. What an entrancing valley we stumbled upon: the emerging springs tints, the rushing torrent, full of newly-melted water, and the sparkling April light etched sharp images in our minds. A couple of years ago we saw the valley in October, a 20-mile drive through a seemingly uninterrupted honour guard of autumn-cloaked broadleaved trees.

Don't bypass Châteauneuf-de-Randon, some 4200 ft above sea-level and at the southern end of the drive: climb to the *place* at the top of the village, typical of many in France. Don't miss, too, the circular **Lac du Bouchet** (once a volcanic crater) in a pretty, wooded setting, 20 km south of Le Puy.

Le Puy is certainly one of the most unusual towns in France. Sharp needles of volcanic rock rise on all sides, several of them with chapels and statues on their summits. The most needle-like has the Chapelle St-Michel d'Aiguilhe on its peak, a Romanesque chapel worthy of the 267-step climb to reach it. Another outcrop has the huge statue of Notre Dame de France on its summit. But it was the cathedral and its famous black Virgin of Le Puy that drew pilgrims to the town. Equally important was the *pierre aux fièvres*, a piece of black stone with, allegedly, miraculous healing powers. The cathedral, a mixture of Byzantine and Romanesque, has cool, quiet cloisters.

Another town, **St-Flour**, west of Le Puy, has long been loved by numerous Britons, partly for its man-made highlights, the cathedral and museums, but also for its impressive site, atop a 100-metre-high "table" of basalt. Not surprisingly the site was strategically important during the many wars that swept cross Auvergne over the centuries.

Vichy is completely different. One of the premier spas in France, the town has its own special place in recent French history. Vichy is an elegant, sophisticated spa with a casino, sports complex and attractive parks, especially those alongside the River **Allier**.

For most tourists "Auvergne" is the area centred on the volcanic peaks of the Monts Dômes and Mont Dore, to the west and south of **Clermont-Ferrand**. The following drive will give you a taste this "different" part of France.

Leave **Royat**, a small, bustling spa, to the south, using the N89. Make the short déviation to Lac d'Aydat and then continue south on the D5 towards **Murol**; the view of the ruined castle below you as you drop down into the valley is an eerie sight. Detour to **St-Nectaire** and admire the grace and beauty of the admirably proportioned Romanesque church.

Allow time to navigate across the lanes to the Gorges de Courgoul. Follow the wooded valley, using the D26, to Compains. Then head north on the D36 to Besse-en-Chandesse, a dour, dark-stoned mountain village, deviating first a few miles west to Lac Pavin, a real beauty and another circular rarity. From Besse continue on the D36 to the Col de la Croix St-Robert. Arguably the D36 is one of the finest mountain drives in France. It's in this terrain that Canteloube's *Songs of the Auvergne*, sung by that angel among singers, Flicka von Stade, seem entirely appropriate and inspiring.

Descend into Le Mont-Dore and then drive north, using the D983. Immediately after the Lac de Guéry, on your left, there are more spectacular views including two rock faces. Through Orcival, an atmospheric medieval village; see the church and the nearby château at Cordès. Continue north-east until you reach the foot of the Puy de Dôme. This 4806-ft-high cone is an astonishing viewpoint; the 4 km, 1 in 8 climb, is a test for any modern car but pity those poor Tour de France cyclists who have to endure the torture of the same ascent.

There's much else to see and do. Let me describe, alas too briefly, two of our most recent visits to the Auvergne.

The first takes you through the forests of the **Monts du Forez** and across the deserted Livradois. Before climbing into the Forez enjoy some of the man-made sites on its eastern flanks, north of **Montbrison** (see Lyonnais map). **Pommiers** has a photogenic site, an austere 12th-century church and a 5th-century bridge. The Renaissance château at **La Bastie-d'Urfé** has especially pleasing two-level, cloister-like terraces. **Champdieu** has a formidable, fortified *église* and a surprisingly elegant, modern structure combining toilets, waiting room, telephone, clock and fountain. What would Gabriel Chevallier have made of this efficient *pissoir*?

Cervières, a couple of minutes away from junction 4 on the A72, is a 12th-century hamlet in a time warp. Walk the narrow streets before heading into the brooding black forests.

My favourite Forez enclave is the wooded terrain to the north-east of Ambert – a moulded jelly of rounded hills, covered with both broadleaved and evergreen trees. To the east the map identifies many *jasseries*; all at high altitude, these ow stone-built structures are now relics of the past. They were once used for the making and maturing of the blue-veined cow's milk cheeses called *fourmes*. Visit the Fromagerie de la Genette of Roger Col, 1.8 km south of **St-Anthème** on the left of the D996 towards Ambert. Buy his new creation: a mini

fourme, "Fourmette du Livradois". The small cylinde
weighing about one pound, is ideal for picnics. (Open Mon t
Sat midday.) On the eastern outskirts of Ambert detour to th
Moulin Richard-de-Bas, where hand-made heavy paper is sti
produced; there's also a museum on paper making.

Don't rush by **La Chaise-Dieu**. The 14th-century *église* is
sober structure with a choir of no less than 144 oak stalls. A
amusing diversion is the Salle d'Echo, behind the church. Ca
at Michel Estienne's showroom of skilfully crafted woode
creations (near Ste-Marguerite, on D4 south-west of La Chais
sign "Artisanat Bois Tourné"). The château at Chavania
Lafayette was the birthplace of La Fayette who, at the age
20 in 1777, was George Washington's second-in-command.

Lavaudieu is the site of a Bénédictine monastery with tin
12th-century cloisters and a rural farm museum. **Brioude**
basilica is a must: hemmed in, the church is a stone-bui
marvel with dozens of differing shades, types and pattern
Last, but not least, don't miss the Musée de la Résistanc
"Joseph LHomenède" at Frugières-le-Pin Gare (south-east
Brioude),the best of all the Resistance museums I've seen.

Our second tour, made in the autumn, started nea
Montsalvy, at the southern *porte* to the Cantal. First, do as w
did and pay a call on Suzy and Nigel Atkins, at their Poteri
du Don, west of Montoursy, a hamlet south-west of Montsalv
Suzy is one of Europe's most gifted potters. For those who'v
been before the descent now has a tarmac surface.

From **Aurillac** follow the signposted "Route des Crêtes" (th
D35). Birds of prey, reddish-brown Salers cattle, glorious view
with ever-changing moods of light, and wild flowers stopped u
in our tracks every few minutes. Detour west to the tin
hamlet of Tournemire and the Château d'Anjony, both s
evocative of Cantal and the high Auvergne mountains. **Saler**
is a stern, forbidding place; be sure to see the extensive view
and the minute Grande Place with its sparkling fountain.

Drive all the roads that descend from the **Pas de Peyr**
(5190 ft), to west, south and north. In the autumn beec
forests resemble mammoth drapes and swathes of golden clot
as if flung down by the gods from the volcanic summits.

From **Murat** drive south, on the D39, to Brézons. The vie
north of the village gets no mention in any guidebook, but th
attractive panorama is, for us, a show-stopper.

The winding **Truyère** is one of France's finest river gorge
Dammed at several points, the biggest lake is to the east of th
Barrage de Grandval. The haunting ruins of the Châtea
d'**Alleuze**, on a rocky pyramid, compare starkly with anothe
more modern man-made marvel, the massive steel Viaduc d
Garabit, built by Eiffel, at the western end of the lake.

The austere, windswept **Monts d'Aubrac** are renowned f
their flora and where cattle outnumber people by thousands
one. **Laguiole**, over 3000 ft above sea-level, is famed for i
gifted son, chef Michel Bras, knives and cheese: *tome* (*tomm*
is the fresh version, used to make *aligot*; *jeune* is a har
cheese, two to four months old; *vieux* has matured for eight
twenty months. **Chaudes-Aigues** is a prosperous little spa
claiming to have the hottest waters in all Europe (82C).

Markets Ambert (Thurs); Aurillac (Wed and Sat); Brioud
(Sat); Châtelguyon (Tues and Fri); Laguiole (Wed and Sat
Murat (Fri); Murol (Wed); Le Puy (Sat); Royat (Tues and Sat
St-Flour (Sat); Salers (Wed); Vic-sur-Cère (Tues and Fri).

Michelin green guides: Auvergne; Vallée du Rhône.

Ardèche (15)

I am well aware that my advice can get repetitive at times: here I go again. I address my plea to all of you who flash up and down the **A7** or N7, totally oblivious to the wooded mountains west of the River **Rhône**. These are the mountains of the Ardèche. I implore you: spend a few days in the area and I guarantee you will not be disappointed.

If time is critical and you really can only manage one day then let me suggest the perfect solution (of course I'm prejudiced): revel in France's best privately-owned railway line, the Chemin de Fer du Vivarais (the ancient name for the Ardèche), a metre-gauge run of 33 km which climbs 250 metres from **Tournon** to **Lamastre**. The railway celebrated its centenary in 1991. What could be better than the summer 10.00 a.m. "steamer" from Tournon, arriving at Lamastre at midday, lunching at Bernard Perrier's Hôtel du Midi (savouring dishes which 60 years ago won chef Barattéro three Michelin stars), and returning at 16.00 hours? For a timetable and English leaflet write to CFTM, rue d'Algérie, 69001 Lyon.

Of the various ways to access the Ardèche mountains the most spectacular is the exhilarating road along the north side of the **Gorges de l'Ardèche**. At several spots you can stop and enjoy views of the River Ardèche far below you; at Pont-d'Arc marvel at a natural stone arch which bridges the river.

To both north and south of the gorge are several underground caves. The most renowned is Aven d'Orgnac (*aven* has the same meaning as our Celtic "avon", a river arising from a natural spring); colossal stalagmites and mighty halls make the cave an impressive sight. Others are the Grottes de la Madeleine and Grottes de St-Marcel (both near the river); the Aven de Marzal (five km north of the Ardèche) and the Aven de la Forestière (just north of the Aven d'Orgnac).

Beyond Vallon-Pont-d'Arc lies dour terrain, the Ardèche version of the *garrigue* (scrub). Around **Ruoms** you'll spot many a vineyard; the grapes are used to make the ever-improving Vin de Pays de l'Ardèche. By **Les Vans**, detouring first through the weird, rocky Bois de Païolive, the landscape improves: often, in the space of a mile or so, you'll encounter olive, cherry and sweet chestnut trees. (Later you'll see plenty of Ardèche's famed chestnut trees.)

One essential deviation is the long, out-of-the-way, dead-end road to the tiny Romanesque church at **Thines**, on a remote, high perch. You will have to devote both time and effort to get to Thines but that will be nothing compared to what was needed centuries ago to build the church.

From Les Vans head north, using the Corniche du Vivarais Cévenol (D10 and D4). In June the **Tanargue** *massif* (along with much of the Ardèche) looks as if it has been splashed with thousands of giant egg yolks: broom is everywhere and, at times, the perfume can be obnoxious. The panorama from the Col de Meyrand is extensive and includes both Mont Viso and Mont Ventoux (see Hautes-Alpes map).

A second entrance to the Ardèche can be made from the Rhône Valley to the south of **Montélimar**. Man-made sites are the attractions on this run: Viviers is the ecclesiastical capital of the area; Alba-la-Romaine has a Roman forum and medieval fortifications; Villeneuve-de-Berg is an old walled town; and both Vogüé and **Aubenas** are renowned for their châteaux.

Both the above routes will lead you to **Vals-les-Bains**, a small, old-fashioned spa. From Vals use the D253 to Chirols;

serried ranks of hills to the west and the River Ardèche to the south. Take the D26 to **Burzet**. After heavy rain the turbulent river views in the village will stop you in your tracks. If you're a hillclimb fan drive the short seven km detour up the D289: the road winds and climbs 2,600 ft from Burzet, a match for the Alps and, not surprisingly, a classic Monte-Carlo Rally stage (Ardèche is full of them).

But, detour or not, return to Burzet and continue up the Valley of Myrtilles (D215). Spare time for the 15-minute walk to the Ray-Pic cascade. Then through the woods to the marshy plateau of Lachamp-Raphaël, to one of the most breathtaking sights. In May Anne and I have gasped at the sheets of wild daffodils, interlaced with yellow marsh buttercups, numerous orchids and scores of different wild flowers. A few weeks later, in mid June, we've been stunned by the same colourful pastures when pillows of intensely dark purple violas have intermingled with wild narcissi and myriad other wild flowers.

Now north-west to the lava cone of **Gerbier de Jonc**; it's a short but lung-testing hike to the top. Below you is the source of the **Loire** and around you an extensive panorama. But I'll lead you to a better one, without the exercise.

Use the D400 to drive to the Croix de Boutières, south of the sleeping dog **Mont Mézenc** (at 5751 ft the area's highest). The immediate landscape to the east is quite remarkable for the many volcanic humps and lumps below you with their interconnecting wooded ridges and valleys; this is how a child would draw a mountain view. The eastern panorama, explained by an observation table, is stunning.

In June the pastures between Les Estables and **Moudeyres** resemble snowfields; in reality wild narcissi. Hidden among them are dense pockets of purple pansies. Stop and be entertained by a meadow orchestra of skylarks and crickets.

In the autumn I would choose to approach the high Ardèche from the north-east, climbing any of the roads that wind up through the dense forests, wearing their gold and russet cloaks, from **Valence**, Tournon or **Annonay**. If the day is clear two viewpoints merit a detour: the panorama east from St-Romain-de-Lerps (north-west of Valence), made more enjoyable by Paul Goichet's observation table of 19 ceramic tiles; and the view west from the Château de Pierre-Gourde, now a mound of ruined stones (south-west of Valence).

Seek out a couple of sites: the Château de Rochebonne on the D478, south of **St-Agrève**, where ruined walls appear to be part of the rocky and isolated strategic perch; and Lalouvesc, on an equally commanding site, with its landmark of a twin-spired basilica (east of **St-Bonnet-le-Froid**).

To the west of the area, in the quiet corners of Velay, the infant Loire provides two chances to paddle in its clear waters: at both **Arlempdes** and Goudet there are fine views and ruined castles. Lac d'Issarlès fills what was once a volcanic crater; the lake has both watersport and bathing facilities. In the hills around **Le Puy** try the yellow and green liqueurs called *Verveine du Velay*; they include over 30 plants, such as wild verbena. Green Puy lentils, too, are on many menus.

Finally, fit in a call to **Hauterives**, north-east of Tain-l'Hermitage, and the amazing Palais Idéal, built of pebbles and stones 100 years ago by the town postman, Ferdinand Cheval.

Markets Annonay (Wed and Sat); Aubenas (Sat); Lamastre (Tues); Ruoms (Fri and Sat); Vals-les-Bains (Thurs); Les Vans (Fri).

Michelin green guide: Vallée du Rhône.

Cévennes (16)

Most of the material on these two pages is taken from the chapter "Captivating Cévennes" in *French Leave Favourites*. There seems little point in trying to conjure up new word pictures of this stunning scenic wonderland. Needless to say the Cévennes is at its best in June when the whole area is a sea of wild flowers, seemingly aflame with burning colours; the new soft greens in the extensive woodlands give the forests a glowing radiance; and the rivers, full of water, are turbulent, thrilling sights. Nature reigns supreme.

I recommend four drives from scores of possibilities; and, to finish, I implore you to make a detour to a superb, man-made ecclesiastical glory. More details later.

Drive 1 From **Millau** head for the world-renowned **Gorges du Tarn**. Try to do the drive in both directions because many scenic aspects are missed if you travel the valley road in one direction only. The drive starts to get interesting at **Le Rozier**. At Les Vignes turn left and climb the snake-like hairpins to the cliffs above the Tarn; at the top use the D46 and continue north to the Point Sublime. The river is far below you; the better vista is to the east, but you also have an eagle's eye view of the 90-degree turn the green Tarn completes to flow southwards (Cirque des Baumes).

Retrace your steps to the Tarn, follow the D907 and continue to **Ste-Enimie**. From there drive south, climbing up the steep D986. In 11 km turn right and aim for the viewpoint at the Roc des Hourtous. Back again towards the D986 but this time descend down the hairpins of the D43 to La Malène. Return to Le Rozier. If you feel like a walk among the many rock faces, cross the Tarn and, before you enter the village, follow the signs for Capluc. Park and enjoy the walks.

Drive 2 Cross the Tarn at Millau and head north-east up the D110 to the Chaos de Montpellier-le-Vieux. The "Chaos" is a collection of weirdly-shaped rocks which litter the ground over an extensive area, as if a giant had walked this way and left utter destruction behind him. There's a signposted path through the rocks; most have fanciful names, like the Devil's Chair, Elephant, Arc de Triomphe and Queen Victoria's Head. Continue north-east on the D110 and the D29.

Head south-east on the D29 and D28 to Lanuéjols, crossing the Causse Noir in the process. This is one of many limestone *causses* in the Cévennes; these plateaux are always dry as water drains away quickly through numerous fissures. Underground streams abound and have played the major role in scouring and blasting out the unusual sculpturing seen in many caves below the surface; the ferocious rivers have also carved out their own brutal sculptures above ground.

Continue east on the D986 through a much changed landscape; dense woods replace the rocky, flat terrain. Visit the Abîme du Bramabiau, where the River Bonheur has cut a subterranean slice through a rugged rock face.

East again to the summit of **Mont Aigoual**, the highest point of the Cévennes National Park; from the observatory on the summit (5141 ft) you get staggering views. Descend to the north and then west to **Meyrueis**. Here you have the choice of two caves: Aven Armand is the most renowned with every imaginable shape of stalagmite and stalactite, enhanced by brilliant lighting; the Grotte de Dargilan (the pink cavern) is impressive, too, particularly the huge bell-shaped sculpture. Now head downstream through the Gorges de la Jonte, a direction I prefer as I believe you see more of the many pink and yellow rock faces and, towards the end of the valley, the strange shapes of the Causse Méjean on your right.

Drive 3 Follow the N9 south-east from Millau across the Causse du Larzac. At Le Caylar turn left and use the D9, D25 and D130 to approach the **Cirque de Navacelles** from the south. *Cirque* means amphitheatre, in this case one of the most unusual in France. From the cliff top the view is amazing: far below you is a *cirque*, formed by a now dried-up meander of the River Vis; today the same stream provides an extra attraction, a colourful cascade. Continue north-east.

At Montdardier the road to **Le Vigan** seems to disappear; a long descent follows into a valley renowned for its orchards. Climb the Col du Minier; apart from the views south the pass is also the watershed between the Mediterranean and the Atlantic. Six km later turn left on to the D151. At Dourbies (a tempting spot: why not give in and have a drink on the café terrace?) use the D151A and D114 to the south of the river. See the weir at **St-Jean-du-Bruel** and the 14th-century covered market at Nant. Back to Millau via tiny Cantobre, snoozing atop a rocky sofa, and the Gorges de la Dourbie.

Drive 4 To **Roquefort-sur-Soulzon** which gave its name to the king of cheeses. Visit, free of charge, the "Société" caves where over half the annual production of Roquefort cheeses mature. Each year 16,000 tons of Roquefort (or six million 2.6 kg "rounds" – *pains*) are sold worldwide.

Pliny wrote in honour of the cheese; Charlemagne adored it; and, during the early Middle Ages, evidenced by documents at Conques, farm rents were even calculated in silver and/or Roquefort. Charles VI, in 1411, provided the patent letter which established the first vintage trademark, giving the town the exclusive right to ripen the cheese in its unique caves.

The Roquefort caves are said to be the best natural "refrigerators" in the world. It's a unique geological site where a mountain top collapsed creating numerous rock faults, fissures and caverns, locally called *fleurines*. The fresh air that blows through them provides the ideal atmosphere for the "penicillium Roqueforti", a microscopic mushroom, to mature within the heart of the creamy rounds of ewe's milk. Salt is added to the surface of the cheese to slow down the growth of mould on the outside, while the inside matures.

Your visit to the caves will be an eye-opener for the way man has capitalised on the quirk of Nature. Built vertically along the northern face of the cliffs, where the numerous *fleurines* emerge as "air corridors", man has constructed a series of enclosed caves; it's on these man-made floors, refrigerated by Nature, where the round blue cheeses ripen, emerging eventually into that sharp, exquisite taste.

Seek out **Belcastel's** superb site on the **Aveyron**; and, downstream, **Najac's** ruined castle high above the river.

Finally, make the most essential of detours to **Conques**. Drive through the Gorges du **Lot**, past picturesque and medieval Espalion, Estaing and Entraygues to the hidden village. The 11th-century *église* is a Romanesque gem: the three spires, high nave, tympanum and famed treasure, including the gold-plated wooden relic, a statue of Ste-Foy enriched with precious stones, makes Conques a three-star wonder.

Markets Albi (Sat); Cordes (Sat); Millau (Wed and Fri); Rodez (Wed and Sat); St-Jean-du-Gard (Tues and Sat).

Michelin green guide: Gorges du Tarn.

Cheese **Cow's milk**

Auvergne (Bleu d') when made on farms at its best in summer and autumn. Strong smell, soft, made in the same way as Roquefort. **Bleu de Laqueuille** is a related cheese

Cantal from the Auvergne. The best comes from **Salers**. The cheese is made from milk of Salers cows. Praised by Pliny. Try it with the fruity Côtes d'Auvergne reds

Causses (Bleu des) a blue cheese with parsley-like veins, hence the term *persillé*. At its best in summer and autumn

Fourme-d'Ambert has a summer and autumn season. A blue cheese from the Auvergne and in the shape of a tall cylinder

Fourme de Montbrison a bitter blue – as is **Fourme de Pierre-s-Haute**

Gapron (Gaperon) a garlic-flavoured, flattened ball

Laguiole related to Cantal. Big cylinders, penetrating bouquet

Loudes (Bleu de) blue-veined and from the Velay hills, near Le Puy

Murol a semi-hard, mild cheese, like St-Nectaire. Made in small disks

St-Félicien a salty-tasting cheese from the hills west of Tournon

St-Nectaire has a purply-brown skin, made in larger disks than Murol. A semi-hard, mild cheese. **Savaron** and **Vachard** are related

Tomme de Cantal a fresh, softish, cream-coloured, unfermented cheese

Goat's milk

Brique du Forez also known as **Chevreton d'Ambert**. A small loaf with a nutty flavour. **Galette de la Chaise Dieu** – a flat cake – is similar

Rigotte de Condrieu soft, small cylinders with no special flavour; available all the year. **Rigotte de Pelussin** is a related cheese

Ewe's milk

Roquefort read my notes on the opposite page

Regional Specialities

Aligot purée of potatoes with Tomme de Cantal cheese, cream, garlic and butter (also read last paragraph on Laguiole in Auvergne introduction)

Bougnette a stuffing of pork, bread and eggs – wrapped in *crépine* (caul)

Bourriols d'Aurillac sweet pancakes, made from buckwheat flour

Brayaude (gigot) lamb cooked in white wine, onions and herbs

Cadet Mathieu pastry turnover filled with slices of apple

Clafoutis baked pancake batter, poured over fruit, usually cherries

Confidou Rouergat ragout of beef, red wine, tomatoes, garlic and onions

Cousinat (Cousina) chestnut soup (*salée* – salted) with cream, butter and prunes and served with bread

Criques grated potato, mixed with eggs and fried – in the form of pancakes. Related to the *truffiat* of Berry

Farçon large *galette* of sausage, sorrel, onions, eggs and white wine

Farinette buckwheat flour pancakes – meat and vegetable filling

Friand Sanflorin pork meat and herbs in pastry

Jambon d'Auvergne a tasty mountain ham

Manouls see *Trénels*

Milliard (Millat, Milla) see *Clafoutis*

Mourtayol a stew with beef, chicken, ham, vegetables and bread

Omelette Brayaude eggs, pork, cheese and potatoes

Perdrix à l'Auvergnate partridge stewed in white wine

Potée Auvergnate stew of vegetables, cabbage, pork and sausage

Pountari a mince of pork fat in cabbage leaves

Pounti small, egg-based savoury soufflé with bacon or prunes

Rouergat(e) Rouergue; the name of the area to the west of Millau

Salmis de colvert Cévenole wild duck, sautéed in red wine, onions, ham and mushrooms

Soupe aux choux soup with cabbage, ham, pork, bacon and turnips

Trénels mutton tripe, white wine and tomatoes

Tripoux stuffed sheep's feet

Truffade a huge *galette* of sautéed potatoes

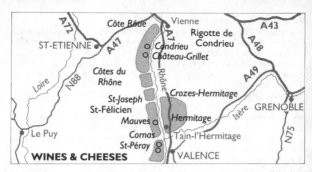

Wines (Great vintages: northern Côtes du Rhône **78 79 82 85 89 90**)
For those visitors based in the northern part of the Massif, look
out for the passable **St-Pourçain** (near Vichy) reds and a fine,
Loire-type white wine. A flourishing VDQS area is **Côtes
d'Auvergne**, near Clermont-Ferrand: among the noteworthy
reds here are **Chanturgue** and **Châteaugay** – both made from
the Gamay grape; and a rosé from **Corent**. From the eastern side
of this northern section of the Massif Central come some
Beaujolais-type reds, the Gamays of the **Côtes du Forez**.

If you are in the Tain area you are in the middle of one of the
best wine-producing parts of France. From Tain-l'Hermitage
(**AC Hermitage**, a wonderful wine and **AC Crozes-Hermitage**,
a less-good, junior brother), **Saint Joseph** and **Cornas**, all north
of Valence and on both sides of the Rhône, you'll enjoy some super,
ruby-red wines, dark and powerful. Only the vineyards on the
granite hill overlooking Tain have the right to the world-famous
Hermitage *appellation*; the vineyards to the north and east
take the Crozes AC. (This area is the northern Côtes du Rhône.)

There are also some great dry whites from this area: a
Hermitage Blanc (the best is reckoned to be **Chante-
Alouette**), a **Saint Péray** white and a **Crozes-Hermitage**
version. For me two highlights of the area are: the **Saint
Péray mousseux** – sheer delight and made by the *méthode
champenoise*; and the little-known **Brézème** red (from a small
vineyard east of Livron-sur-Drôme) made from Syrah grapes.

South-east of Valence, at Die, you will encounter the *demi-sec*
Clairette de Die (local, *naturel* method) and a *brut* version
(*méthode champenoise*), both *mousseux*. There's a dry still
white, too. Near Die are the wines of all shades from **Châtillon-
en-Diois**. East of Montélimar is the **AC Coteaux du Tricastin**
with dry rosés and reds. A century ago they were highly thought
of; their prestige diminished but in the last 30 years they have
risen from a *Vin de Pays* classification to a full AC (1973).

If you are in Millau, or anywhere in the Cévennes, look at
my Languedoc wine notes. You will be offered many good Midi
wines (from Languedoc to the south): **Saint-Chinian**, **Saint-
Saturnin**, **Montpeyroux** and **Faugères** are among the best.

You should also come across the light reds from the north of
Rodez, the newly-promoted **AC Marcillac**. Modest red and
white VDQS wines are made in the Lot Valley, south of
Montsalvy: **Vin d'Estaing** and **Vin d'Entraygues et du Fel**.
Vins de Pays
The **Vin de Pays de l'Ardèche** reds (both Gamay and Syrah
grapes) are fine examples of just how good this classification
can be. Don't be prejudiced: try them.

CLERMONT-FERRAND   Novotel

Very comfortable hotel/Cooking 1
Terrace/Gardens/Swimming pool/Closed parking

Leave A75 at exit 16, Le Brézet (A71 from Paris becomes A75
at exit 15). Hotel on west side of autoroute.
Menus B. Rooms (96) E. Disabled. Cards All.
Post rue Elisée Reclus, 63000 Clermont-Ferrand, P.-de-D.
Tel 73 41 14 14. Telex 392019. Fax 73 41 14 00. Mich 113/E2.
(Bookings: UK 071 724 1000; US toll free 800 221 4542)

MONTELIMAR   Ibis

Simple hotel (no restaurant)
Terrace/Swimming pool/Parking/Good value

A7 Montélimar-Nord exit. Right at N7. Courte-Paille grill.
No rest. Rooms (29) C. Disabled. Cards Access, Visa.
Post 26370 Saulce, Drôme. (En Route p 63)
Tel 75 63 09 60. Telex 345960. Fax 75 63 12 22. Mich 130/A4.
(Bookings: UK 071 724 1000; US toll free 800 221 4542)

ST-RAMBERT-D'ALBON   Ibis

Simple hotel/Cooking 1
Terrace/Parking/Good value

A7 Chanas exit. South on N7, use town bypass, hotel on left.
Menus A-B. Rooms (73) C. Disabled. Cards Access, Visa.
Post 26140 St-Rambert-d'Albon, Drôme. (En Route p 60)
Tel 75 03 04 00. Telex 345958. Fax 75 03 04 07. Mich 130/A1.
(Bookings: UK 071 724 1000; US toll free 800 221 4542)

VALENCE   Climat de France

Simple hotel/Cooking 1
Parking/Good value

Leave A7 Valence-Nord exit. Left at N7, hotel on left.
Menus A-B. Rooms (43) C. Disabled. Cards AE, Access, Visa.
Post 26500 Bourg-lès-Valence, Drôme. (En Route p 61)
Tel 75 42 77 46. Telex 346565. Fax 75 55 62 35. Mich 130/B3.
(Bookings; UK 071 287 3181)

VALENCE   Novotel

Very comfortable hotel/Cooking 1
Terrace/Gardens/Swim pool/Tennis/Lift/Closed parking

Leave A7 Valence-Sud exit. Through toll, over N7, turn right
and join N7, heading north. Hotel on right side of N7.
Menus B. Rooms (107) E. Disabled. Cards All.
Post 217 av. Provence, 26000 Valence, Drôme. (ER p 62)
Tel 75 42 20 15. Telex 345823. Fax 75 43 56 29. Mich 130/B3.
(Bookings: UK 071 724 1000; US toll free 800 221 4542)

Base Hotels

AURILLAC
La Ferraudie

Comfortable hotel
Quiet/Lift/Garage/Parking

Modern and 100 metres or so from the Parc des Sports/Parc Hélitas (follow signs from western N120 bypass).
Rooms (22) C-D. Cards Access, DC, Visa.
Post 15 rue Bel Air, 15000 Aurillac, Cantal.
Tel 71 48 72 42. Mich 126/B3.

CEYRAT
La Châtaigneraie

Comfortable hotel
Quiet

South of Royat and high above the village. Extensive views east. On the D133 west of Ceyrat.
Rooms (16) C-D. Cards Access, Visa.
Closed 1st half May. 1st 3 wks Aug. Sat and Sun.
Post av Châtaigneraie, 63122 Ceyrat, P.-de-D.
Tel 73 61 34 66. Mich 113/D2.

MILLAU
La Capelle

Comfortable hotel
Quiet/Good value

Jane Rouquet, a friendly, helpful owner, and good value count most here. Breakfasts "so-so". Park in the adjacent *place*.
Rooms (46) B-C. Cards Access, Visa.
Closed Oct to Easter.
Post 7 pl. Fraternité, 12100 Millau, Aveyron.
Tel 65 60 14 72. Mich 141/E4.

MILLAU
Jalade

Simple hotel
Lift/Good value

Near station; busy spot. Convenient for Buffet de France.
Rooms (23) C. Cards AE, Access, Visa. (Close to public car park.)
Post 18 bis av. A. Merle, 12100 Millau, Aveyron.
Tel 65 60 62 00. Mich 141/E4.

VIENNE
Midi

Comfortable hotel
Quiet/Gardens/Parking/Good value

To the east of Vienne (D502), at Pont-Evêque. Short, easy 4 km ride to La Pyramide restaurant; cheaper bedrooms too.
Rooms (17) C-D. Cards All.
Closed Xmas to mid Jan.
Post pl. Eglise, 38780 Pont-Evêque, Isère.
Tel 74 85 90 11. Fax 74 57 24 99. Mich 116/B3.

AUMONT-AUBRAC Grand Hôtel & Rest. Guy Prouhèze

Comfortable hotel/Cooking 3
Gardens/Parking

Anne and I first visited the hotel (the Gare in those days) when Guy's father, Raymond, was at the controls. Guy Prouhèze is the fourth generation chef at this much improved and refurbished family hotel; he and his wife, Catherine, celebrated the centenary of *la maison* in 1991. Modern cooking backed up by a regional menu and the odd classic (Aubrac beef with shallots and red wine). Desserts are especially good and three cheers for an enterprising choice of no less than seven menus (both *table d'hôte* and from the full *à la carte* list).
Menus B-F. Rooms (29) C-E. Cards Access, Visa.
Closed Nov to Feb. Sun evg & Mon (not July & Aug).
Post 48130 Aumont-Aubrac, Lozère. (Town now bypassed.)
Tel 66 42 80 07. Fax 66 42 87 78. Mich 127/E4.

BELCASTEL   Vieux Pont

Simple restaurant/Cooking 3
Good value

A sumptuously scenic spot: a huddle of 15th-century houses, dominated by a castle high above the roof tops; a bend in the Aveyron; and a medieval *pont* spanning the 20-yard wide river. Plus Nicole Fagegaltier, born in Belcastel and still in her 20s, a self-taught *cuisinière* inspired by the local hero, Michel Bras. As young as she is, Nicole has fashioned one of the most natural styles of modern cooking we've ever come across. Extensive use of oil (hazelnut, walnut and olive), nuts (hazelnuts, walnuts and almonds) and light reductions: *jus de persil*, *essence de morilles* and *lait d'amandes*. Tasty *galette de pomme de terre* and vegetables. Mas de Daumas Gassac Rosé Frisant Brut is a bargain (see Languedoc-Roussillon). Sister Michèle is an attentive hostess. Rooms? Use Campanile on NW outskirts of 12000 Rodez (Tel 65 42 97 08); or Hôtel Marre at nearby 12390 Rignac (Tel 65 64 51 56).
Menus B-C. Cards AE, Access, Visa.
Closed Jan. Feb. Sun evg & Mon.
Post 12390 Belcastel, Aveyron.
Tel 65 64 52 29. Mich 140/B2.

BRIOUDE   Poste et Champanne

Simple hotel/Cooking 1-2
Parking/Good value

Great value for money is the *raison d'être* for seeking out the Chazal-Barge family hotel (the annexe, around the corner, is quieter). The dining room gets busy; as a result the family are rushed off their feet and Hélène Chazal's cooking, both *Bourgeoise* and regional (*tripoux*; *potée*), can suffer too.
Menus A. Rooms (20) B-C. Cards None accepted.
Closed 2-25 Jan. Sun evg (mid Sept to mid June).
Post 1 bd Dr Devins, 43100 Brioude, H.-Loire. (On N102.)
Tel 71 50 14 62. Mich 127/F1.

BROUSSE-LE-CHATEAU   Relays du Chasteau

Very simple hotel with basic rooms/Cooking 2
Quiet/Parking/Good value

An entrancing riverside village (where the Alrance joins the Tarn): rose-covered walls, a ruined castle and medieval bridge across the Alrance. Young English-speaking chef, Philippe Senegas and his wife, Sybile, are the 4th-generation owners. *Bourgeoise* and classical cooking and some regional dishes.
Menus A-B. Rooms (14) B. Cards Access, Visa.
Closed Mid Dec to mid Jan. Fri evg & Sat midday (Oct to Apl).
Post 12480 Brousse-le-Château, Aveyron.
Tel 65 99 40 15. Mich 151/C4.

CALVINET   Beauséjour

Simple hotel/Cooking 2
Parking/Good value

Renovated throughout and modern bedrooms. Louis-Bernard Puech does a super job mixing classical and regional *plats* with the odd modern creation (*la cuisine d'hier et d'aujourd'hui*). Local produce dominates and there's a wide choice on the *cuisine de terroir* menu. Light-as-air desserts.
Menus A-C. Rooms (10) C. Cards Access, Visa.
Closed Sun evg & Mon. Check ahead for annual holidays.
Post 15340 Calvinet, Cantal.
Tel 71 49 91 68. Fax 71 49 98 63. Mich 126/A4.

LA CHAISE-DIEU   Au Tremblant

Simple hotel/Cooking 1-2
Gardens/Garage/Parking/Good value

A beaming smile and warm welcome from Josette Boyer is a guarantee. *Cuisine Bourgeoise* from husband Jean. The dearer menus list the odd classical dish and the regional menu surprisingly includes *entrecôte marchand de vin*.
Menus A-C. Rooms (27) B-D. Cards Access, Visa.
Closed 12 Nov to 21 Apl.
Post 43160 La Chaise-Dieu, H.-Loire.
Tel 71 00 01 85. Mich 128/B1. (On D906.)

LE CHAMBON-SUR-LIGNON   Clair Matin

Comfortable hotel/Cooking 1
Secluded/Terrace/Gardens/Swim pool/Tennis/Parking

Alain Bard's hotel is a modern chalet-style *logis* in an isolated forest setting. The prime benefits are the facilities listed above, the gym, sauna and solarium and the invigorating terrain to all sides. Cooking? Basic *Bourgeoise*.
Menus B. Rooms (30) D-E. Disabled. Cards All.
Closed 15 Nov to 15 Dec. 5-25 Jan. Wed (Oct to Apl).
Post 43400 Chambon-sur-Lignon, H.-Loire. (On D185 to the E.)
Tel 71 59 73 03. Fax 71 65 87 66. Mich 129/E2.

CHATELGUYON   La Grilloute

Very simple restaurant/Cooking 1-2
Good value

So many of you have been bowled over by Jacqueline Brandibat-Lechevalier's small restaurant, once her husband's bookshop. Born in Casablanca in 1929, she's travelled widely (her father was a pilot with Aérospatiale – later Air France). Not surprisingly her *Bourgeois* repertoire is a touch eclectic: *omelette Mexicaine* and *poulet grillé à l'Indienne* rub shoulders with *terrine maison à l'orange*, *pâté de faisan en terrine* and *pâtisserie maison*. Rooms? No problem in this seasonal spa town; six hotels within a 200-metre walk.
Menus B. Cards Visa. (Park across the road, towards casino.)
Closed 10 Oct to 5 Apl. Tues.
Post 33 av. Baraduc, 63140 Châtelguyon, P.-de-D.
Tel 73 86 04 17. Mich 113/D1.

CHAUDES-AIGUES   Auberge du Pont de Lanau

Comfortable hotel/Cooking 2-3
Terrace/Gardens/Garage/Parking/Good value

Jean-Michel Cornut and his wife have moved five km up the D921 from the family hotel, Aux Bouillons d'Or, to the right bank of the Truyère. The *pont* spans the river, an exciting wooded gorge which I've described elsewhere. There's an adjacent community swimming pool and a man-made lake. Bedrooms are soundproofed. Jean-Michel's repertoire is both classical and neo-classical (*filet de sandre à la vapeur au vin de Cahors et jus de viande* and a gutsy *rable de lièvre rôti son fumet à la crème moutarde* are typical), backed up by some appetising local delights: a delicate *millefeuille au bleu d'Auvergne* and an earthy *rouelle de tripoux sur le lit de lentilles vertes*.
Menus B-C. Rooms (8) C-D. Cards Access, Visa.
Closed 20 Nov to 20 Mar. Tues evg & Wed.
Post Pont de Lanau, 15260 Neuvéglise, Cantal.
Tel 71 23 57 76. Fax 71 23 53 84. Mich 127/D3.

CHAUDES-AIGUES   Aux Bouillons d'Or

Comfortable restaurant with rooms/Cooking 2
Lift/Good value

Jean-Michel Cornut has moved north (see above); his mother, Andrée, remains *la patronne* at the modernised five-storey building in the middle of the town. Chef Didier Vergne's cooking, like the 82C water which rises to the surface at the spa, bubbles on differing hot plates: classical dishes in the main (*aiguillette de canard au poivre vert* and *entrecôte de l'échalote* are typical) and regional *plats* take bit parts (*tripoux du pays*, *coq au vin d'Auvergne*, *tarte au Cantal* and *aligot* all make an appearance). Double-glazed windows.
Menus A-B. Rooms (12) C. Cards Access, Visa.
Closed Nov to Easter.
Post 15110 Chaudes-Aigues, Cantal.
Tel 71 23 51 42. Mich 127/D3.

CONQUES   Ste-Foy

Comfortable hotel/Cooking 1-2
Quiet/Terrace/Gardens/Swimming pool/Lift

I wrote these words 10 years ago for *Hidden France*: an utter gem of a place, creeper-covered and nestling in the shadow of one of France's true jewels, the Eglise Ste-Foy. Nothing has changed, though the old owners, the Cannes, have moved on to their new boutique at the top of the village. New hosts, the Garcenots, have maintained the high standards. They've added a newly-built heated indoor pool, gym and solarium (what next in medieval Conques?). Classical cuisine: the likes of *terrine de foie de volaille maison*, *jambonette de pintadeau au foie gras* and *boeuf sauce Rossini*. Debits? Some rooms slant; the hotel gets very busy; and public parking is 250 metres away.
Menus B-C. Rooms (35) D-F. Cards AE, Access, Visa.
Closed Dec to Feb.
Post 12320 Conques, Aveyron.
Tel 65 69 84 03. Fax 65 72 81 04. Mich 140/B1.

CORDES   Grand Ecuyer

Very comfortable hotel/Cooking 3
Quiet/Terrace

Theatrical? Extravaganza? Extrovert? Yes to all three. There's nothing like this anywhere in France. Cordes and the Gothic house are the first half of the overture: stones and timber, lavish furnishings and stunning views from the 13th-century village in the sky. Then comes the crashing finale. Yves Thuriès (a good enough *cuisinier*; a superb *pâtissier* and *chocolatier*) is, in the words of a reader, an entrepreneur Mrs Thatcher would have been proud to claim for her own. When *in situ* he's the chef/patron but he's often away, demonstrating his fabulous skills with sugar, chocolate, pastry and ice; and he publishes a highly-rated foodie mag. His multi-menu repertoire is neo-classical, his desserts are something else (even Carême would bend his knee to Yves). Marvellous *cave*. Don't miss Yves' Musée de l'Art du Sucre (up the hill).
Menus B-E. Rooms (12) F-F2. Cards All.
Closed Nov to Feb. Rest: Mon (not June-Sept & pub. hols).
Post 81170 Cordes, Tarn. (Parking can be tricky.)
Tel 63 56 01 03. Fax 63 56 16 99. Mich 139/E4.

CORDES   Hostellerie du Vieux Cordes

Comfortable hotel/Cooking 2
Quiet/Terrace

Also owned by Yves Thuriès and run by his brother-in-law. Another medieval building with an unusual, inviting terrace plus distant views. Everything's a lot less over-the-top here, including the cooking, a mix of modern and neo-classical.
Menus A-C. Rooms (21) D-E. Cards All.
Closed Jan. (Parking is equally messy here too.)
Post 81170 Cordes, Tarn.
Tel 63 56 00 12. Telex 530955. Mich 139/E4.

DIEULEFIT   Les Hospitaliers

Very comfortable hotel/Cooking 2-3
Secluded/Terrace/Gardens/Swimming pool/Parking

Five km to the west of Dieulefit is Poët-Laval; high above the
latter is Vieux Village. The hotel is part of the restored
medieval village. The terrace is an original and ingenious
creation. Yvon Morin is the *patron/sommelier*; son Bernard is
le cuisinier. Cooking is neo-classical with some modern brush
strokes. I've received a mixed bag of reports: one letter arrived
saying the hotel was the reader's top favourite; two days later
another reckoned he was unimpressed and that the place was
a bit pretentious. Inconsistency and carelessness crop up as
regular bleats. Retains an entry by a whisker.
Menus C-E. Rooms (23) F-F2. Cards All.
Closed Mid Nov to Feb.
Post Vieux Village, 26160 Poët-Laval, Drôme.
Tel 75 46 22 32. Fax 75 46 49 99. Mich 144/C1.

DONZERE   Hostellerie du Mas des Sources

Very comfortable restaurant with rooms/Cooking 2-3
Secluded/Terrace/Gardens/Parking

An idyllic, delicious *coin*. As you head south down the Rhône
Valley this will be your first real taste of ever-nearing
Provence. The house is typically southern (lots of arches make
the interior especially eye-pleasing), there are vineyards next
door and the modern cooking has a Med feel: olive oil,
tapenade, *thym*, and *olives noires* are some of the telling clues
on the menus. Wine buff Jean-Marie Picard and his wife,
Nicole, are first-class hosts. A spot you'll return to often.
Menus C. Rooms (4) D-F. Cards Access, Visa.
Closed Feb sch. hols. Last wk Dec. Tues evg. Wed (Sept-Apl).
Post Donzère, 26780 Malataverne, Drôme. (Off D144, 3 km to N.)
Tel 75 51 74 18. Fax 75 51 74 63. Mich 144/A2.

GRANE   Patrick Giffon

Comfortable restaurant with rooms/Cooking 3
Quiet/Terrace/Parking/Good value

A *mistral* of welcome change has blown through Grane: Jacques
Giffon handed over the tiller to his son Patrick in 1987. The
happy family environment is unchanged; the small *logis* is still
dominated by the *église*; the flower-trimmed terrace, shaded by
a plane tree, is as cool as ever; but *la cuisine* is filling out with
ambition by the day. Patrick's repertoire is neo-classical and
modern (much influenced by his training at Oustaù de
Baumanière): *fagotin* (bundle) *de saumon de fontaine aux
épinards sauce Clairette de Die*; and *suprême de carrelet à la
crème de morille* are two representative *plats*. Do try a local
red: Jean-Marie Lombard's Brézème (see wine notes).
Menus B-D. Rooms (9) B-D. Cards All.
Closed Feb. Sun evg (Sept to May). Mon (not midday pub. hols).
Post 26400 Grane, Drôme.
Tel 75 62 60 64. Fax 75 62 70 11. Mich 130/B4.

LAGUIOLE   Michel Bras

Very comfortable hotel/Cooking 4-5
Secluded/Lift/Parking

I made my first visit to Laguiole in April 1982. The grey, dour
and undistinguished town of 1,200 souls is at the very heart of
France, on the road to nowhere special. Both the town and
windswept mountainous Aubrac are very much like central
Wales; Laguiole could easily be Llanidloes. To grasp just what
I mean approach from the east, using the D987 from the A75.
(In early spring the pastures are sheets of *jonquils*.)

Since that first taste-tantalising visit I've been back many
times, to discover more about the young genius I had stumbled
upon in remote Aubrac, where cattle outnumber people by
many thousands to one. At the end of my 1982 meal I scribbled
down these words: "For Michel Bras to flourish at Laguiole is
nothing short of a culinary miracle."

What makes this hyper-active, pencil-thin, shy, bespectacled
chef such a culinary powerhouse? When you meet him you
sense his mind is miles away, working at break-neck speed on
several problems at once; his eyes, most certainly, are
constantly on the move. You ask yourself: is Bras a botanist
turned chef, or a chemist converted to cooking? His office, part
of a large kitchen, has always had on its shelves as many well-
thumbed books on horticulture as on cooking. He also has a
deep interest in ancient recipes which made use of Nature's
wild plants and herbs. Yet, remarkably, his training amounted
to no more than a long apprenticeship at his mother's side in
the modest family *pension* and a brief stint in the kitchens of
the Hôtel Fusiès at Lacaune (see Languedoc-Roussillon).

There's not a hint of plagiarism in Bras' cooking; his
inventive brain has no need to crib from other chefs. He long
ago shunned the cooking-by-numbers which prevails at many
of the shrines. He worships Girardet (see Crissier: Jura), the
chef's chef, whom he acknowledges opened his eyes to just what
freedom and spontaneity means to modern masters. Bras, born
in 1946, has shaped and polished a highly individualistic style
of cooking. He has been experimenting, and sometimes making
mistakes, with produce of every kind for well over a decade
and his repertoire includes scores of herbs and flavouring
agents which you'll not encounter anywhere else. (Don't take
Larousse with you: ask Ginette, his wife, to show you her
special notes.) Laguiole is not for classical cuisine fans. Rather
it's a mecca for those of you who want to experience just what
a chef with an utterly open mind, not brainwashed by catering
college dogma, can achieve: culinary common sense, good taste,
healthy eating, technical wizardry, delicate touches, vegetables
galore and sensible portions.

Not everything is perfection for all readers however. One
writer friend, who knows France as well as anyone and who
calls a spade a spade, considers Bras' restaurant to be
pretentious beyond belief. He's also not the first to take
exception to the philosopy of *le patron* written on the menu
(now dropped). Some critics, visiting for the first time since
Bras was "discovered" in 86/87, label his repertoire as
"gimmicky" and the sort that attracts the major guides looking
for scoops. Michel is on to a hiding to nothing: after years of
developing an anything but stereotyped style he now attracts
the curious critic, keen to scoff, thump him about the ears, and

who makes no effort to research just why and how his cooking has developed the way it has.

Service is often hammered; stir-fried is perhaps a better label. Alas, times have changed. If you're chasing three stars rough edges will not do; you've got to pay big bucks to polished professionals to run the front-of-house theatre. Both Bras and Michel Trama (Puymirol) face the same problem.

I'll finish on my favourite hobby horse. For over 10 years I've seen Ginette and Michel strive to write their unique culinary signature in Aubrac, an area still closer to centuries past than anywhere else in France. Today the world beats a path to their door, lit by stars which shine over Laguiole and drawn by *toques* placed on his head.

There's a smell of *déjà vu* in my nostrils; I've seen what follows before. In the Thirties chefs in out-of-the-way spots (André Pic at Le Pin; Joseph Barattéro at Lamastre; Eugénie Brazier at the Col de la Luère; and Marie Bourgeois at Priay) won three Michelin stars at the most modest of restaurants. Bras, then, would have won a third star at his family's *pension*. But not today: now 18 financially demanding words sum up the criteria to win three stars. (Read *Santé Bibendum!*)

Michel's unrelenting passion for his *pays* is nothing short of fanatical, certainly mystical, perhaps even suicidal. He would deny vehemently my suggestion (as all French chefs do) that he's trapped himself in the web of the three-star spiral chase. In April 1992 the couple deserted Laguiole and moved five km east to a new, isolated home 4000 ft above sea-level on the high plateau of the Monts d'Aubrac (a spot not unlike Wales' Plynlimon summit). Prices have climbed with them. If Bras' cuisine is unique then the new hotel is no less so. The couple's "theme" is Aubrac and Mother Nature. Their man-made child is a basalt, granite, glass and metal creation, both jutting out from and encrusted in Aubrac's rocks and soil, an ultra-modern, contemporary building, as hard and brutal and uncompromising as the cruel landscape. Aubrac's remoteness stretches away below you, to the north, west and south. The seemingly never-ending views and 21st-century, high-tech architecture leave you with the feeling you are suspended in a space station. You'll either love the place – or hate it.

Michel and Ginette have made a dramatic statement for their beloved Aubrac. The duo are severely testing their faith in Michel's ability and showing a bold loyalty to their *pays*. The financial commitment is terrifying. (Other two-star chefs, striving for the third – Veyrat and Roellinger for example – have also made recent up-market moves. Their posh properties are at least saleable: who else would buy the Bras' new home?) Fifty-odd years ago a serious restaurant in this spot would have spelt suicide. Today, with the Massif Central's heart now pierced by a toll-free autoroute, access is fast and easy. Will the self-inflicted challenge, remarkable by any standards, culinary or otherwise, crumble into dust, or will the basalt child stand firm and flourish? I hope they win a third star; and, even more so, I pray they remain the unspoilt, gentle and self-effacing couple I've known for so long.

Menus C-F. Rooms (15) F2-F3. Disabled. Cards AE, Access, Visa. (Bras' old hotel (Lou Mazuc), now *sans restaurant*, has cheaper bedrooms (C-F); to save francs book these when reserving.)
Closed Nov-Mar. Sun evg & Mon (Apl-June; Sept & Oct).
Post rte de l'Aubrac, 12210 Laguiole, Aveyron.
Tel 65 44 32 24. Fax 65 48 47 02. Mich 141/D1. (On D15.)

LAMASTRE
Midi & Rest. Barattéro

Comfortable hotel/Cooking 2-3
Gardens/Garage

In the Thirties Joseph Barattéro won three Michelin stars at the modest Midi. After the war his widow (admired by the late Elizabeth David in her *French Provincial Cooking*) worked hard to protect his reputation, helped by her chef Elie Perrier. She died in the early Eighties at which time the Perrier family bought the hotel. Now young Bernard, Elie's son, and his wife, Marie-George, continue the good work. They're an involved, happy couple. Classical cooking with a *menu tradition* paying homage to Joseph's famed *plats*: among them *pain d'écrevisses sauce Cardinal* and *poularde de Bresse en vessie Joseph Barattéro*. Grumbles surface from time to time: total absence of vegetables is a regular chestnut. *Soufflé glacé aux marrons de l'Ardèche* is a well-liked dessert. Good and plentiful coffee.
Menus B-D. Rooms (13) D. Cards All.
Closed 15 Dec-Feb. Sun evg. Mon (not July, Aug & pub. hols).
Post pl. Seignobos, 07270 Lamastre, Ardèche.
Tel 75 06 41 50. Fax 75 06 49 75. Mich 129/F2.

LE LIORAN
Grand Hôtel Anglard et du Cerf

Very comfortable hotel/Cooking 1-2
Quiet/Lift/Parking/Good value

High above Super Lioran; surrounded by pines and with super views of the Monts du Cantal; and super value for the comfort provided; these are the special pluses of the much liked mountain hotel. Jean-Pierre Anglard, *chef de cuisine*, is another experienced classicist: witness his *blanquette de St-Jacques Armoricaine* and a *filet de boeuf mignonnette*. J-P's culinary ambitions have been notched down a peg or two in the last decade; now there's many a *Bourgeois plat* lurking on his menus. But prices, too, have been wound back a notch or two.
Menus A-C. Rooms (38) B-D. Cards AE, Access, Visa.
Closed 9-27 May. 8-30 June. 30 Sept-19 Dec.
Post Super Lioran, 15300 Murat, Cantal.
Tel 71 49 50 26. Fax 71 49 53 53. Mich 126/C2.

MEYRUEIS
Grand Hôtel Europe/Mont Aigoual

Comfortable hotels/Cooking 1
Gardens/Swimming pool/Lifts/Parking/Good value

Frédéric and Stella Robert own two hotels: the Grand and the cheaper Mont Aigoual, 200 metres away. The pool and attractive gardens are at the latter. Both hotels have lifts. Cooking is a mix of basic *Bourgeoise* (*gigot de mouton grillé* and *truite de amandes*) and classical (*contre-filet grillé sauce Bordelaise*). Small but comfortable bedrooms and interesting views from balconies (Grand). Details below include both hotels.
Menus A-B. Rooms (60: for both) B-D. Cards Access, Visa.
Closed Nov to Easter.
Post 48150 Meyrueis, Lozère.
Tel 66 45 60 05 (Grand). 66 45 65 61 (Mont A). Mich 141/F3.

MILLAU   Buffet de France

Comfortable restaurant/Cooking 1-2
Terrace/Good value

Claude Manenc has maintained the high standards set by Albert
Négron at one of France's best station hotels (was Buffet de
Gare). A torrent of menus and both classical and *Bourgeoise*
fare: *chaudrée*, local *charcuterie* and *entrecôte de Roquefort*.
Menus A-B. Cards All. (Rooms? See Millau Base hotels.)
Closed Feb. Tues (not July & Aug).
Post pl. Gare, 12100 Millau, Aveyron. (Park in the *place*.)
Tel 65 60 09 04. Mich 141/E4.

MILLAU   Capion

Comfortable restaurant/Cooking 1-2
Good value

New owners, Patrick (from the Vosges) and Corinne (she's an
Aveyronnaise) Mougeot. Classical (*sole sauce Cardinal* and
gibiers Grand Veneur), Bourgeois (*noisettes de lapin fermier
braisées*) and regional dishes (*tripous Aveyronnais*).
Menus A-B. Cards AE, Access, Visa. (Rooms? See advice above.)
Closed Wed (not July & Aug).
Post 3 r. J.-F. Alméras, 12100 Millau, Aveyron.
Tel 65 60 00 91. Mich 141/E4. (250 metres W of La Capelle.)

MILLAU   Château de Creissels

Comfortable hotel/Cooking 2
Terrace/Gardens/Parking/Good value

Readers like this château hotel with an old tower and medieval
church next door (at night the clock is silent). Bedrooms are
well-appointed, a pleasing counterpoint to the old-world
gentility of the main rooms. Classical and some regional dishes
supervised by Anne Austruy, daughter of *la patronne*.
Menus A-B. Rooms (31) B-D. Cards All. (On D992, 2 km W.)
Closed 2 Jan to 9 Mar. Rest: Tues (out of season).
Post rte St-Affrique, 12100 Millau, Aveyron.
Tel 65 60 16 59. Fax 65 60 24 63. Mich 141/E4.

MILLAU   La Marmite

Comfortable restaurant/Cooking 2
Good value

Three cheers for the indefatigable 78-year-old Albert Négron
and his ever-smiling wife, Janine. After 37 years at the Buffet
de Gare and the Château de Creissels the duo have moved to
yet another Millau home. Authentic *haute cuisine* classics from
the pages of *Larousse*; *Bourgeois* dishes; and a string of
regional pearls: *trénels à la Millavoise, confidou de boeuf à la
Millavoise, aligot* and others (you'll need to refer to the
regional specialities list). Put aside a few extra francs for two
of Albert's peerless *plats*: a *petite marmite du pêcheur* (a fish

soup worthy of a fishing port) and his *bolet* (a toadstool shaped dessert of vanilla and coffee ice cream, lashings of *Chantilly*, and a biscuit top covered in chocolate and rum).
Menus A-B. Cards All. (Rooms? La Capelle one minute away.)
Closed Feb. Sun evg (not high season). Wed.
Post 14/16 bd de la Capelle, 12100 Millau, Aveyron.
Tel 65 61 20 44. Mich 141/E4. (Park in pl. de la Fraternité.)

MONTSALVY   Nord

Comfortable hotel/Cooking 2
Gardens/Parking/Good value

Mauricette Cayron is *la cuisinière*; husband Jean runs the front of house at the modern, much refurbished *logis*. I'm told a garden has been acquired and a pool is planned. Classical, *Bourgeois* and regional dishes (including *choux farci*, *aligot*, *poitrine de veau farcie* and *tripoux au vin blanc*.)
Menus A-C. Rooms (26) B-C. Cards All.
Closed Jan to Mar.
Post 15120 Montsalvy, Cantal.
Tel 71 49 20 03. Fax 71 49 29 00. Mich 126/B4.

MOUDEYRES   Auberge Pré Bossu

Comfortable hotel/Cooking 3
Secluded/Gardens/Parking

A stone and thatched *auberge* built two decades ago. Carlos and Marlène Grootaert, a Belgian couple, have achieved wonders at this remote spot since they bought the property in 1976. English-speaking Carlos champions both neo-classical and modern cooking; he has a special flair for using regional produce in an assured, individualistic style (one example is green Velay lentils in a *gnocchi* creation). Delight in taste-bud teasers such as *saucisson d'escargots* (six small rissoles of *escargots* and *pieds de porc aux orties*), a beefy *bouillon de queue de boeuf* and a gutsy *gâteau de cabri* (young goat).
Menus B-D. Rooms (10) D-E. Cards AE, Access, Visa.
Closed Nov to mid Apl. Rest: Midday (not Sat & Sun).
Post 43150 Moudeyres, H.-Loire.
Tel 71 05 10 70. Fax 71 05 10 21. Mich 129/D3.

NAJAC   Belle Rive

Comfortable hotel/Cooking 1-2
Secl'd/Terr/Garden/Swim pool/Tenn/Parking/Good value

Some site: the *logis* is alongside the Aveyron and high above the valley, across the river, is Najac's ruined fortress. The 5th-generation patron (Louis Mazières) has handed over to the 6th, Jacques. Facilities have moved on; classical/*Bourgeoise* cooking has slipped back. Madame speaks English.
Menus A-C. Rooms (35) C. Cards All.
Closed Nov to mid Apl.
Post 12270 Najac, Aveyron. (Right bank of River Aveyron.)
Tel 65 29 73 90. Mich 139/E3.

NAJAC　　　　　　　　　　Oustal del Barry

Comfortable hotel/Cooking 2-3
Quiet/Terrace/Gardens/Lift

In Najac, at one end of the village square. Five generations of the Miquel family have made their culinary mark in Aveyron, but none of them so successfully as Jean-Marie. He's much influenced by Michel Bras, a local hero. Modern, personalised cuisine (*pousses de pourpier aux langoustines et aux coques, assaisonnées au vinaigre balsamique et huile d'olive* is typical; a wordy mouthful but also mouthwateringly tasty). Desserts are especially good, though their tastes do not always match their visual appeal. Another bonus: a fine cellar. Readers speak warmly of *la patronne*, Catherine.
Menus B-D. Rooms (21) C-E. Cards AE, Access, Visa.
Closed Nov to 6 Apl. Mon (Apl & Oct; but not pub. hols).
Post place du Bourg, 12270 Najac, Aveyron.
Tel 65 29 74 32. Fax 65 29 75 32. Mich 139/E3.

PAILHEROLS　　　　　Auberge des Montagnes

Simple hotel/Cooking 1-2
Quiet/Gardens/Swimming pool/Parking/Good value

A warm-hearted family fusses over you at the 100-year-old farm in an isolated, high-altitude village on the edge of the Monts du Cantal. I've had nothing but praise for André and Denise Combourieu, and papa too. Walking, cross-country skiing, mountain bikes, a gym and games room: exercise the pounds off after you've tucked into the few pounds cost of *Bourgeois* and Auvergnat appetite-quenching menus (*pounti aux pruneaux, truffade* and *tripoux*). Popular British tour operator's base.
Menus A-B. Rooms (18) B. Cards Access, Visa.
Closed Mid Oct to 20 Dec (but not *Toussaint* holiday).
Post 15800 Pailherols, Cantal.
Tel 71 47 57 01. Fax 71 49 63 83. Mich 126/C3.

PONT-DE-L'ISERE　　　　　　　Chabran

Very comfortable restaurant with rooms/Cooking 3-4
Terrace

FL3 readers will chuckle at Chabran's roller-coaster ride: during a five-year span Michelin star two was won, lost and won back again. Bibendum's ins and outs match both my own and readers' ups and downs. One of my meals was *cuisine moderne* perfection; the next a cobbled-up hodgepodge (lousy service; bloody, tough duck; no veg; *sauce poivrade* a shadow of the aromatic, velvet nectar of an earlier visit; and four courses dished up in 60 mins). The trouble is handsome Michel has his fingers in too many pies; self-effacing Rose-Marie soldiers on, defending the fort when hubby's away. Terrific breakfasts. The entry squeaks in by the thickness of a guillotine blade.
Menus B-E. Rooms (12) D-F. Cards All. (En Route p 61)
Closed 2 wks Jan. Sun evg & Mon (not July & Aug).
Post RN7, 26600 Pont-de-l'Isère, Drôme.
Tel 75 84 60 09. Fax 346333. Fax 75 84 59 65. Mich 130/B2.

255

PONTEMPEYRAT

Mistou

Comfortable hotel/Cooking 2-3
Secluded/Gardens/Parking

An 18th-century watermill, well-away from the D498 and in an idyllic wooded, two-acre park alongside the River Ance. (The mill, now generating electricity, was once used to conserve eggs.) Jacqueline Roux is a charming hostess; and her English-speaking husband, Bernard, is a fine chef, with a flair for fish. Neo-classical cooking. Sound cellar with 20 or so half bottles. Next door to a working farm; flies can be a pest. An extremely popular British tour operator's hotel (VFB).
Menus B-C. Rooms (28) C-E. Cards All.
Closed Nov-Easter. Rest: Midday (Sept to June but not w/ends).
Post Pontempeyrat, 43500 Craponne-sur-Arzon, H.-Loire.
Tel 77 50 62 46. Fax 77 50 66 70. Mich 114/C4.

LES ROCHES-DE-CONDRIEU

Bellevue

Comfortable hotel/Cooking 2
Garage/Good value

The best features of the Bouron family hotel are the riverside views and site on the Rhône's left bank. There's a bustling marina beside the hotel. On cool evenings a log fire crackles in the dining room; less cracking is the classical cooking with the likes of *turbot braisé au champagne*, *entrecôte grillée au beurre d'échalotes* and a *voiture du pâtissier*.
Menus B-C. Rooms (18) B-C. Cards All.
Closed 15 Feb-15 Mar. 1-15 Aug. Sun (out of season). Mon.
Post 38370 Les Roches-de-Condrieu, Isère.
Tel 74 56 41 42. Mich 116/A4.

ROYAT

Radio

Very comfortable hotel/Cooking 3-4
Gardens/Lift/Parking

At last the major French guides have picked up the signals transmitting from the Auvergne: Michel Mioche is a chef with volcanic talent. Friendly Michel and his delightful wife, Yvette, have worked wonders with their awkward, high-ceilinged hotel; the art deco styling, now applied to all wavebands, works well. Michel's repertoire is a finely-tuned, sure *mélange* of modern and neo-classical. This is the chef who woke up French *cuisiniers* to the superb contrast of earthy *lentilles vertes du Puy* combined with delicate-tasting fish; the marriage is now commonplace in France. Menu prices have risen steeply; nevertheless the skill and comfort bonuses are Puy de Dôme high. Try an excellent new local white wine from Boudes, west of St-Germain-Lembron. Over and out. (D68 from Clermont; immediately left after high arched rail bridge; left in 100 m. under same line; second right.)
Menus D-F. Rooms (27) E-F. Cards All.
Closed Mid Nov to end Feb. Rest: Sun evg & Mon.
Post 43 r. Pierre-Curie, 63400 Royat-Chamalières, P.-de-Dôme.
Tel 73 30 87 83. Fax 73 36 42 44. Mich 113/D2. (Near station.)

LE ROZIER Grand Hôtel Muse et Rozier

Very comfortable hotel/Cooking 1-2
Secluded/Terrace/Gardens/Lift/Parking

A striking, ultra-modern structure, squeezed between the Tarn and D907, at the southern entrance to the Gorges du Tarn. The Grand was rebuilt in 1982, three years after the original hotel was destroyed by fire. By day the wooded setting catches the eye; at night clever lighting does the same job in an illuminating way. Cooking? No sparks here: little choice and a mix of grills, lighter dishes and classical specialities.
Menus B-D. Rooms (35) D-E. Cards All.
Closed Jan. Feb.
Post à la Muse, 12720 Peyreleau, Aveyron.
Tel 65 62 60 01. Fax 65 62 63 88. Mich 141/E3.

ST-AFFRIQUE Moderne

Comfortable hotel/Cooking 2
Good value

Survival is tough for Jean-François and Yves Decuq at their family hotel in the no-man's land between the Tarn Gorges and the Haut Languedoc Regional Park. They have to try harder and, by golly, they do. The *logis* has been decorated and painted up a treat; the interior is a permanent art exhibition. J-F does the brush work front-of-house; Yves mixes the colours in the kitchen. Cooking is both regional (several Roquefort specialities; the latter is just up the road) and classical.
Menus A-C. Rooms (28) C-D. Cards All.
Closed 20 Dec to 20 Jan. Rest: 5-11 Oct.
Post à la gare, 12400 St-Affrique, Aveyron.
Tel 65 49 20 44. Fax 65 49 36 55. Mich 155/D1.

ST-BONNET-LE-FROID Auberge des Cimes

Comfortable restaurant with rooms/Cooking 3-4
Parking

Régis Marcon, an English-speaking 36-year-old *cuisinier*, is a revelation. How marvellous to encounter this inventive marvel who returned to his native village 12 years ago to take over his mother's simple bistro. In the same mould as Michel Bras, Régis concocts imaginative modern creations and relies very much on local produce. *Le menu entre Velay et Vivarais* dazzles: still etched in our minds is a *tuile de noisette aux grenouilles et aux mousserons*, *crème d'orties* (two thin nut slices sandwiching some baby frogs' legs and *mousserons*, the assembly lying on a bed of sauce); *trifolles* (local potatoes) *farcies aux morilles et foie gras*; and succulent lamb, wrapped in a blanket of *cystre* (hay) and cooked in a bread oven. I implore you: make the detour from the Rhône Valley.
Menus B-E. Rooms (7) C-D. Cards DC, Access, Visa.
Closed 15 Nov to Easter. Sun evg & Wed (Sept to June). Mon midday (July & Aug).
Post 43290 St-Bonnet-le-Froid, H.-Loire.
Tel 71 59 93 72. Fax 71 59 93 40. Mich 129/E2.

ST-JEAN-DU-BRUEL   Midi-Papillon

Simple hotel/Cooking 2
Quiet/Swimming pool/Garage/Parking/Good value

What involved fourth-generation hosts Maryse and Jean-Michel
Papillon are. The site, beside the River Dourbie is one plus; the
new heated pool is another; a third is the newly-acquired
maison Bourgeoise en face de l'hôtel. But, as always, owners
make hotels truly tick. Ask Maryse to show you her album on
the area's wild orchids; the family name is linked with
l'orchidée Papillon. (The whole area is a sea of wild flowers in
late spring.) It's no surprise then to see flowers in the dining
room and the attractively-decorated bedrooms.

Jean-Michel does his bit: he grows his own vegetables; rears
poultry; makes his own *charcuterie, confits, foies gras* and
tripoux; and is a fresh produce fiend. Five bargain menus
(regional, classical and the odd lighter classical dish) with
surprises such as *omble chevalier* and *boudin de truite
saumonée*. Popular British tour operator's base.
Menus A-B. Rooms (19) A-B. Cards Access, Visa.
Closed 11 Nov to Palm Sunday.
Post 12230 St-Jean-du-Bruel, Aveyron.
Tel 65 62 26 04. Fax 65 62 12 97. Mich 141/F4.

ST-VALLIER   Voyageurs

Comfortable restaurant with basic rooms/Cooking 1-2
Good value

Jean Brouchard's formula is simple: some good-value menus;
an air-conditioned dining room; and an uninspiring repertoire
mixing *Bourgeois* basics (*grillade de porc au cumin, gratin de
fruits de mer, entrecôte grillée*) with classical favourites (*filet de
boeuf Béarnaise* is typical). Food is often overcooked. I've had
moans about the basic bedrooms at the *Logis de France*. For
modern rooms use the Ibis instead, a few miles up the N7 (see
Autoroute hotels: St-Rambert-d'Albon).
Menus A-C. Rooms (9) B. Cards All.
Closed 1st 3 wks June. Sun evg & Mon.
Post 2 av. J. Jaurès, 26240 St-Vallier, Drôme.
Tel 75 23 04 42. Mich 130/A1.

SALERS   Le Bailliage

Comfortable hotel/Cooking 1-2
Quiet/Terr/Gardens/Swim pool/G'ge/Parking/Good value

Charles Bancarel has gone from strength to strength at his
logis, now much modernised and with the benefit of a pool; the
contrast with ancient Salers is dramatic (be sure to enjoy the
narrow streets and the views). *Bourgeois* and regional plats:
among the latter *potée, tripoux, truffade, jambon de montagne,
pounti* and both Salers beef and cheese.
Menus A-B. Rooms (30) C-D. Cards AE, Access, Visa.
Closed Mid Nov to end June.
Post 15410 Salers, Cantal.
Tel 71 40 71 95. Mich 126/B2.

SALLES-CURAN   Hostellerie du Lévézou

Comfortable hotel/Cooking 2-3
Quiet/Terrace/Gardens/Parking

A 14th-century château with an imposing tower and a dominating
position which rewards with fine views of the local Welsh-like
terrain. Classical, neo-classical and the odd Rouergue *plat*
from chef/patron David Bouviala (*pavé de rumsteak au deux
poivres, feuilleté de ris d'agneau aux morilles, rouget et St-
Jacques au basilic* and *choux farci Rouergat* are typical.)
Menus B-D. Rooms (20) B-D. Cards All.
Closed Mid Oct to Easter. Sun evg & Mon (15 Sept-15 June).
Post 12410 Salles-Curan, Aveyron.
Tel 65 46 34 16. Fax 65 46 01 19. Mich 140/C3.

SATILLIEU   Gentilhommière

Comfortable hotel/Cooking 1
Quiet/Terrace/Gardens/Swim pools/Tennis/Lift/Parking

Dynamic is the word for both English-speaking *patron*, Jean
Astic, and his ever-improving, ever-growing hotel complex. The
most appreciated feature is the heated indoor pool; there's also
a gym and sauna. Bedrooms are in a collection of buildings.
Cooking? Classical and *Bourgeoise* basics.
Menus A-C. Rooms (51) D. Disabled. Cards Access, Visa.
Closed Nov to Feb. Rest: Fri evg & Sun evg (not July & Aug).
Post 07290 Satillieu, Ardèche.
Tel 75 34 94 31. Telex 345548. Fax 75 34 91 92. Mich 129/F2.

SAULCE-SUR-RHONE   La Capitelle

Simple hotel/Cooking 1-2
Quiet/Terrace

The Bouchers' stone-built Renaissance home has been a hit with
readers (the arched dining room is especially liked). They win
the "patience with children test" prize; several parents have
written about little ones being welcomed with open arms.
Unadventurous classical cooking. (4 km east of the N7.)
Menus B. Rooms (10) C-E. Cards Access, DC, Visa. (ER p 63)
Closed Mid Nov to mid Jan. Tues & Wed midday.
Post Mirmande, 26270 Saulce-sur-Rhône, Drôme.
Tel 75 63 02 72. Fax 75 63 02 50. Mich 130/A4.

SERRIERES   Schaeffer

Comfortable restaurant with rooms/Cooking 2-3
Terrace/Garage/Good value

I revisited this dour-looking place, on the N86 and Rhône right
bank, after including the *logis* in *En Route* (1986). One reader
summarised his feelings this way: "How do they do it; and why
are there so many starred Michelin places at twice the price
that are half as good?" Joëlle Mathe and her husband, chef
Bernard, do sterling work. The interior is much more welcoming

and Bernard's conviction in his classical repertoire is both seen and tasted: exemplary *plats* like *terrine de foie blond* and *escalope de saumon à l'oseille*. (En Route p 60).
Menus B-C. Rooms (12) B-C. Cards Access, DC, Visa.
Closed Jan. Mon evg & Tues (not July & Aug).
Post 07340 Serrières, Ardèche.
Tel 75 34 00 07. Mich 130/A1.

TENCE   Grand Hôtel Placide

Comfortable hotel/Cooking 2-3
Gardens/Parking

What a relief to bring you the news that young Pierre-Marie Placide, the fourth generation, is now the patron/chef at the vine-covered family hotel. His wife, Véronique, a bubbling, English-speaking hostess, is also a welcome rejuvenating tonic. P-M's modern and neo-classical repertoire is much influenced by his spell with Chabran (see Pont-de-l'Isère).
Menus B-D. Rooms (17) D-E. Cards Access, Visa.
Closed Dec & Jan. Sun evg. Mon.
Post av. Gare, 43190 Tence, H.-Loire.
Tel 71 59 82 76. Fax 71 65 44 46. Mich 129/E2.

VALGORGE   La Tanargue

Comfortable hotel/Cooking 1-2
Secluded/Gardens/Lift/Garage/Parking/Good value

The anonymous-looking *logis* is 100 metres or so north of the D24; the large gardens, quiet site and southern outlook more than compensate (in spring a valley of broom, cherry blossom and chestnuts). Amedée Coste's cooking is a mix of *Bourgeoise* and classical. Popular British tour operator's base.
Menus A-B. Rooms (25) C-D. Cards Access, Visa.
Closed Jan to mid Mar.
Post Valgorge, 07110 Largentière, Ardèche.
Tel 75 88 98 98. Mich 143/D1.

VALS-LES-BAINS   Europe

Comfortable hotel/Cooking 2
Lift/Good value

Guide book shorthand is all very well but abbreviations and symbols can't sum up the soul of a place. Shorthand is fine for bricks and mortar; for facilities; for cooking standards; but tells you now't 'bout folk who make the very air hum. Here the pleasure factor is 9 out of 10. Why? Albert (48 years a chef) and Renée Mazet are mine hosts; delightful, amiable folk, full of character and, like their hotel, the epitome of *la vrai France* as she used to be. Top notch *Bourgeoise* cuisine with a three-star dessert trolley (toothsome light *gâteaux*).
Menus B. Rooms (34) C-D. Cards All.
Closed 21 Oct to 9 Apl.
Post 86 rue J. Jaurès, 07600 Vals-les-Bains, Ardèche.
Tel 75 37 43 94. Telex 346256. Mich 129/E4.

VIENNE   La Pyramide

Very comfortable hotel/Cooking 4
Terrace/Gardens/Lift/Garage/Parking

Patrick Henriroux must have felt an awesome burden on his shoulders the day he moved north three years ago with his young family from Mougins (Côte d'Azur). The very name, La Pyramide, is synonymous with legend; this was the home of Fernand Point, the father of modern cooking (see *Who's who*).

We first met Patrick, even now only in his mid-30s, at the insistence of the Battaglia brothers (Mougins and Valbonne). Three dishes on a wet and windy day in 1989 at La Ferme de Mougins convinced us that the boy from Melincourt was set to be a superstar. First, a rarity in France, a starter of seven vegetables, gently steamed and not crunchy; Provence on a plate. (His use of herbs and marinades is masterful.) Then two desserts, among the best we've ever drooled over: *la fleur de chocolat aux griottines* (bitter cherries from Fougerolles) was a marriage of sweet and sour contrasts made in heaven; and a *piano à queue au praliné, amandes et chocolat*, served in the shape of a grand, was a resounding note on which to end the superb meal. I had planned to include him in a major article on "10 Stars of the Future" for the *Sunday Times Magazine* (October 1989) but he moved north a month or two before the feature was due to appear; I had to delete his entry.

Patrick weaves his own modern patterns at Vienne; but he's also having a go at restoring some of Point's classics: *poularde de Bresse truffée en vessie* (order in advance) and *gratin de queues d'écrevisses* are just two. One final word. Young Jean-Claude Ruet is a wizard *sommelier* (he came second in the Meilleur Sommelier d'Europe 1990 competition; Chewton Glen's Gérard Basset was third) and a most helpful soul; quiz him about the Condrieu and Côte Rôtie vineyards.

Menus C-E. Rooms (24) F-F2. Disabled. Cards All. (See Base.)
Closed Feb. 1st wk Mar. Rest: Wed. Thurs midday.
Post 14 bd F. Point, 38200 Vienne, Isère. (W of N7; S of town.)
Tel 74 53 01 96. Telex 308058. Fax 74 85 69 73. Mich 116/A3.

VOLLORE-MONTAGNE   Touristes

Very simple hotel with basic rooms/Cooking 1-2
Terrace/Garage/Parking/Good value

What a contrast this entry is to the one above. Yet, in its own homely, family way the Touristes can please equally well. Don't go with great expectations. Travel instead with open minds and receptive hearts and pocket your prejudices.

At the core of this modest, red-shuttered *logis* is a super family: Daniel Roussel is a nothing-is-too-much trouble host; his wife, Marie-Claire, is the unseen *cuisinière*, beavering away in her spanking new kitchen; teenage daughters Sandrine and Carole help with service. Fare? Basic *Bourgeoise* and *cuisine au beurre*: galantines (*lapin*; *canard*), *truite belle meunière*, *côtes d'agneau* and a light-as-air *forêt noir*.

Menus A-B. Rooms (12) B-C. Cards Access, Visa.
Closed Jan. 3rd wk June. Tues evg & Wed (not July & Aug).
Post 63120 Vollore-Montagne, P.-de-D.
Tel 73 53 77 50. Mich 114/B2.

NORMANDY

- ● Autoroute hotel
- ■ Base hotel
- ▲ Hotel/Rest (rooms)
- △ Restaurant only

0   10   20 Miles

CHERBOURG

Bricquebec
Barneville-
▲**Carteret**

N13

St-Lô

Bayeux ■ **Cresserons** △ Deauville

A13

Roches de Ham
▲
Coutances

Villers-
Bocage ▲

N175

Caen ●

Pavé d'Auge

▲**Goupillières**
▲**Thury-Harcourt**

Hambye

Aunay-sur
-Odon ▲

Orne

Falaise

La Suisse Normande

Putanges-
Pont-Ecrepin

N175

■**Avranches**
■**Ducey** ● Mortain

D962

Domfront

Bagnoles-de-
▲**l'Orne** Alençon

N158

Le Mont-
St-Michel

see page 55

Fougères

Javron △

N12

Sarthe

N138

N12

D178

● Vitré

RENNES

Laval ●

A81

LE MANS

see page 192

For most visitors to France, Normandy, Britain's "partner-in-history", is no more than a long line of invasion beaches, for ever associated with those critical, violent days in June 1944, and ancient towns like **Rouen**, **Caen** and **Bayeux**, each full of man-made sights and all worth exploring.

For some Britons, hell-bent on reaching the Spanish Mediterranean, Normandy is a land to rush through. Their aspirations are basic: heaven is the hell of the "Costas".

Let me try to persuade you to see another face of Normandy – through narrow lanes which lead to wooded hills, easy-going rivers, huge beech forests, carpeted with bluebells in May and cloaked with copper capes in October, and smaller towns, many of which were rebuilt after the devastation of the 1944 summer. In May Normandy is especially delicious: fields are awash with wild yellow irises and apple orchards are laden down with blossom destined to become that fiery apple brandy, Calvados. Brown and white timbered cottages dazzle; chuckle

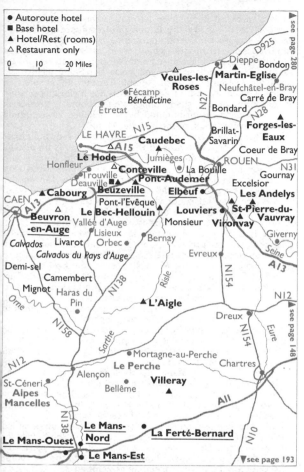

▲ see page 280

Legend:
- ● Autoroute hotel
- ■ Base hotel
- ▲ Hotel/Rest (rooms)
- △ Restaurant only

0   10   20 Miles

Dieppe Bondon
Veules-les-Roses Martin-Eglise
Fécamp Neufchâtel-en-Bray
Bénédictine Carré de Bray
Etretat Bondard
  Brillat- Forges-les-
LE HAVRE Savarin Eaux
  Caudebec Coeur de Bray
Le Hode Jumièges ROUEN
Honfleur Conteville La Bouille N31
Trouville Pont-Audemer Gournay
Deauville Beuzeville Elbeuf Excelsior
Cabourg Pont-l'Evêque Les Andelys
CAEN Le Bec-Hellouin Louviers St-Pierre-du-
Beuvron Vallée d'Auge Monsieur Vauvray
-en-Auge Lisieux Vironvay
Calvados Livarot Orbec Giverny
  Calvados du Pays d'Auge Bernay
Demi-sel Evreux
Camembert
Mignot Haras du
  Pin L'Aigle
  Dreux
  Mortagne-au-Perche
  Le Perche Chartres
N12 Alençon
St-Céneri Villeray
Alpes Bellême
Mancelles
  Le Mans-Nord La Ferté-Bernard
Le Mans-Ouest Le Mans-Est

▲ see page 148
▼ see page 193

at some, where, on the high ridges of thatched roofs, flowering irises have seeded, adding a colourful trimming.

I'll start by summarising a list of the renowned man-made sites, some 900 years old, some more modern-day structures.

Rouen is richly endowed with evidence of man's creative talents: the fabulous Notre-Dame cathedral, several churches, the old quarter with flamboyant half-timbered houses, museums, and the famed rue du Gros-Horloge. Rouen is where Joan of Arc, only 19, was burnt at the stake on May 30, 1431. Upstream from Rouen is **Les Andelys** where the ruins of the once formidable fortress, built by Richard the Lionheart, dominates both the town and **Seine**. **Dieppe** has a lively character: France's oldest seaside resort, the inland harbour and narrow streets make the town the most appealing of the French Channel ports. By comparison, **Le Havre** is a soulless spot.

Etretat and **Fécamp** are quite different: the former a resort, the latter a busy fishing port. Relish the high chalk cliffs

263

that arc east and north from Etretat to the Somme estuary; especially thrilling are the famed *falaises* guarding Etretat. Before you cross the Seine spare time for the abbeys at St-Wandrille and **Jumièges** which, even as a ruin, is still a stunning reminder of the once great Norman structures.

Two modern bridges help you cross the Seine easily: the harp-like Brotonne and the giant Tancarville suspension version. The abbey at **Le Bec-Hellouin** has a glorious setting. Wander through the shady abbey grounds and picture-book village and don't be intimidated by St-Nicholas' Tower; study the plaque before making the 200-step climb.

Pont-Audemer has many fine half-timbered buildings; **Honfleur** and the area around the Vieux Bassin is an artist's delight, as the combination of port, boats, old houses and churches confirm (see the cover); **Deauville**, swish and very chic, is a sportsman's paradise; Caen is a three-star wonder with abbeys, churches, citadel and museums providing days of interest (see page 413); and who could pass through Normandy without marvelling at the tapestry in Bayeux. All these sites are fully described in Michelin's two fine green guides.

What I would like to do now is to describe a tour which meanders in an arc across southern Normandy, passing through the quaintly-named **La Suisse Normande** and detouring south to two unknown areas, the Mancelles "Alps" and **Le Perche**.

Start at **Cherbourg**. Head west, on the D45 to Port Racine, the smallest in France and no bigger than a basketball court. Next gasp at the spectacular sea views from the 400-ft-high cliffs of the Nez de Jobourg. There are several fine beaches to the south; Biville has some of Europe's highest dunes.

Briquebec is a pleasure: not just for the castle and the mighty keep but also for Lefebvres *quincaillerie* near the *hôtel de ville*; in the dark interior you'll trip over everything from horseshoes to beehives, a hardware store *par excellence*. From the heather-covered Mont de Besneville and its three windmills enjoy the views of the Channel Isles.

The river panorama from the cliff top at **Roches de Ham** is quintessential Normandy: here the Vire runs up against a high rock wall covered with oaks and is forced to turn west.

Start your exploration of La Suisse Normande (often called "Little Switzerland") at **Thury-Harcourt**. Walk the Boucle du Hom, where the **Orne** does an almost 360-degree clockwise circle. Follow the signposted Route des Crêtes to the viewpoint above the Pain de Sucre: Normandy personified.

Continue upstream, past Pont-d'Ouilly, along the D167, cross the Orne and climb to the Roche d'Oëtre. The viewpoint, reached through the heady aroma of pines, overlooks the River Rouvre, hardly visible so dense are the forests below you.

At Ménil-Glaise, most easily reached by the lane 400 yards north-east of the cemetery at Batilly, the Orne is at its most seductive. **Bagnoles-de-l'Orne** is like going back to France at the turn of the century: a flower-bedecked spa, lake, spotless streets and encircling woods are pleasing pluses.

Aim next for the **Alpes Mancelles**; alps they are not, deserted they most assuredly are. **St-Céneri**-le-Gérei is an unspoilt pearl with antique houses, an *église* high above the Sarthe, a bridge across the river and a weir humming away upstream. The cool vastness of the Forêt de Perseigne, east of **Alençon**, also appeals. Continue eastwards to Le Perche.

Here rolling hills, forests, pretty views and fortified manor houses dominate the landscape. Among the latter man-made sites are the Château de Feugerets (on the D7, south of **Bellême**); the Manoir de Courboyer, like a vision of Scotland (east of Bellême); and the Manoir de la Vove, north of Courboyer. Call at the rural museum at Ste-Gauburge, east of Feugerets and signposted from the D7, and the two forests near **Mortagne-au-Perche**: the Forêt Réno Valdieu (nose out the *vieux arbres* marked on the map – 100-ft-high oaks with English names like Aberdeen and Oxford); and the Forêt du Perche.

L'Aigle is famous for its super market when, on Tuesday mornings, the whole town is literally taken over. Every conceivable product and animal, from flowers to horses, is on display, each designated to its own special corner in the town, be it a *place* or a *rue*. Finish the tour by exploring the Charentonne Valley, at its best between Anceins and the D819 and from Broglie to **Bernay**. This is "dawdling" country.

There's so little space to tell you about Normandy's 1,001 treats: such as the forests of Eu, Eawy and Lyons between Rouen and Abbeville; the timeless valleys in Bray and Caux (the hinterland behind Dieppe); the National Stud at **Haras du Pin**, east of Argentan; the castle at **Falaise**; numerous châteaux like O, near Haras, St-Germain-de-Livet, south of **Lisieux**, and Balleroy, west of Caen; the Gothic cathedral at **Coutances** and the nearby hidden setting of the ruins of **Hambye** Abbey; the towns of **Avranches**, **Mortain**, **Domfront** and **Orbec**; and the many river valleys.

I'll finish by telling you a little about another very special corner of Normandy. Less than half-a-century ago the region played a unique part in the West's future destiny. On June 6, 1944, the Allies landed at a series of beaches north of Caen, names that have become symbols of courage, bravery and audacity: Utah, Omaha, Gold, Juno and Sword.

Tens of thousands of soldiers, from many nations, lost their lives. There are 18 Commonwealth War Cemeteries alone. For me the most poignant is the tiny Jerusalem Cemetery, alongside the D6 at Chouain, between Bayeux and **Villers-Bocage** – the northern border of the wooded *"bocage"*. Its numerous thickets and primrose-studded high earth banks, topped with trees and hedges, caused great difficulties for Allied tanks.

Jerusalem Cemetery is the last resting place of just 48 souls; the first burial took place on June 10, four days after the D-Day landings. Of the 48 graves at Jerusalem, 47 were soldiers from the British Army and one was a Czech. Legend has it that local villagers staged a "sit-in" to ensure that the remains of the soldiers stayed where they had been initially buried rather than see them moved to a larger cemetery.

Jerusalem is a heart-tugging, emotional corner of sacred Normandy. I always shed a quiet tear when I sit on the small bench in front of the Cemetery Register and read the contents of the slim books behind the brass door. The officers and men came from all parts of Britain: Cornwall to Caithness, London to Ludlow. Don't speed past Jerusalem: stay a while, cry a little and remember always the treasured lives of the many who died for us in bitter campaigns all over the globe.

Markets L'Aigle (Tues); Avranches (Sat); Caen (Tues to Sun); Dieppe (Sat); Domfront (Sat); Honfleur (Sat); Mortagne-au-Perche (Sat); Orbec (Wed and Sat); Pont Audemer (Mon); Pont-d'Ouilly (Sun); Trouville-sur-Mer (Wed and Sun); Villers-Bocage (Wed); Vire (Fri).

Michelin green guides: Normandy Cotentin and Normandy Seine Valley (in English and both excellent guides).

Cheeses Cow's milk

Bondon (also called **Neufchâtel**) from Pays de Bray (north-east of Rouen). Small cylinder, soft and smooth. **Bondard** is related

La Bouille red-speckled, white rind; strong smell, fruity-tasting small disk

Bricquebec made by monks at the abbey of the same name. A mild-tasting, flat pressed disk. Available all the year

Brillat-Savarin mild, creamy disk – a triple-cream cheese. **Magnum** is the same cheese but much older

Camembert soft, milky flavour with a white rind, made as a small, flat disk. Available all the year and super with a Beaujolais wine. Most Camembert is made these days from pasteurised milk. Patrick Rance recommends two farms where cheese is still made, by hand, from raw milk: Robert Durand's farm, La Heronnière (open every day), and the neighbouring La Ferme du Tourdouet (not open weekends), the home of the Delorme family. Leave Vimoutiers (south of Lisieux) on the D246. The farms are beyond the village of Camembert, towards Champosoult

Carré de Bray small, square-shaped, mushroom-smelling cheese

Coeur de Bray fruity-tasting, heart-shaped cheese. Best in summer

Demi-sel mild, fresh and salted – made as a small square

Excelsior best in summer and autumn. Small cylinder, mild and soft

Gournay a one inch thick disk; slightly salty, soft and smooth

Livarot best in autumn and winter. Semi-hard, strong and gold. Spicy flavour; try it with a Riesling. **Mignot** is similar

Monsieur soft, fruity cylinder – strong smell

Pavé d'Auge (Pavé de Moyaux) spicy-flavoured, soft cheese, made in a yellow square. Try it with full-bodied reds

Petit-Suisse available all the year; a small, round, fresh cream cheese

Pont-l'Evêque rectangular or square shape, strong, soft and gold; at its best in summer, autumn and winter. First made in 13th-century

Regional Specialities

Andouillette de Vire small chitterling (tripe) sausage

Barbue au cidre brill cooked in cider and Calvados

Cauchoise (à la) with cream, Calvados and apple

Douillons de pommes à la Normande baked apples in pastry

Escalope (Vallée d'Auge) veal sautéed, flamed in Calvados and served with cream and apples

Ficelle Normande pancake with ham, mushrooms and cheese

Marmite Dieppoise a fish soup with some, or all of the following: sole, turbot, *rouget*, *moules*, *crevettes*, onions, white wine, butter and cream

Poulet (Vallée d'Auge) chicken cooked in the same way as *Escalope Vallee d'Auge*

Tripes à la mode de Caen stewed beef tripe with onions, carrots, leeks, garlic, cider and Calvados

Trou Normand Calvados – a "dram", drunk in one gulp, between courses; claimed to restore the appetite

Wines

There is nothing to say about wines in Normandy but, on the other hand, don't overlook the fact that **Bénédictine** is distilled at Fécamp. And what better compensation could there be than **Calvados**, another *digestive*; distilled apple brandy. There are no less than 10 classified Calvados regions within Normandy but the best is the Appellation Contrôlée **Calvados du Pays d'Auge**. This is a tightly specified area straddling the River Touques – the famous Vallée d'Auge country; see the list of regional specialities above. This particular Calvados must be distilled in stills known as *charentais*; there are two production stages. At home we use Calvados a lot for cooking. Last but not least relish superb **cider**: *cidre bouché* – sparkling; *cidre doux* – sweet.

CAEN   Campanile

Simple hotel/Cooking 1
Parking/Good value

At Caen A13 becomes N413 bypass. On Orne left bank: Hérouville-
Est exit to D515. Exit D515 at Centre Commercial. To right.
Menus A-B. Rooms (70) C. Disabled. Cards Access, Visa.
Post 14200 Hérouville-St-Clair, Calvados. (En Route p 118)
Tel 31 95 29 24. Telex 170618. Fax 31 95 74 87. Mich 32/B1.
(Bookings: UK freephone 0800 897863)

CAEN   Ibis

Simple hotel/Cooking 1
Parking/Good value

At Caen A13 becomes N413 bypass, On Orne left bank: Hérouville-
Est exit to D515. Leave D515 first road right. Ibis to west.
Menus A-B. Rooms (89) C. Disabled. Cards Access, Visa.
Post 14200 Hérouville-St-Clair, Calvados. (En Route p 118)
Tel 31 95 60 00. Telex 170755. Fax 31 06 08 43. Mich 32/B1.
(Bookings: UK 071 724 1000; US toll free 800 221 4542)

CAEN   Novotel

Very comfortable hotel/Cooking 1
Terrace/Swimming pool/Lift/Closed parking

Leave N413 bypass at Caen-Université exit. Hotel to south.
Menus B. Rooms (126) E. Disabled. Cards All.
Post av. Côte de Nacre, 14000 Caen, Calvados. (ER p 118)
Tel 31 93 05 88. Telex 170563. Fax 31 44 07 28. Mich 32/A1.
(Bookings: UK 071 724 1000; US toll free 800 221 4542)

ELBEUF   Campanile

Simple hotel/Cooking 1
Parking/Good value

A13 exit 21 (Cléon). Hotel to west, on north side D7.
Menus A-B. Rooms (42) C. Disabled. Cards Access, Visa.
Post rue de l'Eglise, 76410 Cléon, Seine-Mar. (ER p 115)
Tel 35 81 38 00. Telex 172691. Fax 35 77 69 91. Mich 16/A4.
(Bookings: UK freephone 0800 897863)

ELBEUF   Climat de France

Simple hotel/Cooking 1
Parking/Good value

A13 exit 21 (Cléon). Hotel to east, on north side D7.
Menus A-B. Rooms (34) C. Disabled. Cards AE. Access Visa.
Post 76410 Tourville-la-Rivière, Seine-Mar. (ER p 115)
Tel 35 78 49 48. Telex 771189. Fax 35 78 29 84. Mich 16/A4.
(Bookings: UK 071 287 3181)

LA-FERTE-BERNARD   Climat de France

Simple hotel/Cooking 1
Terrace/Parking/Good value

A11 exit 5. Toll. Right D7. 4 km left. Over N23. On right.
Menus A-B. Rooms (50) C. Disabled. Cards AE, Access, Visa.
Post 72400 La Ferté-Bernard, Sarthe. (En Route p 106)
Tel 43 93 84 70. Telex 723846. Fax 43 93 21 15. Mich 51/F3.
(Bookings: UK 071 287 3181)

LAVAL   Campanile

Simple hotel/Cooking 1
Parking/Good value/Good value

Leave A81 exit 4 (Laval Centre from west; Fougères from east).
Past toll, left at D30, hotel on right.
Menus A-B. Rooms (40) C. Disabled. Cards Access, Visa.
Post rte Fourgères, 53000 Laval, Mayenne.
Tel 43 69 04 00. Telex 722633. Mich 49/F4.
(Bookings: UK freephone 0800 897863)

LAVAL   Climat de France

Simple hotel/Cooking 1
Parking/Good value

As above. D30 4 km, then right (Laval bypass). Hotel on right.
Menus A-B. Rooms (44) C. Disabled. Cards AE, Access, Visa.
Post bd des Trappistines, 53000 Laval, Mayenne. (ER p 109)
Tel 43 02 88 88. Telex 741684. Fax 96 85 40 46. Mich 49/F4.
(Bookings: UK 071 287 3181)

LAVAL   Ibis

Simple hotel/Cooking 1
Parking/Good value

A81 exit 3 (Laval Centre from east; Mayenne from west). Past
toll, left at N162. Ignore bypass, on left towards Laval.
Menus A. Rooms (51) C-D. Disabled. Cards Access, Visa.
Post rte Mayenne, 53000 Laval, Mayenne. (En Route p 108)
Tel 43 53 81 82. Telex 721094. Fax 43 53 11 19. Mich 49/F4.
(Bookings: UK 071 724 1000; US toll free 800 221 4542)

LOUVIERS   Altéa Val de Reuil

Very comfortable hotel/Cooking 1-2
Swimming pool/Tennis/Lift/Parking

A13 exit 19 (Louviers-Nord from south). Hotel east side A13.
Menus B-C. Rooms (58) E-F. Disabled. Cards All.
Post 27100 Val de Reuil, Eure. (ER p 114; previously P.L.M.)
Tel 32 59 09 09. Telex 180540. Fax 32 59 56 54. Mich 34/B1.
(Bookings: UK 071 724 1000; US toll free 800 221 4542)

LE MANS-EST   Campanile-Est

Simple hotel/Cooking 1
Parking/Good value

A11 exit 6 (Le Mans-Est). N224 south. Right N23. Hotel 5 km.
Menus A-B. Rooms (48) C. Disabled. Cards Access, Visa.
Post bd Pablo Neruda, 72000 Le Mans, Sarthe.
Tel 43 72 18 72. Telex 723630. Fax 43 72 91 39. Mich 51/D4.
(Bookings: UK freephone 0800 897863)

LE MANS-NORD   Climat de France

Simple hotel/Cooking 1
Parking/Good value

A11 exit 7 (Le Mans-Nord). Right at N138; hotel to left.
Menus A-B. Rooms (34) C. Disabled. Cards AE, Access, Visa.
Post rte d'Alençon, 72650 St-Saturnin, Sarthe. (ER p 107)
Tel 43 25 31 21. Telex 723645. Mich 51/D4.
(Bookings: UK 071 287 3181)

LE MANS-OUEST   Fimotel

Simple hotel/Cooking 1
Terrace/Lift/Parking/Good value

A11 exit 8 (Le Mans-Ouest), south of A11/A81 junc. N157 to Le
Mans. 4 km right & use bypass (Rocade Sud). Hotel on left.
Menus A-B. Rooms (42) C-D. Disabled. Cards All.
Post rue Pointe, 72100 Le Mans, Sarthe. (En Route p 106)
Tel 43 72 27 20. Telex 722092. Fax 43 85 96 06. Mich 51/D4.

LE MANS-EST   Ibis-Est

Simple hotel/Cooking 1
Parking/Good value

A11 exit 6 (Le Mans-Est). N224 south. Right at N23. 5 km left
at Rocade Sud (bypass). Hotel on left, 1 km after Novotel.
Menus A. Rooms (49) C-D. Disabled. Cards Access, Visa.
Post rue Clément Marot, 72100 Le Mans, Sarthe. (ER p 106)
Tel 43 86 14 14. Telex 720651. Fax 43 84 10 21. Mich 51/D4.
(Bookings: UK 071 724 1000; US toll free 800 221 4542)

LE MANS-EST   Novotel

Very comfortable hotel/Cooking 1
Terrace/Gardens/Swimming pool/Lift/Parking

A11 exit 6 (Le Mans-Est). N224 south. Right at N23. 5 km left
at Rocade Sud. Hotel on left (turn right, then under bypass).
Menus B. Rooms (94) E. Disabled. Cards All.
Post bd R.Schumann, 72100 Le Mans, Sarthe (ER p 106)
Tel 43 85 26 80. Telex 720706. Fax 43 75 31 76. Mich 51/D4.
(Bookings: UK 071 724 1000; US toll free 800 221 4542)

Base Hotels

AVRANCHES   Le Pratel

Comfortable hotel
Quiet/Gardens/Parking/Good value

Small, modern house, ringed by trees and a stunning show of
cyclamen. East side N175 in southern suburbs.
Rooms (7) C-D. Cards AE, Access, Visa.
Closed 26 Feb to 6 Mar.
Post 24 rue Vanniers, 50300 Avranches, Manche.
Tel 33 68 35 41. Mich 30/C4.

BAGNOLES-DE-L'ORNE   Ermitage

Comfortable hotel
Quiet/Gardens/Lift/Parking/Good value

Unusual stone exterior. Quiet side street of handsome spa.
Rooms (39) C-D. Cards Access, Visa.
Closed Oct to Mar.
Post 24 bd P.-Chalvet, 61140 Bagnoles-de-l'Orne, Orne.
Tel 33 37 96 22. Telex 772274. Mich 50/B1.

BAYEUX   Argouges

Comfortable hotel
Quiet/Gardens/Garage/Parking

Marie-Claude Auregan is rightly proud of her 18th-century
hôtel particulier; two buildings well back from the road.
Rooms (25) D-E. Cards All.
Post 21 rue St-Patrice, 14400 Bayeux, Calvados.
Tel 31 92 88 86. Telex 772402. Fax 31 92 69 16. Mich 31/F1.

BEUZEVILLE   Petit Castel

Comfortable hotel
Good value

Owned by M. Folleau (see Cochon d'Or entry; across the road).
Rooms (16) C-D. Cards Access, Visa. (Park in *place*.)
Closed Mid Dec to mid Jan.
Post 53 rue Constant Fouché, 27210 Beuzeville, Eure.
Tel 32 57 76 08. Mich 15/D4. (En Route p 117)

DUCEY   Moulin de Ducey

Very comfortable hotel
Quiet/Lift/Parking

Jacques Dewitte's transformation of the 16th-century mill,
beside the Sélune, is remarkably well done. His father was
once the miller, before fire destroyed the watermill in 1985.
Rooms (28) D-E. Disabled. Cards All.
Post 50220 Ducey, Manche.
Tel 33 60 25 25. Telex 772318. Fax 33 60 26 76. Mich 30/C4.

L'AIGLE Dauphin

Very comfortable hotel/Cooking 2-3

A 17th-century *relais de poste*. The traditional furnishings
and style appeal but the best bonuses come courtesy of the
owner, extrovert Michel Bernard and his vivacious, English-
speaking hostess, Virginie. *Haute cuisine* with due reverence
paid to rich Normandy classics. There's also a cheaper
brasserie (Cooking 1); price band A. Try to stay on Monday
night; Tuesday is the famous market day (see page 403).
Menus B-D. Rooms (30) D-E. Cards All.
Post pl. de la Halle, 61300 L'Aigle, Orne. (Park in *place*.)
Tel 33 24 43 12. Telex 170979. Fax 33 34 09 28. Mich 33/E4.

LES ANDELYS Chaîne d'Or

Very comfortable restaurant with rooms/Cooking 2
Quiet/Parking

A well-organised riverside *relais,* built in 1751 as a toll house
(hence the name, a chain strung across the Seine acting as a
barrier) and now impeccably run by Monique and Claude
Foucault. Classical, neo-classical and regional dishes. Readers
praise the warm welcome; spacious bedrooms; and owners who
don't wince when two-year-olds come down to dinner.
Menus B-D. Rooms (11) D-F. Cards Access, Visa.
Closed Jan. Sun evg and Mon (but not hotel from Apl to Sept).
Post 27 rue Grande, 27700 Les Andelys, Eure. (En Route p 113)
Tel 32 54 00 31. Mich 34/C1.

AUNAY-SUR-ODON St-Michel

Comfortable restaurant with basic rooms/Cooking 1-2
Parking/Good value

A modern stone *logis*. José Lavajo stirs classical, *Bourgeoise*
and *Normande* pots in his kitchen (*cidre*, *vinaigre de cidre*,
crème de cidre and *sabayon au cidre* feature on many *plats*).
Menus A-C. Rooms (7) B-C. Cards Access, Visa.
Closed 15-31 Jan. 15-30 Nov. Sun evg & Mon (not July & Aug).
Post r. Caen, 14260 Aunay-sur-Odon, Calvados.
Tel 31 77 63 16. Mich 31/F2.

BAGNOLES-DE-L'ORNE Bois Joli

Comfortable hotel/Cooking 1-2
Quiet/Gardens/Lift/Parking

A large, handsome red and white Normandy house, surrounded
by trees and 50 yards from the spa's lake. Modest *mélange* of
classical, *Bourgeoise* and regional specialities. Claudine and
Serge Gatti have a formidable *cave*. Some readers have been
disappointed. A caveat: agree prices beforehand, in writing.
Menus B-C. Rooms (20) C-E. Cards All.
Post av. P. du Rozier, 61140 Bagnoles-de-l'Orne, Orne.
Tel 33 37 92 77. Telex 171782. Mich 50/B1.

271

BARNEVILLE-CARTERET   Marine

Very comfortable hotel/Cooking 3
Terrace/Parking

Before your meal relax with an *apéritif* on the terrace which overlooks the tidal estuary and has views of the Cap de Carteret and the distant island of Jersey. Then relish the light modern and neo-classical *panache* of 30-year-old Laurent Cesne, the chef son of the owners, Emmanuel and Bernadette; they run the hotel with both authority and friendliness. Self-taught, the ex-medical student capitalises on the larder of fish and shellfish in his watery backyard. One creation, both rustic and modern, mates pan-fried John Dory with potatoes *écrasée* (crushed); perfection. Menus are in English.

Menus B-D. Rooms (31) D-F. Cards Access, DC, Visa.
Closed 6 Nov to 5 Feb. Sun evg & Mon (Feb & Oct). Mon midday (not Jul & Aug).
Post Carteret, 50270 Barneville-Carteret, Manche.
Tel 33 53 83 31. Fax 33 53 39 60. Mich 12/A3.

LE BEC-HELLOUIN   Auberge de l'Abbaye

Very comfortable restaurant with rooms/Cooking 1-2

A voluptuously pretty 18th-C *maison Normande* (beams, window boxes, the lot). The stunning village is, alas, over-run with tourists. Classical and 3C (cream, cider, Calvados) menus.

Menus B-C. Rooms (8) D. Cards Access, Visa.
Closed 4 Jan to 20 Feb. Mon evg & Tues (Nov to Easter).
Post 27800 Le Bec-Hellouin, Eure.
Tel 32 44 86 02. Mich 33/F1.

BEUVRON-EN-AUGE   Pavé d'Auge

Comfortable restaurant/Cooking 3
Good value

An unbelievably evocative Normandy village; no wonder the community "protects" the superb half-timbered houses. Pavé d'Auge, once the covered market, is owned by the *commune*.

Those of you who have *Favourites* will recall the story of Jérôme and Susan Bansard and their first restaurant (Javron). The young chef, trained by Michel Roux, is going places; Susan, a gentle, self-effacing English lass, is a *pâtissière* second to none. Here *rapport qualité-prix* means just that: quality local produce prepared in eminently sensible modern, good-value ways. Typical are *saumon et grosses langoustines* simply roasted; *perdreau rôti au jus*, served with greens and spuds; and three-star desserts, Susan's creations, such as a *petit vacherin glacé à la confiture du lait, sauce chicorée*. (Rooms? Use the Caen A/R hotels or, at nearby 14390 Cabourg, Le Cottage (sans rest): Rooms (11) C-D; Tel 31 91 65 61.)

Menus B-C. Cards Access, Visa.
Closed 6-28 Jan. 29 Nov-15 Dec. Mon (not midday from Mar to mid Nov). Tues.
Post 14430 Beuvron-en-Auge, Calvados.
Tel 31 79 26 71. Mich 32/C1.

BEUZEVILLE   Auberge du Cochon d'Or

Comfortable restaurant with rooms/Cooking 2
Good value

A much-loved family affair: Charles and Monique Folleau are
now helped by their English-speaking daughter, Catherine, and
her husband, Olivier Martin. Classical and *Normande* cuisine.
(One debit. Wearing shorts? You'll be turned away!)
Menus A-C. Rooms (5) B-C. (See Base hotel.) Cards Acc, Visa.
Closed Mid Dec to mid Jan. Mon.
Post pl. de Gaulle, 27210 Beuzeville, Eure. (Park in *place*.)
Tel 32 57 70 46. Mich 15/D4. (En Route p 117)

CABOURG   Hostellerie du Moulin du Pré

Comfortable restaurant with rooms/Cooking 2
Secluded/Gardens/Parking

The *moulin* (once a forge) and *étang* please; but not as much as
the family who make the place buzz. Jocelyne Holtz, the chef,
makes her own *foie gras*, smokes her own salmon and ducks and
bakes a cracking *tarte aux pommes*. *Le repertoire* is classical,
Normand and grills. Hubby Claude and her mum, Gisèle, run
the dining room; her father, Roger, assists in the kitchen.
Menus C. Rooms (10) B-D. Cards All. (En Route p 118)
Closed 1-15 Mar. Oct. Sun evg & Mon (not Jul/Aug & pub. hols).
Post rte de Gonneville-en-Auge, 14860 Ranville, Calvados.
Tel 31 78 83 68. Mich 32/B1. (SW on D513; then D95A.)

CAUDEBEC-EN-CAUX   Manoir de Rétival

Very comfortable restaurant with rooms/Cooking 3
Secluded/Gardens/Parking

FL3 readers will recall this turreted *manoir*, high above the
Seine, was *sans rest*. Not any more. Jean-Luc Tartarin, in his
mid-20s, is an assertive *cuisine moderne* chef (what a relief in
crème pays); helped by brother Jean-Paul, *le pâtissier*, and by
sister Nathalie, who runs the front of house. Fine views.
Menus B-D. Rooms (5) D-F. Cards All. Cheaper rooms? See below.
Closed 2 wks Feb. 2 wks Oct. Sun (rooms). Mon. Tues midday.
Post 76490 Caudebec-en-Caux, S.-M.
Tel 39 96 11 22. Mich 15/E3. (To E of town; N of D982.)

CAUDEBEC-EN-CAUX   Normotel

Comfortable hotel/Cooking 1
Lift/Parking

New name, new owners and a facelift for the Seine-side hotel
(Marine). Watch the barges chug by from the dining room (at
night they can be a curse). Cheap and cheerful *Bourgeoise*.
Menus A-B. Rooms (29) C-E. Cards AE, Access, Visa.
Closed Jan. Sun evg (mid Nov to mid Mar).
Post quai Guilbaud, 76490 Caudebec-en-Caux, S. -M.
Tel 35 96 20 11. Telex 770404. Fax 35 56 54 40. Mich 15/E3.

CONTEVILLE **Auberge du Vieux Logis**

Very comfortable restaurant/Cooking 3

The delectable brown and white half-timbered cottages of the *logis* catch the eye as you meander along the D312 coast road. Behind the beams wait Yves Louet and his son, Giuillaume, a perfectly-matched tandem in their classical cooking pedalling. Savour past glories: *sole soufflé au Noilly*, *tête de veau Zingara* and *île flottante aux zestes d'orange* are just a trio. What about a real appetite-smasher? Select a low gear and tackle an *andouille de Vire chaud au cidre*; the best there is.
Menus C-D. Cards All. (Rooms? See Beuzeville Base hotel.)
Closed Feb. Wed evg & Thurs.
Post 27120 Conteville, Eure.
Tel 32 57 60 16. Mich 15/D4.

COUTANCES **Cositel**

Comfortable hotel/Cooking 1
Quiet/Parking/Good value

Don't be put off by the name of this *Logis de France*. A large, modern hotel with panoramic views of the town and cathedral from the restaurant. *Bourgeois* and classical *plats* and a pleasing number of fish specialities.
Menus A-B. Rooms (54) C-D. Disabled. Cards All.
Post rte de Coutainville, 50200 Coutances, Manche. (W on D44.)
Tel 33 07 51 64. Telex 772003. Fax 33 07 06 23. Mich 30/C2.

CRESSERONS **La Valise Gourmande**

Comfortable restaurant/Cooking 2-3
Terrace/Gardens/Parking/Good value

Just three kilometres from the coast, La Valise is a restored, wisteria-clad, 18th-century *maison Bourgeoise*. Chef Jean-Jacques Hélie and Jean-Pierre Stéphan (he runs the front of house) have been *in situ* for seven years. J-J's repertoire includes classical and regional dishes and some "specials", recipes handed down by his grandmother. He makes profitable use of local quality farm produce. Typical concoctions include a *clafoutis de moules rognons de veau à la Normande* and an *escalope de ris de veau à la façon Hélie*. Hélie is on the up and up: open *la valisé* and put the contents to the test.
Menus B-C. Cards Access, Visa. (Rooms? See Caen A/R hotels.)
Closed 1-15 Oct. Tues and Wed midday.
Post rte de Lion-sur-Mer, 14440 Cresserons, Calvados.
Tel 31 37 39 10. Mich 32/B1. (SW of Lion-sur-Mer.)
(Head a few km SE to Pegasus Bridge and the Café Gondrée, the first building to be liberated after the airborne landing on the night of June 5/6 1944 (last hour of the 5th British time; 1st hour of the 6th in France). Sisters Arlette (married to a Birmingham solicitor) and Georgette Gondrée battled hard in the late 80s to keep the historic café in their family's hands. The bridge is likely to be replaced soon by a new structure. Read *Pegasus Bridge* by Stephen E. Ambrose: published by Allen & Unwin(UK) and Simon & Schuster(US).)

DOMFRONT   Poste

Simple hotel/Cooking 2
Garage/Parking/Good value

No grumbles about this typical Normandy *relais*. Like so many
others the stone-faced structure is new, courtesy of the 1944
havoc. Yvette Le Prise, *la patronne*, sticks rigidly to classical
and *Normande* paths. She's especially chuffed about *filet de
limande aux nouilles*, described aptly by her as *un marriage
inattendu* (unexpected) *mais un accord parfait*.
Menus A-B. Rooms (26) B-C. Cards All.
Closed Feb-5 Mar. Sun evg & Mon (Oct-mid June; not pub. hols).
Post rue Foch, 61700 Domfront, Orne.
Tel 33 38 51 00. Mich 50/A1.

DUCEY   Auberge de la Sélune

Comfortable hotel/Cooking 2
Gardens/Good value

"The Times is on sale in the village" sign provides the clue that
this is a British tour operator's hotel. A small garden has a
view of the Sélune, a famed salmon river (see pictures). Chef
Jean-Pierre Girres, a classicist, and his wife, Josette, are
proud of their specialities: *pie au crabe* (soup with a pastry
topper) and truite *soufflée à la ducéene* are a couple.
Menus A-B. Rooms (20) C. Cards Access, Visa.
Closed School hols Feb. Mon (Oct to Feb).
Post 50220 Ducey, Manche.
Tel 33 48 53 62. Fax 33 48 90 30. Mich 30/C4.

FORGES-LES-EAUX   Auberge du Beau Lieu

Comfortable restaurant with rooms/Cooking 3
Terrace/Parking

What a terrific bonus to now have Patrick and Marie-France
Ramelet installed in what used to be, in *FL3*, a culinary black
hole. Chef Patrick has savvy; he's carved out a style which
combines classical, modern and regional winners. The spectrum
stretches from a *minestrone de homard légèrement safrané* to a
magret de canard poêlé sauce Rouennaise and an inspired
three-star *assiette Normande* (a Calvados-laced *soufflé*; an iced
Bénédictine parfait; and an apple and cinnamon *feuilleté*).
Menus B-D. Rooms (3) C-D. Cards All.
Closed 9-16 Dec. Feb sch. hols. Wed. Sun evg (Oct to June).
Post Le Fossé, 76440 Forges-les-Eaux, S.-M.
Tel 35 90 50 36. Fax 35 90 35 98. Mich 16/C3. (2 km SE.)

GOUPILLIÈRES   Auberge du Pont de Brie

Comfortable restaurant with rooms/Cooking 1-2
Secluded/Parking/Good value

A fountain of generous compliments has flooded my desk over
the years. A run-of-the-mill plaudit reads: "the reception and

275

kindness of the owners would be hard to equal, far less exceed." The isolated, wooded setting; the close-at-hand River Orne; the super terrain to the south; all are magnetic pluses. But the best of the sparkling bubbly here is, without doubt, the four ladies who make the *auberge* a special vintage.

Véronique Dri is the smiling, helpful *patronne* (what trouble she's been to on behalf of clients); her attractive sister, Danielle, is *la cuisinière*; she's helped in the kitchen by mum, Régine; and sister-in-law, Chantal, assists in the dining room. Both classical and *cuisine Normande* have improved over the years; so have the furnishings. An award-winning *terrine de campagne* is hearty fare and light desserts are welcome. Ask Véronique to show you her notes on the links the site has with William the Conqueror and also the action in August 1944.

Menus A-C. Rooms (10) B-C. Cards Access, Visa.
Closed 1-15 Jan. 15-30 Nov. Wed (Sept to June).
Post 14210 Goupillières, Calvados. (S Caen; D562; W on D171.)
Tel 31 79 37 84. Fax 31 79 87 22. Mich 32/A2.

LE HODE   Dubuc

Very comfortable restaurant/Cooking 2-3
Parking

Another highly competent *cuisinier* who honed his talents on French liners; as a consequence Louis-Philippe Dubuc is an out-and-out classicist and he has every reason to be proud of his impeccable skills. Dive into the menu's *poissons* pool: *blanc de turbot au champagne, saumon d'Ecosse à l'oseille, soupe de poissons de la Méditerranée et sa rouille*; there's now't bland or prissy about their intense flavours. L-P is also a master pastry cook: the saliva glands tickle when I recall his *tarte aux pommes chaude*. Where is Dubuc? Leave the A15 8 km W of the Tancarville crossing; then W on D982. Rooms? Use Ibis at 76700 Harfleur (E of Le Havre; see line below).

Menus B-D. Cards All. (Ibis: Rooms C-D (72); Tel 35 45 54 00.)
Closed 1-15 Mar. 9-23 Aug. Sun evg and Mon.
Post Le Hode, 76430 St-Romain-de-Colbec, S.-M.
Tel 35 20 06 97. Mich 15/D3. (On D982.)

JAVRON   La Terrasse

Very comfortable restaurant/Cooking 2-3
Good value

Prepare yourselves for an exhilarating pleasure and surprise. Readers of *Favourites* will know this used to be the home of Jérôme and Susan Bansard (they've moved to Beuvron-en-Auge). Now Susan's brother, Michael Greenaway, and his wife, Alison, are *les patrons*. Michael, like his sister, was a student at the great Bournemouth Catering College (I told the story in *Favourites*). *Rapport qualité-prix* modern and neo-classical menus. The young couple have refurnished the dining room with terrific flair. They deserve your support.

Menus A-B. Cards AE, Access, Visa. (Rooms? Use Bagnoles Base.)
Closed Jan. Sun evg and Mon.
Post 53250 Javron-les-Chapelles, Mayenne.
Tel 43 03 41 91. Mich 50/B2.

MARTIN-EGLISE   **Auberge du Clos Normand**

Comfortable restaurant with rooms/Cooking 2
Quiet/Terrace/Gardens/Parking

A vine-clad 16th-century *auberge* (once a *relais de poste*) with
bedrooms in an annexe overlooking the gardens and a stream
and opposite a working farm (I emphasise the word working).
The rustic dining room, with tiled floor, fresh flowers and
white table cloths, is unusual in that you can see the chef working
at one end of the *salle à manger*. Classical and *Normande* fare;
hearty and filling *tarte aux moules* and *caneton ma pomme* and
a more refined *turbot sauce crème estragon*. Better than
average breakfasts with enjoyable home-made jam.
Menus B-D. Rooms (9) C-D. Cards AE, Access, Visa.
Closed 1st wk Apl. Mid Nov to mid Dec. Mon evg & Tues.
Post 76370 Martin-Eglise, S.-M.
Tel 35 82 71 01. Mich 16/B2. (SE of Dieppe.)

PONT-AUDEMER   **Auberge du Vieux Puits**

Comfortable restaurant with rooms/Cooking 2-3
Quiet/Gardens/Parking

A superb 13th-century *maison Normande*, originally a tannery,
with a timbered interior that matches the fabulous exterior.
How welcome to be able to say what praise has been lavished
on the owners, Jacques and Hélène Foltz, both of whom speak
excellent English. (They put to shame Mme Pommier at nearby
Le Petit Coq whom readers reckon is positively hostile; no
wonder the chopper has fallen on that expensive roost.) Skilled
classical and *Normand plats* including the celebrated *truite
Bovary au champagne* (the label "Bovary" inspired by Flaubert)
and *canard aux cerises griottes* (both refined treats).
Menus B-C. Rooms (12) B-D. Cards Access, Visa.
Closed 21 Dec to 22 Jan. Mon evg & Tues (not July & Aug).
Post 6 r. N.-D.-du-Pré, 27500 Pont-Audemer, Eure.
Tel 32 41 01 48. Mich 15/D4. (En Route p 116)

PONT-AUDEMER   **Belle Isle sur Risle**

Very comfortable hotel/Cooking 2-3
Quiet/Gardens/Swimming pool/Tennis/Parking

You sit up and take notice when you get a clutch of letters
praising a newcomer to the Normandy hotel scene. Marcelle
Yazbeck is a capable lady: her English is perfect, her taste
impeccable and she's fashioned, over six years, a delectable,
well-named hotel. Built in 1856, the three-storey structure is
on a five-acre island in the Risle; the landscaped grounds, with
1,500 rose bushes and trees a century old, are a delight. Her
chef, Bernard Ibanez, is a *cuisine moderne* advocate: two
polished facets of his skills are *homard, écrevisses et raviole
dans leur coulis* and *pigeon laqué au miel et gingembre, filets
en aiguillettes, cuisses en feuilleté*.
Menus B-F. Rooms (17) F-F2. Cards All.
Post 112 rte de Rouen (N175), 27500 Pont-Audemer, Eure.
Tel 32 56 96 22. Telex 306022. Fax 32 42 88 96. Mich 15/D4.

PUTANGES-PONT-ECREPIN   Lion Verd

Simple hotel/Cooking 1
Good value

The site of the modern, stone-built *logis*, beside the Orne, is a
visual tonic. Chef/patron Jean-Pierre Guillais steers a middle
of the river course: a mix of *Bourgeois*, classical and *Normande*.
Debits? Small bedrooms; some beds are uncomfortable; and
Ginette Guillais, a prolific tapestry weaver, is not the most
welcoming of *patronnes*. Credits? The site and good value.
Menus A-C. Rooms (20) C. Cards AE, Access, Visa.
Closed Xmas to end Jan. (Park in *place* opposite hotel.)
Post 61210 Putanges-Pont-Ecrepin, Orne.
Tel 33 35 01 86. Mich 32/B4.

ST-PIERRE-DU-VAUVRAY   Hostellerie St-Pierre

Very comfortable hotel/Cooking 2
Quiet (see text)/Gardens/Lift/Parking

In *FL3* I described the triangular-shaped, mock-Norman hotel as
a bit of an eyesore. Readers though have liked the Seine-side
site, the fastidiously kept Pommier family hotel, the boat-prow
bar and Alain Pommier's modern and neo-classical cooking.
St-Pierre is a *Relais du Silence*: but, beware, at night the
lights of passing barges can illuminate bedrooms overlooking
the river and the chugging craft can create quite a clatter.
Menus E-F. Rooms (14) E-F. Cards Access, Visa.
Closed Jan. Feb. Rest: Tues and Wed midday.
Post 27430 St-Pierre-du-Vauvray, Eure.
Tel 32 59 93 29. Fax 32 59 41 93. Mich 34/B1. (ER p 114)

THURY-HARCOURT   Relais de la Poste

Comfortable restaurant with rooms/Cooking 1-2
Terrace/Gardens/Parking

The vine-covered *relais* has new owners: the Fremond family.
The Poste will be better for the four fresh pairs of hands at the
controls; the Fouchers found the ride tough going. Jean-
François is the chef: he's a classical fan and has a real
fondness for *homard* and *langouste: à l'américaine, grillé au
beurre d'estragon* and *flambé au cognac*. Sauna and solarium.
Menus B-D. Rooms (9) C-D. Apts (2) F. Cards All.
Closed Mid Jan to mid Feb.
Post 14220 Thury-Harcourt, Calvados.
Tel 31 39 53 55. Fax 31 39 53 55. Mich 32/A2.

VEULES-LES-ROSES   Les Galets

Very comfortable restaurant/Cooking 3

Many *FL3* readers took my advice and made a detour to the
small coastal resort. No serious complaints have come my way.
Visitors appreciate the warm welcome they get from Nelly
Plaisance and the authentic classical cooking of her husband

Gilbert. He also puts his fingers in various other pots: *coq au vin de Bourgogne* and *bouillabaisse de la côte* are two contrasting examples. (Rooms? Use the Altéa at nearby 76460 St-Valéry-en-Caux (8 km): Rooms (153) D-E; Tel 35 97 35 48.)
Menus C-D. Cards AE, DC, Visa.
Closed 5 Jan to 5 Feb. Last wk Nov. Tues evg & Wed.
Post à la plage, 76980 Veules-les-Roses, S.-M.
Tel 35 97 61 33. Mich 15/F1.

VILLERAY   Moulin de Villeray

Very comfortable restaurant with rooms/Cooking 2-3
Secluded/Terrace/Gardens/Parking

The River Huisne forms the essential and pleasing backdrop to the 19th-century cornmill. The beamed dining room, the former engine house, overlooks the old mill wheel. Roland Coldboeuf's repertoire is a classical and neo-classical mix. An intense, richly-sauced *petit pavé de charolais au Chinon* is a *haute cuisine* glory; *agneau rôti au four, raviolis de brebis* a tasty, lighter example of more modern classical dishes.
Menus B-C. Rooms (10) F. Cards All.
Closed Mid Nov to mid Feb. Tues & Wed midday.
Post Villeray, 61110 Condeau, Orne. (N of Nogent-le-Rotrou.)
Tel 33 73 30 22. Fax 33 73 38 28. Mich 52/A2.

VILLERS-BOCAGE   Trois Rois

Comfortable restaurant with rooms/Cooking 2
Gardens/Parking/Good value

The modern *logis*, beside the N175, should have a welcome bonus by the end of 1992: a new bypass will make the site quieter. Henri Martinotti is a classical champ: he's renowned for his *tripes à la mode de Caen*, fish specialities, appetite-busting *tournedos sauté* and an artful *nougat glacé au cointreau*.
Menus B-C. Rooms (14) B-D. Cards All.
Closed Feb. Last wk June. Sun evg & Mon (not pub. hols).
Post 14310 Villers-Bocage, Calvados.
Tel 31 77 00 32. Mich 31/F2. (South-west edge of town.)

VIRONVAY   Les Saisons

Comfortable hotel/Cooking 2
Secluded/Terrace/Gardens/Tennis/Parking

This longtime readers' favourite has new owners. The site has an unobtrusive, natural appeal. The hotel is in fact eight cottages, a mixture of modern and old; they form a ring enclosing, at its centre, a pretty garden and many mature trees, including shady willows. A new chef, Gérard Bouget, has beefed up the cooking, bringing with him a modern spectrum of dishes. Praise, too, for the new manageress, Eliane Di Matteo.
Menus B-D. Rooms (7) E-F. Apts (5) F-F2. Cards AE, Acc, Visa.
Closed Sun evg (but not when Mon is pub. hol). (ER p 114)
Post Vironvay, 27400 Louviers, Eure. (W of N15; E of Louviers)
Tel 32 40 02 56. Fax 32 25 05 26. Mich 34/B1 (shown on map).

NORTH

see page 263
see page 92
see page 148

18

- Autoroute hotel
- Base hotel

0   10   20 Miles

Calais
Dunkerque
Bergues
Cap Gris-Nez
Boulogne-sur-Mer
N42
Hesdin-l'Abbé
St-Omer
A25
Edam Français
Le Touquet
A26
Lille-Ouest
Mimolette Française
Gouda Français
Lille-Sud
Gris de Lille
Montreuil-sur-Mer
Azincourt
A21
Henin-Beaumont
Valenciennes
A23
Hesdin
Crécy
N39
Arras
Maroilles
Le Crotoy
D928
Cambrai
St-Riquier
N43
Abbeville
Beaumont-Hamel
A2
Boulette de Cambrai
N1
Thiepval
Péronne
AMIENS
Somme
St-Quentin
D934
A26
Rollot
D901
Oise
Laon
Beauvais
N31
A1
Compiègne
Soissons
Pierrefonds
N28

"Who could make truly merry in a town that bore the name Péronne?" Those chilling, yet sensitive words were written by Elizabeth Nicholas in her book *The Traveller's Year*.

There's no use pretending that it is easy to make merry anywhere in Flanders or Picardy. A ghostly shroud lies over much of northern France; reminders of inconceivable slaughter are, seemingly, around every corner.

Rose Coombs' *Before Endeavours Fade* will guide you through the killing fields of the 1914-18 War. Motorists speeding along the **A1** autoroute, at the point the **A2** joins it, pass the consecrated ground of the **Somme** in five minutes – yet what countless sacrifices were made in those cold, bleak fields. Seek out the **Thiepval** memorial, described by Elisabeth de Stroumillo as "Lutyens's great pink brick and white stone memorial, rearing like a fugitive bit of New Delhi" above the cemetery. Continue to the far side of the River Ancre to the Memorial Park at **Beaumont-Hamel**, where the battlefield has been left as it was in July 1916 and where there's a monument, a huge bronze caribou, to the Newfoundlanders who lost their lives in the battle. Visit, too, Lutyens's Australian National War Monument at Villers-Bretonneux, east of **Amiens**.

To return to a brighter, more optimistic note, there are scores of happier reminders of the human race's great creative ability. Where better to start than **Arras**, a town with plenty

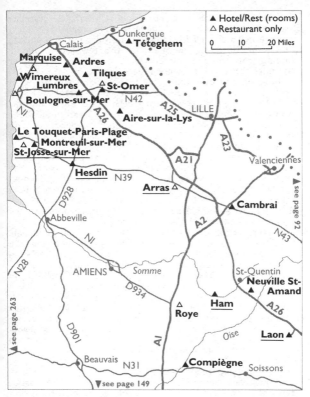

see page 92

see page 263

▼see page 149

of character, a mixture of old and new: see the gigantic Grand'Place, the much smaller Place des Héros, the ancient Abbey of St-Vaast and the *hôtel de ville* with its huge belfry. **Laon**, too, is a personal favourite. Once the capital of France, the town sits majestically on a solitary hill, towering over the surrounding countryside. One of the finest, and oldest, Gothic cathedrals in France is the centrepiece, but any walk through Laon's La Cité rewards you well: ancient houses, old streets and extensive views from the ramparts and cliff-top promenades are just some of the treats.

Compiègne is the site of a great palace, ranking third after Versailles and Fontainebleau. **Pierrefonds** is to the south-east of Compiègne. The awesome, forbidding castle is what we must all imagine a typical medieval version looked like. The feudal château was restored by Viollet-le-Duc in the 19th century and, as with another of his masterpieces, the fortress at Carcassonne, critics say the final result represents what he imagined the structure would look like, rather than being a precise reproduction of the original.

Amiens was terribly damaged during the last war but, miraculously, the Gothic cathedral, one of the largest in the world, was untouched. The nave is massive and, because of its exceptional height, sunlight pours in. Enjoy the stonework and sculptures, the 110 choir stalls, the glorious windows and the celebrated Beau Dieu (a statue of Christ). (I described **Beauvais** cathedral in the Ile de France chapter.)

I have never liked **Lille** much, where driving and parking are testing hurdles. The heart of the town, old Lille, is especially rewarding on Sundays when the streets are quieter; don't miss either the renowned Musée des Beaux-Arts.

I have a particular liking for many of the smaller, more easily explored towns. **St-Omer** is one example. Despite extensive damage inflicted during both world wars, the town retains considerable character. Visit the Basilica of Notre Dame and the Fine Arts Museum at the Hôtel Sandelin. Walk through the town's streets, main square and public gardens. Spare time, too, for the *marais* north and east of the town, an extensive marshland interlaced by 160 km of waterways.

Bergues is missed by most tourists. Hidden behind the town's walled fortifications are a reconstructed belfry, Flemish-style houses and a first-rate municipal museum. To the north of the ramparts is the unusual Couronne d'Hondschoote, originally part of Vauban's star-shaped defence works, but now a leisure walk alongside a canal and lakes.

Between **Calais** and St-Omer is one of man's more hideous "creations", a concrete monstrosity of reinforced concrete called the Blockhaus d'Eperlecques. The blockhouse was planned to be a firing pad for the V2 rockets aimed at London.

Montreuil-sur-Mer was once a port; but the Canche silted up and now the fortified town sits 10 km inland. Its history goes back to Roman times. The special appeal of the town is the ramparts; don't be timid, walk the whole circuit. **Le Touquet**, at the mouth of the Canche estuary, is a swish, sophisticated seaside resort. My family have happy memories of the wide sands; alas, the sea is badly polluted – swimming is dangerous.

South-east of Montreuil is **Hesdin**; many of the *Maigret* TV episodes (with Rupert Davies) were filmed in the town.

There's one man-made treat I would implore you not to miss, the flamboyant Gothic church at **St-Riquier**, north-east of **Abbeville**. The richly carved façade is a mouthwatering appetiser for the even more stunning interior.

Before the final paragraphs, where I detail some of Nature's handiwork, I want to return to battles past. From a small mound, just north of **Crécy**-en-Pontieu, you, too, can survey the same scene Edward III saw on August 26,1346, the start of the Hundred Years War. For the first time, and not the last, the French learned the bitter lesson of the stunning use made of the longbow by the English and Welsh archers. It also marked the day that cannonballs were first used in battle. Agincourt (**Azincourt** on maps) followed 69 years after Crécy. You can see why the French *chevaliers* were massacred by the *l'archer Anglais*; they had no room for manoeuvre, caught as they were between the woods of Azinourt and Tramecourt. A new information centre was opened earlier this year.

Three terrific forests merit your attention. First, the Forêt de Compiègne; not just the unspoilt glades among the vast blankets of trees but also the Clairière de l'Armistice, 7 km east of the town. The railway coach here is a replica of the one in which the 1918 Armistice was signed and in which Hitler, in his vengeful way, received the French surrender in 1940. Second, the Forêt de Retz, which all but rings the town of Villers-Cotterêts, south-east of Compiègne. Third, the Forêt de St-Gobain, west of Laon; enjoy beeches, oaks and pines, small *étangs*, abbeys, numerous small villages and churches.

Several river valleys please in a restful way: follow the right banks of the both the Course, north of Montreuil, and the Canche, south-east of the same town; and drive both sides of the Authie, further south. But the Somme Valley has most to offer. The super 625-acre Parc Ornithologique du Marquenterre, at the mouth of the estuary, is one of Europe's most important sanctuaries for migrating birds. The ports of St-Valery and **Le Crotoy** have provided my family with hours of pleasure; today the same will be true for your children, especially when you tell them about the small-gauge Chemin de Fer de la Baie de Somme which runs between the two villages. And last, the remarkable *hortillonnages* (water-gardens) of Amiens where, for centuries, gardeners have cultivated the marshy land and moved about in gondola-like boats on interlinking canals.

Two final detours: to Nausicaa, the world's largest sea centre in **Boulogne**, terrific for kiddies and adults; and **Cap Griz-Nez**, for views of the white cliffs of Dover.

Markets Abbeville (Thurs and Sat); Amiens (Thurs and Sat); Arras (Wed and Sat); Boulogne (Wed and Sat); Calais (Wed, Thurs, Sat and Sun); Laon (Thurs and Sat); Soissons (Wed and Sat); Le Touquet (Thurs and Sat).
Michelin green guide: Flandres/Artois/Picardie.

Cheeses Cow's milk

Boulette de Cambrai a small, ball-shaped, soft, fresh cheese – flavoured with herbs. Available all the year
Edam Français a red ball without holes or with tiny ones
Gouda Français mild, yellow-coloured, small wheel
Gris de Lille a really salty square of cheese with a strong smell
Maroilles soft, slightly salty and gold. Appears in many regional dishes
Mimolette Française orange-coloured, ball-shaped cheese
Rollot spicy-tasting, soft, small yellow disk; sometimes heart-shaped
(Be certain to visit Philippe Olivier's La Fromagerie at 43 Rue Thiers in Boulogne; his cheese shop is one of France's finest)

Regional Specialities

Carbonnade de Boeuf à la Flamande braised beef with beer, onions and bacon; if only more chefs would prepare this great dish
Caudière (Chaudière, Caudrée) versions of fish and potato soup
Ficelles Picardes ham pancakes with mushroom sauce
Flamiche aux Maroilles see *Tarte aux Maroilles*
Flamiche aux poireaux puff-pastry tart with cream and leeks
Gaufres yeast waffles
Goyère see *Tarte aux Maroilles*
Hochepot a *pot-au-feu* of the North (see *Pepperpot*)
Pepperpot stew of mutton, pork, beer and vegetables
Sanguette black pudding, made with rabbit's blood
Soupe courquignoise soup with white wine, fish, *moules*, leeks and Gruyère cheese
Tarte aux Maroilles a hot creamy tart based on Maroilles cheese
Waterzooï a cross between soup and stew, usually of fish or chicken
(Don't bypass Serge Pérard's exhilarating fish restaurant at 67 rue de Metz in Le Touquet; his *soupe de poissons* is fabulous. Robin Yapp at Mere (my favourite wine supplier) stocks the soup (0747) 860423)

Wines

Champagne to the east and Calvados to the south-west: there is nothing to talk about in the North other than **Genièvre**, a gin drunk as a liqueur, served chilled, and made from grain and juniper berries; and of course, truly excellent beer.

Autoroute Hotels

ARRAS
Campanile

Simple hotel/Cooking 1
Parking/Good value

Leave A26 exit 7 (Arras-Centre). Use N17 to Arras; on right.
Menus A-B. Rooms (42) C. Disabled. Cards Access, Visa.
Post 62223 St-Nicolas-lès-Arras, P.-de-C. (En Route p 123)
Tel 21 55 56 30. Telex 133616. Fax 21 55 46 36. Mich 8/A2.
(Bookings: UK freephone 0800 897863)

CAMBRAI
Ibis

Simple hotel/Cooking 1
Parking/Good value

From A26 take A2 (sign Bruxelles). Leave A2 exit 14 (Cambrai).
Hotel on right, just after toll.
Menus A-B. Rooms (51) C. Disabled. Cards Access, Visa.
Post 59400 Cambrai, Nord. (En Route p 30)
Tel 27 83 54 54. Telex 135074. Fax 27 81 81 66. Mich 8/C3.
(Bookings: UK 071 724 1000; US toll free 800 221 4542)

COMPIEGNE
Ibis

Simple hotel/Cooking 1
Parking

A1 exit 9 (from south); exit 10 (north). On south-east bypass.
Menus B. Rooms (58) D. Disabled. Cards Access, Visa.
Post 18 rue E. Branly, 60200 Compiègne, Oise. (En Route p 24)
Tel 44 23 16 27. Telex 145991. Fax 44 86 48 12. Mich 18/B4.
(Bookings: UK 071 724 1000; from US toll free 800 221 4542)

DUNKERQUE
Campanile

Simple hotel/Cooking 1
Terrace/Parking/Good value

Leave N225 at Bourbourg exit (shortly before it becomes A25),
2 km after leaving Dunkerque bypass. Hotel north of N225.
Menus A-B. Rooms (42) C. Disabled. Cards Access, Visa.
Post 59380 Armbouts-Cappel, Nord.
Tel 28 64 64 70. Telex 132294. Fax 28 60 53 12. Mich 3/D1.
(Bookings: UK freephone 0800 897863)

DUNKERQUE
Mercure

Comfortable hotel/Cooking 1
Quiet/Swimming pool/Closed parking

See above. North of N225 (A25), by lake. Heated indoor pool.
Menus B. Rooms (64) E-F. Disabled. Cards All.
Post 59380 Armbouts-Cappel, Nord. (En Route p 121)
Tel 28 60 70 60. Telex 820916. Fax 28 61 06 39 Mich 3/D1
(Bookings: UK 071 724 1000; US toll free 800 221 4542)

284

HENIN-BEAUMONT   Campanile

Simple hotel/Cooking 1
Gardens/Parking/Good value

Leave A1 exit 17 (Hénin-Beaumont). Hotel to east of A1.
Menus A-B. Rooms (55) C. Disabled. Cards Access, Visa.
Post 62950 Noyelles-Godault, P.-de-C. (En Route p 27)
Tel 21 76 26 26. Telex 134109. Fax 21 75 22 21. Mich 3/F4.
(Bookings UK freephone 0800 897863)

HENIN-BEAUMONT   Novotel

Very comfortable hotel/Cooking 1
Terrace/Gardens/Swimming pool/Closed parking

Leave A1 exit 17 (Hénin-Beaumont). Hotel to west of A1.
Menus B. Rooms (81) E. Disabled. Cards All.
Post 62950 Noyelles-Godault, P.-de-C. (En Route p 27)
Tel 21 75 16 01. Telex 110352. Fax 21 75 88 59. Mich 3/F4.
(Bookings: UK 071 724 1000; US toll free 800 221 4542)

LILLE-OUEST   Mercure Lomme

Comfortable hotel/Cooking 1
Quiet/Terrace/Gardens/Swimming pool/Parking

Leave A25 exit 7 (Lomme). North on N352. Hotel on right, past
Auchan supermarket. Heated indoor pool.
Menus B. Rooms (87) E-F. Cards All.
Post 59320 Englos, Nord. (En Route p 119)
Tel 20 92 30 15. Telex 820302. Fax 20 93 75 66. Mich 3/F3.
(Bookings: UK 071 724 1000; US toll free 800 221 4542)

LILLE-OUEST   Novotel Lomme

Very comfortable hotel/Cooking 1
Quiet/Terrace/Gardens/Swimming pool/Lift/Parking

Leave A25 exit 7 (Lomme). Hotel on south side of A25.
Menus B. Rooms (124) E. Disabled. Cards All.
Post 59320 Englos, Nord. (En Route p 119)
Tel 20 07 09 99. Telex 132120. Fax 20 44 74 58. Mich 3/F3.
(Bookings: UK 071 724 1000; US toll free 800 221 4542)

LILLE-SUD   Climat de France

Simple hotel/Cooking 1
Quiet/Parking/Good value

Leave A1 exit 20 (Faches-Thumesnil from north; Lille-Lesquin
from south). West to island, right on D917; hotel on left.
Menus A-B. Rooms (42) C-D. Disabled. Cards AE, Access, Visa.
Post 59810 Lesquin, Nord. (En Route p 29)
Tel 20 97 00 24. Fax 20 97 00 67. Mich 3/F3.
(Bookings: UK 071 287 3181)

LILLE-SUD
Novotel

Very comfortable hotel/Cooking 1
Terrace/Swimming pool/Lift/Closed parking

Exit details: see previous entry. Hotel on west side of A1.
Menus B. Rooms (92) E-F. Disabled. Cards All.
Post 59810 Lesquin, Nord. (En Route p 29)
Tel 20 97 92 25. Telex 820519. Fax 20 97 36 12. Mich 3/F3.
(Bookings: UK 071 724 1000; US toll free 800 221 4542)

PERONNE
Mercure

Very comfortable hotel/Cooking 1-2
Terrace/Swimming pool/Lift/Parking

On A1 west side (Aire d'Assevillers). Access also from exit 13
(St-Quentin/Péronne): through toll, right at N29, over A1, right
on D146 to Assevillers, where right again.
Menus A-C. Rooms (93) F. Disabled. Cards All.
Post 80200 Péronne, Somme. (En Route p 25)
Tel 22 84 12 76. Telex 140943. Fax 22 85 28 92. Mich 8/A4.
(Bookings: UK 071 724 1000; US toll free 800 221 4542)

ST-QUENTIN
Campanile

Simple hotel/Cooking 1
Terrace/Parking/Good value

Leave A26 exit 10. Take N29 towards St-Quentin; on right.
Menus A-B. Rooms (40) C. Disabled. Cards Access, Visa.
Post 02100 St-Quentin, Aisne. (En Route p 122)
Tel 23 09 21 22. Telex 150596. Fax 23 67 49 55. Mich 8/C4.
(Bookings: UK freephone 0800 897863)

VALENCIENNES
Campanile

Simple hotel/Cooking 1
Parking/Good value

A2 Aérodrome exits: south of A2, between N3 and autoroute.
Menus A-B. Rooms (106) C. Disabled. Cards Access, Visa.
Post Aérodrome, 59300 Valenciennes, Nord.
Tel 27 21 10 12. Telex 810288. Fax 27 21 08 55. Mich 9/D2.
(Bookings: UK freephone 0800 897863)

VALENCIENNES
Novotel

Very comfortable hotel/Cooking 1
Terrace/Gardens/Swimming pool/Parking

Exit details: see above entry.
Menus B. Rooms (76) E. Disabled. Cards All.
Post Aérodrome, 59300 Valenciennes, Nord. (En Route p 31)
Tel 27 21 12 12. Telex 120970. Fax 27 21 06 02. Mich 9/D2.
(Bookings: UK 071 724 1000; US toll free 800 221 4542)

ARRAS Les 3 Luppars

Simple hotel
Lift

Robert de Troy's new venture (ex Chanzy) in the superb Grand'
Place (use its underground car park). Ask to see his cellar.
Rooms (42) C-D. Disabled. Cards All.
Post 49 Grand'Place, 62000 Arras, P.-de-C.
Tel 21 07 41 41. Telex 133007. Fax 21 24 24 80. Mich 8/A2.

BOULOGNE-SUR-MER Urbis

Simple hotel
Lift

On the front (parking). Two min. walk to La Matelote rest.
Rooms (42) C-D. Disabled. Cards Access, Visa.
Post 168 bd Ste-Beuve, 62200 Boulogne-sur-Mer, P.-de-C.
Tel 21 32 15 15. Telex 135248. Fax 21 30 47 97. Mich 2/A3.
(Bookings: UK 071 724 1000; US toll free 800 221 4542)

CAMBRAI Beatus

Very comfortable hotel
Quiet/Gardens/Garage/Closed parking

Mme Gorczynski, the owner, and Philippe, her English-speaking
son, are two big pluses at this refurbished base.
Rooms (32) D. Cards All (En Route p 123)
Post 718 av. Paris, 59400 Cambrai, Nord. (On N44 to south)
Tel 27 81 45 70. Telex 820597. Fax 27 78 00 83. Mich 8/C3.

HESDIN-L'ABBE Cléry

Comfortable hotel
Secluded/Gardens/Tennis/Parking

Handsome 18th-century chateau in a 12-acre park with fine
trees. Elegant furnishings. North of traffic lights on N1.
Rooms (19) D-F. Cards All.
Post 62360 Hesdin-l'Abbé, P.-de-C.
Tel 21 83 19 83. Telex 135349. Fax 21 87 52 59. Mich 2/A3.

MONTREUIL-SUR-MER France

Simple hotel
Parking

An ideal base for the St-Josse-sur-Mer restaurant and a franc-
saving alternative to the Montreuil restaurants' bedrooms.
British owners, Janie Hall and Philip Spear-Bailey, are two
further good reasons for seeking out the character hotel.
Rooms (15) C-D. Cards All.
Post 2 rue Coquempot, 62170 Montreuil-sur-Mer, P.-de-C.
Tel 21 06 05 36. Fax 21 81 22 60. Mich 2/A4.

AIRE-SUR-LA-LYS

Host. Trois Mousquetaires

Comfortable hotel/Cooking 2
Quiet/Gardens/Closed Parking

What varied reports have hit my desk over the years. There's been a 100% thumbs-up record for the ornate 19th-century château, once a fort (note address); for the seven-acre park, lake and river; for super service and the excellent reception from the Mmes Venet; and for the over-the-top interior and richly-furnished bedrooms. The classical and neo-classical cooking (menus in English) from the four hands of MM. Venet is another matter altogether: some readers reckon the grub is good; a few tagged the cuisine pretentious; and others have moaned about over-salting and the serving of cold vegetables.
Menus B-C. Rooms (33) C-F. Cards All.
Closed 20 Dec to 20 Jan. Sun evg & Mon.
Post Ch. du Fort de la Redoute, 62120 Aire-sur-la-Lys, P.-de-C.
Tel 21 39 01 11. Fax 21 39 50 10. Mich 3/D3. (ER p 124)

ARDRES

Château de Cocove

Very comfortable hotel/Cooking 2
Secluded/Gardens/Parking

Restored in 1986, Annick Calonne's 18th-century château is a welcome newcomer to the Pas de Calais. The stone interior is magnificent. The owner is a wine merchant; an extension of the business is the underground *cave* which makes stocking-up, before returning home, a simple affair. Menus in English, describing *plats* which are a mix of modern, classical and neo-classical. Directions: take N43 if heading south (do not use A26); cross A26, left at D217 and keep going left. If heading north, leave A26 at junc 2 and keep going left.
Menus B-D. Rooms (24) E-F. Disabled. Cards All.
Closed Christmas Eve and Christmas Day.
Post 62890 Recques-sur-Hem, P.-de-C. (On D226; N of TGV & A26)
Tel 21 82 68 29. Telex 810985. Fax 21 82 72 59. Mich 2/C2.

ARDRES

Clément

Comfortable hotel (see text)/Cooking 2
Quiet/Gardens/Garage/Parking

Do not stay overnight: no other hotel in *FL3* has been the cause of more gripes about bedrooms than this one. Readers' comments include: dingy, undecorated, small bedrooms and shabby – a few of the more printable comments. What about young François Coolen (the fourth-generation chef at the family hotel) and his modern cum neo-classical repertoire? He and his antiseptic dining room win an entry by a four to one majority. The "Yes" votes included praise for fish in a leek sauce of great delicacy and a good sweet trolley. Among the "No" votes was a thumbs-down for tough, tasteless chicken.
Menus B-D. Rooms (17) C-D. Cards All. (En Route p 125)
Closed Mid Jan to mid Feb. Mon. Tues midday (Oct to Mar).
Post 91, espl. Mar. Leclerc, 62610 Ardres, P.-de-C.
Tel 21 82 25 25. Fax 21 82 98 92. Mich 2/B2.

ARRAS   Ambassadeur

Very comfortable restaurant/Cooking 2-3
Good value

In times past this was the Buffet de Gare. Some station restaurant. A richly-furnished dining room complements the rich *haute cuisine* classics; there's nothing punk about the dishes served at Robert Chaveroche's famous restaurant. In addition to the *plats* from the past you've also got the chance to try some regional stomach fillers: *tarte aux maroilles, ficelles à la Picarde, andouillette d'Arras aux baies de genièvre* among them. A welcome new addition is La Brasserie (open every day); *Bourgeois* dishes in the price range A.
Menus B-C. Cards All. (Rooms? See Base hotel.)
Closed Sun evg. (Parking at nearby bus station.)
Post Buffet de la Gare, 62000 Arras, P.-de-C.
Tel 21 23 29 80. Mich 8/A2.

ARRAS   La Faisanderie

Very comfortable restaurant/Cooking 3

The Dargent family moved lock, stock and barrel from Pommera (see *FL3*) in 1986 to a stunning new home in the greatest of Arras' many man-made glories, the Grand'Place. The 17th-cent brick-arched *cave* was orginally a stable: note the *escalier*, the trough and the tethering hooks. Jean-Pierre Dargent, an inventive modern *maître*, has progressed significantly. Small touches predominate at every stage: witness the six or seven breads (onion, nut, bacon and so on); fresh, flavoursome fish dishes; and one spectacular speciality which remains a laser-burning image: *chevreau rôti en aigre doux, crépine de fressure* (the latter a faggot of roe-deer *abats*). Great wine list with lots of halves. Marie-Laurence, J-P's wife, and her brother, Francis Gaudin, are polished front-of-house professionals.
Menus B-D. Cards All. (Rooms? See Arras Base, 25 yds away.)
Closed Feb school hols. 1st 3 wks Aug. Sun. evg & Mon.
Post 45 Grand'Place, 62000 Arras, P.-de-C.
Tel 21 48 20 76. Mich 8/A2. (En Route p 26)

BOULOGNE-SUR-MER   La Matelote

Very comfortable restaurant/Cooking 3

Tony Lestienne rarely lets the side down at his light, airy restaurant on the promenade just north of the port and opposite Nausicaa. No thundering compliments but no thumps around the ears either. Less invention these days, more a repertoire of personalised neo-classical specialities. Dive into the fish dishes; the *entrées froides et chaudes* include several assured treats and *les poissons'* list provides a dip into a rich sea-water pool of pleasures. The lower-priced good-value menu offers a choice of three *plats* for each of three courses.
Menus B-D. Cards Access, Visa. (Rooms? See Base hotel nearby.)
Closed Xmas to mid Jan. Sun evg. (Park on quayside.)
Post 80 bd Ste-Beuve, 62200 Boulogne-sur-Mer, P.-de-C.
Tel 21 30 17 97. Fax 21 83 29 24. Mich 2/A2.

CAMBRAI

Château de la Motte Fénelon
Rest. Les Douves

Very comfortable hotel/Cooking 1-2
Quiet/Gardens/Tennis/Lift/Parking

Strange: an hotel with a mouthfilling string of words name yet I've had less feedback about the place than any other in the North. Pluses? A series of buildings in a 20-acre wooded park and a quiet site. Debits? Cooking has gone into reverse gear; now primarily classical and inventive no longer (despite management's claims). (NE corner of Cambrai: use N30, turn NE, allée St-Roch, 300 yds past Peugeot garage when heading SE.)
Menus B-C. Rooms (40) C-F. Cards All.
Closed Rest: Sun evg and evgs on public hols.
Post sq. Château, 59400 Cambrai, Nord.
Tel 27 83 61 38. Telex 120285. Fax 27 83 71 62. Mich 8/C3.

COMPIEGNE

Hostellerie du Royal-Lieu

Very comfortable restaurant with rooms/Cooking 2
Quiet/Terrace/Gardens/Parking

The Château de Bellinglise has had the chop: new owners, a major facelift, prices hiked-up; the hotel is a soulless shell which could be anywhere in the world. Not so here, a near neighbour. Angelo Bonechi is not a shy classicist; old style, old traditions and cooking from the past show in the service, furnishings and his repertoire (like a sumptuous turbot in a champagne sauce). The terrace and park are no less enticing. Prices make British equivalents seem like blackmail.
Menus B-D. Rooms (17) D-E. Disabled. Cards All.
Post 9 rue Senlis, 60200 Compiègne, Oise. (On D932A.)
Tel 44 20 10 24. Fax 44 86 82 27. Mich 18/B4. (ER p 24)

HAM

France

Comfortable restaurant with rooms/Cooking 2
Good value

You can't make merry in this consecrated land. Better to come with no great expectations and take quiet pleasure from the vine-covered France in the shadow of the *hôtel de ville*'s high belfry. Jean-Pierre Mailliez walks a classical *rue*, diverting here and there with regional *plats*: *anguille fumée*, *ficelle Picarde* and *tarte aux pommes flambées au calvados* are typical.
Menus A-C. Rooms (6) C. Cards Access, DC, Visa.
Closed 1-15 Aug. Sun evg.
Post pl. H. de Ville, 80400 Ham, Somme. (Park in *place*.)
Tel 23 81 00 22. Mich 18/C2.

HESDIN

Flandres

Simple hotel/Cooking 1-2
Garage/Parking/Good value

The bullets have been flying. Readers left me in no doubt whatsoever: the welcome at the Persyn brothers (a trio) hotel

290

is warm; the cooking has improved; the place is smarter; and
the breakfasts are excellent. Bravo. Classical, *Bourgeois* and
regional *plats* and grills from the *rôtisserie*.
Menus A-B. Rooms (14) B-D. Cards All.
Closed 20 Dec to 10 Jan.
Post 22 rue d'Arras, 62140 Hesdin, P.-de-C.
Tel 21 86 80 21. Mich 7/D1. (In town centre.)

HESDIN   **Trois Fontaines**

Simple hotel/Cooking 1
Quiet/Gardens/Parking/Good value

A newish, whitewashed *logis* where Martine and Patrick Herbin
satisfy in an unassuming way. Modest cooking with a mix of
Bourgeoise, classical and regional specialities.
Menus A-B. Rooms (10) C-D. Disabled. Cards All.
Closed Rest: Mon midday.
Post rue d'Abbeville, Marconne, 62140 Hesdin, P.-de-C.
Tel 21 86 81 65. Mich 7/D1. (500 metres south of Hesdin.)

LAON   **Bannière de France**

Comfortable restaurant with rooms/Cooking 1-2
Garage/Good value

A 17th-century *relais de poste* at the heart of the majestic hill-
top town. Mme Paul Lefèvre lost her husband two years ago;
she battles on courageously, helped by chef Dominique Havot.
Classical specialities with two good-value menus in price band
B. Note garage; otherwise park in nearby *place*.
Menus B-C. Rooms (19) C-D. Cards All.
Closed 20 Dec to 20 Jan. May 1st.
Post 11 rue F. Roosevelt, 02000 Laon, Aisne.
Tel 23 23 21 44. Mich 19/E3.

LUMBRES   **Moulin de Mombreux**

Very comfortable hotel/Cooking 3
Quiet/Gardens/Parking

Anne and I have known the 18th-century *moulin* from the days,
over 20 years ago, when the mill (alongside the River Bléquin)
was first converted into a restaurant. How times change:
regular British trade has meant higher prices; the tills have
tinkled, providing the francs needed to prettify and improve
the interior of the original mill. What's also arrived is an ugly
23-bedroom brick-built annexe which straddles the river. One
consistent grumble from reader after reader: wines are too
dear. Less of the gloom. The fact is the *moulin* is loved by
many; for some this is their favourite French hotel. Jean-Marc
Gaudry's cooking is both classical and neo-classical; and wife
Danièle's welcome is warm and friendly.
Menus C-E. Rooms (24) F. Cards All.
Closed 20-29 Dec.
Post 62380 Lumbres, P.-de-C. (South and west of Lumbres.)
Tel 21 39 62 44. Telex 133486. Mich 2/C2. (En Route p 125)

MARQUISE

Grand Cerf

Comfortable restaurant/Cooking 3
Terrace/Good value

Various changes since *FL3*: Jean-François Lemercier left, to be replaced by Thierry Bernard. He, too, packed his bags and has gone. But the new chef/patron, Stéphane Pruvot, is rather special. A student of Lorrain at Joigny, the young *cuisinier* made quite a name for himself in Paris (Bellecour; *7ème arr.*) His modern, neo-classical cooking complements his new home in the Côte Opale: dishes of vivid tastes and colouring and the lower-priced menus are sparkling *rapport qualité-prix* gems.
Menus B-D. Cards Access, Visa. (Rooms? Use Boulogne Base.)
Closed Sun evg & Mon. (Annual holidays not decided.)
Post av. Ferber, 62250 Marquise, P.-de-C. (On main street.)
Tel 21 87 55 05. Fax 21 33 61 09. Mich 2/A2.

MONTREUIL-SUR-MER   Auberge de la Grenouillère

Very comfortable restaurant with rooms/Cooking 3
Quiet/Terrace/Parking

Frogs are the theme in the converted Picardy-style whitewashed cottages alongside the tree-lined River Canche and below Montreuil's ramparts. (A single dish features *grenouilles*; but be sure to chuckle at the 1930 frescoe in one of the dining rooms.) Roland Gauthier has an impeccable c.v. which shows in his neo-classical and modern repertoire, full of polished, refined *plats*. Few grumbles: the most serious complained of fish not being fresh. Overall, a thumping vote of confidence.
Menus B-D. Rooms (4) D-F. Cards All.
Closed 15 Dec-15 Jan. 10 days Feb. Tue evg & Wed (Sept-June).
Post 62170 Madelaine-sous-Montreuil, P.-de-C. (NW; off D319.)
Tel 21 06 07 22. Fax 21 86 36 36. Mich 2/A4.

MONTREUIL-SUR-MER   Château de Montreuil

Very comfortable hotel/Cooking 3
Quiet/Terrace/Gardens/Garage

Anne and I have followed with exceptional and detailed interest the progress of the young couple who, in March 1982, took over this longtime favourite hotel of ours. Chef Christian Germain, born in a village near Avesnes-sur-Helpe (Champagne-Ardenne), and his vivacious wife, Lindsay, an English "rose", are without any doubt one of my readers' most appreciated hotelier duos. Christian, trained by Michel Roux at Bray, is a talented modern classical (neo-classical) chef. The gardens are an eye-pleasing spectacle, thanks to Francis; but ask to see the hidden *potager du restaurant*, a real retina reeler. On March 12, 1989 fire gutted the interior; after a traumatic year when, at first, all seemed lost, the couple and their precious château resurfaced again.
Menus C-D. Rooms (14) F-F2. Cards Access, Visa.
Closed 15 Dec-early Feb. Mon (not May-Sept). Thurs midday.
Post chaussée Capucins, 62170 Montreuil-sur-Mer, P.-de-C.
Tel 21 81 53 04. Telex 135205. Fax 21 81 36 43. Mich 2/A4.

NEUVILLE ST-AMAND   Château

Very comfortable restaurant with rooms/Cooking 3
Quiet/Gardens/Parking

The Meiresonne château is more akin to a hunting lodge, hidden behind a wall of trees in a seven-acre park. Claude welcomes guests and chef Jean-François (who trained at both Oustaù de Baumanière and Maxim's) is a dedicated classicist with many a modern touch in his repertoire. On one hand an intense and rich *tournedos poêlé à la crème de morilles*; on the other a lighter, more subtle *escalope de saumon d'Ecosse au vermouth*. (Leave A26 at junction 11; follow signs for Laon; at island on N44, right, ascend hill; left to village.)
Menus B-D. Rooms (6) D. Cards All.
Closed 1st 3 wks Aug. Last wk Dec. 1 wk Feb. Sat & Sun evg.
Post Neuville St-Amand, 02107 St-Quentin, Aisne.
Tel 23 68 41 82. Fax 23 68 46 02. Mich 19/D1.

ROYE   La Flamiche

Very comfortable restaurant/Cooking 3

I can give you a Rock of Gibraltar granite guarantee: nowhere else in France will you get a more "royel" welcome than the warm, open-hearted greeting which Christine Klopp lavishes on her clients. (Her father's name and the chef who started the restaurant.) Her husband, Gérard Borck, is proud of his cellar of several hundred varieties (one of the menus offers different wines, by the glass, with each course). The present chef, Thierry Clisson, drives the modern cooking autoroute with several deviations taking in the best of the local *terroir* (*flamichette*; *presse d'anguilles de Somme aux girolles*; and *colvert des Marais*). (Rooms? Motel des Lions: Rooms (43) C-D; Tel 22 87 20 61; at A1 junc 12; 80700 Roye.)
Menus B-D. Cards All. (En Route p 25: Motel and La Flamiche.)
Closed 2nd wk July. Xmas to mid Jan. Sun evg & Mon.
Post pl. H. de Ville, 80700 Roye, Somme. (Park in *place*.)
Tel 22 87 00 56. Mich 18/B2.

ST-JOSSE-SUR-MER   Le Relais de St-Josse

Simple restaurant/Cooking 2
Good value

A reader who lives in St-Josse (a *village fleuri*) gave me the richly rewarding tip about Le Relais in the spring of 1992. Young Etienne Delmer, not yet 30, and his wife, Fabienne, opened just a year ago. The couple deserve great success. The coast needs *rapport qualité-prix* of this sort: what value; what quality; what largesse; what skill. Etienne, with a fine training behind him, is a classical/neo-classical chef: *pièce de boeuf rôti à la moëlle, terrine de sanglier au chutney d'oignons* and *crêpes Suzette* are typical tasty treats.
Menus A-B. Cards Access, Visa. (Rooms? See Montreuil Base.)
Closed 6-28 Jan. Mon. (Park in the big *place* opposite rest.)
Post Grand place, 62170 St-Josse-sur-Mer, P.-de-C.
Tel 21 94 61 75. Mich 2/A4. Between Le Touquet & Montreuil.

ST-OMER   Bretagne

Comfortable hotel/Cooking 1-2 (see text)
Parking/Good value

Francis and Sylvie (once such a talented chef) Beauvalot
decided in the mid-Eighties that chasing stars wasn't for them.
Instead, they now run the hotel as an out-and-out "business"
for Brits. Three restaurants: "Le Best", the most dear, gives
fleeting glimpses why a star was won 10 years ago (mix of
classical and modern); "Petit Best" and "Meava Grill" serve
cheap and cheerful grills and *Bourgeois plats*.
Menus A-B (Pet B/Grill); B (Le B). Rooms (76) C-D. Cards All.
Closed Le B/Pet B: Sat & Sun evg. Grill: Sat midday & Mon.
Post 2 pl. Vainquai, 62500 St-Omer, P.-de-C. (ER p 125)
Tel 21 38 25 78. Telex 133290. Fax 21 93 51 22. Mich 2/C2.

ST-OMER   Le Cygne

Comfortable restaurant/Cooking 2
Good value

A classy classical and *Bourgeois* restaurant at the heart of
St-Omer. Madame is a martinet so no arguing; if you want your
magret de canard to be medium or well done then tough luck
because she insists the bird comes rare and no other way. Keep
out of trouble, let her choose the wines and tuck into good-
value grub: *saucisson chaud de canard, tourte aux fromages,
paillette de truite saumonée fumée, sole façon du chef* and
Olivier cheeses from Boulogne are all first class.
Menus A-C. Cards Access, Visa. (Rooms? Ibis 200 yards away.)
Closed Xmas to 20 Jan. Sat midday. Tues (not public hols).
Post 8 r. Caventou, 62500 St-Omer, P.-de-C.
Tel 21 98 20 52. Mich C/C2. (Park pl. Victor-Hugo; 100 m W.)

TETEGHEM   La Meunerie

Luxury restaurant with rooms/Cooking 4
Quiet/Garage/Parking

If Jean-Pierre Delbé's restaurant was 100 miles to the north-
west he would be the darling of the British media. Instead, La
Meunerie is in the dull Nord, the last place the Parisian media
would look for explosive culinary talent. Wonders never cease
though: at last the major French guides are waking up to the
great skills of chef Jean-Pierre and his ever-smiling,
gregarious wife, Marie-France. Attention to detail is the
couple's great strength: in the modern and neo-classical
specialities; in the flowers; the breads; the cheeses; and in
myriad other ways. Masterful technique and opulent creations
hit you where they count most: in the mouth and eyes. The
bedrooms, designed by J-P himself, are superb with bathrooms
where brilliant use is made of marble and glass (in Britain you
would pay at least double or treble the price).
Menus C-E. Rooms (8) E-F. Cards All.
Closed 25 Dec to 25 Jan. Rest: Sun evg & Mon.
Post 59229 Téteghem, Nord. (E Dunkerque: S of vill, jun D2/D4)
Tel 28 26 14 30. Telex 132253. Fax 28 26 17 32. Mich 3/D1.

TILQUES   Château Tilques

Very comfortable hotel/Cooking 2-3
Secluded/Gardens/Tennis/Parking

Dramatic changes at the 100-year-old château (was called Le
Vert Mesnil): no wonder shoals of praise have come my way.
English owners, European Country Hotels, have beefed up
every aspect of the place, inc' prices. What's most welcome is
the vastly improved classical cuisine; original appetisers and
petits fours, richly sauced *boeuf Rossini* and an unusual
choucroute de poissons au vin de champagne have all pleased.
Menus C-D. Rooms (52) E-F. Disabled. Cards All.
Closed Last wk Dec. Rest: Sat midday. (En Route p 125)
Post 62500 Tilques, P.-de-C. (NW St-Omer; E of N43.)
Tel 21 93 28 99. Telex 133360. Fax 21 38 34 23. Mich 2/C2.

LE TOUQUET-PARIS-PLAGE   Ibis

Comfortable hotel/Cooking 1
Quiet/Terrace/Lift/Parking

Overlooking the beach. Joined to the Novotel by a passageway
which spans an indoor, heated sea-water pool (closed Jan).
Basic Ibis grill; try the St-Josse restaurant instead.
Menus A-B. Rooms (90) D-E. Disabled. Cards Access, Visa.
Post sur la plage, 62520 Le Touquet-Paris-Plage, P.-de-C.
Tel 21 09 87 00. Telex 134273. Fax 21 09 86 10. Mich 2/A4.
(Bookings: UK 071 724 1000; US toll free 800 221 4542)

LE TOUQUET-PARIS-PLAGE   Novotel

Very comfortable hotel/Cooking 1-2
Quiet/Swimming pool (indoor)/Lift/Parking

On the beach. Heated sea-water pool. Cooking? See the notes
on page 4. Try Pérard's fish restaurant (see p 283).
Menus B. Rooms (104) E-F. Disabled. Cards All.
Closed 5-26 Jan.
Post sur la plage, 62520 Le Touquet-Paris-Plage, P.-de-C.
Tel 21 09 85 00. Telex 160480. Fax 21 09 86 10. Mich 2/A4.
(Bookings: UK 071 724 1000; US toll free 800 221 4542)

WIMEREUX   Atlantic

Comfortable restaurant with rooms/Cooking 2
Terrace (brasserie)/Lift/Parking

New owners, Aron and Marie-France Misan, gave the Atlantic
a new lease of life in 1990. (M. Misan worked in London for a
long spell.) Overlooks the beach though not everyone likes the
resort. Classical cooking with a strong emphasis on fish (also a
lobster tank). Brasserie serves simpler, cheaper food.
Menus B-C. Rooms (31) D. Cards Access, Visa.
Closed Jan to mid Feb. Sun evg. Mon (not July & Aug).
Post digue de mer, 62930 Wimereux, P.-de-C.
Tel 21 32 41 01. Fax 21 87 46 17. Mich 2/A2.

POITOU-CHARENTES

Poitou-Charentes offers rewards to all ages: to children, eager to spend their days on beaches or in water; and to older generations, with youngsters now grown-up and off their hands, keen to get away from it all in more deserted landscapes.

The region falls neatly into four parts: **Vendée** is the area in the top half of the map above; **Charentes** is the terrain below; **Poitou** is the countryside in the top half of the page opposite; **Limousin** is the *pays* to the south. I shall devote most space to both Poitou and Limousin, two gorgeous parts of France ignored by far too many tourists.

The Vendée is renowned for its excellent sandy beaches; one of the best is at **Les Sables d'Olonne**. But I have no doubt that Vendée fans would claim that there are dozens of others along the entire length of the coastline and on the Ile de Noirmoutier too (see Brittany map). The hinterland is flat, rising to the gentle hills of the Collines Vendéennes on the left bank of the **Sèvre Nantaise**.

One of the highest points is the **Puy Crapaud** (886 ft), just east of Pouzauges; arguably the extensive views from the summit are the best in the Vendée. Explore the landscape to the north and seek out the Château Puy-du-Fou, due south of **Mortagne-sur-Sèvre**. The largest *spectacle* in Europe is held here every year, from mid June to end August (Fri and Sat). The two-hour *son et lumière* extravaganza tells the story of the Vendée, with the help of lasers, synchronised fountains and other ultra-modern technology.

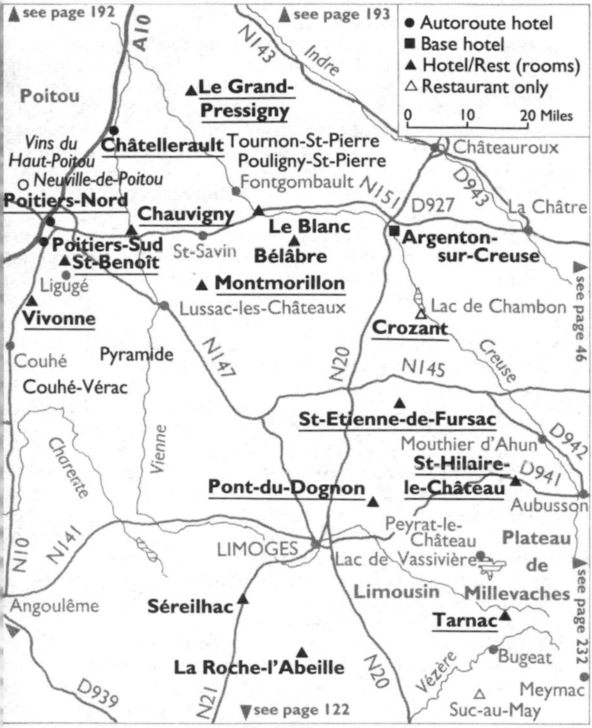
▲see page 192
▲see page 193
● Autoroute hotel
■ Base hotel
▲ Hotel/Rest (rooms)
△ Restaurant only
0 10 20 Miles
A10
N143
Indre
Poitou
▲Le Grand-Pressigny
Vins du Haut-Poitou
Châtellerault
Tournon-St-Pierre
Pouligny-St-Pierre
Châteauroux
○ Neuville-de-Poitou
Fontgombault
N151
D943
Poitiers-Nord
Chauvigny
D927
La Châtre
Le Blanc
Argenton-sur-Creuse
Poitiers-Sud
St-Savin
Bélâbre
▲St-Benoît
▲ Montmorillon
▲see page 46
Ligugé
Lussac-les-Châteaux
Lac de Chambon
Vivonne
Crozant
Couhé
Pyramide
N147
N20
Creuse
N145
Couhé-Vérac
St-Etienne-de-Fursac
Mouthier d'Ahun
D942
Charente
Vienne
St-Hilaire-le-Château
D941
Pont-du-Dognon
Aubusson
Peyrat-le-Château
Plateau de Millevaches
N10
N141
LIMOGES
Lac de Vassivière
▲see page 232
Angoulême
Séreilhac
Limousin
Tarnac
Bugeat
La Roche-l'Abeille
Vézère
Meymac
D939
N21
▼see page 122
N20
Suc-au-May

The area between the Vendée and Charentes is one of the most unusual in France. The **Marais Poitevin** is a vast tract of marshland (*marais* means fen). Here there must be a thousand or more tree-lined canals and streams. Every field is an island to which cows, goats, their milk and their feed, crops and human beings are all moved by punt. Drive along the numerous lanes; better still, take a punt trip from Coulon.

The northern *porte* to the Marais is **Fontenay-le-Comte**, a Renaissance town with the cool Forêt de Mervent-Vouvant on its northern doorstep. South-west of the fens is **La Rochelle**, once a mighty Protestant stronghold and with many historical links. A port of throbbing vitality, the combination of massive medieval towers, old streets, several museums and buzzing life gives it special appeal. A bus boat trip is a must. The islands of **Ré** and **Oléron**, linked by bridges to the mainland and renowned for their clear light, will attract those seeking sandy beaches and small, quiet ports.

After perhaps detouring east to the glorious Eglise St-Pierre at Aulnay, my preference would be to head for **Brouage**, a tiny and mysterious fortified settlement. Built by Richelieu, Brouage was once a port; now the sea is miles away beyond the fens. **Marennes** and the extensive *parcs à huîtres* are famed for their oysters. Be sure to use the coast road through the pines of the Forêt de la Coubre and along La Grande Côte to **Royan**, a bustling seaside resort.

The River **Charente** will attract many visitors. Some will nose out **Cognac** (using the D24 and D82, not the N141) to partake in a *dégustation* or two of the town's special gift to mankind. Others may be intoxicated by **Saintes**, once the Roman capital of western Gaul and still endowed with some fine remains, churches and museums. Others will plump for the proud *ville haute* of **Angoulême**, relishing the cathedral, the invigorating and rewarding Promenade des Remparts and the gardens in front of the *hôtel de ville*.

I would be itching to rush east, to Limousin and two of the most enticing *départements* in France: Corrèze and Creuse. Start with a bang at the **Suc-au-May**, one of the highest points of the wooded Massif des Monedières. From the observation platform on the 2989 ft summit, the panorama extends as far as the volcanic cones of Auvergne in the east.

Next, one of the most eye-catching roads in France. From **Meymac** the D979 to **Bugeat** is signposted as the "Route des Hêtres". For 13 miles, 200-year-old beeches line the road, on one side or other and often on both flanks. Six km before Bugeat make the short detour to the Ruines Gallo-Romaines des Cars. There are two sites. The one 300 yards away, down a track, is intriguing; marvel at the various luxury mod-cons.

Tarnac is a smasher: a tiny 12/13th-century *église*, two oak trees, a fine *pâtisserie* which defies economic logic, and leafy lanes spreading spider's legs in all directions. Take binoculars and a book on plants and flowers. The strangely-named **Plateau de Millevaches** (*vaches* from the Celtic *batz*, meaning spring or source) is one of Nature's paradises; tickle tranquil trout, hum along with dragonflies, savour a picnic and then doze by rustling, hypnotic streams.

The **Lac de Vassivière** is one of the best of man-made lakes. Much of the charm of the 2,500-acre sheet of water comes from the series of coves and forests which encircle the lake. For energetic sports fans there's also a host of water-borne activities. Be sure to cross the bridge to the wooded parkland on the Ile de Vassivière and chuckle at some of the modern sculptures set out on the slopes and in the woods. To the north of the lake is the most alluring of pastoral enclaves. Explore the lanes between **Peyrat-le-Château** and **St-Hilaire-le-Château**. Walk down to the Cascade des Jarreaux (signs say Jarrauds), north of St-Martin-Château.

Aubusson next and the Musée de la Tapisserie. Some of the modern tapestries are stunning walls of colour. Finish your Limousin tour with a crescendo. At **Mouthier d'Ahun** is a 15th-century *église*, part Romanesque, part Gothic. The interior's 300-year-old wooden sculptures are superb, the oak shining as proudly as do the sculptor's skills.

Now head north, following the River **Creuse**, to **Crozant**, at the southern end of another man-made lake, the **Lac de Chambon**. At Crozant are the ruins of a once powerful fortress whose mighty walls, one km long, played an important part in both the Hundred Years' War and the Wars of Religion.

Aim for **St-Savin**, the eastern door to historic Poitou. The finest of the region's numerous Romanesque churches is at St-Savin. Byzantine in origin, the interior, with its many frescoes and decorations, is a show-stopper. Detour west to **Chauvigny**, a picturesque place with a couple of Romanesque churches and three ruined castles. On the far bank of the Vienne, to the north, are two handsome châteaux: Touffou and Dissay. To the east is an appealing triangle of river terrain. The impressive ruins of Angles-sur-l'Anglin's medieval castle is at its heart; and the Romanesque abbey at **Fontgombault** (famed for the Gregorian chants of the Bénédictine monks) is on the far side of the triangle.

Before I finish the introduction let me tell you how Anne and I came to discover the Constable Chandos story. Many years ago, as we approached **Lussac-les-Châteaux** from the south, on the D25 west of the Vienne, we spotted on the map, a couple of hundred yards before the **N147**, the word *mont*. Within seconds we saw the monument itself, sitting in the shadow of a tall chestnut tree. The faded inscription told us it was erected to the memory of Constable John Chandos, mortally wounded at Lussac bridge on December 31, 1369. Who was Chandos?

Sir John was one of England's most outstanding generals. A brilliant tactician, he masterminded the English victory at **Poitiers** on September 19, 1356 (the battlefield is just up the road at Nouaillé-Maupertuis). It was at Poitiers where he turned the hopeless chance of a small army into a triumph over a much larger one. Visit the battlefield (10 km south-east of Poitiers); there's a simple memorial, erected 600 years after the battle, to the soldiers of France, Gascony and England who fell that day. Follow signs for "Champ de Bataille".

Poitiers will appeal to those seeking out ecclesiastical treasures and fine museums. I prefer some of the lesser-known architectural treats which seem to be at every turn in Poitou. Let me give you a handful of examples, all to the south of Poitiers: the 500-year-old Abbey of St-Martin at **Ligugé** with double cloisters; another nearby abbey at Nouaillé-Maupertuis; **Lusignan** with an Eglise Romane and a Maison de Bois, both dating from the 11th century; and, finally, **Couhé**'s covered market hall. Poitou-Charentes is a region you could visit many times over and still not exhaust the endless number of man-made and natural attractions.

Markets Angoulême (Sat and Sun); Challans (Tues and Fri); Cognac (Sat); Fontenay-le-Comte (Wed and Sat); Jarnac (Tues to Sun); Marennes (Sat); Rochefort (Thurs and Sat); La Rochelle (every day); Royan (Tues to Sun); Saintes (Tues to Sun).

Michelin green guides: Poitou/Vendée/Charentes and also Berry/Limousin.

Cheeses Cow's milk

Jonchée from Saintonge area. Fresh cream cheese – served with sugar and cream. **Caillebotte** is a similar cheese

Pigouille small, creamy-flavoured disk – served on straw. Can also be made from goat's or ewe's milk

Goat's milk

Chabichou Poitou area cheese: *laitier* (dairy made) and *fermier* (farm made); small, truncated, upright cylinders; soft and sharp-tasting

Couhé-Vérac soft, nutty cheese made in small squares

Jonchée from Niort area. Mild, soft, creamy – best in summer and autumn. A cheese called **Lusignan**, made as a disk, is similar

La Mothe-St-Héray best in summer and autumn. A small disk, one inch thick. Try it with the reds of Haut-Poitou. **Bougon** is a related cheese

Pouligny-St-Pierre pyramid-shaped; strong smell, soft cheese. A cheese called **Tournon-St-Pierre** is related

Pyramide pyramid-shaped, soft cheese

Ruffec fruity taste, made in a small disk

Taupinière packed and served in chestnut leaves

Ewe's milk

Oléron best in spring; mild, creamy, fresh cheese. Made on Ile d'Oléron; known also as **Jonchée d'Oléron** or **Brebis d'Oléron**

Regional Specialities

Bouilliture (Bouilleture) a freshwater eel stew with shallots and prunes in Sauvignon white wine

Boulaigou thick sweet or savoury pancake

Bréjaude cabbage, leek and bacon soup

Cagouilles (also called **Lumas**) snails from the Charentes

Casserons en matelote squid in red wine sauce with garlic and shallots

Cèpes fine, delicate, flap mushrooms; please do try them

Chaudrée a ragout of fish cooked in white wine, shallots and butter

Chevrettes local name for *crevettes* (shrimps)

Clafoutis pancake batter, poured over fruit (usually black cherries), and then baked; another treat you must not miss

Embeurrée de chou white-heart cabbage, cooked in salted water, crushed and served with butter

Farcidure a dumpling – either poached or sautéed

Farci Poitevin a *pâté* of cabbage, spinach and sorrel, encased by cabbage leaves and cooked in a *bouillon*

Migourée a sort of *chaudrée*

Mique a stew of dumplings

Mogette (Mojette) small pulse beans in butter and cream

Mouclade mussels cooked in wine, egg yolks and cream; can be served with some Pineau des Charentes

Oysters for an explanation of *les claires, belons, gravettes, marennes* and other terms see the *Glossary of Menu Terms* (under *Huîtres*)

Soupe aux fèves des Marais soup of crushed broad beans with bread, sorrel, chervil and butter

Soupe de moules à la Rochelaise soup of various fish, mussels, saffron, garlic, tomatoes, onions and red wine

Sourdons cockles from the Charentes

Tartisseaux fritters

Tourtou thick buckwheat flour pancake

Wines

The countryside of the Charentes offers the world its annual harvest of white grapes – a harvest which eventually matures into **Cognac**, brandy known as the finest on earth. The quality of Cognac varies with the fertility of the soil; this is why there are six districts. The best, **Grande Champagne**, is from the immediate south of Cognac town; the next four districts extend outwards to form a huge circle; the lowest classification is the coastal stretch lying alongside the Atlantic coast. Age is the other vital factor; the maturing process is all important. **Pineau des Charentes** is a liqueur wine (grape juice and Cognac); clear, sweet and heady – drink it cool as an *apéritif*.

Don't miss the chance to try some of the unknown locals of this part of France. The VDQS **Vins du Haut-Poitou** are a revelation: among them a **Sauvignon** white – just like its famous big brother from Sancerre; a **Pinot-Chardonnay** – the renowned white grape of Burgundy; a **Gamay** red – best drunk cool; a dry rosé; and a dry **Chenin** white. Some wine lists will describe the wines as **Poitou** or **Neuville de Poitou** – the main town of the wine-producing area. A recommended grower is Robert Champalou at Marigny-Brizay, north of Poitiers and west of the A10. You will also see VDQS wines of all shades with the marvellous name of **Fiefs Vendéens** (from the Vendée); **Rosé de Mareuil** is from the area around the town of that name.

Vins de Pays

Some really obscure wines will be recommended in the La Rochelle area: **Ile de Ré** and **Blanc de Ré** – so-so dry whites from the Ile de Ré (see map).

CHATELLERAULT Campanile

Simple hotel/Cooking 1
Lift/Parking/Good value

A10 exit 16 (Châtellerault-Nord). East; hotel at N10 junc.
Menus A-B. Rooms (50) C. Disabled. Cards Access, Visa.
Post 86100 Châtellerault, Vienne. Care: old maps say exit 17.
Tel 49 21 03 57. Telex 793038. Fax 49 21 88 31. Mich 82/A3.
(Bookings: UK freephone 0800 897863)

CHATELLERAULT Ibis

Simple hotel/Cooking 1
Lift/Parking

A10 exit 17 (Châtellerault-Sud). North on N10. At N10/D1 junc.
Menus B. Rooms (72) C-D. Cards Access, Visa.
Post 86100 Châtellerault, Vienne. Care: old maps say exit 18.
Tel 49 21 75 77. Telex 791488. Fax 49 02 01 79. Mich 82/A4.
(Bookings: UK 071 724 1000; US toll free 800 221 4542)

NIORT Campanile

Simple hotel/Cooking 1
Parking/Good value

A10 exit 22: Niort from north; St-Maixent from south. Through
toll to N11. Hotel on far side of N11.
Menus A-B. Rooms (48) C. Disabled. Cards Access, Visa.
Post rte de Paris, 79260 La Crèche, Deux-Sèvres.
Tel 49 25 56 22. Telex 791216. Fax 49 05 33 78. Mich 94/B2.
(Bookings: UK freephone 0800 897863)

POITIERS-NORD Campanile

Simple hotel/Cooking 1
Parking/Good value

A10 exit 18 (Futuroscope; new exit). East to N10 (Poitiers);
straight under N10, then keep right to hotel.
Menus A-B. Rooms (70) C. Disabled. Cards Access, Visa.
Post 86360 Chasseneuil-du-Poitou, Vienne. (En Route p 96)
Tel 49 52 85 40. Telex 791534. Fax 49 52 06 07. Mich 81/F4
(Bookings: UK freephone 0800 897863)

POITIERS-NORD France & Rest. Royal Poitou

Comfortable hotel/Cooking 1-2
Lift/Parking

A10 exit 19 (Poitiers-Nord). East to N10. South towards
Poitiers; hotel right side of N10. Care: old maps say exit 19b.
Menus B-C. Rooms (57) D-E. Cards All.
Post 215 rte de Paris, 86000 Poitiers, Vienne. (ER p 96)
Tel 49 01 74 74. Telex 790526. Fax 49 01 74 73. Mich 95/E1.

POITIERS-SUD   Ibis-Sud

Simple hotel/Cooking 1
Lift/Parking

A10 exit 20: Poitiers-Sud (from north). Left N10, on right.
Menus B. Rooms (117) C-D. Disabled. Cards Access, Visa.
Post av. du 8 Mai 1945, 86000 Poitiers, Vienne. (ER p 97)
Tel 49 53 13 13. Telex 791556. Fax 49 53 03 73. Mich 95/E1.
(Bookings: UK 071 724 1000; US toll free 800 221 4542)

POITIERS-NORD   Mercure Relais de Poitiers

Very comfortable hotel/Cooking 1-2
Gardens/Swimming pool/Lift/Parking

A10 exit 18 (Futuroscope; new exit). East to N10 (Poitiers).
South on N10, hotel to right of road. Ugly building.
Menus B-C. Rooms (90) E-F. Disabled. Cards All.
Post 86360 Chasseneuil-du-Poitou, Vienne. (ER p 96)
Tel 49 52 90 41. Telex 790502. Fax 49 52 90 46. Mich 95/E1.
(Bookings: UK 071 724 1000; US toll free 800 221 4542)

POITIERS-NORD   Novotel

Very comfortable hotel/Cooking 1
Terrace/Gardens/Swimming pool/Tennis/Lift/Parking

Exit: see Mercure above. Opposite Mercure on east side N10.
Menus B. Rooms (89) E. Disabled. Cards All.
Post 86360 Chasseneuil-du-Poitou, Vienne. (ER p 96)
Tel 49 52 78 78. Telex 791944. Fax 49 52 86 04. Mich 95/E1.
(Bookings: UK 071 724 1000; US toll free 800 221 4542)

SAINTES   Campanile

Simple hotel/Cooking 1
Parking/Good value

A10 exit 25 (Saintes). Left after toll, then right; on right.
Menus A-B. Rooms (50) C. Disabled. Cards Access, Visa.
Post 17100 Saintes, Char.-Mar.
Tel 46 97 25 25. Telex 790684. Mich 107/D2.
(Bookings: UK freephone 0800 897863)

SAINTES   Ibis

Simple hotel/Cooking 1
Terrace/Swimming pool/Parking

A10 exit 25 (Saintes). Right after toll. 1st right again N150
(sign Royan). On right. Rest closed Sat & Sun (Oct to March).
Menus B. Rooms (71) C-D. Disabled. Cards Access, Visa.
Post rte de Royan, 17100 Saintes, Char.-Mar. (ER p 99)
Tel 46 74 36 34. Telex 791394. Fax 46 93 33 39. Mich 107/D2.
(Bookings: UK 071 724 1000; US toll free 800 221 4542)

ARGENTON-SUR-CREUSE   Manoir de Boisvillers

Simple hotel
Quiet/Gardens/Swimming pool/Parking

An 18th-cent house, a hop-step-and-jump from River Creuse.
Rooms (14) C-D. Cards AE, Access, Visa.
Closed 1st 3 wks January.
Post 11 r. du Moulin de Bord, 36200 Argenton-s-Creuse, Indre.
Tel 54 24 13 88. Mich 97/E1.

CHALLANS   Antiquité

Simple hotel
Quiet/Gardens/Swimming pool/Closed parking

Renovated rooms overlook garden. The family Flaire, all speak
English, also specialise in old fireplaces and *carrelages*. Two of
the children run shops in Atlanta & Jacksonville.
Rooms (16) C-D. Cards All.
Closed Xmas to New Year.
Post 14 r. Galliéni, 85300 Challans, Vendée.
Tel 51 68 02 84. Fax 51 35 55 74. Mich 78/C3.

LA COTINIERE (on Ile d'Oléron)   Motel Ile de Lumière

Comfortable hotel
Secluded/Gardens/Swimming pool/Tennis/Parking

Series of bungalows by sea. Motel? No – otherwise well-named.
Rooms (45) E-F. Cards Access, Visa.
Closed Nov to Mar.
Post La Cotinière, 17310 St-Pierre-d'Oléron, Char.-Mar.
Tel 46 47 10 80. Fax 46 47 30 87. Mich 106/A1.

LA ROCHELLE   Les Brises

Very comfortable hotel
Secluded/Terrace/Lift/Garage/Parking

Five storeys high, exhilarating sea views. Some bathrooms
superb, others pokey. Rest? Readers praise Toque Blanche.
Rooms (48) E-F. Cards Access, Visa. (West of La Rochelle)
Post ch. de la digue Richelieu, 17000 La Rochelle, Char.-Mar.
Tel 46 43 89 37. Fax 46 43 27 97. Mich 92/C3.

LA ROCHELLE   Le Rochelois

Simple hotel
Swimming pool/Tennis/Lift/Garage/Parking

One km west of Les Brises, so same views. Unattractive hotel
but not too expensive. Some rooms have small kitchens. Gym.
Rooms (36) C-D. Disabled. Cards Access, Visa.
Post 66 bd W.Churchill, 17000 La Rochelle, Char.-Mar.
Tel 46 43 34 34. Fax 46 42 10 37. Mich 92/C3.

BELABRE   L'Ecu

Comfortable restaurant with rooms/Cooking 3

I'm delighted that Daniel and Joëlle Cotar's *relais de poste* has
gained deserved recognition from the guides. Classical and
neo-classical specialities: a flavoursome *escalope de sandre au
vinaigre de cidre*, an intensely sauced *filet de boeuf au
Bourgueil* and a light *tarte fine aux pommes à la minute* are
typical. (Their son, Arnaud, worked for Albert Roux.)
Menus B-D. Rooms (6) C-D. Cards All. (Other rooms: see below.)
Closed 2nd half Jan. 2nd half Sept. Sun evg & Mon.
Post 36370 Bélâbre, Indre.
Tel 54 37 60 82. Mich 96/C1. (South-east of Le Blanc.)
An alternative B&B is the most delectable of *chambres d'hôtes*:
an old mill restored by Ren and Willem Wren (Ren's an interior
designer and has worked in the US). Moulin des Chézeaux, 36800
St-Gaultier (W, at Rivarennes); Tel 54 47 01 84; Mich 97/D1.

LE BLANC   Domaine de l'Etape

Comfortable hotel/Cooking 1
Secluded/Gardens/Parking

Delightful Nicole Seiller has made many friends with readers.
The gardens are in fact a 350-acre park. You can fish and boat
on a 40-acre *étang* and horse riding is available all the year.
Dinner only for residents: *Bourgeoise* and modest classical fare
at the low end of price band B (see also L'Ecu above).
Menus B (dinner only). Rooms (30) C-E. Cards All.
Post rte de Bélâbre, 36300 Le Blanc, Indre.
Tel 54 37 18 02. Mich 96/C1. (D10, 6 km SE of Le Blanc.)

BOUHET   Auberge du Vieux Moulin

Comfortable restaurant with rooms/Cooking 1-2
Good value

My *copains* Frank and Shirley Clancy (he designed most of my
book covers; she compiled most of *"So you think you know that
road sign?"*) nosed out this super find near their village home.
Nelly and Stéphane Jacob speak English; both worked in the
UK for a long time. Classical and modern cooking.
Menus B. Rooms (4) B-C. Cards Access, Visa.
Closed Sun evg & Mon (mid Sept to mid June).
Post 17540 Bouhet, Char.-Mar.
Tel 46 68 20 86. Mich 93/E3. (20 km east of La Rochelle.)

BOURCEFRANC   Les Claires

Comfortable hotel/Cooking 2-3
Quiet/Gardens/Swimming pool/Tennis/Parking

This is oyster country: the clue is in the name. Look up
Huîtres in the *Glossary of Menu Terms*. Hardly inspiring *pays*
though the Ile d'Oléron is a short ride away across the toll
bridge (the *péage* is near the hotel). Classical and regional

cooking from Michel Suire and Gérard Touet. Jump into bed with the oyster alternatives (unless, like me, your digestion system had developed an automatic rejection system) and dive into the *poissons* pool; *mouclade* is an absolute must.
Menus B-C. Rooms (48) D-E. Disabled. Cards All.
Post 17560 Bourcefranc, Char.-Mar. (Near D26 toll bridge.)
Tel 46 85 08 01. Telex 792055. Fax 46 85 45 44. Mich 106/B1.

CHALLANS   Le Dauphin

Comfortable restaurant/Cooking 2
Good value

An extremely satisfying discovery, near *la gare* and a short walk from the Base hotel. Martine Daraize runs the *rustique* dining room with an eagle eye; husband Thierry is a competent classicist. One dish is perfection: the perfumed pleasure of a *filet de canard de Challans aux échalotes confites au miel d'acacia* (the Challans area is renowned for its ducks).
Menus A-C. Cards Access, DC, Visa. (Rooms? See Base hotel.)
Closed Sun evg.
Post 40 av. Biochaud, 85300 Challans, Vendée.
Tel 51 93 11 52. Mich 78/C3. (Opposite station.)

CHAUVIGNY   Lion d'Or

Comfortable hotel/Cooking 1
Parking/Good value

You're assured of a warm welcome from the friendly, helpful hosts, Simone and Yves Chartier. Cooking is basic *Bourgeoise* nosh. If you drive a Volvo, or similar, beware the courtyard parking at the rear: one reader counted a 29-point-to-point turn to get his car out. He wondered if it was a new spectator sport? 16 bedrooms are in a modern block at the rear.
Menus A-C. Rooms (26) C. Disabled. Cards Access, Visa.
Closed Mid Dec to mid Jan. Sat (Nov to Mar).
Post 8 rue du Marché, 86300 Chauvigny, Vienne.
Tel 49 46 30 28. Mich 95/F1.

CLISSON   Bonne Auberge

Very comfortable restaurant/Cooking 3-4

An exhilarating find, thanks to an old friend, Colin Pressdee, one of Wales' best chefs. A series of four small dining rooms, under the watchful eye of Chantale Poiron, a delectable hostess. Serge Poiron is an inventive *maître*, though he also makes room on his shelves for a few classics. Simplicity seduces: witness some *queues de langoustines rôties*, a leave-no-morsel *Viennoise de bar, miettes de broche aux épices*, a modern *filet de canard Vendéen aux figues fraîches* and an encore-please *millefeuille au caramel*.
Menus B-D. Cards AE, Visa. (Rooms? Use Gare, 100 metres away)
Closed 15-28 Feb. 8 Aug-1 Sept. Sun evg & Mon (not pub. hols).
Post 1 r. 0. de Clisson, 44190 Clisson, Loire-Atl.
Tel 40 54 01 90. Mich 79/E2. (Park in adjacent *place*.)

CROZANT   Auberge de la Vallée

Comfortable restaurant/Cooking 2
Good value

The "ayes" have rained down in bucketfuls since I tipped this
super *auberge* in a major article. The "eyes" win handsome
dividends too: in the form of the rejuvenating Creuse Valley
and the man-made Lac de Chambon; and in the attractive shapes
of the waitresses dressed in folk costumes Marchois. Jean and
Françoise Guilleminot, helped by daughter Béatrice, complete
the picture with classical and *Bourgeois plats* making
extensive use of local produce: *aloyau Limousin rôti* (prized
beef) and *cèpes du pays* are examples. *Feuilletés au beurre*
feature in many a dish, from starters through to desserts.
Rooms? Use the simple Lac (*sans restaurant*), to the east and
overlooking the Creuse: Rooms (10) B-C. Tel 55 89 81 96.
Menus A-C. Cards AE, Access, Visa. (Rooms? See above.)
Closed Jan. Mon evg & Tues (not July & Aug).
Post 23160 Crozant, Creuse.
Tel 55 89 80 03. Mich 97/E2.

LA FLOTTE (on Ile de Ré)   Richelieu

Very comfortable hotel/Cooking 3
Secluded/Gardens/Swimming pool/Tennis/Parking

Luxury in an elegant ensemble of swish villa and bungalows
overlooking the Pertuis Breton to the north of the Ile de Ré.
Léon Gendre is a savvy hotelier: look after the small details
and you soon have a band of loyal clients. Despite the chef's
name, Dominique Bourgeois, cooking is *haute cuisine* with some
modern touches and local *plats*. A *menu de la mer* includes
mouclade, St-Pierre au beurre d'oseille and an *escalope de lotte
à la vanille*; a representative trio of his repertoire.
Menus C-D. Rooms (37) F-F3. Disabled. Cards Access, Visa.
Closed Rest: 5 Jan to mid Feb.
Post 17630 La Flotte, Char.-Mar.
Tel 46 09 60 70. Telex 791492. Fax 46 09 50 59. Mich 92/C3.

LE GRAND-PRESSIGNY   Espérance

Comfortable restaurant with basic rooms/Cooking 2
Parking/Good value

You'll not find anything bland, prissy or understated here. I
consistently receive praise for the enchanting Paulette Torset
and her hubby, Bernard. Hearty is the word for his classical
cuisine stiffened up by some weightwatchers-beware grub from
another age: a *civet de lapin fermier au vin de rouge de
Touraine* (*en souvenir de nos Grands'-Mères: échalotes, lardons
et champignons*) will keep your wallet unopened for a couple of
days. Ask to see *le potager du restaurant*, one of the best. At
breakfast tuck into Paulette's tasty home-made jams.
Menus A-D. Rooms (10) B. Cards All.
Closed 6 Jan to 6 Feb. Mon (not pub. hols).
Post rte Descartes, 37350 Le Grand-Pressigny, I.-et-L.
Tel 47 94 90 72. Mich 82/B3.

MONTMORILLON　　　　　　　　　France-Mercier

Comfortable hotel/Cooking 2-3
Good value

What an odd-ball mix of reports have come my way about Jean Mercier and his son, Louis. Two readers dispatched Cruise missiles: chop was their verdict. Awful décor and poor lighting. Others praised the long-established France: one reader uses the restaurant as a standard against which he measures others. The family deserve approval for their classical cooking based on regional produce. *Foies-gras* are magnificent; and strong emphasis on lamb and *chèvre* dishes.
Menus B-C. Rooms (25) B-C. Cards All.
Closed Jan. 1 wk June. 1 wk Oct. Sun evg & Mon (not pub hols).
Post 2 bd Strasbourg, 86500 Montmorillon, Vienne.
Tel 49 91 00 51. Fax 49 91 29 03. Mich 96/B2.

MORTAGNE-SUR-SÈVRE France & Rest. La Taverne

Comfortable hotel/Cooking 3
Gardens/Swimming pool (indoor)/Lift/Good value

Guy and Marie-Claude Jagueneau are the fourth generation at the vine-covered hotel, a coaching inn for 400 years. The area is noted for Echiré butter (served as a 10 kg "football" at the table). Guy weighs in, too, with super breads, appetisers, *petits fours* and a faultless show of notable neo-classical and classical *plats*. A simpler restaurant, La Petite Auberge, serves cheaper grub. The pool is a welcome plus at all times.
Menus A-C. Rooms (24) C-D. Cards All.
Closed 27 July to 12 Aug. 20 Dec to 11 Jan. Sat.
Post pl. Dr Pichat, 85290 Mortagne-sur-Sèvre, Vendée.
Tel 51 65 03 37. Fax 51 65 27 83. Mich 80/A2.

PONS　　　　　　　　　　　　　　　Auberge Pontoise

Comfortable hotel/Cooking 3
Terrace/Garage

I've been itching to tell readers about this delectable family *auberge* which I first visited when preparing *En Route* in 1985. I wasn't surprised to see a Michelin star awarded in 1991 for Philippe Chat's assured modern classical repertoire. His wife, Jeanine, has done her bit too: light yet cosy rooms furnished with flair and plenty of flowers in the stylish dining room.
Menus B-D. Rooms (22) C-E. Disabled. Cards AE, Access, Visa.
Closed Sun evg & Mon (15 Sep-June). Mon midday (July-15 Sep).
Post av. Gambetta, 17800 Pons, Char.-Mar. (In Pons: N to N137)
Tel 46 94 00 99. Fax 46 97 33 40. Mich 107/D3. (ER p 100)

PONT-DU-DOGNON　　　　　　　　　　　Rallye

Comfortable hotel/Cooking 1
Secluded/Parking/Good value

Overlooking the River Taurion (here a narrow, winding, man-made lake) the not-so-pretty modern *logis* is a well-liked favourite: for the peace and quiet; above average standards; and for the good value provided by René and Nicole Périéras. *Bourgeoise* cooking with emphasis given to Limousin produce (*cèpes*, *jambon*, *truites* and so on).

Menus A-C. Rooms (20) B-C. Cards Access, Visa.
Closed Mid Oct to Easter. Mon & Tues midday (not high season).
Post Pont-du-Dognon, 87340 St-Laurent-les-Eglises, H.-Vienne.
Tel 55 56 56 11. Mich 110/C1. (NE of Limoges.)

LA ROCHE-L'ABEILLE   Moulin de la Gorce

Very comfortable hotel/Cooking 3-4
Secluded/Gardens/Parking

A preposterously pretty 16th-century *moulin* with an *étang*, cascade and some extravagantly opulent bedrooms (tapestries, antiques, the lot). Jean Bertranet has scuttled some of the hideous combinations he dreamt up a decade ago. His Nineties repertoire is a sensible mix of neo-classical and modern. Desserts, *canapés* and dessert appetisers equal anything the superstar chefs can manage, both in quality and quantity.

Menus B-E. Rooms (9) D-F. Cards All.
Closed 4 Jan to 2 Feb. Sun evg & Mon (mid Sept to Apl).
Post 87800 La Roche-l'Abeille, H.-Vienne. (East of D704.)
Tel 55 00 70 66. Fax 55 00 76 57. Mich 110/B3.

LES SABLES-D'OLONNE   Beau Rivage

Comfortable restaurant with rooms/Cooking 3

Overlooking the beach, the Beau Rivage has won many accolades since *FL3* was published. Maybe, but readers haven't been over-impressed by Joseph Drapeau and his light classical cuisine which, in the main, has a piscatorial influence. One caveat: the bedrooms give me the heebie-jeebies. I dread to think what would happen if there were a fire. (For rooms use Roches Noires, just along the prom, no 12; Tel 51 32 01 71.)

Menus B-E. Rooms (12) C-F. Cards All.
Closed 20 Dec to 20 Jan. 4-14 Oct. Sun evg & Mon.
Post 40 prom. G Clemenceau, 85100 Les Sables-d'Olonne, Vendée.
Tel 51 32 03 01. Fax 51 32 46 48. Mich 92/A1.

LES SABLES-D'OLONNE   La Calypso

Simple restaurant/Cooking 2
Good value

A little Art Deco place where a young couple, Yannick and Joëlle Durand, are slaving away to make a name. Relax in an air-conditioned room and tuck into great value, neo-classical *plats*; super fish specialities are especially appetising. The lower-price menu (around 100 frs) is a steal.

Menus B. Cards AE, Visa.   (Rooms? See above: Roches Noires,
Closed Feb. Sun evg & Mon (Oct-June).   a bracing 5-min walk.)
Post 6 quai Franqueville, 85100 Les Sables-d'Olonne, Vendée.
Tel 51 21 31 57. Mich 92/A1. (Overlooks port; park opp. rest.)

ST-BENOIT   Chalet de Venise

Comfortable restaurant with rooms/Cooking 2
Quiet/Terrace/Gardens/Parking/Good value

Don't be misled by the scruffy exterior. A cool park, shaded by 100-year-old trees, terrace and yard-wide River Miosson are the exterior eye-catchers. Inside, Margaret and chef Serge Mautret seduce with appealing modern cooking: witness a *galette croustillante aux langoustines* and a tasty, unusual *lapin risolle et son jus de vieux Pineau.*
Menus B-C. Rooms (10) B-C. Cards AE, Access, Visa.
Closed Jan. 1st wk Sept. Sun evg & Mon.
Post r. Square, 86280 St-Benoît, Vienne.
Tel 49 88 45 07. Mich 95/E1. (S of Poitiers bypass; W of D741)

ST-ETIENNE-DE-FURSAC   Nougier

Comfortable hotel/Cooking 1-2
Gardens/Garage/Good value

A smart-looking, modern place (used to be called the Moderne), opposite the church and a hop-step-and-jump away from the River Gartempe. Jean-Pierre Nougier walks the classical road: *rognon de veau entier flambé à l'Armagnac, coeur de filet au jus de truffe* and *confit de canard aux cèpes* will ensure you don't leave Nougier with an unfilled hole in your stomach.
Menus A-C. Rooms (12) C-D. Cards DC, Access, Visa.
Closed Dec to Feb. Sun evg & Mon (ex Jul/Aug when Mon midday).
Post 23290 St-Etienne-de-Fursac, Creuse. (S La Souterraine.)
Tel 55 63 60 56. Fax 55 63 65 47. Mich 97/E4.

ST-HILAIRE-LE-CHATEAU   du Thaurion

Comfortable restaurant with rooms/Cooking 3
Terrace/Gardens/Parking/Good value

Here is where, in my opinion, Michelin is guilty of perhaps the worst case of culinary injustice I know of in France. Gérard Fanton, 43 and born in the modest *relais*, is the equal of most one-star chefs I've ever met. He certainly matches any of them for both invention and technical competence; and he beats them all, hands down, for *rapport qualité-prix.*

To do full justice to my cooking rating you'll have to head for his four more expensive menus (B-D); to accept charity feel no shame in electing to order from the two cheapies (A and bottom end of B). The more ambitious menus often include dishes which will leave you scratching your head in wonderment, because they equal anything concocted by rip-off three-star chefs. Super modern cooking with a few Limousin pearls (witness *pâté Creusois aux pommes de terre*). Gérard's wife, dark-haired Marie-Christine, a most unaffected, bright girl, speaks excellent English. The main dining room is now much improved. Snags? Only one; smallish bedrooms.
Menus A-D. Rooms (10) B-C. Cards All.
Closed Xmas week. Jan & Feb. Wed (not May to Sept).
Post 23250 St-Hilaire-le-Château, Creuse.
Tel 55 64 50 12. Fax 55 52 98 75. Mich 111/D1.

Hotels and Restaurants

ST-VINCENT-STERLANGES   Lionel Guilbaud

Comfortable restaurant/Cooking 3
Gardens/Swimming pool/Parking

Readers bullied me into nosing out this Vendée surprise two
years ago. Lionel Guilbaud, together with his wife Josiane,
returned in 1982 to his native *pays*, after a long spell in Paris.
What an immaculate show the duo laid on. On one hand a few
inventive, modern creations; on the other a startling number of
personal interpretations of regional specialities: the *menu
Vendéen* is an unmitigated value-for-money treat. The couple's
great strength, seen at every turn, is quality.
Menus B-D. Cards All. (Rooms? Le Mouton at nearby Chantonnay.)
Closed 1st half Mar. 1st half Oct. Tues evg.
Post 85110 St-Vincent-Sterlanges, Vendée.
Tel 51 40 23 17. Mich 79/F4. (East of La Roche-s-Yon.)

SAINTES   Relais du Bois St-Georges

Very comfortable hotel/Cooking 2
Quiet/Terr/Gardens/Swim pool (indoor)/Garage/Parking

A fabulous *relais* by any measure. West of Saintes and near
the A10 exit, the 37-acre park and *étang* add an extra sparkle
to the man-made comforts: two pavilions house the bedrooms
(the more expensive have individual themes); the indoor pool is
superb; and the classical cooking is entirely adequate (one
spicy variant: tandoori chicken and basmati rice). Another
plus: Bettina Tegeder speaks faultless English. (Right after
toll; 1st right (N150); right at Ibis; right at D137.)
Menus B-E. Rooms (31) F-F2. Disabled. Cards Access, Visa.
Post r. Royan (D137), 17100 Saintes, Char.-Mar. (ER p 99)
Tel 46 93 50 99. Telex 790488. Fax 46 93 50 99. Mich 107/D2.

SEREILHAC   La Meule

Very comfortable restaurant with rooms/Cooking 3
Gardens/Parking

Since *FL3* appeared many readers have written praising the
talents of *cuisinière* Nicole Jouhaud, a lady I had bypassed on
my previous travels. But no longer. I can confirm the N21 now
has at least one redeeming feature: the neo-classical and rich
gutsy Périgord specialities of an extremely capable chef. (Less
expensive rooms? Use the nearby Motel des Tuileries.)
Menus C-D. Rooms (10) D-E. Cards All.
Closed 20 days Jan. Sun evg & Tues (Nov to Easter).
Post 87620 Séreilhac, H.-Vienne.
Tel 55 39 10 08. Fax 55 39 19 66. Mich 110/A2.

SOUBISE   Le Soubise

Comfortable restaurant with rooms/Cooking 2
Gardens/Parking/Good value

I've long been a fan of Lilyane Benoit but even I find it hard to
310

believe that the attractive blond *cuisinière* has been cooking for 38 years. Her repertoire is less ambitious now, a mix of classical and regional: among the latter are *cotriade* and a perfumed cheese dessert, based on *Jonchée*, in an almond sauce. Two gripes: service is haughty; and, apparently, if a client wants salad instead of cheese a swop is not allowed.
Menus B. Rooms (23) B-D. Cards Access, DC, Visa.
Closed 2nd half Jan. Oct. Sun evg & Mon (not July & Aug).
Post 17780 Soubise, Char.-Mar.
Tel 46 84 92 16. Fax 46 84 91 35. Mich 106/B1.

TARNAC   Voyageurs

Simple hotel/Cooking 1-2
Quiet/Good value

Jean Deschamps is the second generation chef at the modest *logis*. With his friendly wife, Ghislaine, the couple have won an enviable reputation with readers since I wrote about them in a major article. Classical and *Bourgeoise* cooking.
Menus A-B. Rooms (17) B-C. Cards Access, Visa.
Closed 20 Dec-10 Jan. Feb sch hols. Sun evg & Mon (Oct-May).
Post 19170 Tarnac, Corrèze. (Park in nearby *place*.)
Tel 55 95 53 12. Fax 55 95 40 07. Mich 111/E2.

VELLUIRE   Auberge de la Rivière

Comfortable restaurant with rooms/Cooking 1-2
Quiet

The site is everything: at the northern *portes* of the Marais Poitevin and alongside the River Vendée. The vine-covered modernised *auberge* is stylishly furnished and decorated. Robert Pajot is *le patron*; his wife, Luce, is an able exponent of classical and *Bourgeoise* cooking. Her fish dishes are exemplary.
Menus A-C. Rooms (11) D. Cards Access, Visa.
Closed Nov sch hols. 20 Dec-31 Jan. Sun evg & Mon(ex Jul/Aug).
Post 85770 Velluire, Vendée. (11 km SW of Fontenay-le-Comte.)
Tel 51 52 32 15. Mich 93/D2.

VIVONNE   La Treille

Simple restaurant with basic rooms/Cooking 2
Terrace/Gardens/Good value

A nondescript village with the luck of having a N10 bypass. But don't whistle past for, hidden in Vivonne opposite the park, is a dedicated couple I love dearly: Geneviève Monteil is the most helpful *patronne* I know; and her classicist hubby, Jacquelin, does as much as anybody to protect and promote regional dishes. You'll need to refer constantly to the regional specialities list: *mouclade*, *embeurrée de choux*, *farci Poitevin*, *mojettes* and *bouilliture* are just a few.
Menus A-B. Rooms (4) A-B. Cards AE, Access, Visa.
Closed 2nd half Feb. 2nd half Oct. Wed.
Post av. Bordeaux, 86370 Vivonne, Vienne. (ER p 97)
Tel 49 43 41 13. Mich 95/D2. (Parking no problem.)

PROVENCE

see page 233
see page 232
see page 138
see page 177
see page 104

20

Montélimar
N102
Rhône
D993
D104
Nyons
D994
Ardèche
Gorges de
l'Ardèche
Buis-les-Baronnies
Vaison-la-Romaine
Bollène
Mont Ventoux
Orange
Alès
Carpentras
A7
Pont
du Gard
Avignon-Nord
Gordes **Roussillon**
N106
Fontaine de Vaucluse
Apt
Avignon-Sud
L'Isle-sur-la-Sorgue
N570
Cavaillon Bonnieux
Nîmes
Lubéron
St-Rémy-de-Provence
Fontvieille
Durance
A51
A9
A55
Mausanne-
Arles **les-Alpilles** **Salon-de-Provence**
Aigues-Mortes
N568
Aix-en-Provence
Camargue
Marignane
A8
A52
Stes-Maries-de-la-Mer
A55
MARSEILLE
Cassis
A50
● Autoroute hotel
■ Base hotel
Méditerranée
0   10   20 Miles
Bandol

"Provence is a country to which I am always returning, next
week, next year, any day now, as soon as I can get on a train."
The late Elizabeth David's words captured succinctly the
fascination that Anglo-Saxons have for Provençale life and
landscapes: brilliant, sensuous light; the reds, ochres and
terracottas of both earth and roof tiles; the scent of wild
flowers, lavender and thyme; shady plane trees, pencil-slim
cypresses and aromatic pines; open-air markets full of produce
with varying perfumes, textures and colours; and food which is
the epitome of common sense and natural tastes.

Many years ago, Simon Elmes, the producer of *Bookshelf*,
introduced me to the works of Marcel Pagnol. The latter's
evocation of Provence, in the earlier decades of this century, is
heady stuff; the two-parter *Jean de Florette* and *Manon des
sources* are now popular classics. The film adaptations of the
novels are masterpieces: their stories of harsh life in the
southern hills of *la langue d'oc* is the essence of what most
French folk ache for, a return to the land, to Nature and to
simple living (with a swimming pool of course). (For "French"
read Anglo-Saxons, too.) Many of us face the same dilemma:
we want to embrace the conveniences of modern-day life, but,
at the same time, our genes remind us constantly of our past
peasant roots. No wonder the French love their second homes.

Few tourists experience Provence at its most cruel. Some
have seen what effect drought can have on both the land and
communities. But have you endured, as we have in mid-winter,
the maniacal *mistral*, sent, roaring and raving, from the
vengeful north to drive southerners mad?

Where do you head for first? There are many riches, both
man-made and natural. I'll start with the latter. Pagnol

▲ see page 233
◄ see page 232
see page 138 ►
◄ see page 177
see page 104 ►

Montélimar

N102

Ardèche Rhône

D104

N106

Alès

D993

D994

N75

Séguret ▲ Vaison-la-Romaine
▲

Orange

Tavel ▲ Gigondas ▲ ▲ Barroux

Castillon-du-Gard △ ▲ Monteux Roussillon
Villeneuve-lès-Avignon ▲ Gordes ▲ △

Avignon Apt

NIMES ▲ Noves L'Isle-sur-la-Sorgue

N570 A7

Fontvieille ▲ ▲ Les Baux-de-Provence
Arles N113 ▲ Durance

A9 A55 Salon-de-Provence

N568 Aix-en-Provence

A8

Stes-Maries-de-la-Mer

A55 Carry-le-Rouet MARSEILLE

A52

A50

▲ Hotel/Rest (rooms)
△ Restaurant only

0   10   20 Miles

Méditerranée

country, east of **Marseille**, includes the Massif de la Sainte
Baume: forests; the pilgrim's cave linked, by legend, with Mary
Magdalene; and the panorama from St-Pilon are three
attractions. See, too, the nearby lunar landscape of the
Montagne Ste-Victoire, Cézanne's *pays*, east of **Aix**; and the
long, deep coves of Les Calanques, protected by high cliffs
(west of **Cassis**). Then head for the Vaucluse.

First to the sulking, sleeping giant of the Montagne du
Lubéron. The massif is a regional nature park, at its most
flamboyant in late spring. Walk the southern slopes and gasp
at the glades of wild flowers: jonquils, irises, grape hyacinths,
dianthus and numerous other varieties blanket the mountain
which itself wears a thick coat of scrub (*garrigue*) and
wildwood. On the northern, mistral-prone slopes, villages like
Ménerbes, Oppède-le-Vieux and **Bonnieux** have changed
dramatically since we first saw them decades ago. Bonnieux
has become too precious, not unlike some Cotswold villages,
and is full of evacuees from northern Europe.

You'll have noted the many orchards in the **Durance** Valley
as you headed north – harvests for **Apt**, renowned for
crystallised fruits. Visit **Roussillon** with its red and ochre
cliffs. **Gordes** has a Vasarély Museum and, dotted around in
the nearby hills, are examples of *bories* – dry-stone, beehive-
shaped dwellings which date back to the Stone Age. After
heavy rain the resurgent spring at the **Fontaine de Vaucluse**
is superb. Seek out also the giant water wheels of **L'Isle-sur-
la-Sorgue**, further downstream.

On to a second hypnotic mountain, the extinct volcanic cone
of **Mont Ventoux**, 6263 ft above sea-level. Drive to the sun-
parched summit in high summer and recall the tragic death of

cyclist Tommy Simpson on the climb in the 1967 Tour de France. All the hills and dales to the north of Ventoux are tonics: drive east from **Buis-les-Baronnies**, famed for its herb market, to the Col de Perty. Visit Nyons, the olive capital, and **Vaison-la-Romaine**, a small-scale Pompeii.

To the far west, on the right bank of the **Rhône**, is more exhilarating terrain. The **Gorges de l'Ardèche** are best seen from the road connecting Pont-St-Esprit and Vallon Pont-d'Arc. The nearby Aven d'Orgnac is a three-star wonder, an exciting cave with colossal stalagmites and halls.

Two remaining natural sites compete to catch your attention. First the jagged outcrop of hills, the Chaîne des Alpilles, to the south of **Avignon**. Walk the single street of **Les Baux**, destroyed by Richelieu in 1632. Marvel at the mighty chambers cut from solid limestone just north of the village. Marvel, too, at the extensive Roman ruins of Les Antiques, between Les Baux and **St-Rémy**. Then continue south, to the lagoons and salt marshes of the **Camargue**, a zoological and botanical nature reserve which is famed for its wild flowers, white horses, bulls, herons, flamingoes and other wild life.

What of Provence's man-made treasures? They come thick and fast; I can only list a few. Buy a Michelin green guide.

Not surprisingly ancient Rome plays a significant part. **Arles** has happy memories for both of us: the arena is older than Rome's Colosseum; the Théâtre Antique must once have been a handsome semi-circular auditorium (relax in the adjoining small and pretty park); and, from a dozen centuries later, the cloisters of St-Trophime are exquisite.

Nîmes is also extravagantly endowed: a gigantic Roman arena, perhaps the best preserved of all; the Maison Carrée, a small but perfectly balanced temple; and the Jardin de la Fontaine, created 200 years ago. Avignon has a papal palace within its walls and much else besides: museums, *églises* and old streets galore. **Orange** is the home of the best preserved and most handsome of all Roman theatres and a splendid Triumphal Arch. The **Pont du Gard** aqueduct and bridge is just as breathtaking, truly one of the wonders of the world and quite sensational, in both engineering and architectural terms.

Drive, if you must, to the heart of Marseille and its bustling old port; I'd plump instead for aristocratic **Aix-en-Provence**, a city of fountains and shady streets, ancient houses and museums. And I'd not miss **Aigues-Mortes** with its ramparts and towers and a great circular keep; it was once a port until the sea receded.

Finally, some tips about four interesting shops. If you want excellent olive oil seek out the village of Mouriès, on the road between **Salon-de-Provence** and St-Rémy. On the Salon side, just past the Esso garage, turn right for the *"Moulin à huile d'olives coopératif"* (open Wed and Sat afternoons and Sun morning); take a container. In St-Rémy *"L'Herbier de Provence"* is full of heady aromas; and the *"Lilamand"* enterprise specialises in *fruits confits*. La Riboto, the Novi restaurant at Les Baux, stocks both the best local wines and the finest marinaded olives you'll ever taste.

Markets Aix-en-Provence (Mon, Tues and Thurs to Sun); Arles (Wed and Sat); Avignon (Tues to Sun); Buis-les-Baronnies (Wed); Cavaillon (Mon); Carpentras (Fri); Fontvieille (Mon and Fri); St-Rémy-de-Provence (Wed and Sat); Salon-de-Provence (Wed and Fri to Sun).
Michelin green guide: Provence (in English).

Cheeses **Goat's milk**
Please also see neighbouring regions for details of their cheeses
Picodon de Valréas soft, nutty-tasting, small disk
> **Ewe's milk**
Brousse du Rove creamy and mild-flavoured cheese; best in the winter
Cachat also known as **Tomme du Mont Ventoux**. A summer season;
very soft, sweet and creamy flavour

Regional Specialities
Please see the specialities listed in the Côte d'Azur

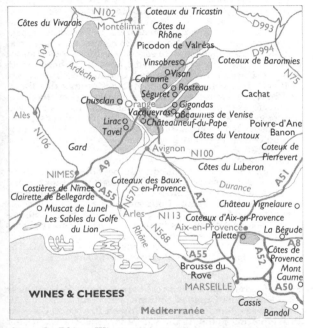

Côtes du Rhône Wines (Great vintages: northern Côtes du Rhône
78 79 82 85 89 90; southern Côtes du Rhône **78 79 90**)
At the northern end of the Rhône Valley, near Vienne, is the **Côte
Rôtie** – the home of fine, heady red wines. The home also of two
superb whites, **Condrieu** and **Château-Grillet** (see Lyonnais).
　　Further south, from Tain-l'Hermitage (**AC Hermitage**, a
wonderful wine and **AC Crozes-Hermitage**, a less-good, junior
brother), **Saint Joseph** and **Cornas**, all north of Valence, you will
find some ruby-red wines, dark and powerful. The best of the
Rhône reds are made from the Syrah grape. There are also
great dry whites from the same area: a **Hermitage Blanc** (the
best is **Chante-Alouette**), a **Saint Péray** white and a **Saint
Péray mousseux**. Some whites take the **Crozes-Hermitage**
AC. Refer to Ardèche (Massif Central) wine map and notes.
　　South-east of Valence, at **Die**, you'll find the lovely **Clairette
de Die mousseux**; Clairette grapes for the *brut* version and
mainly Muscat for the *demi-sec*. Near Die are the wines of all
shades from **Châtillon-en-Diois** (see Hautes-Alpes map). To the
south of Valence, near Montélimar, is the **AC Coteaux du**

315

Tricastin and its rosés and reds (see Massif Central notes).

From the southern end of the Rhône Valley come some of the best wines in the region, particularly at **Châteauneuf-du-Pape** (with its own AC), a strong, full-bodied red. **Gigondas** (with its own AC) and **Vacqueyras** are both red and very similar to Châteauneuf-du-Pape; the **Lirac** red is now considered important and look out, too, for the very rare white.

Tavel was the pioneer among rosés and nearby Lirac makes another famous one; both are among the best. The Tavel rosé, slightly orange in colour, is made from the Grenache grape.

A fine wine from the pretty area just west of Mont Ventoux is **Muscat de Beaumes de Venise**, a delicious, honey-sweet dessert wine (made from the Muscat grape). A similar wine comes from nearby **Rasteau** (made from the Grenache grape).

Many cheaper wines, mainly reds, come from the fringe areas on both the eastern and western edges of the Rhône Valley: among them the **Côtes du Ventoux** and **Côtes du Lubéron** (both AC) and **Côtes du Vivarais** and **Coteaux de Pierrevert** (both VDQS). Another small AC area is **Coteaux des Baux-de-Provence** – wines of all shades but rarely seen other than locally: for example the Château d'Estoublon rosé is excellent (the property is west of Maussane); so are the reds of the Domaine de Trévallon (north of Les Baux on the D27) and the Mas du Cellier (owned by Englishman, James Baring; south of the D99 between St-Rémy-de-Provence and Eygalières).

The *generic* AC classifications for the whole Rhône area are **Côtes du Rhône** and **Côtes du Rhône-Villages**. 14 villages can show their names coupled with the former AC: **Chusclan** and **Laudun** in the *département* of Gard; **Cairanne**, **Vacqueyras**, **Rasteau**, **Valréas**, **Visan**, **Roaix** and **Séguret** in Vaucluse; **St-Maurice-sur-Aygues**, **Rousset**, **Rochegude**, **St-Pantaléon-les-Vignes** and **Vinsobres** in Drôme; wines of this type pass the tough test of having at least 12.5 per cent alcohol as against the 11 per cent of the Côtes du Rhône-Villages AC. The main grape for all these southern reds is the Grenache.

Provence Wines

Fresh, fragrant whites and rosés are made at **Palette** (near Aix – look out for **Château Simone**, a property within this AC area), **Cassis**, **Bandol**, **Coteaux d'Aix-en-Provence**, **Côtes de Provence** and **Bellet** (in the Var Valley; see Côte d'Azur). For details of **Costières de Nîmes** and **Clairette de Bellegarde** – shown on the map – see Languedoc-Roussillon.

Many fine reds originate from the areas above: **Château Vignelaure**, near Rians, is especially good; as are the **Bandol** reds (try the Domaine de Terrebrune).

Vins de Pays

You will encounter sound wines, of all shades. **Vin de Pays des Sables du Golfe du Lion** (around Aigues-Mortes) is good; so is the **Vin de Pays du Vaucluse** (the *département* name). Two other area classifications are **Les Maures** (near St-Tropez; Côte d'Azur) and **Mont Caume** (Toulon).

If you see the label **Vin de Pays d'Oc** this will mean the wine can have originated in any of five *départements*: Ardèche, Drôme, Var, Bouches-du-Rhône or Vaucluse; or four *départements* to the south-west – see Languedoc. Labels may give the *département* name or, in the case of Gard, it may be identified by one of no less than 11 small area names – **Coteaux du Salavès** is just one. **Vin de Pays des Coteaux de Baronnies** (Drôme) borders some of the best Rhône areas.

AIX-EN-PROVENCE   Ibis

Simple hotel/Cooking 1
Terrace/Gardens/Lift/Parking/Good value

Leave A8 Aix-Est/Les 3 Sautets exit. Left at island, left next island, cross over A8, hotel on left (south side of autoroute).
Menus A-B. Rooms (83) C-D. Disabled. Cards Access, Visa.
Post 13100 Aix-en-Provence, B.-du-R. (En Route p 70)
Tel 42 27 98 20. Telex 420519. Fax 42 38 50 76. Mich 159/E3.
(Bookings: UK 071 724 1000; US toll free 800 221 4542)

AIX-EN-PROVENCE   Novotel Beaumanoir

Very comfortable hotel/Cooking 1
Terrace/Swimming pool/Lift/Parking

Exit details as above. Don't cross over A8; on north side.
Menus B. Rooms (102) E. Disabled. Cards All.
Post 13100 Aix-en-Provence, B.-du-R. (En Route p 70)
Tel 42 27 47 50. Telex 400244. Fax 42 38 46 41. Mich 159/E3.
(Bookings: UK 071 724 1000; US toll free 800 221 4542)

AVIGNON-SUD   Climat de France La Cristole

Simple hotel/Cooking 1
Parking/Good value

A7 Avignon-Sud exit. Right at N7. Continue on N7; hotel (first of two Climats) on right, after Citroën garage.
Menus A-B. Rooms (40) C. Disabled. Cards AE, Access, Visa.
Post Clos de la Cristole, 84145 Montfavet, Vaucluse. (ER p 65)
Tel 90 88 15 00. Telex 431063. Mich 158/B1.
(Bookings: UK 071 287 3181)

AVIGNON-SUD   Ibis

Simple hotel/Cooking 1
Swimming pool/Closed parking/Good value

See above. Near Climat. Rest shut Sat lun & Sun (Nov to Mar).
Menus A-B. Rooms (96) C-D. Disabled. Cards Access, Visa.
Post Clos de la Cristole, 84140 Avignon, Vaucluse. (ER p 65)
Tel 90 87 11 00. Telex 432811. Fax 90 87 70 88. Mich 158/B1.
(Bookings: UK 071 724 1000; US toll free 800 221 4542)

AVIGNON-SUD   Mercure

Very comfortable hotel/Cooking 1-2
Terrace/Swimming pool/Lift

See above. On left past Novotel, Ibis and both Climats.
Menus B-C. Rooms (105) F. Disabled. Cards All.
Post rte Marseille, 84000 Avignon, Vaucluse (ER p 65)
Tel 90 88 91 10. Telex 431994. Fax 90 87 61 88. Mich 158/B1.
(Bookings: UK 071 724 1000; US toll free 800 221 4542)

AVIGNON-SUD
Novotel Avignon Sud

Very comfortable hotel/Cooking 1
Terrace/Gardens/Swimming pool/Closed parking

See previous entry. On left of N7, past Ibis & Climats.
Menus B. Rooms (79) E. Disabled. Cards All.
Post rte Marseille, 84000 Avignon, Vaucluse. (ER p 66)
Tel 90 87 62 36. Telex 432878. Fax 90 88 38 47. Mich 158/B1.
(Bookings: UK 071 724 1000; US toll free 800 221 4542)

AVIGNON-NORD
Novotel Avignon Nord

Very comfortable hotel/Cooking 1
Terrace/Gardens/Swim pool/Tennis/Lift/Closed parking

A7 Avignon-Nord exit. Through toll, keep right. West of A7.
Menus B. Rooms (100) E. Disabled. Cards All.
Post 84700 Sorgues, Vaucluse. (ER p 66; previously Sofitel)
Tel 90 31 16 43. Telex 432869. Fax 90 32 22 21. Mich 158/B1.
(Bookings: UK 071 724 1000; US toll free 800 221 4542)

BOLLENE
Campanile

Simple hotel/Cooking 1
Parking/Good value

A7 Bollène exit. After toll left, north on D26; on right.
Menus A-B. Rooms (30) C. Disabled. Cards Access, Visa.
Post 84500 Bollène, Vaucluse. (En Route p 64)
Tel 90 40 44 44. Telex 432017. Fax 90 40 07 63. Mich 144/B2.
(Bookings: UK freephone 0800 897863)

MARIGNANE
Climat de France

Simple hotel/Cooking 1
Parking/Good value

A7 Marignane/Aéroport exit. Head west, keeping right in 2 km.
Hotel on right, opposite spur to airport terminal and Sofitel.
Menus A-B. Rooms (80) C. Disabled. Cards AE, Access, Visa.
Post 13127 Vitrolles, B.-du-R. (En Route p 68)
Tel 42 75 23 00. Telex 402031. Mich 159/D4.
(Bookings: UK 071 287 3181)

MARIGNANE
Sofitel

Luxury hotel/Cooking 1-2
Terrace/Gardens/Swimming pool/Tennis/Lift/Parking

A7 Marignane/Aéroport exit. Head west, keeping right in 2 km.
Hotel on right of spur road to airport terminal.
Menus B. Rooms (180) F. Disabled. Cards All.
Post 13700 Marignane, B.-du-R. (En Route p 68)
Tel 42 78 42 78. Telex 401980. Fax 42 78 42 70. Mich 159/D4.
(Bookings: UK 071 724 1000; US toll free 800 221 4542)

NIMES Ibis

Simple hotel/Cooking 1
Lift/Parking/Good value

Leave A9 Nîmes-Ouest exit (also junc. A9/A54). Through toll;
keep going right to Ibis and other hotels.
Menus A. Rooms (108) C-D. Disabled. Cards Access, Visa.
Post Parc Hôtelier, 30900 Nîmes, Gard. (ER p 81)
Tel 66 38 00 65. Telex 490180. Fax 66 29 19 56. Mich 157/E2.
(Bookings: UK 071 724 1000; US toll free 800 221 4542)

NIMES Novotel Nîmes Ouest

Very comfortable hotel/Cooking 1
Terrace/Gardens/Swimming pool/Closed parking

See exit details above.
Menus B. Rooms (96) E. Disabled. Cards All.
Post Parc Hôtelier, 30900 Nîmes, Gard. (ER p 81)
Tel 66 84 60 20. Telex 480675. Fax 66 38 02 31. Mich 157/E2.
(Bookings: UK 071 724 1000; US toll free 800 221 4542)

ORANGE Campanile

Simple hotel/Cooking 1
Parking/Good value

A7/A9 Orange exit. Through toll, left at D17, left again.
Menus A-B. Rooms (43) C. Disabled. Cards Access, Visa.
Post rte Caderousse, 84100 Orange, Vaucluse.
Tel 90 51 68 68. Telex 431885. Fax 90 34 04 67. Mich 144/B4.
(Bookings: UK freephone 0800 897863)

ORANGE Ibis

Simple hotel/Cooking 1
Terrace/Swimming pool/Parking/Good value

As above; north of D17. Rest shut Sun lun & Sat (Nov to Feb).
Menus A. Rooms (72) C-D. Disabled. Cards Access, Visa.
Post rte Caderousse, 84100 Orange, Vaucluse.
Tel 90 34 35 35. Telex 432752. Fax 90 34 96 47. Mich 144/B4.
(Bookings: UK 071 724 1000; US toll free 800 221 4542)

SALON-DE-PROVENCE Ibis

Simple hotel/Cooking 1
Terrace/Gardens/Swimming pool/Parking/Good value

From A7 west on A54: Salon-Sud from north; Salon from south.
At toll right (Pélissanne). On right. Rest shut Sat/Sun lunch.
Menus A. Rooms (60) C-D. Disabled. Cards AE, Access, Visa.
Post 13300 Salon-de-Provence, B.-du-R. (En Route p 67)
Tel 90 42 23 57. Telex 441591. Fax 90 42 10 17. Mich 158/C3.
(Bookings: UK 071 724 1000; US toll free 800 221 4542)

Base Hotels

ARLES   D'Arlatan

Very comfortable hotel
Quiet/Gardens/Lift/Garage

A 15th-century delight in a quiet side street. Well liked. Some
rooms smallish. No lounges. Gardens/courtyard cool pluses.
Rooms (31) E-F. Cards All.
Post 26 rue du Sauvage, 13631 Arles, B.-du-R.
Tel 90 93 56 66. Telex 441203. Fax 90 49 68 45. Mich 158/A2.

ARLES   La Roseraie

Simple hotel
Quiet/Gardens/Closed parking/Good value

A big favourite. Mme Villa, a "pleasant martinet", runs a tight
ship. She's also proud of her prize-winning flowers.
Rooms (12) C-D. Cards All. (2 km south-east of Arles)
Closed Mid Oct to mid March.
Post Pont de Crau, 13200 Arles, B.-du-R.
Tel 90 96 06 58. Mich 158/A2.

BANDOL   Golf-Hôtel

Simple hotel
Fairly quiet/Gardens/Parking

On the beach west of Bandol. The hotel's toes are in the sands
of the Plage Renecros; ideal for children.
Rooms (20) D-E. Cards Access, Visa.
Closed Nov to Easter.
Post plage Renecros, 83150 Bandol, Var.
Tel 94 29 45 83. Telex 400383. Mich 160/B4.

FONTVIEILLE   St-Victor

Very comfortable hotel
Secluded/Gardens/Swimming pool/Parking

A new discovery. An elevated site to the south of the D17, on
the road to Arles. Daudet's *moulin* and museum to the east.
Rooms (10) E-F. Cards All.
Post ch. des Fourques, 13990 Fontvieille, B.-du-R.
Tel 90 54 66 00. Mich 158/B2.

GORDES   Le Gordos

Comfortable hotel
Quiet/Swimming pool/Parking

Modern stone building on the southern approach to the village.
Rooms (18) F. Cards AE, Access, Visa.
Closed Nov to Feb.
Post 84220 Gordes, Vaucluse.
Tel 90 72 00 75. Mich 159/D1.

L'ISLE-SUR-LA-SORGUE   Les Névons

Comfortable hotel
Quiet/Swimming pool/Lift/Garage/Parking/Good value

The waterwheels town. South of the main street, near the River
Sorgue. Handsome trees; pity about the ugly concrete hotel.
Rooms (26) C-D. Cards Access, Visa.
Closed Mid Dec to mid Jan.
Post ch. Névons, 84800 L'Isle-sur-la-sorgue, Vaucluse.
Tel 90 20 72 20. Mich 158/C1.

MAUSSANE-LES-ALPILLES   Pré des Baux

Comfortable hotel
Quiet/Gardens/Swimming pool/Closed parking

Another marvellous find. Single storey with rooms overlooking
the pool and gardens. South of the main road. Cool and quiet.
Rooms (10) E-F. Disabled. Cards Access, Visa.
Closed Jan to Easter.
Post r. Vieux Moulin, 13520 Maussane-les-Alpilles, B.-du-R.
Tel 90 54 40 40. Mich 158/B2.

MAUSSANE-LES-ALPILLES   Touret

Comfortable hotel
Quiet/Swimming pool/Parking/Good value

West of the village. Unresponsive, unfriendly owners.
Rooms (16) C-D. Cards Access, DC, Visa.
Post 13520 Maussane-les-Alpilles, B.-du-R.
Tel 90 54 31 93. Fax 90 54 42 44. Mich 158/B2.

ORANGE   Mas des Aigras

Comfortable hotel
Secluded/Gardens/Swimming pool/Tennis/Parking

Recommended by many readers (base for British tour operator).
The gardens and small stone Provençal *mas* appeal, as does
the site, to the west of the N7 and north of Orange.
Rooms (7) D-E. Cards Access, Visa.
Post ch. des Aigras, 84100 Orange, Vaucluse.
Tel 90 34 81 01. Mich 144/B3.

ROUSSILLON   Résidence des Ocres

Comfortable hotel
Quiet/Garage/Parking/Good value

Useful for David restaurant. Air-conditioned bedrooms.
Rooms (16) C-D. Cards Access, Visa.
Closed Mid Nov to 21 Dec. 13 Jan to mid Feb
Post rte de Gordes, 84220 Roussillon, Vaucluse.
Tel 90 05 60 50. Mich 159/D1.

Base Hotels

ST-REMY-DE-PROVENCE
Canto Cigalo

Comfortable hotel
Secluded/Gardens/Closed parking/Good value

Recommended by many readers. Dominique and Claude Flogeac's base is a haven of peace; the gardens have been especially appreciated. East of the town and south of the D99.
Rooms (20) C-D. Cards Access, Visa.
Closed Mid Nov to Feb.
Post ch. Canto Cigalo, 13210 St-Rémy-de-Provence, B.-du-R.
Tel 90 92 14 28. Mich 158/B2.

ST-REMY-DE-PROVENCE
Soleil

Comfortable hotel
Quiet/Gardens/Swim pool/G'ge/Cl'd parking/Good value

An oasis of calm, consistently liked by readers. A flourishing family affair which I've seen develop over 20 years. Joseph Denante's daughter, Françoise, now runs the hotel with her husband, Guy Monset. South of the town, away from the road.
Rooms (18) C-D. Cards AE, Access, Visa.
Closed Mid Nov to mid March.
Post av. Pasteur, 13210 St-Rémy-de-Provence, B.-du-R.
Tel 90 92 00 63. Mich 158/B2.

ST-REMY-DE-PROVENCE
Van Gogh

Comfortable hotel
Quiet/Gardens/Swimming pool/Parking/Good value

A more modern building than the Soleil; to the east of St-Rémy and north of the D99. Shame about the inadequate breakfasts and the utterly anonymous owners. Three restaurants have been regularly applauded: Bistrot des Alpilles and La Gousse d'Ail in the town; and the Bistrot de Paradou at Paradou, just west of Maussane-les-Alpilles. (See page 479: Aux Deux Soeurs.)
Rooms (18) C-D. Cards Access, Visa.
Closed Mid Nov to Feb.
Post av. J.Moulin, 13210 St-Rémy-de-Provence, B.-du-R.
Tel 90 92 14 02. Mich 158/B2.

STES-MARIES-DE-LA-MER
Mas des Rièges

Comfortable hotel
Secluded/Gardens/Swimming pool/Closed parking

The best of my new base hotels in Provence. Literally an island of tranquillity just north of the town (off D85A), the latter tagged by a reader: "Often looks like a French version of Margate in full spate." Single storey where the pool is both a sun and perfume trap. The Camargue at its most alluring.
Rooms (16) E. Cards AE, Access, Visa.
Closed Nov to Easter.
Post rte de Cacharel, 13460 Stes-Mairies-de-la-Mer, B.-du-R.
Tel 90 97 85 07. Mich l57/E4.

BARROUX   Géraniums

Comfortable hotel/Cooking 1-2
Quiet/Terrace/Gardens/Parking/Good value

The views, *les terrasses*, medieval village and good value are
the reasons for seeking out Agnes and Jacques Roux's *logis*:
the Dentelles de Montmirail are to the N; the sullen cone of
Ventoux to the E. Take dark glasses: the colour pink over-
whelms you. Smallish bedrooms and a cavernous dining room
with zero charm. *Bourgeoise*, classical and Provençal *plats*.
Menus A-C. Rooms (22) B-C. Cards All.
Closed 5 Jan to 15 Feb. Wed (Oct to Mar).
Post 84330 Barroux, Vaucluse. (NE of Carpentras.)
Tel 90 62 41 08. Fax 90 62 56 48. Mich 144/C3.

LES BAUX-DE-PROVENCE   Mas d'Aigret

Comfortable hotel/Cooking 3
Quiet/Terrace/Gardens/Swimming pool/Parking

Patrick and Janet Rance (the duo who created that masterpiece,
The French Cheese Book (see p 19) and who live nearby) led me
to this tremendous hotel a few months after Englishman Pip
Philipps (Patrick Ivor) and his French wife, Chantal, bought
the property in 1989. Like Lindsay Germain at Montreuil, it's
Pip who makes the place buzz. Pip, Chantal, her brother Fred
Laloy, and a brilliant young modern *maître* of a chef, Pascal
Johnson, are a formidable *équipe*. On the eastern flanks of Les
Baux, the 250-year-old farmhouse (*mas*) has its back in the
limestone rocks; indeed many of the rooms are troglodyte. The
modern cooking is most certainly up to Michelin one-star
standard and exceptional use is made of regional produce. The
mas is a popular British tour operator's base hotel.
Menus C-E. Rooms (14) E-F. Cards All.
Closed Jan to end Feb. Rest: Wed midday.
Post 13520 Les Baux-de-Provence, B.-du-R. (To E; on D27A.)
Tel 90 54 33 54. Fax 90 54 41 37. Mich 158/B2.

LES BAUX-DE-PROVENCE   La Riboto de Taven

Very comfortable restaurant with rooms/Cooking 3
Secluded/Terrace/Gardens/Parking

The intriguing name gives one clue to the restaurant's appeal:
taven in Mistral's works is a "fairy"; *la riboto* a "feast of the
table". The garden, a riot-of-colour oasis in the Val d'Enfer
(Hell), is dominated by rock faces to both sides.
    Jean Pierre and Claire Novi (who made many English
friends during their years at Southbourne and Gordleton) have
returned to his parents' long established home (Louisette, his
mother, was born in the house, once a farm), teaming up with
his delectable sister, Christine, who runs the dining room, and
her husband, Philippe Thème. The two men man the stoves
(with minimal help) and, aided by an enterprising supply of
local vegetables grown specially for them, conjure up a *cuisine
libre* of modern and Provençale specialities.
    One new surprise: two huge, stunning troglodyte bedrooms.

323

Hotels and Restaurants

Ask to see them even if you don't stay: marvel at the fossils and the Roman reservoir. "Treated like Royalty" and "passed the patience test with children" are among some of the more unusual plaudits sent my way. Bibendum: why no red rocking chair symbol? If Oustaù earns one, so should Riboto.
Menus D-E. Rooms (3) F. Cards All.
Closed 15 Jan-15 Mar. Tues evg (not high season). Wed.
Post 13520 Les Baux-de-Provence, B.-du-R.
Tel 90 54 34 23. Fax 90 54 38 88. Mich 158/B2.

CARRY-LE-ROUET   L'Escale

Very comfortable restaurant/Cooking 3-4
Terrace/Gardens

Dany and Gérard Clor's Thirties-style restaurant has one of the most impressive settings on the French Mediterranean. A series of terraces overlook the port and distant views stretch as far as Cap Croisette, beyond Marseille. Dany is a sparkling hostess and Gérard's neo-classical cooking complements her personality. Enjoy the fish *plats*; the choice is tantalising. Save some extra francs and tuck into the chef's *bouillabaisse* (minimum 2 persons; about 300 francs each); a formidable price but a superb repast. No bedrooms, alas, but several hotels at Marignane (Marseille airport), an easy, 9-mile drive. See A/R hotels; there's also a Novotel and Ibis. (En Route p 68.)
Menus D-F. Cards Access, Visa. (Rooms? See above.)
Closed Nov-Jan. Mon *midi* (Jul/Aug). Sun evg & Mon(rest of yr).
Post 13620 Carry-le-Rouet, B.-du-R.
Tel 42 45 00 47. Fax 42 44 72 69. Mich 159/D4.

CASTILLON-DU-GARD   Serge Lanoix

Comfortable restaurant/Cooking 4

My confidence in Serge Lanoix is total: he's a chef who is certain to become a huge culinary talent. Bras, Silva, Jeunet, Henriroux: all were first encountered before the major guides woke up to their extraordinary talents. Lanoix is another.
   I first met English-speaking Serge at Gevrey-Chambertin seven years ago, after he had taken over at the Rôtisserie following the death of Céline Menneveau. In 1989, with help and encouragement from his mother, he set off on his own, converting a small medieval ruined "manger" into a stylish restaurant home. Freedom and maturity (he's still on the right side of 40) have unleashed locked-away genius. Anne and I were rendered speechless by a series of audacious modern dishes: a roasted *foie gras de canard*, soft on the inside and served with pumpkin, apple and elderberries; a *homard* soup with *rouille*; an out-of-this-world *boudinets de truffes noires et blanches* (from nearby Alès) in a *bouillon* of truffles; and the tenderest *chevreuil*. Who wants to waste money at three-star shrines when talent like this exists? (Rooms? See A/R & Base hotels; a longish but safe and easy drive to several of them.)
Menus B-D. Cards All. (ER p 80; next door to Vieux Castillon.)
Closed 1-10 Nov. 2 Jan-2 Feb. Tues & Wed midday (Oct to Mar).
Post 30210 Castillon-du-Gard, Gard. (Parking no problem.)
Tel 66 37 05 04. Fax 66 37 25 94. Mich 157/F1.

FONTVIEILLE   La Regalido

Very comfortable hotel/Cooking 3
Quiet/Terrace/Gardens/Parking

I'm still wondering how so many beguiling pluses can be packed into such a tiny area. The converted oil mill is hemmed in on all sides. Yet both the bucket-of-colour garden and the stylish interior are hard to beat; the sheer compactness of Regalido (re-awakened flame of the fire) concentrates the senses wonderfully well. Classical cooking with four menus: fish; regional; *haute cuisine*; and, a surprise, *Du Sud-Ouest*.
Menus C-E. Rooms (14) F-F2. Cards All.
Closed Dec. Jan. Rest: Mon (not evg July-Sept). Tues midday.
Post 13990 Fontvieille, B.-du-R.
Tel 90 54 60 22. Telex 441150. Fax 90 54 64 29. Mich 158/B2.

GIGONDAS   Les Florets

Comfortable restaurant with rooms/Cooking 2
Secluded/Terrace/Gardens/Parking/Good value

A trickle of gripes over 10 years has spoilt what would have been a first-class record. Readers love the shaded terrace in the heat of the afternoon and, under lights, at dinner; the service is mixed with "off-hand" surfacing regularly; and the grub – classical, regional and *Bourgeoise* – ranges from OK to very good. The Bernard family also sell their own wines.
Menus B. Rooms (13) D. Cards All.
Closed Jan. Feb. Tues evg (not high season). Wed.
Post 84190 Gigondas, Vaucluse. (E of village.)
Tel 90 65 85 01. Fax 90 65 83 80. Mich 144/C3 (shown on map).

GORDES   La Mayanelle

Comfortable restaurant with rooms/Cooking 1-2
Quiet/Good value

Don't be put off by the exterior. You walk down a flight of stairs to the dining room. French cuisine as she exclusively was just three decades ago: classical and regional with no punkish monstrosities. Original raw flavours; honest, copious servings; *tapénade* and *salade Niçoise*; and a stunning view of both the sulking Lubéron and Mayle's Ménerbes terrain.
Menus B-C. Rooms (10) C-D. Cards All.
Closed 3 Jan to 3 Mar. Tues.
Post 84220 Gordes, Vaucluse.
Tel 90 72 00 28. Mich 159/D1.

L'ISLE-SUR-LA-SORGUE   Mas de Cure Bourse

Comfortable restaurant with rooms/Cooking 2-3
Secluded/Terrace/Gardens/Swimming pool/Parking

The *mas* (farmhouse) is lost in the maze of rich market-garden fields to the south-west of the town; once a *relais de poste* and now the home of *cuisinière* Françoise Donzé. Neo-classical and

regional *plats* and a welcome number of light fish dishes: try her seafood salad; a *filet de rascasse coulis de crabe*; and a goat's cheese, coated in hazelnuts and deep fried.
Menus B-C. Rooms (13) D-F. Cards All. (See also Base hotel.)
Post 84800 L'Isle-sur-la-Sorgue, Vaucluse.
Tel 90 38 16 58. Mich 158/C1. (S of D25; W of D31 bypass.)

MONTEUX   Blason de Provence

Comfortable hotel/Cooking 2
Terrace/Gardens/Swim pool/Tennis/Parking/Good value

1988 brought a happy change at this attractive hotel (in *FL3* La Genestière): new owners arrived. English-speaking Joan and Roger Duvillet are keen as mustard, determined and charming. I receive only the occasional negative report: far more typical is the comment "we were thoroughly spoilt". Classical cooking; the two lower-priced menus (B) are good value for money.
Menus B-C. Rooms (20) C-D. Cards All.
Closed Jan. Rest: Sat midday & Sun evg out of season.
Post 84170 Monteux, Vaucluse. (E of town, towards Carpentras.)
Tel 90 66 31 34. Fax 90 66 83 05. Mich 144/C4.

NOVES   Auberge de Noves

Luxury hotel/Cooking 3
Secluded/Terr/Gardens/Swim pool/Tennis/Lift/Parking

If the Garden of Eden is in France, then search no further than Noves. Expensive? Of course. But many readers are unanimous: this is their number one favourite. Even if you can't stay (plenty of nearby Base hotels) then try a lunch on the exquisite terrace; worth every penny. English-speaking André Lalleman, the perfect *patron*, now has the help of his young son, Robert, in the kitchen. A long training has set him up well. Neo-classical cooking which is consistently delicious (sometimes too complicated but time will bring increased confidence, the prerequisite for *faites simple*).
Menus D-E. Rooms (23) F2-F3. Disabled. Cards All.
Closed Jan to mid Feb. Rest: Wed (not evgs 15 Mar-15 Oct).
Post 13550 Noves, B.-du-R. (NW of village; on D28.) (ER p 65)
Tel 90 94 19 21. Telex 431312. Fax 90 94 47 76. Mich 158/B1.

ROUSSILLON   David

Comfortable restaurant/Cooking 1-2
Terrace/Good value

Jean David's restaurant sits atop one of the pupil-piercing red and ochre cliffs which make the village so famous. Classical and *Bourgeoise* cuisine and there's also a so-called regional menu (*daube de boeuf à la provençale* and so on). Good value applies only to the two B menus. Colourful views.
Menus B-D. Cards Access, DC, Visa. (Rooms? See Base hotel.)
Closed 25 Nov to 18 Dec. 3 Feb to 8 Mar. Mon & Tues.
Post place de la Poste, 84220 Roussillon, Vaucluse.
Tel 90 05 60 13. Mich 159/D1.

STES-MARIES-DE-LA-MER   Mas de la Fouque

Very comfortable hotel/Cooking 2
Secluded/Terrace/Gardens/Swimming pool/Tenn/Parking

An ultra-swish, ultra-modern, single-storey, whitewashed ranch in its own 13 acres of the Camargue. Relax and do your bird and flamingo watching alongside the hotel's own *étangs*. Exercise? Then riding (on some of the famed white horses) is on tap, literally almost from your bedroom doorstep. All this opulent convenience has a price: swallow hard before you refer to the room price bands. Cooking is straightforward classical and neo-classical, based on produce such as Sisteron lamb and Angus beef. The ubiquitous *tarte Tatin* makes an appearance, having migrated south from the *étangs* of the Sologne.
Menus C-D. Rooms (13) F2-F4. Cards All. (See also Base hotel.)
Closed 4 Jan to 20 Mar. Rest: Tues (not pub. hols).
Post 13460 Stes-Maries-de-la-Mer, B.-du-R. (D38, 4km to NW.)
Tel 90 97 81 02. Telex 403155. Fax 90 97 96 84. Mich 157/E3.

STES-MARIES-DE-LA-MER   Pont de Gau

Comfortable restaurant with rooms/Cooking 2
Terrace/Parking/Good value

When you get a dozen or so separate letters of recommendation from readers about a restaurant you have to sit up and take notice. I did better: I paid a call on Jean Audry to find out just why so many of you (from Scotland to the US) had raved about his good-value, unassuming and discreetly furnished *logis* where flowers are everywhere. But the unseen kitchen is an even bigger draw. Vivid regional and classical *plats*, on a quartet of menus, are mouthwatering: *gambas au Noilly-Prat, faux filet sauce diablotin* and a *croustillant d'agneau au beurre d'herbes* were all the evidence we needed to confirm why readers return so often. Another bonus: the *logis* is next door to the Information Centre for the Parc Ornithologique.
Menus A-C. Rooms (9) C. Cards AE, Access, Visa.
Closed 5 Jan-22 Feb. Wed (mid Oct to Easter except sch. hols).
Post 13460 Stes-Maries-de-la-Mer, B.-du-R. (D570, 5 km N.)
Tel 90 97 81 53. Fax 90 97 84 54. Mich 157/E3.

SALON-DE-PROVENCE   Abbaye de Sainte-Croix

Very comfortable hotel/Cooking 3
Secluded/Terrace/Gardens/Swimming pool/Parking

Parts of the restored abbey date back 800 years. There's a strong sense of peace and tranquillity in the cool interior; the exterior is a touch more dramatic with sensational views south. Cooking is what I term Relais & Châteaux fastidious: classical and neo-classical with little to fault and little to excite. A welcome short wine list features the best local *châteaux* and *domaines*; there's nothing dull about the *cave*.
Menus C-F. Rooms (19) F-F2. Cards All. (Also see A/R hotels.)
Closed Nov to Feb. Rest: Mon midday.
Post 13300 Salon-de-Provence, B.-du-R. (5 km to E; D17 & D16.)
Tel 90 56 24 55. Telex 401247. Fax 90 56 31 12. Mich 158/C2.

SALON-DE-PROVENCE — Le Mas du Soleil

Very comfortable restaurant with rooms/Cooking 3
Quiet/Terrace/Gardens/Swimming pool/Parking

That much-loved, unassuming, modest couple, Francis Robin and his gentle wife Christiane, have a new home: all brightness and light in a modern refurbishment of a 19th-century house. The spacious, glass-lined, marble-floored dining room is a world away from the cramped dining room at their old home. As relatively shy as Francis is, that doesn't stop him discussing your meal with you beforehand. His repertoire is as wide as ever: neo-classical and modern side-by-side with classics. He's at his best when working with fish: the *plats* are light, creative and some are laced with the tastes of Provence. The remarkable *fromages* from Gérard Paul's refrigerator-cool, treasure chest of a cheese shop are still on offer; so is the *Grand Chariot des Douceurs*, one of the best of its kind. The bedrooms are extremely comfortable. (Off D17 to E.)
Menus C-D. Rooms (10) F. Disabled. Cards AE, Access, Visa.
Closed Sun evg & Mon. (Also see Autoroute hotel.)
Post 38 ch. St-Côme, 13300 Salon-de-Provence, B.-du-R.
Tel 90 56 06 53. Fax 90 56 21 52. Mich 158/C2.

SEGURET — La Table du Comtat

Very comfortable restaurant with rooms/Cooking 2-3
Secluded/Swimming pool/Parking

The stunning views outshine the cooking: to the west, far over the Rhône (cross fingers and hope for a sky-on-fire sunset); to the south the wooded Dentelles de Montmirail. Franck (the chef) and Josiane Gomez' home clings to a rockface; the cooking, a lot less precarious but often over-complicated, is classical and neo-classical. The herb-scented lamb (*gigot ou côte d'agneau*) is hard to beat; put your knife and fork there.
Menus C-E. Rooms (8) F. Cards All.
Closed Feb. 24 Nov-4 Dec. Tues evg & Wed (not high season).
Post 84110 Séguret, Vaucluse. (SW of Vaison-la-Romaine.)
Tel 90 46 91 49. Fax 90 46 94 27. Mich 144/C3.

TAVEL — Hostellerie du Seigneur

Simple restaurant with basic rooms/Cooking 1-2
Terrace/Good value

Ange and Juliette Bodo are great favourites: rightly so, as they've been put to the test at least twice, when the help they've given readers in trouble has gone well beyond the call of duty. *Bourgeoise* fare with a Tavel rosé used as both an *apéritif* (mixed with Campari and Martini *rouge*) and with a *pruneaux au Tavel* dessert. Relish the couple (from Nice), their art gallery dining room, the 15th-century house and the smallest *place* in France which acts as car park and terrace.
Menus A-B. Rooms (7) B-C. Cards Access, Visa.
Closed Dec to mid Jan. Thurs. (Dinner? Vital to book ahead.)
Post 30126 Tavel, Gard. (Note: new A9 A/R exit nearby.)
Tel 66 50 04 26. Mich 144/A4.

VAISON-LA-ROMAINE   Le Beffroi

Comfortable hotel/Cooking 1-2
Terrace/Gardens/Parking

Let's get the snags unravelled first: ruddy (that's not the word one reader used) bells are a nuisance at night; and parking can be tricky (only 11 places). What then are the pluses? First, the 5 Es: Yann and Catherine Christiansen's 16th-century house is enchanting; the furnishings elegant; the setting exquisite; the views exhilarating; and the humming birds working the flowers exciting. Cuisine is Provençale and classical. Vaison, too, isn't exactly dull: for me the old Roman town is a small-scale Pompeii; and, as an extra bonus, there's the sinister hulk of Mont Ventoux to the south-east. No wonder then that readers return, snags and all.

Menus B-C. Rooms (20) B-F. Cards All. (S & W of Pont Romain.)
Closed Dec-15 Mar. Rest: Mon and Tues midday (not July/Aug).
Post Haute Ville, 84110 Vaison-la-Romaine, Vaucluse.
Tel 90 36 04 71. Telex 306022. Fax 90 36 24 78. Mich 144/C3.

VILLENEUVE-LES-AVIGNON   Le Prieuré

Luxury hotel/Cooking 3
Terrace/Gardens/Swim pool/Tennis/Lift/Closed parking

Another of the superb Relais & Châteaux Provençal showpiece hotels. The former convent was bought in 1943 by Roger Mille; 30 years later a new wing, the Atrium, was added in the courtyard. Today, clients have much to appreciate and admire: the welcome of Marie-France Mille; the rose-scented and herb-perfumed gardens; the elegant ambience; the friendliness of the place; the pool; the softly-lit terrace for evening dining; no wonder so many are seduced. Chef Serge Chenet is a *cuisine moderne* disciple. He capitalises heavily on the regional larder of textures and tastes; there's hardly a dish which doesn't feature a herb of some sort. Breakfast? A serve yourself buffet plus the chance to polish off what's left from the previous evening's dessert trolley. Who's for tennis?

Menus D-E. Rooms (26) F-F2. Cards All. (Also see next entry.)
Closed 4 Nov-13 Mar. (N of Philippe-le-Bel landmark tower.)
Post pl. Chapître, 30400 Villeneuve-lès-Avignon, Gard.
Tel 90 25 18 20. Telex 431042. Fax 90 25 45 39. Mich 158/B1.

VILLENEUVE-LES-AVIGNON   Résidence Les Cèdres

Simple hotel/Cooking 1
Terrace/Gardens/Swim pool/Closed parking/Good value

No longer a base *sans restaurant*. Evening meals only are now available: *Bourgeoise plats* with no prizes awarded for culinary talent. What appeals? The old house, the handsome cedar trees, the "folly", the modern bungalows and the pool. I suggest Les Cèdres is still used as a base.

Menus B (dinner only). Rooms (24) D. Cards Access, Visa.
Closed 15 Nov to 15 Mar. (At Bellevue; NW of D900.)
Post 39 av. Pasteur, 30400 Villeneuve-lès-Avignon, Gard.
Tel 90 25 43 92. Telex 432868. Fax 90 25 14 66. Mich 158/B1.

SAVOIE

see page 162

I am often asked which is my favourite part of France. As the years roll by I find giving an answer becomes more and more difficult. I've got to know so much of that lovely country and I feel guilty giving my vote to one specific area.

Guilt or not, I continue to give this one word answer: Savoie. This will not surprise any of you who have read the handful of books I've written about France. Perhaps the first ten years of my life, spent in the high Himalayas, have left me with an insatiable love for lofty heights.

Here I have space for just 1,985 words. What a pity: I could write pages about the region. I'll highlight three particular areas of which I am especially fond; alas, I am well aware I've turned my back on many other super mountain corners.

Where do I start? Let's commence with a Wagnerian overture. First, seek out the Auberge du Bois Prin at **Chamonix**. For some this chalet hotel will be too expensive for an overnight stay; but I'm certain all of you could afford a drink, coffee or cup of tea on the terrace. Sit and relax: study the towering mountain curtain above you. To the far left is the sharp pyramid tooth of the legendary Aiguille du Dru (silhouetted by the even higher Aiguille Verte); you may remember seeing TV coverage of the fearsome climb. As your eyes move right you'll see a "molar" formed like the letter "M". To its right are two more *aiguilles* (needles): the right-hand one, set further back, is the dreaded Aiguille du Grépon.

In front of you is the Aiguille du Midi (the summit is easily reached these days, courtesy of a cable car); to the right, the dominant dome of **Mont Blanc** fills the sky. Consider the "arithmetic" of both the jagged line and rounded dome: the mountain wall looming above you rises nearly four km above the sun-trap terrace, yet is only five to eight km away. Only in

330

the Himalayas can you better those statistics.

Alternatively, drive north from Chamonix, cross the Swiss border and climb past Finhaut to the skyscraper high concrete wall of the **Barrage d'Emosson**. Here you're not far short of 7000 ft above sea-level and your reward is a spellbinding panorama of the entire Chaîne du Mont Blanc.

Before deserting the Chamonix Valley let me list a few other diversions. First, a trip through the Mont Blanc Tunnel to the **Val Ferret**. Long ago I penned these words: "the loveliest terrain is more often than not found by using dead-end roads that, apparently, go nowhere." This is a supreme example. Relish the Doire torrent, the Grandes Jorasses, the other side of the Mont Blanc *massif* and the rejuvenating tonic of isolation from both man and his machines.

There's a lot more to see and do in and around the Chamonix Valley: facilities include both a golf course and a fabulous sports complex (including an all-seasons ice rink); various cable-car, rack-railway, chair-lift and ordinary railway services (try the line to **Martigny**); and numerous walks and drives (our favourite is across the border in Switzerland, to the exquisite lake at **Champex**, south of Martigny).

(It is a pity that the vast majority of winter sports enthusiasts never see the high-altitude ski resorts in summer: they would be shocked by the appalling damage being done to the mountain slopes. Nature is paying a heavy price for man's savage mauling of the delicate mountain environment.)

Where next? Let me introduce you to a slightly different scenic landscape: the mountains, valleys and single lake, **Lac d'Annecy**, which lie in a semi-circle to the north of deadbeat **Albertville** (the home of the 1992 Winter Olympics).

To understand the terrain drive to the Crêt de Châtillon,

331

south of **Annecy**. The 5574-ft-high summit is a superb viewpoint: below you is Lac d'Annecy; to the far south are the icy peaks of the Massif des Ecrins (see Hautes-Alpes map); and, to the east, the dominating dome of Mont Blanc.

In early June the marshy pastures one km south of the Crêt are peppered with lapis lazuli-tinted gentians. On the night of April 15, 1943, these same pastures, identified by bonfires, were witness to a daring wartime mission. Peter Churchill, a British SOE agent, parachuted from a Halifax and landed on the mountain top, to be met by his future wife, the legendary Odette Sansom, and a group of the local *maquis*. Within hours both were captured at nearby St-Jorioz.

Now head south to the largely ignored mountain fastness of **Les Bauges**. Call first at the local tourist office at **Le Châtelard** (SI des Bauges; post code 73630) for copies of several useful leaflets. Especially good is a leaflet which explains the background to the Réserve Nationale de Faune du Massif des Bauges which lies between Le Châtelard and Albertville. The leaflet map identifies 17 marked trails, of varying lengths and difficulty, which snake into the heart of the small circle of high protected terrain.

I'll identify a handful of the walks. The first must is the drive up the Vallon de Bellevaux, a dead-end wooded valley with roaring river and the start of several walks. Next, access the reserve from Doussard, near the southern end of Lake Annecy; drive to and walk in the similarly wooded Combe (valley) d'Ire. The St-Ruph valley is reached from **Faverges**, to the north-east; here there are more woods, a river landscape and a waterfall at Seythenex. And, from the Abbaye de **Tamié**, two walks take you through the forests high above the celebrated monastery (use the abbey car park).

Keen walker or not be certain not to bypass Tamié Abbey. A new *Centre d'Accueil* has been built on the hillside: an audio visual presentation explains the history of the Cistercian monastery; you can buy the renowned cheese made at the abbey; and you can also purchase tapes of the soothing chants recorded by the monks in their church. Better still find time for one of the many daily services. Vespers is ideal; lasting half an hour the service is primarily song and always leaves one with a deeper understanding of the simple, spiritual life led by the monks. (Summer: Sun 17.00; other days 18.15.)

In May and June the valley below the abbey, towards Faverges, is renowned for its wild flowers. Scores of varieties fill the meadows between Tertenoz and Les Combes.

For the finest views of Lake Annecy climb the Col de la Forclaz, high above the eastern shore. At the summit you are offered the chance to "Fly like a bird on two-seat hang glider with Instructor." Better you than me. **Talloires**, with its world-famous lakeside setting, is an exotic spot. No trains, no busy main road and a protective wooded headland to the north; what more could the resort want?

Before leaving the area I'll identify some detours. **Thônes** is a delight. Three km north-west of the town is a Resistance Museum and a roadside cemetery where hundreds of patriots who died in the tragic battle with 5,000 German and French Vichy *miliciens* on the **Plateau des Glières** are buried. If you want to see the site of the battle, which took place on March 26, 1944, then access to the plateau is from Thorens-Glières; the highly scenic drive ends at the Col des Glières where there's a monument and maps explaining the story.

From Thônes use the pretty Col de la Croix Fry to reach the **Col des Aravis**. This latter pass, together with the Col des Saises and the nearby Signal de Bisanne (both east of Albertville) reward you with ever-closer views of Mont Blanc. South of Beaufort minor roads lead you through **Arèches** to Boudin where, as you climb the hairpins to the Col du Pré, you have a perfect view of old traditional chalets.

Now to the self-contained visual joys locked within the secretive **Chartreuse**. The road journey from **Grenoble** to **Chambéry** is less than 60 km; the A41, hugging the Isère's right bank for much of the way, allows you to cover the distance in 30 minutes, if you so wish. The longer, more time-consuming alternative takes you through a wonderland, a world away from the crash and bash of Grenoble and Chambéry.

What's the best time of the year to enjoy the idyllic *massif*? I've seen the Chartreuse during each season but I reckon it's at its most captivating in the spring and autumn. In April and May the roaring streams are full of cold foaming water, the woods are alight with the first hints of green and the meadows are sheets of wild flowers. In September the same pastures are swathed in lilac-tinted autumn crocuses and, in October, your eyes feast on the rich shades of dying leaves.

Let me give you another classic example of a road that goes nowhere. Drive from the Col de Porte, 18 km north of Grenoble, in a north-westerly direction, to the point called "Bergeries" (sheepfolds) on the map. Stunning views await you. Energetic walkers can climb the steep slopes of the **Charmant Som**, 6125 ft above sea-level. (Botanists should quiz the lady who owns the sheepfolds; she's an expert on mountain plants.)

I mentioned earlier the important visual impact made by mountain streams in the *massif*. Two deserve your undivided attention: the strangely-named Guiers Vif and Guiers Mort. Start at their sources. Descend through narrow, wooded gorges as both streams fall steeply to the west. The tracks high above the two Guiers are exhilarating drives: the D45 north of the Vif is an intoxicating scenic bonus, especially near Corbel; so is the taxing forest climb south of the Mort.

Nose out some of the numerous "white" roads on the map; the following is just one example. From **St-Pierre-de-Chartreuse** head south and, after a climb of about a dozen km, you reach the edge of the eastern escarpment of the *massif* with extensive views over the Isère Valley (the road is unsurfaced near the summit of the Col du Coq). The best viewpoint is at the Bec du Margain; there's a funicular to the valley floor at St-Hilaire and, at **Le Touvet**, there's a small château with a man-made water cascade, a miniature Chatsworth.

The Chartreuse is not richly endowed with man-made architectural gems. Some, however, are worth seeking out. Just north of the Guiers Mort is the world-renowned Couvent de la Grande Chartreuse, a barracks-sized monastery hidden in wooded mountains. No wonder Saint Bruno chose the isolated site over 900 years ago as the first home of the Carthusian Order. You cannot visit the monastery but La Correrie, at its southern entrance, is a museum which depicts the way of life of the Carthusian monks in an informative way.

(Chartreuse, the world-famous liqueur, is made at the distillery at Voiron, not at the monastery itself. Apart from the powerful green and yellow varieties, try some others, too: *myrtille, framboise, génépi* (made from mountain plants) and a *liqueur du 9e centenaire*, made to celebrate the nine centuries since St-Bruno founded the monastery.)

Something different, and very modern, is the Eglise de Saint-Hugues, just south of St-Pierre. The church is a celebration of contemporary sacred art; the artist, Arcabas, created the paintings from 1953 to 1973.

What else is there? **Evian**, an attractive spa on the southern shores of Lac Léman; nearby **Thonon**, another lakeside resort; **Aix-les-Bains** and **Lac du Bourget**, not forgetting the handsome Hautecombe Abbey across the lake; the old, arcaded streets of Annecy and the town's shady park and gardens alongside Lac d'Annecy; the summer and winter resorts of **Megève** and **St-Gervais** (a spa); the high passes on the Italian border, the **Col du Petit St-Bernard**, the mighty **Col de l'Iseran** and the **Col du Mont Cenis**; and other cols to the east of Grenoble, particularly **la Croix de Fer**.

Markets Annecy (Tues, Sat and Sun); Chamonix (Sat); Evian (Tues and Fri); Faverges (Wed); Thônes (Sat).

Michelin green guide: Alpes du Nord.

Cheeses Cow's milk

Abondance from the hills and valleys encircling the town of the same name. Best in summer and autumn. Small, firm wheel

Beaufort at its best in winter, spring and summer. A hard, cooked cheese, equivalent to Gruyère, but with no holes

Beaumont mild, creamy, hard disk. Related to Tamié

Chambarand made by monks near Roybon. A mild, creamy-tasting, small disk. Ideal with the light wines of Savoie

Colombière from the Aravis area; mild-flavoured, flat disk

Fondu aux Raisins (Fondu au Marc) big disk of processed cheese and covered in grape pips

Reblochon best in summer and autumn. Semi-hard, gold colour with a mild and creamy flavour. Made in flat, small disks.

St-Marcellin available all the year. Small, mild-flavoured disks

Ste-Foy (Bleu de) a blue-veined cheese, made in a flat cylinder. Best in summer and autumn. **Bleu de Tignes** is a related cheese

Sassenage a summer and autumn season. A soft, spicy-flavoured, blue-veined cheese, related to Bleu de Gex (see Jura region)

Tamié (Trappiste de Tamié) made by monks at the monastery of the same name, south of Lake Annecy; light rind, pressed, uncooked disk

Tomme de Savoie a semi-hard, flat cylinder with a slight nutty smell. A summer and autumn season. Has many relations – all called **Tomme**

Vacherin d'Abondance mild, soft and the size of a thick pancake. At its best in winter. Ideal with Crépy or a Chautagne wine

Goat's milk

Chevrotin des Aravis a small, flat cylinder with a summer and autumn season. Mild, no particular smell. From Aravis area

Persillé des Aravis blue-veined, sharp-tasting, tall cylinder. Also known as **Persillé de Thônes** and **Persillé du Grand-Bornand** (nearby towns)

Regional Specialities

Farcement (Farçon Savoyard) potatoes baked with cream, eggs, bacon, dried pears and prunes; a hearty stomach filler

Féra a freshwater lake fish

Fondue hot melted cheese and white wine

Gratin Dauphinois a classic potato dish with cream, cheese and garlic

Gratin Savoyard another classic potato dish with cheese and butter

Lavaret a freshwater lake fish, like salmon

Longeole a country sausage

Lotte a burbot, not unlike an eel

Omble chevalier a char, it looks like a large salmon trout

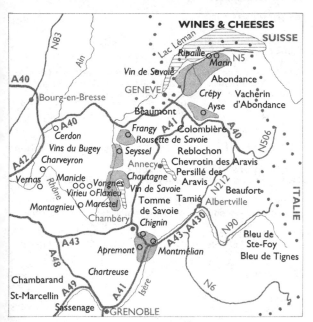

WINES & CHEESES

Wines

Whites and Rosés

There are many good value whites and rosés. The whites from **Seyssel** are delicate and flinty (**Clos de la Peclette** is the best). Another fine white is **Crépy**, made from the Swiss Chasselas grape type; this is an AC wine, from the general area south of Lake Geneva. The **AC Vin de Savoie** applies to white wines: of these, **Chignin**, **Apremont** and its close neighbour **Abymes** – Abîmes on the maps – (both on the northern slopes of the glorious Chartreuse Massif) are fresh, light and dry; so is the wine called **AC Roussette de Savoie**. **Roussette de Frangy**, north-east of Seyssel, is a pleasant, subtle wine, as is **Marestel**. These last three are made from the Altesse grape type.

Reds

Montmélian and the neighbouring **Chignin** – both south of Chambéry – are tasty reds and are made from the Mondeuse grape. Another red is **Chautagne**, made from the Gamay grape, from the vineyards south of Seyssel. These three share the **AC Vin de Savoie**. Often reds will be listed on menus as Mondeuse or Gamay – their *varietal* names.

Sparkling wines

Look out for the **Seyssel mousseux, Vin de Savoie mousseux, Vin de Savoie pétillant, Mousseux de Savoie** and **Pétillant de Savoie**. Other sparklers are the rare **Vin de Savoie Ayze mousseux** and **pétillant** (Ayse on the maps). Remember you are near **Chartreuse** country: don't miss those knockout green and yellow liqueurs (see bottom of p 333). See *French Leave Cocktails* for Chambéry *vermouths*.

Vins de Pays

These will be labelled by *département* names: **Haute-Savoie, Savoie** and **Isère**.

ALBERTVILLE Ibis

Simple hotel/Cooking 1
Lift/Parking

A43/A430 to junc. with N90; to north (signs Gilly-sur-Isère).
Menus A-B. Rooms (75) D. Disabled. Cards Access, Visa.
Post 73200 Albertville, Savoie. (Hotel south-west of town.)
Tel 79 37 89 99. Telex 319194. Fax 79 37 89 98. Mich 118/C2.
(Bookings: UK 071 724 1000; US toll free 800 221 4542)

ALBERTVILLE Le Roma

Very comfortable hotel/Cooking 1
Terrace/Gardens/Swimming pool/Tennis/Lift/Parking

As above; hotel south side of N90, 1 km from town. Le Roma now
quite a business enterprise. Some rooms have small kitchens.
Menus B. Rooms (140) D-F. Disabled. Cards All.
Post 73200 Albertville, Savoie. (Hotel south-west of town.)
Tel 79 37 15 56. Telex 980140. Fax 79 37 01 31. Mich 118/C2.

ANNECY Campanile

Simple hotel/Cooking 1
Parking/Good value

A43 Annecy-Sud exit. Through toll, join N508 (from left) and
immediately right, crossing over N508 (hotel on far side).
Menus A-B. Rooms (49) C. Disabled. Cards Access, Visa.
Post 74960 Cran-Gevrier, H.-Savoie. (En Route p 148)
Tel 50 67 74 66. Telex 385565. Fax 50 57 49 34. Mich 118/B1.
(Bookings: UK freephone 0800 897863)

ANNECY Climat de France

Simple hotel/Cooking 1
Parking/Good value

As above. Through toll, join N508 (from left) and immediately
right; but now south, right at church, hotel on right (D16).
Menus A-B. Rooms (44) C. Disabled. Cards AE, Access, Visa.
Post 74960 Cran-Gevrier, H.-Savoie. (En Route p 148)
Tel 50 69 31 03. Telex 309394. Fax 50 69 14 38. Mich 118/B1.
(Bookings: UK 071 287 3181)

ANNECY Mercure

Very comfortable hotel/Cooking 1
Terrace/Swimming pool/Parking

As above, but stay on N508. Join N201 (Chambéry). On right.
Menus B. Rooms (69) F. Disabled. Cards All.
Post rte Aix-les-Bains, 74000 Annecy, H.-Savoie. (ER p 148)
Tel 50 52 09 66. Telex 385303. Fax 50 69 29 32. Mich 118/B1.
(Bookings: UK 071 724 1000; US toll free 800 221 4542)

ANNEMASSE   Campanile

Simple hotel/Cooking 1
Terrace/Parking/Good value

A40 exit 14 (Annemasse). On right of N206, north of A40.
Menus A-B. Rooms (42) C. Disabled. Cards Access, Visa.
Post 74100 Annemasse, H.-Savoie. (ER p 144; by Renault gar.)
Tel 50 37 84 85. Telex 309511. Fax 50 37 02 04. Mich 104/C3.
(Bookings: UK freephone 0800 897863)

ANNEMASSE   Mercure

Very comfortable hotel/Cooking 1
Terrace/Swimming pool/Lift/Parking

As above. Use N206 north. Left after river crossing, on left.
Menus B. Rooms (78) F. Disabled. Cards All.
Post 74240 Gaillard, H.-Savoie. (En Route p 144)
Tel 50 92 05 25. Telex 385815. Fax 50 87 14 57. Mich 104/C3.
(Bookings: UK 071 724 1000; US toll free 800 221 4542)

BONNEVILLE   Supotel

Comfortable hotel/Cooking 1
Fairly quiet/Swimming pool/Tennis/Parking

A40 Bonneville exit from west; La Roche-sur-Foron exit from
east. Hotel on west side of A40, north of N203. Use as
overnight stop for Vougy restaurant (to east of Bonneville).
Menus A-B. Rooms (52) D. Disabled. Cards All.
Post 74800 St-Pierre-en-Faucigny, H.-Savoie.
Tel 50 03 86 55. Telex 309825. Fax 50 03 77 23. Mich 105/D4.

CHAMBERY   Ibis

Simple hotel/Cooking 1
Parking

A43 Chambéry exit. Right at N201 (A41) expressway. Leave at
exit 6 (ZI des Landiers). Hotel on east side of expressway.
Menus A-B. Rooms (88) D. Disabled. Cards Access, Visa.
Post 73000 Chambéry, Savoie. (En Route p 156)
Tel 79 69 28 36. Telex 320457. Fax 79 96 39 91. Mich 118/A3.
(Bookings: UK 071 724 1000; US toll free 800 221 4542)

CHAMBERY   Novotel

Very comfortable hotel/Cooking 1
Terrace/Gardens/Swimming pool/Lift/Closed parking

As above. Novotel opposite Ibis, on east side of expressway.
Menus B. Rooms (103) E. Disabled. Cards All.
Post 73000 Chambéry, Savoie. (En Route p 156)
Tel 79 69 21 27. Telex 320446. Fax 79 69 71 13. Mich 118/A3.
(Bookings: UK 071 724 1000; US toll free 800 221 4542)

Autoroute Hotels

GRENOBLE-EST   Climat de France

Simple hotel/Cooking 1
Parking/Good value

A41 Meylan Est/Zirst exit. Left at x-roads, north A41; on right.
Menus A-B. Rooms (38) C. Disabled. Cards AE, Access, Visa.
Post 38240 Meylan, Isère. (En Route p 152)
Tel 76 90 76 90. Telex 305551. Fax 76 41 01 68. Mich 131/E1.
(Bookings: UK 071 287 3181)

GRENOBLE-EST   Ibis

Simple hotel/Cooking 1
Terrace/Lift/Parking

Leave A41 Rocade-Sud exit. South on *rocade* (bypass). Cross
River Isère; leave exit 1 (Domaine Univ.). Ibis to west.
Menus A. Rooms (81) D. Disabled. Cards Access, Visa.
Post r. Condamine, 38610 Gières, Isère.
Tel 76 44 00 44. Telex 308855. Fax 76 51 03 58. Mich 131/E1.
(Bookings : UK 071 724 1000; US toll free 800 221 4542)

PONTCHARRA   Climat de France

Simple hotel/Cooking 1
Terrace/Tennis/Parking/Good value

Leave A41 Pontcharra exit. Through toll, hotel on right.
Menus A-B. Rooms (24) C. Disabled. Cards Access, Visa.
Post 38530 Pontcharra, Isère. (En Route p 150)
Tel 76 71 91 84. Telex 320529. Fax 76 71 99 30. Mich 117/F4.
(Bookings: UK 071 287 3181)

SALLANCHES   Ibis

Simple hotel/Cooking 1
Terrace/Parking/Good value

A40 Sallanches exit from north; on right. Use N205 from south.
Menus A-B. Rooms (53) C-D. Disabled. Cards Access, Visa.
Post av. de Gèneve, 74700 Sallanches, H.-Savoie. (ER p 146)
Tel 50 58 14 42. Telex 385754. Fax 50 47 88 61. Mich 105/E4.
(Bookings : UK 071 724 1000; US toll free 800 221 4542)

VOREPPE   Novotel

Very comfortable hotel/Cooking 1
Terrace/Gardens/Swimming pool/Lift/Closed parking

Leave A48 Veurey exit (from north at main toll); Voiron exit
(from south). Novotel on east side of A48.
Menus B. Rooms (114) E. Disabled. Cards All.
Post 38340 Voreppe, Isère. (En Route p 157)
Tel 76 50 81 44. Telex 320273. Fax 76 56 76 26. Mich 131/E1.
(Bookings : UK 071 724 1000; US toll free 800 221 4542)

338

ANNECY   **Motel le Flamboyant**

Comfortable hotel
Garage/Parking

English-speaking owners. 20 rooms have small kitchens. From
north-east corner of lake use D129 (rue de Verdun); on left.
Rooms (32) C-D. Disabled. Cards All.
Post 52 r. Mouettes, 74940 Annecy-le-Vieux, H.-Savoie.
Tel 50 23 61 69. Telex 309284. Fax 50 27 97 23. Mich 118/B1.

ST-ALBAN-DE-MONTBEL   **St-Alban-Plage**

Comfortable hotel
Quiet/Gardens/Parking/Good value

Two buildings, between road and tranquil Lac d'Aiguebelette.
Delectable, English-speaking owner, Jeannine Duport.
Rooms (16) C-E. Cards Access, Visa. (Meals? See Novalaise.)
Closed Oct to April.
Post 73610 St-Alban-de-Montbel, Savoie. (En Route p 156)
Tel 79 36 02 19. Mich 118/A3.

ST-GERVAIS-LES-BAINS   **L'Adret**

Simple hotel
Quiet/Good value

Chalet-style, on inside of hairpin bend, south-west of spa.
Rooms (15) B-D.
Closed Easter to May. 25 Sept to 20 Dec.
Post ch. La Mollaz, 74170 St-Gervais-les-Bains, H.-Savoie.
Tel 50 93 50 60. Mich 119/D1.

ST-JULIEN-EN-GENEVOIS   **Le Soli**

Simple hotel
Quiet/Lift/Parking/Good value

Away from main roads. Useful for Diligence rest. (100 yards).
Rooms (27) C. Cards AE, Access, Visa.
Closed Xmas to New Year. (En Route p 143)
Post rue M.Paget, 74160 St-Julien-en-Genevois, H.-Savoie.
Tel 50 49 11 31. Fax 50 35 14 64. Mich 104/B3.

TALLOIRES   **Les Prés du Lac**

Very comfortable hotel
Secluded/Gardens/Parking

Superb: tranquil, lakeside setting & gardens; light, airy rooms;
and bubbly, English-speaking owner, Marie-Paule Conan.
Rooms (16) F-F2. Cards All.
Closed 5 Nov to 6 Feb.
Post 74290 Talloires, H.-Savoie.
Tel 50 60 76 11. Telex 309288. Fax 50 60 73 42. Mich 118/B1.

Hotels and Restaurants

(Please also refer to the hotels and restaurants on the eastern edge of the Lyonnais; in the southern hills of the Jura; and in the area around Grenoble, part of the Hautes-Alpes.)

ALBERTVILLE   Chez Uginet

Comfortable restaurant/Cooking 2-3
Terrace/Good value

Young Eric and Josie Guillot have had a hard act to follow: previous chef/patron, Alain Rayé, was a huge favourite. Eric paddles a modern cooking course at his restaurant alongside the fast-flowing River Arly. Especially noteworthy is the Savoyard menu of modernised traditional dishes: *agnelots* (ravioli) *pochés au bouillon de poule parfumé au foie gras*; and *pascalines (crêpes) d'agneau aux champignons Mondeuse* are typical. Value-for-money menus.
Menus B-D. Cards Access, DC, Visa. (Rooms? See A/R hotels.)
Closed 24 June to 9 July. Tues. (E of river; bridge to N.)
Post Pont des Adoubes, 73200 Albertville, Savoie.
Tel 79 32 00 50. Fax 79 31 21 41. Mich 118/C2.

ALBERTVILLE   Million

Very comfortable hotel/Cooking 3-4
Terrace/Gardens/Lift/Garage

Fluent English-speaking chef/patron, Philippe Million, is the 7th generation of the family at this much refurbished and improved town-centre hotel. A gentle, intelligent man; those appealing traits show in his work. Assured, refined modern, neo-classical and Savoyarde specialities. His light fish interpretations are among the best of their kind: among them a *filet de perche légèrement fumé galette parfumée* and *féra rôtie, crème de jeunes poireaux, la quenelle de grenouilles*.
Menus B-E. Rooms (28) E-F. Cards All.(Nr N212 N exit of town.)
Closed 26 Apl-16 May. 20 Sept-5 Oct. Rest: Sun evg & Mon.
Post 8 pl. Liberté, 73200 Albertville, Savoie.
Tel 79 32 25 15. Telex 306022. Fax 79 32 25 36. Mich 118/C2.

LE BOURGET-DU-LAC   Ombremont

Very comfortable hotel/Cooking 3
Secluded/Terrace/Gardens/Swimming pool/Lift/Parking

Sensational is the word to describe the views of the Lac du Bourget far below you and the wall of Mont Revard across the lake. Any meal on the terrace must rank as one of the most spectacular in France. Monique Carlo is a passionate *patronne*; her exceptional good taste shows at every turn. Neo-classical cooking: typical examples are *filet de lavaret à l'étuvée de poireaux, beurre de tomates au Génépi* (see the bottom of page 333), *papillote de langoustines aux champignons* and a heady *soupe de cerises au vin Chautagne*.
Menus C-E. Rooms (13) F-F3. Cards AE, Access, Visa.
Closed 2 Jan-5 Feb. (Cheaper rooms? See Chambéry A/R hotels.)
Post 73370 Le Bourget-du-Lac, Savoie.(N on N504; tricky turn.)
Tel 79 25 00 23. Telex 980832. Fax 79 25 25 77. Mich 117/F2.

CHAMONIX   Albert 1er

Very comfortable hotel/Cooking 4 (see text)
Terrace/Gardens/Swim pool/Tennis/Lift/Garage/Parking

If Anne and I were asked to say which hotel family we respect,
admire and have grown to love most, then, after only a brief
number of seconds we would, in unison, shout "Carrier". We've
known Mum and Dad, Andrée (truly an angel) and Marcel (the
salt of the earth), for 25 years. Today, their eldest son, Pierre
Carrier, is the chef/patron at Albert 1er. His brother Denis
runs the newer enterprise, the Bois Prin. The boys are the 7th
generation Carriers to have lived in the valley.

We've watched Pierre grow from a boy of ten to become, at
35, one of the best of the younger generation of French chefs.
Indeed, two of the finest meals we've had in the last few years
have been at Albert 1er. Witness a *filet mignon de veau au foie
gras et au jus de truffe*, the best veal dish we've ever savoured;
a *filet de bar rôti sa peau* in a red wine sauce with a
mysterious Carrier ingredient; or a *poire farcie aux pruneaux
au vin et son briochon perdu* (the latter, dipped in *crème
anglaise* is fried, a posh "French toast"). Twice a day Pierre
and his team prepare set meals for *pension* clients and what
treats they are: inexpensive and available to visitors. The
cooking rating of 4 is given for the neo-classical and modern
masterpieces on the gastronomic and à la carte menus.

Pierre and his ex-champion skier wife Martine – both speak
good English – have added extra facilities: a gym, sauna and
jacuzzi. Admire, too, Lionel Wibault's (a Chamonix guide)
paintings, explosions of colour, and the wood panelling in one
of the dining rooms (*arolle*: a rare evergreen pine). (Cheaper
rooms? Use the simple Vallée Blanche (*sans rest*): Lift & small
kitchens; Rooms (18) D-E; All cards; Tel 50 53 04 50; Fax 50 55
97 85; Post 36 rue Lyret; Irish owner, Patricia Byrne.)
Menus B-E. Rooms (17) F. Cards All. (Near main station.)
Closed 10-25 May. 19 Oct-3 Dec. Rest: Wed midday.
Post 74400 Chamonix-Mont-Blanc, H.-Savoie.
Tel 50 53 05 09. Fax 50 55 95 48. Mich 105/F4.

CHAMONIX   Auberge du Bois Prin

Very comfortable hotel/Cooking 2-3
Secluded/Terrace/Gardens/Lift/Garage/Parking

I've already devoted 18 lines at the start of the regional
introduction to the sensational views from the terrace, garden
and all 11 bedrooms of the flower-strewn chalet-hotel. Please
also read the entry above for details of the Carrier family.

Denis and Monique Carrier, both of whom speak excellent
English, are *les patrons*. Denis, originally the award-winning
sommelier at Albert 1er, has developed into a highly competent
chef; his repertoire includes both neo-classical and Savoyarde
specialities. Use the facilities at Albert 1er; and admire, too,
Marcel's remarkable high-altitude vegetable garden at Bois
Prin (which supplies produce for both the hotels).
Menus B-E. Rooms (11) F-F2. Cards All. (Nr Le Brévent *gare*.)
Closed 10-26 May. 26 Oct-11 Dec. Rest: Wed midday.
Post aux Moussoux, 74400 Chamonix-Mont-Blanc, H.-Savoie.
Tel 50 53 33 51. Fax 50 53 48 75. Mich 105/F4.

CHAPARON   La Châtaigneraie

Comfortable hotel/Cooking 1-2
Secluded/Terrace/Gardens/Tennis/Parking/Good value

The man-made and natural benefits of this alluring family
hotel are reason enough to visit Chaparon. The *logis* is a mile
or so from the west bank of Lake Annecy and the views east
are a further plus. But, better still, the biggest bonus is the
friendly Millet family, led by English-speaking Martine and
Robert (the chef), an open-hearted and helpful duo who cannot
do enough for clients. Cooking is competent classical and
Bourgeoise: Robert's repertoire ranges from *brochette de boeuf
au grill*, to *jambonette de volaille farcie sauce poivre vert* and
an *omble chevalier aux noisettes*. Some rooms have small
kitchens. Popular British tour operator's base (VFB). (Follow
Chaparon signs from N508 Brédannaz traffic-lights.)
Menus A-C. Rooms (25) C-D. Cards All.
Closed Mid Oct to Jan. Sun evg & Mon (Oct to Apl).
Post Chaparon, 74210 Faverges, H.-Savoie. (Directions above.)
Tel 50 44 30 67. Fax 50 44 83 71. Mich 118/B1.

ELOISE   Le Fartoret

Very comfortable hotel/Cooking 1-2
Secluded/Terr/Gardens/Swim pool/Tennis/Lift/Parking

The family Gassiloud *logis* has become too much of a business
complex. 40 bedrooms mean the place is frankly too busy at
times. Nevertheless, the dead-end village ensures peace and
quiet; there's plenty of good walking; extensive views; the A40
(N of junc. 11) is close; and the cooking, whilst winning no
prizes, is copious *Bourgeoise* and classical fare: *escalope de
truite de mer crème d'épinard, filet de canard sauce Madère*
and *crème caramel* are typical of the spectrum.
Menus B-C. Rooms (C-E). Cards All. (En Route p 143)
Post Eloise, 01200 Bellegarde-sur-Valserine, Ain. (5 km SE.)
Tel 50 48 07 18. Fax 50 48 23 85. Mich 104/A4.

FAVERGES   Florimont

Comfortable hotel/Cooking 2
Terrace/Gardens/Lift/Parking/Good value

Let's give the family Goubot another chance: see my comments
about their old hotel, the Alpes, on page 268 in *FL3*. Madame
Marie-Josèphe Goubot is as stern and unsmiling as ever; her
son, Jean-Christophe, is now the gaffer in the kitchen; and his
wife, Marie-Claire, provides a much happier, warmer welcome
for clients seeking out the family's new modern *logis*. Their old
place, first recommended in *Hidden France*, went up in smoke;
the Florimont, to the north-east of Faverges and on the N508,
is as bright as a button. *Bourgeois* and classical dishes: *filet de
féra meunière, contrefilet garni, tournedos aux morilles et
petites crêpes, tarte maison* and similar.
Menus B-D. Rooms (27) D-E. Disabled. Cards All.
Post 74210 Faverges, H.-Savoie. (3 km NE; on N508.)
Tel 50 44 50 05. Telex 309369. Fax 50 44 43 20. Mich 118/C2.

FAVERGES   Gay Séjour

**Simple hotel/Cooking 2-3
Secluded/Terrace/Parking/Good value**

A consistently appreciated readers' favourite. For many
reasons: the quiet location, between Lake Annecy and the
inspiring Tamié Abbey; the 17th-century Savoyarde farmhouse
(ask to see the watercolour painted decades ago); and for the
utterly splendid family Gay. You'll meet several generations:
first the heart and soul of the place, the generous-spirited
Bernard (taught to cook by his grandmother Jeanne who started
the enterprise six decades ago); his mother Andrée who keeps
the hotel spotless; and, more than likely, his teenage son,
Pierre, who will probably be lending a hand in the kitchen.

In the 10 years I've known the *logis* I've seen Bernard's
cooking become more and more ambitious. Neo-classical and
Savoyard *plats* using excellent produce: numerous dishes
capitalise on fish sent overnight from Brittany and the
piscatorial treasures from Lake Annecy.
Menus B-D. Rooms (12) D-E. Cards All. (D12 S from Faverges.)
Closed 27 Dec to end Jan. Sun evg & Mon (not school hols).
Post Tertenoz, 74210 Faverges, H.-Savoie.
Tel 50 44 52 52. Fax 50 44 49 52. Mich 118/C2.

NOVALAISE   Novalaise Plage

**Comfortable hotel/Cooking 1-2
Quiet/Terrace/Parking/Good value**

A modern *logis* close to the much-loved Base hotel owned by
the delectable Jeannine Duport. The Plage is a chalet-style
lakeside hotel with its own sandy beach. Christiane Bergier is
a helpful *patronne*. Cooking is a mix of *Bourgeoise* and
classical. Much the best catches are the likes of *friture de lac,
truite rosée* and *filet de lavaret au beurre blanc*.
Menus B-C. Rooms (12) B-D. Cards Access, Visa.
Closed Oct to Mar. Tues (not high season). (En Route p 156)
Post 73470 Novalaise, Aiguebelette-le-Lac, Savoie.
Tel 79 36 02 19. Mich 117/E3. (W bank of Lac d'Aiguebelette.)

ST-JULIEN-EN-GENEVOIS   Diligence & Taverne du
Postillon
**Comfortable restaurant/Cooking 2-3
Good value (see text)**

You can save francs here by using the brasserie where cooking
standards are 1-2. I suggest you descend to the Taverne, the
more serious Favre restaurant. Young Christophe is the boss
these days; his repertoire is both neo-classical and classical
with many a gutsy *plat*: *côte de boeuf à la Mondeuse, turbot
aux algues dans sa carapace de gros sel* and a *gratin d'oranges
au Grand-Marnier* are typical. His wife, Marie-Antoinette, and
mother, Christianne, run the busy front-of-house operation.
Menus B (brasserie) & C-D (Taverne). Cards All. (See Base.)
Closed 1-21 Aug. Xmas-15 Jan. Sun (not midday Sept-June). Mon.
Post av. Genève, 74160 St-Julien-en-Genevois, H.-Savoie.
Tel 50 49 07 55. Mich 104/B3. (On N201, nr church & parking.)

ST-JULIEN-EN-GENEVOIS   Hôtel Rey

Comfortable hotel/Cooking 2
Terr/Gardens/Swim pool/Tennis/Lift/Parking

At the summit of the Col du Mont Sion. Gilbert Rey and his
wife have made many friends. Readers have liked their warm,
friendly personalities; the amenities; and have spoken
generously of the Clef des Champs restaurant in a separate
building. Chef Gilbert walks the neo-classical cooking path; his
range of lighter fish specialities is especially welcome.
Menus B-C. Rooms (31) D. Cards Access, Visa.
Closed 4-25 Jan. 21 Oct-12 Nov. Rest: Thurs & Fri midday.
Post Col du Mont Sion, 74350 Cruseilles, H.-Savoie. (S; N201.)
Tel 50 44 13 29. Fax 50 44 05 48. Mich 104/B4. (ER p 143)

ST-PAUL-EN-CHABLAIS   Bois Joli

Comfortable hotel/Cooking 1-2
Secluded/Gardens/Tennis/Parking/Good value

A super tip from Jacques Marchal (Chez Nous restaurant,
Plymouth). In the camera-friendly, wooded hills south-east of
both Evian and St-Paul. You'll need no second mortgage to
enjoy the classical and neo-classical cooking of the Birraux
family. Typical dishes: *medaillons de lotte sauce Dugléré* (see
sole in *Glossary*) and *noisettes d'agneau et son jus à l'estragon*.
Menus B-C. Rooms (24) C-D. Disabled. Cards Access, DC, Visa.
Closed Mid Mar to mid Apl. Mid Nov to mid Dec.
Post La Beunaz, 74500 St-Paul-en-Chablais, H.-Savoie.
Tel 50 73 60 11. Fax 50 73 62 28. Mich 105/E2.

ST-PIERRE-DE-CHARTREUSE   Beau Site

Comfortable hotel/Cooking 1
Swimming pool/Good value

A smart, modernised building in the higher part of St-Pierre.
No serious complaints but no special praise either. *Bourgeois*
dishes. Anonymous owners. Some rooms have small kitchens.
The welcome pool regularly earns bonus points from readers.
Menus A-B. Rooms (31) D. Cards Access, Visa.
Closed Mid Oct to mid Dec. Sun evg & Mon (not high season).
Post 38380 St-Pierre-de-Chartreuse, Isère. (Park in *place*.)
Tel 76 88 61 34. Fax 76 88 64 69. Mich 117/E4.

ST-PIERRE-DE-CHARTREUSE   Chalet Hôtel du
                                                            Cucheron

Simple restaurant with rooms/Cooking 1-2
Secluded/Terrace/Parking/Good value

Can I give you yet another reason for driving up into the
secretive Chartreuse? Nothing is too much trouble for the most
kind-hearted owners of the chalet, André and Colette Mahaut.
Among many small touches this one is typical of their anything
but stingy attitude: during a coolish autumn spell radiators
were left on without any pestering from a reader. Cooking?

Expect no miracles and tuck into hearty *Bourgeoise* fare: *truite meunière, selle d'agneau grillée aux herbes, fromage blanc* and *pâtisseries*. Vicka, the Great Dane with the glowing blue coat, has died; there's a one-year-old black replacement (take care!).
Menus A-B. Rooms (7) B. Cards All. (North of St-Pierre.)
Closed Mid Oct to Boxing Day. Tues (not school hols).
Post Col du Cucheron, 38380 St-Laurent-du-Pont. Isère.
Tel 76 88 62 06. Fax 76 88 65 43. Mich 117/F4.

TALLOIRES   Hermitage

Very comfortable hotel/Cooking 2
Secluded/Terr/Gardens/Swim pool/Tennis/Lift/Parking

Neither I nor readers think much of Talloires' lakeside "managed" hotels. This family *logis*, in a glorious position high above the lake, wins an entry by a modest margin. Jean-Jacques and Jacques Chappaz paint a classical cooking canvas with the odd Savoyarde speciality adding a splash of colour.
Menus B-E. Rooms (34) E-F. Cards All.
Closed Nov to Jan. (E of Talloires and above D909A.)
Post chemin de la cascade d'Angon, 74290 Talloires, H.-Savoie.
Tel 50 60 71 17. Telex 385196. Fax 50 60 77 85. Mich 118/B1.

THONES   Nouvel Hôtel du Commerce

Comfortable hotel/Cooking 2
Lift/Garage/Good value

Don't be misled by the name and don't be put off by the exterior of the *logis* in the centre of Thônes. Behind the façade is a terrific hotel. First the welcome from attractive Christiane Bastard-Rosset. Next the assertive cooking from her husband, Roby. Primarily classical cuisine but he makes a sterling effort to promote Savoie. In the evening he lays on a *fondue Savoyarde, raclette* (and with *jambon fumé*) and a *fondue Bourguignonne*. Hungry? Try *farcement Savoyard*: are you full?
Menus A-C. Rooms (25) C-D. Cards Access, Visa.
Closed 1-15 May. 26 Oct-2 Dec. Rest: Mon (not high season).
Post rue Clefs, 74230 Thônes, H.-Savoie. (Near church.)
Tel 50 02 13 66. Mich 118/C1.

VOUGY   Capucin Gourmand

Very comfortable restaurant/Cooking 3
Parking

Guy and Christine Barbin's chalet-style home has two dining rooms; one blue, one white. (She's a friendly lass and is trying hard to polish up her English.) Assured neo-classical dishes: *rable de lapin aux olives noires et purée d'artichaut, pigeon des Dombes rôti à l'estragon* and *filet de féra braisé à l'Ayze* are typical of Guy's light and restrained touch.
Menus C-D. Cards All. (Rooms? See Bonneville A/R hotel.)
Closed 1st wk Jan. 16 Aug to 7 Sept. Sun evg & Mon.
Post rte Bonneville, 74130 Vougy, H.-Savoie.
Tel 50 34 03 50. Mich 105/D4. (N of N205; 7 km E Bonneville.)

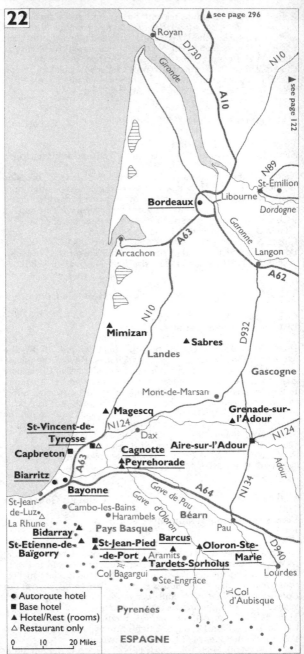

22

see page 296

see page 122

Royan

Gironde

D730

A10

N10

N89

St-Emilion

Bordeaux

Libourne

Dordogne

Garonne

Langon

A62

A63

Arcachon

D932

N10

Mimizan

Sabres

Landes

Gascogne

Mont-de-Marsan

Magescq

N124

Grenade-sur-l'Adour

St-Vincent-de-Tyrosse

Dax

N124

Capbreton

Cagnotte

Aire-sur-l'Adour

Adour

Peyrehorade

Biarritz

A63

A64

N134

Bayonne

Gave de Pau

St-Jean-de-Luz

Cambo-les-Bains

Gave d'Oloron

Béarn

La Rhune

Harambels

Pau

Pays Basque

Bidarray

Pau

St-Etienne-de-Baïgorry

St-Jean-Pied-de-Port

Barcus

Oloron-Ste-Marie

Aramits

D940

Tardets-Sorholus

Col Bagargui

Ste-Engrâce

Lourdes

Col d'Aubisque

Pyrénées

• Autoroute hotel
■ Base hotel
▲ Hotel/Rest (rooms)
△ Restaurant only

0   10   20 Miles

ESPAGNE

346

Why do so many Britons think that there's nothing beyond the southern border of "Dordogneshire"? They seem content to share the Dordogne with tens of thousands of their countrymen, all resident aliens, already encamped there. Why are they oblivious to the pastoral pleasures beyond the **Lot**? The Southwest is one of the most appealing of French regions; the landscape is green and restful and its people are the most open-hearted, friendly and generous in France.

The region, once part of Aquitaine, is composed of several different areas: **Pays Basque** is the south-western corner, alongside the Atlantic and much influenced by Spain; **Béarn** is the terrain around and to the south of Pau; **Landes** is the great line of sandy beaches that run arrow-like north from the Pays Basque, backed up by the enormous pine forests in the hinterland; and Gascony (**Gascogne**) is the mass of gentle hills and valleys between Béarn and the River **Garonne**. To top all that the region also includes the best of the high **Pyrénées**, the mighty mountain barrier between France and Spain. A geographical quirk is that the southern part of the region is on the same latitude as the Côte d'Azur; the "green" tag comes courtesy of the Gulf Stream.

Following this introduction are two additional articles. The

347

first is Selwyn Powell's fascinating account about Béarn which appeared in *French Leave Favourites*. The second is a short piece about the annual Tour de France cycle race.

What does the region offer? Start in **Agen**. The Agen Museum houses the Vénus de Mas, a famed Greek marble statue, and several of Goya's paintings. Then head south to the tiny *cité* of **La Romieu** with its college and two fine examples of Gasconne towers. From there complete a short anti-clockwise tour. **Nérac** comes first, a market town with a park and riverside promenades. On to delectable **Fourcès**; this tiny circular *bastide* was built by the English. Nearby Montréal, built by the French, is on a perched site. Don't miss **Larressingle**, a miniature fortified hamlet the size of two tennis courts. Finally, **Condom** is handsomely sited above the River **Baïse**; the town has a Gothic cathedral with fine cloisters, old streets and an Armagnac museum.

From Condom head upstream, past the 12th-century Abbaye de Flaran and then east to **Lectoure**, high above the River **Gers**. The town has a splendid site, attractive promenades, extensive views, a museum and a cathedral. **Auch** is a bustling town; one exceptional treasure is the Cathédrale Ste-Marie, with marvellous choir stalls and stained-glass windows. **Toulouse**, further east, is a traffic madhouse: endure the crush to see the basilica and the Jacobins church.

Three small *bastides*, west of **Mirande**, will please just as much: Bassoues, with a daunting *donjon* (keep) but, beware, there are over 200 steps to the top; Marciac; and Beaumarchés. Detour to the viewpoint at Puntous de Laguian, on the **N21**, midway between Mirande and **Tarbes**: to the south is the 100-mile-long Pyrénées wall. Spare time for **Plaisance**, a deadbeat little place but the home now of a glorious, cathedral-sized organ, built by young Daniel Birouste. I told the story of this tremendous enterprise in *Favourites*: suffice it to say, that despite numerous setbacks during the construction of the organ, the little town now benefits hugely from the superhuman efforts of both Daniel and Betrand Lazerme, the organist. Each year numerous concerts are held. For details write to Ars Organorum, 32160 Plaisance.

Now to **Pau** and Béarn. Henri IV was born in Pau château, today a pantheon to his memory. The town is endowed with many other charms; among them its cool parks and the classic Boulevard des Pyrénées with its dramatic view of the majestic mountain range to the south.

Follow the banks of the **Gave de Pau** (*gave* means river) to the Grottes de **Bétharram**; there are five levels in the underground series of limestone caves where water plays an important part. Further upstream is **Lourdes**: the events of 1858, when Bernadette first saw the Virgin Mary in a cave alongside the *gave*, is known by all.

From Lourdes several excursions are a must. The **Cirque de Gavarnie** is an unforgettable sight, savage mountains at their overpowering best. Vertical rockfaces rise in several tiers to a total height in excess of 11,000 ft above sea-level. Almost as thrilling is the neighbouring Cirque de Troumouse. The Pyrénées' finest viewpoint is the 9400-ft-high **Pic du Midi de Bigorre**, just north of the **Col du Tourmalet**. The panorama includes, to the south, the wild, snow-covered peaks of the Massif de Néouvielle. You can access the *massif* by road; from St-Lary-Soulan, follow the Neste de Couplan torrent, up to the trio of lakes below the lofty summits.

If you're heading east towards the Med there's a trio of detours you must make. First to the medieval walled village of **St-Bertrand-de-Comminges** with its amazing *cathédrale*, part Romanesque, part Gothic. Next to the dead-end Vallée de la Pique, south of **Bagnères**-de-Luchon and a scenic wonderland. Finally, up yet another road that goes nowhere and voted one of the best in France by readers, the deserted **Col de Pause**, south of **St-Girons**.

I'll return to my tour of Béarn. From Pau head south-west to **Oloron-Ste-Marie** and the 13th-century Eglise Ste-Marie (the Romanesque west door is stunning). Beyond Oloron is *The Three Musketeers* country: Aramis took his name from **Aramits**; nearby Lanne was the home of Monsieur de Porthau – he gave his name to Porthos; and Trois-Villes lent its name to Tréville. Athos is north-west of Sauveterre-de-Béarn.

Beyond the latter, on the road to **St-Jean-Pied-de-Port**, you enter the Pays Basque. Share the pilgrims' road to Santiago de Compostela in northern Spain; you'll spot many a pilgrimage site, clearly marked by the shell sign of St-Jacques. For me the best of the sites is the unusual 12th-century church at Harambeltz (**Harambels** on the map), 21 km north-east of St-Jean. The interior is a richly-decorated surprise. (Ask at the adjacent farm for the key.) St-Jean is a picturesque place where the river and old houses alongside the stream combine attractively. Look out for the high, unusually shaped walls used for the Basque game of *pelota*; St-Jean is one of the strongest centres of the sport.

One must: seek out the D347 between **Tardets-Sorholus** and **Barcus**. Half-way along the route stop: the view south is one of the most eye-pleasing mountain panoramas in France, a landscape of cones, sugar-loaves and mounds.

Follow the Nive to **Cambo-les-Bains**, a small spa and typically Basque. To the east are the underground caves of Isturits and Oxocelhaya. The most famous Basque towns are **Biarritz**, my favourite French resort; bustling **Bayonne**; and the old port of **St-Jean-de-Luz**. **La Rhune** is a legendary summit – a 360-degree panorama of mountains and sea. Between Cambo and the coast are numerous villages; the timbered houses all wear a colourful red and white livery.

The Landes stretches north from Biarritz. The most notable features are the uninterrupted line of sandy beaches, over 100 miles long, and the giant pine forests in the hinterland. In autumn carpets of heather are colourful bonuses.

The southern *porte* to the forest is **Dax**, on the banks of the **Adour**. Apart from its museum and cathedral I remember its *fontaine chaude*, where hot spring water bubbles out of the ground. Water also plays a feature in the many *étangs* (pools) which lie just behind the beaches.

What else remains to be seen? There's **Arcachon**, a sheltered inland resort beside a huge bay and famed for its oysters. Nearby is Europe's highest sand dune, rising nearly 400 ft above the ocean. **St-Emilion** is a personal favourite, much the most atmospheric of the southern wine towns (don't miss its underground church carved out of the limestone). And, finally, if you can cope with the hectic traffic, **Bordeaux** is the most graceful and proud of French cities.

<u>Markets</u> Aire-sur-l'Adour (Tues); Condom (Wed); Mézin (Thurs); Nérac (Sat); Oloron-Ste-Marie (Fri); Pau (Mon to Sat); Plaisance (Thurs); St-Jean-Pied-de-Port (Mon). Michelin green guide: Pyrénées Aquitaine.

Bliss in Béarn   **Selwyn Powell**

"What made you come here?" they all ask, Binns included.
"And do you like it?" It was, quite clearly, our Guardian Angel
who chose the place, and we like it for lots of reasons. Because
of the people, the climate, the scenery, the "browsing and
sluicing" as Wodehouse called it. "But in the North..." "Oh,
they are French; we are Béarnais. Not at all the same thing."

Henri IV (the only good French king. Or, perhaps, not good,
but best-loved) thought Paris was worth a Mass when they
offered him the Kingdom of France on condition that he
became a Roman Catholic. That was, in addition to the King of
Navarre. He was born in the Château de **Pau** which is now a
pantheon to his memory. Round here they wonder if he chose
right. They are not really fond of "Paris", meaning the seat of
government. They enjoy it only as a place to visit.

So let us examine our reasons for liking it here in this part
of non-France. First, the people. At all levels, from the
humblest to the grandest, they are kind and friendly and
helpful. The day we arrived it was pelting and after Pickfords
had unloaded one of their pantechnicons it was parked in a
muddy field. It sank up to the axles. "My employers won't be
pleased when I go back by train without it," said the
disconsolate driver. A couple of hours later a small man in
streaming oilskins came up to me. "I've put it back on the hard
road," he said. "But how, and how did you know?" "I have the
only four-wheel-drive tractor in the district. I farm three
kilometres up the road. I heard you were in trouble." He
wouldn't take any reward or payment. (About how he knew:
they know everything!) "I'm your neighbour and you were in
trouble." It is true: a neighbour will always help.

Even in the middle of a fearful family feud, your cousin with
whom you are daggers drawn will drive your wife ten miles to
town to visit you in hospital. Once, when an English family
was away on holiday at fruit-picking time, they came back to
find their trees stripped, and on the kitchen table was a bowl
of ten franc notes. The fruit had been taken to market for them
without a word and the sale proceeds left in the bowl.

Now, after ten years, we know dozens of people over a
largish area. They are all utterly charming and very
hospitable. Of course there is one exception. "Oh, him," they
say. "He is *un espèce de salaud*! Don't go near him."

Aquitaine was English for 300 years and the French fought
like tigers to get it back, and then in the 19th century the
English conquered it, or part of it, again. You will notice in
Biarritz the Avenues Reine Victoria and Edouard VII; in Pau
there is the Pau Golf Club, founded in 1856 and still a fine
example of clubs established by the British all over the world.
To this day they possess the gold medal presented by the Duke
of Hamilton in 1857; while at the Cercle Anglais (originally the
English Club) the chimney-piece in the salon is adorned by a
bust of "Granny Queen", and there are photographs of her
descendants Queen Elizabeth and the Duke of Edinburgh, and
of the present Prince of Wales and his wife whom they insist
on calling "Lady Dee". My wife and I may be the only English
members now; but at the monthly dinners the silver and table
linen are monogrammed EC and menu cards and invitations
are printed on the original stationery.

The climate of Pau was described by an English (or was he
Scottish) doctor, Sir Alexander Taylor, when he settled there
after the Carlist wars in 1836. He considered this the mildest

place in Europe and the most beneficial for invalids. We are not invalids, but we, too, enjoy the mild, short winters, and summers that are not too blazingly hot. The countryside is always green and there is hardly any frost or snow. Occasionally there are little slips: the spring of 1985 with intense frosts over a long period ("the coldest for 101 years") and the fearful drought of the same year's summer; an unprecedented tempest in 1976, blowing down thousands of trees and stripping nearly every roof, but these really are exceptions. Usually we are able to drink our Christmas or New Year's Day *apéritifs* in the sunshine in the garden; in the summer we live in the blissfully midge-less out-of-doors.

From our house you can see the Pyrénées like a frieze along the skyline and, as we drive into Pau, they rise dramatically in front of us. There are peaks of up to 10,000 ft or so and the Spanish frontier is only an hour and a half away. They rise sharply on the French side, then fall gently away for a hundred miles to the south. By October the first snows have fallen up there, soon most of the passes will be closed and then the skiing starts. The other day we had an autumn picnic facing this lovely panorama, a mile or so beyond the frontier, each high peak topped with white. It was superb, and, as always, we feel "abroad". Here, in France, we are at home. In spring and early summer there are wild flowers that even Alpine enthusiasts have to admit are "just as good". Wherever you look, the slopes are splashed in almost vulgar profusion.

As well as mountains, we have the sea. A gleaming white beach stretches the 250 kilometres from the Gironde to Spain, washed by the least polluted sea, and waves that provide the best surfing in Europe, while the beaches, like the mountain slopes, are almost vulgar with a multicoloured profusion of umbrellas and bikinis and stunning bathing beauties.

About the food and drink: I should refer you to Binns, but there is a lot to be said for living within 30 kilometres of one of the world's best restaurants, while our reward for going to church on Sunday at St-Andrew's, Pau, is to be able to stop at one of the roadside stalls on the way home and buy a couple of dozen *fines claires de Marennes* for a fraction of what oysters cost in some other parts of the world.

It is only when you cross the Channel with your car that you remember how narrow and winding and traffic-filled the English main roads are. Here you can drive almost alone on straight country roads, with only the cowslips and the orchids and the enticing scent of cider-apples to distract you. You can wander for days through Les Landes or the Gers, looking at little fortified villages, many of them built by the English 600 years ago, among woods that are growing the oak for wine casks, and vineyards and châteaux whose names are magic on the labels of bottles far too expensive to drink.

Our *jardin anglais*, made with much toil and almost unaided, though hardly *anglais* at all, is immensely admired by all our French friends. Gardening on this rock-like clay and in this climate makes a nonsense of most of what you knew before, but it is very rewarding. There is never a week in the year when some shrub is not in flower. We had a list of over a hundred flowers in a bowl at Christmas. Seasons are utterly different: snowdrops in December, iris stylosa in October.

All in all this is a wonderful place to live, and we haven't had a moment's regret in ten years at that fateful decision made by our Guardian Angel.

Tour de France

Every July I follow, with consumate interest, the annual progress of the Tour de France cycle race. No other sporting event compares with the heroic efforts of the Tour de France cyclists: the race is the epitome of bravery and endurance.

My interest goes deeper than most because I know the terrain they cover so well, the risks they must take, and the deep depths of human energy they must draw on. How do they do it?

The tour lasts for three weeks and is literally a "tour" of France. Every year the route includes dozens of muscle-sapping climbs in either the Alps or Pyrénées, or both. (In 1992 the high Pyrénées were bypassed, the first time in 80 years.)

During the Eighties English-speaking riders have emerged as both winners of the event or as strong contenders to win: the American Greg LeMond and Irishman Stephen Roche have both won the epic race; others like Irishman Sean Kelly, Scotsman Robert Millar, Australian Phil Anderson, American Andy Hampsten and Canadian Steve Bauer have all made an impact. Anglo Saxons do not appreciate how famous these riders are in Europe. We are fortunate that each year Channel 4 brings us daily TV coverage: bravo Brian Venner and Phil Liggett.

I've chosen this region to highlight the tour because it gives me the chance to identify several of the most demanding, and scenic, roads used in the Pyrénées. Each time the route is varied but every inch is a scenic wonderland; you don't have to be on a bicycle to enjoy the varying landscapes.

Often a stage will finish with a killing climb that comes at the end of what is already an exhausting day's cycling. Think about it: the riders have already covered 150 miles of mountain *cols* but then, at the end of eight hours' cycling, they are expected to finish the stage with a spell of further pedal torture. The organisers are a sadistic lot.

One finishing point of this type is at Superbagnères, south-west of **Bagnères**-de-Louchon. The place is normally a winter-sports' resort but, in July, it provides a snow-free, 4000-ft-climb from Bagnères, 19 km away. The resort itself is over 6000 ft above sea level.

Another mountain-top finish is at Luz Ardiden, west of **Luz-St-Sauveur**. This winter-sports' resort is at a slightly lower altitude than Superbagnères but, nevertheless, the final climb of 3,300 ft is covered in a distance of only 7½ miles. A third, used for the first time in 1991, is Val Louron, south-east of Arreau (at the foot of the Col d'Aspin).

The organisers usually permutate any three of the four highest passes in the Pyrénées. From west to east they are: the **Col d'Aubisque** (between Laruns and **Argelès-Gazost**); the **Col du Tourmalet** (east of Luz-St-Sauveur); the **Col d'Aspin** (much the prettiest pass); and the **Col de Peyresourde** (west of Bagnères-de-Louchon).

Finally, the Tour de France organisers are not afraid of sending the cyclists along some of the most obscure roads. For example, they think nothing of incorporating the narrow roads that run south-east from **St-Jean-Pied-de-Port**, through the Forêt d'Iraty, across the **Col Bagargui**, on to **Ste-Engrâce** and then further east on the newly-completed road which joins the D132 just north of Arette-Pierre-St-Martin. For those of you who really do like to get away from it all, leaving other people far behind, then these are the roads that you should seek out. The terrain is all very much my sort of "mapoholic" territory. I love it; you will too.

Cheeses **Cow's milk**
Belle des Champs from Jurançon; white, mild and an aerated texture
Bethmale a hard cylinder from the valleys south of St-Gaudens
Fromage des Pyrénées a mild, semi-hard, large disk with a hard rind
Passe-l'An a strong, hard cheese; made as a huge wheel
Goat's milk
Cabécous small, flat cheese. Mild, nutty flavour. At its best in winter
Ewe's milk
Esbareich in the form of a big, flat loaf. A summer and autumn season;
ideal with Madiran. Related cheeses: **Laruns**, **Amou** and **Ardi-Gasna**
Iraty a strong-flavoured, pressed loaf. Contains some cow's milk

Regional Specialities
Besugo *daurade* – sea-bream
Chorizos spicy sausages
Confit de canard (d'oie) preserved duck meat (goose)
Cousinette (Cousinat) vegetable soup
Echassier a wading bird of the Landes
Garbure (Garbue) vegetable soup with cabbage and ham bone
Gâteau Basque a shallow, custard pastry – often with fruit fillings
Grattons (Graisserons) a *mélange* of small pieces of rendered down
duck, goose and pork fat; served as an appetiser – very filling
Hachua beef stew
Jambon de Bayonne raw ham, cured in salt. Served as paper-thin slices
Lamproie eel-like fish; with leeks, onions and red Bordeaux wine sauce
Lou-kenkas small, spicy sausages
Loubine (Louvine) grey mullet (like a sea-bass)
Ortolan a small bird (wheatear) from the Landes
Ouillat (Ouliat) Pyrénées soup; onions, tomatoes, goose fat, garlic
Palombes (Salmis de) wild doves and wood pigeons from the Landes
and Béarn, sautéed in red wine, ham and mushrooms
Pastiza see *Gâteau Basque*
Ramereaux ring doves
Salda a thick cabbage and bean soup
Tourin (Tourain) see *Ouillat*. (*Touron*: see Languedoc-Roussillon)
Tourtière Landaise a sweet of Agen prunes, apples and Armagnac
Ttoro (Ttorro) a Basque fish stew

Southwest Wines (see map on next page)
In the countryside near **Jurançon** (south of Pau) you'll find
both sweet and dry whites; other whites are the oddly-named
Pacherenc du Vic-Bilh and the VDQS **Tursan**. **Madiran**
reds are my personal favourites; Tursan, too, makes some reds.
Buzet, north of Condom, produces both reds and whites. The
reds of the AC **Côtes de St-Mont** are much improved; and a
newish VDQS is the **Côtes du Brulhois**, on the left bank of
the Garonne. Meaty reds come from the AC **Côtes du
Frontonnais** and VDQS **Vin de Lavilledieu** areas.
In the south-west corner try **Irouléguy** wines: reds, whites
and rosés. From the area around Orthez come **Béarn** and
Béarn Bellocq wines, again of all shades. **Armagnac**,
France's oldest brandy, is one of the region's marvels. The
Basques make a liqueur called **Izarra** (star) – one yellow, the
other green. **Floc** (Armagnac and grape juice) is an *apéritif*.
Vins de Pays
In the Southwest these will be classified by the names of
départements: **Landes**, **Gers** or **Pyrénées-Atlantiques**.
Alternatively, in the Gers area, you will see **Vin de Pays des
Côtes du Condomois** (from the hills around Condom), **Côtes
de Montestruc** and **Côtes de Gascogne** (reds and rosés).

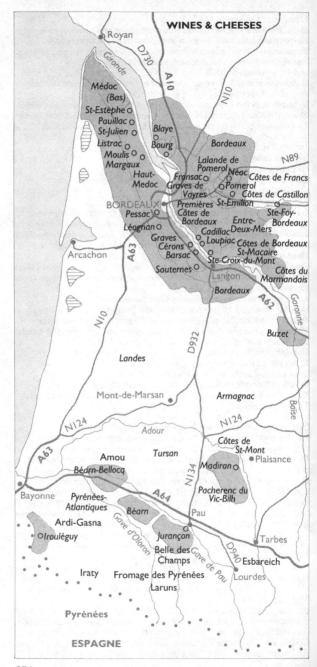

WINES & CHEESES

Royan
Gironde
D730
A10
N10

Médoc
(Bas)
St-Estèphe
Pauillac
St-Julien
Blaye
Listrac
Bourg
Moulis
Margaux
Bordeaux
Haut-
Medoc
N89
Lalande de
Pomerol
Fronsac
Néac
Côtes de Francs
Graves de
Pomerol
Côtes de Castillon
Vayres
Premières
St-Emilion
BORDEAUX
Côtes de
Ste-Foy-
Pessac
Bordeaux
Bordeaux
Léognan
Entre-
Cadillac
Deux-Mers
Graves
Loupiac
Côtes de Bordeaux
Cérons
St-Macaire
Barsac
Ste-Croix-du-Mont
Sauternes
Côtes du
Langon
Marmandais
Bordeaux
A62
Garonne

Arcachon
A63
N10
Buzet

Landes
D932
Mont-de-Marsan
Armagnac
Baïse
N124
N124
Adour
Côtes de
Tursan
St-Mont
Amou
Madiran
Plaisance
Béarn-Bellocq
N134
Bayonne
Pyrénées-
Pacherenc du
Atlantiques
Béarn
Vic-Bilh
A64
Pau
Ardi-Gasna
Gave d'Oloron
Irouléguy
Jurançon
Tarbes
Belle des
Gave de Pau
Champs
Esbareich
Iraty
Fromage des Pyrénées
Lourdes
Laruns
D940

Pyrénées

ESPAGNE

354

Bordeaux Wines

One faces an impossible task in summarising an area where, usually, whole books are devoted to the complex subject. But try I will – especially for those of you who know nothing of the complexities of the Bordeaux classification system. A classic red Bordeaux (called *claret* in the UK) is dryer than red Burgundy, has a longer life, is less heavy in alcohol and is really only drinkable when accompanied by food.

There are five great wines areas. The first four – Médoc, Graves, St-Emilion and Pomerol – produce reds:

Médoc, the largest area and divided into Bas-Médoc and Haut-Médoc. (In **Haut-Médoc** is the very famous village of **Pauillac**, from where three of the five world-renowned, great red châteaux wines come.)

Graves (which means gravelly soil), the second largest area. Whites also are made here.

St-Emilion and **Pomerol**, much smaller areas and both on the banks of the Dordogne.

Sauternes is the fifth area, famous for its white wines.

Some of the best-known wines in the world come from the vineyards of Bordeaux: among the reds are **Château Lafite**, **Château Latour** and **Château Mouton-Rothschild** (all in Pauillac); **Château Margaux** in the Haut-Médoc; and **Château Haut-Brion** from Pessac (Graves). These five are at the top of the pyramid, the *Premiers Crus* (First Growths). It is a white from Sauternes, **Château d'Yquem**, that has a special rank above even those five, *Grand Premier Cru*. Dozens of other château follow, split into levels of prestige, rather than excellence of quality – see the lists that follow two pages on. Thankfully, there are many clarets towards the bottom of the pyramid (see *Crus Bourgeois*) which are sensibly priced; the Bordeaux area produces a high proportion of quality wine for all of us, whatever the size of our pockets.

We need to understand how the *Appellation Contrôlée* system works in Bordeaux. Think of a pyramid: the wines from a specific vineyard, perhaps just as big as a football field, sit at the top and are the most expensive. The bottom of the pyramid represents those wines from any part of the whole region, the ones that do not have a pedigree in the form of their own individual AC status. In Bordeaux, unlike Burgundy, an individual château does not have its own AC; it will share the *commune*, or even the region's, AC classification. Do not imagine the term château always means a fine, imposing building; more often than not it refers to vineyards making up an estate, the only building perhaps being a humble shed, half-buried, where the wine is stored. How does the Bordeaux *Appellation Contrôllée* system work?

1 The bottom of the pyramid. A bottle label with **AC Bordeaux** or **AC Bordeaux-Supérieur** (this means higher alcohol strength, not superior quality) is wine that has come from anywhere in the region; it will be from the fringe areas and will be cheaper. Often, alas, it's nasty wine.

2 A label with **AC Médoc** indicates it comes from that general area to the north-west of Bordeaux, on the west bank of the Gironde. This will be both dearer and better wine. It is likely it will be from the Bas-Médoc – which is considered to be inferior to Haut-Médoc.

3 Moving up the pyramid, a label with **AC Haut-Médoc** will signify the wine was produced in that specific part of the Médoc considered superior for vineyard quality. These wines will be further up the quality and price scale.

All three examples are *generic* wines, those carrying the name of a geographical area, though many of them, even some at the bottom of the pyramid, may still carry a château name.

4 A label with **AC Pauillac** means the wine was made in that *commune* within the Haut-Médoc. It will be getting expensive and will be an excellent claret. Most labels will be carrying a château name as well, from the humble to a few like AC Pauillac Château Lafite; this label would indicate that not only have you a specific vineyard in Pauillac but also one of the top five reds in Bordeaux.

Reds (Great vintages: **45 47 49 53 55 61 66 70 73 75 82 83 89 90**)
There are dozens of clarets available at relatively modest cost. Clearly the first three examples I have mentioned qualify and some from the fourth. So do wines from other Haut-Médoc *communes*: from north to south, **Saint Estèphe**, **Saint Julien**, **Listrac**, **Moulis** and **Margaux**; all have their own AC.

Wines from other areas qualify: **Graves**, **Pessac-Léognan** (Graves *communes*), **Pomerol** (**Château Pétrus** is perhaps the top claret) and **Saint Emilion**. The latter has two AC classifications: the lower rating of **Saint Emilion**; and **Saint Emilion Grand Cru** (divided into two: 11 châteaux take the **Premier Grand Cru Classé**; 60-odd others are **Grand Cru Classé**). Saint Emilion is bordered by five smaller *communes*, all having their own AC with the addition of the words **Saint Emilion**: **Lussac**, **Montagne**, **Parsac**, **Puisseguin** and **Saint Georges**. Other reds from lesser-known areas are (from north to south): **Premières Côtes de Blaye**, **Bourg**, **Côtes de Bourg** (better), **Côtes de Fronsac**, **Fronsac**, **Côtes Canon Fronsac**, **Lalande de Pomerol**, **Néac**, **Bordeaux Côtes de Francs** and **Côtes de Castillon** (both east of St-Emilion).

Other areas are the **Premières Côtes de Bordeaux** (three dozen *communes* can show their village names) on the east bank of the Garonne; **Graves de Vayres**; **Bordeaux Haut Benauge** (part of the Entre-Deux-Mers territory). **AC Bordeaux** and **AC Bordeaux Supérieur** are the most common reds.

Rosés
Rarely seen are the **Bordeaux Clairet** and **Bordeaux Supérieur Clairet** – wines with a shorter fermentation period and thus dark rosé in colour; equally rare are the **AC Bordeaux Rosé** and the **AC Bordeaux Supérieur Rosé**.

Whites (Great vintages: **45 47 49 53 55 61 67 70 71 76 88 89 90**)
The white wines of Bordeaux have gone through a significant transition during recent decades. Because of both the increasing demand for dry wines and the crippling costs of producing sweet, dessert wines, growers have responded by making crisp, light whites – lovely wines and cheap, too. Dry white wines will normally be in green bottles, sweet ones in clear glass.

Of the various whites made from the Sauvignon Blanc grape, look out for the crisp drys of **Entre-Deux-Mers**, **Entre-Deux-Mers-Haut Benauge** and **Graves de Vayres**. A white **AC Bordeaux** will be a dry alternative, as will **Blaye**, **Côtes de Blaye**, **Côtes de Bourg** and **Graves**. From **Côtes de Bordeaux Saint Macaire**, north of Langon, **Premières Côtes de Bordeaux** and **Ste-Foy-Bordeaux** come both dry and sweet wines.

For those of you with a sweet tooth the golden **Sauternes**, **Barsac**, **Cérons**, **Loupiac**, **Sainte Croix-du-Mont** and **Cadillac** will be the answer (the Sémillon grape is the most common – ideal with its high sugar content). **Bordeaux Supérieur** and **Graves Supérieur** are medium-sweet alternatives. There are two AC sparklers: **Bordeaux mousseux** and **Crémant de Bordeaux**.

Great Growths (Grands Crus) of the Médoc – 1855 list

Château	AC taken	Château	AC taken
Premiers Crus		**Troisièmes Crus** (continued)	
Lafite-Rothschild	*Pauillac*	Malescot-St-Exupéry	*Margaux*
Latour	*Pauillac*	Marquis d'Alesme-Becker	*Margaux*
Margaux	*Margaux*	Palmer	*Margaux*
Haut-Brion (not in Médoc)	*Pessac*	**Quatrièmes Crus**	
	(Graves)	Beychevelle	*St-Julien*
Mouton-Rothschild (1973)	*Pauillac*	Branaire-Ducru	*St-Julien*
Deuxièmes Crus		Duhart-Milon	*Pauillac*
Brane-Cantenac	*Margaux*	Lafon-Rochet	*St-Estèphe*
Cos d'Estournel	*St-Estèphe*	La Tour-Carnet	*Haut-Médoc*
Ducru-Beaucaillou	*St-Julien*	Marquis-de-Terme	*Margaux*
Durfort-Vivens	*Margaux*	Pouget	*Margaux*
Gruaud-Larose	*St-Julien*	Prieuré-Lichine	*Margaux*
Lascombes	*Margaux*	St-Pierre	*St-Julien*
Léoville-Barton	*St-Julien*	Talbot	*St-Julien*
Léoville-Las-Cases	*St-Julien*	**Cinquièmes Crus**	
Léoville-Poyferré	*St-Julien*	Batailley	*Pauillac*
Montrose	*St-Estèphe*	Belgrave	*Haut-Médoc*
Pichon-Longueville and Pichon-		Camensac	*Haut-Médoc*
Longueville-Lalande	*Pauillac*	Cantemerle	*Haut-Médoc*
Rauzan-Gassies	*Margaux*	Clerc-Milon	*Pauillac*
Rausan-Ségla	*Margaux*	Cos-Labory	*St-Estèphe*
Troisièmes Crus		Croizet-Bages	*Pauillac*
Boyd-Cantenac	*Margaux*	Dauzac	*Margaux*
Calon-Ségur	*St-Estèphe*	du Tertre	*Margaux*
Cantenac-Brown	*Margaux*	Grand-Puy-Ducasse	*Pauillac*
Desmirail	*Margaux*	Grand-Puy-Lacoste	*Pauillac*
Ferrière	*Margaux*	Haut-Bages-Libéral	*Pauillac*
Giscours	*Margaux*	Haut-Batailley	*Pauillac*
d'Issan	*Margaux*	Lynch-Bages	*Pauillac*
Kirwan	*Margaux*	Lynch-Moussas	*Pauillac*
Lagrange	*St-Julien*	Mouton-Baronne-Philippe	*Pauillac*
Langoa-Barton	*St-Julien*	Pédesclaux	*Pauillac*
La Lagune	*Haut-Médoc*	Pontet-Canet	*Pauillac*

Then follow about 200 *Crus Bourgeois* properties – making quality wines at lower prices than the classified growths listed above. Until recently there were two additional classifications – *Cru Grand Bourgeois* and *Cru Bourgeois Exceptionnel*: the EC objected to these terms and now all of them are called *Crus Bourgeois*.

Premiers Grands Crus of St-Emilion

11 châteaux share this 1985 classification.

Category A (2): Ausone, Cheval-Blanc. *Category B (9)*: Beauséjour-Duffau-Lagarrosse, Bel-Air, Canon, Figeac, Clos Fourtet, La Gaffelière, La Magdelaine, Pavie, Trottevieille. (Beauséjour-Becot demoted 1985.)

Classed Growths of the Graves

Red wines Bouscaut, Haut-Bailly, Carbonnieux, Domaine de Chevalier, Fieuzal, Olivier, Malartic-Lagravière, La Tour-Martillac, Smith-Haut-Lafitte, Haut-Brion (see Médoc list) and its excellent white wine as well, La Mission-Haut-Brion, Pape Clément, Latour-Haut-Brion.

White wines Bouscaut, Carbonnieux, Domaine de Chevalier, Olivier, Malartic-Lagravière, La Tour-Martillac, Laville-Haut-Brion, Couhins.

1855 Classification of Sauternes and Barsac châteaux

Grand Premier Cru – the only one in Bordeaux: Yquem.

Premiers Crus: Climens, Coutet, Rayne-Vigneau, Suduiraut, Guiraud, Haut-Peyraguey, Lafaurie-Peyraguey, La Tour-Blanche, Rabaud-Promis, Rieussec, Sigalas-Rabaud. *Deuxièmes Crus*: Brousset, Caillou, d'Arche, de Malle, de Myrat, Doisy-Daëne, Doisy-Dubroca, Doisy-Védrines, Filhot, Lamothe, Nairac, Romer, Suau.

AGEN
Campanile

Simple hotel/Cooking 1
Terrace/Parking/Good value

A62 exit 7 (Agen). Right towards Agen, cross river, on right.
Menus A-B. Rooms (50) C. Disabled. Cards Access, Visa.
Post ZAC d'Agen Sud, 47000 Agen, L.-et-G.
Tel 53 68 08 08 Telex 573118. Fax 53 98 32 46. Mich 137/D3.
(Bookings: UK freephone 0800 897863)

BAYONNE
Campanile

Simple hotel/Cooking 1
Parking/Good value

Leave A63 exit 6 (Bayonne). On west side of N117.
Menus A-B. Rooms (52) C. Disabled. Cards Access, Visa.
Post av. du Grand Basque, 64100 Bayonne, Pyr.-Atl.
Tel 59 55 95 95. Telex 570772. Fax 59 55 54 61. Mich 148/B3.
(Bookings: UK freephone 0800 897863)

BIARRITZ
Ibis Biarritz Aéroport

Simple hotel/Cooking 1
Terrace/Parking/Good value

Leave A63 exit 4 (Biarritz). At N10 turn right, proceed northeast; hotel on left of N110, opposite airport.
Menus A-B. Rooms (83) C-D. Disabled. Cards Access, Visa.
Post 64 av. d'Espagne, 64600 Anglet, Pyr.-Atl.
Tel 59 03 45 45. Telex 560121. Fax 59 03 33 55. Mich 148/B3.
(Bookings: UK 071 724 1000; US toll free 800 221 4542)

BIARRITZ
Novotel Biarritz Aéroport

Very comfortable hotel/Cooking 1
Terrace/Gardens/Swimming pool/Tennis/Lift/Parking

See Ibis above for exit details.
Menus B. Rooms (85) E-F. Disabled. Cards All.
Post 64 av. d'Espagne, 64600 Anglet, Pyr.-Atl.
Tel 59 03 50 70. Telex 572127. Fax 59 03 33 55. Mich 148/B3.
(Bookings: UK 071 724 1000; US toll free 800 221 4542)

BORDEAUX
Campanile Bordeaux le Lac

Simple hotel/Cooking 1
Parking/Good value

A630 (Bordeaux bypass) exit 4 (Bordeaux le Lac) from Paris; exit 4b (Centre Hôtelier du Lac) from south. North of A630.
Menus A-B. Rooms (132) C. Disabled. Cards Access, Visa.
Post Cent. Hôt. du Lac, 33300 Bordeaux, Gironde. (ER p 103)
Tel 56 39 54 54. Telex 560425. Fax 56 50 19 58. Mich 121/D3.
(Bookings: UK freephone 0800 897863)

BORDEAUX Climat Bordeaux le Lac

Simple hotel/Cooking 1
Parking/Good value

Leave A630 (Bordeaux bypass, the continuation of A10 from Paris) at exit 4 (Bordeaux le Lac) when coming from Paris; exit 4b (Centre Hôtelier du Lac) from south. North of A630.
Menus A-B. Rooms (70) C. Disabled. Cards AE, Access, Visa.
Post Centre Hôtelier du Lac, 33300 Bordeaux, Gironde.
Tel 56 50 50 00. Fax 56 50 09 66. Mich 121/D3.
(Bookings: UK 071 287 3181)

BORDEAUX Ibis Bordeaux le Lac

Simple hotel/Cooking 1
Terrace/Parking/Good value

See Climat above for exit details. At Centre Hôtelier.
Menus A-B. Rooms (119) C-D. Cards Access, Visa.
Post Cent. Hôt. du Lac, 33300 Bordeaux, Gironde. (ER p 103)
Tel 56 50 96 50. Telex 550346. Fax 56 39 63 52. Mich 121/D3.
(Bookings: UK 071 724 1000; US toll free 800 221 4542)

BORDEAUX Mercure Bordeaux le Lac

Comfortable hotel/Cooking 1-2
Terrace/Lift/Closed parking

See Climat and Ibis above for exit details.
Menus B-C. Rooms (108) E-F. Disabled. Cards All.
Post Cent. Hôt. du Lac, 33300 Bordeaux, Gironde. (ER p 103)
Tel 56 50 90 30. Telex 540077. Fax 56 43 07 55. Mich 121/D3.
(Bookings: UK 071 724 1000; US toll free 800 221 4542)

BORDEAUX Mercure Pont d'Aquitaine

Very comfortable hotel/Cooking 1
Terrace/Swimming pool/Tennis/Lift/Closed parking

See all hotels above for exit details. (Previously Sofitel)
Menus B. Rooms (100) F. Disabled. Cards All.
Post Cent. Hôt. du Lac, 33300 Bordeaux, Gironde. (ER p 103)
Tel 56 50 90 14. Telex 540097. Fax 56 50 23 95. Mich 121/D3.
(Bookings: UK 071 724 1000; US toll free 800 221 4542)

BORDEAUX Novotel Bordeaux le Lac

Very comfortable hotel/Cooking 1
Terrace/Swimming pool/Lift/Closed parking

See all hotels above for exit details.
Menus B. Rooms (176) E-F. Disabled. Cards All.
Post Cent. Hôt. du Lac, 33300 Bordeaux, Gironde. (ER p 103)
Tel 56 50 99 70. Telex 570274. Fax 56 43 00 66. Mich 121/D3.
(Bookings: UK 071 724 1000; US toll free 800 221 4542)

Base Hotels

AIRE-SUR-L'ADOUR   Adour Hôtel

Comfortable hotel
Quiet/Swimming pool/Garage/Closed parking/Good value

A new security-conscious building on the right bank of the
River Adour. Rooms cheaper than Oudill's bedrooms (Grenade).
Rooms (31) C. Disabled. Cards Access, Visa.
Post 28 av. 4 Septembre, 40800 Aire-s-l'Adour, Landes.
Tel 58 71 66 17. Fax 58 71 87 66. Mich 150/B2.

CAPBRETON   Océan

Comfortable hotel
Lift/Parking

I discovered the Océan when researching *En Route*. Not on the
front but overlooking the channel which links the sea to inland
étangs. Built in Thirties style of sea-going ship.
Rooms (52) C-E. Cards Access, DC, Visa.
Closed Nov to 9 Apl. Mon evg & Tues (Oct to May).
Post av. G.Pompidou, 40130 Capbreton, Landes. (En Route p 168)
Tel 58 72 10 22. Mich 148/B2.

PAU   Bilaa

Comfortable hotel
Secluded/Lift/Parking/Good value

A modern, ugly-looking concrete box. But don't be put off.
Friendly patron. Tranquil site six km to the west of Pau.
Rooms (80) C-D. Cards AE, Access, Visa.
Closed Xmas to New Year.
Post chemin de Lons, 64230 Lescar, Pyr.-Atl.
Tel 59 81 03 00. Telex 541856. Fax 59 81 15 24. Mich 150/A4.

ST-JEAN-PIED-DE-PORT   Plaza Berri

Simple hotel
Quiet/Good value

Small house in south-east corner of the walled town. Adjacent
to *pelota* court. Parking easy. Rooms cheaper than Pyrénées.
Rooms (8) C.
Post av. Fronton, 64220 St-Jean-Pied-de-Port, Pyr.-Atl.
Tel 59 37 12 79. Mich 166/C2.

ST-VINCENT-DE-TYROSSE   Côte d'Argent

Comfortable hotel
Quiet/Gardens/Lift/Parking/Good value

Smart colourful building – and a lounge too. West of N10.
Rooms (23) C. Cards All.
Post rte Hossegor, 40230 St-Vincent-de-Tyrosse, Landes.
Tel 58 77 02 16. Mich 148/C2.

(No change from *FL3*: still my favourite culinary region.)

AGEN   Hostellerie des Jacobins

Comfortable hotel/Cooking (see text)
Quiet/Parking

I'm writing these words with a heavy, sad heart – just a few days before I go to press. A phone call from a reader has brought the unwelcome news that Serge Bujan, a most lovable and caring hotelier, has passed away after a long illness. The hundreds of readers who've sought out Jacobins (previously a *sans restaurant* base and a huge favourite) will already know of the style and furnishings from another age which give the hotel such character. Gisèle, Serge's widow and an angel of a lady, soldiers on – helped by her daughter and grandson.

You'll note the reference above to "cooking". For some years the plan has been to open a dining room. Who will be the chef? Stéphane, Gisèle's grandson, a lad she and Serge brought up as their own. He's had a long, rigorous culinary training; I've met him and I've seen his classical menus but I've not been able to sample his repertoire. Naturally, the start of the project has been delayed. Dining room or not you will still be able to use Jacobins as a base. (From the A62, use N21 & N113 on Garonne's R bank; turn R just past Chamber of Commerce.)
Menus B-D. Rooms (14) C-F. Cards All. (En Route p 165.)
Closed Rest: 1-15 Nov. Mon midday. Sat. (By Jacobins church.)
Post 1 ter pl. Jacobins, 47000 Agen, L.-et-G.
Tel 53 47 03 31. Telex 571162. Fax 53 47 02 80. Mich 137/D3.

ARGELES-GAZOST   Miramont

Comfortable hotel/Cooking 2
Gardens/Parking/Good value

An unusually-styled smart hotel with a colourful garden and opposite a circular park. Readers rate Mme Pucheu one of the friendliest *patronnes* in France. Husband Louis, the chef, is a classicist who makes good use of regional produce.
Menus A-B. Rooms (29) B-C. Cards Access, Visa.
Closed 20 Oct to 22 Dec. Mon (Jan to Mar but not school hols).
Post rue Pasteur, 65400 Argelès-Gazost, H.-Pyr.
Tel 62 97 01 26. Mich 168/B3.

ARGELES-GAZOST   Thermal

Comfortable hotel/Cooking 1
Secluded/Gardens/Parking/Good value

You don't have to have an ailment to qualify as a visitor at this fort-like 100-year-old *logis* with its own thermal spring. Gardens? No, a 20-acre wooded park with fine views. Readers like Gisèle Coiquil, the hotel's *directrice*. Jean Coiquil's cooking is basic *Bourgeoise*. Annexe rooms have small kitchens.
Menus A-B. Rooms (30) B-C. Cards Access, Visa.
Closed 11 Oct to 17 May. (At Beaucens; 5 km SE on D100 & D13.)
Post Beaucens-les-Bains, 65400 Argelès-Gazost, H.-Pyr.
Tel 62 97 04 21. Mich 168/B3.

BARBOTAN-LES-THERMES — La Bastide Gasconne

Very comfortable hotel/Cooking 3
Quiet/Terr/Gardens/Swimming pool/Tennis/Lift/Parking

One of the Guérard/Barthélémy quartet of spa hotels. A vital improvement here is that "Hubert" and his wife, Joëlle, have arrived to take over the running of both the kitchens and the front of house. Now 60, Hubert's culinary working life has led him up all sorts of avenues; he's a passionate modern cooking fan with a repertoire bubbling with an innovative mix of mainly Nineties *plats* and some neo-classical dishes. A menu labelled *Repas Impromptu* is a fine example of *rapport qualité-prix*. Hubert is most certainly not a Guérard clone. Bravo! La Bastide (in this case the word means small country house or farm) is a pleasant, pleasing hotel in a quiet, homely spa.
Menus B-D. Rooms (34) E-F. Cards AE, Access, Visa.
Closed Nov to 22 Mar.
Post Barbotan-les-Thermes, 32150 Cazaubon, Gers.
Tel 62 69 52 09. Telex 521009. Fax 62 69 51 97. Mich 150/C1.

BARBOTAN-LES-THERMES — Château Bellevue

Comfortable hotel/Cooking 2
Quiet/Terrace/Gardens/Swimming pool/Lift/Parking

Michèle Consolaro's château, at Cazaubon south of the spa, has many admirers. Readers have liked the elegant mansion, the large park and its century-old cedars. Chef Bruno Roussel's cuisine is primarily neo-classical. Raise your beret to both Bruno and Michèle for introducing and persevering with a *Menu Tout Poisson* (all fish menu): that's just what Gers needs.
Menus B-D. Rooms (25) C-E. Cards All.
Closed 2 Jan to 22 Feb. Tues evg & Wed (Dec).
Post 32150 Cazaubon, Gers. (3km SW of Barbotan-les-Thermes.)
Tel 62 09 51 95. Telex 521429. Mich 150/B1.

BARCUS — Chez Chilo

Comfortable hotel/Cooking 2
Gardens/Parking/Good value

A super find to the west of Oloron-Ste-Marie, at the heart of *The Three Musketeers* terrain. Rarely explored, there's now an extra good reason for heading into this largely-ignored *pays*. Pierre (a rallying nut) and Martine Chilo are the third generation *patrons* (a family renowned locally for their rugby links). She's as proud as a punchy prop of her eight new bedrooms, built to her design; cracking they are too, worth the extra francs charged. Pierre's cooking play is a mix of mainly classical, some *Bourgeoise* and regional: the spectrum of dishes includes *pigeonneau rôti à l'ail doux, côte de porc, pintade forestière, île flottante* and *panaché de desserts du pays Basque*. (Don't miss the D347 drive to the south.)
Menus A-B. Rooms (15) B-E. Disabled. Cards Access, Visa.
Closed Mid Jan to mid Feb. Sun evg & Mon (not high season).
Post 64130 Barcus, Pyr.-Atl.
Tel 59 28 90 79. Fax 59 28 93 10. Mich 167/E2.

BIDARRAY   **Pont d'Enfer**

Simple hotel/Cooking 1-2
Quiet/Terrace/Gardens/Parking/Good value

Readers have nothing but complimentary praise for the modest Dufau family *logis*, clothed in the standard red and white livery of the area. One big plus: the hotel is on the left bank of the Nive, away from the hellish D918. Another bonus is the terrace beside the river and bridge. At places like this value for money is paramount and you'll not nose out better *Bourgeoise* grub: *truite amandine, mouton grillé, omelette au jambon, crème caramel* and so on. In addition a handful of local specialities appeal: *poulet sauté Basquaise, piperade au jambon* and *gâteau Basque* are a typical tummy-filling trio.
Menus B. Rooms (17) B-D.
Closed Nov to Easter.
Post 64780 Bidarray, Pyr.-Atl.
Tel 59 37 70 88. Mich 166/B1.

CAGNOTTE   **Boni**

Simple hotel/Cooking 2
Terrace/Swimming pool/Parking/Good value

Another good find. The tip came from a reader who had enjoyed the gentle hill walking at the southern end of the otherwise flat, forested Landes *département*. Annie Demen is the capable *cuisinière*. A mix of classical and *Bourgeoise* cooking and some reworked regional recipes; shellfish and fish (*merlan, sole, langoustines, moules* and similar) play an important part in her repertoire. That's no surprise as husband Jacques is a wholesale fishmonger. He speaks some English.
Menus B-C. Rooms (10) B-C. Cards AE, Access, Visa.
Closed Jan. 26 Oct-9 Nov. Rest: Mon midday (Oct to mid June).
Post 40300 Cagnotte, Landes. (8 km NE of Peyrehorade.)
Tel 58 73 03 78. Fax 58 73 13 48. Mich 149/D3.

CASTERA-VERDUZAN Rest. **Florida & Hôtel Ténarèze**

Simple restaurant with rooms/Cooking 2
Terrace/Good value

A longtime favourite of readers. Castéra-Verduzan is a minute thermal spa on the road from Auch to Condom. The light stone-built Florida is the home of Bernard Ramounéda, the third generation chef/patron; his grandmother started the business in 1935 and was continued by his mother Paulette. In winter a fire crackles in the dining room fireplace; in summer the tiny terrace is shaded by a chestnut tree umbrella. Classical, neo-classical and regional offerings: *foie gras en terrine, pot au feu de canard confit, fleur de courgette à la mousse de saumon frais, canette aux pêches* and *trois chocolats* are a sample quintet. The hotel is run as a separate business.
Menus B-C. Rooms (24) B. Cards All (R); Access, Visa (H).
Closed Feb. Sun evg & Mon (not high season).
Post 32410 Castéra-Verduzan, Gers.
Tel 62 68 13 22(R) 62 68 10 22(H).Fax 62 68 14 69.Mich 151/E2.

ENCAUSSE-LES-THERMES · Marronniers

Comfortable restaurant with basic rooms/Cooking 2
Quiet/Terrace/Gardens/Parking/Good value

I first recommended the unspoilt, well-named Marronniers a decade ago. The setting is enticing: alongside the Job, the big bonus is the shady terrace between the building and the river. Equally important is the all-critical human part of the equation: Michel, the chef, and Christiane Estrampes have never let the side down. A warm, friendly welcome is assured from *la patronne*; and copious, enjoyable fare (classical and *Bourgeoise*) from Michel's kitchen is just as certain. Among the two cracking good-value menus are some highlights: *cassoulet Commingeois* (don't miss St-Bertrand-de-Comminges), *saumon frais braisé au Jurançon* and *gâteau des Prélats*.

Menus A–B. Rooms (10) B. Cards Access, Visa.
Closed 2-31 Jan. Sun evg & Mon (not high season).
Post 31160 Encausse-les-Thermes, H.-Gar.
Tel 61 89 17 12. Mich 169/F2. (South of St-Gaudens.)

GRENADE-SUR-L'ADOUR · Pain Adour et Fantaisie

Very comfortable restaurant with rooms/Cooking 4
Terrace/Parking

Not yet 40, Didier Oudill has already chalked up almost 25 years' working experience in kitchens, half of that span at the right hand of the legendary Michel Guérard. First at the Pot au Feu in Asnières, when he was a strip of a lad at 15; later at nearby Eugénie. Didier and Janine, his wife, went solo in 1987 with the simplest of philosophies: "Clients come first, clients come second, clients come third."

The evidence of that noble thinking is all around you. Didier's two lower-priced menus (one B, Mon-Fri; one C) are largesse; bear in mind they include TVA (VAT) at 18.6% and 15% service. Small details here are supreme. Appetisers give you the first clue to the chef's laser-sharp eye for not cutting corners; the *petits fours*, the best anywhere, confirm that he's a prince among chefs. Didier's talents are highly individualistic; neo-classical, modern and regional creations flow from his kitchen in a spectacular cascade. Among many highlights we recall a dramatic *rouleaux de printemps à la friture d'ognoasses et la suprême de caneton cuit rosé en cocotte* and an audacious feather-light *dacquoise moelleuse aux avelines, poêlée d'abricots au gros sucre et glace au caramel*.

The interior is a pleasing combination of spacious rooms, proud stonework and warm panelling and the riverside terrace is one of the best. This should be the model for all two-star and three-star shrines; there's no penguin stiffness about the service and there's a humm of excitement in the air. Perhaps Didier can win a third star without changing one iota. Cynic that I now am I'll not put any money on that wishful thought. 1991 saw the opening of 11 super bedrooms in an adjacent 18th-century, half-timbered house overlooking the River Adour.

Menus B–E. Rooms (11) F. Disabled. Cards All. (See Aire Base.)
Closed 4-8 Jan. Mon (rest). Sun evg (not July/Aug). Pub hols.
Post 7 pl. Tilleuls, 40270 Grenade-sur-l'Adour, Landes.
Tel 58 45 18 80. Fax 58 45 16 57. Mich 150/A2.

MAGESCQ   Relais de la Poste

Very comfortable hotel/Cooking 3-4
Quiet/Terr/Gardens/Swim pool/Tennis/Garage/Parking

The Basque-style Relais is a formidable family enterprise.
Bernard Coussau and his son, Jean, cook impeccable classical
plats, all of which profit from the rich Landes larder and the
bountiful Biscay waters. *Foie gras chaud de canard aux raisins*
and *lou magret de canard, sauce Landaise* are *terroir* dishes;
chevreuil sauce Grand Veneur, *sole aux cèpes* and *tournedos de
boeuf de Chalosse et sa sauce aux truffes* are refined examples
of their classical skills. A second son, Jacques, is both a
polished *maître-d'hôtel* and knowledgeable *sommelier*.
Menus C-D. Rooms (10) F. Cards All.
Closed 11 Nov-23 Dec.Mon *midi*(Jul/Aug).Mon evg & Tue(Sep-Jun).
Post 40140 Magescq, Landes. (The N10 bypass is most welcome.)
Tel 58 47 70 25. Telex 571349. Fax 58 47 76 17. Mich 148/C2.

MIMIZAN   Au Bon Coin

Very comfortable restaurant with rooms/Cooking 3
Quiet/Terrace/Gardens/Garage/Parking

An idyllic spot among the perfumed Landes' pines and with its
lawns edging on to the still Etang d'Aureilhan. The restaurant
is aptly named and has been extensively swished up during the
15 years we've known Bon Coin. Jean-Pierre and Jacqueline
Caule regularly win plaudits. His cooking is both modern and
neo-classical: *terrine de langoustines, saumon et sole* and *petits
crabes farcis* are light concoctions; *pot au feu de la mer* is a
more hearty signature speciality of the very capable chef.
Breakfasts? One reader wrote: "Superlative; the best
anywhere, ever." If only more French chefs would emulate J-P.
Menus B-D. Rooms (8) E-F. Cards AE, Access, Visa.
Closed Feb. Sun evg & Mon (not July & Aug).
Post 40200 Mimizan, Landes. (N of Mimizan on D87.)
Tel 58 09 01 55. Fax 58 09 40 84. Mich 134/A3.

OLORON-STE-MARIE   Darroze

Comfortable hotel/Cooking 2
Gardens/Lift/Good value

Guy and Fanfan Darroze battle on at their refurbished family
hotel in a quiet corner alongside the *mairie* (the hotel was
previously called Béarn). Guy lost both his brother Luc and his
mother in 1990/91. His cooking flows with the classical and
neo-classical streams: *patisson braisé au foie gras, rognons de
veau aux langoustines* and *tulipe de mousse au chocolat et sa
crème au gingembre* are typical. Fanfan speaks English and
the couple work hard to lay on interesting detours for clients:
visits to Jurançon and *foie gras* producers; and a *promenade*
with an ornithologist are just two examples.
Menus B-C. Rooms (30) C-E. Cards All. (Park in *place*.)
Closed 2nd half Jan. Fri & Sat midday (Nov to Apl).
Post 4 pl. Mairie, 64400 Oloron-Ste-Marie, Pyr.-Atl.
Tel 59 39 00 99. Fax 59 39 17 88. Mich 167/F2.

PEYREHORADE
Central

Comfortable hotel/Cooking 2-3
Lift/Good value

The hotel bears no resemblance to the place François Barrat ran a decade ago. In 1987 Sylvie de Lalagade and her husband Patrick bought the property. They've given the place more than just cosmetic plastic surgery; the light, colourful furnishings and décor are a vast improvement. And, better still, two years ago Sylvie's brother, Eric Galby, took over the kitchens. He spent many years at the Bonne Auberge at Clisson (Poitou-Charentes); he learnt a lot from Serge Poiron. Modern and neo-classical cooking with an appetising touch.

Menus A-B. Rooms (17) D. Disabled. Cards All. (Park in *place*.)
Closed Last wk Feb. 1st half Mar. Sun evg & Mon(not July/Aug).
Post pl. A. Briand, 40300 Peyrehorade, Landes.
Tel 58 73 03 22. Telex 571301. Mich 149/D3.

PLAISANCE
La Ripa Alta

Simple hotel/Cooking 2-3
Good value

Maurice Coscuella's roller-coaster ride resembles a fast car drive in the Cotswold's big-dipper Bottoms (page 45 *Best of Britain*). Up came the star, deservedly; down went standards, out went the star. Generous-hearted, English-speaking Maurice and his gentle wife, Irène, have had their problems in the last few years, both health and other headaches. I've taken off the rose-tinted specs one reader said I was wearing; see my rating. His cooking is innovative modern; not always with the polish of the past but still damm good value.

Menus A-D. Rooms (10) B-D. Cards All.
Closed Mid Nov to end Dec. Rest: Mon (mid Sept to mid Mar).
Post 32160 Plaisance, Gers. (Opposite church; park in *place*.)
Tel 62 69 30 43. Fax 62 69 36 99. Mich 150/C3.

POUDENAS
La Belle Gasconne

Comfortable restaurant with rooms/Cooking 2-3
Gardens/Swimming pool/Parking

Hurrah: the six rooms are at last ready and waiting in the *moulin* across the road and alongside the Gélise (see *FL3* and *Favourites*). Marie-Claude Gracia is a remarkable chef by any measure; strong brown eyes give the clues to her quiet determination and indefatigable character. A mother of five, she and her hubby, Richard, have an intuitive sympathy for their *pays*. Tuck into truly authentic regional and classical treats: prize-winning *foies gras*; rich, gutsy *civet de canard*; home-made *fromageon*; yummy Agen *prune* tart; the list is long. One debit: readers claim inconsistency which, alas, was confirmed by us on our last visit when the couple were away.

Menus B-C. Rooms (6) E-F. Cards All.
Closed 1-15 Jan. 1-15 Dec. Sun evg & Mon (not high season).
Post 47170 Poudenas, L.-et-G.
Tel 53 65 71 58. Mich 136/B4.

PUYMIROL   L'Aubergade

Very comfortable hotel/Cooking 4-5
Terrace/Garage

Two-star chefs face a perverse dilemma. Their food may match, or even better, any three-star chef's efforts. But to join the club they must gamble: they have to put their money where their mouths are. More precisely they must borrow Fort Knox sums to meet Michelin's non-culinary criteria. If the gamble succeeds fame and fortune are assured. However, with perhaps one exception, Jacques Pic, the accolade changes the individuals, their families and restaurants: not one of the latter can match the pleasure they gave in pre-three-star days.

Will the same changes affect the next generation of chefs near the top of the three-star spiral? Clément, Bardet, Silva, Bras and Oudill may, one day, reach the summit. Will they, their families and restaurants change for the worse? Will the same fate engulf Trama at L'Aubergade?

Michel and Maryse, with their young family, arrived at the *bastide* in 1978. A year later, after a total renovation, they opened the 13th-century restaurant. By 1981 Michel had won a first star, by 1983 the second. (Gault Millau took years to recognise his talents; as they did with Robuchon, too.)

Trama is passionate, outspoken, self-taught, a V12 engine of powerful energy and talent. I first met Michel in 1982 but I recall, more vividly, a long heart-to-heart I had with him in 1985. His determination to win a third star was, and still is, all consuming. His concern was would he achieve his ambition in out-of-the-way Puymirol? Would Toulouse be better? For his family's sake he decided to stay put. But he needed an hotel. By 1989 he had masterminded the addition of ten ultra-modern, high-tech bedrooms in the house next door. The kitchens and dining rooms were also given an expensive revamp.

The gamble has been taken. But now he incurs sky-high, three-star costs without the flood of income guaranteed by the accolade. Bedroom prices are dear: one reader wonders if Trama is trying to earn back his investment all at once.

Back to the culinary basics. Trama, like Bras and Robuchon, is a one-off. His ultra-modern, contemporary style (*la cuisine en liberté*) requires vast amounts of time-consuming skills. He's a construction and presentation addict and his technical ability is peerless: witness the succession of cones, cubes, pyramids, textures and tastes. His knife work would please a neuro-surgeon and many a *plat* is spiced with a dash of fun.

Michel's inventiveness is unique: *déclinaison de canard*, an *hors d'oeuvre* of seven or eight differently-prepared morsels of duck; *cristalline de pomme verte*, made from Granny Smith apples, epitomises his rare skills; and *hamburger de foie gras chaud*, the *foie gras* sandwiched between a thick slice of potato and an equally matched in thickness *cèpe*, are three examples of his brilliance. The list is endless. Some readers reckon his cooking is "gimmicky"; and others now tie the same label to the bedrooms. Best of luck Michel and Maryse: I hope you reach the summit; but I pray even more that you keep your feet planted firmly on the precarious peak.

Menus C-E. Rooms (10) F2. Disabled. Cards All. (See also p 361.)
Closed Feb. Mon (Oct to Easter but not on pub. hols).
Post 52 rue Royale, 47270 Puymirol, L.-et-G. (East of Agen.)
Tel 53 95 31 46. Fax 53 95 33 80. Mich 137/E3.

RISCLE   Paix

Very simple hotel with basic rooms/Cooking 1
Good value

As basic as they come but that doesn't stop Michel Caupenne
dressing up the façade with two dozen colourful window boxes.
Cooking is cheap and cheerful regional and *Bourgeoise*, beefed
up with *salmis de palombes* and *confit de canard grillé*.
Menus A-B. Rooms (16) A-B.
Closed 26 Aug to 5 Sept. Last 3 wks Oct.
Post 32400 Riscle, Gers. (Parking no problem.)
Tel 62 69 70 14. Mich 150/B2.

SABRES   Auberge des Pins

Comfortable hotel/Cooking 2
Quiet/Terrace/Gardens/Parking

Typical Landais flower-strewn, chalet-style hotel surrounded
by pines. Super for children: sand-pit, swing, nearby *piscine*,
and a mini railway to the Marquèze Ecomusée. Michel Lesclauze
and Suzanne, his mother, cook classical and regional fare.
Menus A-D. Rooms (26) C-F. Disabled. Cards Access, Visa.
Closed Jan. Sun evg & Mon (not high season).
Post 40630 Sabres, Landes. (Follow signs for town's *piscine*.)
Tel 58 07 50 47. Fax 58 07 56 74. Mich 134/C3.

ST-ETIENNE-DE-BAIGORRY   Arcé

Comfortable hotel/Cooking 2
Secluded/Terrace/Gardens/Swim pool/Tennis/Parking

The setting, beside the swirling Nive des Aldudes, is superb.
Praise, too, for the Arcé family, represented by Emile and his
son Pascal (5th generation). Sadly, groans about the classical
and regional cooking (heavy, greasy and indigestible) land on
my desk from time to time. Popular UK tour operator's base.
Menus B-C. Rooms (20) C-E. Cards Access, Visa.
Closed Mid Nov to mid Mar.
Post 64430 St-Etienne-de-Baïgorry, Pyr.-Atl.
Tel 59 37 40 14. Fax 59 37 40 27. Mich 166/C2.

ST-GIRONS   Eychenne

Very comfortable hotel/Cooking 2
Quiet/Terrace/Gardens/Swimming pool/Parking

Arguably English-speaking Michel Bordeau (a famed French rugby
player) and his wife, Sylvette, are consummate hoteliers. But,
like the entry above, the hotel just scrapes in. Some gripes
about service ("seemed as if customers in the way"). Classical
and regional cuisine. Popular UK and US tour operators' base.
Menus B-D. Rooms (48) B-E. Cards All.
Closed 22 Dec-31 Jan. Sun evg & Mon (Nov-Mar; not pub. hols).
Post 8 av. P.Laffont, 09200 St-Girons, Ariège. (E; nr bypass.)
Tel 61 66 20 55. Fax 61 96 07 20. Mich 170/B3.

ST-JEAN-PIED-DE-PORT   Pyrénées

Very comfortable hotel/Cooking 3-4
Terrace/Gardens/Swimming pool/Lift/Garage/Parking

Firmin Arrambide, in his mid-40s, has progressed remarkably since I enthused, over a decade ago, about his innovative modern and regional cooking. Born in St-Jean, he's the third generation chef at the family hotel. The building, now much extended and modernised, has all the usual R&C mod-cons. Lighting in both bedrooms and corridors needs improving: Anne had a very nasty fall in a darkened passage-way last year.

Firmin's repertoire includes widely-differing conundrums of choice: a punchy regional *garbue aux choux*; a classic *pièce de boeuf grillée à la Béarnaise* (where better to savour the silky sauce); and modern canvases, typical of which is an inspired marriage of fish and the local sweet red peppers. Vegetables (shaped, stuffed, sophisticated and savourless) and desserts are less successful. Raymonde, Firmin's mother, has retired, much to readers' relief. Service is slick. St-Jean can be noisy; the bedside ear-plugs could be welcome in high season.

Menus C-E. Rooms (20) F-F2. Cards AE, Access, Visa.(See Base.)
Closed 5-28Jan. 20Nov-22Dec. Mon evg(Nov-Mar).Tue(15 Sep-Jun).
Post pl. Ch. de Gaulle, 64220 St-Jean-Pied-de-Port, Pyr.-Atl.
Tel 59 37 01 01. Telex 570619. Fax 59 37 18 97. Mich 166/C2.

ST-VINCENT-DE-TYROSSE   Le Hittau

Comfortable restaurant/Cooking 3
Terrace/Gardens/Parking

Le Hittau is described as an 18th-century *bergerie* (manger) but, in reality, is a Landaise wooden-built *maison* in a tree-filled garden. Max Dando is a classical cooking disciple capitalising on the treasure chest of regional produce: *foie gras*; *pigeon de pays à l'ail doux confit*; *St-Pierre au vin rouge*; and an immigrant from the Sologne, a scrumptious *tarte Tatin*. Brother Philippe is a polished *maître-d'hotel*. The roaring fire is welcome on coolish autumn days.

Menus B-D. Cards All. (Rooms? See Base hotel; 2 minutes away.)
Closed 1 Feb-15 Mar. Mon(not evg July/Aug). Sun evg(Sept-Jun).
Post 40230 St-Vincent-de-Tyrosse, Landes.
Tel 58 77 11 85. Mich 148/C2. (200 metres S of N10; E of town.)

TARDETS-SORHOLUS   Pont d'Abense

Comfortable restaurant with rooms/Cooking 1-2
Quiet/Terrace/Gardens/Parking/Good value

A big favourite. Why? Four winning shots: the caring Ibars (*15-l'oeuf*); the shady garden and *jardin fleuri* (*30-l'oeuf*); the quiet Basque house west of the Saison (*40-l'oeuf*); and classical/regional fare which ensures tummies are kept full to the brim (Game). (*L'oeuf*? That's how tennis got its "love".)

Menus A-C. Rooms (12) B-C. Cards Access, Visa.
Closed 20 Nov to 10 Jan. Thurs (not high season).
Post Abense-de-Haut, 64470 Tardets-Sorholus, Pyr.-Atl.
Tel 59 28 54 60. Mich 167/E2. (S&W of Tardets & River Saison.)

CORSICA

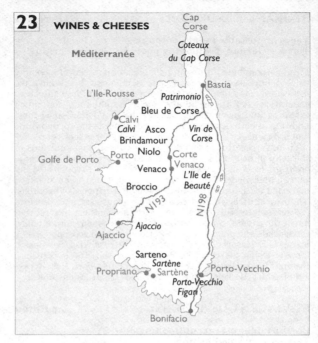

23   **WINES & CHEESES**

Cap Corse

Coteaux du Cap Corse

Méditerranée

Bastia

L'Ile-Rousse

Patrimonio

Bleu de Corse

Calvi

Asco   Vin de Corse

Brindamour

Niolo

Porto   Corte

Golfe de Porto   Venaco

Venaco   L'Ile de Beauté

Broccio

N193   N198

Ajaccio

Ajaccio

Sarteno

Sartène

Propriano   Sartène

Porto-Vecchio

Porto-Vecchio

Figari

Bonifacio

Few visitors to France are ever lucky enough to share in the exciting spectacle of spotting the distant island of Corsica from the mainland. The atmospheric conditions that create this rare sight occur infrequently. You need a crisp, cold, winter's day and to be high up in the Alpes Maritimes; the island lies 100 miles to the south of the Côte d'Azur.

I have only had the good fortune to visit the island once, far too many years ago. There are few roads but what exciting rallying stages they make: no wonder an annual event is tagged the "Rally of the 10,000 Curves". Perhaps one day I'll make the time to explore the island at a more gentle pace and then I can prepare a full regional chapter for Corsica.

Rallyists may rush the island's roads but the tourist must drive like a snail. Today Corsica is called the "Scented Isle"; the Greeks named the island *kalliste*, "the most beautiful"; Byron wrote "the purple of ocean is deepest in dye". The coast roads twist and turn in tortuous succession. The high mountain lanes dive left and right, up and down; no straight is more than 100 yards long. The roads wind across forests of pine, chestnut and beech, and through the air of the *maquis*, perfumed by rosemary, lavender, juniper and other herbs.

The spectacular landscape around **Corte** and **Venaco** is a must; the D84 from Corte to **Porto** is a special highlight. Both the hinterland and the coast around Porto (the **Golfe de Porto**) is recommended time after time by readers. So is the long drive around **Cap Corse**; and don't bypass the detour up the D31 from **Bastia** to San-Martino-di-Lota, for one reader the "dream of southern paradise (no streets, just terraces and tiny little areas which pass for squares)."

Other much-liked areas include: the terrain to the south of **L'Ile-Rousse**; the coast surrounding **Porto-Vecchio**; and the medieval town of **Sartène**, perched high above **Propriano**. Michelin green guide: Corse.

Cheeses Goat's milk

Brindamour also known as **Fleur du Maquis**. A small square, covered with the herbs rosemary and savory. Best season in summer. Some versions of neighbouring **Asco** are similar

Niolo similar shape to Brindamour but with no herb covering. Very sharp taste; can also be made with ewe's milk. **Asco** is a related cheese

Sarteno an uncooked, pressed and flattened ball with a sharp taste. Often made from ewe's milk

Venaco can also be made from ewe's milk. Same shape as Niolo. Strong, sharp smell and taste. Cured in caves

Ewe's milk

Broccio (Brocciu) a fresh cheese made by heating and beating the milk. Packed in small baskets. Often served with cream and sugar. Used in many Corsican desserts

Corse (Bleu de) a blue cheese made in tall cylinders. Used to be cured at Roquefort (see Massif Central: Cévennes) but now on the island. Similar taste to that world-famous sharp-tasting cheese

Regional Specialities

Aziminu the Corsican *bouillabaisse*. Large *rascasse* (called *capone* or *capoum*), red peppers and pimentos are among the local ingredients

Canistrelli an almond cake flavoured with *anis*

Cédrat a sour lemon-like fruit used in sweets and liqueurs

Falculelle (Falculella) a cheesecake using Broccio cheese

Fiadone an orange-flavoured flan made with Broccio cheese

Fritelle chestnut flour fritters

Panizze a fried cake made from chestnut flour (or cornmeal)

Piverunata (Pebronata) a stew of kid (young goat), or beef, or chicken – in a sauce of red peppers, garlic and tomatoes

Pulenta (Polenta) in Corsica this is usually made from chestnut flour – similar in appearance to the Italian boiled commercial version ·

Stufatu the Italian influence is strong in Corsican cooking – especially pasta. This dish is macaroni with mushrooms and onions

Torta castagina a tart covered with crushed almonds, *pignons*, *raisins secs* and a dash, or two, of rum

Ziminu a pimento and red pepper sauce for fish

Wines

There are eight *appellation contrôlée* names for the island's wines. The most basic wine is **Vin de Corse**. This Vin de Corse prefix forms part of five of the classifications – followed by local area names: **Coteaux du Cap Corse** (near Bastia); **Sartène**, **Figari**, **Porto-Vecchio** (all in the south) and **Calvi**. **Ajaccio** and **Patrimonio** (near Bastia) are the other two. You'll find dry whites, fruity rosés (the best comes from grapes macerated for one night) and strong reds.

Look out for the sweet Muscat and Malvoisie (Malmsey) grape type wines. Cap Corse (Corsica's northern finger) also gives its name to a well-known *apéritif*.

Enjoy the Corsican versions of *eaux-de-vie* – colourless liqueurs distilled from fermented fruit juices: *arbouse* – strawberry tree fruit, a Corsican rarity. Relish *cédratine* – a sweet liqueur made from *cédrat*, a sour lemon-like fruit.

Vins de Pays

These are called **L'Ile de Beauté**.

FRANCE A LA CARTE

Some of you may have seen one of the first books I wrote and published over a decade ago – *France à la Carte*. Assembling that little book gave me as much pleasure as any of my more heavyweight tomes. The concept was simple. I wrote scores of chapters on different "themes"; I gave the reader a choice so "à la carte" seemed an apt label. Every chapter, on the facing page, had a map; place names in **bold** print in the text were identified on the map – making it easier for readers to locate them on a larger-scale *carte*. The words "à la carte" seemed doubly appropriate. Hence the title.

For this new edition of *French Leave* I have included an 80-page section which gives me the chance, once again, to bring to your notice dozens of different "themed" subjects. One-third of the chapters, in the section that follows, is entirely new. The remainder appeared in *France à la Carte*; I have rewritten some of these completely and the rest have been edited and improved by additional material.

I hope you'll skip through the pages, stopping to read the odd chapter which takes your fancy. I would like to think all of them will prove interesting and that some will lead you down new paths of exploration. (Please read "Roads that go Nowhere": a short insight into idiosyncratic "Binns".)

Contents

BOOKS & BOOKSELLERS

I have found the problem of persuading bookshops to stock my titles increasingly difficult as each year has passed since I started my do-it-yourself publishing venture. In their defence there are numerous reasons why an individual bookshop cannot stock every book published. But for readers the problem is this: how can one discover details of all the books available on France and the French – whatever the theme or subject?

Compass Books has created an invaluable directory for both Francophiles and publishers alike: a catalogue of the hundreds of books on France which can be ordered either from them or from a local bookshop. Three cheers for their masochistic sorting and sifting, digging and delving. I would have given my eye teeth for the directory during the last four decades.

Booksellers have an impossible task. In 1980, when I started, about 40,000 new titles were published in the UK each year; today the figure is about 60,000. That yearly avalanche, coupled with the almost bottomless pit of back titles, means that most bookshops can only stock a token number of books on France. Whether you are a mapoholic or a Francophiliac book addict, somewhere within the Compass directory you'll find the titles you need to help you on your travels.

Every page contains a publishing surprise, identifying the existence of books quite new to me or bringing back instant reminders of titles I've treasured over the years: for example Charlie Waite's evocative photographic masterpiece *Landscape in France* or Zelden's *The French* – a revealing insight into the intricate spider's web complexities of the French nation.

The catalogue is split into many parts. The first covers sixteen themed sections: from general guide books and pictorial titles to children's books and humour; from eating out and cookery to hotel, restaurant, guest house and self-catering accommodation; from art, history and architecture to all types of outdoor interests. The second half lists guides and special interest titles, region by region. You really have no idea of just how many books are available on the French regions until you peruse the pages of this section. Finally, there are details of the numerous language titles available and the various IGN and Michelin local and regional maps.

As both a publisher and author I know better than most just what the problems are in trying to communicate to the world at large the existence of one's work. Media publicity is all important; obviously in view of what I said earlier. To be honest one would prefer to sit back and let the books sell themselves. What innocent naïvety! I know that Compass has found it difficult to get support from the editors of national newspapers. How sad: you would have thought that their readers would be only to keen to know of the existence of a catalogue which provides all the answers.

Not all of us have access to the capital's specialist "travel" bookshops: Chapter Travel at 126 St. John's Wood High St, London NW8 7ST (tel 071-586-9451); Stanfords at 12-14 Long Acre, London WC2 (tel 071-836-1321); and The Travel Bookshop (13 Blenheim Cres, London W11 2EE (tel 071-229-5260). Whether we live in London or not we need the Compass catalogue. We can study it at leisure and then pick the books we want – buying them either from Compass or a local bookshop. Compass Books is at 15 Bertie Ward Way, Dereham, Norfolk NR19 1TE (tel 0362-691623). A copy of their catalogue should be the essential first purchase for all travellers bound for France. Send £1.00 (refunded on first order over £10).

ARTISTS

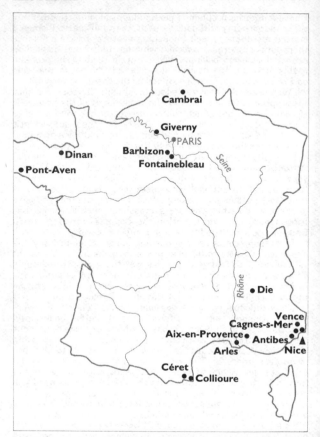

One of the great interests in my life is to paint and draw. Unhappily, lack of time has allowed me to do only a tiny amount of work during the last 35 years. I did put aside 60 days to do the pencil drawings for *French Leave Favourites*. That reveals how time consuming drawing is. Those 60 images filled less than 30 pages; writing the equivalent number of words would have occupied me for less than ten days.

What I have been able to do during the last four decades is to absorb the character, style, light and feel of many parts of France – areas renowned for their scenes, so brilliantly captured by artists through the simple mediums of paints, pencil and ink. Where are some of these places?

First, let's start with three Englishmen. Some of you will already know that Edward Whymper has always been one of my heroes: a courageous and skilled climber, he was also a superb engraver. His book, *Scrambles Amongst the Alps*, will give you an inkling of his talent. The reprints of his original work are rather poor but the book remains in a class by itself.

Next, Russell Flint. One of his favourite areas was the Drôme Valley around **Die**. Flint's work is much admired by my great friend, Denis Pannett; the latter's watercolours, including some Drôme scenes, have done much to brighten up my own books – especially *French Leave Favourites*.

Now south. The Côte d'Azur is endowed with the work of men who created their masterpieces in the brilliant light of the south. Auguste Renoir lived at **Cagnes-sur-Mer**; first at the post office, then at Les Colettes, the house, now a museum, in which he spent the last 12 years of his life.

Picasso did much of his work on the Côte d'Azur. The Musée Picasso, at the Château Grimaldi in **Antibes**, houses some of his best creations; it includes all the paintings and ceramics he produced in the autumn of 1946 when he lived at the château. At nearby Vallauris, the potter's town, made famous by Picasso, are clear signs of the influence he had on the development of ceramics and pottery skills.

Paul Cézanne used to visit Renoir at Les Colettes. He worked in the magical light of **Aix-en-Provence**. Montagne St-Victoire, to the east, featured in dozens of his paintings.

Perhaps the most famous of all the artists who found inspiration in Provence was Van Gogh. **Arles**, and the terrain surrounding the town, especially in spring, is alive with living reminders of the strong images this talented genius captured on canvas: flowers, trees, fields and houses.

Matisse, too, revelled in the southern light. **Nice** has a Matisse Museum; and Vence has his famous (for some readers infamous) decorations at the Chapelle du Rosaire, just north of the town. Matisse was born at Le Cateau, east of **Cambrai**. A museum at the latter contains some of his work.

There are numerous museums in the south worth taking the time to search out. The National Museum at Nice houses some of Marc Chagall's work. Biot has the Fernand-Léger Museum; St-Paul, south of **Vence**, is the home of two museums, the Provençal and the Maeght Foundation. Grasse has two museums and Draguignan has an excellent Municipal version.

At the other end of the French Mediterranean coast is the tiny town of **Céret**, inland from the evocative, colourful port of **Collioure**. Both towns, and the landscape between them has always been a magnet for modern painters. Famed for its clear light, Collioure became, at the turn of the century, a favourite of the Fauvist artists, and Braque, Chagall, Matisse and Picasso all painted here. The Musée d'Art at Céret has works by all those artists and many others.

The Seine and Loing rivers form the eastern and southern borders of the Forest of **Fontainebleau**; **Barbizon** is on the northern edges of the *forêt*. The latter village gave its name to the Barbizon School – painters like Théodore Rousseau who specialised in painting sombre scenes of the forest and nearby country vistas. The Impressionists gained their inspiration from the rivers mentioned earlier and, occasionally, from the forest. The Seine and the Oise, north of Paris, also inspired many of the celebrated artists of the same school. Claude Monet, Sisley, Degas, Renoir, Manet, Pissarro – the roll call of artists is formidable. Elsewhere, in the Ile de France introduction, I have referred to **Giverny** and Claude Monet's home beside the Epte. All the rivers and forests of the Ile de France are at their best in the spring and autumn.

Pont-Aven is the most famous of the many Brittany schools of painters: this small town inspired many, particularly Paul Gauguin. **Dinan**, and the River Rance below the town, are also favourite subjects of many landscape artists.

A chapter as short as this can only be the tiniest of morsels, an appetiser to what could easily be a gargantuan feast on the subject. First, I'll remind you of a handful of French authors where you can either visit houses associated with them or see countryside immortalised in their work. Later, I'll list a few books, from hundreds in my possession, where "foreign" writers have captured the very essence of France.

Nohant A sleepy Berry backwater – once the home of George Sand (1804-76). The "cigar-smoking workaholic" – 80 novels and 12,000 letters – was known as "la bonne dame de Nohant"; every corner of the village, from her house to the small chapel, is devoted to her memory. Open most of the year.

La Devinière The birthplace of Rabelais (1494-1553). The son of a Chinon lawyer ("the finest town in the world"), he laughed his way through life and became one of the world's greatest promoters of laughter. There's a small museum at the village, at the heart of Gargantua country. Open Feb to Nov. Closed Sun & holidays & Wed (Oct to mid Mar).

Balzac (1789-1850) spent great periods of his life at the château in **Saché**. Today the house is dedicated to his life and work with letters, manuscripts, proofs, original editions and portraits. Open all year (not Wed – Oct to mid Mar).

Edmund Rostand (1868-1918), author of *Cyrano de Bergerac*, lived in the Villa Arnaga at **Cambo-les-Bains**, a super spa in the Pays Basque. Open May to Sept; Apl & Oct p.m. only.

Colette (1873-1954), the creator of Claudine, Chéri and Gigi, lived in several parts of France. There's no finer informal autobiography than Robert Phelps' *Earthly Paradise* (Penguin p/b). Equally, there's no more evocative account of her many varied musings on French cuisine than the glorious *Colette Gourmande* (Albin Michel) – written by Marie-Christine and Didier Clément (**Romorantin** – Loire; Grand Hôtel Lion d'Or). An English edition is expected soon.

Elsewhere I've referred to the work of Marcel Pagnol (**Provence**), to Emmanuel Le Roy Ladurie's **Montaillou** (Languedoc-Roussillon: Penguin p/b), to **Belley's** Brillat-Savarin (Lyonnais and "Who's who in French cuisine"; Penguin p/b) and several others.

What of "foreign" writers? A host of differing books are readily available, either from booksellers or from libraries. I've mentioned some books elsewhere but I'll list a few more which have given me great pleasure.

Travels Through France and Italy. An account, in 1763, of a journey by Tobias Smollett. Idiosyncratic, prejudiced, all trumpets and percussion, critical of everything.

A Little Tour in France. An 1882 tour by Henry James. This is in a minor key – strings and flutes compared with Smollett's verbal fireworks. Some claim this as one of the most readable travel books ever written.

Two Towns in France by the late Mary Frances Kennedy (M.F.K.) Fisher. A revealing account of aspects of French life: topography, history, personal memories – all crafted around vivid portraits of **Aix-en-Provence** and **Marseille**.

Dirk Bogarde is a master of two crafts: acting and writing. His *An Orderly Man* is an outstanding autobiography; particularly interesting is the account of his years spent at his home among the olive trees to the east of **Grasse**.

Hannibal's Footsteps by Bernard Levin is an exhilarating tale of the author's personal footsteps – from **Aigues-Mortes** to **Le Pain de Sucre** – following the momentous journey across France by Hannibal and his army in 218 B.C. For me this is the most readable travel book I've ever picked up.

Marina Warner's *Joan of Arc* is a riveting read, a masterful insight into the life and myth of the French heroine, from **Domrémy-la-Pucelle** (her birthplace is open all year) to **Rouen** (where she was burnt at the stake on May 30, 1431).

Edward Whymper's *Scrambles Amongst the Alps*. Many of you know of my great admiration for this genius of a climber and engraver. Among mountain books "in a class by itself".

SOE in France by M.R.D.Foot. A monumental work – 550 pages of intricate detail, recounting the history of the Special Operation Executive and its heroic work in France during 1940-45. An essential read, together with the others mentioned elsewhere, for all of you interested in the Resistance.

Finally, one writer, John Ardagh, has made an exceptional effort in his *Writers' France* to develop the idea of linking authors' books, both French and foreign, with topography: among them Pagnol and Provence; Mauriac and the **Landes;** Chevallier and **Beaujolais**; Goethe and **Alsace**; Stevenson and the **Cévennes**; and many others.

COMPOSERS

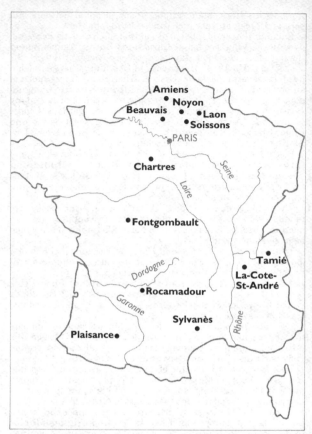

Every year I make it my business to get hold of leaflets which give details of French musical festivals. Every year I scratch my head, perplexed by the remarkable absence of any significant number of events laid on to celebrate the work of French composers – whether they be orchestral or soloist works, organ or choral music. The numbers are minuscule.

I am equally perplexed by the almost complete absence of any reference to music among any of the heavyweight tomes written by intellectuals analysing France and the French.

Choral music, a great British tradition, is almost dead in France. Not that life is easy these days for our renowned cathedral schools. During the last few years there has been a severe falling-off in the numbers of children applying for places at the schools. All of you will know of the cathedral choirs, all with household names, which maintain the British choral tradition. But other educational establishments, outside the church, do remarkable work – in both public and state schools. Of the latter no teacher comes more gifted and inspired than Ian Hooker, who achieves minor miracles with the choir at Dr. Challoner's Grammar School in Amersham, Bucks.

In defence of French standards I wonder how many readers appreciate that Napoleon "guillotined" all the choir schools in France, over 400 in number. That, coupled with the secular nature of French primary schools, ensures that liturgical music across the Channel remains in a sorry state.

Less of the doom and gloom. One pillar of the French music scene has strong foundations: organ composition – from minor little fantasies to major symphonies. If you haven't heard the work of some of the "French Romantics" (organist-composers working, roughly, from the mid 19th century to the mid 20th century) then do put the omission right: Charles-Marie Widor, Louis Vierne, Alexandre Guilmant, Joseph Bonnet and Eugène Gigout composed some splendid organ works. Without exception all of them were organists at churches in Paris. Fauré, too, was both a composer and organist. Try to find time to hear some of the great cathedral organs: the instrument at **Chartres** is superb. Closer to home, in Picardy, there are many fine cathedral organs – at **Amiens, Noyon, Laon, Soissons and Beauvais**. (Laon holds a festival of classical French music during the first half of October every year.)

At a different level seek out the dreary little town of **Plaisance** in Gers. In *French Leave Favourites* I told the story of how two 22-year-old friends – Daniel Birouste, an organ builder, and Bertrand Lazerme, an organist – first conceived, and then contrived to build, a cathedral-sized organ in the town's church. Today the instrument is finished; what an electrifying experience it is to glory in its rich sound. Within a year or two Daniel will have repeated the exercise at the Abbaye de **Sylvanès**, 60 km south of Millau.

One composer's work does regularly appear on the programmes of French musical festivals: Poulenc. Even so I think more of his choral work is probably performed here in Britain than in France. There's a Francis Poulenc Museum in **Rocamadour**. In 1936 the composer re-discovered his Christian faith at the shrine of the Black Virgin in Rocamadour; the spiritual experience he underwent was the inspiration for his *Litanies à la Vierge Noire de Rocamadour*.

Another quite different aspect of French religious music is the work done at the abbeys and monasteries. One example is the Romanesque abbey at **Fontgombault** where it is a joy to listen to the Gregorian chants. Another inspirational abbey is at **Tamié**; I've relished the chants of the monks on many occasions and I've acquired many tapes of their singing which I play over and over again back home and in the car.

Thankfully, there are other ways of experiencing the works of French composers – on record, tapes and CDs. I take numerous tapes with me on my car travels. Many of them seem easier to absorb in French terrain. An example is Canteloube's *Chants d'Auvergne*; they seem more appropriate when played in remote mountainous country – and Frederica (Flicka) von Stade's interpretation is a tingling thrill.

If you cannot find festivals celebrating the music of French composers then tapes will have to do. I regularly take the following in the car: Massenet's *Scènes Alsaciennes* and *Manon Lescaut*; Bizet's *L'Arlésienne*; Fauré's various work – from his *Requiem* to *La Bonne Chanson*; the varied compositions of Berlioz (there's a Musée Hector Berlioz at **La Côte-St-André**, south-east of Vienne); Debussy's musical "impressionismn; and Saint-Saëns's varied output, from the *Carnival of the Animals* to his opera *Samson and Delilah*.

FESTIVALS

France is a land of fêtes, fairs, carnivals and festivals – of every kind imaginable: historic pageants (covered elsewhere), folk festivals, gastronomic fairs, solemn concerts, classical music, jazz, drama, dance, street theatre, puppets . . .!

On these two pages I have concentrated mainly on musical festivals – of all kinds. For further details of 100 or more festivals, of all kinds, held annually in France, write to the French Government Tourist Office for a copy of their "Festive France" English-language guide: send £1, in postage stamps, to cover p&p (also ask for the "Touring Traveller in France").

Vienne *Jazz Festival*. First 2 wks July. 12 concerts held in the Théâtre Antique. All types of jazz, all sorts of artists both famous and unknown. Info: Theâtre de Vienne, 4 rue Chantelouve, 38200 Vienne. Tel 74 85 00 05.

Strasbourg *Strasbourg International Music Festival*. Mid June to mid July. Founded 60 years ago, the oldest festival in France. Famous soloists and orchestras. Info: Wolf Musique, 24 rue de la Mésange, 67000 Strasbourg. Tel 88 32 43 10.

Sarlat *Drama Festival*. Last wk July, first wk Aug. Forty years old and now one of France's premier drama festivals.

Open-air venues, range of established and new work, famous and up and coming actors and authors. Info: Festival de Sarlat, BP 53, 24202 Sarlat Cedex. Tel 53 31 10 83.

Dijon *International Folkloriade and Wine Festival.* First wk Sept. Dozens of folk groups compete for medals. 2,000 dancers and musicians. Info: FMDP, Cellier de Clairvaux, 27 bd de la Trémouille, 21025 Dijon Cédex. Tel 80 30 37 95.

Rennes *Nightfall Festival.* First wk July. 15 sites – squares, cloisters, gardens, medieval streets – host drama, music, jazz and dance. Info: Office du Tourisme, 8 pl du Maréchal Juin, 35000 Rennes. Tel 99 30 38 01.

Chartres *Organ Festival.* Sundays in July, Aug, and first half Sept. 16.45 hours. Recitals on the great cathedral organ. Entry free. Info: Assoc. des Grandes Orgues de Chartres, 75 rue de Grenelle, 75007 Paris. Tel (1) 45 48 31 74.

Noirlac *Summer in Noirlac.* Second half July. Classical and sacred music Performed in the Cistercian Abbaye de Noirlac (south of Bourges). Info: Les Amis de l'Abbaye de Noirac, 5 rue de Séraucourt, 18000 Bourges. Tel 48 21 22 17.

Charleville-Mézières *World Festival of Puppet Theatre* (triennial – last one 1991). Second half Sept. Puppeteers from all over the world. Info: Festival de Marionnettes, 7 pl Winston Churchill, 08000 Charleville. Tel 24 56 44 55.

St-Guilhem-le-Désert *St-Guilhem-le-Désert Musical Season.* Mid June to end Aug. Reputed for Baroque music. The Romanesque abbey has a fine 18th-century classical French organ. Info: Saison Musicale de St-Guilhem-le-Désert, 165 rue Michel-Ange, 34000 Montpellier. Tel 67 63 14 99.

Prades *Pablo Casals Festival.* Last wk July, first 2 wks Aug. Held at the monastery at St-Michel-de-Cuxa. Soloists, chamber orchestras and choristers. Info: Festival Pablo Casals, BP 24, 66502 Prades Cédex. Tel 68 96 33 07.

Nancy *"Nancy Jazz Beat".* Mid Oct. 20 years old, this eclectic festival features dozens of shows and scores of groups – in Nancy and elsewhere in Lorraine. Info: Nancy Jazz Beat, 6 passage Sébastien Bottin, 54000 Nancy. Tel 83 37 83 79.

Souillac *"Sim Copans" Souillac Jazz Festival.* Mid July. American and European musicians bring jazz to town. Info: Bureau du Festival, BP 16, 46200 Souillac. Tel 65 37 80 90.

Confolens *International Folk Festival.* Mid Aug. Hundreds of artists from 15 nations bring dance and traditional music to the small town, north-west of Limoges. Info: Festival Int. de Folklore, BP 14, 16500 Confolens. Tel 45 84 00 77.

Aix-en-Provence *International Arts and Music Festival.* Last 3 wks July. World-famous festival, synonymous with the great names of music and song, art and literature. A bonus is the exquisite town. Info: Festival d'Aix, Palais de l'Ancien Archevêché, 13100 Aix-en-Provence. Tel 42 17 34 00.

Orange *Les Chorégies d'Orange.* End July, early August. A connoisseurs festival – of operas, concerts and oratorios; held in the incomparable Théâtre Antique. Info: Chorégies d'Orange, BP 180, 84105 Orange Cédex. Tel 90 34 24 24.

Finally, let me use this as an excuse to remind you, once again, of the inspiring cathedral-sized organ in the deadbeat town of **Plaisance** in Gers. Concerts are held in the church throughout the year. Info: Ars Organorum, 32160 Plaisance. Tel 62 69 30 25. By the time this guide is published the great new organ at **Sylvanès** should be finished, or near completion (a renowned festival is already established here). Info: Abbaye de Sylvanès, 12360 Camarès. Tel 65 99 51 83.

FISHING

No fisherman am I: but I know the rivers of France especially well. So, whether you are a serious participant, fishing to actually catch something, or one who is just happy to dabble and dally, content to sit against a tree and watch the swallows and sand-martins dart and dive, or, a third sort, just pleased to lose yourself along river-banks, enjoying the pleasures of a French picnic and a water-cooled bottle of wine – then all of you will gain by making detours to the best streams in France. It is no coincidence that all the fishing areas which follow are set in blissful country – with fine, local cuisine and some close to bargain basement wine-making areas. There's more to fishing than catching fish!

Salmon fishing is at its best in the streams flowing down from the western Pyrénées. The most famous is the **Gave d'Oloron**, from Peyrehorade to Sauveterre; the river is at its best in February and March. April and May see the next stretch of the Gave at its best from Sauveterre to Navarrenx. The 40 kilometres upstream from the latter to Oloron-Ste-Marie are at their peak in June, July and August.

Trout fishing, too, in the Pyrénées is excellent; there are

numerous sporting streams. Some of the best trout and char water is in the Gave d'Ossau (flowing into the Gave d'Oloron); from Oloron to its source near the Spanish border.

As popular as the Ossau is, the neighbouring Gave d'Aspe is even more highly rated for trout and char (south of Oloron).

In Brittany, far to the north, the best salmon fishing is found in the **Aulne**, a lovely estuary and river south-east of Brest. During the first three months of the year salmon are caught as far upstream as Châteaulin; from April to July the next section of the river, to Châteauneuf-du-Faou, is at its best; the upper stretches, in enticing inland Brittany, provide the finest sport at the end of the season.

Trout, too, can be fished in the tributaries of the Aulne, and in the **Blavet** and the **Aven** which flow south to Hennebont and Pont-Aven. The streams and lakes near Huelgoat are renowned for trout, perch and carp. All are near hotels.

Normandy is richly endowed with trout streams. In **Calvados** country are the **Orne** – best in its upper reaches; the Dives; the Touques – upstream from Lisieux; and the **Risle** – from Pont-Audemer to Brionne. The Charentonne, too, a tributary of the Risle, is highly rated. Certainly this is all pastoral, timeless *pays*; seductive all year round. In **Caux** country, north of the Seine, many relatively tiny streams like the Yères, Saâne and Durdent, provide excellent sport.

In the far north-east of France, the **Meuse** and many of its tributaries offer some of the finest trout fishing in Europe. Between Toul and Verdun are a fair number of *étangs*.

Further south the wooded hills of the mysterious **Morvan** in Burgundy attract many fishermen to the streams and lakes of the regional nature park. The Yonne, Cure and Cousin are the principal rivers within the park; to the west, on the other side of the A6 autoroute, are the Serein and Armançon.

The *département* of **Doubs** in the Jura is another magnet: there are no better streams than the Loue and Lison, south of Besançon – and that's just as true of the Dessoubre and Doubs, the latter forming the border with Switzerland for much of its length. Read the Jura introduction for a host of other reasons for visiting this most self-effacing of regions.

The Alps offer two differing types of sport; the mountain trout streams and the special treasures of the lakes.

Of the streams and rivers, those in the Dauphiny Alps are particularly renowned. South of **Grenoble** is the Drac; to the west, in the Vercors, is the Bourne, fed by many streams; to the north-west the Chartreuse with its two strangely-named torrents, the Guiers Vif and the Guiers Mort.

To the south of the Vercors, the upper reaches of the **Drôme** and one of its tributaries, the Bez, are both highly thought of: both **Die** (beside the Drôme) and Châtillon-en-Diois (on the Bez) are renowned for their excellent wines, particularly the sparkling Clairette de Die. What could be better than local wines cooled in local streams – in succulent country?

Of the various lakes in the French Alps, **Annecy** and Lac du **Bourget** are perhaps the most rewarding. The lakes yield piscatorial treasures unknown anywhere else in France. The menus of many restaurants in the region are built around these delicious fish: salmon trout, some a metre long and weighing 15 kilograms; *omble chevalier*, the most subtle and finest tasting of all freshwater fish (a char, it looks like a large salmon trout); *féra*; *lavaret*; *brochet* and *lotte* (a burbot, not unlike an eel). Fisherman or not, enjoy them all.

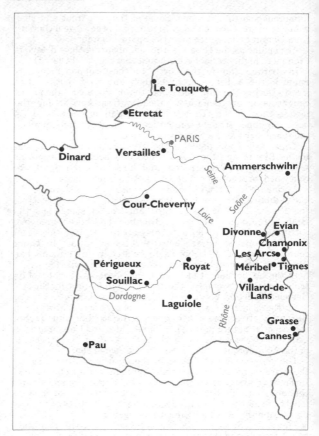

One of the more enterprising products published by Michelin in the last year or so is map number 199 "Golf France". Based on the exemplary 989 map, Monsieur Bibendum manages to locate, by the use of "flags", over 400 courses in France – both private and public and both nine and eighteen hole. Addresses and telephone numbers are provided for all the courses.

The impact of the map is immediate. Today there's not an area in France without one or more courses. I know many of my friends and a huge number of readers are golf addicts. Well, map 199 is the perfect holiday planner. Organise your route on a golf course basis, hopping from one flag to the next.

In my time I've enjoyed golf immensely – but now lack of time and detached retinas have put a stop to wishful thinking. Nevertheless, any map fascinates and this one is a winner. Let me give you some golfing ideas: initially, I'll highlight courses which I have not seen personally but, which, by just glancing at the map, I realise are located in ideal touring terrain; I'll finish by describing some of the courses I've known in earlier playing days – all in idyllic country.

What a surprise to spot a course bang in the middle of the

Vercors: a nine-holer at Corrençon-en-Vercors, just south of **Villard-de-Lans**. I can think of nothing nicer than combining a tour of the high mountain fortress with a quick round.

The same would be true in Alsace. In the introduction to the region I explained some of the treats in store for visitors to the Vosges and the wine villages at the foot of the high hills. What could be more enjoyable than say an autumn break in the area, staying at Les Remparts in Kaysersberg and playing the 18-hole course west of **Ammerschwihr**.

The Ile de France has a huge number of courses to entice visiting golf nuts: dozens ring Paris and there's a particularly wide choice in the St-Germain-en-Laye and **Versailles** area. Near the latter is the French Golf HQ.

For those of you who want to mix châteaux bashing with ball thumping then the perfect answer is available at the Château de Cheverny 18-hole course at **Cour-Cheverny**. Four major châteaux are within a few minutes drive.

Laguiole, at the heart of France, is the home of a superb French chef, Michel Bras (see Massif Central); within a few kilometres of his hotel are two nine-hole courses.

Surprisingly, the Dordogne has few courses; the map shows only five between **Périgueux** and **Souillac**. On the other hand most of the high Alpine ski resorts have the summer magnet of a golf course: Flaine, **Les Arcs**, **Tignes** and **Méribel** among them. And so the pleasure goes on: each flag on the map is, for me, a visual scene of the local terrain.

Now for links I've known in past playing days. All offer a sporting challenge and all provide a scenic dividend.

Few readers will know that, after Blackheath and Calcutta, the course at **Pau** was the third to be built outside Scotland. The course, 135 years old, is on the right bank of the Gave.

Nearer home, the links at **Le Touquet** is another renowned French course, sitting among pine woods and dunes south of the resort. Another seaside course is at **Etretat**, high above the sea, atop the famous white cliffs. Playing here is akin to teeing off in Scotland. The same is true of yet another bracing seaside links at St-Briac-sur-Mer, west of **Dinard**.

Divonne overlooks Lake Geneva and has distant views of Mont Blanc; the 18-hole course here is in wooded, hilly terrain. **Evian** is on the other side of Lake Geneva; the 18-hole course is another scenic beauty. Most views are northwards; Mont Blanc will not put you off your stroke at Evian!

In **Chamonix** you'll be able to claim, after every poor shot, that you were distracted by the spectacular panoramas: *aiguilles* are on every side and, looming over you to the south, is the snoozing dome of Mont Blanc. Chamonix is a sportsman's paradise – the home of a superb sports centre which includes a covered, open-all-year-round ice rink.

Royat, too, west of Clermont-Ferrand, and at the heart of the volcanic Auvergne peaks, sports three scenic courses: one a nine-holer near the spa; the other two, 18 and nine, are at the foot of the infamous Puy de Dôme.

Finally, numerous courses have sprouted up all over Provence and the Côte d'Azur; there must be at least three dozen now. Between **Grasse** and **Cannes** are six courses. Three I know: two east of Mougins and a stylish links at La Napoule, just across the road from the Mediterranean; the other three are in an arc to the south of Grasse. All in all, I hope I have given you a few ideas for some sporting days on your next holiday.

LEGS AND BOTTOMS!

Walking

For the walker France is a treasure-chest of possibilites. The choice is wide: from the easier terrain of Burgundy, Brittany and the Loire, to the ultra difficult Alps and Pyrénées.

I've never been able to dedicate a whole holiday to walking; time has always been the enemy. However, I have spent many hours on shorter walks in every part of the country. I'll give you a few ideas – from scores of alternatives.

Both the **Chartreuse** (see Savoie) and the **Vercors** (see Hautes Alpes) are ideal; I'd rate the terrain as fairly difficult. So is the countryside around **Lac d'Annecy** (see Savoie) – both to the south (Les Bauges; see the regional introduction) and east. The mountains encircling **Chamonix** and the Ecrins National Park, north-west of **Briançon**, are more difficult; the latter is loved by naturalists.

For those of you who want easier alternatives, without the monotony of dead-flat landscapes, then inland Brittany around **Huelgoat** is ideal: woods, moorlands, rivers, rocks and viewpoints (see Brittany). So is "Little Switzerland" in Normandy (around **Thury-Harcourt**) and Burgundy's

Morvan; in both the scenery is pastoral and gentle but with no extensive moorlands. All are at their best in the spring.

In Provence two ranges provide get-away-from-it-all areas – both are within minutes of main roads: the Montagne du Lubéron (south-east of **Avignon**) and the rocky outcrop of hills, the Chaîne des Alpilles (south of Avignon).

The Massif Central provides all sorts of alternatives; the region is especially rewarding for those of you who love wild flowers. The R. L. Stevenson Trail through the Cévennes has become a classic walk; there's a book by George Osborn who recounts his own version of following Stevenson's footsteps (GTBS Publications). Read the three Massif Central introductory chapters: **Auvergne**, **Ardèche** and **Cévennes**.

Another possibility is the **Vosges** hills in Alsace. An enterprising group of 12 hoteliers, "Horizons d'Alsace", has a proven package where clients can permutate overnight stops between any of the hotels, walking from one to another in the knowledge that their luggage is taken for them to their next base. All the hotels are in a semi-circle of terrain to the west of Kaysersberg. Further details from 20 rue Ch. de Gaulle, 68370 Orbey (Tel 89 71 25 25; Fax 89 71 30 75).

There's a wide choice of organised walking holidays; I refer you to *The Active Traveller in France*, published by The French Government Tourist Office, 178 Piccadilly, London W1V 0AL (send £1 to cover post and packing), for specialist tour firms. The guide lists scores of tour operators and a host of alternative activity holidays. For those of you who want to do your own thing I recommend two excellent books: Rob Hunter's *Walking in France* (Oxford Illustrated Press) and Adam Nicolson's *Long Walks* in France (Weidenfeld and Nicolson).

In the saddle

This includes two types of activity holidays. One requires you to turn the pedals yourself, whilst you sit on the saddle of a bicycle; the other requires little effort on your part as you'll be atop a horse on a different sort of saddle. I know from your large number of letters that both these holidays give you all a lot of pleasure, especially cycling.

Touring with a cycle is becoming more and more popular. Many of you take your own bikes. Areas like the **Loire** Valley (especially the **Sologne**), the **Marais Poitevin** (see Poitou Charentes), the **Vendée** and western Brittany provide easy, flat landscapes with a varied choice of scenery. Alternatively, you could take the "steamer" from Tournon to Lamastre (see **Ardèche**) and free-wheel all the way back. *The Active Traveller in France* lists numerous firms who organise everything for you: two have often been praised by readers – Susi Madron's Cycling Holidays and Alastair Sawdray's Tours.

Horse riding is an easier way of using a saddle. There's a wide choice of terrain. The **Camargue** would figure in any list (see Provence). But what about **Le Brionnais** – gentle hills and numerous Romanesque churches (see Lyonnais)? Or the **Limousin** where two green *départements*, Corrèze and Creuse, must be the ultimate in riding country. With this sort of saddle holiday you'll not want to take your own horse. Again I refer you to *The Active Traveller* for a list of specialist firms.

Skiing

I've kept away from putting my toes in even the shallow end of this specialist pool. It would need a book to do justice to the subject. As a starter you can't do better then ask the FGTO to send you *The Winter Traveller in France*.

MONTE-CARLO RALLY COUNTRY

PARIS

Loire

Chambéry
Chartreuse
●7
Ardèche ● ●Grenoble
● 6 Vercors
5 8
4
Montélimar ●
3
Alpes- 2
Maritimes1 ●
● Grasse

Rhône

Most of you will have no interest whatsoever in motor sport. A few of you will be passionately interested – perhaps even competitors, past or present. All of you, with few exceptions, will be motorists and, hopefully, all of you will be eager to see the scenic attractions that abound in France. I promise you all, whichever way you qualify, that any time you set aside in visiting the various stage suggestions I list below will not be wasted: that's a guarantee.

So many of you have written and told me of your adventures. I have especially welcomed those letters from motoring novices who grasped the nettle, did some basic navigating and lapped up hours of exciting scenic motoring; without exception they all admitted they had found a new holiday interest for future years. What bad habits I've started!

The Monte-Carlo Rally is a January event, run, usually, on snow and ice in the best mountain terrain in Europe – country interlaced with thousands of minor roads. I have identified just a few of the many "stages" used on the Rally. The countryside surrounding the stages all happens to be super scenic stuff – so seek them out. Another plus is that you'll be using the roads when the weather is much kinder.

You will be intrigued and fascinated by just what the competing drivers and navigators, and their cars, have to cope with – usually on hard-packed snow and ice. You will be taking it easy, stopping frequently to admire a scenic aspect; they will be averaging speeds far in excess of anything you can safely do. The roads are "closed" to other traffic for the cars; that's not so for you. Don't try to emulate them.

The stages are grouped into three area of south-east France: the Maritime Alps, between Digne and Grasse; the Ardèche; and the Chartreuse and Vercors, north and south of Grenoble.

Maritime Alps: among a dozen or more I'm describing three.

Stage 1. From **Grasse** head north-west to the crossroads called Les 4 Chemins, east of Thorenc. Start here. Ascend the Col de Bleine. Descend, then east through Le Mas and Aiglun. Eight km later left, past Sigale to Pont des Miolans (finish).

Stage 2. Start at Pont des Miolans. West to Collongues, Briançonnet and finish at St-Auban. (What are "clues"? See Côte d'Azur introduction.) Now head for the Var Valley and Entrevaux by retracing your steps to Briançonnet and using the Col de Buis (I first found this through road decades ago when the map showed it as a footpath) and the Col de Félines.

Stage 3. West of Entrevaux is Annot. Start here; climb the Vaire Valley, finishing at the junction just south of Pont de Villaron. In winter competing cars then turn south. You may have the appetite to try the Col d'Allos, to the north – an old favourite of the Alpine Rally. Don't miss the dead-end climb from Allos to the Lac d'Allos; 45 mins walk to lake.

Ardèche: any map of the area will show you instantly why this area is such competitive motoring country. A maze of twisty mountain roads in terrain at its best in spring.

Stage 4. From **Montélimar** head west to Aubenas. West of the latter is La Souche. Start here. Climb the Col de la Croix de Bauzon. At the D239 turn north finishing just past the Col du Pendu. Before you leave the area detour south to the vast panorama from the Col de Meyrand.

Stage 5. Vals-les-Bains is just north of Aubenas. Find Burzet to the north-west of the spa. Start here, using the D215 to the north. Climb past the waterfall of Ray-Pic (a 15-minute walk). At the D122 turn right to finish at Mézilhac. (Before you start from Burzet do the hillclimb north-west, on the D289: this, too, is often used as a stage.)

Stage 6. At the end of stage 5, at Mézilhac, head south to Antraigues. Start here. East through Genestelle and on D218 to the Col de la Fayolle. Now use the D261 down the Auzène Valley, finishing at Le Moulinon in the Eyrieux Valley.

Chartreuse: across the Rhône to **Chambéry**.

Stage 7. Take the D912 south from Chambéry. The stage starts at Bellecombette. Climb the Col du Granier and keep going south. Climb the Col du Cucheron, then the Col de Porte. Finish at Le Sappey-en-Chartreuse. Glorious country – some of the best in France. Take your time. I'm not going to tell you the standard time for this stage; it would turn your hair as white as the ice covering the roads in winter.

Vercors: south-west of **Grenoble**.

Stage 8. Take the N75 south of Grenoble. At Vif follow the D8 to St-Barthélemy. Start here: Col de l'Arzelier; St-Andéol; Col des Deux; Gresse-en-Vercors; Col de l'Allimas. In front of you is the hypnotic, flat-topped Mont Aiguille. Finish at St-Michel-les-Portes. This stage needs careful map reading.

SPECTACLES

Spectacle: the French word always needs further elaboration just as *château* covers a wide range and type of buildings. In this chapter I'm considering *spectacles historiques:* in English we would call them "pageants" – defined by a dictionary as "elaborate public spectacles, especially those where there are processions in costume".

The French have developed pageants into quite an art form, more often than not backed up with high-tech use of *son et lumière*. In Britain we have relatively few pageants: is it the weather or our inhibitions which put the brakes on our efforts to celebrate past historical events? In France organisers of *spectacles historiques* have simple objectives: to recall and record their tumultuous history – always evocatively and with no signs of any embarrassment whatsoever.

The range and number of *spectacles* is amazing. I can only find space here to describe, briefly, fourteen: for further information contact the addresses given (telephone numbers supplied as well). All performances are in the evening.

Ailly-sur-Noye (Eighteen km south of Amiens.) *Terre de Picardie "Rivière du Temps"*- On Fri and Sat – last wk Aug, three wks Sept. A cast of 1,500 relate the history of Picardy; water plays a big part. Info: Terre de Picardie, 1 rue du Dr Binant, 80250 Ailly-s-Noye. Tel 22 41 06 90.

Amboise *A La Cour du Roy François.* 389 inhabitants of the Loire town lay on a lavish show at the château, recalling the flamboyant history of the royal palace. 20 performances from end June to early Sept. Info: Office de Tourisme, quai Gén.-de-Gaulle, 37400 Amboise. Tel 47 57 01 37.

Autun *Il etait une fois Augustodunum.* Half a dozen shows in July and Aug tell the Gallo-Romain history of France. Held in the town's Roman theatre. Info: Office de Tourisme, 3 av Charles-de-Gaulle, 71400 Autun. Tel 85 86 30 00.

Cour-Cheverny *Cheverny: "Rêves en Sologne".* The story of a family, a château and the Sologne. 600 roles, 2,000 costumes, fountains, fireworks. 17 shows in July and Aug. Info: Assoc Louis XII, 5 rue A. Gerbault, 41000 Blois. Tel 54 42 79 72.

Courcouronnes (South of Paris and Orly, near A6.) *Le Fil d'Ariane.* Fifteen acres, water, lasers and 2,000 actors feature in this musical spectacle. Info: Le Lac en Fête, 2 rte de Versailles, 91080 Courcouronnes. Tel 64 97 89 07.

Elven (North-east of Vannes.) *Tristan et Yseult.* Held during July and August at the Fortresse de Largoët, to the west of the small village. Info: Tristan et Yseult, rue Robert de la Noe, 56250 Elven. Tel 97 53 52 79.

Flagnac (In the Lot Valley, east of Figeac.) *Hier, Un Village.* A simpler affair – the history of a hamlet in a gorgeous section of the Lot. Six shows in July and Aug. Info: Office de Tourisme, 12300 Decazeville. Tel 65 43 18 36.

La Clayette (West of Mâcon.) *Le Rêve de Marie Jacquet presente par "Chantemerle".* Six performances in July and Aug at the Château de la Clayette. Info: Groupe "Chantemerle", 26 rue du Château, 71800 La Clayette. Tel 85 28 23 02.

Le Lude (On the Loir, north-east of Tours.) *Les Féeries de l'Histoire.* By all accounts the supreme *spectacle* and the ultimate in *son et lumière.* Fri and Sat from third wk in June to third wk in Aug. At the château, alongside the Loir. Info: B.P. 35, 72800 Le Lude. Tel 43 94 67 27.

Le Puy-du-Fou (South-east of Nantes.) *Jacques Maupillier, Paysan Vendéen.* Said to be the largest *spectacle* in Europe. An evocation of Vendée life: lasers, synchronised fountains, the lot. Fri & Sat – June to Sept. Info: "Jacques Maupillier", 30 rue G. Clemenceau, 85590 Les Epesses. Tel 51 57 65 65.

Rocamadour *Les Lumières du Temps.* Three evenings in early Aug. From the valley floor you look upwards for the show – at the evocative village clinging to the steep rock face above you. 800 kw of light, fountains, fireworks, lasers. Info: "Les Lumières du Temps", 46500 Rocamadour. Tel 65 33 67 77.

Saint Fargeau (East of Gien, west of Auxerre.) *Spectacle Historique du Château de St-Fargeau.* Another *spectacle* claiming to be one of the greatest in Europe. On Fri and Sat in July and Aug; late start 22.00 hours! Sumptuous, dramatic; readers say "don't miss it". Info: Château de St-Fargeau, 89170 St-Fargeau. Tel 86 74 05 67.

Solignac (South of Limoges.) *Les Lumières de la Briance.* Six shows at end July, early Aug. 2,000 years of Briance Valley history – from Romans to Saracens and Normans. Info: Les Lumières de la Briance, 87110 Solignac. Tel 55 00 42 31.

Vendôme *Le Loir, Les Méandres de l'Histoire.* In July and August. A "fresco" of Loir history. Info: Le Loir, etc., 11 rue Marcille, 41100 Vendôme. Tel 54 77 10 60.

My family has never tackled a water-borne holiday on the other side of the Channel though we have, in the past, done just that on the Norfolk Broads. Certainly, both my brother and my son are avid sailing and cruising enthusiasts. My brother has his own traditional gaff-rigged sloop on the Broads and he hardly misses a weekend out on the craft; no wonder as he lives in Norfolk. My son, too, has tried his hand at various types of sailing and counts among his most enjoyable holidays his numerous canal cruising adventures.

So, family, friends and a multitude of readers have all reported back to me on their French sailing adventures. I think it's fair to say that everyone who has taken the tiller has enjoyed the experience immensely. Adventure is the plus on any boating holiday; they're also good for a laugh and they always produce an exciting moment or two, or three!

Four areas in France are particular favourites. I'll give you a brief outline of the quartet but, first, let me recommend that you write to the French Government Tourist and ask for *The Active Traveller in France*. This lists the names and addresses of a score of companies in the boat hire business. I know one of the operators well and I recommend them wholeheartedly: VFB Holidays of Cheltenham.

Burgundy

Much the most popular area with readers is Burgundy. There are two starting points which figure in most canal-cruising holidays: **St-Florentin** and **Auxerre.**

The former provides access to the Canal de Bourgogne. This famous waterway allows you to cruise to **Dijon** and onwards south-east to the River Saône. Not far from the point the canal joins the river, at **St-Jean-de-Losne**, there's a further starting, or finishing, centre for tours at Pontailler. This "port" gives access to both the Canal de l'Est, which heads north-east to **Epinal** and beyond; and south-west to **Digoin**, via the Canal du Centre. The St-Florentin to Dijon section of the Canal de Bourgogne passes some terrific sites: the châteaux at Tanlay and Ancy-le-Franc, the Cistercian Abbaye de Fontenay, the perched village of Châteauneuf, a restored medieval gem, and many others (see Burgundy introduction).

Auxerre is the starting/finishing port for the Yonne and the Canal du Nivernais. You can go as far south as the River Loire but most holidaymakers have to be satisfied with Clamecy or Corbigny. Certainly this is a part of France I know well and there's nothing more scenically pleasing than the section between Vermenton and Clamecy; seek out Mailly-le-Château.

Midi

The alternative options are tantalising. The Canal du Midi conects **Toulouse** with **Sète** on the Mediterranean – passing on the way **Carcassonne**. You can also detour to Narbonne. From Sète the Canal du Rhône à Sète links the Canal du Midi with the River Rhône. One interesting aspect of this waterway is that it makes use of the large *étangs* behind the coast: the most renowned is the Bassin de Thau, famed for its oysters and mussels. **Aigues-Mortes** is an essential port of call – a medieval fortified jewel.

The Canal Latéral à la Garonne heads north from Toulouse and eventually joins the River Garonne near Langon, south of **Bordeaux**. The sections between Toulouse and **Agen** and Agen to Le Mas-d'Agenais are the most popular.

Brittany

The River Vilaine and the Canal de Nantes à Brest provide the best cruising. The two waterways connect at the key town of **Redon**. Two centres, both near Redon, cater for the hire of cruisers. Malestroit is on the canal, to the north-west (not far from the picture-postcard pretty château at **Josselin**); and Arzal is situated at the mouth of the Vilaine. The cruising alternatives are varied as any Brittany map will confirm.

Alsace

The Canal de la Marne au Rhin links the rivers Moselle and Rhine. The section from near **Sarrebourg** to **Saverne** is especially scenic, cutting as it does through the wooded hills of the northern Vosges (see Alsace). An equally appealing scenic treat is the Canal des Houillères de la Sarre; this leaves the Marne-Rhine waterway just east of Sarrebourg and winds past *étangs* and through woods northwards towards Germany.

Other areas

These include the western Loire, the River Charente in Poitou Charentes, the Saône-Rhône rivers to the Med, the Camargue, Champagne and the Côte d'Azur. Several operators specialise in luxury cruises where all the hard work is done for you by the resident crew; not cheap but cruising in the grand style.

ETANGS

Etang is the French word for pond or pool. There are several areas in France where many hundreds of *étangs* pepper the landscape; they're invariably full of wildlife and are surrounded by interesting countryside.

One of the finest examples, and the first my wife and I explored, is the triangle of flat countryside between Lyon, Bourg-en-Bresse and Mâcon – **Les Dombes.** For the ornithologist the area is a real paradise. We can remember breaking a journey south to allow our son, no more than ten or eleven then but very much a budding bird-watcher, to quietly watch the goings-on. That stop lasted hours longer than originally planned; we were as absorbed as much as he was.

There's an excellent bird sanctuary (a small-scale Slimbridge) at Villars-les-Dombes. So many readers have written and spoken warmly of their visits to the bird reserve. Both Vonnas and Châtillon-sur-Chalaronne are renowned *villages fleuris*; the labels are entirely justified as both are a mass of flowers throughout the summer. We particularly like the latter: the half-timbered buildings, the stream through the middle, the market and the triptych. This is in the town hall on the first floor; just enter and ask to see it.

Another area we love dearly is a similar bit of country, the **Sologne**. There's one difference though: much of the Sologne is covered with thick woods – silver birch, chestnut and pine and both heather and broom. The combination of water and woodland makes it a wildlife eden, well-known for its game, freshwater lake and river fish and wildfowl. Strange regiments of rounded earth molehills in the fields protect the young asparagus stalks of early spring. Sologne is the place to come to eat freshly-cut bundles of asparagus, sumptuous *pâtés* and the celebrated *tarte Tatin*, an upside-down caramelised apple tart named after two ladies from Lamotte-Beuvron.

Typical of La Sologne is a pocket which lies west from Romorantin-Lanthenay on the D59, where soon the road is matched by reflections in the pond water gleaming to the right. Stop to look at the sluice gates positioned beside the road, put there to empty and clean the ponds occasionally – an essential requirement with all *étangs*. Beyond that, you soon arrive at another pool, the Etang de Paris, its surface encrusted with water lilies. Look out for herds of goats; their milk is used to produce the local *chèvre* cheese, which may be tingling fresh or gobsmacking dry in flavour.

South-west now to the **Marais Poitevin**, north of La Rochelle. Not so much *étangs* here as a thousand canals and tree-lined streams (*marais* means fen). Every field is an island – where cows, goats, their milk and their feed, and all crops are moved by punt. You can make punt trips from Coulon.

The **Camargue** is, perhaps, the best known of all the regions where *étangs*, and the wildlfie they spawn and protect, predominate. The area is a regional nature park and part of it is a zoological and botanical reserve. No wonder: flora and fauna, horses, bulls, birds of all types, water and seclusion everywhere. We've been fortunate to see huge flocks of pink flamingos on several occasions. To the north is Roman Provence; Arles is very much our favourite. Aigues-Mortes is a fortifed medieval wonder; once a port, now miles inland as the sea has long since receded. Saintes-Maries-de-la-Mer is the town long associated with gypsies (festival May 24/25).

The Parc Régional de **Brière**, north of St-Nazaire and La Baule, is not so much *étang* terrain as a small circle of marshland, criss-crossed by canals and channels. Use the D50 across the marshes and make certain you detour to one of several "islands", the Ile de Fédrun. To the west seek out the salt pans; there's no better salt produced anywhere.

I'll finish by describing two off-the-beaten-track areas both of which are rarely explored by tourists.

To the north-east of Nancy, before you reach **Sarrebourg**, is a long line of forests and *étangs*. Much the most interesting feature of this small enclave in the Parc Régional de Lorraine is the Canal des Houillères de la Sarre.

Further south, between Remiremont and Belfort, and part of the Parc Régional des Ballons des Vosges, is another wooded area peppered with tiny pools. In spring the valleys are pin-cushions of fruit blossom, primarily cherry. Don't miss the many distilleries in **Fougerolles**. Call on Roger and Agnes Coulin. Have a look at the numerous delights on their shelves: *kirsch* (cherry) and other *eaux-de-vie* – *framboise sauvage*, *abricot*, *quetsche*, *prune*, *mirabelle*, *reine-Claude*, *poire William*, *myrtille*, *fraise*, *gentiane*, *coing* and *mûre*. There's never a dull moment in France, wherever you are!

FORESTS

Life has treated me with great favour. It has been my good
fortune to see the great forests and mountains of the
Himalayas, the Rockies in western North America and the
superb technicolour eastern seaboard of Canada and the
United States. Britain has tiny forests in comparison but they,
too, are marvels of Nature. For example, take the Chilterns.
Every few years, when the weather conditions are just right,
the autumn spectacle makes the heart beat faster. France is
richly endowed with perhaps the finest forests in Europe. As
the years have rolled by and I've seen more and more of that
glorious country, the more I have grown to appreciate and love
the seemingly never-ending richness of its woods and forests.

Where do I start? The subject merits several pages. Perhaps
one of the best is also one of the smallest, hidden in the very
heart of France, the Forêt de **Tronçais** (south of **Bourges**).
The forest is a tapestry of rich, proud and handsome oaks. Its
future will be as interesting as its past. Careful regeneration
since the last war, and thinning-out in the decades to come,
will ensure that in future centuries some magnificent
specimens will be growing there.

Fontainebleau is at its best when the trees wear their autumn cloaks. Oak, beech, and Scots pine flourish in this giant green lung of Paris. The vast forest is encircled by so many roots of French history; easy to reach it's covered by tracks and paths which open up many seductive vistas. Barbizon, on the northern edges, has a long association with artists and is a special attraction. The outcrops of rocks are another interest – much used in training rock climbers.

The beech forests of France are as breathtaking as the woods in the Chilterns. The best are in Normandy and the finest of all are the forests surrounding Lyons-le-Forêt (east of **Rouen**) and the Forêt d'Eawy (south of **Dieppe**). I have seen the beech glades in spring – carpets of bluebells stretching in all directions; the same glades, in autumn, become copper sheets which blanket the ground below the trees.

Southern Normandy has its fair share of large forests. Sandwiching **Alençon** are the Forêt d'Ecouves and the Forêt de Perseigne; we especially like the latter, a cool haven and with some splendid beech specimens. Two unknown forests are in Le Perche, to the north-east of Alençon: the Forêt du Perche and the Forêt Reno Valdieu. In the latter the map identifies some *vieux arbres* – 100ft high oaks with the names Aberdeen, Oxford and Forestry Commission.

Every year Anne and I are stopped in our tracks by some new scenic surprise. So it was a couple of years ago, in October, when we had the Monts du Cantal to ourselves (west of **St-Flour**). See for yourself the beech forests in the Falgoux and Jordanne valleys (west and south of Puy Mary). Much the most unusual of French beech forests, the Cantal versions resemble mammoth drapes and swathes of golden cloth, flung down by the gods from the volcanic summits, rolls 2,000 to 3,000 ft long! We cannot recommend Cantal enough.

Several great forests are to the north-east of Paris: **Compiègne** is the most famous. Perhaps you will just want to lose yourself in its glades; a shame, as much history surrounds you. There's the palace at Compiègne; the forbidding castle at Pierrefonds; and the railway coach, a replica of the one in which the 1918 Armistice was signed and in which Hitler, in his vengeful way, received the French surrender in 1940 (Clairière de l'Armistice, 7km east of Compiègne).

Other forests north of Paris are the Forêt de St-Gobain, west of **Laon**; the Forêt de Retz, south-west of Soissons; and a trio, the Forêt de Chantilly, the Forêt d'Halatte and the Forêt d'Ermenonville (a special favourite of mine) – all near **Senlis**. At weekends all the forests are crowded.

Far to the east is the best of all the pine forests of France – the Forêt de la Joux, north-east of **Champagnole**. The forest is criss-crossed by roads which make it easy to see the huge specimens, only bettered in the Rockies. One particular tree you should seek out is the "Sapin Président" with a circumference of over four metres (see Michelin map).

One particular small forest in the Alps is another old favourite of ours – the Forêt de Boscodon. This is to the south of **Briançon**, near the Lac de Serre-Ponçon. The forest covers high mountain-sides and the trees are of mixed varieties. Use forestry roads (RF) to the Fontaine de l'Ours; you'll encounter two super viewpoints *en route*.

On the west coast is the largest of all French forests, the **Landes**. Man-made and just a century old, the pine forests were planted to save the land from becoming a vast desert.

GARDENS

For many years I have been unfairly prejudiced about France's gardens. In Britain we are unbelievably spoilt. The sheer variety and quantity of our gardens is mind boggling: vast parks, formal and wild gardens, tiny cottage plots – the wide choice is helped no end by the annual "Yellow" guide.

Slowly but surely, on my travels around France, I have woken up to the fact that there is indeed a wide spectrum of gardens across the Channel. My objective here is to give you a few clues about a selection of French gardens, some famous and some virtually unknown. Try to obtain a copy of an excellent leaflet from the French Government Tourist Office called "Visit a Garden in France"; 128 gardens are listed.

First, I'll highlight some of the more famous gardens which I have visited over the years. Later I'll let you into the secret of a talented author and some of the "secret" gardens she's discovered across the length and breadth of France.

Parc du Touvet Château du Touvet, 38660 **Le Touvet**. Tel 76 08 42 27. Some of you will recall the drawing I did in *Favourites* of this miniature Chatsworth, high above the Isère on the eastern slopes of the Chartreuse. Partly formal with

cascades, chestnuts and extensive views. Open mid April to
end June on Sun p.m. only; July to Oct on Sat & Sun p.m.
Giverny Musée Monet, 27620 **Giverny**. Tel 32 51 28 21.
Monet's garden, the subject of so many of his paintings; water-
lilies, of course, dazzle – but so does much else. Open every day
from Apl to Oct – except Mon.
Villandry Château de Villandry, 37510 **Villandry**. What a
rare mixture: several formal *jardins* but the ornamental
kitchen garden is a knockout. Open every day, 9.00 to sunset.
Vaux-le-Vicomte Domaine de Vaux-le-Vicomte, 77950 Maincy
(north-east of **Melun**). Le Nôtre's fabulous masterpiece.
Symmetry and "sculptured" gardens are the overpowering
sensations. Open every day except Christmas Day.
Château de La Roche-Courbon 17250 **St-Porchaire**. Tel 46 95
60 10. A perfect harmony of small château, water, trees and
formal garden. Open every day.
Château de Hautefort 24390 **Hautefort**. Terrific site for both
the château and its classical terraced gardens – matched by
equally super views. Open every day Apl to mid Nov; rest of
the year Sun p.m. only.

Some months after the publication of this guide Pavilion will
publish *Secret Gardens of France* by Mirabel Osler. She writes
wonderfully – in a Nevile Shute style, a master storyteller
whose words compel you to carry on and make putting down
her books an impossibility.

Anne and I have been fortunate enough to be privy to her
latest book at the manuscript stage. She has spent years
nosing out some of France's "secret" gardens. The location of
some will remain a secret; others can be visited. I've listed
below the briefest of details of six of the latter. On the
following two pages Mirabel gives you a *dégustation* of just one
of the many gardens featured in her new book.
Les Roses Anciennes André Eve, 28 Faubourg d'Orléans, 45302
Pithiviers (north-east of Orléans). Tel 38 30 01 30 (office
hours). A long, narrow town garden absolutely stuffed to
overflowing with old roses grown with lush abandon and
sensuality. Open on Mon and Sat in June and Sept.
Château Beauregard Marquise de Beauregard, Chens-sur-
Léman, 74140 **Douvaine**. Tel 50 94 04 07. Surrounded by
magnificent trees on the shores of Lake Léman and redolent of
French formality. Open first 10 days in July and Sept.
Le Labyrinthe aux Oiseaux Yvoire, 74140 **Douvaine**. Tel 50 72
88 80. A small, walled medieval garden, built as a "garden of
the five senses". Open every day from May to end Oct.
Association Les Roses Anciennes de la Bonne Maison Odile
Masquelier, 99 ch. de Fontanières, La Mulatière, 69350 **Lyon**.
Tel 78 42 42 82. A large garden on the hills of Lyon (the
suburb is on the right bank of the Saône, near its confluence
with the Rhône) made with fastidious refinement and expert
knowledge. Open Mon from Mar to July and in Sept.
Host. de St-Caprais rue St-Caprais, 91770 **St-Vrain**. Tel (1) 64
56 15 45. Arlette Malgras's restaurant courtyard is the
ebullient floral production of an extremely passionate
gardener. Closed mid July to mid Aug and Sun evg and Mon.
See next two pages. Michelin rating: "*restaurant avec
chambres*". Meals are adequate – nothing to rave about.
Pépinières Planbessin Colette Sainte-Beuve, **Castillon**, 14490
Balleroy (between Bayeux and Balleroy). Tel 31 92 56 03. A
first-class nursery with its own large, exquisite garden
displaying the versatility of both planting and design.

GARDENS

She said it used to be a sad place   **Mirabel Osler**

We had drifted by sheer chance into the courtyard of Arlette Malgras's restaurant. A courtyard absolutely sizzling with fervid colours. We had come because we were visiting Courson-Monteloup for the flower show. Accommodation was almost impossible to find, with Germans, Dutch, Belgians as well as French enthusiasts filling any available space. Some instinct of Tasmin's had led us to the Host. de St-Caprais, with only five bedrooms, located about six miles south-east from Courson, and the courtyard, as we entered under the arched entrance, bowled us over with throbbing floral discord. But what utter enchantment to find hidden in the unprepossessing territory which lies amid the urban sprawl between Paris and Etampes and the A6 and A10 autoroutes.

Until twelve years ago Arlette worked in a bank. Her husband worked in a restaurant in Paris, in the avenue Victor Hugo. Originally the property they bought at St-Vrain, a village of 2,000 inhabitants, consisted of two houses. From these they have made a large restaurant, with just a few bedrooms. "We didn't want it to look too much like a restaurant, you see. We wished to preserve the character of the place and the style of an old house." They have succeeded.

She and her husband had made the garden out of a cobbled courtyard. "There was nothing before – in fact it was a sad place!" Arlette cried waving her arms at our surroundings. It was hard to believe now; dolefulness had been banished, not a shadow of sobriety remained. As we sat having lunch in a galaxy of simmering colours – scarlet, magenta and carmine; livid purple, orange, chrome and ultramarine – Madame Malgras told us how they had begun by laying down the small grass lawns, very neat, and very vivid, before making the first flower bed. "My husband designs and I have *la main verte.*"

The result was a knockout. Geraniums, petunias, campanulas, roses and pinks, button-shaped daises, miniature pine trees, laurels, conifers and a weeping birch, surrounded four round dining tables with pink tablecloths standing under striped umbrellas. Pansies swarmed; their royal petals, yellow and velvety purple, filled the foreground where golden conifers were backed against the walls. Ivy, used as ground cover, formed a sober background to lobelias, fuchsias and begonias.

In the centre of the garden was a very large pot held together by strands of wire. Its green glaze, streaked with yellow, was crazed by old age, and earthenware showed through small chipped blemishes. "The pot was here when we arrived, when we bought the house, and I kept it because I adore it! Look!" We did. It was jammed with puce geraniums.

At the end of the courtyard furthest from the restaurant was a large raised terrace with steps leading up to it. Here the sun beat relentlessly against the high wall of the neighbouring building, reflecting back from the stone floor so that the area was a continual dilemma to Arlette. "Palm trees – I lost several on the terrace. It was too hot." I suggested rather mundanely that perhaps overhead vines would make a green shaded area for her pots, but she had her sights fixed on something far more theatrical. A fountain. "A big fountain in the middle. I've been looking in the antique shops for an old cast iron one." Her eyes sparkled. "With a gargoyle and with flowing water. What freshness! My husband's told me he could do that for me . . . so, *enfin*, it's possible."

Her husband, between hours of cooking, was as keen to

construct things as Arlette was to fill every space with flowers. "You see the pool there? My husband made it. We went to find the stones in the country, in a quarry, and he built all that." The pool was full of brown, beige, gold and blue fish gliding, twisting and catching the light in sudden flashes of fluorescence. They were not for eating but for decoration, though occasionally predatory musk rats did invade the pool which meant an excursion had to be made to find replacements. On one side of the lawn was a natural underground spring which made sporadic gushing noises as it rose to the surface, filling the pool with fresh water and the courtyard with soothing sound of rainfall.

After twenty-four hours of staying in this heavenly place, we had come to terms with Madame's priorities. We began to understand. For miles around people came to the restaurant for their anniversaries, christenings, business presentations and for weddings – *les noces*. Bookings were being made continually in advance and it was easy to understand why. Monsieur Malgras's cooking was fine, but the floral arrangements were irresistible. Naturally, in those circumstances, comfort in the bedrooms was irrelevant. Arlette Malgras was not to be deflected – though at first we did try.

We had been supplied with a leather-bound edition of the complete works of Molière, and a white bust of Beethoven standing on a tiny table just inside the bedroom door, and the lack of a bathroom shelf was irrelevant because there was no tooth glass; towels had to lie across the cistern, and there was no plug to the wash basin. "Try the bath plug," Madame suggested. We have, it's too big. "Tomorrow I'll buy one." But it never came. A bulb for the bedside light? A pillow? *"D'accord, d'accord"* came her placatory promises. They never appeared, naturally; Arlette Malgras's heart was elsewhere. Plumbing and light bulbs were trivia to someone who had her sights set on filling every pot and vase with high-pitched flowers whose colour decibels reached visual dissonance.

These arrived each morning from the florist. "Every day I do about twenty or thirty vases for the house. It's a lot of work, but I love it. I'd like to buy masses of flowers." Looking around I thought she had already reached the Plimsoll line. "Masses of plants, masses and masses. But we are limited for space – so I have them in the house!" You might think she was talking of discreet little posies for each dining table, but she was not. Her vases were filled with dynamic explosions of hi-tech ingenuity. Yet it required only a slight readjustment to achieve a different attitude of mind to all this turbulence. The vases, the garden were magnificent.

The trouble is, we are stuck with this one word, "garden", to describe the discreet garden of Maryvonne Sentuc, municipal gardens made from bedding plants, Anne Simonet's hill-top courtyard, Villandry, or the garden at the Château Beauregard on the shores of Lac Léman. The word is inadeqaute; totally unsubtle and unrevealing. What we need in English are a few nouns to use as alternatives to "garden" so that the great span of these creative places can be adequately named.

Here, in the courtyard, Arlette's garden had reached visual amplitude. What were a few shortcomings in the bedrooms compared with what was pulsating downstairs? I would go again at the drop of a hat for the joy of sharing with someone her extravagant delight in what had been effervescing in her mind for years and now was gratified by flowers.

MARKETS

For almost 40 years Anne and I have been bowled over by the variety and number of markets we've encountered on our travels across France. The sheer range of produce which we've seen, and occasionally tasted, has been breathtaking – and mouthwatering too. Kaleidoscopes of colour have dazzled our eyes; myriad aromas and perfumes have teased our sensitive noses; and the tantalising tastes and textures have ranged across the entire spectrum of possibilities.

During the last few years I have assembled a foot high pile of literature on French markets. I have also nosed out numerous markets – to dig deeper and see for myself some of the oddities that turn up in every *département*. At the end of each regional introduction I've listed a few of the principal markets; each list could have been ten times longer!

What follows is a limited selection of some of the markets I've enjoyed over the years. Get the French Government Tourist Office's "Touring Traveller in France" booklet. This lists all the regional tourist offices in France; write to them for more specific information on local markets.

Anne and I first saw **Nice** flower market over 30 years ago.

We've returned often but that first encounter left indelible impressions. You, too, will be overwhelmed by the spectacle. (Cours Saleya – eastern end of Promenade des Anglais; every morning except Mon – go early.)

Cannes The flower market is another colourful sight (every morning except Sun). The general market (Marché Forville) and the rue Meynadier (its shops almost entirely devoted to food) are immediate neighbours. All three are north of the port.

L'Aigle The Normandy town's market is rated *"le 3e marché de France"*. Every Tues morning the centre of the town stops to accommodate the show: *charcuteries et boucheries* in Place St-Martin; *poissons et crémeries* in rue de l'Abreuvoir; *fruits et légumes* in Place Boislandry....and on and on. (Write to the Hôtel Dauphin for a special leaflet; see Normandy.)

Romorantin Elsewhere, in the Loire introduction, I have written in detail about some of the local producers.

Tranzault (north-west of La Châtre – in Berry terrain). A rare market of "forgotten" vegetables; 3rd Sun in October.

Grasse This is the market Anne and I have visited, and used, more than any other in France. Small and compact, the market fills the Place aux Aires at the heart of Grasse. Best on Sat (held every morning except Mon).

Clermont-l'Hérault Typical of hundreds of markets held in non-tourist towns where local folk congregate for their day out. Every Wed morning. *Charcuterie* from Lacaune; cheeses from Aveyron and Rouergue; oysters from Thau; dozens of different olives; numerous dried fruits, herbs and grilled nuts.

Kaysersberg Refer to the Alsace introduction for further details of the Christmas market held every Fri, Sat and Sun during the four weekends prior to Christmas.

Every region, every *département*, has its own traditional market. The Pays Basque is typical. **St-Jean-Pied-de-Port** has its weekly market on Mon. On the last Sun in Sept the *"Ardi Gasna"* market and fair is held (see Southwest cheeses); tastings, sales and shepherds. Nearby **St-Etienne-de-Baïgorri** has a gastronomic and crafts market on the first Sun after July 14th and the first Sat and Sun after August 15th. These provide an ideal way of seeing and tasting Basque produce and specialities. **Espelette**, near Cambo-les-Bains, is as typical a Basque village as any – its houses proudly displaying their red and white livery. The village is famous for red peppers. In the early autumn blankets of red peppers cover many a whitewashed wall, drying in the benevolent sun. The annual *"Fête de Piment"* is held during the last w/e in Oct.

Aups and the surrounding terrain is renowned for *truffes* (truffles). Paul Bajade (Chênes Verts; see Côte d'Azur) is a master truffle chef. There's no better *marché aux truffes* than the Aups version: every Thurs (10.30) from Nov to March.

St-Trivier-de-Courtes is reputed for farms with Saracen chimneys (see Lyonnais) and its *"Journée du Poulet de Bresse"* (first w/e in Sept). An amazing range of poultry.

Three Ardèche markets in tiny hamlets: St-Joseph-des-Bancs (Wed morning in Oct and Nov) and St-Julien-du-Gua (Wed and Fri from mid Oct to mid Nov) are both north of **Vals-les-Bains** and both hold a *marché aux châtaignes* (sweet chestnuts); **St-Martial** (east of Gerbier de Jonc) has a *champignons* (mushrooms) fair on the Thurs before All Saints Day.

Finally, a "new" market at **Brive**: on the first Sat in July a *marché aux fruits rouges*, combined with a *concours gastronomiques* (dishes created from red fruits).

REGIONAL NATURE PARKS

Some of the happiest memories my wife and I have of France came as a result of us making the effort to discover for ourselves the surprises which Mother Nature keeps to herself. Make a start by searching out the numerous regional and national parks. I'll start with the regional parks.

The first park which you'll encounter, assuming you use either Calais or **Boulogne**, is made up of three parts: the gentle hills to the east of Boulogne, known as Le Boulonnais; the *marais* (fen), criss-crossed by canals, to the north of **St-Omer**; and the Forêt de Raismes-St-Amand-Wallers, on the north-west side of **Valenciennes**, on the Belgium border.

Normandy has a couple of parks: the smaller of the two is **Brotonne** – the woods and Seine estuary to the west of Rouen; the other is **Normandie-Maine** which stretches south-west and west of Alençon and includes the hillier parts of the region (the escarpment around Bagnoles is especially nice).

Brittany has a duo – each so different from the other: the **Armorique** includes both the high moorland of the Argoat (see the Brittany introduction) and the coast south of Brest; **Brière** is the marshland north of La Baule – at its best in May and June when yellow irises are in bloom.

The two regions I've called Alsace and Champagne-Ardenne have a quartet of regional parks. **Montagne de Reims** includes both the wooded hills to the south of Reims and part of the Marne Valley on either side of Epernay. **Forêt d'Orient** is to the immediate east of Troyes and encircles the huge manmade lake of the same name. **Lorraine** is divided into two sections: one is the wooded hills to the east of the Meuse, north-west of Nancy (seek out the American Memorial on the high Butte de Montsec); the other is to the west of Sarrebourg – woods and *étangs* and crossed by two canals. **Vosges du Nord** is the high wooded hills north of Saverne.

Burgundy is the home of the **Morvan** Regional Park. I've referred to this calm, green *parc* many times, studded as it is with wooded hills, lakes, streams and old villages.

The lower western seaboard of France has two unusual parks: the **Marais Poitevin**, north of La Rochelle (see Etangs); and the vast **Landes de Gascogne** (south of Bordeaux) which, as big as it is, is still only about one-quarter of the Landes pine forest (see Forests and Southwest).

From Gascony head east now to the **Haut Languedoc** park, west of Montpellier. What a cool surprise this one is, its high green hills a world apart from the dry scrub of the Med coast, just kilometres away (see Languedoc-Roussillon). Continuing around the Med coastline you soon come to the **Camargue**, south of Arles; I've described this one in *Etangs*.

Provence has a second Parc Régional: the **Lubéron** park includes the entire Montagne du Lubéron – at its best in late spring when wild flowers are at their finest (north of Aix-en-Provence). Read the Provence introduction.

Further up the Rhône Valley, to the south-west of Lyon, is the **Mont Pilat** park. We remember this one in the autumn when, on a cloudless, clear day, the light was utterly flawless.

Crossing the Rhône and entering the Alps brings you to two of the best of all France's regional parks. First **Vercors**, east of Valence. Read the introduction to Hautes-Alpes for further details. This high limestone fortress is a magnetic citadel; no wonder it became the very symbol of French Resistance. This was *maquis* terrain: *Mort pour La France* say the carved words on the numerous monuments; no finer words can be used for an epitaph. Go once: return often!

The second regional park in the Alps is **Queyras**, south-east of Briançon – remote Hannibal terrain (see Hautes-Alpes).

One of the newest of the regional nature parks is **Haut Jura**, the high, wooded hills of the Jura to the north and south of St-Claude. Read the introduction to the Jura.

The **Volcans d'Auvergne** park is in the northern Massif Central. This includes the extinct volcanic cones of the ranges called Dômes and Dore and the Monts du Cantal.

Last, but not least, most of mountainous inland **Corse** (Corsica) and the superb coast near Porto is a regional park.

In addition to the regional nature parks there are six national parks – the only real difference is that the latter are in uninhabited areas. The newest is **Mercantour**, north of Nice and along the Italian border. Others include **Ecrins**, north-west of Briançon; **Vanoise**, the high peaks south of Val d'Isère; **Cévennes**, the wooded limestone mountains north of Montpellier; **Pyrénées**, the highest central section of the range, south of Tarbes; and the smallest of the lot, the **Ile de Port-Cros**, in the Med, south-east of Hyères.

If you are lucky enough to be able to choose any season of the year to take your holiday you are indeed fortunate. Apart from missing the crowds outside the months of July and August, the time of the year can influence your decision about which region to visit. Many parts of France are lovely at any time but especially so in the spring, autumn and winter.

Spring and early Summer

All mountain country is at its most alluring. The air is clear and sharp, the torrents and cascades are at their fullest, the first blossoms and green tints are beginning to appear and pastures are full of wild flowers.

The **Pyrénées** is one example: Anne and I have seen the countryside near **Pau** in early April, fruit blossom everywhere and snow still thick on the mountains – a visual wonderland which July and August cannot emulate.

To the north of Pau is **Gascony**. In April and May we have seen primroses, daffodils, tulips, bluebells, lilacs and roses – all flowering together. The new tints on the awakening trees seem to permutate every shade of yellow, green and brown – from limes and emerald to sand and coffee.

The hinterland of the **Côte d'Azur** and **Provence** – *l'arrière pays* – is a delight. **Moustiers-Ste-Marie** and the nearby Gorges du Verdon combine to show what man and Nature can contrive together. The hills from **Rians** (east of Aix-en-Provence) to **Grasse** are attractive in early summer: wild flowers carpet the meadows and at lower altitude every garden, wall, terrace and field are a different colour.

Where else can you enjoy the awakening best of spring? **Finistère**, the western-most part of Brittany, and **Normandy** are a mass of apple blossom. In Normandy primroses line the roadsides and wild yellow irises wave in the pastures; further west both gorse and broom compete for your attention. In the **Chartreuse** and **Vercors** the roaring streams are full of ice-cold water; splashes of new greens act as honour guards to the rushing torrents. The **Vosges**, the **Jura** and the mountains of the **Massif Central** are all gorgeous.

In May and June we have marvelled at the wild flowers in the high pastures south of **Royat**, in the wooded glades of the Monts du Forez, in the marshy meadows of the Ardèche, in the remote fastness of **Bugey**, on the dry slopes of the Lubéron and on the Alpine slopes to the south of Lac d'Annecy.

I recall, too, the perfume of the lilacs alongside the River **Lot**; the herb-scented air in the hills around Cotignac (east of Rians); the overpowering smell of freshness in the upper reaches of the **Aude** Valley . . .spring is perfection!

Autumn

The beech forests north of the **Seine** (near **Rouen**) and those of the **Ile de France** are among our most vivid memories. But so are the gigantic beech swathes tumbling down the slopes of the Monts du **Cantal**; and the Jura's vast forests, primarily broad-leaved, when they wear their autumn clothes, Kaffe Fasset designs of random hues and shades.

We remember, too, the Alpes Maritimes (Côte d'Azur). In the autumn every mountainside is a massive canvas of colour. If I were to paint the myriad landscapes Anne and I have encountered in the past, you would accuse me of gross exaggeration. Steep slopes are covered with heavy dustings of multi-coloured confetti. Most spectacular are the thousands of "smoke trees" (*cotinus*) resembling fires of red-hot coals.

We have vivid memories of the Chapeauroux Valley, from Châteauneuf-de-Randon to the point the stream joins the Allier at Chapeauroux (south of **Le Puy**): one sunny October day the entire 20-mile run was akin to being in a Walt Disney wonderland. The same colour-scapes give both the Chartreuse and the Vercors extra appeal in the autumn.

Any of the wine villages and wine country are at their best when the grapes are being harvested for the new vintage. **Alsace** and the Jura both produce their own delectable light wines: Alsace has its picturesque villages, the Jura has pastures full of lilac-coloured autumn crocuses. **Beaujolais** and the **Loire** have their own scenic attractions: the former its hills, woods and nearby man-made sites – like Cluny, Pérouges, Charlieu and others; and the Loire its châteaux.

Winter

Winter allows you to see scenes with a new perspective; trees and hedges are leafless, like bare bones, and you glimpse, for the first time, sights not seen in summer.

Try the Ile de France. The Côte d'Azur, Gascony and the sheltered spas and villages in the foothills of the Pyrénées at the Med end of the range are amazingly mild in winter.

SPAS

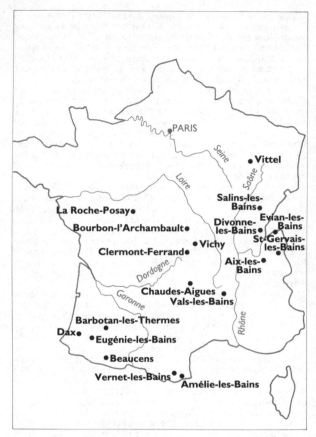

Throughout the centuries, "taking the waters" has been a custom known to our forefathers; indeed, many of the famous medicinal springs in France were enthusiastically used, and their praises sung, by the Romans, 2,000 years ago.

An ever increasing number of people over the years have discovered the therapeutic qualities of the springs. But whether you are taking the waters or not, all the spas listed below have some tourist appeal. Cures are no doubt helped by the many scenic attractions close at hand and by the clear air, the lack of noise and the parks, gardens and pools.

The first three are in the Alps – each adjacent to a host of varied scenic and man-made pleasures.

St-Gervais-les-Bains is under the shadow of the massive Mont Blanc. Above the town, in the hills to the east, is Le Bettex: drive there on a clear day (especially the afternoon) and enjoy one of the greatest of all Alpine views. Or take the tramway from St-Gervais to Le Nid d'Aigle.

Aix-les-Bains sits on the eastern bank of the Lac du Bourget; Lamartine wrote his famous poem about Elvire here. On the opposite shore is the Cistercian Hautecombe Abbey, founded by Saint Bernard in 1125. Above Aix is Mont Revard; from the summit, reached by car, there are panoramic views.

Evian-les-Bains is an attractive lakeside town – forever associated with the pure spring water which, in bottles, must travel to every country in the world. For me, the countless lanes in the foothills to the south are a special attraction. For others, steamer trips on the lake would appeal more.

The Jura and Vosges have a variety of spas. Much the most prosperous in the Jura is **Divonne-les-Bains**, on the doorstep of Genève and Lac Léman and with a backdrop of hills. A casino, sports complex, boating on the lake, golf and "French" prices make the resort popular with both tourists and the Swiss. **Salins-les-Bains** is a bit more basic; near Arbois, the spa has been famed for its salt since Roman times. Local vineyards are the extra plus in this self-effacing spa.

The Vosges spas are all to the west of the high ridge of hills. **Vittel**, of course, is world renowned; green, elegant and exceedingly prosperous. To the south-east of the town are some smaller spas: Bains-les-Bains, Luxeuil-les-Bains and Plombières – all at their best in the spring.

The Massif Central contains many spa towns. Several are grouped around **Clermont-Ferrand**: Néris-les-Bains, Châtelguyon and **Vichy**, another famous spa which has become a household name, are to the north; Royat, La Bourboule, Le Mont-Dore and St-Nectaire to the south – all among the extinct volcanic cones of the Auvergne. On the borders of the Auvergne, in the Loire Valley, are two contrasting spas: tiny, untouched by tourists, Sail-les-Bains and Montrond-les-Bains. There are numerous man-made treats to distract you: the Romanesque churches at Blesle, St-Nectaire (the finest of them all) and Brioude (see the Auvergne introduction) and the sombre abbey at La Chaise-Dieu.

Further south, in Cantal, is **Chaudes-Aigues** (the town claims the hottest waters in Europe); and, in the Ardèche, are two unpretentious spots, **Vals-les-Bains** and Neyrac-les-Bains (12 km to the west). The latter is "all French" – no tourists here. The Hôtel Du Levant, a touch run-down, is like France as it used to be – especially at Sunday lunch with large platters of cold meats and cheeses, from which you help yourself.

In the south, dotted among the Pyrénées, are several spas. **Vernet-les-Bains** and **Amélie-les-Bains** are in sheltered valleys at the Med end of the range: both have dry climates and mountains surrounding them; and both are near the sea.

Further west, south of Lourdes, are several small spas; perhaps the tiniest is at **Beaucens**, on the road to Gavarnie.

Just north of the Pyrénées, on the borders of Gascony and the Landes, are several varying spas. **Dax**, a biggish place, has fountains bubbling forth hot spring water. A touch more fashionable, and certainly smaller, is **Barbotan-les-Thermes**. As swish and chic as you can find anywhere in the thermal world, is Michel Guérard's three-star hotel and restaurant at **Eugénie-les-Bains**. Here you can take the cure and choose between his *cuisine gourmande* or, requiring more discipline this, the slimming agony of *cuisine minceur*.

Right at the heart of France are a couple of unknown spas, both of which give easy access to equally unassuming scenic and man-made sights. **La Roche-Posay** is in the north-east corner of Poitou; **Bourbon-l'Archambault** is on the borders of both Berry and the Bourbonnais. The neighbouring terrain is pastoral perfection with many historical treasures.

WILD FLOWERS

In the first edition of *French Leave* I wrote: "No wonder the coronation dress for Queen Elizabeth II was based on a design of the scores of wild flowers of France." I made one mistake in that sentence: instead of scores, read hundreds.

Where do I start? Anne and I have stumbled across myriad sites in France where we've been forced to stop in our tracks, willing admirers of the exuberant displays laid out in front of us. Nature fashions many priceless treasures – wild flowers among them. Brother Roger of Taizé put it simply and succinctly: "the constant need to admire is satisfied."

I'll start in Auvergne. One hot Midsummer's Day, on the D106 near Perrier (in the Monts du Forez, north-east of **Ambert**), we counted, within a few minutes, a score of different types. Later, above the tree-line, on the Col des Supeyres, we thrilled at the sight of even more varieties.

On another occasion, in the middle of October, we were heading north-east on the deserted "Route des Crêtes" (the D5 from **Aurillac** towards the Monts du Cantal). Gale-force winds had cleared the sky. To our great delight and surprise, we came across the tiniest of tricolour pansies glistening in the autumn air together with campion, scabious, harebells, hardy cranesbill, wild lavatera and verbascum.

In June, at the heart of the Parc National des Cévennes, I've encountered glittering numbers of wild flowers; the more remote and minor the road, the more handsome the reward. I recall in my mind's eye, even today, the D114 between Dourbies and **St-Jean-du-Bruel**; the countless varieties formed an honour guard alongside the narrow, winding road.

But the Ardèche has given us the biggest thrills. In May we have taken the roads north from **Vals-les-Bains** and Burzet and, on reaching the marshy plateau south of the Gerbier de Jonc, we've gasped at the sheets of wild daffodils, interlaced with yellow marsh buttercups, numerous orchids and scores of other wild flowers. A few weeks later, in mid June, and a decade on, we have been stunned by the same pastures ablaze with pillows of dark purple violas, intermingling with wild narcissi and myriad other wild flowers.

A little further north, on the western flanks of Mont Mézenc, between Les Estables and **Moudeyres**, the pastures have resembled snow fields; in reality wild narcissi and, hidden among them, dense pockets of intense purple pansies.

We remember Bugey vividly – for many reasons; but most of all we recall an early June day when we climbed south from the concrete viaducts of the A40, near **Nantua**, up the D55 to the Col de Bérentin. Our mouths dropped: could those be lingering fields of snow, not yet melted? No: they were gargantuan duvets of wild narcissi. So dense, Anne and I picked armfuls in minutes. A few weeks earlier, vast swathes of yellow jonquils flood the same Plateau de Retord.

Further west, in the valley below Tamié Abbey and heading north towards **Faverges** (more specifically in the meadows between Tertenoz and Les Combes), it's possible to identify a hundred or more varieties in May – assuming you have the time and patience, and knowledge, to do the counting.

In early June, atop the **Crêt de Châtillon**, on the marshy plateau south of the summit, we've marvelled at the lapis lazuli-tinted gentians peppering the spongy pastures.

I remember, too, when I have been driving on my own in the hills around **Lacaune**. One Sunday evening in June I used the D607 north from the town. The sides of the road were ribbons of wild flowers, of every variety imaginable. I counted at least 20 family groups busily collecting blooms.

We've seen free "shows" in the most unlikely of places: on the G51 west of the Col du Canadel, high above **Le Lavandou** and the Med; in the hills around **Cotignac** and Fox-Amphoux, the air saturated with the scent of herbs and flowers; in the valley below Thorenc and the **Col de Bleine**; and on the descent from the Col du Bel-Homme down into **Bargemon**.

In the high Pyrénées, near **Luz-St-Sauveur**, I've taken colour photographs of tiny wild daffodils waving in the wind; in September Anne and I have admired lilac-shaded autumn crocuses sparkling in the autumn light of the **Vercors** and **Chartreuse**; in April, in **Bresse** terrain, we've been cheered on by crowds of cowslips; in early spring, in Normandy's *bocage* (south-west of **Caen**), we've been welcomed by thousands of primroses, sunning themselves on the slopes of the high banked hedges and, later, in May, we've had escorts of wild yellow irises as we headed towards "La Suisse Normande". My pen has to stop now; pity, the possibilities go on and on . . . !

BATTLEFIELDS

My selections cover many centuries in time: all of them require you to use your imagination. But then all history requires that of you. With the help of large-scale maps, studied intelligently, and perhaps more detailed accounts of the battles themselves, a picture of each of them will form more clearly in your mind; some lasted just hours, some months and some years.

Crécy. From a small mound, just north of Crécy-en-Ponthieu (one km on D111), you can survey the same scene Edward III saw on August 26, 1346. Crécy was the start of the Hundred Years War and for the first time, and not the last, the French learned the bitter lesson of the stunning use made by the English – and the Welsh – of the longbow. The battle also marked the day that cannonballs were first used in battle; a pile lies in a small museum at the village. (I recommend Robin Neillands' book, *The Hundred Years War*.)

Poitiers. On September 19, 1356, one of the outstanding English victories of the Middle Ages was at Poitiers. The battle was fought at La Cardinerie, near the village of Nouaillé-Maupertuis, south-east of Poitiers. There's a simple monument to the men who fell that day – the soldiers of France, Gascony, and England. Follow signs on the western D142 exit that say "Les Bordes" and "Champ de Bataille". The monument was erected in 1956 – 600 years after the battle. Edward, the Black Prince, took the credit for the victory but the real hero was his general, Sir John Chandos; he was the unsung mastermind who won the day. (Read the concluding paragraphs in the introduction to Poitou-Charentes.)

Agincourt. On October 25, 1415, 69 years after Crécy, another spectacular and bloody battle was lost by the French at Agincourt (Azincourt on the maps), just 30 km to the north-east of the site of Edward III's victory. The spot is marked on the D104 and, even today, you can see why, once again, the French nobles were massacred by Henry V's longbowmen: they had no room for manoeuvre, trapped as they were between the woods of Azincourt and Tramecourt.

Verdun. A unique name that means so much to France: a symbol of French valour and suffering. To the north-east of Verdun are the tragic reminders of the bitter battles that raged there during the First World War: the Fort de Douaumont, the Fort de Vaux, the Fort de Souville, monuments, cemeteries and the chilling Ossuaire de Douaumont. This is sacred, sombre ground; the scars of Verdun influenced French thinking profoundly during the ensuing decades.

Somme. Elizabeth Nicholas wrote: "Who could make truly merry in a town that bore the name Péronne?" To the west, in the land to the north of the river Somme, surrounding Albert, was the scene of the worst bloodshed of the 1914-18 war. Motorists speeding along the A1 autoroute, at the point the A2 joins it, pass this consecrated ground in less than five minutes and yet what countless sacrifices were made in those cold, bleak fields. Stop one day at the memorials at Thiepval and Beaumont-Hamel and contemplate the awful sufferings of previous generations. (Of several specialist books I recommend *Before Endeavours Fade* by Rose Coombs.)

Dunkirk. If you use Calais or Dunkerque as ports of embarkation, don't sit out the last hours in the terminal car parks. Spend the time in the lanes of the canal and dyke-lined terrain to the south of Dunkerque. You'll get, first hand, a vivid picture of what an important part that marshy piece of Flanders played in the successful evacuation from Dunkerque: in the way the landscape helped the retreating forces to defend their positions during those few vital days; and how the fear of the marshes influenced the Germans in their decision, made on May 23, 1940, to temporarily stop their tanks at the River Aa, to the west of the port.

D-Day Landings. On the Normandy coast, north of Bayeux and **Caen**, are the D-Day beaches of Utah, Omaha, Gold, Juno and Sword (west to east). See the Arromanches museum; and, under no circumstances, miss the new "Mémorial pour la Paix" in Caen, which tells the story of the Second World War in Europe (just to the north of the Caen bypass). At Bénouville is Pegasus Bridge, where, on the night of June 5/6, 1944, ahead of the landings, airborne troops parachuted down. Normandy suffered terribly during those first few weeks. Arm yourself with one of the many books that tell the story of those days: then follow the battles that raged for St-Lô, Caen, Cherbourg, Mortain and Falaise. Numerous cemeteries, throughout Normandy, remind you of the high price the Allies paid for victory. (*Normany-Overlord. Holt's Battlefield Guide* is a must.)

JOURNEYS OF JOAN OF ARC

Hammond Innes, writing about **Chinon**, made the telling comment that it was in the fortress there that the death knell of English power in France was sounded, when "Jeanne La Pucelle" met her Dauphin for the first time.

There is no more absorbing way of bringing history alive than by reading Joan's story and following her footsteps, or parts of them, during her short, majestic and inspiring life. It is well worth finding the time to trace once again the various journeys she made during two momentous years.

A caveat: all history gets bent – shaped and twisted to suit the purposes of the sculptor; this is just as true of events that took place this century! You can be certain then that much of Joan's "story", 500 years later, is myth. She was, and has been, cast in many roles: warrior, saint, witch, patriot and other symbolic guises. Perhaps the most revealing, most intriguingly researched account of her life is Marina Warner's *Joan of Arc* (published by Weidenfeld & Nicolson).

Start at **Domrémy-la-Pucelle** where she was born, on January 6, 1412. The house is there, much restored, but the living room and its fireplace, her bedroom, the garden – none of these can have changed much. On a hill nearby, at Bois Chenu, south of the village, where she first heard the voices, a basilica has been built in her honour.

At the tender age of 17 she successfully persuaded Robert de Baudricourt, at Vaucouleurs, 20 km north of Domrémy, to send her to see her Dauphin. The Porte de France, through which Joan rode on February 23, 1429, to start her momentous journey, is still there. The Hundred Years' War raged on.

She travelled for 11 days: passing through Joinville (she slept at nearby St-Urbain on the first night) and then on to **Clairvaux**, now a prison, but once such an important abbey. (You should not miss visiting the home of another legend, General de Gaulle, at nearby Colombey-les-deux-Eglises.) She went on, passing through **Auxerre** (later returning through the town with Charles on their way to his coronation at Reims), Gien and Loches – all steeped in French history.

Few take the trouble to locate **Ste-Catherine-de-Fierbois**, just off the N10, 25 km south of Tours. You can still see the place where Joan spent the night and the old church where, legend tells us, Charles Martel's sword was found. His sword? Hardly, as some 700 years had elapsed since his death.

Today, the fortress at Chinon is in ruins but much of the town Joan saw still stands. She rode under the Tour de l'Horloge, stayed first at the Grand Carroi and later in the Château du Coudray, the western part of the castle. She arrived on March 6, 1429; the following day she successfully identified the Dauphin in a "line-up" of his courtiers. First she was sent to **Poitiers** to be examined by doctors. At last the Dauphin, not surprisingly, as **Orléans** was in mortal danger, sent her up the Loire with her own army.

She recaptured Orléans. There's not much there today that remains from Joan's time. But, at **Sully**, upstream on the Loire, there is; she was a guest at the castle there twice. It was during her first visit, after the battles of Orléans, Beaugency and Patay (where Talbot was captured), that she persuaded the Dauphin to go to **Reims** to be crowned. The coronation of Charles VII took place at Reims on July 17.

It is not difficult to relive that coronation in the magnificent Gothic cathedral. Your imagination will help you to envisage the stirring-moment when she threw herself at the feet of her king. Joan was captured by the English at **Compiègne**; she was shut outside the town gates by her own soldiers, in their haste to retreat. Remains of the ramparts, near the superb Palais, are still there to this day.

Rouen is where Joan, only 19, was burnt at the stake on May 30, 1431. 500 years later, some of the most distinguished people in the UK, Catholics and non-Catholics alike, supported an appeal to provide a window in her memory in Rouen Cathedral. In 1956, 500 years after her trial was declared null and void and she was proclaimed innocent, the window, by Max Ingrand, was dedicated on the re-opening of Rouen Cathedral after the war (the building was badly damaged).

The English who watched her die shouted: "We are lost; we have burnt a Saint." In the years that followed the French began to think of themselves as Frenchmen, not Burgundians, Normans and Armagnacs. By 1453, the English had been routed from France; only Calais remained in their hands.

Only a few days, in this modern age, would be needed to follow Joan's steps. Allow a week; there are many other sights to see and absorb on your journey.

For over a thousand years pilgrims have flocked from all over Europe to Santiago de Compostela in northern Spain. Its Romanesque cathedral is supposedly sited above the tomb of Saint James (*Santiago* in Spanish: *Compostela* meaning "field of the star") – reputed to have been beheaded by Herod Agrippa in A.D. 44. Mystery or myth, the magnet of Compostela has drawn millions of pilgrims over the centuries.

The four main starting points in France were at **Paris**, **Vézelay**, **Le Puy** and **Arles**. Each of the routes followed a general line towards the Spanish border in the south-west corner of France, though all of them had small variations. All the alternatives, without exception, passed through many of the great religious centres in southern France.

I'll describe two of the roads in some detail, locating the more magnificent ecclesiastical centres *en route*. I'll also pinpoint a couple of the unknown chapels, ones rarely seen by today's tourists. Most pilgrimage sites are marked with the "scallop" shell sign of Saint James.

Le Puy is one of the most unusual towns in France. Sharp needles of volcanic rock rise on all sides, several of them having chapels and statues on their summits. The cathedral, a strange mix of Byzantine and Romanesque, is a favourite of mine; the cloisters are particularly cool and quiet.

The next important religious stopping point was **Conques**. Hidden in the hills south of the River Lot, this jewel among Romanesque churches (Eglise Ste-Foy) is a remarkable building – its "treasure" even more so. Sainte Foy was a young Christian martyr; her relics were at Agen, where they reputedly worked miracles. Legend has it that a monk from Conques worked faithfully at Agen for ten years, then removed the relics to Conques, where they have since remained. One of the items making up the treasure is a statue of Ste-Foy, carved in yew and covered with gold and precious stones.

From Conques the route continued south-west, through the Romanesque town of **Moissac** and past the Cistercian abbey at **Flaran**. Trace the road on a map and you'll see that all manner of historical sites are passed: Espalion and Estaing in the Lot Valley, Cahors and the nearby caves at Pech Merle.

From Vézelay the route headed south-west, through **La Charité-sur-Loire** and **Bourges**. One alternative road went west through **Brantôme** and **Périgueux**; another kept slightly east and aimed for **Rocamadour**. The village has a spectacular site, clinging to the north side of a steep valley. A statue of the Virgin Mary, carved from oak and now the colour of ebony, has always been the pilgrims' goal: included among them have been two Kings of England, Henry II and John and, more recently, the composer Poulenc.

From Rocamadour the route passed through Conques, Rodez and Millau to the Cistercian abbey at **Sylvanès**. Elsewhere, in the introduction to Languedoc-Roussillon, I've told you about a modern-day project here, the building of a cathedral-sized organ. Onwards, through **Castres** and **Foix** to the cathedral, part Romanesque, part Gothic, at **St-Bertrand-de-Comminges**. In Roman times this small place was part of a town that boasted a population of 50,000. Herod was exiled here by Caligula. Further west, **Oloron-Ste-Marie** boasted two churches which were important to the pilgrims: the 13th-century Eglise Ste-Marie and the Church of Ste-Croix.

The Arles route included stops at Castres, **Toulouse** and **Auch**. Do spare time for the cathedral at Auch; its choir stalls are reckoned to be among the finest in France.

The Paris route kept to the west; past **Orléans** and **Tours** to **Parthenay**, in Poitou. Here the name St-Jacques is given to a bridge, gate and an old street. **Poitiers** and Melle were important stops; so was Aulnay with a Romanesque church and its great number of fine sculptures. Onwards through **Saintes**, once the capital of Western Gaul, and still full of man-made treasures, particularly its Romanesque churches.

Most of the routes converged at **St-Jean-Pied-de-Port**, the gateway to Spain. In the vicinity of this splendid Basque town, to the north-east, is the church at Harambeltz (Harambels on the map) – a 12th-century gem. Ask at the farm for the key. Michelin maps for the south-west are covered with the symbol for a "chapel" – many in isolated spots and, more likely than not, lying on the pilgrimage routes. Find **Plaisance** in Gers. To the east are numerous symbols. One unmarked site, the Chapelle du Ban, is a 12th-century empty shell surrounded by Armagnac vines and sitting in the shade of two ancient oak trees; you'll find it 400 metres east of Fromentas, itself about eight km north-east of Plaisance.

THE RESISTANCE & SOE

No other subject has generated more letters from my readers, over the years, than my many references to the Resistance. All the references have been positive accounts of incredible bravery and amazing actions. But we should remind ourselves that not every Frenchman or woman was a Resistance hero or heroine. Traitors lived under every stone. Most French people collaborated passively. We shouldn't be too smug: what would have occurred here if Germany had over-run Britain?

There's not space here to debate that question further or to develop the myth which asks us to believe that everyone in France was a member of a *maquis* group. I would rather stay with the positive aspect and bring to your attention some of the more renowned *maquis* battles and also one or two unheralded accounts of equally redoubtable resistance.

Life is full of surprises. I thought I had uncovered most Resistance stories. But a couple of years ago, quite by chance, Anne and I came across the newly-opened Musée de la Résistance "Joseph LHomenède" at Frugières-le-Pin Gare (south-east of **Brioude**). I've seen many museums in France devoted to the Resistance but this is the *pièce de résistance* –

utterly fascinating and filled with memorabilia of every type imaginable. Joseph was the leader of the local Livradois *maquis*; his home was the adjacent Café Fayolle. Ask for access at the café. The lady who opens up the museum is Jacqueline, Joseph's daughter. Put aside two hours at least!

I've had more letters about one remote, hard-to-find spot than any other in France. I refer you to the Burgundy introduction and my brief outline of the "Maquis Bernard" story. Seek out Le Boulard, south-west of **Montsauche**, and follow the signs to the "Cimitière Franco-Anglais". I first discovered this inspiring and poignant spot in April 1982. Then there was nothing to tell me the background detail of this most inspiring of corners. Bit by bit, over the years, I gleaned snippets of the story: from the local mayor and *maquis* members, from ex-SAS agents and from readers. Today, huge boards explain the events of 1943/44. The story of the Morvan Resistance is told at a museum based at the Maison du Parc at St-Brisson, north-east of Montsauche (June to Sept).

Much the most famous of all Resistance actions is the battle which took place in the **Vercors**. One book, *Tears of Glory*, relates the story of the Vercors quite superbly. Alas, it's out of print (a lamentable action by Pan); but get hold of a copy of the hardback (Macmillan) from your library. Michael Pearson's subtitle for his book, "The Betrayal of Vercors 1944", is a revealing pointer to the events that took place after D-Day. Visit the Vercors: the museum at Vassieu, the cave and memorial at the Grotte de la Luire, the rebuilt villages (all razed to the ground in 1944), the D215 from Villard to Valchevrière. Read, too, my Hautes-Alpes introduction.

Another of the renowned Resistance battles, once more a tragic defeat, was fought on the high Plateau des Glières, to the north-east of **Annecy**. Hundreds, too, died here, defeated by 5,000 Germans and French Vichy *miliciens*. Access is from Thorens-Glières; at the Col des Glières there's a monument and maps which explain the battle. To the south, in the valley west of **Thônes**, there's a museum and cemetery.

I refer you to the Lyonnais introduction and my references to the various *maquis* groups of Bugey. Memorials abound: there's a huge monument at **Cerdon**, alongside the N84; another more poignant, smaller version, is on the D8 just west of Luthézieu, itself north of **Virieu-le-Grand**.

Some say the **Sologne** *maquis* was the most formidable in France. Here the local Resistance groups, together with SOE agents, caused mayhem for the Germans. Some spectacular sabotage actions took place in the Sologne and in towns like Tours and Orléans. I refer you to the Loire introduction and my reference to a new book by Stella King, *Jacqueline: Pioneer Heroine of the Resistance*. Also note the reference to the **Lorris** *maquis* and the action which took place in the Orléans forest in August 1944 (right bank of the Loire).

I have referred already to two books, both of which are accounts of the work of the SOE and the Resistance. But others, too, are essential references: the monumental *SOE in France* by M.R.D.Foot is a 550-page wonder (ask your library for a copy); or, alternatively, the paperback published by Grafton called *F Section SOE* (by Marcel Ruby) an easier read; and Max Hastings' *Das Reich* (Pan p/b) – read the Dordogne introduction for a précis; and, finally, the most inspiring book of all, *Odette – The Story of a British Agent*, by Jerrard Tickell (Chivers Press).

ANCIENT ABBEYS

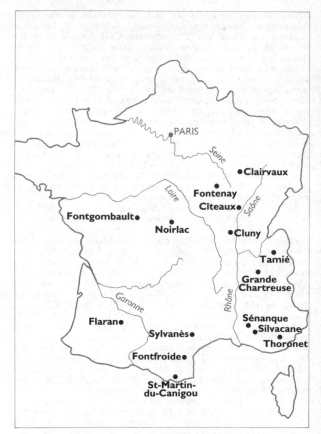

There are dozens throughout France deserving of your time: my selection is made from just a few that span the centuries. They range from ruins to vast impressive buildings: some are easy to find, others are well off-the-beaten-track.

Cluny, from the 9th to the 12th century, was the spiritual hub of the Christian World. Today, little remains of Cluny Abbey which, until the building of St-Peter's in Rome, was the largest Christian church in Europe. The 11th century was a time of incomparable prestige for the Benedictine Order of Cluny and for their *églises romanes*. Cluny's influence – spiritual, intellectual and artistic – was far-reaching; it radiated from Burgundy, throughout France and into the rest of Europe. Its hundreds of "children" (dependent abbeys and priories) kept alive the Christian faith during periods of history when it came close to dying. Only your imagination can bring alive the past glory of the site; but both the small town and the Musée Orchier are interesting enough to warrant a detour. Some examples of sculpture and statuary are in the museum but better examples of the Cluniac school are found at Vézelay, Autun, Semur-en-Auxois and Avallon.

The 12th century, under the influence of Bernard of Clairvaux, was the century of the monks of **Cîteaux**. This was the first of the Cistercian abbeys; like Cluny, only ruins remain, lying among the reeds, of this once powerful abbey. Cîteaux, too, had hundreds of "children", spread throughout Europe. Founded at the end of the 11th century it took Saint Bernard to build up its strong and real influence throughout Europe. A present-day order of the Cistercians is based at Cîteaux: every Sunday morning you can hear their Gregorian chants in the chapel (east of Nuits-St-Georges).

In 1146 it was Saint Bernard who preached so effectively for the Second Crusade to take place. **Clairvaux** (east of Troyes) was his abbey: today it is the site of a prison. Saint Bernard was the arch enemy of Abelard who courted Heloïse so passionately. Their story is mentioned in "Hilltop Sights & Sites" but, coincidentally, Abelard died at Cluny.

Saint Bernard's influence was colossal: he was the arbiter of Europe and between Popes. He led the development of the Cistercian order from Cîteaux, where he died in 1153.

Fontenay was founded in 1118 by two of Saint Bernard's uncles and is a perfect example of the flowering of the Cistercian influence. Fontenay was the second "daughter" of Clairvaux and there is no finer place for you to grasp just why Burgundy, the mother of all the arts, became so important. That Burgundian influence lasted hundreds of years; today, Fontenay survives and remains, after much restoration, in marvellous condition. Be sure not to miss it.

Other Cistercian abbeys should be included on your travels around France. Three are in Provence: **Sénanque**, near Gordes, east of Avignon; **Silvacane**, in the Durance Valley, south of the Lubéron; and, my favourite, **Thoronet**, east of Brignoles. Other favourites are the abbeys at **Noirlac**, south of Bourges, and famed for both its majestic example of medieval monastic architecture and an annual music festival; **Flaran**, in the Baïse Valley south of Condom and Agen; **Sylvanès**, in a quiet valley south of Millau and soon to be the home of a massive new organ (see Languedoc-Roussillon); and **Fontfroide**, near Narbonne – in an isolated site where silence, gardens, cloisters and an old abbey combine to inspire.

Other abbeys should also be included on your itinerary. One of my favourites is the abbey at **Tamié**, in the tranquil hills south of Lac d'Annecy. This, too, is Cistercian though sometimes the monks are called "trappistes". Read the Savoie introduction for some of the varied reasons why you should seek out the abbey. **Fontgombault**, alongside the River Creuse and east of Poitiers, was built at the end of the 11th century. The abbey church is a fine example of Romanesque skill; visitors can hear Gregorian chants every morning.

St-Martin-du-Canigou is a tiny abbey, built in the 10th century, and sits high above Vernet-les-Bains at the eastern end of the Pyrénées. The climb is exhausting but the rewards more than outweigh the effort required.

Finally, I will never miss an opportunity to persuade you to visit the seductive Massif de la Chartreuse – some of the finest mountain country in France. The **Grande Chartreuse** – in reality a monastery, not an abbey – is set in idyllic scenery. Founded in 1035 by Saint Bruno of the Carthusian Order, the buildings have been destroyed and rebuilt many times during the centuries. You cannot visit the monastery but enjoy La Correrie, a museum explaining the life of the monks.

CHEESE & OTHER TASTINGS

Yet again, a chapter of 80 lines is just not enough to begin to do justice to the innumerable culinary treats seemingly around every corner in France. What follows is a small selection of some of the more memorable treats I've relished.

Perhaps the most impressive, larger-than-life character I've met anywhere in France is Marc Streitz. A decade ago, when his mother died, Marc returned to the 2,000 olive trees she had so lovingly nursed for over 30 years. "To put my fingers back in the earth – a much better way of life than being a bad architect," Marc laughingly explains.

His olives and olive oil are second to none. So is his "new" business – supplying quality, young vegetables, grown 100 per cent naturally, to a handful of lucky chefs within a ten minute drive of the estate. I can still taste the delicate savours of his different tomatoes, carrots, *petits pois* and numerous others – not forgetting the herbs, some most unusual and rare. Where do you find him? Head south from **Valbonne** for one km on the D3; 100 metres past the Auberge Fleurie (see Côte d'Azur) turn right and continue for 500 metres; Marc's estate, the Colline de Peirabelle, is on the right.

Other olive oil suppliers we've used over the years are at the Moulin d'Opio at Opio (east of **Grasse**); and the Moulin à huile d'olives Coopératif at Mouriés, between St-Rémy and **Salon-de-Provence** (open Wed & Sat p.m. & Sun p.m.).

Talking about olives perhaps the most tasty, delicious ones we've ever encountered are those served at La Riboto de Taven in **Les Baux**. The olives are soaked in olive oil and then marinated in fresh Provençal herbs and a "secret" ingredient. You can buy them, and local wines, from the restaurant.

Let's stay in the south. All my family have a sweet tooth – or two! Not surprisingly then we all adore the crystallised fruits of Provence. It's a revelation to see how the fruits and jams are made. Visit the Confiserie des Gorges du Loup at Pont-du-Loup (alongside the river between Grasse and Vence). Like the perfumeries at Grasse, guided tours are free and in English: but a caveat – you'll fall for their wares.

Finally, before leaving the Côte d'Azur, head for Pégomas, south of Grasse, and the evocative La Bolognaise (Chez César & Pierrette) – a treasure trove of Italian goodies: *raviolis, pâtes fraîches, gnocchis, pâtes vertes, cannellonis, lasagnes, tortellonis* and goodness knows what else – all home made.

Heading north we remember stumbling, literally, on the Château d'Andert, just off the D32 from Contrevoz to **Belley**, in Bugey. A superb panorama, splendid château and hostess Martine Schmidt all appeal – but so do the home-made *cassis* products, especially the *jus naturel* version which contains neither sugar nor alcohol. Happy memories!

Visit one of the Franche-Comté farms with their huge chimneys (called *tué* or *tuyé*): La Ferme des Guinots, south-east of the crossroads at Les Cerneux-Monnots, on the D414 from **Charquemont** to Le Russey; it's the first farm on the right side of the D457. You'll gasp at the sheer number of hams and sausages that can be smoked in the high, dark cavern. Try tasty morsels on the spot: *saucisse de Morteau* (also called *Jésus de Morteau*), *jambon de tuyé* and *brési*.

In the Morvan, seek out Chez Millette at Planchez, south of **Montsauche** – the most rustic café imaginable. Authentic fare cooked by *madame: jambon de Morvan, rosette* (pork sausages), *boudin blanc* and *crapinaude* (bacon pancakes).

I guess I have seen two to three dozen cheesemakers over the years, in the middle of their arduous daily grinds. Two were especially memorable. The first in the Jura: the Sancey Richard Fromagerie du Mont d'Or at Metabief, near **Malbuisson**. Arrive at 9.30 a.m. any day, except Sunday, and witness, from special galleries, the making of three supreme cheeses: Comté, a huge hard wheel; Morbier, an LP-sized record with an ash streak through the middle; and Mont d'Or, a creamy CD-sized *fromage*, made from November to March.

The second was the redoubtable Paul Bogey at his one-man Fromagerie de Doucy-en-Bauges (east of **Le Châtelard**). Again, arrive between 8.30 to 9.00 a.m. to see him at the critical stage of his relentless daily production of three 40-kilo "wheels" (1,500 litres of milk are needed to make them).

Among hundreds of cheese shops three stand out: Philippe Olivier's La Fromagerie at 43 rue Thiers in **Boulogne**; the refrigerator-cool magasin of Gérard Paul in the bd G.-Clemenceau, Salon-de-Provence; and Roger Casoni's "L'Etable" in the rue Sade, **Antibes** – his *chèvre* selection is both an eye-opening and a kick-in-the-mouth experience. Please also read the final paragraph in "Etangs".

FORTIFIED TOWNS

There are many dozens of fortified towns throughout France. Some are huge places, some are tiny; some restored, some in ruins. But not one of the handful I've chosen to highlight in this chapter will disappoint you.

Carcassonne: is there a more romantic skyline anywhere in France? The impressive fortress is massive, the largest in Europe. Before you absorb the details of the man-made skills within the walls of La Cité, view it from the banks of the River Aude; the perspective sets the scene perfectly for your walking efforts to come. If time is your enemy and you are "flying" past Carcassonne on the A61 autoroute, then at least stop at the excellent rest area to the west of the town; the view of the fortress is as good as any. It is said that the architect Viollet-le-Duc used a bit too much imagination (as he did at Pierrefonds on the edges of the forest at Compiègne) in his restoration work. Perhaps, but your imagination will be failing you if your senses are not aroused by his handiwork.

Briançon is the highest "town" in Europe. Above the modern town is the old Ville Haute and a citadel – designed by Vauban, the military architect and engineer – with three rows of impressive ramparts. The Grande Rue in the Ville Haute is a medieval treasure. The views from the citadel are extensive.

Embrun is south of Briançon and it, too, sits above the Durance. Embrun was once an important fortified town and ecclesiastical centre; its church is probably the finest in the Dauphiny Alps. You'll never get bored in terrain like this: the Forêt de Boscodon and Lac de Serre-Ponçon to the south and the Queyras Regional Park to the north-east.

Montreuil-sur-Mer, the full name, was once a port; but the River Canche long ago silted up and Montreuil now sits ten km inland. The history of the town goes back to Roman times but its main importance came in the 13th and 14th centuries. Victor Hugo, in his epic *Les Misérables*, and Laurence Sterne, in *A Sentimental Journey*, both wrote of the town; for me its special pleasure is the ramparts. Do the whole circuit.

Pérouges has intrigued Anne and me for over two decades. Four centuries ago it was a busy place; three centuries later it had all but disappeared. The last 60 years have seen the tiny *ville* restored. Pérouges is the most perfect of fortified towns; although hardly a town now, more a village. Nothing clashes, nothing jars the eye. We always try to walk the narrow, cobbled lanes before dusk – when they're deserted; twilight enhances the fine setting and you find it easier to visualise the place all those centuries ago.

Aigues-Mortes, like Montreuil, was also once a port. From the ramparts of this astonishing fortified town the blue Mediterranean can be seen a few kilometres to the south; again the result of silt building up over the centuries. There was a village here in Roman times but it was Saint Louis, at the time of the Crusades, who made the town so important. He built the circular keep, the impressive Tour de Constance, with five metre thick walls. His son, Philip the Bold, organised the building of the extensive walls, towers and gates.

Entrevaux is a fine example of how important a small fortified town like this must have been centuries ago. You can grasp the importance of the strategic site by climbing to the south up the Col de Félines: to the north is the remarkable aspect of the medieval village, on the far bank of the Var, linked by an umbilical zigzag wall to a citadel high above the collection of houses. Another Vauban enterprise.

Noyers is a medieval dream, all but surrounded by a loop of the River Serein. Built 500 years ago the town has narrow streets, tiny squares and walls with 16 towers.

Brouage, south of Rochefort, is the third fortified town now isolated from the sea. This one has an air of mystery; history seems to seep from its massive walls. Built by Richelieu, the once famous port is small and compact.

There are dozens of *bastides* (fortified towns) in the south and west of France. All of them were built 700 to 800 years ago by the Kings of both England and France. Most have a common design: rectangular in shape with fortified walls, and streets, within the walls, which run at right-angles to each other. In the centre is a fortified church and, nearby, a main square with covered arcades. One good example is **Monpazier**. Built in 1284 by Edward I, Monpazier is, for me, much the best of them. The arcaded square at its heart is a joy – with perfectly proportioned stone buildings. This is a must!

Further south, south-west of Agen, is a minute, circular *bastide*, **Fourcès**; one word sums it up – fantastic. Nearby, too, is **Larressingle**, the smallest of all *bastides*.

As I start writing these short chapters, I realise that 80 lines is hardly enough to do justice to the subject at hand. This chapter is an ideal example. There are scores and scores of places, throughout France, which could be included here. Some of the missing hilltop sights and sites are included elsewhere in this "themed" section of the book; others have been incorporated into the regional introductions.

I'll start in the far south, in the hinterland of the Côte d'Azur and Provence – *l'arrière pays*. Here there are dozens of "perched" villages, with houses clustered around a church – some high on the tops of hills, others, lower down, on their flanks. All have narrow streets with houses which almost touch. Their shaded "squares" vary from the minute, like Bargemon, to biggish ones at Cotignac and Fayence; all have fountains and "umbrellas" of chestnuts and plane trees.

Peillon embodies the essence of the French Mediterranean. An air of timelessness pervades the huddle of houses, an oasis of calm perched atop huge vertical slabs of rock. The village is minutes from the coast yet remains hidden from the ever creeping tentacles of Nice's ghastly suburbs. Medieval

Bargème is quite different; seven km east of Comps, the isolated hamlet is no more than a ruined castle and church.

Laon is at the opposite end of the country. Once the capital of France, the town sits majestically on a solitary hill, towering over the surrounding countryside. One of the finest Gothic cathedrals is the centrepiece, but any walk through the town is rewarding: ancient houses, old streets and extensive views from the ramparts and cliff-side promenades.

Provins is a town which is unknown to most tourists. Its site does not lie on any of the recognised north-south routes and few travellers pass the town on the east-west road; as a consequence they all miss this intriguing old place. The huge ramparts, built by the English during the Hundred Years War, are still there. To the north is Champagne country; to the south is a steep slope bordered by the Durteint and Voulzie streams; to the east is the Church of St-Ayoul, where Abelard once taught his students. South-east of Provins, seven km beyond Nogent-sur-Seine, on the D442, are the ruins of Le Paraclet alongside the Ardusson. This was the hermitage to which Abelard was banished. When he left he gave it to Heloïse; she, in turn, became the abbess there. Their story has become immortalised. Abelard died at Cluny but was buried at Le Paraclet. Now the two of them are buried together in the Père Lachaise Cemetery in Paris – together with Balzac, Bizet, Chopin, Molière, Proust, Oscar Wilde and many others.

Haut-Koenigsbourg is a fantastic castle, perched like an eagle on its eerie high in the Vosges – overlooking the vast plain of Alsace, the Rhine and the Black Forest, far to the east in Germany. The castle was restored in 1900 by Kaiser Wilhelm II; a marvellous place for children and adults alike – a Grimm's fairy-tale castle if ever there was one.

The River Armançon loops in a giant circle around the massive walls of the old Burgundian town of **Semur-en-Auxois** – making it into all but an island. Gigantic towers, precipitous views, tree-lined avenues – Semur has everything. Burgundy at its best, as it was centuries ago.

Châteauneuf. How many of you have motored down the A6 and, just south of the exit to Pouilly and Dijon, admired the small fortified village perched high above the autoroute to the left? Next time, instead of sitting there admiring the site, why not leave at the Pouilly exit and explore the tiny place. The hamlet has been saved from dereliction not by the State but by individuals who were appalled by the thought that ancient Châteauneuf could die. The views are extensive and the narrow streets and old houses are absorbing pleasures.

Les Baux-de-Provence is a haunting, ghost-ridden village, perched on a hilltop in the Chaîne des Alpilles, one of the strangest outcrops in France. Over 300 years ago it was a flourishing place; Louis XIII ordered the town destroyed. Les Baux gave its name to bauxite, discovered hereabouts. Seek out the nearby "Cathédrale d'Images": since long before the time of the Romans, man has used the limestone from here and other quarries in the Chaîne – its dazzling whiteness can be seen in buildings as far apart as Genève and Marseille. Now the "cathedral" is used for high-tech audio-visual spectacles.

Domme is a hilltop village, high above the left bank of the River Dordogne. The view of the river far below is a classic vista – one of the finest in France. Domme, a *bastide*, had its shape adapted to suit the contours of the rocky hill. Also see the Dordogne introduction for other local attractions.

PRIVATELY-OWNED RAILWAYS

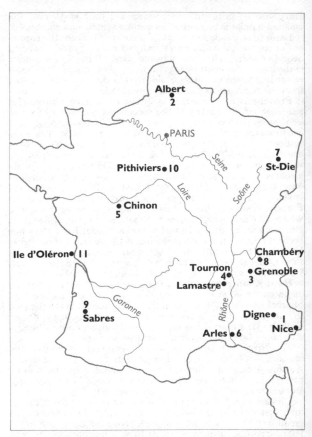

During the last two decades there has been a steady growth of interest throughout France in reviving old railway lines. Though none of them match the best of the privately-run lines in Britain (the Severn Valley Railway from Bridgnorth to Kidderminster and the Ffestiniog Railway from Porthmadog to Blaenau Ffestiniog are just two examples that both I and my son know intimately), nevertheless, dozens are there to be enjoyed, a few of them having steam-driven engines. Alas, many are only open at weekends. I have given as much information as I can; check opening times with French Railways at 179 Piccadilly, London W1 or the French Government Tourist Offices in your own country. Or enquire locally.

Chemins de Fer de Provence (1). This is an important and major link between **Digne** and **Nice**. Diesel cars ply the metric gauge line – scenically exciting and full of technical interest. At weekends during the summer a steamer ("Train des Pignes" – pines) uses the track between Annot and Puget-Théniers in the Var Valley. My advice is to try the service for a limited distance – say St-André-les-Alpes to Annot and return; then make use of your car to enjoy the numerous scenic attractions in the mountains astride the Var.

Chemin de Fer Touristique Froissy-Dompierre (2). A short seven km run on a 60 cm track. South of the River Somme, just west of the Al autoroute and south of **Albert**. Steamers only on Sundays and fête days; otherwise diesels.

Chemin de Fer de St-Georges-de-Commiers à La Mure (3). A 30 km run, full of exciting sections. The railway starts at the SNCF connecting station at St-Georges (just a few km south of **Grenoble**, in the Drac Valley) and then, as a *voie métrique*, winds its way up to La Mure. Super views of the Drac Valley and the Vercors peaks. Sundays only in summer.

Chemin de Fer du Viverais (4). Don't miss this on any account. Much the best "small" line in France, coming close to matching the Ffestiniog run in Wales. A metre-gauge railway of 33 km from **Tournon** (where it shares the SNCF station) in the Rhône Valley, following the Doux Valley on a climb of 250 metres to **Lamastre**. All this is Ardèche country. The railway celebrated its centenary in 1991. What could be better than the summer 10.00 a.m. "steamer" from Tournon, arriving at Lamastre at midday, lunching at Bernard Perrier's Hôtel du Midi (relishing dishes which 60 years ago won chef Barrattéro three Michelin stars), returning at 16.00 hours. A leaflet in English, giving details of services, is available from CFTM, 8 rue d'Algérie, 69001 Lyon. (An alternative – for cycling nuts: if you've got your bikes with you why not let the train take the strain from Tournon to Lamastre – and then return, freewheeling all the way, back to the Rhône? Bikes go free.)

There are limited services in April, May, September and October. In June and September trains run every day except Monday. During July and August there's a service every day, with additional trains at weekends and on public holidays. The single steamer train leaves Tournon at 10.00 a.m., returning from Lamastre at 16.00 hours. The journey lasts two hours.

Chemin de Fer Touristique Chinon-Richelieu (5). A 20 km run on standard gauge track during summer weekends. A steam and autorail line surrounded by historical countryside.

Chemin de Fer Touristique des Alpilles (6). From the SNCF station at **Arles**, this short steam run of nine km takes you to Fontvieille. Summer Sundays only.

Chemin de Fer Touristique de la Vallée du Rabadeau (7). From Senones to Etival, the latter on the line from Nancy to **St-Dié** (on the western flanks of the Vosges). A 10 km steam line open every weekend in summer; alternate weekends in April, May and September.

Chemin de Fer Touristique du Bréda (8). A standard gauge run from Pontcharra, in the Isère Valley (south-east of **Chambéry**), through the Gorges du Bréda, to La Rochette. Steam trains run from June to September; enquire locally for days and times. This line runs through mountain terrain.

Chemin de Fer Touristique des Landes de Gascogne (9). Steam trains run on Sundays and public holidays from Easter to Oct from **Sabres** to Marquèze (north-west of Mont-de-Marsan), where there is an ecological museum.

Musée des Transports de Pithiviers (10). A museum, full of old rolling stock and a short 60 cm gauge line; the latter is open on Sundays from May to Oct (north-east of Orléans).

Tramway Touristique de St-Trojan (11). On the **Ile d'Oléron**, at the western end of the bridge which connects with the mainland (south of La Rochelle). A six km, 60 cm gauge line, runs from Easter to September every day.

TGV

TGV is "Train à Grand Vitesse" or high speed train. Some readers will recall I first wrote about the then new TGV system in 1981, prior to the opening of the TGV Sud-Est line. Now, over ten years later, I'm bringing you up-to-date on TGV developments. Nothing demonstrates more dramatically how third-rate Britain's transport infrastructure has become. Railways, autoroutes, bypasses: we've been left behind.

First, some background. French railways (SNCF) has made tremendous progress during the last 20 years in the use of electric locomotives and gas turbine turbotrains on both major and minor lines. Much the most startling development was the introduction, at the end of 1981, of new "bullet" trains with traction from self-commutating synchronous motors (today each TGV trainset has a continuous power rating of 8,800 kW).

The TGV trains can use existing tracks but they run best on specially-built lines. What a best it is: at speeds of up to 270 kilometres per hour on the **Paris-Lyon** (TGV Sud-Est) service; and up to 300 k.p.h. on the TGV Atlantique run. The quickest running time from Paris to Lyon is two hours.

The special track is the key. Because of shock waves as two

trains pass each other, the twin tracks are some five metres apart. Sharp curves are completely avoided; the tightest curve has a radius of four kilometres. Gradients are no problem: a 1 in 28 climb reduces running speeds to 200 k.p.h. Whether you use the service or not it really is an eye-opening sensation to stand on a bridge over the line and watch a TGV flash under you. The Michelin Atlas identifies all TGV lines.

(Richard Hardy, an old friend, worked for British Rail for 42 years. I've reprinted on the next two pages the fascinating piece he wrote for *Favourites*.)

Now for the reality. First, let me provide basic details of the existing TGV network. Later, I'll describe the future.

The TGV Sud-Est started life in September 1981. Services use the Gare de Lyon in Paris and connect with Lyon main-line stations. New stations were built at **Le Creusot** (Montchanin) and **Mâcon**. But TGV trains continue beyond Lyon to several towns, including Nice (6h 58m); and from Dijon (using a branch to Montbard) to Lausanne (3h 41m).

The TGV Atlantique service commenced operations three years ago. At the moment the special tracks only connect Paris (Montparnasse) with **Le Mans** and **Tours** (there's a new station outside **Vendôme**). The two towns are less than an hour from Paris; Brest is just under four hours away and Bordeaux a couple of minutes less than three hours.

What of the near future? Obviously the line which interests us most is the TGV Nord service. Use the A1 autoroute and you can see the construction work being finalised: from Paris (Gare du Nord) to **Lille** (a new station) and on to **Calais** (the station will be at Frethun). Another new station, **Gare Picarde**, will be opened near junction 13 on the A1. TGV Nord will be ready in 1993 – to link up with the opening of the Channel Tunnel. Paris to London will be a three hour trip.

Other new tracks are being constructed. The most interesting by far is the line to the east of Paris, in effect a "bypass" of the capital, linking the TGV Nord and TGV Sud-Est tracks. There will be new stations at **Roissy**/Charles-de-Gaulle Airport and **Marne-la-Vallée**/Euro Disney; this first part of "L'Interconnexion" will be ready by June 1994. Roissy to Lyon 2h; Roissy to London 3h. QED London to Lyon 5h.

The second part of "L'Interconnexion" – an east-west route, running through the suburbs south of Paris and connecting both the TGV Nord and TGV Sud-Est with TGV Atlantique – will be ready by the spring of 1995. Tours and Le Mans will be about 1½ hours from Roissy and 4½ hours from London.

Another ambitious "bypass" enterprise is also underway – a loop to the east of Lyon and extending all the way down to **Valence** (with a new station at Satolas airport, to the east of Lyon). When this new branch opens in 1994, **Marseille** will be about four hours from Roissy. Eventually special tracks are planned to link Valence with **Avignon**, Marseille and **Cannes**. But the controversial plans have caused uproar. Everyone in Provence is up in arms. A French minister suggested the proposals should have been kept quiet – adding: "If you want to drain the swamp, you don't tell the frogs."

For the start of the new millennium other ambitious plans should have become reality: an extension to Bruxelles and further links to Amsterdam and Cologne; a new TGV Est line to Strasbourg and beyond to Stuttgart; and a line from Calais to **Amiens** and then connecting with the TGV Nord track. Will we have our own high-speed line across Kent by year 2000?

TGV

Vaporiste et Technicien   **Richard Hardy**

It is a warm summer evening in 1961 at **Aulnoye** in Northern France. Steam traction has nearly done on this section but tonight, André, René and I are going to draw wonderful work from our old locomotive, the S2, which has but a month to go before she is laid aside for ever. André, the *mécanicien*, is five foot tall, a little gold-toothed, pink-faced ball of fire of 48 who knew all about the Railway Resistance in the War, a marvellous driver, artistic in his use of the brake; René is one of the best of firemen, tall, strong, quiet and immensely experienced. *L'Equipe* Duteil/de Jongh come from the historic depot of La Chapelle, under the shadow of Montmartre.

I know the road so André motions me to take charge of the locomotive. It is hot in the cab but when we are moving the wind will freshen us up although the fire will become blindingly white, requiring constant attention over the enormous grate; our faces will soon be black with coal dust and certainly the bucket of water containing bottles of *citron* will be needed for we shall have to work very hard tonight.

We are away with a huge, packed train of 780 tonnes and the S2 soon gets into her stride. One does not need to press her with that load, but nevertheless, because we are late and time must be regained, we are going to reach our maximum permitted speed of 120 k.p.h. quickly and then hold it, uphill and downdale. This will need constant and careful adjustment of the controls and speed of firing, an intimate knowledge of the route, gradients and position of the signals, for in the lefthand corner of the cab, under my only lookout window, lies the speed recorder which tells me everything I want to know but also charts our speed: *L'Espion* – the spy!

And now the light has gone, a wall of blackness lies ahead of the long boiler for no headlights probe the darkness: stations flash by, one's head outside in the wind to pick up, as soon as they appear, the green signals that beckon us on, our old engine tearing into it, René in his element, for we are living parts of our machine which depends on the skill and courage of its crew. We are in a world of our own, cut off from authority, from our passengers, from every living soul except those in distant places who control the signals.

We stop only once, at **St-Quentin**, running up the long platform as fast as possible to save a few seconds, for every little counts. On again into the night, Tergnier, Noyon, Compiègne and then, as we approach the great junction near Creil, first yellow, then red lights bar the way but the road clears as we pass slowly through the station. We have lost some of the time we regained from Aulnoye, so now the S2 is opened out to shoulder her load, thundering up the long rise, spitting sparks of defiance high into the sky. On through Chantilly, over the viaducts, she gradually accelerates to 100 k.p.h. before we reach the summit near Survilliers, passing under "le pont de soupirs", momentarily illuminated by the open fire door. And now our work is done and we can spin silently, but ever vigilantly, down to **Paris**.

As we climbed through Chantilly, André had served a good Bordeaux, bought specially for the occasion. Having uncorked, tasted and approved the wine, very much at room temperature, we drank to the great days of steam and to our own good fortune. At length, we drew quietly to a stand in the Gare du Nord. We have covered 134 miles in 132 minutes and, as we looked down on the passing throng, we knew we had reached the end of a momentous railway era.

And what lay ahead? 21 years later, we are in the Gare de Lyon with Roger, our *conducteur*, a man who knew not steam traction but who is dedicated to the TGV with which he will travel at up to 270 k.p.h. Whereas André stood at his work, in overalls, cap and scarf, Roger sits comfortably at his controls, brake to his left hand, power regulator in the centre, vigilance devices to the right. He wears a blue smock over smart but casual clothes. Whereas André and René looked outside their cab to sight signals in fog, wind or rain, Roger works in an air-conditioned silence, his vision unencumbered, each signal repeated on the panel in front of him, with an automatic power device to ensure speed limits are not exceeded. He can telephone the *poste de commandement* in Paris to report an incident at a speed of 270 k.p.h. and the *poste* can contact him at will. How utterly different this new world is: clinical, regulated, incredible, exciting – and fast! André was a *vaporiste* – Roger is very much a *technicien*.

By the end of 1981, a TGV line had been cut across France, a country where the railways are regarded as a national asset and treated accordingly. Through the south-eastern suburbs of Paris our speed was limited to a mere 160 k.p.h. Then we were clear of restrictions and on the new TGV line. Roger had started quietly, almost imperceptibly until the motion had become discernible, so different from the sonorous exhaust, the rotating parts and the hiss of steam. But once on the new line, he wound on the power, notch by notch, and one experienced the fantastic surge as speed mounted rapidly to 270 k.p.h., to be held effortlessly uphill and downdale. Gone was the anticipation needed to face an adverse gradient for the power is always there for the asking, drawn from overhead wires at 25,000 volts, enabling us to climb gradients of 1 in 28 at about 200 k.p.h. – banks which would have reduced the S2 to a crawl. For this railway has been built as no other in the world – straight, long banked curves, sweeping gradients and but two stations between the Gare de Lyon in Paris and **Lyon**.

The ride is perfect, conversation a simple matter, cab cool and clear, no draughts, no vibration, almost tame until one looks down or one passes another TGV at a combined speed of 540 k.p.h. But never for a moment does Roger's concentration waver: he may sit relaxed, calm, hand on the controller but, every 50 seconds, he must make a movement of some sort to defeat the ever watchful vigilance devices which, along with the "deadman's" control, have the power to apply the brakes if he fails, momentarily, to acknowledge their existence.

Le Creusot, Mâcon, the only stations on the line, the latter passed at a full 270 and, at last, Lyon lies ahead. The air brake is applied inaudibly, almost invisibly, by two fingers of Roger's left hand and we come gently to a stand. We have come like a bat out of hell but you would never have believed it. We had covered 267 miles in two hours; a new world and, for the passengers, comfort, silence and freedom from the stress of high speed driving on the A6 autoroute.

Roger will step down on arrival, clean and smart, will hang his smock in the locker and drive home to lunch but, on that night in 1961, it took André half an hour to wash and change before going home by train, tired and hungry. But he loved his work and he was proud to be known as a *gueule noire*.

(Richard has written two autobiographical books: *Steam in the Blood* and *Railways in the Blood* – publisher Ian Allan.)

WINE DEGUSTATIONS

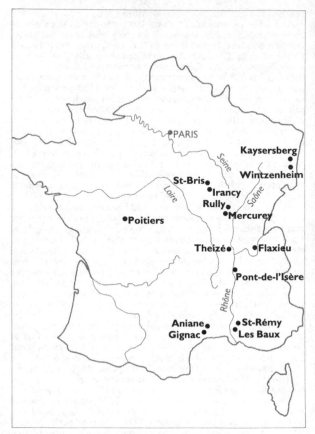

Over the years I have had more than a few *dégustations* on my travels across France. None of the tastings has ever been conducted too seriously; nor have any been long drawn-out affairs. I've always been driving, and, in addition, there's never been enough time to dally. Excuses, excuses!

I'm not going to devote any space to the classics of Burgundy or Bordeaux. Real experts do enough of that, writing prodigious numbers of words about them. Some scribes dream up the most amazing gobbledegook to describe wines. Finding enough different adjectives to describe topography, food or wine is always difficult. But what vivid psychedelic minds some wine writers have: where do they find the words?

I am going to describe just a handful of the lesser-known, good-value regional wines which I've enjoyed over the years – allowing myself, at the end, to name a trio of the more famous wine makers; famous to me but perhaps not known well enough by some readers. In more or less every case a local chef has introduced me to the wine makers. Do the same: if you enjoy a local wine, ask the chef to make an introduction.

First, Beaujolais. We all know the fruity Gamay guzzler;

occasionally awful, sometimes surprisingly drinkable. In the far south of the area, away from the renowned *appellations* of the big boys, is the village of **Theizé** – the home of Antoine Pein. Some say Beaujolais became a fancy name in the early 70s; well, New Yorkers got to know of Antoine Pein's handiwork as long ago as 1964 when Surmain (Mougins, Côte d'Azur) introduced his wines to Lutèce customers. Pein makes reds of course; but also try a *blanc moelleux* (sweet) and a sparkling white made by the *méthode champenoise*.

Now north, to unknown Burgundy, to the largely-ignored villages of **St-Bris** and **Irancy**. Call on two proprietors in the latter: the down-to-earth, larger-than-life Colinot family – their basement *cave* is opposite the town hall; and the modern premises of Bernard Cantin, in the shadow of the handsome village church. His little "bar" is a picture – literally; a wall painting of the church, wood sculptures and some fossil finds add extra appeal to your *dégustation*. Try rosés and reds from Irancy and whites from St-Bris; all are good value.

Midway between Irancy and Theizé is **Mercurey**. Snap up some real quality bargains here. Call, first, on the one-man business of Michel Juillot. His reds are from the Clos des Barraults (the 78 red is a magical potion) and his Chante Fluté white is one of my favourite tipples. In nearby **Rully**, sniff out Jean François Delorme at his lair, the Domaine de la Renarde. Reds are perfumed delights – with no bitterness. Whites – an *Aligoté* and a *crémant* – are light and fruity.

Languedoc-Roussillon next. The celebrated Mas de Daumas Gassac is hardly unknown these days. Its humble *vin de pays* bottle label insults the contents. Both reds and whites are among the best of all French wines. The story of how and why this has come about is intriguing: visit the vineyard, between **Gignac** and **Aniane** and find out for yourself. The same goes for the up-and-coming young wine maker, Jullien Olivier, at the Mas Jullien, Jonquières, north-west of Gignac.

East to Provence. Is there a more pleasant, quaffable rosé than the Château d'Estoublon version? The property is just west of Maussane, itself south of **Les Baux**. I've introduced many a reader to the reds of the Domaine de Trévallon – on the D27 north of Les Baux; and to James Baring's Mas du Cellier, south of the D99 between **St-Rémy** and **Eygalières**.

The classification "Vins du Bugey" usually leaves even the most supercilious *sommelier* speechless: ask them to explain it. I guarantee immediate respect. Visit **Flaxieu** and the home of Camille Crussy. Savour sparklers, Chardonnay whites and both reds and rosés. Other suppliers are in nearby Vongnes: Le Caveau Bugiste and Eugene Monin et fils.

The VDQS Vins du Haut-Poitou are an example of how good "unknown" wines are. Visit the *viticulteur*, Robert Champalon, at Marigny-Brizay, north of **Poitiers** and west of the A10. Wines are identified by grape types: Sauvignon, Pinot-Chardonnay and Chenin whites and a Gamay red.

Of the more illustrious wine-makers I've met three, and their wares, have made a big impact. The Hermitage vineyards of Chave have been in the family's hands for 500 years; his *cave* is at Mauves, across the Rhône from **Pont-de-l'Isère**. Colette Faller is at **Kaysersberg**; her *vendanges tardives* vintages must be made in heaven. A gentle giant, English-speaking Olivier Humbrecht, weaves his spell at the Domaine Zind-Humbrecht in **Wintzenheim**; many consider his Alsace Grand Cru wines the finest in the region.

CIRQUES

One definition of *cirque* is "circus"; but that's not the meaning when applied to this subject title. Another use of the word means an "amphitheatre" of hills or mountains.

France is richly endowed with *cirques*; inspiring sights they are too, from small-scale versions to giant examples which fill the sky with rock faces climbing high above you. Some can only be seen from the valley below – unless, that is, you are a skilled rock climber. Others can be viewed from both the valley floor and from the tops of the high cliffs lining their steep sides. I'll start in the Jura.

Though the Jura versions are not the most spectacular of France's *cirques*, they are, nevertheless, my favourites. Start your exploration with a bang – at the startling viewpoint, the Roche du Prêtre, 35 miles east of Besançon and close to the junction of the D461 and D41. To your right is the dramatic **Cirque de Consolation**; far below, nestling under a pin cushion of tree tops, is the 17th-century abbey of Notre Dame de Consolation. If luck is with you, you may spot a *milan royal* (kite) gliding in the swirling thermals of the *cirque*. Don't linger. Retrace your steps on the D461 and use the D39 to descend to the delectable abbey park and River Dessoubre.

Now head south-west to the **Cirque de Baume**. View it first from the belvedere at the southern end, high above the natural amphitheatre. Then descend and drive to the head of the valley, where there's a pretty waterfall gushing out of the rock face and tumbling over mossy rocks. This is a resurgent stream (*reculée*), one of many in the Jura – where water disappears underground miles away, high above a *cirque*, to reappear in caves or falls at the bottom of the rock faces.

The most famous is the **Cirque du Fer à Cheval** (east of Arbois). Visit the Grande Source de la Cuisance at the Grottes des Planches, where subterranean pathways share space with the turbulent stream. (Other resurgent streams are the Source du Lison, west of **Pontarlier**, where two caves feed the river; and the Source de la Loue, north of the town: both are thundering roars of water.)

The Alps have their own versions of *cirques*. In Savoie is another **Cirque du Fer à Cheval**, east of Samoëns. This is quite different from its Jura namesake. Surrounded by high mountains, I retain a vivid impression in my memory of the day I first saw the *cirque* – late in the spring when literally dozens of cascades were shooting forth melted snows from alpine glaciers and snowfields. In the Vercors, south-west of **Grenoble**, is the **Cirque d'Archiane**. Here a stunning sight confronts you: a vast semicircle stone wall rears high above the valley. Chuckle, too, on the D224, at the immaculate small box hedges beside the road: who, out here, keeps them so trim?

Perhaps the strangest of French *cirques* is the hardest one to pin down on a map, and consequently the most difficult to seek out: the **Cirque de Navacelles**, south-east of **Millau**. From the cliff tops on either side of the *cirque* the views below are thrilling: around you is the "amphitheatre" – a giant circle of stone scooped out over the centuries by the River Vis; and, at the bottom, water provides a refreshing cascade into an emerald pool at the base of the fall. Not too far away, west of Clermont-l'Hérault, is the **Cirque de Mourèze**; here a vast number of weird rocks litter the ground.

For me the Jura *cirques* are the most pleasing on the eye; they're not so savage and their edges are lined by the refreshing green duvets of the Jura forests. Hundreds of kilometres away, at the heart of the lofty Pyrénées, are two totally different *cirques*, one the most famous in France.

You have to drive many, many miles out of your way to reach the **Cirque de Gavarnie**, south of Lourdes. Vertical rock faces – rising in several stages, and each one as much as 500 metres high – surround you on three sides. The highest point of the gigantic, all-enveloping circle of mountains is 11,000 feet above sea-level; in reality the "wall" towers 6,500 ft over you. The floor of the valley is a mass of rocks, like the remains of a battlefield. In spring, when the melting snows pour forth their watery torrents, a dozen or more cascades are at their best. Nature provides many fabulous sights on the face of the earth and this is surely one of them. From the car park you can reach the foot of the *cirque* easily – courtesy of donkeys. One problem though: the owners charge rip-off prices. The alternative is to walk: allow two hours each way.

Just a few kilometres away, to the east, is a second formidable mountain wall, the **Cirque de Troumouse**. The access toll road is narrow, winding and difficult, climbing to a height of over 7,000 ft above sea-level.

GORGES: FAMOUS ONES

Among European countries, France stands alone in its vast variety of spectacular canyons, gorges and river valleys. They are spread throughout the mountainous regions of the country: some are world famous and these are the gorges I've listed in this chapter. Among the lesser-known ones are several which are well worth bringing to your attention: seek them out as they'll not fail to please – see the next chapter.

The most breathtaking and impressive of the famous gorges is the **Grand Canyon du Verdon** – a small-scale Grand Canyon of Colorado. Small-scale or not, in Europe the gorge has no rival: 20 km long and a deep scar in the limestone plateau, at places the valley floor is nearly 700 metres below the viewpoints lining the cliff-top edges.

Starting at the western end near Moustiers-Ste-Marie, I suggest the road circuit of the Grand Canyon is made in a **clockwise** direction – because then the gorge is always on your right-hand side and this makes it easier to park your car at the viewpoints and your passengers get better views. The gorge is heavily wooded with deciduous trees; in late autumn the steep flanks are a luminous, spellbinding sight.

When you reach La Palud be certain to use the 23 km "Route des Crêtes"; this circuit brings you practically back to the village. Soon after, immediately beyond the Point Sublime, turn right down the short dead-end road to the Couloir Samson. At the Pont de Soleils head south, via Trigance, to join the Corniche Sublime: a series of exciting viewpoints follow – at the Balcons de la Mescla, the Pont de l'Artuby, the Pilon de Fayet, Les Baouchets (walk the latter two sections on foot) and the Col d'Illoire. At many points on the circuit the Verdon River is nearly 2,000 ft below you: you require little imagination to visualise the astonishing view. Serious walkers are well catered for – but I cannot stress enough that the paths are only for those of you who are well equipped and who understand the risks entailed. Take care!

Elsewhere I have written about some of the man-made sites in the area: Aups, Comps, Cotignac, Fox-Amphoux, Barjols, Tourtour and Villecroze – villages ignored by most tourists.

Due west from the Verdon, on the other side of the Rhône, is the **Vallée de l'Ardèche** – from Vallon-Pont-d'Arc, south-east, to Pont-St-Esprit, where the River Ardèche joins the Rhône. On the northern side of the gorge, high above the river, is a new, thrilling road, one of the most rewarding drives in France. The river is much the best in early spring, when the rushing waters, unharnessed, are in flood. Elsewhere I have described some of the numerous underground caves near the river edges (see Ardèche); visit one or more but be sure, too, to spare time for the Pont-d'Arc, a natural stone arch across the river, and the many viewpoints.

At the southern end of the Massif Central are the **Gorges du Tarn** (see Cévennes). They are equally enthralling whether viewed from the roads on the cliff edges or those alongside the Tarn. From Millau head upstream to Le Rozier; the drive starts to get interesting from this point on. At Les Vignes turn left and take your car up the snake-like hairpins to the cliffs above the river; at the top use the D46 and continue north to the Point Sublime. The vistas are superb: the better view is to the east. From Ste-Enimie drive south, climbing up the steep D986. After 11 km turn right and aim for the viewpoints at the Roc des Hourtous. Descend on the D43 to La Malène from where you can take a boat trip on the river.

The **Vercors** is a great favourite of mine (see Hautes-Alpes). Within the limestone mountain fortress are some astonishing natural sights. The spring and autumn colours of the trees are both equally pleasing, though spring is perhaps the best time to use the roads which pass through the various gorges. One is the amazing Grands Goulets where the tiny, but powerful, River Vernaison, punches through a rocky barrier at Les Barraques-en-Vercors. Somehow man has built a leech-like road alongside the torrential stream as it hurtles down the narrow ravine. Equally dramatic is the road that hugs the floor of the dark Gorges de la Bourne – west of Villard-de-Lans; steep cliffs, coming so close together that they nearly touch, overhang the claustrophobic, bumpy tarmac ribbon.

Finally, the **Gorges du Loup** – seen by more tourists than any of the others, simply because the Loup is within a few miles of the main towns on the Côte d'Azur. Drive the route starting from Vence and descending into Pont-du-Loup. Continue north up the valley and return south again, climbing up to Gourdon. Just before the village enjoy the impressive panorama of both mountains and river far below.

GORGES: LESSER-KNOWN ONES

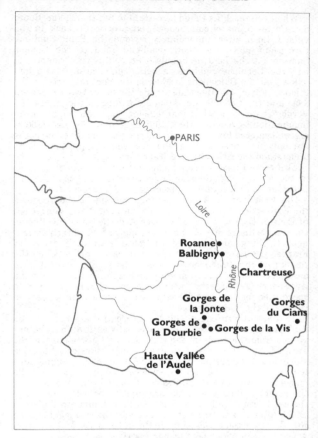

The following are among the less well-known gorges, found off-the-beaten-track. Few tourists will have seen them, for the simple reason that, assuming they knew of the gorges, I doubt whether they would have made the navigation effort required to seek them out. Don't make the same mistake.

The River Loire provides one example of what I mean. Every visitor to France will know of the wide, relatively dull river which flows (just!) through the middle of the legendary châteaux countryside. Further upstream, beyond Orléans, the river is still as boring, its main purpose being to provide the cooling waters for ghastly nuclear power stations. The real Loire only gets interesting south of Roanne.

Ten years ago, after researching *Hidden France*, I described the gorges between **Roanne** and **Balbigny** with these words: "You will get a pleasant surprise indeed." Today, I could use exactly the same sentence. The surprise would be a touch different though. The gorges have been flooded! One credit is that the long, winding lake is not unattractive; some of the character of the narrow river valley has been retained. The sight of a new marina and ugly bridge below Bully is a shock.

And the "new" lake view from St-Maurice will please most tourists but does the vista do the same for locals? They must curse the long detour to see their friends on the right bank. And the "island" château at La Roche comes as a real poke in the eye: once well above the river now the high walls are lapped by the lake's waters. Despite man's wretched handiwork Nature still comes out on top.

North of Grenoble is one of the best parts of France – the entrancing, secretive mountains of the **Chartreuse** Massif. Within its high walls the Chartreuse has many hidden charms missed by most tourists, hell-bent on their blinkered motorway speeding. Among the secrets are two gorges: the Gorges du Guiers Vif; and, further south, the Gorges du Guiers Mort.

Explore both of them. Start with the River Guiers Vif at its source, six km south-east of St-Pierre-d'Entremont. Drive its entire length until you reach Les Echelles. Then climb the Guiers Mort Valley up to St-Pierre-de-Chartreuse. Both are narrow, boulder-strewn and surrounded by cool, dark woods and verdant countryside. They are at much their best in early spring when the new greens add brightness and light to the pure water of the crashing torrents – in full flood during April and May. In autumn the water flow is much reduced but the forests dazzle in a different, eye-catching way.

Far to the south, just before the Alps fall sharply into the Mediterranean, are the **Gorges du Cians**. Follow the Var Valley northwards from Nice, to a point 15 km before Entrevaux where the River Cians flows in from the right. Now drive north up the D28 for a truly memorable adventure, the Gorges du Cians. Steep cliffs on both sides, almost touching, overhang the narrow road; dark rocks add extra splendour to the river as it falls steeply down towards the Var. Though different from the famous Verdon, I find the Cians gorges a real extrovert show. The road is narrow: take great care.

Near neighbours of the Tarn, but rarely visited, are the **Gorges de la Jonte**, the **Gorges de la Dourbie** and the **Gorges de la Vis**. Follow the Jonte downstream – a direction I much prefer as I believe you see more of the many pink and yellow-tinted rock faces and, towards the end of the valley, the strange twists and turns of the Causse Méjean; you also finish with a view of Peyreleau. Much of the Dourbie runs through the huge forests of the Cévennes: see the weir at St-Jean-du-Bruel, the covered 14th-century market at Nant and isolated Cantobre, sitting contentedly on a saucer of sturdy rock. Much of the Vis runs through dry terrain; you'll have the roads to yourself. Don't miss the Cirque de Navacelles.

Further south is a river valley which has given readers as much pleasure as any in France. The **Haute Vallée de l'Aude**, from its source near Mont-Louis, downstream to Quillan, is full of scenic attractions – especially the section from Puyvalador to Axat: high mountains, some glorious forests and splendid gorges all unite to put on an impressive show. I once spent an idyllic April day soaking up the pleasures of the enchanting valley. The clear, blue sky helped of course. But what pleased most was the way that colours and sounds combined to excite the senses. Even today, a decade later, I still have a clear picture in my head – with sound! There were the numerous new tints on the trees; the thundering rush of the Aude, in flood as the snows melted and fed the hungry torrent with clear, pure water; huge splashes of snow on the mountain tops; and a turquoise sky.

GROTTOES & CAVES

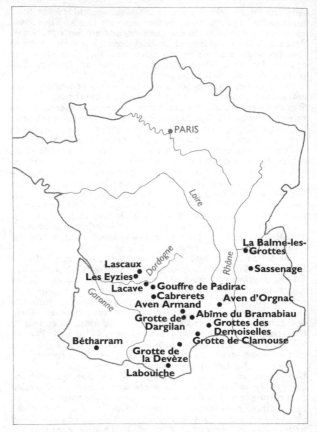

France has so many "surface" attractions that I imagine one would have to be satisfied to see just part of the total in a normal lifetime. "Underground" attractions abound too: France has more than its fair share of caves, caverns and grottoes all of which are in the southern half of the country.

They fall into three types: the caves of prehistoric men, some decorated by our forefathers; the massive underground caverns, some as large as modern-day symphony halls and studded with bizarre stalagmites and stalactites; and, finally, the grottoes which, whilst not calling for the skills of pot-holers, will, nevertheless, require a fair bit of effort if they are to be explored by the average visitor.

The most legendary of the prehistoric caves in the Dordogne area is **Lascaux**. I regret bitterly that Anne and I, in those early years of the 60s, didn't visit Lascaux before the cave was closed to the public on April 30, 1963. Today, there's a truly fantastic facsimile called Lascaux II – just 300 metres away from the original cave (closed Mondays).

The magical paintings fill me with a massive feeling of mystery. What made the Magdalenian hunters enter the subterranean cave? What were the gigantic problems facing early man in the cruel, harsh world outside the sanctuary of the dark cavern? It must have been a world of unimaginable fear and an unbearably lonely one at that – surrounded by multitudes of animals including elephants and rhinoceros. Yet early man, seventeen thousand years ago, had the ingenuity to create those paintings, full of vitality and technical wizardry. What a treasure the four boys from Montignac opened up for the world on September 12, 1940; all because a small dog, Robot, fell through a hole in the ground. Just go!

Further down the Vézère Valley is **Les Eyzies**, the "University of Prehistory". The skull of Cro-Magnon man was found in the cave-riddled limestone walls above the village. In the neighbourhood are several important caves where you can view paintings and carvings from prehistoric times.

Further south, near **Cabrerets**, and just north of the Lot Valley, is the Grotte du Pech-Merle. This famous place, apart from wall paintings and carvings, has some outstanding natural stone formations; stalagmites and shapes like saucers, plates and wheels fill the caves with unusual interest.

Of the various caverns to be seen in the Dordogne area much the most exciting is the **Gouffre de Padirac**, where, hundreds of metres underground, you can travel for several kilometres on a punt on the dark subterranean waters. The *gouffre* is a staggering world of stalagmites, stalactites, lakes and rivers – all enhanced by modern lighting. But one caveat: at those depths you feel the cold – so take suitable clothing!

Back at Les Eyzies is the Grotte du Grand Roc – a much simpler affair, with no water or long underground descents but, nevertheless, still rewarding all visitors with a marvellous display of natural rock carvings.

Further east, near the Gorges du Tarn, are two exceptional grottes: **Aven Armand** is breathtaking – with every imaginable shape of stalagmite and stalactite, enhanced superbly by brilliant lighting; the **Grotte de Dargilan** (the pink cavern) is renowned for a huge "bell-shaped sculpture".

Further east still, to the south of the River Ardèche, is the **Aven d'Orgnac** (*aven* has the same meaning as the Celtic *avon* – a river arising from a natural spring); colossal stalagmites and mighty halls make this cave an impressive sight. To the south-west, completing a triangle with the three caves just described, are two in the Hérault Valley. The **Grotte des Demoiselles** is another of the great "dry" caverns: a funicular takes you to the entrance of a vast underground hall – over 50 metres high and housing one especially notable stalagmite, the Virgin and Child, for all the world like a man-made statue. Downstream is the **Grotte de Clamouse** with various curious shapes, some unusually coloured.

Of the grottoes where water plays a significant part in adding to their interest, those at **Bétharram** (just west of Lourdes in the Southwest) and at **La Balme-les-Grottes** (near the Rhône and east of Lyon) are particularly absorbing. A third, similar grotto, is the subterranean river at **Labouiche**, just north-west of Foix, in the eastern Pyrénées.

There are many other grottoes and caves – both "wet" and "dry". A few are listed below (and the nearest town). Among the "wet" caves are: **Abîme du Bramabiau** – east of Millau; and **Sassenage**, near Grenoble – an "erosion" cavern. Among the "dry" caves are: **Lacave**, just north of Rocamadour (Dordogne); and **Grotte de la Devèze**, west of Béziers.

ISLANDS

France suffers particularly badly when its islands are
compared with those lying off the coast of the United Kingdom.
Are there any islands to match the majestic versions adjacent
to the Western Highlands in Scotland?

One exception of course is **Corse** (Corsica). Elsewhere I've
listed the cheeses, regional specialities and wines of the island
– together with the briefest outline of its topographical assets.
The island has some of the wildest, most exciting terrain to be
found anywhere in Europe. Is there any mountain road in
Corsica without a bend every 100 yards?

Some parts of Corsica deserve special mention. The D18 and
D84 run from Corte to Porto, past Calacuccia and through the
vast forests of Valdo-Niello and Aitone. The dead-end drive up
the Vallée d'Asco (north-west of Corte). The deserted
mountainous district called La Castagniccia to the north-east
of Corte. The mountains to the south of L'Ile-Rousse. The Golfe
de Porto is another terrific favourite: from the Golfe de
Girolata to the north to the amazing natural sculptures on the
red granite coast called Les Calanches to the south. The road
which, like a bandage, encircles Cap Corse, Corsica's northern

"finger". The D31 which leave Bastia to the north and winds its way up to San-Martino-di-Lota. And much more.

After Corsica there remains just a handful of possible alternatives that are worth highlighting: two are off the coast of Brittany; four are situated in the Bay of Biscay between **Nantes** and **Royan**; and several tiny islands, compared with Corsica, bask in the Mediterranean.

In making the sea trip to the **Ile d'Ouessant** (Ushant) there is no more dramatic and effective way of grasping why this north-west corner of Brittany's coast is so dangerous. In the summer months the waters are at their quietest; in the worst of the winter, the sea is thundering, dangerous and cruel. The island is just seven kilometres long and the northern coastline is famous for its rocky shores. The island is part of the Armorique Regional Park; the sea birds that nest on the cliffs are the highlight for any naturalist making the trip.

To the south-east, much further down the Brittany coast, is **Belle-Ile**: there's no better place in France if you want real peace and quiet. A variety of differing scenes will intrigue you: rocky cliffs; quiet beaches; small valleys; fine trees; a sheltered east coast; and the island's most famous sight, the Apothicairerie Grotto. The name comes from the cormorants' nests that line the rocky cliffs; unusual, too, is the blue-green colour of the sea in the narrow inlet.

South of the Loire are two smallish islands. **Ile de Noirmoutier** is reached by a toll bridge; you'll enjoy sandy beaches, some woods and little else. **Fromentine** is at the point the bridge leaves the mainland; the port also serves as the departure point for a second island called **Ile d'Yeu**. The southern end of this island is renowned for rocky headlands called the Côte Sauvage (a common label along the coasts of France). There is much else to appreciate: small ports, sandy beaches and a general air of picturesque charm.

Further down the French coast are two more islands, both bigger than Belle-Ile. The southernmost of the two is **Ile d'Oléron**, France's second largest island. Both are famous for luminous light, sunsets, oysters and shrimps, sands and sea air. Oléron is my favourite, reached by a three kilometre long *pont-viaduc*. The **Ile de Ré**, to the west of **La Rochelle**, is now reached by a viaduct, opened in 1988. Smaller than Oléron, I find the island less interesting.

In the Mediterranean there are several individual islands, and groups of islands, worth seeking out.

The **Château d'If**, near **Marseille**, is famous for the legendary Count of Monte Cristo, from Dumas's classic story. The island and fortress have always made an effective prison.

The **Ile de Bendor**, off Bandol, is a minute affair, developed by Monsieur Ricard of *apéritif* fame: a Provençal village, museum and zoo make the islet an interesting port of call for all holiday-makers to Bandol and Sanary.

Further east are the **Iles d'Hyères**, also called the "golden isles". The Ile de Porquerolles, quickly and easily reached from the mainland, is the best one to visit; sandy beaches and fine views reward visitors. The heavily wooded Ile de Port-Cros, to the east, is unusual in being a national park.

The **Iles de Lérins** (the Ile Ste-Marguerite is the closer of the two to Cannes – the other is Ile St-Honorat) provide extensive views of the coast around Cannes. Both are well wooded with pines and provide plenty of shady walking. Ste-Marguerite has a fortress; St-Honorat a monastery.

LAKES

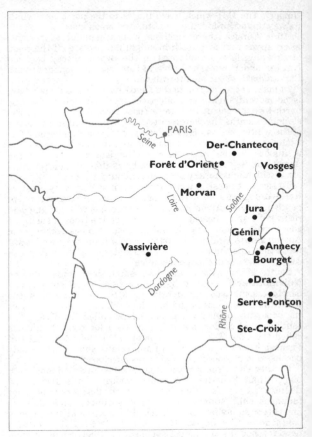

Lakes return many benefits to those who seek them out: scenic pleasures; fishing; boating – in various forms; swimming; and other water sports are just a few of the dividends. Whilst I don't think there's a lake in France that can emulate some of the priceless jewels we have in our islands, nevertheless, there's a pretty comprehensive range across the Channel in France: some man-made, others fashioned by Nature.

I'll start with my three favourites – the first being the smallest of small lakes. **Lac Genin** is an unspoilt emerald, protected by a circular couch of wooded cushions – beech, pines and spruce. A display board tells you about the local flora and fauna. During the week you're likely to have the lake to yourself; or you may have to share it with some goldcrests hovering around your head like humming birds. Where is the lake? East of Nantua, north of the A40 (see Jura).

The second natural lake is **Lac d'Annecy**. Drive right around the lake shore. The best views are from Duingt, on the west shore, and from the hill just above Talloires, as you descend into the world-renowned small resort. If you want a wider perspective then ascend the Semnoz mountain to the west or the Col de la Forclaz to the south-east. No train lines and a not-too-busy road make the eastern shore especially attractive. There's only one scenic eyesore: on the western side, just south of Duingt, there's a gargantuan mouthful gouged out of the mountainside – an absolutely hideous quarry.

My third favourite is a man-made lake – one of the best I know: **Lac de Vassivière**. I'll wager you'll not easily find any evidence of how man dammed the lake in the years after the last war. Much of the charm of the 2,500-acre sheet of water comes from the series of coves and inlets, from the forests that encircle the lake and from the sensible way the French have commercialised the amenities available – not always true elsewhere. The lake's southern arc is the most appealing.

For the sportsman or woman there's much to enjoy: several sandy beaches, riding, sailing, canoeing, pedalos, wind surfing and water skiing. For the less energetic there are gentle walks, motor boats, fishing and even water-bus trips in streamlined modern craft based on the western banks.

The **Lac du Der-Chantecoq**, near St-Dizier, is considered Europe's largest artificial lake – some 12,000 acres of water. You'll find woods, beaches, water sports and motorboat rides and a museum village at Ste-Marie-du-Lac-Nuisement.

A neighbour, to the south-west, is the 5,750-acre **Lac de la Forêt d'Orient**; there's sailing and bathing at Mesnil-St-Père and a wildfowl nature reserve in the north-east corner.

The **Vosges** has a fair selection of lakes. Gérardmer is the largest and the busiest; Longemer the most attractive; the nearby Retournemer the smallest; and Lac Blanc and Lac Noir the most tranquil – both on the eastern side of the range.

The **Jura** has a much bigger selection of lakes. Among the man-made varieties is the snake of Lac de Chaillexon, where the River Doubs has been dammed near Morteau; and the long winding Lac de Vouglans, where the River Ain is held back behind a barrage – west of St-Claude. But I prefer the natural Lac de St-Point, south of Pontarlier and close to the Swiss border. Roads run down either side and Malbuisson is a pleasant centre. To the south-west is a handful of small lakes in the Hérisson Valley – to both sides of Ilay. The other water "magnet" in the neighbourhood of Ilay is a succession of two dozen or more cascades; the River Hérisson falls over 250 metres in three kilometres. Read the Jura introduction.

There's **Lac du Bourget**, the other big lake in the French Alps. I'm not too struck by this one – though the roads that climb to the tops of mountains on both sides of the lake provide exceptional panoramas. South of Grenoble is the man-made lake in the **Drac** Valley; at the northern end is the inevitable dam. The eastern bank, tagged the Corniche du Drac, is worth following. Further south-east the first of the many dams built to harness the "white power" of the River Durance has created the **Lac de Serre-Ponçon**; some superb forests are nearby and new roads (use the D3) encircle the lake. Another man-made sheet, the **Lac de Ste-Croix**, is at the western end of the Grand Canyon du Verdon; view it from the D19.

Within the boundaries of the **Morvan** Regional Nature Park are several lakes, unknown to the vast majority who rush down the A6 and N6. The Lac de Pannesière-Chaumard, Lac des Settons (especially nice) and Lac de Chaumeçon have quiet roads around their banks and plenty of refreshing terrain to all sides. When these lakes are "full" they're nice enough; equally, I've seen them empty – depressing sights.

MOTOR MOUNTAINEERING

I like this title – taken from a book I read a year or two ago, published over 70 years earlier, about touring in Europe. The last two chapters of this section in *French Leave Encore* are subjects dear to my heart. You'll have grasped that fact long ago from reading the regional introductions. I could devote scores of pages to the two subjects. Here, I'll have to be content with just passing references to some of the best "motor mountaineering" that France can offer.

I'll start with the **Route des Grandes Alpes** – both the official version and my own. I got the bug for motoring, rallying and navigating over 35 years ago; Anne and I were heading for these high mountain roads as soon as we bought our first car – an Austin A30 which cost £30. Since then I must have driven almost every road in the French Alps.

I have savoured the spell of these mountains at all seasons and at all times of the day and night. The suggestions which follow are at their best in early autumn and are suitable for all of you. Do them from south to north; then the sun is always behind you. And, if you can, climb a high pass at night; the heavens seen at altitude is a thrill indeed.

The official "Route des Grandes Alpes" starts at **Nice** and tracks a south-north line of high cols. Follow the Var for every inch of its life, over the **Col de la Cayolle**, the Col de Vars and the **Col d'Izoard** to Briançon. Then over the Col du Lautaret and **Col du Galibier**, up the Arc Valley and across the **Col de l'Iseran**, descending to Bourg-St-Maurice. Next, the Cormet de Roselend, the Col des Saisies and through northern Savoie, past Morzine to Thonon and **Evian**.

All that's O.K. as far as it goes – but the Cayolle is not the best of the three alternatives north of the Var: the highest is the **Col de la Bonette**, 2802 metres high (9193 ft); the best for me, when combined with a detour to the Lac d'Allos, is the **Col d'Allos**. At Briançon I would cross into Italy and make the descent of the **Col du Mont Cenis**; a much better alternative than the Galibier. And, at Bourg, I would head back into Italy, over the **Col du Petit St-Bernard**, then decide whether to pass through the Mont Blanc tunnel or take the "old" road across the Col du Grand St-Bernard. Either way I would finish at the **Barrage d'Emosson**. For details of the latter, and other dead-ends, see the next page.

The trouble is, once you've seen one of those ultra-high, treeless tracts called "cols" (passes) you've seen them all. What I would do is to head north from Grasse, rather then Nice. Over the Col de Bleine, east past Le Mas and through Sigale to Puget-Théniers in the Var Valley. Up the superb Gorges du Cians and back to Annot. After the Allos, and the lake detour, I'd aim for Savines-le-Lac, and Serres.

This would then allow one to head north on the N75. At Clelles I'd double back over the Col de Menée, cross the Col de Pennes and then, via the Col de Rousset, enter the **Vercors**. (Read the Hautes-Alpes introduction.) On through the **Chartreuse** and **Les Bauges**, the climb and descent of the Semnoz, past Thônes, over the Col des Aravis, the Col des Saises and the Cormet de Roselend to Bourg. Into Italy, through the Mont Blanc tunnel and finish at Emosson. (Read the Savoie introduction and next chapter for further details.)

I realise you'll have to do a lot of map work to follow all the alternatives listed above – but it's worth the effort.

I've never had the same enthusiasm for the Pyrénées as I have for the Alps. But, more and more, as I've seen every pass, detoured up every dead-end – both valleys and mountain tops – I've come to appreciate these southern peaks more and more. My **Route des Pyrénées** is a rewarding drive.

Start in the Tech Valley, at **Céret**. Take the D618 north. Then up the N116 to Mont-Louis. Avoid the obvious route to Ax-les-Thermes. Instead, follow the Aude downstream to **Axat**, the Rebenty Valley and Gorges du Rebenty, past Montaillou, and the Route des Corniches (D2), above the River Ariège, to Tarascon. Over the **Col de Port** and the Col de Portet d'Aspet, then south to Bagnères-de-Luchon (Luchon).

I described much of what follows in the "Tour de France" section in the Southwest introduction; please read it. Over the Col de Peyresourde, **Col d'Aspin** (the best of the Pyrénées passes), **Col du Tourmalet** (detour to the Pic du Midi de Bigorre) and descend to Argelès-Gazost. Next, follow the **Col d'Aubisque**, down to Laruns, north on the D934 to Bielle, and west over the Col de Marie-Blanque. Through Arette, south on the D132 and, just before the Spanish border, right on the new road (D113), past Ste-Engrâce, over the **Col Bagargui** and finishing at **St-Jean-Pied-de-Port**.

ROADS THAT GO NOWHERE

From the very first day I embarked on my do-it-yourself publishing venture I realised my work would have to be exceptionally subjective – to allow my personal interests, emotions and prejudices, fallible as they undoubtedly are, to dominate my writing. Nine books and 2,016 pages later, I remain as conscious of that objective as ever.

To survive against the publishing giant of Michelin (and others) I knew I would have to accept the breadcrumbs left on the table or, putting my point another way, I would have to be content with filling in the mortar between the Bibendum bricks. Twelve years on, I admire the tyre man's products more than ever; I also realise, more than ever, that I must continue to be idiosyncratic – to the point of eccentricity.

I have always tried to ensure that every page I've written has transmitted my enthusiasm, whatever the subject, to my readers. If I feel unenthusiastic or bored stiff, or begrudge money spent, then the same feelings will be shared by you! I *can* be as acerbic and jaundiced as anyone. The trouble is cynicism fills up too much valuable space; better to ignore, or bypass, places where time or money has been wasted.

So, here we are at the very end of *Encore*, with a subject that fits the idiosyncratic label to a tee. Dyed-in-the-wool readers, doing a "Binns", will already know that the best parts of any country are always found at the end of roads that go nowhere. France is full of them; here's a *dégustation*.

I'm going to remain odd-ball to the end. The finest view of French mountains is not to be found within France but from a spot across the frontier, in Switzerland. Head north from **Chamonix**, cross the frontier and, almost immediately, turn left for Finhaut, driving higher and higher until you arrive at the massive **Barrage d'Emosson**, literally a metre or two on the Swiss side of the border. The top of the dam, which you'll stand on, is not far short of 7000 ft above sea-level. Your reward is a spellbinding panorama of the entire Chaîne du Mont Blanc. In addition you may be lucky enough to see all the mightiest peaks of the Bernese Oberland and, within 200 metres of descending from the dam, the distant Matterhorn; revel in the dazzling array of mountains.

Drive 100 miles due south, to the Parc Régional du Queyras. Three dead-ends await you here. The first climbs south from the brooding and formidable fort at **Château Queyras** to the Sommet-Bucher, 7400 ft high; the panorama is extensive with the Massif des Ecrins to the west and Mont Viso to the east. The second must is the climb to **St-Véran**, at 6700 ft the highest *commune* in Europe; time stands still here and, unlike so many other spots in the Alps, the village remains unspoilt (don't continue to the very end of the road – to what were, once, a marble quarry and copper mine). The third is the climb up the Guil Valley – as far as you can go, to the spot where a collapsed bridge has been left unrepaired. It's a short walk to the Petit Belvédère (allow 30 minutes there and back); a much longer hike to the Belvédère du Cirque (allow four hours for the return trip). Superb is the word for the terrain and views (Mont Viso, 12601 ft high, dominates the skyline).

This is the way Hannibal and his army passed 2,000 years ago. I've always accepted Sir Gavin de Beer's research on the likely route as the most plausible – though I know that Bernard Levin, in following the general's footsteps, crossed into Italy at Le Pain de Sucre, a few miles to the south (where there's a modern-day "road" across the frontier).

Now head south-east to the Parc National du Mercantour. From **Nice** aim north, up the Var and Vésubie valleys to **St-Martin-Vésubie**; then north again to Le Boréon and right, as far as you can go. This is a walker's paradise; set off up the valley and who knows – you may be lucky enough to spot some chamois, marmots or even, at higher altitude, the *lièvre variable* (brown coat in summer, white in winter).

When you return south, just before the confluence of the Vésubie and Var, turn right and ascend the winding road to **Madone d'Utelle**; the road climbs over 3,000 ft from St-Jean in just 15 kilometres. First you pass through cool, green woods; then, at the summit, the hillside covering is dry scrub. At the summit there's an observation platform under a strange umbrella-like roof. Will you be lucky and see Corsica?

The Pyrénées, too, has many versions. **Gavarnie** is, of course, supreme; so is the toll road to the three-star **Pic du Midi de Bigorre** panorama (both south of Lourdes); and, an unknown "Road that goes Nowhere" *par excellence*, the exhilarating remote **Col de Pause**, south of **St-Girons**. I need another book to do justice to the myriad French "dead-ends".

Glossary of Menu Terms

A point medium rare

Abatis (Abattis) poultry giblets

Abats offal

Ablette freshwater fish

Abricot apricot

Acajou cashew nut

Acarne sea-bream

Achatine snail (from Far East)

Ache celery

Acidulé(e) acid

Affiné(e) improve; ripen, mature (common term with cheeses)

Africaine (à l') African style: with aubergines, tomatoes, *cèpes*

Agneau lamb

Agneau de pré-salé lamb fed on salt marshes

Agnelet young lamb

Agnès Sorel thin strips of mushroom, chicken and tongue

Agrumes citrus fruits

Aïado lamb with herbs and garlic

Aiglefin haddock

Aigre-doux sweet-sour

Aigrelette sharp sauce

Aiguillette thin slice

Ail garlic

Aile (Aileron) wing (winglet)

Aillade garlic sauce

Aïoli mayonnaise, garlic, olive oil

Airelles cranberries

Albert white cream sauce, mustard, vinegar

Albuféra *béchamel* sauce, sweet peppers

Alénois watercress-flavoured

Algues seaweed

Aligot purée of potatoes, cream, garlic, butter and fresh Tomme de Cantal (or Laguiole) cheese

Allemande a *velouté* sauce with egg yolks

Allemande (à l') German style: with sauerkraut and sausages

Allumette puff pastry strip

Alose shad (river fish)

Alouette lark

Alouette de mer sandpiper

Aloyau sirloin of beef

Alsacienne (à l') Alsace style: with sauerkraut, sausage and sometimes *foie gras*

Amande almond

Amande de mer small clam-like shellfish with nutty flavour

Amandine almond-flavoured

Amer bitter

Américaine (à l') Armoricaine (à l') sauce with dry white wine, cognac, tomatoes, shallots

Amourettes ox or calf marrow

Amuse-bouche appetiser

Amuse-geule appetiser

Amusette appetiser

Ananas pineapple

Anchoïade anchovy crust

Anchois anchovy

Ancienne (à l') in the old style

Andalouse (à l') Andalusian style: tomatoes, sweet red peppers, rice

Andouille smoked tripe sausage

Andouillette small chitterling (tripe) sausage

Aneth dill

Ange angel

Ange à cheval oyster, wrapped in bacon and grilled

Angevine (à l') Anjou style: with dry white wine, cream, mushrooms, onions

Anglaise (à l') plain boiled

Anguille eel

Anis aniseed

Anis étoile star anise (a star-shaped fruit)

Ansé basted with liquid

Arachide peanut

Araignée de mer spider crab

Arc en ciel rainbow trout

Ardennaise (à l') Ardenne style: with juniper berries

Arête fish bone

Argenteuil asparagus flavoured (usually soup)

Arlésienne stuffed tomatoes *à la provençale,* eggplant, rice

Armoricaine see *Américaine*

Aromates aromatic; either spicy or fragrant

Arômes à la gêne Lyonnais cow's or goat's cheese soaked in *marc*

Artichaut artichoke

Asperges asparagus

Assaisonné flavoured or seasoned with; to dress a salad

Assiette (de) plate (of)

Aubergine aubergine, eggplant

Aulx (plural of *ail*) garlic

Aumônière pancake drawn up into shape of beggar's purse

Aurore (à l') pink sauce, tomato flavoured

Auvergnate (à l') Auvergne style: with cabbage, sausage and bacon

Aveline hazelnut

Avocat avocado pear

Avoine oat(s)

Azyme unleavened (bread)

Baba au rhum sponge dessert with rum syrup

Baguette long bread loaf
Baie berry
Baigné bathed or lying in
Ballotine boned and stuffed poultry or meat in a roll
Banane banana
Bar sea-bass
Barbarie Barbary duck
Barbeau barbel
Barbeau de mer red mullet
Barbue brill
Barigoule (à la) brown sauce with artichokes and mushrooms
Baron de lapereau baron of young rabbit
Barquette boat-shaped pastry
Basilic basil
Basquaise (à la) Basque style: Bayonne ham, rice and peppers
Bâtarde butter sauce, egg yolks
Bâtarde pain crusty white loaf
Batavia salad lettuce
Bâton stick-shaped bread loaf
Baudroie monkfish, anglerfish
Bavaroise bavarois mould, usually of custard, flavoured with fruit or chocolate. Can describe other dishes, particularly shellfish
Bavette skirt of beef
Baveuse runny
Béarnaise thick sauce with egg yolks, shallots, butter, white wine and tarragon vinegar
Béatilles (Malin de) sweetbreads, livers, kidneys, cockscombs
Beaugency *Béarnaise* sauce with artichokes, tomatoes, marrow
Bécasse woodcock
Bécassine snipe
Béchamel creamy white sauce
Beignet fritter
Beignet de fleur de courgette courgette flower in batter
Belle Hélène poached pear with ice cream and chocolate sauce
Belon oyster (see *Huîtres*)
Berawecka Christmas fruit bread stuffed with dried fruit, spices and laced with *kirsch*
Bercy sauce with white wine and shallots
Bergamot variety of pear or orange
Bergamote orange-flavoured sweet
Berlingot mint-flavoured sweet
Berrichone *Bordelaise* sauce
Bêtisse hard mint
Betterave beetroot
Beuchelle à la Tourangelle kidneys, sweetbreads, morels, cream and truffles

Beurre (Echiré) butter. (Finest butter from Poitou-Charentes)
Beurre blanc sauce with butter, shallots, wine vinegar and sometimes dry white wine
Beurre noir sauce with browned butter, vinegar, parsley
Biche female deer
Bière à la pression beer on tap
Bière en bouteille bottled beer
Bifteck steak
Bigarade (à la) orange sauce
Bigarreau type of cherry
Bigorneau winkle
Billy By mussel soup
Biscuit à la cuiller sponge finger
Bisque shellfish soup
Blanc (de volaille) white breast (of chicken): can describe white fish fillet or white vegetables
Blanchaille whitebait
Blanquette white stew
Blé corn or wheat
Blé noir buckwheat
Blettes Swiss chard
Blinis small, thick pancakes
Boeuf à la mode beef braised in red wine
Boeuf Stroganoff beef, sour cream, onions, mushrooms
Boletus type of edible fungi
Bombe ice cream
Bon-chrétien variety of pear
Bonne femme (à la) white wine sauce, shallots, mushrooms
Bonne femme (à la) potato, leek and carrot soup
Bordelais(e) (à la) Bordeaux style: brown sauce with shallots, red wine, beef bone marrow
Bouchée mouthful size (either a tart or *vol-au-vent*)
Boudin sausage-shaped mixture
Boudin blanc white coloured; pork and sometimes chicken
Boudin noir black pudding
Bouillabaisse Mediterranean fish stew and soup
Bouilliture eel stew (see *matelote d'anguilles*)
Bouillon broth, light consommé
Boulangère sauce of onions and potatoes
Boulette small ball of fish or meat
Bouquet prawn
Bouquet garni bunch of herbs used for flavouring
Bourdaloue hot poached fruit
Bourdelot whole apple pastry
Bourgeoise (à la) sauce of

carrots, onions and diced bacon

Bourguignonne (à la) Burgundy style: red wine, onions, bacon and mushrooms

Bouribot duck stewed in red wine

Bourrache borage, a herb used in drinks and salads

Bourride creamy fish soup with *aïoli*

Bourriole sweet or savoury pancake

Boutargue grey mullet roe paste

Braisé braised

Brandade de morue salt cod

Brassado (Brassadeau) doughnut

Bréjaude cabbage and bacon soup

Brème bream

Brési thin slices dried beef

Bretonne sauce with celery, leeks, beans and mushrooms

Brioche sweet yeast bread

Broche (à la) spit roasted

Brochet pike

Brochette (de) meat or fish on a skewer

Brouet broth

Brouillade stewed in oil

Brouillés scrambled

Broutard young goat

Brugnon nectarine

Brûlé(e) toasted

Brunoise diced vegetables

Bruxelloise sauce with asparagus, butter and eggs

Bucarde cockle

Buccin whelk

Bugne sweet pastry fritter

Cabillaud cod

Cabri kid (young goat)

Cacahouète roasted peanut

Cacao cocoa

Caen (à la mode de) cooked in Calvados and white wine

Café coffee

Cagouille snail

Caille quail

Caillé milk curds

Caillette pork and vegetable faggot

Cajasse sweet pastry (sometimes made with black cherries)

Cajou cashew nut

Calissons almond and crystallised fruit sweetmeats

Calmar inkfish, squid

Campagne country style

Canapé a base, usually bread

Canard duck

Canard à la presse (Rouennaise) duck breast cooked in blood of carcass, red wine and brandy

Canard au sang see above

Canard sauvage wild duck

Caneton (canette) duckling

Cannelle cinnamon

Capilotade small bits or pieces

Capoum scorpion fish

Caprice whim (a dessert)

Capucine nasturtium

Carbonnade braised beef in beer, onions and bacon

Cardinal *béchamel* sauce, lobster, cream, red peppers

Cardon cardoon, a large celery-like vegetable

Cari curry powder

Caroline chicken consommé

Carpe carp

Carré d'agneau lamb chops from best end of neck

Carré de porc pork cutlets from best end of neck

Carré de veau veal chops from best end of neck

Carrelet flounder, plaice

Carvi caraway

Casse-croûte snack

Cassis blackcurrant

Cassolette small pan

Cassonade soft brown sugar

Cassoulet casserole of beans, sausage and/or pork, goose, duck

Caviar d'aubergine aubergine (eggplant) purée

Cebiche raw fish marinated in lime or lemon juice

Cedrat confit a crystallised citrus fruit

Céleri celery

Céleri-rave celeriac

Cendres (sous les) cooked (buried) in hot ashes

Cèpe fine, delicate mushroom

Cerfeuil chervil

Cerise (noire) cherry (black)

Cerneau walnut

Cervelas pork garlic sausage

Cervelle brains

Cévenole (à la) garnished with mushrooms or chestnuts

Champignons (des bois) mushrooms (from the woods)

Chanterelle apricot-coloured mushroom

Chantilly whipped cream, sugar

Chapon capon

Chapon de mer *rascasse* or scorpion fish

Charbon de bois (au) grilled on charcoal

Charcuterie cold meat cuts

Charcutière sauce with onions, white wine, gherkins

Charlotte sponge fingers, cream, etc.
Charolais (Charollais) beef
Chartreuse a mould form
Chasse hunting (season)
Chasseur sauce with white wine, mushrooms, shallots
Châtaigne sweet chestnut
Chateaubriand thick fillet steak
Châtelaine garnish with artichoke hearts, tomatoes, potatoes
Chaud(e) hot
Chaudrée fish stew
Chausson pastry turnover
Chemise (en) pastry covering
Cheveux d'ange vermicelli
Chevreau kid (young goat)
Chevreuil roe-deer
Chevrier green haricot bean
Chichi doughnut-like fritter
Chicon chicory
Chicorée curly endive
Chiffonnade thinly-cut
Chinoise (à la) Chinese style: with bean sprouts and soy sauce
Chipirones see *calmars*
Choisy braised lettuce, sautéed potatoes
Choix (au) a choice of
Choron *Béarnaise* sauce with the addition of tomatoes
Chou (vert) cabbage
Choucroute (souring of vegetables) usually white cabbage (sauerkraut), peppercorns, boiled ham, potatoes and Strasbourg sausages
Chou-fleur cauliflower
Chou-frisé kale
Chou-pommé white-heart cabbage
Chou-rave kohlrabi
Chou-rouge red cabbage
Choux (au fromage) puffs (made of cheese)
Choux de Bruxelles Brussels sprouts
Choux (pâte à) pastry
Ciboule spring onion
Ciboulette chive
Cidre cider
Citron (vert) lemon (lime)
Citronelle lemon grass
Citrouille pumpkin
Civet stew
Civet de lièvre jugged hare
Clafoutis tart (usually cherry)
Claires oysters (see *Huitres*)
Clamart with petits pois
Clou de girofle clove (spice)
Clouté (de) studded with
Clovisse small clam
Cocherelle type of mushroom

Cochon pig
Cochonailles pork products
Coco coconut; also small white bean
Cocotte (en) cooking pot
Coeur (de) heart (of)
Coeur de palmier palm heart
Coffret (en) in a small box
Coing quince
Colbert (à la) fish, dipped in milk, egg and breadcrumbs
Colin hake
Colvert wild duck
Compote stewed fruit
Concassé(e) coarsely chopped
Concombre cucumber
Condé creamed rice and fruit
Confiserie confectionery
Confit(e) preserved or candied
Confiture jam
Confiture d'oranges marmalade
Congre conger eel
Consommé clear soup
Contrefilet sirloin, usually tied for roasting
Copeaux literally shavings
Coq (au vin) chicken in red wine sauce (or name of wine)
Coque cockle
Coque (à la) soft-boiled or served in shell
Coquelet young cockerel
Coquillages shellfish
Coquille St-Jacques scallop
Corail (de) coral (of)
Coriandre coriander
Cornichon gherkin
Côte d'agneau lamb chop
Côte de boeuf side of beef
Côte de veau veal chop
Côtelette chop
Cotriade Brittany fish soup
Cou (d'oie) neck (of goose)
Coulemelle mushroom
Coulibiac hot salmon *tourte*
Coulis (de) thick sauce (of)
Coupe ice cream dessert
Courge pumpkin
Courgette baby marrow
Couronne circle or ring
Court-bouillon aromatic poaching liquid
Couscous crushed semolina
Crabe crab
Crambe sea kale
Cramique raisin or currant loaf
Crapaudine (à la) grilled game bird with backbone removed
Crapinaude bacon pancake
Craquelot herring
Crécy with carrots and rice

Crème cream

Crème (à la) served with cream or cooked in cream sauce

Crème à l'anglaise light custard sauce

Crème brûlee same, less sugar and cream, with praline (see *brûlée*)

Crème pâtissière custard filling

Crème plombières custard filling: egg whites, fresh fruit flavouring

Crémets fresh cream cheese, eaten with sugar and cream

Crêpe thin pancake

Crêpe dentelle thin pancake

Crêpe Parmentier potato pancake

Crêpe Suzette sweet pancake with orange liqueur sauce

Crépinette (de) wrapping (of)

Cresson watercress

Cressonière purée of potatoes and watercress

Crête cockscomb

Creuse long, thick-shelled oyster

Crevette grise shrimp

Crevette rose prawn

Cromesquis croquette

Croque Monsieur toasted cheese or ham sandwich

Croquette see *boulette*

Crosne Chinese/Japanese artichoke

Croustade small pastry mould with various fillings

Croûte (en) pastry crust (in a)

Croûtons bread (toast or fried)

Cru raw

Crudité raw vegetable

Crustacés shellfish

Cuillère soft (cut with spoon)

Cuisse (de) leg (of)

Cuissot (de) haunch (of)

Cuit cooked

Cul haunch or rear

Culotte rump (usually steak)

Cultivateur soup or chopped vegetables

Dariole basket-shaped pastry

Darne slice or steak

Dartois savoury or sweet filled puff-pastry rectangles

Datte date

Daube stew (various types)

Daurade sea-bream

Décaféiné decaffeinated coffee

Dégustation tasting

Délice delight

Demi-glace basic brown sauce

Demi-sel lightly salted

Diable seasoned with mustard

Diane (à la) peppered cream sauce

Dieppoise (à la) Dieppe style: white wine, cream, mussels, shrimps

Dijonnaise (à la) with mustard sauce

Dijonnaise (à la belle) sauce made from blackcurrants

Dinde young hen turkey

Dindon turkey

Dindonneau young turkey

Diot pork and vegetable sausage

Dodine (de canard) cold stuffed duck

Dorade sea-bream

Doré cooked until golden

Doria with cucumbers

Douceurs desserts

Douillon pear wrapped in pastry

Doux (douce) sweet

Dragée sugared almond

Du Barry cauliflower soup

Duxelles chopped mushrooms, shallots and cream

Echalote shallot

Echine loin (of pork)

Echiquier in checkered fashion

Eclade (de moules) (mussels) cooked over pine needles

Ecrasé crushed (as with fruit)

Ecrevisses freshwater crayfish

Ecuelle bowl or basin

Effiloché(e) frayed, thinly sliced

Emincé thinly sliced

Encornet cuttlefish, squid

Encre squid ink, used in sauces

Endive chicory

Entrecôte entrecôte, rib steak

Entremets sweets

Epaule shoulder

Eperlan smelt (small fish)

Epice spice

Epinard spinach

Epis de maïs sweetcorn

Escabèche fish (or poultry) marinated in *court-bouillon*; cold

Escalope thinly cut (meat or fish)

Escargot snail

Espadon swordfish

Estouffade stew with onions, herbs, mushrooms, red or white wine (perhaps garlic)

Estragon tarragon flavoured

Esturgeon sturgeon

Etrille crab

Etuvé(e) cooked in little water or in ingredient's own juices

Exocet flying fish

Façon cooked in a described way

Faisan(e) pheasant

Fane green top of root vegetable

Far Brittany prune flan

Farci(e) stuffed
Farine flour
Faux-filet sirloin steak
Favorite a garnish of *foie gras* and truffles
Favouille spider crab
Fécule starch
Fenouil fennel
Fenouil marin samphire
Féra lake fish, like salmon.
Ferme (fermier) farm (farmer)
Fermière mixture of onions, carrots, turnips, celery, etc.
Feuille de vigne vine leaf
Feuilleté light flaky pastry
Fève broad bean
Ficelle (à la) tied in a string
Ficelles thin loaves of bread
Figue fig
Filet fillet
Financière (à la) Madeira sauce with truffles
Fine de claire oyster (see *Huîtres*)
Fines herbes mixture of parsley, chives, tarragon, etc.
Flageolet kidney bean
Flamande (à la) Flemish style: bacon, carrots, cabbage, potatoes and turnips
Flambé flamed
Flamiche puff pastry tart
Flan tart
Flétan halibut
Fleur (de courgette) flower (courgette flower, usually stuffed)
Fleurons puff pastry crescents
Flie small clam
Florentine with spinach
Flûte long thin loaf of bread
Foie liver
Foie de veau calves liver
Foie gras goose liver
Foies blonds de volaille chicken liver mousse
Foin (dans le) cooked in hay
Fond (base) basic stock
Fondant see *boulette*: a bon-bon
Fond d'artichaut artichoke heart
Fondu(e) (de fromage) melted (cheese with wine)
Forestière bacon and mushrooms
Fouace dough cakes
Four (au) baked in oven
Fourré stuffed
Frais (Fraîche) fresh or cool
Fraise strawberry
Fraise des bois wild strawberry
Framboise raspberry
Française (à la) mashed potato filled with mixed vegetables

Frangipane almond custard filling
Frappé frozen or ice cold
Friandises sweets (*petits fours*)
Fricadelle minced meat ball
Fricandeau slice topside veal
Fricassée braised in sauce or butter, egg yolks and cream
Frisé(e) curly
Frit fried
Frite chip
Fritot fritter
Frittons see *grattons*
Friture small fried fish
Frivolle fritter
Froid cold
Fromage cheese
Fromage de tête brawn
Fruit de la passion passion fruit
Fruits confits crystallised fruit
Fruits de mer seafood
Fumé smoked
Fumet fish stock
Galantine cooked meat, fish or vegetables in jelly, served cold
Galette pastry, pancake or cake
Galimafrée (de) stew (of)
Gamba large prawn
Ganache chocolate and *crème fraîche* mixture used to fill cakes
Garbure (Garbue) vegetable soup
Gardiane beef stew with red wine, black olives, onions and garlic
Gardon small roach
Gargouillau pear tart or cake
Garni(e) with vegetables
Garniture garnish
Gasconnade leg of lamb roasted with anchovies and garlic
Gâteau cake
Gâtinaise (à la) with honey
Gaufre waffle
Gayette faggot
Gelée aspic jelly
Géline chicken
Gendarme smoked or salted herring: flat, dry sausage
Genièvre juniper
Génoise rich sponge cake
Gentiane liqueur made from gentian flowers
Germiny sorrel and cream soup
Germon long-fin tuna
Gésier gizzard
Gibelotte see *fricassée*
Gibier game
Gigot (de) leg of lamb. Can describe other meat and fish
Gigot brayaude leg of lamb in white wine with red beans and cabbage
Gigue (de) shank (of)

Gingembre ginger
Girofle clove
Girolle apricot-coloured fungi
Givré frosted
Glacé iced. Crystallised. Glazed
Glace ice cream
Gnocchi dumplings of semolina, potato or *choux* paste
Godard see *financière (à la)*
Gougère round-shaped, egg and cheese *choux* pastry
Goujon gudgeon
Goujonnettes (de) small fried pieces (of)
Gourmandises sweetmeats; can describe *fruits de mer*
Gousse (de) pod or husk (of)
Graine (de capucine) seed (nasturtium)
Graisse fat
Graisserons duck or goose fat scratchings
Grand Veneur sauce with vegetables, wine vinegar, redcurrant jelly and cream
Granité water ice
Gratin browned
Gratin Dauphinois potato dish with cream, cheese and garlic
Gratin Savoyard potato dish with cheese and butter
Gratiné(e) sauced dish browned with butter, cheese, breadcrumbs, etc.
Gratinée Lyonnaise clear soup with port, beaten egg and cheese (grilled brown)
Grattons pork fat scratchings
Gravette oyster (see *Huîtres*)
Grecque (à la) cooked vegetables served cold
Grelette cold sauce, based on whipped cream, for fish
Grenade pomegranate
Grenadin thick veal escalope
Grenouille (cuisses de grenouilles) frog (frogs' legs)
Gribiche mayonnaise sauce with gherkins, capers, hardboiled egg yolks and herbs
Grillade grilled meat
Grillé(e) grilled
Grilot small bulb onion
Griotte (Griottine) bitter red cherry
Griset mushroom
Grisotte parasol mushroom
Grive thrush
Grondin gurnard, red gurnet
Gros sel coarse rock or sea salt
Groseille à maquereau gooseberry

Groseille noire blackcurrant
Groseille rouge redcurrant
Gruyère hard, mild cheese
Gyromitre fungi
Habit vert dressed in green
Hachis minced or chopped-up
Hareng herring
    à l'huile cured in oil
    fumé kippered
    salé bloater
    saur smoked
Haricot bean
Haricot blanc dried white bean
Haricot rouge kidney bean
Haricot vert green/French bean
Hochepot thick stew
Hollandaise sauce with butter, egg yolk and lemon juice
Homard lobster
Hongroise (à la) Hungarian style: sauce with tomato and paprika
Hors d'oeuvre appetisers
Huile oil
Huîtres oysters
    Les claires: the oyster-fattening beds in Marennes terrain (part of the Charente Estuary, between Royan and Rochefort, in Poitou-Charentes).
    Flat-shelled oysters:
    Belons (from the River Belon in Brittany);
    Gravettes (from Arcachon in the Southwest);
    both the above are cultivated in their home oyster beds.
    Marennes are those transferred from Brittany and Arcachon to *les claires,* where they finish their growth.
    Dished oysters (sometimes called *portugaises*):
    these breed mainly in the Gironde and Charente estuaries; they mature at Marennes.
    Fines de claires and *spéciales* are the largest; *huîtres de parc* are standard sized.
    All this lavish care covers a time span of two to four years.
Hure (de) head (of). Brawn. Jellied
Ile flottante unmoulded soufflé of beaten egg white and sugar
Imam bayeldi aubergine with rice, onions and sautéed tomatoes
Impératrice (à la) desserts with candied fruits soaked in kirsch
Indienne (à l') Indian style: with curry powder
Infusion herb tea

Italienne (à l') Italian style: artichokes, mushrooms, pasta
Jalousie latticed fruit or jam tart
Jambon ham
Jambonneau knuckle of pork
Jambonnette (de) boned and stuffed (knuckle of ham or poultry)
Jardinière diced fresh vegetables
Jarret de veau stew of shin of veal
Jarreton cooked pork knuckle
Jerez sherry
Jésus de Morteau smoked Jura pork sausage
Joinville *velouté* sauce with cream, crayfish tails and truffles
Joue (de) cheek (of)
Judru cured pork sausage
Julienne thinly-cut vegetables: also ling (cod family, see *lingue*)
Jus juice
Kaki persimmon fruit
Lait milk
Laitance soft roe
Laitue lettuce
Lamproie eel-like fish
Langouste spiny lobster or crawfish
Langoustine Dublin Bay prawn
Langue tongue
Languedocienne (à la) mushrooms; tomatoes, parsley garnish
Lapereau young rabbit
Lapin rabbit
Lapin de garenne wild rabbit
Lard bacon
Lard de poitrine fat belly of pork
Lardons strips of bacon
Laurier bay-laurel, sweet bay leaf
Lavaret lake fish, like salmon trout
Lèche thin slice
Léger (Légère) light
Légume vegetable
Lieu cod-like fish
Lièvre hare
Limaçon snail
Limande lemon sole
Limon lime
Lingue ling (cod family)
Lit bed
Livèche lovage (like celery)
Longe loin
Lotte de mer monkfish, anglerfish
Lotte de rivière (de lac) burbot, a river (or lake) fish, like eel; liver a great delicacy
Lou magret see *magret*
Loup de mer sea-bass
Louvine (loubine) grey mullet, like a sea-bass (Basque name)

Lyonnaise (à la) Lyonnais style: sauce with wine, onions, vinegar
Macédoine diced fruit or veg
Mâche lamb's lettuce; small, dark, green leaf
Macis mace (spice)
Madeleine tiny sponge cake
Madère sauce *demi-glace* and Madeira wine
Madrilène Madrid style: with chopped tomatoes
Magret (de canard) breast (of duck); now used for other poultry
Maigre fish, like sea-bass
Maigre non-fatty, lean
Maillot carrots, turnips, onions, peas and beans
Maïs maize flour
Maison (de) of the restaurant
Maître d'hôtel sauce with butter, parsley and lemon
Maltaise an orange flavoured *hollandaise* sauce
Manchons see *goujonnettes*
Mandarine tangerine
Mangetout edible peas and pods
Mangue mango
Manière (de) style (of)
Maquereau mackerel
Maraîchère (à la) market-gardener style: *velouté* sauce with vegetables
Marais marsh or market-garden
Marbré(e) marbled
Marc pure spirit
Marcassin young wild boar
Marché market
Marchand de vin sauce with red wine, chopped shallots
Marée fresh seafood
Marengo tomatoes, mushrooms, olive oil, white wine, garlic, herbs
Marennes (blanche) flat-shelled oyster (see *Huîtres*)
Marennes (verte) green shell
Mareyeur fishmonger
Marinade, Mariné(e) pickled
Marinière see *moules*
Marjolaine marjoram
Marjolaine almond and hazelnut sponge cake with chocolate cream and praline
Marmite stewpot
Marquise (de) water ice (of)
Marrons chestnuts
Marrons glacés crystallised sweet chestnuts
Massepains marzipan cakes
Matelote (d'anguilles) freshwater red wine fish stew (of eels)

Matignon mixed vegetables, cooked in butter

Mauviette lark

Médaillion (de) round piece (of)

Mélange mixture or blend

Melba (à la) poached peach, with vanilla ice cream, raspberry sauce

Mélisse lemon-balm (herb)

Ménagère (à la) housewife style: onions, potatoes peas, turnips and carrots

Mendiant (fruits de) mixture of figs, almonds and raisins

Menthe mint

Mer sea

Merguez spicy grilled sausage

Merlan whiting (in Provence the word is used for hake)

Merle blackbird

Merlu hake

Merluche dried cod

Mérou grouper (sea fish)

Merveilles hot, sugared fritters

Mesclum mixture of salad leaves

Meunière (à la) sauce with butter, parsley, lemon (sometimes oil)

Meurette red wine sauce

Miel honey

Mignardises *petits fours*

Mignon (de) small round piece

Mignonette coarsley ground white pepper

Mijoté(e) cooked slowly in water

Milanaise (à la) Milan style: dipped in breadcrumbs, egg, cheese

Millassou sweet maize flour flan

Mille-feuille puff pastry with numerous thin layers

Mimosa chopped hardboiled egg

Mique stew of dumplings

Mirabeau anchovies, olives

Mirabelles golden plums

Mirepoix cubes carrot, onion, ham

Miroir smooth

Miroton (de) slices (of)

Mitonée (de) soup (of)

Mode (à la) in the manner of

Moelle beef marrow

Mojettes pulse beans in butter

Moka coffee

Montagne (de) from mountains

Montmorency with cherries

Morilles edible, dark brown, honeycombed fungi

Mornay cheese sauce

Morue cod

Morvandelle (jambon à la) ham with a piquant cream sauce, wine and wine vinegar (from Burgundy)

Morvandelle rapée baked eggs,

cream and cheese, mixed with grated potato (from Burgundy's Morvan)

Mostèle (Gâteau de) cod mousse

Mouclade mussel stew

Moule mussel

Moules marinière mussels cooked in white wine and shallots

Mourone Basque red bell pepper

Mourtayrol stew with beef, chicken, ham, vegetables and bread (from the Auvergne)

Mousse cold, light, finely-minced ingredients with cream and egg whites

Mousseline *hollandaise* sauce with whipped cream

Mousseron edible fungi

Moutarde mustard

Mouton mutton

Mulet grey mullet

Mûre mulberry

Mûre sauvage (de ronce) blackberry

Muscade nutmeg

Museau de porc (de boeuf) sliced muzzle of pork (beef) with shallots and parsley in *vinaigrette*

Myrtille bilberry (blueberry)

Mystère a meringue desert with ice cream and chocolate; also cone-shaped ice cream

Nage (à la) *court-bouillon*: aromatic poaching liquid

Nantua sauce for fish with crayfish, white wine, tomatoes

Nappé sauce covered

Nature plain

Navarin stew, usually lamb

Navets turnips

Nègre dark (e.g. chocolate)

Newburg sauce with lobster, brandy, cream and Madeira

Nid nest

Nivernaise (à la) Nevers style: carrots and onions

Noilly sauce based on vermouth

Noisette hazelnut

Noisette sauce of lightly browned butter

Noisette (de) round piece (of)

Noix nuts

Noix (de veau) topside of leg (veal)

Normande (à la) Normandy style: fish sauce with mussels, shrimps, mushrooms, eggs and cream

Nouille noodle

Nouveau (nouvelle) new or young

Noyau sweet liqueur from crushed stones (usually cherries)

Oeufs à la coque soft-boiled eggs

Oeufs à la neige see *île flottante*
Oeufs à la poêlé fried eggs
Oeufs brouillés scrambled eggs
Oeufs durs hard-boiled eggs
Oeufs moulés poached eggs
Oie goose
Oignon onion
Oison rôti roast gosling
Omble chevalier freshwater char; looks like large salmon trout
Ombre grayling
Ombrine fish, like sea-bass
Omelette brayaude omelette with bacon, cream, potatoes and cheese
Onglet flank of beef
Oreille (de porc) ear (pig's)
Oreillette sweet fritter, flavoured with orange flower water
Orge (perlé) barley (pearl)
Origan oregano (herb)
Orléannaise (à l') Orléans style: chicory and potatoes
Orly dipped in butter, fried and served with tomato sauce
Ortie nettle
Ortolan wheatear (thrush family)
Os bone
Oseille sorrel
Osso bucco à la Niçoise veal braised with orange zest, tomatoes, onions and garlic
Ouillat Pyrénées soup; onions, tomatoes, goose fat, garlic
Oursins sea-urchins
Pageot sea-bream
Paillarde (de veau) grilled veal escalope
Paille fried potato stick
Pailletté (de) spangled (with)
Paillettes pastry straws
Pain bread
    bis brown bread
    de campagne round white loaf
    d'épice spiced honey cake
    de mie square white loaf
    de seigle rye bread
    doré bread soaked in milk and eggs and fried
    entier/complet wholemeal
    grillé toast
Paleron shoulder
Palmier palm-shaped sweet puff pastry
Palmier (coeur de) palm (heart)
Palombe wood pigeon
Palomête fish, like sea-bass
Palourde clam
Pamplemousse grapefruit
Pan bagna long split bread roll, brushed with olive oil and filled with olives, peppers, anchovies, onions, lettuce
Panaché mixed
Panade flour or bread paste
Panais parsnip
Pané(e) breadcrumbed
Panier basket
Panisse fried chickpea or maize fritter
Pannequets like *crêpes*, smaller and thicker
Pantin pork filled small pastry
Paon peacock
Papeton fried or puréed aubergines, arranged in ring mould
Papillon small oyster (butterfly) from the Atlantic coast
Papillote (en) cooked in oiled paper (or foil)
Paquets (en) parcels
Parfait (de) a mousse (of)
Paris-Brest cake of *choux* pastry, filled with butter cream, almonds
Parisienne (à la) leeks, potatoes
Parmentier potatoes
Pascade sweet or savoury pancake
Pascaline (de) see *quenelle* (of)
Passe Crassane variety of pear
Passe-pierres seaweed
Pastèque watermelon
Pastis (sauce au) aniseed based
Pâté minced meats (of various types) baked. Usually served cold
Pâte pastry, dough or batter
Pâte à choux cream puff pastry
Pâte brisée short crust pastry
Pâte d'amande almond paste
Pâté en croûte baked in pastry crust
Pâtes (fraîches) fresh pasta
Pâtés (petits) à la Provençale anchovy and ham turnovers
Pâtisserie pastry
Pâtisson custard marrow
Patte claw, foot, leg
Pauchouse see *pochouse*
Paupiettes thin slices of meat of fish, used to wrap fillings
Pavé (de) thick slice (of)
Pavot (graines de) poppy seeds
Paysan(ne) (à la) country style
Peau (de) skin (of)
Pêche peach
Pêcheur fisherman
Pèlerine scallop
Perce-pierre samphire (edible sea fennel)
Perche perch
Perdreau young partridge
Perdrix partridge

Périgourdine (à la) goose liver and sauce *Périgueux*
Périgueux sauce with truffles and Madeira
Persil parsley
Persillade mixture of chopped parsley and garlic
Petit-beurre biscuit made with butter
Petit gris small snail
Petite marmite strong consommé with toast and cheese
Petits fours miniature cakes, biscuits, sweets
Petits pois tiny peas
Pétoncle small scallop
Pets de nonne small soufflé fritters
Picanchâgne (piquenchâge) a pear tart with walnut topping
Picholine large green table olives
Pied de cheval large oyster
Pied de mouton blanc cream-coloured mushroom
Pied de porc pig's trotter
Pigeonneau young pigeon
Pignon pine nut
Pilau rice dish
Pilon drumstick
Piment (doux) pepper (sweet)
Pimpernelle burnet (salad green)
Pintade (pintadeau) guinea-fowl (young guinea-fowl)
Piperade omelette or scrambled eggs with tomatoes, peppers, onions and, sometimes, ham
Piquante (sauce) sharp-tasting sauce with shallots, capers, wine
Piqué larded
Pissenlit dandelion leaf
Pistache green pistachio nut
Pistil de safran saffron (*pistil* from autumn-flowering crocus)
Pistou vegetable soup bound with *pommade*
Plateau (de) plate (of)
Pleurote mushroom
Plie franche plaice
Plombières sweet with vanilla ice cream, *kirsch,* candied fruit and *crème chantilly*
Pluche sprig
Pluvier plover
Poché(e) Pochade poached
Pochouse freshwater fish stew with white wine
Poêlé fried
Pogne sweet brioche flavoured with orange flower water
Poire pear

Poireau leek
Pois peas
Poisson fish
Poitrine breast
Poitrine fumée smoked bacon
Poitrine salée unsmoked bacon
Poivrade a peppery sauce with wine vinegar, cooked vegetables
Poivre noir black pepper
Poivre rose red pepper
Poivre vert green pepper
Poivron (doux) pepper (sweet)
Pojarsky minced meat or fish, cutlet shaped and fried
Polenta boiled maize flour
Polonaise Polish style: with buttered breadcrumbs, parsley, hard-boiled eggs
Pommade thick, smooth paste
Pomme apple
Pommes de terre potatoes
  à l'anglaise boiled
  allumettes thin and fried
  boulangère sliced with onions
  brayaude baked
  château roast
  dauphine croquettes
  duchesse mashed with egg yolk
  en l'air hollow potato puffs
  frites fried chips
  gratinées browned with cheese
  Lyonnaise sautéed with onions
  vapeur boiled
Pomponette savoury pastry
Porc (carré de) loin of pork
Porc (côte de) pork chop
Porcelet suckling pig
Porchetta whole roasted young pig, stuffed with offal, herbs, garlic
Porto (au) port
Portugaise (à la) Portuguese style: fried onions and tomatoes
Portugaises oysters with long, deep shells (see *Huîtres*)
Potage thick soup
Pot-au-crème dessert, usually chocolate or coffee
Pot-au-feu clear meat broth served with the meat
Potée heavy soup of cabbage, beans, etc.
Potimarron pumpkin
Potjevleisch northern terrine of mixed meats (rabbit, pork, veal)
Pouchouse see *pochouse*
Poularde large hen
Poulet chicken
Poulet à la broche spit-roasted chicken
Poulet Basquaise chicken with

tomatoes and peppers

Poulet de Bresse corn-fed, white flesh chicken

Poulet de grain grain-fed chicken

Poulette young chicken

Poulpe octopus

Pounti small, egg-based, savoury soufflé with bacon or prunes

Pourpier purslane (salad green, also flavours dishes); a weed

Pousse-pierre edible seaweed

Poussin small baby chicken

Poutargue grey mullet roe paste

Praire small clam

Praline caramelised almonds

Praslin caramelised

Pré-salé (agneau de) lamb raised on salt marshes

Primeur young vegetable

Princesse *velouté* sauce, asparagus tips and truffles

Printanièr(e) (à la) garnish of diced vegetables

Produit (de) product (of)

Profiterole *choux* pastry, custard filled puff

Provençale (à la) Provençal style: tomatoes, garlic, olive oil, etc.

Prune plum

Pruneau prune

Purée mashed

Quasi (de veau) thick part of loin of veal (chump)

Quatre-épices four blended ground spices (ginger, cloves, nutmeg and white pepper)

Quatre-quarts cake made with equal weights of eggs, butter, sugar and flour (four-quarters)

Quenelle light dumpling of fish or poultry

Quetsche small, purple plum

Queue tail

Queue de boeuf oxtail

Quiche (Lorraine) open flan of cheese, ham or bacon

Râble de lièvre (lapin) saddle of hare (rabbit)

Raclette scrapings from specially-made and heated cheese

Radis radish

Ragoût stew, usually meat, but can describe other ingredients

Raie (bouclée) skate (type of)

Raifort horseradish

Raisin grape

Raïto sauce served over grilled fish (red wine, onions, tomatoes, herbs, olives, capers and garlic)

Ramequin see *cocotte (en)*

Ramier wood pigeon

Rapé(e) grated or shredded

Rascasse scorpion fish

Ratafia brandy and unfermented Champagne. Almond biscuit

Ratatouille aubergines, onions, courgettes, garlic, red peppers and tomatoes in olive oil

Ratte de Grenoble white potato

Raves (root) turnips, radishes,etc.

Ravigote sauce with onions, herbs, mushrooms, wine vinegar

Ravioles ravioli

Ravioles à la Niçoise pasta filled with meat or Swiss chard and baked with cheese

Ravioles du Royans small ravioli pasta with goat cheese filling (from the terrain under the western edges of the Vercors)

Régence sauce with wine, truffles, mushrooms

Réglisse liquorice

Reine chicken and cream

Reine-Claude greengage

Reinette type of apple

Réjane garnish of potatoes, bone-marrow, spinach and artichokes

Rémoulade sauce of mayonnaise, mustard, capers, herbs, anchovy

Rillettes (d'oie) potted pork (goose)

Rillons small cubes of fat pork

Ris d'agneau lamb sweetbreads

Ris de veau veal sweetbreads

Rissettes small sweetbreads

Rivière river

Riz rice

Riz à l'impératrice cold rice pudding

Riz complet brown rice

Riz sauvage wild rice

Robe de chambre jacket potato

Robert sauce *demi-glace,* white wine, onions, vinegar, mustard

Rocambole wild garlic

Rognon kidney

Rognonnade veal and kidneys

Romanoff fruit marinated in liqueur; mostly strawberries

Romarin rosemary

Roquette salad green

Rosé meat cooked to pink stage

Rosette large pork sausage

Rossini see *tournedos*

Rôti roast

Rouelle (de) round piece or slice

Rouget red mullet

Rouget barbet red mullet

Rouget grondin red gurnard

(larger than red mullet)

Rouille orange-coloured sauce with peppers, garlic and saffron

Roulade (de) roll (of)

Roulé(e) rolled (usually *crêpe*)

Rousette rock salmon; dog fish

Roux flour, butter base for sauces

Royan fresh sardine

Rutabaga swede

Sabayon sauce of egg yolks, wine

Sablé shortbread

Sabodet Lyonnais sausage of pig's head, pork, beef; served hot

Safran saffron (see *pistil de*)

Sagou sago

Saignant(e) underdone, rare

Saindoux lard

St-Germain with peas

St-Hubert sauce *poivrade*, bacon and cooked chestnuts

St-Jacques (coquille) scallop

St-Pierre John Dory

Saisons (suivant) depending on the season of the year

Salade Niçoise tomatoes, beans, potatoes, black olives, anchovy, lettuce, olive oil, perhaps tuna

Salade panachée mixed salad

Salade verte green salad

Salé salted

Salicornes marsh samphire (edible sea-fennel)

Salmigondis meat stew

Salmis red wine sauce

Salpicon meat or fish and diced vegetables in a sauce

Salsifis salsify (vegetable)

Sanciau thick sweet or savoury pancake

Sandre freshwater fish, like perch

Sang blood

Sanglier wild boar

Sanguine blood orange

Sanguines mountain mushrooms

Santé potato and sorrel soup

Sarcelle teal

Sarrasin buckwheat

Sarriette savory, bitter herb

Saucisse freshly-made sausage

Saucisson large, dry sausage

Saucisson cervelas saveloy

Sauge sage

Saumon salmon

Saumon blanc hake

Saumon fumé smoked salmon

Sauté browned in butter, oil or fat

Sauvage wild

Savarin *un baba au rhum*

Savoyarde with Gruyère cheese

Scarole endive (chicory)

Scipion cuttlefish

Seiche squid or cuttlefish

Sel salt

Selle saddle

Selon grosseur (S.G.) according to size

Serpolet wild thyme

Sévigné garnished with mushrooms, roast potatoes, lettuce

Smitane sauce with sour cream, onions, white wine

Socca chickpea flour fritter

Soissons with white beans

Soja (pousse de) soy bean (soy bean sprout)

Soja (sauce de) soy sauce

Sole à la Dieppoise sole fillets, mussels, shrimps, wine, cream

Sole Cardinale poached fillets of sole in lobster sauce

Sole Dugléré sole with tomatoes, onions, shallots, butter

Sole Marguéry sole with mussels and prawns in rich egg sauce

Sole Walewska *mornay* sauce, truffles and prawns

Sorbet water ice

Soubise onion sauce

Soufflé(e) beaten egg whites, baked (with sweet or savoury ingredients)

Soupière soup tureen

Sourdon cockle

Souvaroff a game bird with *foie gras* and truffles

Spaghettis (de) thin strips (of)

Spoom frothy water ice

Strasbourgeoise (à la) Strasbourg style: *foie gras, choucroute*, bacon

Sucre sugar

Suppion small cuttlefish

Suprême sweet white sauce

Suprême boneless breast of poultry; also describes a fish fillet

Sureau (fleurs de) elder tree (flowers of); delicious liqueur

Tacaud type of cod

Talleyrand truffles, cheese, *foie gras*

Talmousse triangular cheese pastry

Tanche tench

Tapé(e) dried

Tartare raw minced beef

Tartare (sauce) sauce with mayonnaise, onions, capers, herbs

Tarte open flan

Tarte Tatin upside down tart of caramelised apples and pastry

Telline small clam

Tergoule Normandy rice pudding

with cinnamon

Terrine container in which mixed meats/fish are baked; served cold

Tête de veau vinaigrette calf's head *vinaigrette*

Thé tea

Thermidor grilled lobster with browned *béchamel* sauce

Thon tunny fish

Thym thyme

Tiède mild or lukewarm

Tilleul lime tree

Timbale mould in which contents are steamed

Tomate tomatoe

Topinambour Jerusalem artichoke

Torte sweet-filled flan

Tortue turtle

Tortue sauce with various herbs, tomatoes, Madeira

Toulousaine (à la) Toulouse style: truffles, *foie gras*, sweetbreads, kidneys

Tournedos fillet steak (small end)

Tournedos chasseur with shallots, mushrooms, tomatoes

Tournedos Dauphinoise with creamed mushrooms, *croûtons*

Tournedos Rossini with goose liver, truffles, port, *croûtons*

Touron a cake, pastry or loaf made from almond paste and filled with candied fruits and nuts; also see *ouillat*, a Pyrénées soup

Tourte (Tourtière) covered savoury tart

Tourteau large crab

Tourteau fromager goat's cheese *gâteau*

Tranche slice

Tranche de boeuf steak

Traver de porc spare rib of pork

Tripes à la mode de Caen beef tripe stew

Tripettes small sheep tripe

Tripoux stuffed mutton tripe

Trompettes de la mort fungi

Tronçon a cut of fish or meat

Trou water ice

Truffade a huge sautéed pancake, or *galette*, with bacon, garlic and Cantal cheese

Truffe truffle; black, exotic, tuber

Truffée with truffles

Truite trout

Truite (au bleu) trout poached in water and vinegar; turns blue

Truite saumonée salmon trout

Tuiles tiles (thin almond slices)

Turbot (turbotin) turbot

Vacherin ice cream, meringue, cream

Valenciennes (à la) rice, onions, red peppers, tomatoes, white wine

Vallée d'Auge veal or chicken; sautéed, flamed in Calvados and served with cream and apples

Vapeur (à la) steamed

Varech seaweed

Veau veal

Veau à la Viennoise (escalope de) slice of veal coated with egg and breadcrumbs, fried

Veau Milanaise (escalope de) with macaroni, tomatoes, ham, mushrooms

Veau pané (escalope de) thin slice in flour, eggs and breadcrumbs

Velouté white sauce with *bouillon* and white *roux*

Velouté de volaille thick chicken soup

Venaison venison

Ventre belly or breast

Verdurette *vinaigrette* dressing with herbs

Vernis clam

Véronique grapes, wine, cream

Verte green mayonnaise with chervil, spinach, tarragon

Vert-pré thinly-sliced chips, *maître d'hôtel* butter, watercress

Verveine verbena

Vessie (en) cooked in a pig's bladder; usually chicken

Viande meat

Vichy glazed carrots

Vichyssoise creamy potato and leek soup, served cold

Viennoise coated with egg and breadcrumbs, fried (usually veal)

Vierge (sauce) olive oil sauce

Vierge literally virgin (best olive oil, the first pressing)

Vigneron vine-grower (winemaker)

Vinaigre (de) wine vinegar or vinegar of named fruit

Vinaigre de Jerez sherry vinegar

Vinaigrette (à la) French dressing with wine vinegar, oil, etc.

Viroflay spinach as a garnish

Volaille poultry

Vol au vent puff pastry case

Xérès (vinaigre de) sherry (vinegar)

Yaourt yogurt

Zeste (d'orange) rubbing from (orange skin)

So you think you know that road sign?

Absence d'accotements no verges
Absence de glissières latérales no protective barriers
Absence de marquage no road markings
Absence de signalement horizontal no road markings
Absence de signalement vertical no road signs
Accotement étroit narrow verge
Accotement non stabilisé soft verges
Affaissement subsidence
Aire parking area
Allumez vos feux switch on lights
Arbres inclinés trees leaning over the road
Arrosage et boue watering, mud on the road
Atelier d'entretien maintenance workshop
Attachez vos ceintures fasten your seat belts
Attente de marquage no road markings
Attention(!) look out (!)
Attention aux travaux danger, road works
Autoroute péage toll motorway
Autres directions other directions
Bande d'arrêt d'urgence emergency hard shoulder
Bande d'arrêt d'urgence déformée emergency hard shoulder, bad surface
Betteraves beet harvesting, mud on the road
Bifurcation road divides
Bis short for *bison futé* (crafty bison); alternative routes across France avoiding traffic congestion. Free maps, showing marked routes (green arrows with word *bis*), available from tourist offices or, better still, buy Michelin map 911.
Bouchon bottleneck, traffic jam
Boue mud
Brouillard fog or mist
Carrefour crossroads
Cédez le passage give way
Centre d'entretien maintenance centre
Centre ville town centre
Chantier roadworks
Chantier mobile mobile roadworks
Chausée déformée bad road surface
Chausée inondable road liable to flooding

Chute de pierres danger, falling rocks or stones
Circulation alternée single line traffic, alternately
Convoi exceptionnel large load
Dans l'agglomération built-up area
Déviation diversion
Eboulements landslides
En cas de pluie when raining
Enquête de circulation traffic census
Essence petrol/gasoline (2 star)
Eteignez vos phares switch off headlights
Fauchage mowing
Feux traffic lights
Feux clignotants flashing lights
Fin de ... end of ...
Flèches vertes green arrows (secondary route)
Gendarmerie traffic and local police
Gravillons loose chippings
Hauteur limitée height limited
Hors des cases (accompanied by sign) no parking outside bays
Hors gabarit not the normal size (height or width). Used in conjunction with additional sign
Interdiction de stationner parking prohibited
Interdit prohibited
    aux piétons no entry to pedestrians
    du ler au 15 du mois no parking from 1st to 15th of month
    du 16 à fin de mois no parking from 16th to end of month
    sauf aux livraison no entry except for deliveries
    sauf aux riverains no entry except for residents
    sauf services no entry except for service vehicles
    sur accotement no stopping on verges
Itinéraire bis see *bis*
Itinéraire conseillé recommended route
Itinéraire obligatoire compulsory route
Lacet sharp bend
Laissez libre la bande d'arrêt d'urgence do not obstruct hard shoulder
Libre service self-service
Mairie town hall
Mouvements de chars heavy vehicles

Nappe d'eau puddles on road
Nappe de fumée smoke patches
Ni vitesse ni bruit drive slowly and quietly
Nids de poules pot holes
P parking
P.T.T. (P et T) post office and telephone
Par temps de pluie during rain
Passage à niveau level crossing
Passage protégé you have right of way
Péage toll
Piétons pedestrians
Pique-nique picnic area
Pique-nique jeux d'enfants picnic area with children's playground
Piste cyclable cycle track
Poids lourds heavy vehicles
Priorité à droite give way to traffic coming from your right
Prochaine sortie next exit
Prudence take care
Rainurage grooves in road
Ralentir slow down
Rappel reminder (accompanied by instruction: e.g. speed limit)
Renseignements information
Respectez les feux obey traffic lights
Risque de brouillard possible fog
Risque d'inondation flooding risk
Risque de verglas possible risk of ice (usually black ice) on road
Rocade bypass road
Route barrée road closed
Route bombée badly cambered road (usually bumps in road)
Route glissante slippery road
Sans plomb unleaded fuel
Sens interdit no entry
Sens unique one-way street
Serrez à droite keep to the right
Servez-vous help-yourself (fuel: petrol, gasoline and diesel)
Signal automatique automatic signal

Sortie exit
   de camions lorries emerging
   de carrière quarry exit
   d'engins machinery or plant emerging
   de secours emergency exit
   d'usine factory exit
   du véhicules traffic exit
Stationnment alterné semimensuel parking alternates halfmonthly
Stationnement gênant park tidily; do not obstruct
Stationnement interdit no parking
Super petrol/gasoline (4 star)
Toutes directions all directions
Travaux roadworks
Travaux cachent les hommes roadworks obscuring men
Traversée de véhicules vehicles crossing the road
Trou hole in the road
Troupeaux cattle
Trous en formation holes developing
Un train peut en cacher au autre (seen at level crossing) one train may be concealing another coming in the opposite direction
Véhicules lents slow vehicles
Véhicules lents serrez à droite slow vehicles keep to the right
Véhicules lents voie de droite slow vehicles use right hand lane
Vendange grape harvesting
Vent latéral cross wind
Vent violent strong cross winds
Verglas fréquent often icy
Virages bends
   en d'envers bends with opposite or reverse camber
   sur (km) bends for (km)
Voie sans issue no through road
Zône bleue parking for permit (disc) holders only in a blue zone (you need a disc, obtained locally from newsagents)

(The above compiled with the assistance of Shirley Clancy)

DO wear seats belts (front & rear); put under-tens in the back
   pull right off the carriageway on open roads
   take a complete set of spare bulbs for your car
   come to a complete halt at stop signs (creeping will not do)
   take a red warning triangle for emergency breakdowns
   observe speed limits:
   built-up areas 50 km/h (31 mph) (town name starts limit; **bar** through town name is the derestriction sign)
   ordinary roads 90 km/h (56 mph) (if **wet** 80 km/h, 50 mph)
   dual carriageways & toll-free autoroutes 110 km/h (68 mph) (if **wet** 100 km/h, 62 mph)
   other autoroutes 130 km/h (81 mph) (if **wet** 110 km/h, 68mph)

Index of Wines

Please also read Wines of
France *(pages 20, 21 and
22) and the chapter called*
Wine Dégustations *in the*
France à la Carte *section
of the book (page 434).
The latter provides you
with a selection of not-so
well-known growers, all of
whom are worth seeking
out on your travels.*
Santé!

Index of Cheeses

472

Bin(ns) Ends

The Author's Burden (Charles Colton 1780-1832)
There are three difficulties in authorship: to write anything
worth the publishing; to find honest men to publish it; and to
get sensible men to read it. ("Buy" would be a better word.)

I've bypassed one "difficulty" by becoming a do-it-yourself
publisher. That, however, brings two additional difficulties: (1)
how do you tell "sensible men", and women, about your book
and (2) how do you persuade bookshops to stock copies? I've
never really solved those two problems. Anyone who thinks that
books sell themselves is both innocent and naive. You need a
fertile imagination to conjure up ways of winning publicity
(articles, features, interviews and reviews). Solve that and you
crack the problem: prospective buyers read or hear of your book
and hopefully ask shops to order a copy or, better still, persuade
them to stock the title. Anyway, that's the theory. (Note: well
over 1,000 new titles are published every week.)

Another dilemma Is there any better **buy** than a good-value
guide? For year after year a hardback edition can be read and
re-read, used and re-used; the guide can be lent to friends and
lent again. A bottle of wine, once drunk, has gone for ever; a
meal, once eaten, is just a memory. They, too, can be shared
with friends – but only once. That's the dilemma with a
borrowed book: fine for friends but not for the author.

Earlier this year I gave some moral support to another do-it-
yourself publisher, Colin Corder. His *Some of my best friends*
are French is a corker, a thoroughly entertaining A-Z crammer
on the French and France. Try to persuade a bookshop to stock
the book and get a copy for you; failing the former buy direct
from Colin, 6 St Albans Rd, Codicote, Hitchin, Herts SG4 8UT
(£9.95; Shelf Publishing; p&p f.o.c.; UK Sterling cheques).

Aux Deux Soeurs

Readers who have *Best of Britain* will know how Anne and I
followed the fortunes of the Café Pélican and its founder,
Carolyn Hall, with more than passing interest (p 130). We've
known the Hall family for 30 years: Jim and Mabel and their
children, Carolyn, Andrew and Julie. Now Carolyn has a new
interest: looking after her delectable 25-acre property, Aux
Deux Soeurs, on the northern slopes of the Alpilles to the west
of St-Rémy-de-Provence. Two parts of the property, The Lodge
and The Cottage, are available for rental. For details write to
Carolyn Hall, Aux Deux Soeurs, Le Vieux Chemin d'Arles,
13150 St-Etienne-du-Grès, B.-du-R. (Mich 158/B2).

Département abbreviations used in postal addresses (Numbers
are the first two digits in the postal codes (last two on car
plates). Whenever "H" is used this means Haute; "B" is Bas.)
04 Alpes-de-H.P: Alpes-de-Haute-Provence. **06** Alpes-Mar:
Alpes-Maritimes. **13** B.-du-R: Bouches-du-Rhône. **17** Char.-
Mar: Charente-Maritime. **22** C.-d'Armor: Côtes-d'Armor. **28** E.-
et-L: Eure-et-Loir. **31** H.-Gar: Haute-Garonne. **35** I.-et-V: Ille-
et-Vilaine. **37** I.-et-L: Indre-et-Loire. **41** L.-et-Ch: Loir-et-Cher.
44 Loire-Atl: Loire-Atlantique. **47** L.-et-G: Lot-et-Garonne. **49**
M.-et-L: Maine-et-Loire. **54** M.-et-M: Meurthe-et-Moselle. **62**
P.-de-C: Pas-de-Calais. **63** P.-de-D: Puy-de-Dôme. **64** Pyr.-Atl:
Pyrénées-Atlantiques. **66** Pyr.-Or: Pyrénées-Orientales. **71** S.-
et-L: Saône-et-Loire. **76** S.-M: Seine-Maritime. **77** S.-et-M:
Seine-et-Marne. **82** T.-et-G: Tarn-et-Garonne. **90** Ter.-de-
Belfort: Territoire-de-Belfort.

French Leave *Cocktails*

Apéritifs of France Enjoy three main types:

1) Alcohol-based Most common are the *anis* (aniseed) types: **Berger Blanc** and **Pernod 45** (coloured); these contain no liquorice. The *pastis apéritifs* do have liquorice: **Berger Pastis, Pernod Pastis 51** and **Ricard 45**. Drink them with cool water (not ice), one part to five parts water; initial content of 45 per cent is then reduced to something like an acceptably safe level.

Other alcohol-based drinks are the *amers, bitters* and *gentianes;* all 20 per cent. Extracts of various plants are used. **Picon** and **Mandarin** are *amers,* long drinks of one part to two parts water. *Bitters* are extra bitter: e.g., **St-Raphaël Bitter. Suze** and **Aveze** are gentian based.

2) Wine-based (*aromatised wines*) Some are *quinquinas* (tropical tree bark); usually red, drunk straight or as a long drink with soda. Main ones are based on Roussillon wines: **Ambassadeur, Byrrh, Dubonnet, St-Raphaël.** Alcohol content is 16 to 18 per cent.

Others are *vermouths;* usually white, dry and aromatised by bitter substances; reds are white wine coloured with caramel. Main centres are Chambéry (Savoie) and Languedoc: examples **Noilly-Prat, Clarac, Valtoni, Cazapra** and **Chambérizette** (this is Chambéry *vermouth* laced with strawberry juice, a real delight).

3) Natural sweet wines (*vins doux naturels*) – **Liqueur wines** See regions: Languedoc-Roussillon, Poitou-Charentes, Provence.

The types and shades of wines

White wine is made from white or red grapes; the skins are removed at the start of the wine-making process.

Rosé is wine from red grapes; juice is separated from skins after a brief period, fermentation is completed without them. *Vin gris* (grey) is pale pink; skins and juice are kept apart at pressing.

Red end product of red grape juice and skins which ferment together.

Dry wine is the end product of allowing fermentation to run its whole course; all sugar converts to alcohol.

Sweet wine results when fermentation is prematurely stopped, while sugar remains; this done by filtration or adding sulphur dioxide.

Sparkling wine results when juice is bottled before fermentation is complete; this finishes in the bottle, hence the carbon dioxide bubbles.

Méthode champenoise is difficult, lengthy process; fermentation is helped by adding yeast and sugar. Dom Pérignon invented the process. Madame Cliquot developed the technique of keeping the liquid clear and sparkling. To compensate dryness, a *dosage* (sweetening) is added.

Brandies Cognac is the end product of distilled white wine: first heated, the vapour is collected and condensed; process is repeated. Armagnac is distilled once. **Fines** are brandies from wine-making areas.

Marc is pure spirit, distilled from grape-pulp after pressing.

Eaux-de-vie read wine notes in Alsace region.

Still and sparkling waters of France

Badoit a sparkling water from St-Galmier, west of Lyon (Lyonnais).

Evian a pure, still water. From Evian on Lake Geneva (Savoie).

Perrier a sparkling water. From the Vergèze spring, between Lunel and Nîmes (Provence); gases of volcanic origin mix with spring waters.

Vichy another sparkling spring water. From Vichy (see Auvergne).

Vittel a still water from the spa, south of Nancy (see Alsace).

Volvic a still water from the Auvergne.

French Government Tourist Offices (Maison de la France)

Australia: BNP Bldg, 12th floor, 12 Castlereagh St, Sydney, NSW 2000.

Canada: 1981 Av McGill Collège, Suite 490, Montréal, QUE H3A 2W9; 1 Dundas St West, Suite 2405, Box 8, Toronto, ONT M5G 1Z3.

UK: 178 Piccadilly, London W1V 0AL. USA: 645 North Michigan Av, Chicago, Illinois 60611-2836; Cedar Maple Plaza, 2305 Cedar Springs Rd, Suite 205, Dallas, Texas 75201; 9454 Wilshire Blvd, Beverly Hills, California 90212; 610 Fifth Avenue, Suite 222, New York, NY 10020.

LES BAUX